BELGIUM
NETHERLANDS
LUXEMBURG
WEST GERMANY
AUSTRIA
LICHTENSTEIN
SWITZERLAND
ITALY
MEDITERRANEAN SEA
Rhine
Lille
Reims
Metz
Nancy
Strasbourg
Châlons s. Marne
LORRAINE
ALSACE
CHAMPAGNE
Marne
Aube
Troyes
Seine
St Quentin
Mulhouse
Belfort
Besançon
FRANCHE COMTÉ
Dijon
Saône
Doubs
Chalon s. Saône
BOURGOGNE
BURGUNDY
Yonne
NIVERNAIS
Nevers
BOURBONNAIS
Allier
Loire
AUVERGNE
Lyon
Rhône
Lot
Montpellier

France

A COMPANION TO FRENCH STUDIES

Methuen's Companions to Modern Studies

GERMANY: *A Companion to German Studies*
Edited by Malcolm Pasley

SPAIN: *A Companion to Spanish Studies*
Edited by P. E. Russell

THE UNITED STATES: *A Companion to American Studies*
Edited by Dennis Welland

France

A COMPANION TO FRENCH STUDIES

SECOND EDITION

edited by D. G. Charlton

METHUEN & CO. LTD

LONDON AND NEW YORK

First published in 1972
by Methuen & Co. Ltd
11 New Fetter Lane, London EC4P 4EE

Second edition 1979
Published in the USA by
Methuen & Co. Ltd
a division of Methuen, Inc.
733 Third Avenue, New York, NY 10017

Printed in Great Britain
by Richard Clay (The Chaucer Press) Ltd
Bungay, Suffolk

ISBN 0 416 72300 4

Contents

List of Illustrations

The illustrations fall in a separate section between pages 498 and 499

Sir Anthony Blunt and the publishers wish to thank the following for permission to reproduce the illustrations that appear in this book:

Burrell Collection, Glasgow Art Gallery and Museum, for nos. 19 and 22; Courtauld Institute Galleries for nos. 1, 2, 3, 5, 6, 13, 14, 24, 25, 26, and 27; Duke of Sutherland Collection on loan to the National Gallery of Scotland for no. 7; Fitzwilliam Museum, Cambridge, for no. 23; Musée des Beaux-Arts, Brussels, for no. 12; Musée du Louvre for nos. 4, 15, 16, 18, 20 and 21; Museum of Modern Art, New York, for no. 32; National Gallery, London, for nos. 17 and 28; National Gallery of Art, Washington, Chester Dale Collection, for no. 30; National Museum, Stockholm, for no. 10; Royal Collection for no. 8 which is reproduced by gracious permission of Her Majesty the Queen; Sotheby's, for photograph of no. 34; State Hermitage Museum, Leningrad, for no. 29; The Tate Gallery, London, and A.D.A.G.P., Paris, for no. 33; University of Glasgow, Hunterian Museum, for no. 11; Wallace Collection for no. 9; Wallraf-Richartz Museum, Cologne, for no. 31.

Preface to the First Edition

This volume seeks to provide a detailed introduction and guide to the history and culture of France from the time of the Renaissance to the present day – to a civilization which in its sustained duration and richness equals that of England in the modern world and those of Greece and Rome in ancient times. It is addressed both to the many general readers for whom France is of persisting cultural interest and to students in universities and schools who wish a wider knowledge and evaluation of her heritage, whether their more specialized study is of French literature, history, thought, music, fine arts or politics. To examine one aspect of any civilization in isolation imposes an inadequate understanding of even that aspect – and still more of the significance of the civilization as a whole. This work aims to help its readers to avoid any such restricted approach and to appreciate more fully the range and the wealth of activity and sensibility that collectively comprise *la civilisation française*. Each area is by design treated in its own terms and in the light of contemporary scholarly knowledge, but the interdependence of the parts, the unity of the whole, will be apparent to the reader in every chapter. Select bibliographies are provided after each chapter for those who wish further reading.

Even so full a volume as this cannot include everything that calls for attention. Regretfully accepted omissions include the history of the French language (which demands a much more extended treatment than would have been possible here), the history of science and technology in France, and its geography (passing background information excepted). The choice has gone in favour of a fuller discussion of a more limited, though still extensive range of subjects; hence, above all, the hard decision had to be made to exclude treatment of medieval France. Had France died in the late fifteenth century it would still retain a permanent and fascinating place in the history of the human spirit, but it requires another book – of no less size – to describe and appraise its major role in European history, literature, art, architecture, theology and philosophy during the Middle Ages. To reconcile inevitable limitations of space with the goal of providing a detailed and reasonably comprehensive treatment within each chapter has therefore dictated that the starting-point for this volume should be the full achievement of a French national unity and the rise – though even here the medievals are precursors – of the Renaissance.

After a brief introductory chapter to set the scene for what follows, Chapter 2 surveys the history, literature and thought of the period of the Renaissance in France. The succeeding seven chapters are concerned in turn with French history and society (3 and 4), French thought (5 and 6) and French literature (7, 8 and 9) over the period from around 1600 to the present day and with fullest attention going to the distinctively modern era of post-Revolutionary France. Chapters 10 and 11 are respectively devoted to French art and architecture and to French music over the whole period covered by this volume, whilst Chapter 12 concludes it by concentrating upon the politics, society and institutions of contemporary France.

This work replaces, on the decision of the publishers, a similar one edited by the late Professor R. L. Graeme Ritchie which has proved of great usefulness to countless readers for more than thirty years. In acknowledging the fine achievement of Professor Ritchie and his fellow contributors, the present editor can only hope that this replacement will be found no less illuminating and helpful. He is greatly indebted to the distinguished scholars who have contributed to this volume and believes that the learning, lucidity and authority of their chapters give grounds for claiming that, like its predecessor, it provides a highly informative companion and work of reference for all serious students of France.

D. G. C.

University of Warwick
June 1971

Preface to the Second Edition

For this second edition the chapters have been revised, where necessary, in the light of new scholarship and interpretation, and in particular all those concerned with contemporary France have been updated to include recent events and developments. In addition, the short bibliographies of the original *Companion* have been replaced by more extended bibliographical essays, and Professor Sir Anthony Blunt's chapter now has the benefit of illustrations (which previously appeared only in an 'offprinted' volume on *French Art and Music since 1500*, Methuen, 1974). The widely regretted death of Edward Lockspeiser has finally led to the decision to ask Dr Hugh Macdonald to prepare an entirely new chapter on French music. I am grateful to him for undertaking this task, to my other fellow contributors, and to Mr Anthony Forster and Mrs Linden Stafford of Methuen for their constant helpfulness.

D. G. C.

University of Warwick
April 1978

1 Introduction

D. G. CHARLTON

The historian Michelet described France as a personality presenting many different faces. Diversity and contrast are indeed inescapable features of its geography, its people and its history alike, and it is thus small wonder that its civilization and culture should display so outstanding and complex a richness, as the later chapters of this volume make clear. In this brief introduction, which seeks to set the scene for the detailed treatment of France since the Renaissance that follows, the theme of variety imposes itself.

This is evident, at the most basic level, in the very geographical realities of France. It is firmly linked with the Mediterranean and its peoples by virtue of its southern frontiers, running from the often changing border with Italy near Menton, along the Côte d'Azur and Provence, past the plains of the Rhône delta and skirting Spain the length of the Pyrenees. Again and again military invasion and cultural influence have come from the south – from the Greeks, the Romans, the Arabs, the Italians – moving past La Turbie or in from Spain to Aix-en-Provence and Marseille, on to Avignon, Arles and Nîmes, and up the valley of the Rhône to Lyon and the north. The French language, French history, French culture are inexplicable without reference to the consequences of this Romance and Mediterranean element. The western frontier is very different – moving north from the foothills of the Pyrenees near Saint-Jean-de-Luz along the sand-dunes of the Landes and out to the rocky promontory of Brittany stretching far into the storms of the Atlantic. For centuries this was the distant, untamed extremity of the country, not even, in the case of Brittany, part of France itself. The present-day visitor will find medieval castles – at Combourg, Josselin, Fougères and elsewhere – but few great churches (despite the deep Breton piety) or Renaissance châteaux. Its major historical monuments remain the prehistoric alignments at Carnac, and even the place-names still reflect the Celtic more than the Romance. Yet if remote from the urban activity of Paris, Lyon and even the Loire, the ports of this western fringe – Bordeaux, La Rochelle, Saint-Nazaire, Brest and others – have been the base from which French explorers have moved out into the non-European world, to French Canada, the West Indies, the African colonies and the Pacific. And French culture has in turn been affected by these trans-oceanic links, notably during the Renaissance 'age of discovery', the eighteenth century – so impressed by the travel-lore of Bougainville and other adventurers – and since. The north-west sea-coast of France, from the Île d'Ouessant to Dunkirk, faces in the same direction – receiving the ocean liners at Cherbourg and Le Havre and with Rouen being second only to Marseille in importance as a port – but also towards Britain and northern Europe. Normandy resembles Sussex, the Paris basin that of London, and the undulating landscape of the Pas-de-Calais continues that of Belgium and of Kent. France is both close to and yet separate from England in relationship as much as in geography: the contacts are numerous but often marked by tension. From these French coasts the armies of Julius Caesar and William of Normandy sailed to conquer the Britons, and upon them landed a succession of alien invaders – amongst others, the Vikings to pillage ninth-century Paris, Henry Plantagenet of England, the English soldiery of the Hundred Years War and (this time to liberate) the Allied armies of 1944. And in cultural terms likewise the Anglo-French relation has been ambivalent – close in the Middle Ages and the time of Erasmus, of Lockean philosophy, of Romantic literature, but no less marked by recurrent misconceptions and suspicion.

Yet France, bordered to north, south and west by sea or high mountains, lies open to Central Europe on her eastern side, and most obviously so to the north-east. Further south, the Alpine and Jura mountains provide a defensive barrier along the frontier with Italy and Switzerland, but despite the Vosges and the hilly country to their north the French have throughout their history been deeply conscious that their country lacks natural defences on this one part of its hexagonal outline. From the earliest times these areas have suffered the passage of military men. Even during the later Roman Empire (we know little before that) there came the Visigoths, who occupied the lands from Spain to the Loire, the Burgundians from the Vistula, settling in Savoy, the Ostrogoths, the Alemanni and – most successful of these barbarian invaders – the Franks, Germanic tribesmen sweeping down from the region of the Zuyder Zee and bequeathing their name to the country they occupied. They were led from A.D. 481 by Clovis, king of the Franks, who successively defeated the Romans and subdued the other barbarian groups, chose Paris as his capital, and was first of the Merovingian dynasty which ruled in France to 638 (and retained the throne in name if not in power to 751). At other times it was the French themselves who were the invaders, moving into the Lowlands or Germany and thereby hoping for greater security from the east. The greatest of the Carolingian dynasty, Charlemagne, king of the Franks from 768 (sole king from 771), set an example to be followed by Louis XIV, Napoleon and others. By continuous wars, above all against the Saxons, he created an empire extending from the Atlantic to the Elbe and was crowned Emperor of the West in 800 by Pope Leo III. Indeed, the German invasion and occupation in 1940 and the French occupation of part of Germany in 1945 are only the latest illustrations of a recurrent military pattern, and parallel with it has gone a cultural and intellectual exchange between France and her eastern neighbours that, in its more peaceful way, has been hardly less important.

If France's frontiers are windows, as it were, on to four quite different geographical and cultural areas, its internal life and its peoples are equally varied. There is, for example, not one French climate but several – ranging from the rainy, misty, but mild, almost frost-free weather of the Atlantic seaboard to the extreme continental-type variation between summer heat and winter cold found in the east around Strasbourg or Nancy, and from the subtropical summers and mild winters of the sheltered coasts of the Mediterranean to the greyer, more 'English' climate of Picardy or the harsh snow-bound winters of the High Alps.

The landscape is equally diverse. Although one most often connects France with rich agricultural lands of the kind found in the Île de France or the plain of Beauce (one source of the Frenchman's feeling for his 'soil'), in fact one-sixth of France's land-area of just over 200,000 square miles is mountainous and produces few crops – the Massif Central, the Alps, much of the Vosges and Juras, the Pyrenees – and even these high areas, one may add, offer very different kinds of mountain scenery. The deserted marshlands of the Camargue; the cliffs of Calais or Normandy; the volcanic peaks of the Puys; the bare windswept hills of Brittany; the vineyard slopes of the valley running from Dijon to the south; the geologically young, jagged folds of the Alps; the green softness of the valley of the Loire as it flows past Tours and

Angers; the sun-bleached hills and plains of Provence; the almost tideless sands of the Mediterranean resorts; the highest tidal range in western Europe (at Saint-Malo) – and its highest mountain also – and the long rollers moving in from the Bay of Biscay to break on the coast around Biarritz: all these are examples of the diversity that composes the French scene.

The people – or, rather, peoples – of France offer a parallel mixture. There is no French 'race'; the French comprise and interfuse three main ethnic groups: Nordic (tall and fair, chiefly living in the north and east); Mediterranean (the dark, small 'Latins', dominant above all in the south); Alpine (medium-built, usually dark-haired 'Celts', occupying the central area of the country and the east). The earliest inhabitants of whom we know, who have left the evidences of their life and art 20,000 years and more before Christ, when the ice-sheets still covered northern Europe, in the caves of Dordogne, around Les Eyzies and Lascaux; the Gauls, Celtic people from Central Europe, who moved in perhaps around 12,000 B.C.; the Greeks who founded the port of Marseille about 600 B.C. and have left their traces at Saint-Blaise and Glanum (and in the Greek vase of Vix); the Romans who settled in Provence (*c.* 120 B.C.), followed by Caesar's army from 58 B.C.; the eastern 'barbarians' in the centuries of the Dark Ages: all these have contributed to the racial 'mix' we describe as 'French'.

Given the sources of diversity and difference we have noted, it is not surprising that the unification of France should have been slowly achieved – often, over the centuries, appearing to be won only to be lost again. After the victory of Caesar over Vercingetorix in 52 B.C. the Romans established a political unity for the first time – stretching to include even Brittany after the defeat of the Breton fleet in the Gulf of Morbihan. Many monuments of this Roman civilization still remain in France, as any traveller knows: the Pont du Gard, the Maison Carrée at Nîmes, the arena at Arles, the theatre at Orange and others – not excluding some of the long, straight roads along which he drives to reach them. But by the fourth century the Empire was in decline, and the fifth century saw the successive invasions of the barbarians from the north and east, culminating in the triumph of Clovis and the creation of a new military authority. Yet the unity imposed by the kings of the Franks was never total and was always precarious. By the seventh century they no longer ruled either the Bretons or the country south of the Loire, the duchy of Aquitania. Local wars between competing nobles were frequent in the Frankish lands, and by the early eighth century new invaders – Moslems from Africa – had not only conquered Spain but occupied southern France as far as Arles. Then, once again, new military leaders imposed themselves and a fresh unity was enforced by the remarkable Carolingian family, deriving from the area around Metz, of Pépin d'Héristal, ruler as *maire du Palais* to the Merovingian king from 687 to 714, and his son Charles Martel (714–41). Charles brought wide regions of France to obedience and drove the Moslems from the south after his victory at Poitiers in 732. His son, Pépin le Bref, in alliance with the Pope, further extended the kingdom, compelled the submission of Aquitania, and took the throne as the first Carolingian king. All Gaul was again under a single authority, and Pépin's own son, Charlemagne, consolidated its stability and, as already noticed, extended it far beyond the frontiers of France: the King of the Franks became Emperor of the West. Within France he had a still more lasting influence. It was he who formalized the link of Church and State – a link of mutual self-interest, each strengthening the other's power – which lasted to the nineteenth century – from the papal coronation of Charlemagne in 800 to the *sacre* of Charles X in 1824; to give only one example, he ordered all his subjects to pay the local priest a tithe, a tenth part of all their crops – an obligation (an economic consolidation of the Church) only swept finally away after 1789. He also revived the tradition of intellectual culture in France, bringing learned men from other countries, notably England and Italy, encouraging the reform of writing in the script that would ultimately be perpetuated in our printed alphabet, favouring libraries of manuscript copies of the works of the ancients and the formation of ecclesiastical schools.

Yet again, however, the unity was short-lived. On the death of Charlemagne's son, Louis, the Carolingian Empire was divided by the Treaty of Verdun (843), and power was increasingly dispersed amongst local noblemen and church authorities. The disintegration of central control was further hastened by new invasions – by the Norsemen, who four times pillaged Paris, settled in Rouen from 912 and gave their name to Normandy; by the Saracens who sailed up the Rhône and struck as far north as Savoy; by the Huns, driving into Lorraine and Burgundy and even to Toulouse. The dynasty survived amid growing disorder and internal conflict to 987, but thereafter the nobles rejected the Carolingian heir of Louis le Fainéant in favour of Hugues Capet – the first of the dynasty that was to prevail in France for almost 900 years: in the direct line to 1328, in the Valois branch to 1589 and in the Bourbon branch to 1848.

But throughout the Middle Ages the Capetian kings never ruled over a unified country. They firmly controlled the area around Paris – and perhaps the Paris-centredness of France to the present day is related to this fact. Beyond that prosperous northern region, however, their dominance fluctuated constantly. The development of feudalism – more organized in northern France than other countries, it seems – divided power amongst countless lords and local rulers. And though in the feudal hierarchy they were theoretically subordinate to the king, his control was no greater than his possessions and military strength and the extent to which they recognized his overlordship and the sacred quality bestowed by his coronation; many a count or duke in reality ruled his lands as sovereign. Moreover, the very success of William of Normandy in invading England and becoming its king was to rebound in the following century when the Plantagenets succeeded to the English throne. Henry II inherited Normandy as well as England from his grandfather and Anjou and Touraine from his father and gained Aquitaine through his wife. For 300 years the English king controlled parts of France – and at times the inhabitants of the two great southern states of Toulouse and Aquitaine seemed almost foreigners to the French. Philippe II, king from 1180 to 1223, regained Normandy and Anjou (1203–6) and defeated the coalition of the princes in 1214, and the Albigensian crusade (1209–13) restored Languedoc to French rule. Over the following two centuries marriage, inheritance and military campaigns gradually extended the lands governed by the French monarchy – but it was only after the destruction and sufferings of the Hundred Years War (1337–1453) that the English were at last removed from everywhere save Calais. Nor was this slow movement to national unity an uninterrupted trend. Set-backs were numerous – defeat at Crécy (1346), defeat at Poitiers (1356) after which the French king even ceded half his kingdom to the English, defeat at Agincourt (1415) whereafter the English king had to be recognized as ruler of the whole region north of the Loire; and if Jeanne d'Arc helped to relieve Orléans and led Charles VII to be crowned at Reims, she was also captured and burnt by her enemies (1431). But after the victory of Castillon in 1453 unification came rapidly. Through convenient deaths Louis XI gained Anjou, Provence and Burgundy. The marriage of Charles VIII to Anne de Bretagne added Brittany in 1491 (formally united a little later). Already in 1484 – though the event is no more than symbolic perhaps – the very first meeting of the Estates-General from the whole kingdom had been convened in Tours. By 1494 the king felt confident enough to invade Italy to support his claim to the throne of Naples. With his reign at the close of the fifteenth century the country of France had at long last attained territorial unity within what broadly remain its present frontiers and had also gained the relative security in which could flower most fully the civilization of the French Renaissance.

Not, of course, that the emergence of French culture awaited the sixteenth century; even the French 'Renaissance' itself is situated by some modern scholars hardly less in the fifteenth century than in the age of Rabelais and Marguerite de Navarre that followed. We must in fact now note that though France's military and territorial unity were long delayed, its role as an intellectual and cultural force was of international significance for centuries before. Through all the invasions and conflicts we have noted and all the devastation they imposed, through the recurrent outbreaks of disease and famine, and although life for the majority was harsh, French pre-eminence in the cultivation of the mind and the arts was perhaps even more marked in the Middle Ages than in the centuries since. In the age when learning and civilization were European far more than 'national', Paris in particular was the great centre for scholars and students from every Western country – and as well as that of the Île de France, thriving cultures existed in southern France, Burgundy and Normandy. Not that the narrower patriotism of modern times should mislead us. For example, though French was to become the language of the medieval English courts and palaces and of much poetry in England, the scholars called to his court by Charlemagne to establish his École Palatine, an academy of learning and literature, were not French but English (notably Alcuin), Norman, Pisan, Spanish and Italian, and a similar internationalism continued throughout the Middle Ages.

The internationalism – and the very existence – of medieval European civilization was due above all to the Christian Church – a platitude, but of major importance. In the early fourth century Constantine had proclaimed himself a Christian. Prior to that isolated foreigners had preached the Gospel in Gaul, but it was only with the adoption of Christianity as the official religion of the Roman Empire that the Church could begin to establish the position – first in the towns, then in the country districts – which it was to preserve tenaciously through all the changes of the following centuries. Successive kings (we have already remarked) allied themselves with the Church, and the Church gained in return added wealth, influence and security and was able progressively to extend its general dominance – through the local impact, most basically, of its priests, through the vigour and appeal of its teachings, through – above all – its role in education. For if the Crusades, from 1096 onwards, were the most obvious military consequence of the Christian preoccupations that underrun the whole medieval period, even more lasting were their cultural and intellectual manifestations. These are visible, in the literal sense, in the art and architecture of the period: in the great Romanesque abbeys, mainly built in the eleventh and twelfth centuries, of Caen, Poitiers, Le Puy, Toulouse, Cluny (before its destruction) and (most moving of all) Vézelay, set on the pilgrims' route to Compostella; in the superb Gothic cathedrals of Chartres, Reims, Bourges, Strasbourg, Albi, Amiens and Notre-Dame-de-Paris, erected in the twelfth and thirteenth centuries; in the sculptures which decorate these churches; in the work of the artists who were subsidized for the same religious ends, whether decorating manuscripts, designing stained glass, or, later, painting frescoes and providing altar-pieces. And though any survey of medieval French literature is outside the scope of this introductory chapter, one can at least note in much of it a parallel religious inspiration – notably in the miracle and mystery plays which represent the main types of medieval drama, in many at least of the *chansons de geste*, to some extent in such prose chronicles as Villehardouin's *Conquête de Constantinople* and Joinville's *Histoire de Saint Louis* – an inspiration, morover, that is sometimes implicit also in the more secular themes of literature at this age, themes of love, chivalry and military valour, for example. But the supreme achievement of the Church during these centuries, one may well think, was to re-establish education and learning, to foster the search for knowledge and truth, to promote what has proved the most enduring of all medieval creations (which has outlived feudalism and government by kings and nobles and may be thought even to have superseded the Church in modern times, for good or ill, as society's intellectual mentor) – the university. And here too, though the first European university was at Bologna, it was in France, and most especially at Paris, that the university movement in the Middle Ages was best exemplified.

The medieval educational achievement has its original foundations in the school created by Charlemagne and run by Alcuin and soon supplemented by the establishment of monastic schools, to which external pupils were admitted as well as oblates, of which the most important was at Reims. These monastic schools were to be the chief centres of education into the eleventh century, but thereafter primacy passed to the cathedral schools, notably those at Laon, Chartres, Sens, Rouen and elsewhere, and at Paris. And it was out of the cathedral school of Paris, made famous throughout Europe by such masters as Guillaume de Champeaux (d. 1121) and, above all, Pierre Abélard (1079–1142), one of the founders of scholastic theology and a philosopher of markedly independent intelligence, that there emerged the University of Paris. It came into being about 1170 – as a guild of masters who were licensed to teach – and its first statutes date from early in the following century. Already, moreover, it was a *universitas* in the sense of being in its emphasis a place of widely ranging higher education and study, as well as being a corporation of teachers. It included faculties of law and arts in addition to theology, and a faculty of medicine was added a little later, and though Paris was outstanding in theology from the time of Abélard and Peter Lombard to that of Thomas Aquinas and beyond, the seven liberal arts as a whole – grammar, logic and rhetoric (the trivium); arithmetic, music, geometry and astronomy (the quadrivium) – formed the basis of the education provided. 'Never before in any time', wrote an observer in 1210, 'or in any part of the world, whether in Athens or in Egypt, had there been such a multitude of students' – to the point that students in the faculty of arts were divided by the mid-thirteenth century into four 'nations' (the French, the Normans, the Picards and the English – including Germans and others). And to house them numerous colleges were founded – some sixty between 1137 and 1360 – of which the best-known, the college founded by Robert de Sorbon about 1257, originally for sixteen bursars in theology, four from each 'nation', was centuries later (after a stormy history of mainly conservative theology) to become the headquarters and a synonym for the University as a whole. Soon, too, as a natural consequence, by virtue of its libraries and its numerous booksellers controlled by the University, Paris became (as another witness enthuses) 'the paradise of the world' for books: 'there are delightful libraries, more aromatic than stores of spice; there abundant orchards of all manners of books . . .' The university movement was advancing in the provinces also – with the great law school at Orléans, the University of Toulouse, founded in 1229 to combat the Albigensian heresy, and universities at Montpellier, Angers, Avignon, Grenoble, Orange and elsewhere developing between the late thirteenth and late fourteenth centuries. But it was Paris that was supreme, not only in France but throughout Europe, its greatest intellectual centre, the meeting-place of its best minds, attracting and gaining further reputation from such teachers as Roger Bacon, Albertus Magnus, Bonaventura, Aquinas, Siger of Brabant and others in the thirteenth century and Duns Scotus and Meister Eckhart in the early fourteenth. Here more than anywhere else in the West, for two centuries and more – in the small, cramped, dirty, turbulent area of the Latin Quarter around the old Rue du Fouarre, that 'straw-littered street' evoked in Dante's *Divine Comedy* – intellectual culture was preserved and extended, the learning of the classical world rediscovered and reinterpreted, new thought worked out in such controversies as those between Abélard and St Bernard of Clairvaux or Aquinas and Siger and in many works of both pious and disputatious argument.

It falls outside the range of this Introduction to describe the achievements of Paris and the other medieval universities. In some ways their role may be thought conservative and even narrowing, seeking to consolidate the role of theology as queen of the sciences, prepared to subordinate all other learning to the ends of Catholic religion and to the achieving of salvation in the world-to-come, jealous of their own independence but intolerant of others – albeit these attitudes follow understandably from the tenets of medieval religion. Yet in other ways, one may think, they also anticipated what was to come with the Renaissance and later ages. On the one hand they were bulwarks of the Faith, training, for example, the canon and civil lawyers who formed the bureaucracy of Church and State; on the other they allowed a freedom of discussion on theological and many other matters far greater than was possible outside. Hence the seeming disillusionment of the Papacy at the work of universities, some of which it had helped to found – as when a papal legate of 1290, the future Boniface VIII, openly attacks the Paris professors as 'more foolish than the ignorant, men who have poisoned by their teaching not only themselves but also the entire world'. Indeed the University of Paris in the later Middle Ages became increasingly the opponent of the Papacy and a supporter of the Gallicanism of the French monarchy. And within that University itself the theologians were more and more outnumbered by the masters in the faculty of arts, through which every student had to pass and which was – then as perhaps still – a home for ideological unrest. The tension had been evident for many decades – since the early thirteenth century when the 'artists' had moved from the Île de la Cité and the control of the Chancellor of Notre-Dame to a new base on the Left Bank. By the mid-fourteenth century, as against 25 masters in theology, the same number in medicine, and even fewer in canon law, there were over 400 masters of arts. And dispute thrived amongst the theologians themselves. Even Aquinas was attacked by the Franciscans and other conservatives of 1265 as a dangerous innovator – ironically, given the twentieth-century attribution of orthodoxy to Thomist philosophy, but also with some justice. For Aquinas, no less than Abélard before him, made reason an arbiter of faith and has even been dubbed a precursor of the rational philosophy of Descartes and a 'father of the Enlightenment'. He not only read avidly such Arab thinkers as Averroes and Avicenna and numerous translated Greek and Jewish works; even more he rejected all obscurantism, and to Augustine's stress on emotion and the will he opposed the primacy of the intellect. Furthermore, if he and others anticipated the rationalism of the modern age, medieval thinkers also foreshadowed its empiricism and laid the bases for the development of the natural sciences. A stress upon observation was already contained within the nominalist arguments of the early twelfth century against the 'realism' of Anselm, and the scientific movement more explicitly founded in the following century by Robert Grossteste at Oxford was extended there, in Paris, and elsewhere by Roger Bacon, Duns Scotus, William of Ockham and others, and was enriched by the influx of Arab and Jewish scientific ideas in particular.

Yet, even in the later Middle Ages, the tensions between reason and faith, between religion and science, between orthodoxy and free inquiry, between sacred doctrine and secular learning (and also between Papacy and emerging nation-state), were little more than tensions and existed within a relatively stable and coherent world-view. The leading fifteenth-century thinker Nicholas of Cusa (1401–64), for example, was a cardinal as well as a mathematician and scientist, seeking to unite science and theology as fully as had his Spanish precursor Ramon Lull (1235–1315), still confident that Platonism and Christianity were compatible – a confidence inherited in the next decades by such scholars as Ficino and Pico della Mirandola and still alive in the mid-sixteenth century in Marguerite de Navarre and her Neoplatonist friends. So strong and inclusive was the medieval Christian synthesis that even the more adventurous minds thought not in terms of irreconcilable oppositions but of temporary discrepancies to be dissolved. And in the end Catholic faith still prevailed: Pico, for instance, might study Eastern philosophies, alchemy and cabalism, as well as Plato and write an optimistic treatise on 'the dignity of man' – but he died in the arms of the puritanical Florentine Dominican, Savonarola.

All the same, in the final decades of the fifteenth century new factors and forces were at work: the Greek scholars moving to the West with numerous manuscripts of Greek and Latin works; the first printing press in France, set up in Paris in 1470 by Guillaume Fichet, initiating a rapidly widening diffusion of texts, translations and works of scholarship; the growing influence in France of the 'Italian Renaissance' and its attitudes. Journeys of discovery, moreover, were revealing a hitherto unknown world beyond the familiar area of Europe and the Near East: Diaz reached the Cape of Good Hope in 1486 and Vasco da Gama sailed past it to reach Malabar in 1498; Columbus sighted America in 1492 and the Cabot brothers Newfoundland in 1497, and in 1520 Magellan rounded South America and went on into 'the Peaceful Sea'; what have been termed 'the new horizons of the Renaissance' were geographical as much as intellectual. And above all, perhaps, the final emergence of France as a unified nation was important, and not least by favouring the patronage of learning and the arts by François I and others. Any clear line between the Middle Ages and the Renaissance is idle to seek or to draw; the medievals, we have noted, prefigured some basic modern approaches, and the sixteenth and seventeenth centuries in particular retained many elements persisting from medieval Christianity. But gradually the discrepancies between the old faith and the new knowledge widened to become oppositions, and the tensions deepened into overt conflicts; and as slowly but as surely as France had achieved its national unity it moved in its culture and intellectual life also towards a new age.

Bibliography

The following suggestions for further reading are as selective and introductory as this chapter itself; many of the works named contain far fuller bibliographies, to be consulted by those interested in specific subjects. In addition, a very useful list of select bibliographies on all the subjects treated in this volume, and on other aspects of France also, is found in J. Pemberton, *How to Find Out About France: A Guide to Sources of Information* (Oxford, 1966).

On the geography of France, helpful works in English include H. Ormsby, *France: A Regional and Economic Geography* (London, 1931), and I. B. Thompson, *Modern France: A Social and Economic Geography* (London, 1970); and major studies in French are P. Vidal de la Blache, Vol. I, in E. Lavisse, *Histoire de France depuis les origines jusqu'à la Révolution*, 9 vols (Paris, 1911), J. Brunhes and P. Deffontaines, Vols I and II, in G. Hanotaux, *Histoire de la nation française*, 15 vols

(Paris, 1920–35), P. George, *Géographie économique et sociale de la France*, 3rd ed. (Paris, 1949), and E. Granger, *La France: son visage, son peuple, ses ressources* (Paris, 1932).

On French history, its whole span is surveyed in the basic works by G. Hanotaux, *Histoire de la nation française*, 15 vols (Paris, 1920–35), and E. Lavisse, *Histoire de France depuis les origines jusqu'à la Révolution*, 9 vols (Paris, 1911), shorter accounts being provided by R. Pernoud, *Histoire du peuple français: des origines au moyen âge* (Paris, 1953), E. R. Curtius, *The Civilisation of France* (London, 1932), and C. Seignobos, *Histoire sincère de la nation française*, 6th ed. (Paris, 1946). On the earliest period, good accounts are given by O. Brogan, *Roman Gaul* (London, 1953), C. Jullian, *Histoire de la Gaule*, 8 vols (Paris, 1908–26) – an authoritative work – and R. Latouche, *From Caesar to Charlemagne* (London, 1968). The earlier Middle Ages are well treated in M. Bloch, *Feudal Society* (London and New York, 1961), and F. L. Ganshof, *Feudalism* (New York, 1961), as well as in chronologically wider studies such as G. Duby, *The Chivalrous Society* (London, 1977), J. Evans, *Life in Medieval France* (London, 1925), F. Heer, *The Medieval World* (London, 1925) – a major work of synthesis – and H. Pirenne, *Medieval Cities: Their Origins and the Revival of Trade* (Princeton, NJ, 1952). A. Luchaire, *Social France at the Time of Philip Augustus* (Harper Torchbooks, Evanston and London, 1967), deals well with the period of Philippe II; Joinville and Villehardouin, *Chronicles of the Crusades* (London, 1963), is evocative source-reading. The later Middle Ages are best approached through P. S. Lewis, *Later Medieval France* (London, 1968), and J. Huizinga, *The Waning of the Middle Ages* (London, 1924), is a long-standing classic of cultural history, whatever reservations later scholars have had. On medieval anticipations of the Renaissance, a standard work is F. Simone, *The French Renaissance* (London, 1969). The fundamental study of the medieval university movement remains H. Rashdall, *The Universities of Europe in the Middle Ages*, 3 vols (Oxford, 1936).

The best accounts of medieval thought for English readers are D. Knowles, *The Evolution of Medieval Thought* (London, 1962), G. Leff, *Medieval Thought: St Augustine to Ockham* (London, 1958), and E. Gilson, *History of Christian Philosophy in the Middle Ages* (London, 1955), and of its greatest representative F. C. Copleston, *Aquinas* (London, 1956).

General and authoritative studies of medieval French literature are provided by R. Bossuat, *Histoire de la littérature française: le moyen âge* (Paris, 1962), P. Le Gentil, *La Littérature française du moyen âge* (Paris, 1968), and P. Zumthor, *Histoire littéraire de la France médiévale* (Paris, 1954); J. Crosland, *Medieval French Literature* (Oxford, 1956), is a useful shorter survey in English. C. H. Haskins, *The Renaissance of the Twelfth Century* (Cambridge, Mass., 1927), is a major work on its period. On medieval theatre, G. Cohen, *Le Théâtre en France au moyen âge*, 2 vols (Paris, 1928), is basic, and G. Frank, *The Medieval French Drama* (Oxford, 1954), is a sound treatment in English. On the troubadours and the tradition of courtly love, one should consult R. Boase, *The Origin and Meaning of Courtly Love* (Manchester, 1976), H. Davenson (= H.-I. Marrou), *Les Troubadours* (Bourges, 1961), L. Topsfield, *Troubadours and Love* (Cambridge, 1975), and – from a more literary viewpoint – L. M. Paterson, *Troubadours and Eloquence* (Oxford, 1975), and A. Jeanroy, *La Poésie lyrique des troubadours*, 2 vols (Toulouse, 1934). A contrasting tradition, as regards its view of women, is represented by medieval *fabliaux*, for which P. Nykrog, *Les Fabliaux* (Copenhagen, 1957), has perhaps largely superseded J. Bédier, *Les Fabliaux*, 6th ed. (Paris, 1964). On medieval poetry as a whole A. Jeanroy, *Les Origines de la poésie lyrique en France au moyen âge*, 4th ed. (Paris, 1965), remains basic, supplemented by P. Champion, *Histoire poétique du XVe siècle*, 2 vols (Paris, 1966), for that later period. Epic poetry, and especially the *chanson de geste*, is treated in J. Bédier, *Les Légendes épiques*, 4 vols, 2nd ed. (Paris, 1917–21), I. Siciliano, *Les Chansons de geste et l'épopée: mythes, histoire, poèmes* (Torino, 1969), and, for English readers, J. Crosland, *The Old French Epic* (Oxford, 1951). On the Arthurian legend, one should begin from J. D. Bruce, *The Evolution of Arthurian Romance to 1300*, 2 vols (Göttingen, 1923), and R. S. Loomis, *The Arthurian Tradition and Chrétien de Troyes* (New York, 1949). Finally, a helpful introduction to its subject is offered by J. M. Ferrier, *Forerunners of the French Novel* (Manchester, 1954).

As regards other areas of medieval French culture, one should consult on music T. Gerold, *La Musique au moyen âge* (Paris, 1932). A readable general survey of its subject is provided by J. Evans, *Art in Medieval France* (London, 1948). Two fundamental studies are by E. Mâle, *L'Art religieux du XIIe siècle en France* (Paris, 1922) and *L'Art religieux du XIIIe siècle en France* (Paris, 1898), a general survey is given by P. Mantz, *La Peinture française du IXe au XVIe siècle* (Paris, 1897), and more particularized works are M. Aubert, *La Sculpture française au moyen âge* (Paris, 1947), L. Dimier, *Les Primitifs français* (Paris, 1911), and G. Ring, *A Century of French Painting 1400–1500* (London, 1949).

2 The Renaissance in France: History, Thought and Literature

A. H. T. LEVI

Renaissance, Humanism and Reform

In the context of French studies, the term 'Renaissance' is conventionally used to indicate the whole spectrum of cultural phenomena by which the sixteenth century differed from the centuries immediately preceding it. Unless some newly emerging series of personal and social values can be seen to relate to one another the changes to be observed in philosophy, theology, religion, education, music and architecture, art and literature, social organization, economic and political life, the term 'Renaissance' would have to be taken as mere shorthand for an unconnected assortment of cultural innovations during an arbitrarily chosen period. The difficulty has always lain in identifying the new values and perspectives that relate to one another developments in so many different branches of cultural life.

Discussion takes for its starting-point Jacob Burckhardt's *The Civilisation of the Renaissance in Italy* (1860) which defended the view, in its full form long since abandoned, that the Renaissance was a definite period, marking the end of the superstitious Middle Ages, which manifested unlimited individualism in political life and the visual arts. In the course of subsequent controversy, different dates have been assigned to the Renaissance to accord with different theories about its nature. In French studies, interest has come to centre on the sense in which the Renaissance can be said to mark a break with the Middle Ages and on the extent to which the cultural developments in northern Europe were independent of the Renaissance in Italy.

Almost as controverted as the nature of the Renaissance has been the related problem of 'humanism'. As a substantive the word first occurs in the nineteenth century. However, the terms *studia humanitatis* and *studia humaniora* were used from the early fourteenth century, and probably derived from a library classification for non-theological books. The teachers of the humanities were originally concerned with grammar, poetry and rhetoric and then, from the early fifteenth century, with moral philosophy. The term 'humanist' was used to designate first these teachers and then their students. It occurs from the late fifteenth century, often in lists of similar words like 'Thomist' and 'Scotist'. By this date the connection between the humanist and specifically classical literature is clear. The initial opposition between *humanitas* and *divinitas* as subjects for study was beginning to be overcome. But it was not until the sixteenth century that humanists like Erasmus and Budé connected the study of classical literature with *paideia*, the antique ideal of an education in which a knowledge of all the disciplines mediated *humanitas* in the sense of moral formation. It is this specifically sixteenth-century view of the function of the study of the humanities with which we are concerned in an attempt to define the ideals and values underlying the northern Renaissance.

It would, however, be mistaken to believe that humanism as such was a creation of the sixteenth century in France. The influence of Petrarch (1304–74) never died away in France. The humanism of Petrarch's Avignon lived on in the entourage of particular patrons and certainly influenced Jean Gerson (1363–1429), the great chancellor of the University of Paris who wrote theological, mystical and political treatises and defended Christine de Pisan's advanced position in the first phase of the *Querelle des femmes*. In the late fifteenth century, there existed an important circle of 'monastic' humanists who acknowledged Gerson's authority and who were themselves either monks or at least favourable to the monastic ideal. They included Nicolas de Clamanges, Guillaume Fichet, Robert Gaguin, Jean Trithème, Jean Raulin and Josse Clichtowe. For many of them, monastic peace was also the peace conducive to study.

What changed in the early sixteenth century was the consciousness of the humanists themselves, now aware of the whole vistas of human potential opened up by the classical ideal and confident enough to go well beyond their immediate predecessors, who had never had a confrontation with the established late medieval scholasticism. Almost from the turn of the century a new generation of humanists deliberately strove to widen the norms of religious orthodoxy. Erasmus's greatest achievement was to be the anchoring of an apparently heterodox and pagan ideal firmly in the Church's own revelation by demonstrating the compatibility of what he called the *Philosophia Christi* with the Pauline epistles and the Sermon on the Mount.

It was as if a fire which had long been smouldering suddenly burst into flame. The resulting upheaval, social, political and religious, was for all its hidden causes and remote antecedents a specifically sixteenth-century phenomenon in France. Its effects included the Reformation and the Counter-Reformation. They included wild millenarianist obsessions and the delicate imaginative explorations of advanced social and personal values conducted by Thomas More in *Utopia* (1516) and Erasmus in the series of essays added to the *Adages* in 1515. The initial confidence was total. Toleration, the abolition of war, class and property, were all seriously examined. Reaction set in with the neo-Stoicism of late sixteenth-century France and with seventeenth-century Jansenism. But the eighteenth-century belief in progress was the fruit finally culled from the Renaissance, and even the nineteenth-century Romantics, who 'rediscovered' the Renaissance in their own quest for self-definition, were intent on emphasizing, however one-sidedly, some of the values it contained. However disturbing the upheaval in the sixteenth century, it gave birth to the dialectical process from which modern France has emerged.

The Renaissance has often been taken to be essentially a 'renaissance des lettres', and it is important to understand how its progress can be measured not so much in terms of the 'influence' of classical authors as by the way in which they were exploited to different ends in the sixteenth century. It was only in the mid-century that the Pléiade generation firmly established in France the Greek humanism of Erasmus and won for Homer a place above Virgil in the hierarchy of poets. In the late fifteenth century Greek had been taught only unofficially and inadequately in France. But in the early years of the new century the most devoted humanists were already turning to Greek studies, in spite of the theological suspicion that attached to attempts to go behind the official Latin 'vulgate' version of the scriptures or to upgrade the theological status of the early and often Neoplatonist Greek fathers. Even Budé, the greatest of France's early Greek scholars and one of Erasmus's comparatively few supporters in France, had to write an apologia to defend himself against the suspicion of Lutheranism.

The major Latin authors were reasonably well known in the Middle Ages. Greek humanism took root in France comparatively late. But what the humanists described as a 'rebirth' or a 'reflowering', whose inception they dated from Petrarch, always took its inspiration from some remote but idealized past period. The monastic humanists had looked to the twelfth-century sources of their spirituality to combat the decadence of monasticism and the scandals of a pluralist and absentee clergy. The humanist wing of the Parisian scholastics sought to reinstate the thirteenth-century synthesis of Thomas Aquinas to combat the later medieval contention that religious perfection was not necessarily correlative to moral aspiration or intrinsic to moral achievement. The evangelical humanists based their programme on a return to the moral elevation of scripture and the early Fathers in their effort to combat the apparently arbitrary religious observances and logic-chopping theology favoured by the late medieval scholastics. The rebirth itself gave rise to a new interest in ancient authors and a new educational ideal, but its effects were much wider and certainly extended into religion. In 1549 Calvin could ascribe the rebirth of the arts and the sciences to divine inspiration: 'Dieu a resuscité les sciences humaines . . . il nous a remis les arts et les sciences en leur entier.'

The idea that something of quite fundamental importance was being restored with the humanist educational reform was very widespread. The letter from Gargantua to Pantagruel inserted into *Pantagruel* by Rabelais in 1532 sums up the enthusiasm. In 1516 Jean Despautère asserted in the preface to his *Ars versificatoria* that it was Petrarch 'who not without divine inspiration . . . opened war on the barbarians; and, recalling the Muses who had fled, vehemently excited the study of eloquence.' Jacques Lefèvre d'Étaples, the mystical commentator on Aristotle who devoted the last years of his life to the vernacular dissemination of scripture, had in 1503 associated the return to Aristotle's text with 'probity of behaviour, propriety of life and every sort of virtue'. In the same year the Parisian printer Josse Bade had again associated the knowledge of scripture and interior moral values with the 'rebirth' of true eloquence. The whole intellectual synthesis of Erasmus was to depend on the association of an elegant humanist style and textual criticism on the one hand with evangelical religion and the primacy of moral values over external rites on the other. Even in so far as it concerned a new attitude to classical texts, the early French Renaissance was largely moral and religious in its significance.

During the late Middle Ages, the scholastics had increasingly emphasized the transcendence of God, the inability of man to fathom his purposes and the derivation of the moral law from his arbitrary will. To some extent this view could call on the authority of the later writings of Augustine, composed while the civilization he knew was crumbling around him and gloomy about the powers of unaided human nature. It was not until the thirteenth century that a full-scale attempt was made to alter the perspectives left by Augustine to the Western Church. By regarding human reason as a derivative reflection of the eternal mind of God, Aquinas built into his intellectual system a correlation between the mind's need for an explanation of its experience and the truth revealed by God, as also between divine law, necessarily 'rational' because a product of divine reason, and the rational values towards which human nature, itself also derivatively 'rational', aspired for its fulfilment.

Aquinas's theory was too audaciously naturalist to win acceptance in the medieval schools, and it was under the influence of theological constraints that Scotus, Ockham and such 'nominalist' theologians as Gregory of Rimini and Gabriel Biel reacted against Aquinas to emphasize the arbitrary nature of revelation and law. Not surprisingly, the early Renaissance scholastics attempted a full-scale rehabilitation of Aquinas. By the end of the sixteenth century, his *Summa Theologica* had everywhere replaced the twelfth-century *Sentences* of Peter Lombard as the basis for the lecture-commentaries which were the backbone of theological instruction.

The late fifteenth century, however, had advocated religious practices which were no longer experienced as morally elevating, and had accepted the great nominalist principle, 'To those who do what lies within them, God does not deny grace'. Since the effects of grace had become non-moral and non-empirical, the result at the level of popular religion was a state of considerable psychological tension in which 'works' were multiplied without reference to their morally fulfilling effects in order that grace should not be denied. The characteristic forms of devotion developed in the late fifteenth century make intellectually tolerable and devotionally meaningful the repetition of identical acts, as in the Rosary, the Litanies, the Stations of the Cross and the Angelus. The growth at the same period of the doctrine that 'indulgences' might benefit the souls of the dead, suggesting that a man's eternal fate might be affected by the actions of somebody else and not be solely dependent on his moral status, reinforced the impression that salvation was not solely determined by moral stature. The result, naturally enough, was a religion often based on the fear of death and a psychological tension which too easily bred in turn a quasi-superstitious repetition of observances in order to secure a salvation not measurable in terms of moral achievement.

The need to shift this emphasis to promote more exclusively interior dispositions had become acute by about 1500. At that date, the success of Ludolph the Carthusian's meditations of the life of Christ had been established. The 'return to scripture' had already begun. All over Europe the humanists, to some extent confirming the work of earlier mystical writers, were to turn within five or six years to work on the text of scripture, the Pauline theology of the redemption and the spiritual values of the gospels. In 1516 Erasmus produced the first printed Greek text of the New Testament, called the *Novum Instrumentum* to emphasize its religious aims, and prefaced by a call for the vernacular dissemination of scripture which showed a daring confidence in the natural aspirations of redeemed humanity.

In France, Jacques Lefèvre d'Étaples (*c.* 1450–1536) began to turn his attention to the text of scripture when he moved to Saint-Germain in 1507. In 1509, he published five versions of the Latin psalter and in 1512 he translated and commented on the epistles of St Paul. He still worked on Aristotle and the medieval mystics and in 1522, after he had moved to the diocese of Meaux, he was to publish a series of gospel commentaries called the *Commentarii Initiatorii*. But thereafter he was to be exclusively concerned with the vernacular dissemination of scripture. In 1530, he published the first French translation of the whole Bible. The first Protestant translation was published by Olivétan in 1535.

Lefèvre was invited to Meaux by Guillaume Briçonnet, recently appointed bishop and intent on reforming not only his own diocese but, through the influence of Marguerite, sister of the king, François I, the whole of France. Under Lefèvre, he assembled a team of the finest humanists he could find. Briçonnet himself subsequently reacted against some of the 'Lutheran' tendencies which appeared at Meaux. One of his team, Guillaume Farel, went over to the Swiss reform, while another, Pierre Caroli, was for a time a Calvinist. But most of the scholars assembled at Meaux remained faithful to Rome and were protected by Marguerite when the Franciscans succeeded in having the reform suppressed in 1525, while the king was a prisoner in Madrid after the disastrous battle of Pavia and Marguerite had gone to intercede with the emperor.

The central evangelical humanist contention throughout Europe was that human perfection, and even religious perfection, was a product of moral achievement and not a non-empirical divine gift separable from any ethical status. One literary source widely used to support this view was the commentary on Plato's *Symposium* by the Florentine Marsilio

Ficino (1469). This commentary adopted the Plotinian myth that there are four degrees in the created cosmos, characterized by progressively less unification. Man's progress towards unification, which brings with it the beatifying union with God, is achieved through a series of steps and can be initiated by any one of four 'furores' (poetic or musical, prophetic, religious and erotic). It was an implication of this view that religious perfection was at the term of a natural movement of the affections. Ficino realized that his view implied the salvation of the ancient pagans, in spite of their lack of Christian belief, and in an important letter he proclaimed the sanctity of Socrates. His commentary on the *Symposium* established the *trattato d'amore* as a new literary genre, immensely influential in France. It was the first theoretical treatment of love to maintain squarely that the instinctively based affection was compatible with the spiritually fulfilling love acknowledged by many medieval authors. And Ficino's Augustinian apologetic in defence of immortality meant that his orthodoxy was not immediately in peril.

Ficino's view was slightly modified by Pico della Mirandola, even better known in sixteenth-century France. Pico, more eclectic than Ficino, pointed out that man could, by exercising his own autonomous and self-determining moral choice, either join the ranks of the angels or reduce himself to the level of the beasts. It was Pico more than anyone else who influenced the early Erasmus, and it was Pico's view of free will that Erasmus was later to defend against Luther. The mediator of Pico's view was John Colet, who first enthusiastically encouraged Erasmus to work on the text of scripture and who was himself deeply influenced in his evangelism by Ficino, although he later turned directly to St Paul.

Erasmus, however, was conscious of the difficulties in the Neoplatonist view, as developed from Ficino through Pico and Colet. At a period when religious 'faith' was universally equated with orthodox belief, the 'justification' dependent on faith could not, by definition, have been achieved by pagans. The salvation of the pagans became the key question. To admit it meant holding that justification was the product of moral achievement, and not of orthodox belief and practice.

Such sporadic attempts as had earlier been made to account for the possible salvation of ancient pagans and unbaptized babies had hinged not on ethical achievement but on such hypotheses as a sudden illumination at the hour of death. Even Aquinas had been unwilling to allow the possibility of non-culpable ignorance of the Christian revelation, although it may be said in excuse that in the thirteenth century the Americas had not yet been discovered. Ficino admitted the salvation of Socrates. In 1512, Lefèvre, with the Americans in mind, suggested that those who lived in accordance with the laws of nature and of God might be saved. In 1522, Erasmus's *Convivium Religiosum* gently probes the possibility of pagan virtue and suggests, after Ficino, the possible sanctity of Socrates. In 1523, Erasmus's preface to Cicero's *Tusculan Disputations* goes further in accepting Cicero's sanctity. The scholastics could continue in the sixteenth century to use torture in order to extract that external conformity to norms of behaviour and belief which, in their view, would 'save' heretics. The principle of the evangelical humanist opposition to them was precisely the view that human perfection, including religious perfection, was interior and moral. The difficulty was that such a view, by implying the possibility of grace for the pagans, dissociated religious justification from credal belief and so had implications which went beyond the bounds of orthodoxy.

But the evangelical humanists' belief in intrinsic human perfectibility also explains their opposition to the reformers. All the reformers were in rebellion against the late medieval religion of psychological tension in which the performance of 'works', if sufficiently intense, was thought to guarantee salvation without real reference to interior moral dispositions, or at any rate without sufficient emphasis on the importance of interior religious dispositions. The reformers, however, unlike the evangelical humanists, went so far in their opposition to theories of 'merit' as to deny to men any autonomous power of self-determination to good. Grace and justification, being gratuitous gifts of God, were not in man's own power to achieve. The reformers, that is, denied free will.

Technically, the problem could only be solved by regarding 'nature' itself as redeemed and therefore as capable of accepting grace in virtue not of its own powers but of its redeemed aspirations. This solution avoids allowing grace to be 'merited' while also leaving its acceptance in man's autonomous power. But it also involves allowing this power to pagans, and so separates grace from belief. The religious disputes of the early sixteenth century, although they spread out far beyond this central dilemma, were none the less caught up in the impossibility of reconciling a theory in which grace did not primarily depend on merit with one which allowed to man the power of self-determination to good. Any attempt to understand the scholastics, reformers and evangelical humanists of the sixteenth century must be based on an awareness of the existence of this central dilemma.

Erasmus had agreed with much that Luther had said about indulgences in the 1517 theses. When he finally came out against Luther, Erasmus picked, at the suggestion of Henry VIII, the absolutely central issue of free will. To Erasmus's diatribe *On Free Will* (1524), Luther answered with his treatise *On Unfree Will* (1525). Much more than Eucharistic theology, this was the centrally dividing doctrinal issue behind the schism and the only criterion for deciding, in the early sixteenth century, to which side anyone by right belonged.

The relationships between Renaissance, humanism and Reformation are subtle and complex. In the technical sense at least, Calvin was a humanist. His first published work was a commentary on a text of Seneca. It is generally true to say that, in France, a specifically Latin and Ciceronian humanism went hand in hand with reformatory ideas until about the middle of the century. But the Pléiade originated in a counter-reformatory group, and Ronsard's somewhat ostentatiously Greek and Erasmian humanism, like his poetic theory, was to some extent defined against the earlier tradition. In the first half of the century Rabelais, overwhelmingly the most important French author, is untypical in his total adhesion to Erasmian ideas. The king's sister Marguerite, who became queen of Navarre in 1528, moved from an almost Lutheran position in the 1520s towards a serious interest in Ficino before her death in 1549. The picture is distorted, too, by the fact that French studies necessarily give relatively greater attention to what happens to have been written in French. But the choice of French or Latin was sometimes haphazard, and there is a serious risk that the programmatic use of the vernacular might seem more significant than it was, because vernacular literature has attracted much more attention than Latin. Behind the authors, often untypical, and the texts of the French Renaissance loom a whole series of major historical problems about the nature of the sixteenth-century Renaissance in France and its relation to the very different sorts of 'humanism' which can be observed. It would be a mistake to offer solutions which are too firm, since discussion is still taking place. But this chapter attempts to provide some background to the major texts by trying to identify the issues and currents in whose light texts and events have to be understood and evaluated.

Art, Education and Early French Humanism[1]

During the fifteenth century, the kings of France had lived much more in the châteaux of the Loire than in a Paris still clustered within a mile of Notre-Dame. The dauphin son of Charles VI, born in 1403, escaped from Paris with his life in 1418 and removed the seat of government to Poitiers before making Bourges his capital in 1422. Only after the campaign of Joan of Arc, the relief of Orléans in 1429 and the taking of Paris in 1436 could he return as Charles VII. Within four weeks he left again for the Loire.

By the time his son Louis XI succeeded him in 1461, the Hundred Years War was over, the English had been driven back to Calais and the power of the feudal overlords was clearly waning. When Louis XI died in 1483, it had virtually been crushed, and France was almost unified into a single kingdom. The final consolidation of France into a single nation occurred under Charles VIII, who died in 1498 at Amboise where he had largely rebuilt the château. Louis XII, who made Blois his principle residence, reigned from 1498 to 1515.

The visual arts normally cross boundaries more slowly than ideas and values, and it is to the Italian campaigns of Charles VIII and Louis XII that we owe the introduction into France of the first clear break with medieval tradition in architecture and decoration. When Charles VIII left Italy, he brought with him to Amboise Italian works of art in considerable quantities. He also brought twenty-two craftsmen from Renaissance Italy. The upper part of the Tour des Minimes at Amboise and the frame of the upper door of the Tour Hurtault show clearly Italianate influence, the first traces in the heart of France of what we now call the Renaissance style of architectural decoration.

[1] In 1564 an edict fixed the beginning of the year on 1 January. This is the 'new style' of dating. The 'old style' had reckoned the year from Easter to Easter, but it had been employed only sporadically from the beginning of the sixteenth century. The result is that any date in February, which is before Easter, might be given as, say, 1534 new style but 1533 old style. In this chapter, dates have been given according to the new style. Where they differ by being one year in advance of dates given in reference books, it may be assumed that the works of reference are keeping to the old style. Unhappily, major problems of Renaissance chronology are still caught up in the difficulties of knowing which style is being used. Dates of publication of books, in particular, are often copied from title pages, which may employ old style dating. Wherever a date is known to have been according to the old style but to have been copied from a book published before Easter, this chapter has used the new style.

The death of Charles VIII stopped work at Amboise, but by December 1498 Louis XII had started building at Blois. We know that he transferred workmen from Amboise, and the interior façade of his generally traditional wing at Blois exploits a number of Italian decorative motifs. More interesting is the château at Gaillon in Normandy, dating from 1509–10. The Cardinal of Amboise, archbishop of Rouen and powerful Minister of Louis XII, had brought workmen from Amboise and Blois. But only when they were replaced from 1506 by local workmen less impervious to change were the traditional windows, decorated with ornamental columns and semicircular pediments, to create the first Renaissance façade in France.

The final triumph of the Italian decorative style was the magnificent wing at Blois built by François I, begun before the end of 1515 and left unfinished in 1524 when François left for Pavia. By 1515 the Italians had themselves abandoned their delicate ornamental style to return to classical severity under the influence of Raphael and Bramante. The exterior of the François I wing at Blois shows the influence of Bramante's work for Leo X, but it was to become in France the model for a style of decoration already obsolete in Italy and soon in France to be transposed into less decorative and more purely architectural terms.

The Loire was the preferred region of the upper nobility and of the poets and musicians they patronized. Paris remained the centre of intellectual life. Its university was the most important in Europe and it was the centre of theological orthodoxy. Estimates of student numbers vary wildly, but something between four and twelve thousand may reasonably be assumed for the early sixteenth century, with a city population of around 300,000. Most of the colleges had regional affiliations, but some of them specialized in teaching for the three graduate faculties of theology, canon law and medicine. The fourth graduate faculty, civil law, had been banished to Bourges and Orléans in the middle of the fourteenth century because it attracted too many students away from theology.

The only undergraduate discipline was arts, consisting of grammar, poetry, rhetoric and philosophy, but including a little mathematics and geography. The arts course normally finished at the age of eighteen, although Ramus at the Collège de Prêles boasted of getting his students through by fifteen. Thereafter it took about seven years for a doctorate in medicine or canon law and twelve or more for a doctorate in theology, taught exclusively in four of the colleges. The Dominican convent of St Jacques was the first to replace the *Sentences* of Peter Lombard with the *Summa* of Aquinas as the basis for commentary. The arts subjects were taught by graduate students. In 1362, the only date for which we have figures, there were 25 professors of theology, 11 of canon law, 27 of medicine and 449 of arts.

Students lived in halls of residence, generally sharing a room with a *magister*, or in town lodgings. Instruction was by lecture-commentaries, with frequent 'repetitions' in college and occasional disputations. Many students worked their way through the course by doing domestic chores. Some found patrons or benefices. Life was hard, food poor, discipline harsh and holidays short, especially in such foundations as Montaigu, reformed by Standonck in the fifteenth century largely in order to provide an educated entry into the secular clergy. Food cost two or three times as much in Paris as in the country, streets were used as drains and sewers, water was drawn from sixteen public fountains, everyone ate with his fingers and one was wise not to go out at night.

Printing came to Paris only in 1470, after presses had been established in a dozen other European towns, at the private instigation of Guillaume Fichet, librarian of the Sorbonne. Recently returned from Milan, he taught philosophy and theology in the mornings and commented on classical texts in the evenings. He was supported by Jean Heynlin, prior of the Sorbonne, and the press, manned by three Swiss, printed its first two dozen books in Roman characters. These included only three theological works, alongside Sallust, Cicero, Bessarion, Valla, Virgil, Juvenal and Terence. Fichet's own *Rhetoric* was printed, and, in a preface which compared Paris to Athens, proclaimed the importance of uniting rhetoric to philosophy and emphasized the importance of the ancient authors whose neglect had caused all the disciplines to languish. When Ramus was made a *lecteur royal* in 1552, he was programmatically named professor of eloquence and philosophy, still fighting the battle inaugurated by Fichet for the primacy of humanist values, represented by 'rhetoric' or 'eloquence', over the rough polemical style of scholastic 'philosophy'. But by 1552, the victory of 'eloquence' was assured. Budé had already gone much further than Fichet in associating the primacy of eloquence with the fully humane values of the education mediated by the cycle of liberal arts.

Fichet returned to Italy with Cardinal Bessarion in 1472. In 1473, the printers left the Sorbonne to start up on their own, switching to the production of theological and legal books in Gothic type. Guillaume Tardif, Fichet's most notable disciple after Gaguin, advised on the production of a thin stream of humanist books in semi-Roman type alongside the theological and liturgical works. At Lyon, where the first book printed in French appeared in 1476, the type was Gothic and no humanist works were published. By 1480 only nine French towns had presses and very few of them had printed humanist titles.

Fichet had been a theologian, humanist and diplomat. Of those who carried on his tradition, the most important was Robert Gaguin (1433–1501), general of the Maturins from 1473, humanist, diplomat and dean of the faculty of canon law. He formed round himself a group of humanists and reformers and, like the other Paris theologians, supported Pico della Mirandola. One of his close associates was the reforming preacher Jean Raulin, master of the Collège de Navarre from 1481, who left in 1497 to join the Benedictines at Cluny. His circle also included Guy Jouenneaux, who had commented on Valla's *Elegantiae* before joining the reformed Benedictine monastery of Chézal-Benoît in 1492, where he was soon to be joined by his humanist musician brother.

The small circle of humanists slowly expanded, not without quarrels. Filippo Beroaldo came to Paris from Bologna in 1476, a Neoplatonist philosopher who had published Virgil. Hieronymus of Sparta arrived in Paris the same year, to keep himself by copying manuscripts and teaching Greek. His pupils, who included Reuchlin, Erasmus, Budé and Beatus Rhenanus, do not always speak highly cf him, but Lefèvre d'Étaples became his friend. The humanist group was severe on ecclesiastical abuse, orthodox in theology and often mystically inclined. Their ideas on educational reform were still timid and their humanism did not permeate beyond the faculty of arts. Lefèvre joined the group before leaving for Italy to investigate the humanist Aristotelianism of Eramlao Barbaro and the more eclectic philosophy of Pico della Mirandola. By 1492 he was back, commenting on Aristotle at the Cardinal Lemoine College and already interested in the great Neoplatonist mystics. He was to edit the Pseudo-Denis (1499), Ramon Lull (1499) and Nicholas of Cusa (1514).

Lefèvre's early commentaries on Aristotle had endowed that author with a hidden mystical meaning, a *secreta analogia*, and Lefèvre himself wrote a disquisition on natural magic. In the 1499 edition of the Pseudo-Denis he identified the first convert of St Paul at Athens with Denis the first martyr of France, thereby asserting apostolic continuity for the French Church, consolidating the spiritual relationship between Athens and Paris and investing Neoplatonist theology with Pauline authority, as if to parallel the energetic attempts of other Neoplatonist humanists to demonstrate that the doctrine of Moses was passed on to

Plato through all or any of Orpheus, Hermes, Zoroaster and Pythagoras.

Lefèvre continued to edit Aristotle until, after the 1503 *Organon* with its prefatory diatribe against the Parisian terminists, the *Metaphysics* appeared in 1515. But from very soon after the turn of the century, his mind was in fact dominated by the Neoplatonist mystics, and especially by the advocate of *docta ignorantia*, Nicholas of Cusa, whom Lefèvre was to edit after Ruysbroeck, John of Damascus, the late antique Neoplatonist books known as the *Corpus Hermeticum* and believed by some Renaissance scholars to be older than the Bible, and some of the twelfth-century Victorines. Meanwhile, however, he had turned to the text of scripture. After moving to Saint-Germain-des-Prés in 1507, he published in 1509 the *Psalterium Quincuplex* containing five versions of the Psalms and a commentary entirely devoted to the mystical sense of the text. In 1512 followed the Latin translation of St Paul with a long commentary on the Vulgate text which, because it was clearly faulty, seemed to Lefèvre not to have been the work of St Jerome. At this date Lefèvre, who was to influence Luther before he was influenced by him, defends works as well as faith, upholds relics, pilgrimages, ascetical practices and the cult of Mary.

Lefèvre had from the beginning been associated with the monastic reformatory humanism of Gaguin. But he also sounded a new note of impatience at the abstract logic-chopping of late medieval scholasticism and extended the battle into the realms of moral and religious experience and even, with his scriptural activities, to theology itself. The Sorbonne theologians, technically competent defenders of an abstract intellectual system which they identified with ecclesiastical orthodoxy, were not in general pastorally concerned. Their leader in the 1520s, Noël Beda, was a resolute opponent of Lefèvre as he was of Erasmus, Berquin and, of course, Luther.

But Lefèvre also and increasingly moved on from the spirit of monastic humanism as it existed around 1490. The collaborator who had helped him for thirty years with the Aristotelian commentaries, Josse Clichtowe, became a practical reformer who, by 1513, was defending the monastic vows against Erasmus. He thought that a learned clergy with a more liturgical spirituality would put right what was wrong with the Church. From 1519 he was almost totally taken up with apologetic against Luther and Erasmus. Although he supported Lefèvre's *Disceptatio* of 1517 arguing that Mary Magdalen, the sinner of Luke VII and the sister of Lazarus were three different people, their outlooks were no longer the same. When Lefèvre moved to Meaux the break with Clichtowe was complete, and it may well have been Clichtowe who inspired Briçonnet's anti-Lutheran decrees of 1523.

But if Lefèvre went further than those humanists who, like Clichtowe, remained faithful to the spirit of Gaguin, he remained a mystic, even a spiritual dreamer, who never achieved the ironic articulateness of Erasmus. He no doubt did more than Erasmus for the vernacular dissemination of scripture, but his critical faculties were much less well developed. His refusal to consider the faulty Vulgate to be the work of Jerome argues an unreasonable regard for that Father's authority which Erasmus was unable to share. Lefèvre erroneously defended the authenticity of the writings of the Pseudo-Denis, later correctly rejected by Erasmus as earlier by Valla. Lefèvre even held that St Paul, if he was married, had a vow of chastity with his wife and could not have had a dispute with St Peter. Erasmus's critical mind allowed him no such easy ways out.

After the suppression of the Meaux reform, Lefèvre ended his life in the entourage of Marguerite at Nérac and at Blois. Marguerite herself was born in 1492, two years before her brother, François I. Her first husband died in 1525, by which time she had already written the *Dialogue en forme de vision nocturne*, which clearly reflected the theological views of Lefèvre as transmitted by Briçonnet. Brantôme tells us that Marguerite was afraid of death. The *Dialogue* was between herself and an eight-year-old niece she had lost in 1524. It draws on Dante and Petrarch, is mostly in Dante's *terza rima* and shows strong Neoplatonist influence. In the poem her niece assures Marguerite that death is painless and the body a prison for the soul which retains no memories of earthly life. All that is human and mortal must be consumed in the transcendent love which welcomes suffering. The path to salvation is faith, not works, and grace alone restores free will to fallen man. There is no salvation for pagans, however virtuous.

The *Dialogue* was first published in 1533, in the second edition of a 1531 collection of verse called the *Miroir de l'âme pécheresse* whose reformatory content provoked the Sorbonne. And in the Lent of 1533, Marguerite invited to preach before her Gérard Roussel, one of Lefèvre's collaborators in the Meaux reform. The situation was serious. The theology faculty had condemned works of Lefèvre and Erasmus, the *parlement* had banned vernacular translations of scripture and the burnings for 'blasphemy' had already begun. The 1533 collection of verse published by Marguerite contained a transposition of the well-known hymn to the Virgin, *Salve Regina*, into a hymn in honour of Christ, as well as a psalm translation by Marot.

Marguerite's collection of verse was put on the list of prohibited books. Early in October a skit on Marguerite and Roussel was performed at the Collège de Navarre. The king intervened and the theologians, led by Noël Beda, were forced to rescind the prohibition of Marguerite's book. Then on 1 November Nicolas Cop, an evangelical humanist from Sainte-Barbe who was rector of the university, preached a provocatively evangelical sermon at the Mass opening the academic year. Denounced by the irate theologians, Cop found it prudent to leave Paris, as also did the humanist reforming principal of Sainte-Barbe, Andrea de Gouvea, and the young humanist lawyer Jean Calvin. In October 1534 blasphematory pamphlets about the Mass (the *placards*) were posted up and down the kingdom, and especially on the door of the king's bedroom at Amboise. François I, hitherto concerned to protect the humanists, was now forced to regard the reformatory current as productive of political and social disruption and began the active suppression of heresy. In March 1536 appeared the first Latin edition of Calvin's *Institutes of the Christian Religion*. Schism had broken out in France.

Vernacular Literature to 1540

Among the books prohibited in 1533 is one which had appeared a year earlier over the name of Alcofribas Nasier, entitled *Pantagruel*. The author, disentangled from his anagram, was François Rabelais (*c.* 1494–1553), former Franciscan, former Benedictine, evangelical humanist, doctor, soon to become the most illustrious practitioner of the satirical novel that France has ever known.

Pantagruel started out as the continuation of the popularly successful *Grandes et Inestimables Chronicques de l'énorme géant Gargantua*. The tone is at first the same, although wit and learning quickly take precedence over irreverence and obscenity and a serious satirical undertone swiftly develops, making the novel unintelligible to the unlearned on any but the most superficial level. The obligatory episodes of the giant story, like that with the bells, are retained, but Rabelais quickly becomes bored with the routine popular money-spinner he apparently set out to write, and he parodies his own frivolous intentions with layer under layer of serious meaning, until only the most careful literary analysis can reveal on how many levels any particular episode has a reference. Rabelais clearly enjoys the game he has invented. He writes with immense vigour and energy, and he delights in sending up what he believes in as well as what he wants to attack, more to provide himself with a defence than to confuse the issue, which generally remains clear, but also no doubt with a sense of satisfaction at his own technical virtuosity, which was considerable. *Gargantua* (1535 is the likely date of the first edition, although 1534 is often supposed) continues to pretend to be a giant story, although the humour is already much more integrated into the narrative, serious satire predominates and the burlesque scarcely attempts any longer to conceal the serious imaginative exploration of humanist ideals in education, pacifism (with oblique but adverse reference to the behaviour of France's enemy, the emperor Charles V), and man's capacity for self-determination. From the *Third Book* onwards, the characters no longer depend on gigantic stature, Pantagruel becomes the spokesman for Rabelais and the humour is almost totally integrated into the narrative. The novel turns out to contain not only multiple layers of reference and meaning, but also a good deal of complex self-parody, being at once comic and serious about the same subjects, although at different levels.

For modern readers, there is too much Renaissance obscenity. Rabelais is both too coarse and too ingenious. There are too many feats of verbal ingenuity, puns, lists, non-languages. Some of the humour is pedantic. Only scholars can take delight in recognizing the source of Pantagruel's itinerary to Utopia or the allusion contained in the description of Gaster as the world's first master of arts. But underneath the coarse humour and the sophisticated wit, the pedantry and the overwhelming energy of the novel lies an extremely serious and important work of literature. The difficulties of access are considerable. But seldom can whole series of values have been so ruthlessly criticized and explored or projected in a single work as they are in Rabelais. Imaginatively, it probably achieves more than Shakespeare's tragedies or Beethoven's quartets. It is certainly one of the half dozen great masterpieces of European literature.

The work of Rabelais, which adheres closely to the ideas and values of Erasmus, incorporates a type of Renaissance 'satire' typified by More's *Utopia* which contains little irony but is essentially an imaginative projection and exploration of a new series of values. More, like the Renaissance authors of other Utopian legends, such as those concerned with the classical golden age and the Isles of the Blest, was exploring an ideal social order and ideal personal values which would promote social harmony. *Utopia* is not a blueprint but an experimental exploration into how humanist values might be combined to achieve a harmonious and peaceful society. Rabelais owes a good deal to More. He frequently refers to *Utopia*. He includes a full-scale mock encomium at the beginning of his *Third Book*. He deliberately conceals his use of Lucian as a source. But the all-important Thélème episode of *Gargantua* is the same sort of experimental dream as that conducted by More.

The sources of comedy in *Pantagruel* remain largely burlesque. Recondite authorities are quoted in learned languages in support of banalities and obscenities. A verbal ingenuity and imaginative exuberance create a superstructure of fantasy over a cutting satirical wit aimed especially at legal procedures and scholastic argument. The evangelical humanism becomes clearer towards the end of the book, although the original text of Pantagruel's speech to his prisoner in chapter 28 attacking the efficacy of meritorious works was prudently modified in later editions. The Pauline prayer before the battle with Loup Garou in the following chapter, however, subsists as an expression of the religion of Pantagruel and of Rabelais. The book ends with Epistemon's account of the underworld, certainly inspired by Lucian, and with the traditional episode, also Lucianic, of the giant's mouth, which Rabelais deliberately sends up by using incompatible scales of space and time.

Gargantua is much less episodic in structure. The birth of the giant, his education, a war and a scene with bells are all included, but the chapters group themselves round three centres of humanist interest, education, peace and the individual's power of self-determination. The famous last line of the prefatory verse

Pour ce que rire est le propre de l'homme

is an erudite joke alluding to the scholastic logicians whose invariable example of a logical *proprium* (not pertaining to a definition but always and only present when the definition was realized) was the *risibilitas* of the *animal rationale*.

The prologue to *Gargantua* takes up the theme of drink prominent in *Pantagruel*, and hints at its later serious transformation into the Neoplatonist Bacchic *furor*, with all its religious associations. Rabelais alludes to the *Symposium* of Plato and he goes on to develop the Erasmian image of the Silenus figures, frivolous outside but precious within. Erasmus, slightly transposing the image, had added Christ to the list. Rabelais is not warning the reader of any allegorical meaning for his novel, but he may well be humorously hinting at a semi-serious intention, the 'sustantificque mouelle' beneath the comedy.

Gargantua takes the side of François I against Charles V so wholeheartedly that it can no longer be considered as audacious a text as used to be thought. But the provocative evangelical humanism was toned down in subsequent editions to accord with the king's new policy of religious repression. The book starts with the accounts of Gargantua's birth and education, in a section culminating in chapter 23, where Ponocrates puts into practice the humane education sketched in chapter 8 of the earlier book, in which the restored study of ancient languages allied to evangelical religion is seen as the path to wisdom and virtue. The second section, on war, is recounted with even more moral comment, including another letter from father to son (chapter 29) setting forth a love of peace and allowing a just war only after exhausting every other possible resource and, even then, shedding as little blood as possible. The relationship of fathers to sons is something Rabelais always takes seriously. It enables us to identify his own attitude with that of Grandgousier here, and with that of Gargantua (and hence also with that of Pantagruel) in the *Third Book*. The humanism of Grandgousier towards his prisoners is emphasized and the whole section on peace and war ends with Gargantua's remarkable harangue to his defeated opponents (chapter 50).

The final section, the Thélème episode, is more dense and more complex. Thélème is obviously an anti-monastery, created (chapter 52) by reversing all the established monastic vows and regulations. Instead of poverty, chastity and obedience, there is luxury, marriage and freedom. Rabelais uses this technique of reversing what is normal for comic effect, as in the Chicquanous episode of the *Fourth Book*. But, at least on the surface, Thélème is a satire on monastic life. More deeply, however, it is an exploratory dream which probes into the possibility that human nature and human instinct, given every possible advantage of talent, birth, upbringing and environment, might provide reliable guides to human fulfilment. The result of totally free choice is also social harmony (chapter 57). Rabelais is exploring imaginatively the possible conditions under which man is perfectible intrinsically, in accordance with his natural desires and instincts and not simply by abnegating them. More deeply still, however, Rabelais, who quotes Erasmus's polemic against Luther in his famous 'Fay ce que voudras' passage, is in the Thélème episode taking Erasmus's side in defending an autonomous power in man of self-determination. The very word

Thélème means will, and Rabelais leaves no doubt that he thinks it implies genuinely free choice, whatever the difficulties might have been in reconciling the power of free choice with the gratuity of grace.

Rabelais did not publish his *Third Book* until 1546. Erasmus and Lefèvre d'Étaples had both died in 1536. The French reformers, and even the evangelical humanists, had broken with Erasmus. Lefèvre's team had always mistrusted him. The French Ciceronians deeply resented the brilliantly satirical *Ciceronianus* of 1528, in which Erasmus seemed to have reduced Budé to the same level as the printer Josse Bade. The French humanists, all of them interested in vernacular writing, protected by Marguerite de Navarre, leaned further towards Luther than Erasmus. Some of them approached syncretism.

In 1538, Bonaventure des Périers, the author of an important collection of *contes*, published the enigmatically Lucianic *Cymbalum Mundi*. He had worked with Olivétan on the first Protestant Bible in French (1535) and had collaborated with Dolet in the production of his great Latin dictionary (1536 and 1538). In 1550 Calvin included him amongst those who had turned their back on the gospel. Henri Estienne gives a lurid and highly suspect account of his suicide.

The interpretation of the *Cymbalum* is still disputed. It is clearly a satire on various human attitudes. It is not an atheist declaration, although the famous second dialogue certainly shows a weakening of dogmatic commitment and a movement towards syncretism. The *Cymbalum* can still be interpreted as an evangelical document, although not to the taste of Calvin in 1550. The disputed question is not so much whether the *Cymbalum* is sceptical as whether it is simply anti-intellectual. It is perfectly possible that a concern with religious values in a situation of dogmatic dispute should produce a sort of satirical agnosticism about dogmas which none the less is a vehicle for serious religious concern.

Étienne Dolet (1509–46) was in many ways similar to des Périers, although a more ardently Ciceronian humanist and a more actively reformatory publisher. Dolet published against Erasmus a dialogue defending the cult of Cicero (1535) and the famous *Commentarii Linguae Latinae* (1536 and 1538). In 1538, he opened a printing press in Lyon. By 1542 he had published thirty-six titles, of which only three had religious relevance, but in six months of 1542 fourteen of thirty-four new titles were works of piety. Works of Calvin and Melanchthon were among his stock. It is ultimately on account of his publishing and bookselling activities that he was executed in 1546, although the actual charge of heresy arose from a perfectly innocent translation of the pseudo-Platonic *Axiochus* in which, it was alleged, Dolet had denied the immortality of the soul by slightly expanding the Greek text.

It does seem, however, that Dolet's commitment to evangelical piety was accompanied by a diminished belief in the possibility of dogmatic certainty, to judge at least from some of the passages of personal reflection in the *Commentarii*. In Dolet and Bonaventure des Périers, there are no more than germinating seeds of religious scepticism. But they are sufficient to show how scepticism could and did develop, like the reform, from the movement already apparent in the late fifteenth century to attach more importance to interior values, moral, spiritual and social, than to dogmatic commitment as such.

The confidence of the early Renaissance was not so much in the powers of reason as in the aspirations of nature. The particular forms taken by the Renaissance, or the Reformation, in France could not have been predicted and were anyway not unified. But once it was generally felt that in certain circumstances human beings could trust their own natures to guide them towards their spiritual and moral fulfilment a whole series of strains and tensions with fifteenth-century scholastic orthodoxy was bound to be generated. It is these strains and tensions which lie behind the events as they actually took place. They do not explain the Reformation, or incipient religious scepticism, but they can be seen to underlie these phenomena, like so many others in the early sixteenth century.

Plato and Poetry to 1560

Until about 1540, humanism and evangelical reform had nourished one another. Calvin was a humanist. The first edition of the *Institutes* refers to the 'philosophy of Christ'. Théodore de Bèze, his successor at Geneva and principal lieutenant, was also an accomplished humanist. But by 1540 the word 'humanist' is ambiguous. The French reformers, like the Catholic faculties of Louvain and Douai, remained 'humanist' in the sense of deriving their theology from scriptural and patristic sources which they read in the original languages. But in neither Louvain nor Geneva was there any trust in human nature's power to guide man to his moral perfection and fulfilment.

The humanist tradition which did trust natural aspirations developed after 1540 in close association with a wave of Neoplatonism which originated in the circle of Marguerite de Navarre, and crossed a cultural barrier to nourish the poets of the Pléiade. It was also associated with the advanced position in the *Querelle des femmes*, itself reflected in the beginnings of social emancipation and a new way of writing about love.

The first translations of Plato began to appear soon after 1540 in the entourage of Marguerite. The *Lysis* was translated by Bonaventure des Périers, the *Crito* by Simon Vallambert. Dolet's translations of two apocryphal dialogues appeared in 1544 and in 1546 Richard Le Blanc's translation of the *Io* was published, in the same year as the Siméon du Bois translation of the Ficino commentary on the *Symposium*. Christian Platonism was not new in France. The Lyon doctor Symphorien Champier had already exploited it in a whole series of works, and Charles de Bouelles had drawn on it. But there is a wholly new flavour after 1540.

Dolet had published at Lyon in 1542 the poem of the Parisian Antoine Héroët, *La Parfaite Amie*. In 1536 Héroët, who had received a pension from Marguerite, had composed a poetic version of the Androgyne legend from Ficino's translation of the *Symposium*. The *Parfaite Amie* puts into the mouth of a woman the idealized Ficinian view of love as perfective and conducive to beatitude, although also instinctive and productive of *volupté*. It is not a poem of the highest literary merit, but it is not surprising that the advanced Neoplatonism of Ficino should reappear in sixteenth-century France in the context of an advanced position on the role of women. It is not surprising, either, that the advanced position in the *Querelle des femmes* should be particularly associated, like Ficinian Neoplatonism, with the town of Lyon. Lyon was near enough to Italy to be a natural clearing-house for cultural importations from the south, while the proximity of Geneva made it an increasingly important centre for cultural and religious activity. The absence of either a *parlement* or a university contributed to a distinctly liberal, even radical, atmosphere, and the consequent influx of poets, scholars and humanists, among them many patronized by Marguerite de Navarre, made Lyon for a time the liveliest centre of cultural activity in France.

The moral and intellectual inferiority of women was still argued by most of the scholastics and a few humanists. Agrippa of Nettesheim's *De nobilitate et praecellentia foeminei sexus* (1509, published 1529) had gone so far as to argue the superiority of women, perhaps with less than total seriousness. Among the other champions of marriage and women's rights were Erasmus, Bouchard, François de Billon and Rabelais, although Rabelais could also mock the feminist misunderstandings of

Plato which derived from Ficino. Of great influence, too, was the French version of Castiglione's *Il Cortegiano* which contained a somewhat attenuated version of Ficino's doctrine. *Il Cortegiano* appeared in French in 1537. In 1542 Bertrand de la Borderie published his reactionary *Amie de cour* attacking the Petrarchan view of love as an emotion of sighing and suffering and which reduced women's power to the level of sexual seduction. The provocation was quickly taken up by the advanced party, particularly by Charles Fontaine, who was to defend Marot's usage against the Pléiade, in the *Contr'Amie de cour* and then by Héroët, as later by Gilles Corrozet in *Le Compte du rossignol* (1546).

It was at Lyon in 1544 that appeared the first complete cycle of poems in French devoted to singing the vicissitudes of the poet's love for one woman, Maurice Scève's *Délie*, a series of 449 ten-line stanzas arranged in groups of nine under fifty different emblems. The lady was probably Pernette du Guillet, herself a poet of distinction, but the poetic stylization of Scève's work diminishes the importance of such scanty biographical information as we have. Broadly speaking, Scève belongs to the Petrarchan tradition popular in Italy and widely adopted by neo-Latin poets in France, many of whom were associated with Lyon. Scève indeed pays homage to Petrarch himself at the beginning and end of his sequence and he draws on a large common stock of Petrarchan images and conceits, although he exploits them in conjunction with a new and almost systematic psychology of the emotions. The emblems with their attached mottoes seem only loosely connected with the stanzas and, although the *Délie* was at first considered primarily as an emblem book, its interest today rests on the sometimes masterly poetic effects achieved by the interplay of images, rhythms and syntax.

In the course of the sequence the poet resigns himself to a love which, while reciprocated, can never be satisfied. At the outset love's birth is described as sudden and overwhelming. The final *dizains* draw heavily on Speroni's *Dialoghi* (1542) and are more openly Platonist in inspiration. The sequence ends with the affirmation,

> Aussi je voy bien peu de differencе
> Entre l'ardeur, qui noz coeurs poursuyura,
> Et la vertu . . .

In spite of the stylized Petrarchan images and the abstraction of much of the language, the real emotion which infuses the best of the *dizains* announces the Pléiade, for whom the emotional content of poetry was to be all-important.

In the early years of the century, French poetry had been dominated by the courtly tradition of elegant and witty, but trivial, allegorical or merely encomiastic verse as practised by Jean Marot, Crétin, Molinet, Gringore and Meschinot. The name *rhétoriqueurs* applied to these poets was intended to be pejorative, and much of their poetry consisted in a sort of verbal acrostic, depending for its effect on puns and intricate metrical patterns. There was, however, a gradual movement towards the adoption of classical forms. Jean Lemaire de Belges (1473–1524?), who admired Petrarch and made a fleeting reference to poetic inspiration, continued the late fifteenth-century effort to found French culture on antique tradition in his prose work *Les Illustrations de Gaule* (1511–13), which earned him considerable fame. His *Concorde des deux langages*, an allegory urging the harmony of French and Italian cultures, is partly in *terza rima*. Lemaire was clearly influenced by Ovid, whose *Héroïdes* were translated into French by Octavien de Saint-Gelais in 1497. The nephew of Octavien, Mellin de Saint-Gelais (1491–1558), was a more important, if somewhat precious, poet and one of the first to adopt the sonnet form in France.

The most important poet in the *rhétoriqueur* tradition, however, was undoubtedly Clément Marot (1496–1544). Boileau's contemptuous dismissal of his 'badinage élégant' is an injustice. He certainly composed a considerable number of poetic trivia, but he was also a serious humanist and religious poet, and even his lighter work is distinguished for its qualities of wit, grace and delicacy. His great achievement was to adapt himself to such classical forms as the eclogue, the epigram and the *épître* in place of the complex traditional forms inherited from the Middle Ages. Marot entered the service of Marguerite in 1519 before succeeding to his father in the king's service in 1526. After the *Placards* of 1534, Marot went into exile at the brilliant court of Ferrara, and when he returned to France in 1536 he had acquired a much greater familiarity with the Latin poets, especially Juvenal and Martial. In 1542 Dolet published Marot's satirical *Enfer*, possibly without his permission, and Marot retreated swiftly to Geneva, where Calvin encouraged him to continue his translation of the psalms.

Marot's poetry became simple, direct and clear as well as graceful and witty, infused in his best pieces with real emotion. Technically, his development is important and his work links the *rhétoriqueur* tradition to the Pléiade. In the full sense, he was neither humanist nor Lutheran. But his intimate religious poetry, his extension of the epigram into the sonnet, his grace and charm explain why Ronsard, for instance, keen to proclaim his own revolution, was unable to decide whether Marot was a glorious predecessor or a poet whose techniques epitomized what the revolution was against.

Also in the realm of religious verse, but now much less close to the reform, were the spiritual confessions of Marguerite de Navarre, the three books of *Prisons*. After the 1533 *Miroir*, Marguerite published no major work until her secretary, Antoine du Moulin, edited in 1547 the *Marguerites de la Marguerite des Princesses*, a substantial volume containing many short poems, some comedies and the long poem *La Coche*. The prose *Heptaméron*, originally intended to run to a full hundred stories, was published only posthumously (incompletely by Boaistuau in 1558 and completely by Gruget in 1559). The *Dernières Poésies*, which completely alter Marguerite's poetic stature, were only published in 1896.

The third and by far the longest book of the *Prisons* from the *Dernières Poésies* is much the most important item in the volume. Marguerite recounts her efforts to acquire learning in poetry, the liberal arts, philosophy and theology before finding satisfaction in the Bible and gradually achieving liberation from the 'cuyder de sçavoir' in the word which breaks the bonds of sin, consoles the living and brings eternal life to the dead, 'Je suys qui suys'. In the course of the ensuing meditation on this revelation Marguerite averts swiftly to the understanding of it mediated by the hermetic books, with which she is clearly acquainted. They had been published by Lefèvre in Ficino's translation. But if Marguerite's mysticism still shows the influence of Lefèvre, she now draws an important new conclusion from the idea of a primitive hermetic illumination by the Holy Spirit outside the Judaic revelation. The 'cognoissance naïfve . . . qui tout homme illumine' leads directly to an implied affirmation of pagan virtue. Socrates, whose death speech is almost translated, died illumined by 'ceste charitable clarté de Dieu'. Marguerite has rejoined the Lefèvre of 1512 and gone back on the *Dialogue*'s rejection of pagan virtue. She manifests, too, a new admiration for Plato.

Prose Literature of the Mid-Century

The *Heptaméron* is a collection of *contes* linked by a series of conversations between the 'devisants' who discuss the moral, social and religious issues raised by one another's stories. In so far as it is a collection of *contes*, the *Heptaméron* is important for a new seriousness, an interest in psychology, a care for *vraisemblance* and the alternation of long and short, sad and gay, subtle and coarse material. The narrative technique is swift and direct, and there are clear references to real people and events. The treatment of the aristocracy is better than that of other classes. There is localization without precise detail and some effort at realism about customs and dress. Both realism and psychological acumen mark an advance on previous collections of *contes*.

But the real interest of the volume centres very largely on the discussions after each *conte*. There are signs in the composition of the work that the first five days (fifty *contes*) were written in 1546–7. Writing was probably interrupted on the death of Marguerite's brother, François I, in April 1547. The remaining portion of the book probably dates from after October 1548. Marguerite and her husband Henri are fairly clearly identified with the characters Parlamente and Hircan. The overwhelming probability is that the other characters were also real and contributed a number of the stories which they narrate. In particular Oisille, the wise old evangelical humanist, seems likely to have been Louise de Daillon, the grandmother of Brantôme. The religious pattern is much stronger from the beginning of the sixth day. The end of the volume is hurried, and the comparatively simple rules for the order of narrators are broken.

Modern criticism suggests that the *Heptaméron* reflects a real discussion in the entourage of Marguerite rather than a stylized and imaginary one. The characters' points of view therefore become more important. Hircan, Parlamente's husband, shows interest in honour, military prowess and hunting. He despises the women he loves and is the spokesman for simple male supremacy, cynical, brutal and the only character to have a good word to say for the Franciscans. Parlamente, on the other hand, tentatively gropes towards the Ficinian view of love. Dagoucin stands by the courtly code in which love is purely the projection of a moral aspiration on to an idealized object. It may not even be declared: 'je n'ose penser ma pensée, de paour que mes oeilz en revelent quelque chose.' Saffredent disagrees: 'Il me semble que c'est beaucoup mieulx faict d'aymer une femme comme femme, que d'en ydolatrer plusieurs comme on fait d'une ymaige.' Parlamente thinks that no one has ever loved God perfectly 'qu'il n'ait parfaictement aymé quelque creature en ce monde'. Saffredent later ironically argues that a true lover cannot commit serious sin with the object of his love, 'veu que c'est ung degré pour monter à l'amour parfaicte de luy, où jamais nul ne monta, qu'il n'ait passé par l'eschelle de l'amour de ce monde'.

The confrontation of ethical values in the dialogue links between the *contes* lifts the *Heptaméron* to the status of a literary exploration of the meaning of human experience of quite special interest. It probes not only into the meaning of love but also into the distinction between guilt and scandal, the malice of hypocrisy and the fundamental principles of evangelical humanism.

Some of the important prose writers between 1540 and 1562, like Ramus, wrote only in Latin. The chief interest of others was theology and religious controversy. Sebastien Castellio (1515–63) reacted against the burning of Michel Servet for heresy at the end of a prosecution led by Calvin and wrote his *Conseil à la France désolée* (1562). He was attacked by Bèze and refrained from publishing his reply. But his thoroughgoing attack on any attempt to force consciences is important. Louis Le Roy (1510–77), best known for his translations of Aristotle and Plato, was an important political thinker whose works reflect a gradual move away from Neoplatonist optimism as France moved towards the wars of religion. Among the prose writers whose work had reflected Neoplatonist optimism at its height were Pontus de Tyard (1521–1605) and Jacques Peletier du Mans (1517–82).

Pontus de Tyard's philosophical dialogues, and in particular his *Solitaire premier* (1552), reproduce the whole panoply of Ficinian theory on both love and poetic inspiration. The Solitaire enters into ecstasy when he finds his Pasithée measuring an ode, in French, to the music of her lute, so combining at least four activities of special significance in the mid-century tradition of Neoplatonist poetic theory (the classical form, the idea of 'measuring', the vernacular, the combination of poetry and music). Jacques Peletier du Mans illustrates another sort of Neoplatonist inspiration, owing more to Cusa than to Ficino. Inspired by the antique ideal of moral formation mediated by encyclopedic knowledge, in which all the disciplines are united by the mind of the knower, he elaborated a theory in which the mathematical principles underlying the cosmos could be mentally reconstructed on the basis of the proportions contained in the human memory. Poetry and music therefore became the means by which man accomplished his task of reconstituting within himself the spiritual form of the cosmos, thereby uniting himself with nature and with God, and achieving his own spiritual perfection. This is a particular articulation of an altogether new view developing about the status of the poet and the moral and religious significance of his activity. It also explains the quite general importance attributed in the sixteenth century, by Ronsard as well as others, to the 'scientific' poetry which strove to reconstitute in the mind and reveal to the hearer the secret order of the universe.

One of the literary *genres* to which the revival of interest in Plato gave birth was naturally the Platonic dialogue. The mid-century saw a great increase in the number of philosophical dialogues, although none of them is of major imaginative significance. The most important among the numerous authors are perhaps Guy de Bruès, who attempted in an important series of dialogues to establish the mind's capacity for reaching certainty, and Louis le Caron (1534–1613), who much more typically aspired to lead men to virtue. Both authors were loosely associated with the mid-century poetic movement led by Ronsard, and Bruès shows some signs of having been influenced by the thought of Ramus.

In some ways the *Third Book* of Rabelais (1546) is itself the prototype for the vernacular philosophical dialogues. The giants are now most of the time ordinary mortals, at least in stature. The comedy has become more subtle, more intellectual, more closely integrated into the narrative. Pantagruel throughout, and Gargantua when he appears, are figures of wisdom and insight. The comedy is still prodigious. But underneath Panurge's desire to know whether to get married and, if he does so, to be assured that he will not be cuckolded, lies a serious attempt to define a new series of values and an ideal way of living. Evangelical humanism still exercises a strong influence, as does Erasmus personally, but there begins to emerge a joyous and energetic personal ideal which, based on the Epictetan contempt for fortuitous things, leads to a trust in God coupled with a confident power of personal self-determination. This ideal is summed up under the name of 'Pantagruelism' and several times defined, notably in the prologue to the *Fourth Book* (1552), as a 'certaine gayeté d'esprit conficte en mespris des choses fortuites'.

Even more than *Gargantua*, the *Third Book* and the *Fourth Book* communicate to the reader on all sorts of different levels. The *Third Book* opens for instance with an amusing harangue by Panurge in praise of debt, a good example of a Lucianic mock encomium and of the ability of Rabelais to achieve comic effects by turning all that is normal, sane and reasonable upside down. Underneath the comedy, however, are serious allusions to the evangelical virtues and to the Neoplatonist circle of love which, because it binds the world together and the world to God, is known as the *vinculum mundi*. Similarly in the *Fourth Book*, the storm episode, clearly a comic elaboration of Erasmus's rather dry colloquy *The Shipwreck*, reveals underneath the comedy a quite serious moral message about prayer and trust in God.

The *Third Book* is dedicated to Marguerite de Navarre and it includes much comic philosophical discussion woven round the theme of Panurge's quest. The *Fourth Book* is a travelogue which at times draws near to being a collection of satirical parables. It seems unlikely that the fifth and last book is all by Rabelais, but some very recent criticism suggests that some or even most of it may be, not least on account of the brilliance of such episodes as the *Isle sonante* and the *Chats fourrés* which satirize respectively the Church and the judiciary. The whole work is the product of one of the most powerful and energetic imaginations of any period. It combines pure fantasy with deadly serious satire, self-parody with the coarsest comedy, serious learning with immense wit, humanist concern with an energetic feeling for the ridiculous and the grotesque. Rabelais never ceases to relish and to laugh at his own cleverness. Reading him carefully is to follow him as author through the initial wave of boredom with his own giant story, in spite of its boisterous fun, to become fascinated with him by the way in which he could turn comedy into a vehicle at different levels for communicating profound convictions and exploring deeply the whole spectrum of personal and social experience, as it required to be explored for his generation.

The Pléiade to 1560

If there are few rivals to Rabelais for the title of France's greatest novelist, and none who can pretend to his range of interest and technique, the mid-sixteenth century also saw a great galaxy of French poets, of whom the greatest was undoubtedly Pierre de Ronsard (1524–85), the central figure of what came, on account of a passing reference by Ronsard in 1556, to be called the 'Pléiade'. Ronsard is today best known for his love lyrics and his nature poetry, both of them fresh, sensitive, delicately and exactly communicating his feelings in all their spontaneous individuality. He regarded himself above all as a scholar-poet. He accepted as axiomatic the morally and even religiously enriching nature of the experience mediated in and by poetry, especially when set to music, and he attached much importance to the imitation of classical authors and the exploitation of antique myths. His real poetic achievement may lie outside the elaboration of his Neoplatonist poetic theory and his complex deployment of classical learning, but his poetry cannot finally be understood without some reference to the considerable body of poetic theory which appeared to him to justify his creative activity.

Both Ronsard and Du Bellay (1522–60) knew Jacques Peletier du Mans (named by Ronsard as a member of the 'Brigade' of seven from 1552). Although Ronsard started by writing in Latin and Du Bellay continued to write Latin poems throughout his short life, it was from Peletier that both absorbed the idea of enriching their own vernacular, primarily by imitating in it the great poets of antiquity. In 1544 Ronsard joined the household of Lazare de Baïf, ex-ambassador to Venice, to work with Lazare's son Jean-Antoine (1532–89) under Dorat, the second person to be a really important influence on Ronsard's poetic development. It was Dorat who taught Ronsard to envelop moral truth in antique fable and to cultivate the Pindaric ode.

In 1547 Dorat moved to the Collège de Coqueret with Ronsard and Jean-Antoine de Baïf, who were now joined by Du Bellay. The Brigade existed in embryo. Its attitude to Scève and Marot was to be equivocal. To Dolet's views it was opposed on almost all points. Dolet sympathized with the reform. Ronsard's satirical *Discours*, however moderate and tolerant they start off, are all polemically Catholic, while Baïf spent much of his life translating the psalms to oust the 'heretical' translations of Marot and Bèze. Dolet was a Latin humanist. Ronsard somewhat ostentatiously vaunted his preference for the Greeks. Dolet wrote a treatise on translation. Ronsard and Du Bellay insisted on 'imitation'. Dolet wrote in Latin. The manifestos of the Brigade insisted on the enrichment ('illustration') of the vernacular.

In 1548 Thomas Sebillet (1512–89) issued his *Art poétique*, the first major treatise on poetic practice since Fabri's *Art de pleine rhetorique* (1521). Sebillet confines himself to codifying the usage of Marot and Scève, but on several important points, and notably on the religiously and morally elevating role of the inspired poet, the distinction between art and inspiration and the introduction of the ode and the sonnet, he steals the thunder of Ronsard's group, while continuing to give information about the complex rhyme schemes of the *Chant Royal* and to admire the *rhétoriqueurs*. Ten months later came the reaction from Du Bellay in the group's first manifesto, the *Défense et illustration de la langue française* (1549) prefacing Du Bellay's *Olive*. A great deal derives from the Italian Speroni, and more than a little comes from Cicero and Quintilian. The real originality of the *Défense* lies in the emphasis it puts on the need for the poet to move his hearers emotionally. It insists on the need to enrich the vernacular and on the doctrine of imitation, but it does not satisfactorily resolve the problem of reconciling the need for inspiration with the need for the poet to be a scholar. Both needs were felt strongly by the Pléiade, but their reconciliation on the plane of theory was rarely to prove adequate.

The *Défense*, like Ronsard's theoretical writings, in the end gropes towards a new form of poetry more than it legislates for one. In practice, Ronsard's imitation differs from translation largely in that he re-feels and often re-situates or modifies the images he takes from ancient authors. In practice, too, inspiration means something very close to emotion. In spite of the insistence on the necessity for scholarship, Du Bellay can say in the *Défense*: 'celuy sera veritablement le poëte que je cherche en nostre langue, qui me fera indigner, apayser, enjouyr, douloir, aymer, hayr, admirer, etonner, bref, qui tiendra la bride de mes affections, me tournant ça et la à son plaisir. Voyla la vraye pierre de touche . . .' Du Bellay is here remembering Cicero, and much of his own poetry is not primarily distinguished by its emotional power. The Pléiade poets were not romantics. But Du Bellay's assertion, taken in conjunction with Ronsard's views on inspiration, mean that emotion in the poet is becoming an important criterion of aesthetic achievement. It also explains in passing the important connection in the sixteenth century between poetry and rhetoric. Following Aristotle, the sixteenth century poetic theorists included under the term rhetoric the theory of how to arouse and appease the various passions in an audience.

Ronsard's own lyric poetry combines a freshness of emotional inspiration with a careful imitation of antique authors. At times the Greeks are of more interest to him, in fact as well as theory. The influence of Pindar, Anacreon and the poets of the Greek anthology broke over him in seemingly irresistible waves. But the influence of the Latins, and especially of Horace, Virgil, Catullus, Propertius and Tibullus, was constant and perhaps more important, although increasingly diffused. The early Petrarchan imagery is left behind as Ronsard's verse loses an early stiffness and replaces a style heavily dependent on classical allusions with what Ronsard called his 'beau style bas'. Neither Petrarch nor the classics could in the end provide Ronsard with a means of poetic expression adequate to explore his own attitudes and sentiments. There is no doubt much poetic affectation in the somewhat stylized way in which Ronsard depicts his relationship with Hélène de Surgères in the final cycle of love sonnets, but they have a very real emotional depth, and the poetic technique has become supple, personal and mature. It is the relationship which is stilted, not the poetic technique which now owes to Petrarch only some of its decorative motifs.

The nature poetry, renowned for its freshness, its regional roots and its ecstatic pleasure in the countryside of the lower Loire valley, shares some of the characteristics of the love poetry. It is intimate and, for all its close derivation from the antique, it remains precisely aware of the physical and sensuous qualities of landscape. In many ways it paved the way for the introduction of the pastoral in France.

Ronsard himself, however, never regarded the poetry of nature and love as sufficient to justify the high moral status he ascribed to poetic activity and on account of which so much of his verse refers to and loudly invited musical accompaniment. The early Pindaric odes had adapted the Greek form for singing the praises of athletic heroes into a vehicle for praising the achievements of artists, statesmen and scholars. The *Hymnes* and the *Poèmes* carry on this encomiastic function while often also fitting in to the Neoplatonist tradition of Peletier du Mans. Ronsard belongs to the mainstream of scientific poetry in his attempt mentally to reconstitute the spiritual truths of the cosmos and the moral realities of human life, and to communicate them under the guise of fable and myth. But his use of the alexandrine to develop moral and philosophical subjects, his learning, his seriousness of moral purpose and his technique transformed the genre into something more exciting and more important. It is generally considered that the unfinished patriotic epic, the *Françiade*, written in decasyllables, was a failure. It does, however, show us how Ronsard's moral purpose was also extended into a patriotic one and how keen he was to establish, with so many Renaissance patriots, antique derivation for French Renaissance culture. Not surprisingly, Ronsard's religious commitment is made clear in the *Discours*, written at and just after the outbreak of the wars of religion. These satirical poems again mark a wholly new departure in the writing of satirical verse and demonstrate a flexibility in the exploitation of the alexandrine sufficient to raise polemical verse into poetic achievement of the highest order.

Du Bellay's inspiration was not so much lyrical as satirical and elegiac. There is here even something of the verbal skill of an earlier generation, though now allied to a rigorous control of sonnet form and neoclassical genres. The delicate nostalgia of the *Antiquités* and the *Regrets* (both published in 1558) owes less to Petrarch than did Du Bellay's earlier poems, and both collections show exquisite mastery of the elegiac and satirical sonnet forms. They are lyrical in a sense different from that in which the term can be applied to Ronsard's love poetry. Behind the nostalgia, there is always a philosophical reflection, almost a meditation, which gives the poems point and strength. Du Bellay, surprisingly, also wrote in Latin and translated Virgil. He preferred the Latins to the Greeks. Had he lived beyond 1560 (in which year he was thirty-eight), we might now see the Pléiade not as a group inspired by Dorat and led by Ronsard, but as a real constellation of independently original poets.

As it is, the Pléiade was a group of seven poetic innovators constituted by Ronsard and those with whom he wished to be associated. The kernel was the original Coqueret trio, Baïf, Ronsard and Du Bellay. Dorat and Nicolas Denisot were close associates. The publication of Ronsard's first odes made him the leader of the new school in 1550. In that year Guillaume des Autels and Pontus de Tyard, both from Lyon, made contact with the group. In 1551, it is Charles de Sainte-Marthe. Thereafter the production of Jodelle's tragedy *Cléopâtre captive* (1553) brought Jodelle, Grévin and Belleau into the group. In 1553, Ronsard names these and several others. In the end he lists six poetic companions, the final list of the Pléiade, Du Bellay, Tyard, Baïf, Peletier, Jodelle, Belleau. The Pléiade is a myth. It was a mutable list generally of seven names, chosen from a possible score of poets who were associated with the general aims of Ronsard, or with some of them, and never including some of the most distinguished. Its final achievement was totally to liberate French poetry from the constraints and the timid classicism of the *rhétoriqueurs*.

The Wars of Religion

François I had died in 1547, two months after Henry VIII. He was succeeded by his second son Henri II, husband of Catherine de Medici. In 1548 Jeanne d'Albret, daughter of Marguerite de Navarre, married Antoine de Bourbon. Their child was to become Henri de Navarre, later Henri IV. In 1548, too, the dauphin son of the new king Henri II became engaged to Mary Stuart. Henri II's reign lasted until 1559. In that year he concluded the treaty of Cateau-Cambrésis with Philip II of Spain, so ending the Italian wars. His sister married the Duke of Savoy and Philip II of Spain married his daughter, Elizabeth de Valois. Henri II died as the result of an injury sustained at a tournament to celebrate the double marriage which cemented the peace.

François II acceded to the throne, son of Catherine de Medici and Henri II. He was fifteen, married to Mary Stuart and dominated by his wife's uncles, the Guise family. In 1560 Protestant conspirators were hanged from the balcony at Amboise, and François II died. He was succeeded by his even younger brother, Charles IX, aged 10. His mother, Catherine de Medici, was regent. In 1561, Catholics and Protestants came together at Poissy, but the struggle had become political, and the outcome of the talks was not successful. In 1562, the January edict permitted the Protestants to practise their religion outside the large urban centres. But in 1562 the entourage of the Duc de Guise massacred some hundreds of Protestants at Vassy. The wars of religion had broken out.

The wars of religion were also a power struggle in which religion became a pretext. On one side was the Catholic faction led by the Guise family, who clearly contemplated strengthening their own position against the king by achieving Spanish domination of France. Many of the lesser nobility saw their interests furthered by the reform and the Huguenot rebellion. In the middle there eventually emerged a party of *politiques* who returned to the earlier policies of Catherine de Medici under the chancellorship of Michel de l'Hôpital. They were mostly drawn from the magistracy, were predominantly but by no means exclusively Catholic, favoured religious toleration and cultivated a neo-Stoic system of values not unrelated to intellectual scepticism and demonstrably a defensive adaptation of the optimistic Neoplatonism of the mid-sixteenth century.

The wars themselves were sporadic but bitter. The first one lasted from 1562 until the peace of Amboise in 1563, which gave Orléans back to the king. Hostilities broke out again in 1567–8, when the Protestants, who had attempted to capture Charles IX, were defeated by Montmorency, who was himself killed. The Protestants were again defeated at Jarnac in 1569 when their leader, Condé, was assassinated. He was succeeded by Henri de Béarn, the later Henri de Navarre and Henri IV. In 1570 the peace of Saint-Germain gave four towns to the Protestants. Two years later Catherine de Medici married her daughter, Marguerite de Valois, to the new Protestant leader, now king of Navarre, although any hopes of consequent pacification were undone by the notorious massacre of St Bartholomew in that year, the principal victim being the Protestant Coligny. Henri de Navarre and the young prince Condé had to abjure Protestantism.

In 1573 the Catholics besieged in vain the Protestant strongholds of Sancerre and La Rochelle and in the following year Charles IX died, to be succeeded by his brother, the third son of Henri II, who had been king of Poland for a year and now became Henri III of France. In 1576

Henri de Navarre escaped from the court and reverted to Protestantism. The Catholic League was officially constituted, with the king its titular head, although it was in fact dominated by the Guise family. Further battles took place in 1577 and 1580. Then in 1584 Henri III's younger brother, the last son of Henri II, died. The natural heir to the throne became Henri de Navarre, which considerably intensified the bitterness of the wars, from 1585 almost continuous. The only possible solution looked like being the reconversion of the legitimate heir to Catholicism. The Catholic faction would not willingly have tolerated a Protestant heir, and any attempt to bypass the legitimate succession would certainly have ended in Spanish domination. From 1585 the prospects of settlement seemed depressingly slight. In that year, Henri III revoked all privileges accorded to the Protestants, although he also broke with the League and declared his wish for the succession to pass to his legitimate heir. In 1588 Henri III was forced to leave Paris for Chartres when Henri de Guise took over the capital. Later that year, during an Estates-General at Blois, Henri III had two of the three Guise brothers murdered. In 1589 Catherine de Medici died and Henri III was himself assassinated. The war between Henri de Navarre and the League continued until, in 1593, Henri de Navarre definitively abjured Protestantism for the second time and was finally accepted throughout France as king in 1594. In 1598 the Edict of Nantes granted relative freedom to Protestants and marked the final settlement of the wars of religion. The *politiques* had prevailed.

The cultural effects of the political and religious troubles, as of their eventual cessation, were dramatic. It is true that the court of Catherine and of Henri III was given to cultural pursuits, to magnificent entertainments, music, masques and discussions on the arts and on morals. The most glorious of all French tapestries date from this period. But the literature of the wars of religion shows a serious change of direction in imaginative needs. No one any longer explored the morally enriching effects of instinctive experience as the mid-century exploiters of Ficino had done. Montaigne scoffed at the Ficinian view of love. La Noue (1531–91) regarded the scenes of exalted sensual love in the *Amadis* romances (published in France in the 1540s by Herberay des Essarts) as corruptive. The *Monophile* of the lawyer Étienne Pasquier (1529–1615) took an anti-feminist view which once more regarded love as a simple 'passion'. The *Printemps* of Agrippa d'Aubigné (1552–1630) included poems in which the two sorts of love, the morally perfective and the instinctive, were again opposed to one another. Ronsard used

Neoplatonist imagery about love and juxtaposed a spiritual view of love's effects with expressions of physical passion. But increasingly he took an earthy view of love and its satisfaction, and increasingly he turned away from the Ficinian perspectives of an earlier generation. One of the most vicious of his posthumous sonnets attacks Ficino's popularizer, Leone Ebreo. Significantly at this date, it was in Italy, England and Spain that the imaginative exploration into the morally perfective effects of instinctive love continued until, after the wars of religion, the pastoral suddenly and tardily took root in France.

It is not only in the literature of love that the reversal of direction in imaginative exploration is striking. No one any longer seriously examined the possibility that human perfection, including religious perfection, was intrinsic to moral achievement. In 1588, for all his tolerance and intellectual uncertainty, Montaigne did not doubt that Plato's soul, because pagan, was 'grande d'humaine grandeur seulement'. For Montaigne philosophy appeared pardonably to be only a 'poësie sophistiquée'. He points out how the legitimacy of rebellion against 'tyranny' for the defence of religion had been a Protestant doctrine until Henri de Navarre became heir presumptive, after which the Protestants promptly repudiated it and the Catholics immediately embraced it.

It was not the religious conflict alone which caused the reaction of cultural retreat. Indeed, in modern times the religious conflict has come increasingly to look like a pretext for a crisis that had been building up even during the reign of François I. When the Treaty of Cateau-Cambrésis put an end to the wars between France and Spain, both countries were bankrupt. The wars had been fought on funded debts, providing annuities (*rentes*) for those who invested in them. In 1555 Henri II had contracted a very large series of short-term loans at an annual rate of interest of 16 per cent. In 1557, a few months after Philip II, he defaulted. Both countries needed peace because they could not afford to go on fighting. When Henri II died, the debt was forty million *livres* (say four million pounds of contemporary English money, or about fifteen times the annual income of Elizabeth of England at the beginning of her reign). The kings of France could and did impose taxation by decree, but the result of the *taille* was a social unrest which was expressed in the religious conflict. Offices were created for sale, which meant that the king lost control of a bureaucracy he could not afford to pay and who recouped themselves from their social inferiors until they could buy up the estates of the lesser nobility living on fixed *rentes*, ruined by price inflation, bereft of a social function and debarred from trade. The unrest of the lesser nobility as well as of the populace found its outlet in the wars of religion.

When Henri II died, his wife Catherine de Medici was forty-nine, immensely rich and possessively maternal. Power devolved on Catherine when the fifteen-year-old François II became king, and stayed there when he was succeeded in 1560 by his ten-year-old brother Charles IX. But her famous chancellor Michel de l'Hôpital (1506–73) was one of the outstanding statesmen of sixteenth-century France. A lawyer who became chancellor in 1560, he was a Catholic with a Protestant wife, a constant advocate of tolerance, peace and moderation, increasingly distressed at Catherine's move towards the League and forced by her to resign a few months after the massacre of St Bartholomew (23–4 August 1572). He died six weeks after resigning. It was the chancellor's policies which inspired the early *Discours* of Ronsard. Later they were to be adopted by the *politiques*.

Polemical and Humanist Literature from 1560

Ronsard's polemical *Discours* were in fact a logical development from the moralizing and religiously didactic *Hymnes*. Their spirit differs from that of Erasmian humanism in Ronsard's preoccupation with national achievements and concerns, but the *Discours* start with a very moderately counter-reformatory tone still capable of bitterness at ecclesiastical abuse. As the wars break out, the *Discours* become more coruscating. The stilted images and stylized decorative elements of baroque begin to appear alongside mannerist gestures and adjectives.

The greatest polemical achievement in Protestant poetry was undoubtedly that of d'Aubigné, whose *Les Tragiques* is already recognizably baroque. Ronsard, when pressed, wrote polemically. D'Aubigné was a professional soldier who prolonged his work in a long, uneven, but often splendid quasi-epic poem which deals with the sufferings and final vindication of the Huguenot people of God.

Les Tragiques consists of seven books. It was begun in 1575 and generally finished by 1589, although not published until 1616. As a poem it is certainly too long and its imagery is too stylized. Events on earth, and especially at the Valois court, are seen from the viewpoint of the Old Testament God of vengeance against a backdrop of eternity. The ocean complains of the blood drained into it by the rivers and the elements themselves protest at what is happening on earth. The poem develops without much taste or economy but with polemical vigour into a wide cosmic panoply in which d'Aubigné's vision is energetically communicated with the help of baroque, or even mannerist, imagery. The Muse who is invoked is the Muse not of poetry but of tragedy. The poem contains lists, curses, prayers, appeals, lyrical interpolations and much satirical bitterness. Catherine de Medici is the object of a furious attack, and the picture of a homosexual Henri III surrounded by his 'mignons' (in fact his personal bodyguard) is only slightly more restrained.

The Protestant side of the schism produced a series of important authors. The most important poets were d'Aubigné and du Bartas (1544–90), who wrote chiefly scientific and learned verse. But the Protestant contribution to the literature of the wars of religion was largely made by such moralists and historians as Bèze (1519–1605), Calvin's lieutenant at Geneva, La Primaudaye, the soldier historians Monluc (1502–77) and La Noue (1531–91). Some important authors, such as Jean Bodin (1530–96) and Jean de la Taille (1540–1608), were of uncertain religious conviction.

The one overpowering genius of the period, who ranks with Rabelais and Racine among the most powerful authors ever to write in French, was Michel de Montaigne (1533–92). He both transcended the polemic of the religious wars and was conditioned by it. He was Catholic, *politique*, conservative, neo-Stoic and of a cast of mind much better called relativist than sceptical. He was the third child, but the eldest to survive, of a business family recently ennobled by the purchase of the Montaigne estate. His mother came from a converted Jewish family. A brother and a sister were Protestants. He was brought up gently, at first with tutors who spoke Latin but no French, and then at the prestigious Collège de Guyenne. From 1557 to 1570 he served in the lower chambers of the Bordeaux *parlement*, which had executive and administrative as well as legal functions. It was there that he met La Boétie (1530–63), a poet and political thinker of conservative religious and social views, with whom he formed an intimate friendship. Two years after La Boétie's death Montaigne married and, since preferment at Bordeaux was denied to him on account of the presence of close relatives in the upper chambers of the *parlement*, in 1571, at the age of thirty-eight, he retired.

In 1578 he became ill with the kidney stone, from which his father had died, but in 1580 he served in the king's army, besieging the Protestant citadel at La Fère. Later that year he set out on his formative

Italian journey. He heard in Italy in 1581 that he had been appointed mayor of Bordeaux, which he remained for four years. Politically he worked to mediate between Henri de Navarre and Henri de Guise. He regarded the wars of religion as being primarily a political struggle but took the view that the reformers' innovations were the cause of the political and social strife in the country.

Montaigne himself fell back on a neo-Stoic relativism, fascinated with the mutability of human behaviour and experience. The chapters of his book, known as the *Essais* and intended to be personal reflections on his reading, experience and speculative interests, grew from the early compilations of examples on the pattern of a commonplace book into an extended, and not unaffected, self-portrait which he crammed with allusions and quotations, and which proceeded more by additions and associations than by logical development. If the book remains so intensely personal, it is because Montaigne uses its successive chapters as so many attempts to sound his own reactions and analyse his own experience. It is in this sense that each chapter is an *essai* or an attempt. What Montaigne ultimately succeeded in doing was to transform erudite historical and moral compilation and commentary, which had already been mixed with personal whimsy, into the totally new genre known, after Montaigne, as the *essai*, and to move from the speculative and didactic treatment of important moral issues to the projection of a humanist sensibility in a self-portrait.

The first edition of the *Essais* appeared in 1580. In 1588 the third book was added to the first two, in which numerous additions were also made. In 1595 a posthumous edition appeared, incorporating many further additions made by Montaigne in the margins of a 1588 copy before his death. There are comparatively few deletions, and it has become conventional to print the 1595 text, indicating what portions of it date from 1580 and 1588. The first chapter in which Montaigne clearly overflows the limits of the genre in which he had been writing is the twentieth of the first book, 'Que philosopher, c'est apprendre à mourir'. The title is taken from Cicero and is significant because, throughout the early chapters, Montaigne attempts to overcome his fear of pain and death by having recourse to stoic reflections. The definitive rejection of the pure neo-Stoic ethic comes only in the second book with the rejection of the legitimacy of suicide in the 'Coutume de l'île de Cea' (II, 3). But the neo-Stoicism merges quite smoothly into the intellectual relativism which particularly characterizes Montaigne's middle period, in which he is fascinated by the influence of custom, upbringing and prejudice on human ideas and behaviour and by what he calls 'le branle' of human experience, although nowhere does he ever in the end deny absolute moral values or the validity of rational norms in ethics.

In the longest and most famous of the chapters (II, 12), Montaigne sets out rather against his will to defend the thought of Raimond Sebond, an early fifteenth-century Spanish theologian who had undertaken to prove by reason all the major Christian dogmas and whose book Montaigne had translated into French at his father's request. Montaigne is clearly from the outset out of sympathy with Sebond, and he incorporates into his defence a great deal of presumably already existing material which compares man's autonomous capabilities unfavourably with those of animals and which points to the changing views the great philosophers have held about human nature. But there is no contradiction in Montaigne's thought. Montaigne denies any autonomous power of self-perfection in man and regards grace as that by which man is lifted beyond the animal realm. Reason, when aided by grace, is still the infallible rational power of the ancient Stoics. It is only because Sebond's detractors are presumed by Montaigne to lack grace that he can defend Sebond by pointing to what he regards as the feebleness of unaided reason, of man 'sans secours estranger, armé seulement de ses armes, et despourveu de la grace et cognoissance divine'. It is for Montaigne man without grace who is capable of neither virtue nor truth.

In the third book, Montaigne's chapters become more personal, intimate and rambling. They reflect Montaigne's own success in adapting himself to the 'forme sienne', the 'forme maistresse', which allows him simply to be himself. The affectations drop away, and one of the important chapters of the third book ends with a moving and serious, if still ironic, panegyric of self-knowledge. He addresses his reader, 'tu es le scrutateur sans connoissance, le magistrat sans jurisdiction et, après tout, le badin de la farce'. Few phrases more succinctly sum up Montaigne's view of what he was the first to refer to as 'la condition humaine'.

Montaigne knew from 1580 that the interest of his book lay in the self-portrait. Nevertheless some of his contemporaries condemned it, preferring to appreciate the many moral aphorisms which the book contains. He was sometimes compared to Plutarch. But he illustrates the way in which Neoplatonist doctrines could merge into neo-Stoic and Epicurean views perfectly compatible with relativism and even

Augustinianism. These labels can denote different sensibilities, but they are extremely dangerous when applied to late sixteenth-century authors, since no one of them on the purely conceptual level excludes any other. Montaigne disbelieved in intrinsic human perfectibility. He did not allow the granting of grace to pagans and he was insistent on the close union of body and soul. Yet many of his conceptual affirmations are clear derivatives from mid-century Neoplatonism. Cultural changes have finally to be measured in terms of sensibilities rather than of ideas.

Guillaume du Vair (1556–1621) is another author to illustrate the same point. He is a certain, if neglected, source for Descartes who combined a purely scholastic description of man's passions, or affective states, with a great deal of neo-Stoic phraseology. He was clearly influenced by the Florentine spiritual tradition. He advocated the suspension of judgement in all matters of possible doubt and his thought contains clearly Epicurean elements. Like so many of the late sixteenth-century humanists, he belonged to the magistracy. His major works, *De la sainte philosophie*, *La Philosophie morale des stoïques* (1585?), *De la constance et consolation ès calamités publiques* (1594), all show the characteristically defensive moral attitudes of the major humanists during the wars of religion, stoic in their mistrust of passion, humanist in their refusal to deny autonomous rights to however corrupt a nature, sceptical in their dogmatic commitments and concerned in their desire to promote Christian and humane behaviour. Du Vair's works were plagiarized by Pierre Charron (1541–1603), who was even more indebted to Montaigne; Charron's famous *De la sagesse* (1601) was largely a systematization of views extracted from Montaigne, philosophically uncertain and imaginatively uninteresting. But it carried much influence, and is historically important as a chain in the link between sixteenth-century neo-Stoicism and the scepticism which began to develop in the seventeenth century.

Among the other important authors of the wars of religion were Jean Bodin (1503–96) and Guy du Faur de Pibrac (1529–84). Both were eclectics. Bodin is important for his thoroughgoing criticism of legal theory on the basis of historical development and the geographical circumstances of different nations with different laws. He is also the author of a famous religious dialogue, frankly syncretist in tone, known as the *Heptaplomeres*, of a critical *Methodus* for assessing the probability to be given to the assertions of different historians, a treatise of natural theology and an important treatise on political philosophy in which he favours a powerful hereditary monarchy. Pibrac was a friend of Bodin's who composed a sort of moral code in a long series of *quatrains* and whose conservatism was commended by Montaigne. For many years, Pibrac's *quatrains* were considered to contain the basic ingredients of the gentlemanly ethic in France.

The wars of religion saw the emergence of a new school of historical writing, not yet fully critical, but capable of producing work still utilized by modern historians. Apart from the historians already mentioned, Estienne Pasquier calls for comment on account of his nationalistic, episodic, but none the less objective and critical *Recherches de la France* (1560–1621), which also contains remarks on the history of French literature. But the greatest historian of all, Jacques-Auguste de Thou (1553–1617), wrote in Latin the history of his own time (1543–1607) with scrupulous avoidance of partisanship and a remarkably dispassionate account of the wars of religion. Both Pasquier and de Thou were lawyers. Both sympathized with the *politiques*, and both represented the finest sort of critical humanism from which was to emerge the seventeenth-century opposition to Richelieu's political and intellectual establishment.

There were other genres, too, of considerable importance in the imaginative assessment of the experience and prospects of those who lived during the wars, among them tragedy and satire. French Renaissance tragedy was a serious elegiac genre which has too often been compared to the classical tragedy of Racine, created to explore quite different imaginative needs in a totally different cultural context. Indeed, the incommensurability of the two sorts of tragedy argues strongly against the study of literature in historical genres at all.

Renaissance tragedy was seldom what we should call dramatically viable. It grew out of the rhetorical exercises through which students in the Collèges were trained to move the passions of their hearers. It was still therefore a form of rhetoric rather than of drama. Most Renaissance tragedies consisted of a series of tableaux, and the tragedy was manifested in the often stoic fortitude with which the chief characters reacted to the blows of fate. As a genre, it parallels neo-Stoicism as a creation of the religious wars. The characters neither develop nor interact on one another. They lament, they preach, and they go stoically towards their pre-ordained fate. A chorus generally comments on their guilt or innocence, and they talk much more to the audience than to one another. But the best of these tragedies have a lyrical and elegiac grandeur still effective today.

In 1548 the biblical mystery plays which had become crude and often impious were stopped by decree, although the morality plays, which generally drew on non-biblical material, were allowed to continue. But the end of the mystery plays left a gap, only slowly to be filled by the legitimate theatre, itself undecided about the propriety of biblical and modern subjects for many years. De Bèze used a biblical theme for his *Abraham sacrifiant* (1550), but specifically sacred Renaissance tragedy did not establish itself with real success, partly because it could neither totally escape religious associations nor totally escape the profane associations of the stage.

More successful, and no less morally edifying, was the regular neo-classical tragedy which exploited subjects from classical, and later even modern, history. Jodelle's *Cléopâtre captive* (1553) was the first regular neoclassical tragedy written by a Frenchman in French and was acclaimed by the Pléiade as a great victory. Among the other important authors of tragedies were Jacques Grévin (1538–70), whose *Mort de César* added *vraisemblance* by putting the chorus into soldiers' uniforms and so giving them some reason to appear on stage, Jean de la Taille (1540–1608), who introduced formal Aristotelian theory into France, emphasizing the need to move the audience emotionally, Robert Garnier (1534–90) whose poetry lifts *Les Juives* from the ordinary level of Renaissance tragedy and who wrote the first great tragi-comedy in France (*Bradamante*, 1582), and Antoine de Montchrestien (1575–1621) whose *L'Écossaise* not only used a modern subject, Mary Stuart's death, but whose poetry sometimes announces a *préciosité* to come.

All of them are indebted to Seneca, and all attempted to exploit the devices of imitative rhetorical ornamentation in order to elaborate within a series of stylized forms the elegiac presentation of dignified and tragic emotions. Only de la Taille attempts true dramatic confrontation, but his *Saul le furieux* (1572) is not so successful on other levels. Taken as elegiac poetry, however, presented in a series of stylized *tableaux*, Renaissance tragedy is undoubtedly moving, and it certainly preserves for us the mood and the imaginative preoccupations of an unhappy period in the history of France.

The other genre brought into prominence by the wars of religion was satire, a term used in the sixteenth century of virtually any form of moral discourse, from the homily to personal invective, whether or not it used irony and whether or not it was based on classical models. In 1548 Sebillet described Marot's *coq-à-l'âne* genre as satire, on account both of its moral aims and its logical inconsequence. In the following year Du Bellay's *Défense* rebelled against allowing to Marot the literary skill of the classical satirist. Satire, being a classical category, was something whose modern reincarnation the Pléiade wished to reserve to themselves. In 1554 Claude de Boissière's *Art poétique* included both satire on the classical model and the *coq-à-l'âne* under the heading of 'propos non liez, couvertement reprenant les vices d'un chacun'. When the *Satire Menippée* appeared in 1594, its printer appended a note to say that satire had three meanings, a 'poème de médisance', any mixture of prose and verse, and any derivative of the ancient satyr plays.

Much humanist satire derives from the Greek satirical dialogues of Lucian, famed for his irreverence about the gods and his fusion of the sacred with the frivolous. Various of his dialogues were translated by Erasmus and More. From Lucian derives the mock encomium, a form used by Erasmus in the *Praise of Folly* (1511), as also by More and Rabelais among others. The influence of Lucian on Rabelais is especially strong, but it is also clear in the *Cymbalum Mundi*.

'Menippean' satire is that which attacks values and attitudes rather than persons, although the printer of the *Satire Menippée* took it simply to mean cynical. The *Satire Menippée* is a composite pamphlet issued by the *politiques* to discredit the League, whose principal figures it cruelly ridicules. It ends, however, by breaking the ironic mould for the sensible and moderate final harangue presenting the *politique* view.

The 'Renaissance' can scarcely be said to extend beyond the end of the wars of religion. The following period in French cultural history is known either as pre-classical or, perhaps a shade more appropriately, as baroque. Satire with Mathurin Régnier (1573–1613) turned its attention to types and portraits. Tragedy gave way to pastoral drama and tragi-comedy. D'Urfé's neo-Stoic *Épîtres morales* were followed by his lengthy and imaginatively searching pastoral novel *L'Astrée*. There was a renewed vogue for Ficino on love among secular and religious moralists alike, and a perceptible advance in religious scepticism. Literary treatments of love were again, and overwhelmingly, concerned to explore the spiritually perfective potentialities of instinctive experience. The power of man's will to determine his fate and control his reactions was examined with a buoyancy quite alien to an earlier generation. The Renaissance itself was over, but the underlying value-shift which it had announced, probed, proclaimed, challenged and shelved, reasserted itself with renewed vigour. In spite of future challenges, it was to widen the bounds of ecclesiastical orthodoxy and to establish itself beyond any doubt.

Bibliography

GENERAL

During the late nineteenth and early twentieth centuries, the interpretation of Renaissance authors was coloured by the conflict which then existed between the religious and academic worlds in France. Rabelais and Montaigne (together with Erasmus, Goethe, Shakespeare and Cervantes) were critically explored for their defiance of orthodox religion. The pendulum swung too far, and a series of works in the 1930s then demonstrated the authentic Catholicism of Montaigne, while Lucien Febvre successfully argued in 1942 the sincerity of the religious belief of Rabelais. The great critics of earlier generations have now therefore to be read with care, whatever their scholarly achievements.

On the general history of sixteenth-century French literature, there are some good modern surveys, notably including I. D. McFarlane's *Renaissance France 1470–1589* (London, 1974), particularly useful for the rich bibliography, and the ancillary material listing reference works, useful reviews and other established *instruments de travail*; the less stimulating volume by R. Morcay and A. Muller, *La Renaissance* (Paris, 1961); and the less comprehensive paperback volume in the series 'French Literature and its Background' entitled *The Sixteenth Century*, edited by J. Cruickshank. *France in the Sixteenth Century* (Englewood Cliffs, NJ, 1969) by Donald Stone is also a useful introduction. The classical work on changing attitudes to the French Renaissance is W. K. Ferguson's *The Renaissance in Historical Thought* (Cambridge, Mass., 1948).

For the non-literary aspects of sixteenth-century French history, the best recourse in the first instance is to the standard collections, the *Histoire de France* by E. Lavisse, the *New Cambridge Modern History*, the relevant volume of A. Fliche and V. Martin, *Histoire générale de l'Église*, the Oxford *History of Music*, Sir Anthony Blunt's volume on French art 1500–1700 in the Pelican *History of Art*, and the various specialized economic histories, including F. Mauro, *Le XVIe Siècle européen: Aspects économiques* (Paris, 1966). Much, however, has also to be gleaned from more specialist works which can scarcely be listed here, but which consist of studies devoted to single individuals or institutions. The most important periodical devoted to the literature of sixteenth-century France is the *Bibliothèque d'Humanisme et Renaissance*.

RENAISSANCE, HUMANISM AND REFORM

On the nature of the Renaissance in France, the best modern book is F. Simone, *The French Renaissance*, trans. H. Gaston Hall (London, 1969). Other fundamental works dealing specifically with the evangelical humanism of the French Renaissance include A. Renaudet, *Préréforme et humanisme (1494–1517)*, rev. ed. (Paris, 1953), especially important for Lefèvre d'Étaples, and Lucien Febvre, *Au cœur religieux du XVIe siècle* (Paris, 1957). Much of the best work on evangelical humanism is to be found in monographs devoted to specific authors such as Lucien Febvre's *Autour de l'Heptaméron: Amour sacré, amour profane* (Paris, 1944), M. A. Screech, *L'Évangélisme de Rabelais* (Geneva, 1959), W. Kaiser, *Praisers of Folly* (Cambridge, Mass., 1963), F. Wendel, *Calvin, the Origins and Development of his*

Religious Thought (London, 1963), and Quirinus Breen, *J. Calvin: A Study in French Humanism* (Hamden, 1968). The nature of evangelical humanism and its relationship both to the Renaissance and to the Reformation emerge clearly also from much of the critical work on Erasmus and his colleagues. See especially R. H. Bainton, *Erasmus of Christendom* (New York, 1969), the introduction by A. H. T. Levi to Betty Radice's Penguin translation of *The Praise of Folly* (London, 1971), A. H. T. Levi, *Pagan Virtue and the Humanism of the Northern Renaissance* (London, 1974), Sears Jayne, *John Colet and Marsilio Ficino* (London, 1963), Margaret Mann's *Érasme et les débuts de la Réforme française 1517–30* (Paris, 1934), and the same critic's study of the *Adages* of Erasmus (Cambridge, 1964). The most important account of late medieval spirituality is to be found in H. A. Oberman's somewhat dense *Gabriel Biel: The Harvest of Medieval Theology* (Cambridge, Mass., 1963).

ART, EDUCATION AND EARLY FRENCH HUMANISM

Most help will be gained from works already mentioned. There are important studies of individual colleges of the University of Paris, such as Quicherat's three-volume *Histoire de Sainte-Barbe* (Paris, 1860). Detailed information can also be obtained from W. Ong, *Ramus, Method and the Decay of Dialogue* (Cambridge, Mass., 1958). On the history of printing in Paris, there are several studies of individual printers, and a definitive series entitled *Imprimeurs et libraires parisiens du XVIe siècle* is being prepared by J. Veyrin-Forrer and others (1965–). The most important material on the history of Greek studies in Paris is contained in A. Lefranc's *Histoire du Collège de France* (Paris, 1893) and in an article by L. Delaruelle, *L'Étude de grec à Paris de 1514 à 1530* published in the *Revue du XVIe siècle* in 1922. Important information on Parisian humanism is also contained in such works not so far mentioned as E. Rice's edition of the *Prefatory Epistles* of Jacques Lefèvre d'Étaples (New York and London, 1972), D. O. McNeil's *Guillaume Budé and Humanism in the Reign of Francis I* (Geneva, 1975) and the two-volume study of Josse Clichtove by J.-P. Massaut (Paris, 1968) which shows some anti-Erasmian bias. On the Meaux reform and the religious position of Marguerite de Navarre, the most important works are still those by Lucien Febvre referred to above. Much useful material is to be found in collected volumes such as *Humanism in France in the Late Middle Ages and the Early Renaissance*, ed. A. H. T. Levi (Manchester, 1970), *The Renaissance Heritage*, ed. D. Haggis and others (London, 1968), and *French Renaissance Studies 1540–70*, ed. P. Sharratt (Edinburgh, 1976).

VERNACULAR LITERATURE TO 1540

The best introduction to Rabelais among the many available is perhaps the short biography *Rabelais* by A. J. Krailsheimer (Paris, 1967), the author also of an important study, *Rabelais and the Franciscans* (Oxford, 1963). Lucien Febvre's densely allusive but epoch-making study, *Le Problème de l'incroyance au XVIe siècle: la religion de Rabelais* (Paris, 1942), and Walter Kaiser's *Praisers of Folly* (Cambridge, Mass., 1963) made serious advances in Rabelais studies. A more recent work of considerable interest is D. Coleman's *Rabelais* (Cambridge, 1971). Much important work has appeared in the sporadically published *Études rabelaisiennes*, in particular including *L'Évangélisme de Rabelais* (Geneva, 1959) by M. A. Screech, the author also of *The Rabelaisian Marriage* (London, 1958).

The *Cymbalum Mundi* of Bonventure des Périers has been well edited with an intelligent introduction by Peter Nurse (Manchester, 1957). Lucien Febvre's *Au cœur religieux du XVIe siècle* (Paris, 1957) is again important for the religious discussions of the period and includes a good account of Étienne Dolet.

PLATO AND POETRY TO 1560

On the sixteenth-century *Querelle des femmes*, see the introduction by F. Gohin to his edition of Antoine Héroët's *La Parfaite Amie* (Paris, 1909). On Agrippa of Nettesheim, see Charles G. Nauert, *Agrippa and the Crisis of Renaissance Thought* (Urbana, Ill., 1965). The classic study on early sixteenth-century Neoplatonism, now rather out of date, is A. Festugière's *La Philosophie de l'amour de Marsile Ficin et son influence sur la littérature française du XVIIe siècle* (Paris, 1941), but *Platonism in French Renaissance Poetry* by R. V. Merrill and R. J. Clements (New York, 1957) is also a useful guide.

There is a fine edition of Scève's *Délie* by I. D. McFarlane (Cambridge, 1966) with ample critical comment, and Henri Weber's *La Création poétique au XVIe siècle* (Paris, 1956) is an unmatched source of critical comment on all major sixteenth-century poets. Marot's editor C.-A. Mayer is also the author of a study *Clément Marot* (London, 1972), which should, however, be read in conjunction with M. A. Screech's *Marot évangélique* (Geneva, 1967). Hans Staub's *Le Curieux Désir* (Paris, 1967) contains an important analysis of Scève's *Microcosme*, and the scientific poetry of the sixteenth century is well analysed by A.-M. Schmidt, *La Poésie scientifique en France au XVIe siècle* (Paris, 1939), and is interestingly discussed by D. B. Wilson in *French Renaissance Scientific Poetry* (London, 1974).

PROSE LITERATURE OF THE MID-CENTURY

The fundamental work on the *Heptaméron* is to be found in Pierre Jourda's two-volume study *Marguerite d'Angoulême* (Paris, 1930), but Lucien Febvre's *Autour de l'Heptaméron* (Paris, 1944) is also important, and much earlier criticism has become out of date with the publication by A. J. Krailsheimer of his article 'The *Heptaméron* Reconsidered' in *The Renaissance Heritage*, ed. D. Haggis and others (London, 1968). Interest in Sebastien Castellio has recently been increasing, but the standard work remains the biography of F. Buisson (Paris, 1892). There is a study of the *Life and Works of Louis le Roy* by W. Gundersheimer (Geneva, 1966). On Pontus de Tyard, see Kathleen Hall, *The Philosophical Dialogues of Pontus de Tyard* (Oxford, 1963), and on Jacques Peletier du Mans there is an important study by Hans Staub in *Le Curieux Désir* (Paris, 1967).

THE PLÉIADE TO 1560

The standard work on the Pléiade is the four-volume *Histoire de la Pléiade* by H. Chamard (Paris, 1939–40). On Pléiade poetic theory, see Grahame Castor, *Pléiade Poetics* (Cambridge, 1964). The most helpful introductory work on Ronsard's poetry is the collection of essays edited by T. C. Cave, *Ronsard the Poet* (London, 1973). More specialist studies of merit include, among many others, P. de Nolhac, *Ronsard et l'humanisme* (Paris, 1921), and I. Silver, *Ronsard and the Greek*

Epic (St Louis, 1961). The best edition of Ronsard, which has copious notes, is that by P. Laumonier completed by R. Lebègue and I. Silver, 18 vols (Paris, 1914–70), but there are several useful anthologies, of which the best, in two volumes, is edited by T. C. Cave and G. Castor. On Ronsard as poet of nature and love, see D. B. Wilson, *Ronsard, Poet of Nature* (Manchester, 1961), and F. Desonay, *Ronsard poète de l'amour*, 3 vols (Brussels, 1951–9).

There are surprisingly few standard or useful critical works on other members of the Pléiade, but on Du Bellay V.-L. Saulnier's introductory *Du Bellay, l'homme et l'œuvre* may be usefully consulted. Many works deal with biography, with the development of different poetic genres, and with individual aspects of French poetry. The most immediately helpful is probably *Descriptive Poetry from Blason to Baroque* by D. B. Wilson (Manchester, 1967).

THE WARS OF RELIGION

On Pasquier, see L. Clark Keating's *Étienne Pasquier* (New York, 1972). On d'Aubigné there are a number of excellent if often specialist studies. *D'Aubigné poète des tragiques* (Caen, 1968) by J. Bailbé is of considerable interest.

POLEMICAL AND HUMANIST LITERATURE FROM 1560

Several studies have recently been devoted to the poetry of the period, notably including T. C. Cave's *Devotional Poetry in France c. 1570–1613* (Cambridge, 1969), M. Jeanneret, *Poésie et tradition biblique au XVIe siècle* (Paris, 1969), and P. A. Chilton, *The Poetry of Jean de la Ceppède* (Oxford, 1977).

From the vast literature on Montaigne, the work of Donald Frame, author of a biography (London, 1965), and of an important study, *Montaigne's 'Essais'* (Englewood Cliffs, NJ, 1969), must be singled out. There is also a carefully balanced critical assessment by R. A. Sayce, *The Essays of Montaigne: A Critical Exploration* (London, 1972), an important study by Frieda S. Brown, *Religious and Political Conservatism in the 'Essais' of Montaigne* (Geneva, 1963), and an important work by M. Baraz, *L'Être et la connaissance selon Montaigne* (Paris, 1968).

On sixteenth-century French tragedy, in which interest is increasing, the most important available studies include those by Gillian Jondorf, *Robert Garnier and the Theme of Political Tragedy in the Sixteenth Century* (Cambridge, 1969), and Richard Griffiths, *The Dramatic Technique of Antoine de Montchrestien: Rhetoric and Style in Tragedy* (Oxford, 1970), and the two major works of R. Lebègue, *La Tragédie religieuse en France 1514–73* (Paris, 1929) and *La Tragédie française de la renaissance*, 2nd ed. (Paris, 1954).

Very little of interest has been written about sixteenth-century satire, but on the humanism of the late sixteenth century in France it is important to consult J. H. Franklin, *Jean Bodin and the Sixteenth-Century Revolution in the Methodology of Law and History* (New York, 1963).

3 French History and Society from the Wars of Religion to the Revolution

ROGER METTAM

The thirty years before the accession of Henri IV to the French throne in 1589 were torn by social and religious conflict, erupting from time to time into bitter spells of civil war – the 'wars of religion' as they have been styled. During the preceding half of the sixteenth century much of Europe had been involved in the Italian wars, a series of international confrontations which had inspired Frenchmen to forget their internal differences and unite behind their two strong kings, François I and Henri II. When the wars were ended by the Peace of Câteau-Cambrésis in 1559, the same year in which Henri II met his untimely and accidental death, the country was deprived of a national purpose and dissident elements came to the fore. All the constituents of civil war were present in the succeeding years: a dissenting religious minority, whose influence had grown unchecked during the Italian wars but whose very existence was abhorrent to a Catholic monarch bearing the title of 'Most Christian King'; a series of weak or child rulers, and at times the regency of a woman and a foreigner – the Queen-Mother Catherine de Medici; powerful aristocratic factions and privileged social groups who were eager to gain authority by supporting the feeble crown against other opponents.

These 'wars of religion' were thus only partly concerned with conflicting faiths, although the combatants were always quick to emphasize the divine mission which justified their political actions. Parties formed and reformed, individuals changed sides with frequency, but a pattern can nevertheless be imposed on their battles because the core of each faction remained fairly constant. On the one hand was the ultra-Catholic party of the Guise family, who were ever amenable to the demands of the Spanish and who constituted themselves into the

Catholic League. At the other extreme were the Protestants and their supporters, ultimately led by Henri of Navarre, the most obvious candidate for the crown when Henri III should die. In the centre was the steadily increasing *politique* party, preferring peace and religious toleration to civil war and the persecution of heretics.

Whether the next king were to be a Navarre or a Guise, his first priority would have to be the establishment of a secure throne, dependent on none of these sectional interests. Yet it was not easy to devise national policies and create a single centralized government which all Frenchmen would willingly accept. France was too fragmented a collection of provinces to have any common aspirations, save against an external enemy. In certain areas, where the representative provincial Estates still met or where great and independent aristocrats held the post of governor, the royal administration seemed scarcely to acknowledge some of the directives issued by its sovereign. Only a laborious process of attrition would erode the various forms of opposition which existed throughout the kingdom and would free the crown from restraint. In the two hundred years between the accession of Henri IV and the outbreak of the Revolution, that process continued unceasingly and never achieved its target.

The history of seventeenth- and eighteenth-century France is dominated by this conflict between centralized royal government and local privilege. The crown tried steadily to extend its control over all aspects of life within the kingdom, while social groups and administrative institutions sought to preserve their varying degrees of independence and their traditional rights. The authority of the monarch was accepted unquestioningly, as long as it was confined to those matters which were generally regarded as its legitimate concern. When the royal ministers attempted to encroach upon provincial power, or stealthily to undermine the privileges of individuals, resistance was strong and widespread.

If the sphere of royal influence was thus limited, within it the absolutism of the Bourbons was unchallenged. No one suggested any means of restricting or replacing the executive power of the crown, partly because there were no individuals or institutions in the State who were fitted for the role. Those who had the ability would not have had the necessary popular support. Theorists reminded the king that France had an ancient constitution and a code of fundamental laws which he was morally bound to observe, but this was not an effective way of restraining the monarch. Nor could a petition against a particular edict be relied upon to move the hard hearts of the Paris ministers. The only way of opposing the many unpopular policies evolved by the central government was simply for the royal agents in the provinces to refuse to implement them. Throughout the years of the *ancien régime* the French crown, unlimited in its power of decision, never managed to impose its will wholeheartedly on its officials or on the country.

French Society in the Seventeenth Century

If the privileged groups in French society regarded the central government with suspicion, they showed little more affection for each other. Such social antagonisms resulted from the ill-defined nature of their rights and duties, which led to frequent disputes. Yet, whatever the tensions between them, these various smaller units – the parish, the town, the guild, the sovereign court, the province – seemed to the ordinary subject to be more easily comprehensible and relevant to his needs than the State, whose policies brought him so little benefit and so much hardship.

The First Estate of the realm, the clergy, was more frequently among the supporters of the crown than were the other two Estates. Although the higher churchmen were usually drawn from noble families, they received their benefices from the king, and were normally appointed because they had a reputation for loyalty and intelligence. Continued support of the crown was essential for further promotion within the hierarchy. The humble *curés* of the parishes were men of very different background, who had more in common with their parishioners than with their clerical superiors, but all played a crucial role in moulding the society of this highly religious age. The Church possessed fiscal privileges, of course, but it was more willing to pay its traditional 'free gift' to the crown than were the provincial Estates. The ruler, God's representative in the kingdom by Divine Right, exploited the wealth of the Church from time to time, and protests from an allegedly hard-pressed clergy resulted; but the monarch was also their only hope of defence against the attacks of the *parlements*, who consistently sought to abolish the few remaining powers of the ecclesiastical courts and were ever watchful lest Rome interfere in the affairs of France through the agency of the Church.

The nobility were even less amenable to the extension of royal power and proved a more effective obstacle. The term *noblesse* referred to a wide range of people, united only by their privileges, especially their exemption from direct taxation. Nobility was either inherited or acquired – by royal favour, by outstanding military achievements or by long or distinguished service in the bureaucracy. Because of the social prestige associated with it, especially when reinforced by landed wealth, the men of the rich middle classes preferred to spend their profits on buying an office which sooner or later gave them noble status than to invest them in further commercial enterprises. They were then compelled to abandon all their former economic pursuits in favour of the profits of office and the estates which they now purchased, because trade and business were forbidden to the noble by law, and the men who practised them were heartily despised by the aristocratic élite. It was a perpetual problem for royal ministers that their cherished economic schemes lacked the support of the wealthiest men in the kingdom. Even though the laws forbidding nobles to trade were modified, most of them still disdained to enter this profession which the ancestors of some noble houses had followed successfully in the not too distant past.

The influence of the nobility was everywhere in French society. In the localities they had power over the peasantry, over municipal officials and even over royal agents. In the *pays d'états*, those provinces where the representative Estates still met, they had an opportunity in these assemblies to voice the views of their order. The higher aristocrats took a lead in provincial affairs, and might have the ear of the king or his ministers at court as well. Although many had fallen from favour in consequence of their role in the civil wars of the sixteenth century, and others would do so after the Frondes of Louis XIV's minority, there were always some nobles at court whom the kings trusted and asked for advice, despite the rise of new kinds of counsellor, and always a few who, as provincial governors, were still important and powerful royal agents in difficult provinces. The nobility were essential to the State because they provided the officers of the army and, if a few men rose from the ranks by merit alone, continued to do so during the reign of Louis XIV. Indeed that monarch, more than his two predecessors, reduced the percentage of humbler families who entered the nobility, believing firmly in maintaining the purity of his social élite.

Nobility was thus the goal in seventeenth-century France. It was discussed endlessly in the *salons* and formed the subject of the most famous plays. It was generally believed that nobles were superior beings and it therefore followed that, while they were treated with unusual respect and fairness in the courts of law, they were, if convicted, considered more guilty and were more severely punished than commoners who committed the same crimes. The aristocrat was allowed to wear finery which was forbidden to others, and his privileges were upheld by the king, even though royal agents in the localities might be attempting to undermine them surreptitiously.

The greatest nobles of all, the princes of the blood royal, were a particularly serious threat to the crown, even though their position in society was so unique that they had very little in common with other social groups, including other nobles. If they came to the fore at moments of crisis, their selfishness and arrogance rapidly disillusioned their supporters. After their behaviour in the civil wars and in the Frondes, together with their constant plotting against ministers and during minorities, Louis XIV determined to keep them under surveillance at court, showered with prestigious court offices, but detached from the spheres where their patronage was most effective. He strongly preferred the company of aristocrats to that of the new financial and trading classes on whom his revenues and the prosperity of his State depended, and was able to surround himself with large numbers of them once the court moved to its permanent home at Versailles in 1682. Yet, although a man's rank within the nobility usually determined the level of ceremonial office which the king granted to him, it bore no relation to his influence in political affairs. The favoured advisers of the king might include men of varied social backgrounds, but no kind of pedigree gave one any certainty of entering their exclusive circle. Royal favour could not be predicted. Many nobles chose instead to remain in the provinces where their influence was assured.

A distinction is often made between the *noblesse d'épée* and the *noblesse de robe*, but this is somewhat misleading. Many members of the *épée* – nobles by birth or of distinguished, if recent, military origins – did indeed despise the professional bureaucrats of the *robe*, and lived by the traditional landed wealth and military talents of their class. Others, whose financial situation was more precarious, resented that they could not afford to compete with middle-class men in purchasing these posts in the bureaucracy for themselves. A third group did buy offices or marry into leading *robe* families, and it is here that the boundary between the two kinds of nobility becomes blurred. *Robe* and *épée* might describe a man's profession, but conveyed less clear evidence about his family background.

The *noblesse de robe*, whatever their origins, formed the greatest threat to the extension of royal absolutism, even though they, as royal officials, were also its agents. The upper levels of this bureaucracy were men of immense social prestige, who wielded great power either in the sovereign courts in Paris or in the *parlements* and administrative departments of the provinces, and who married into other influential families in their institution or locality. Of all the bureaucracies evolved by the 'Renaissance states', this was the largest, and in France there was no 'country' party to challenge its power, not only because there were no effective national representative assemblies through which to do so, but because the bureaucrats tended to side with groups in the localities in opposing the policies of the royal ministers in the central government.[1]

In the early seventeenth century there was no alternative to an administrative system of this kind, which had developed fast under the later Valois and was as efficient as any of those kings might have expected. Officials passed on their posts to a relative, probably a son, who, although he had received no more specialized training than his predecessor, had at least been associated with the office before he took charge of it. Secondly there were the financial benefits which this system brought to the royal treasury, and which hard-pressed governments exploited at the cost of efficiency. If the purchase of office and subsequent ennoblement were the ambitious aims of the wealthy merchants, so too they provided the crown with a way of taxing men who were exempt from many other taxes. A proportion of the original purchase price went to the crown, after which the office-holder paid annual dues for the right to bequeath it to his descendants, and was often forced to lend money to the king at uneconomic rates. The officials largely paid themselves out of the revenues and fees they handled, which encouraged them to work harder and saved the crown a salary bill, although the central government's inadequate sources of information could not discover how often an illegal share of these profits was retained by the official. Corruption became more tempting when the ministers, seeking urgent funds, created more and more

[1] A comparison of the role played by the bureaucracy in various 'Renaissance states', as he calls them, and in the revolts of mid-seventeenth-century Europe was made by Professor H. Trevor-Roper in *Past and Present*, 16 (1959). This stimulating attempt to propound a theory of a general crisis, together with criticisms of his analysis, may be most conveniently found in Trevor Aston (ed.), *Crisis in Europe 1560–1660: Essays from 'Past and Present'* (London, 1965).

offices, all of which found eager buyers, but which antagonized existing office-holders who saw their work and its rewards divided up and shared with others. Yet, although prices of offices rose, the legal and illegal perquisites and the social prestige more than compensated for the initial outlay.

Below the privileged strata of clergy and nobility were many other stratified levels. At the top were the bourgeois, the chief citizens of the towns, exempt from direct taxation but having certain duties as well as privileges. The bourgeois of Paris were especially favoured and could be tried only by the courts of their own city. There was frequently tension between these more exalted men and the humbler townsmen who lived alongside them, made worse by the closed corporations of craftsmen and merchants which gave the leading citizens complete and selfish control over the economic life of their town or city. The townsmen paid certain dues to the municipality which was responsible for much of its own local administration, while in the countryside the peasant might pay seigneurial dues to the local lord in addition to the heavy burden of taxation imposed on him by the crown. The peasantry suffered badly during much of the seventeenth century, some being forced to abandon their land and join the bands of vagabonds who roamed the countryside or made the streets of the towns unsafe. Survival was a precarious business. If the average woman had twelve children, six would die within a year, while plague, starvation through bad harvests and other hazards would reduce still further the number who reached maturity. Forty was an unusual age to achieve. The distance from normal existence to starvation was so short that one bad crop could bring disaster to an entire province.

Direct taxation thus weighed heavily on these lower and poorer levels of society, because so many other groups were exempt from it. A perennial problem for the royal ministers was how to tap the wealth of the privileged for the benefit of the State, especially as the increase of indirect taxes often further crippled the humbler subject at the same time as it reached his superiors.

Henri IV and Louis XIII

Henri IV gained his kingdom by degrees. Named as heir by the dying Henri III in 1589, deprived by the hand of death of his closest rival for the throne, the Cardinal de Bourbon, in 1590, he returned to the true faith of the Catholic Church in 1593, and finally entered his capital in

1594, conspicuously refraining from taking revenge on those who had opposed him. The League was in disarray, with its allies drastically depleted, and many of its members therefore decided to support the king in his attempt to establish internal peace, whatever religious disunity remained. When Henri declared war on Spain in 1595, which ended with what was, for France, the desirable Treaty of Vervins in 1598, he had the backing of most of the French nation. Now, with his great minister Sully, the restoration of the kingdom could begin.

Many of the royal ministers of the seventeenth century shared common aims, even if they achieved varying degrees of success in pursuing them. They sought to introduce expert knowledge into the administrative machinery and to direct it more closely from the centre, to inquire into and systematize the use of the country's resources, and to replace the many different provincial standards of taxation, justice, weights and measures by nationally acceptable codes and tables. In economics there were the tasks of uniting the disparate provinces into a viable whole, of improving tax assessment and collection, of reducing or avoiding fiscal exemptions, and of planning royal expenditure so that the ministers were not having perpetual recourse to short-term emergency taxation as a way of meeting unforeseen expenses. There was the permanent fear of war, which always threw the royal finances into crisis, and there was the Huguenot community which, if it were docile in 1598, could not but alarm ministers who remembered the religious wars in their own country and saw similar conflicts continuing elsewhere.

The rise of more expert, professional administrators could be clearly seen in the central government before the accession of Henri IV, but it was to be a very slow process to introduce them into provincial and municipal institutions. At the centre the secretaries of state continued to accumulate power during the first half of the seventeenth century, even though their influence declined at times. The secretary of state was one of the 'new men' whom French kings frequently employed, hoping to reinvigorate the administration by placing a newly and rapidly promoted servant, and therefore a grateful one, in authority over selfish office-holders. Louis XI and François I had tried this remedy, but each new layer of men became just one further stratum in the bureaucracy, as self-seeking as the rest.

Under the great ministers who dominated French government from 1598 until 1661 – Sully, Richelieu and Mazarin – the secretaries were influential members of the central conciliar system, loyally carrying out their duties and forming a kind of inner cabinet in which they gave constant advice. The ministers and secretaries screened the king from the public in the sense that they took the blame for unpopular policies, and preserved the integrity of the crown. Although Louis XIII by no means relinquished all power into Richelieu's hands, the young Louis XIV was nevertheless hailed as the monarch who came to save France after a half century of ministerial tyranny. But when, on Mazarin's death in 1661, he made a point of underlining his determination to be his own first minister, the policies continued unchanged, except that they could be prosecuted more fiercely now that they were the personal wishes of a divinely ordained monarch. Kings and ministers alike believed in a State whose interests overrode all others, and to whose greater glory all personal considerations must be sacrificed. The inhabitants of provincial France found the resulting policies bewildering, for the good of the State was seldom compatible with their own advancement.

The ministry of Colbert (1661–83) saw the greatest progress in the reform of finance, the economy and the administration, but the ground had already been laid by his predecessors. Sully wrestled with the finances after the civil wars, although the economic state of the country was not so bad as is sometimes claimed, and introduced some kind of budgeting, even if the reliability of these forecasts of State expenditure declined during the regency for Louis XIII. Sully is to be praised more for his plans to order the finances and the bureaucracy than for his success. Foreign policy and defence had to be given priority, but his schemes for the clearer delineation of France's frontiers, the building of a large fleet, the expansion of the economy, the construction of roads, bridges and canals, the accurate assessment of the resources of the country, and, above all, the establishment of a powerful monarchy, at the head of a national Church, free from the independent power of nobles who plotted against ministers like himself, and supported by a bureaucracy which served the interests of the crown in preference to its own – all these aims were to be adopted by his successors.

A noticeable characteristic of the first quarter of the seventeenth century was a more general revival of interest in economics. A number of pamphlets and learned works, of which Montchrestien's *Traicté de l'œconomie politique* (1615) was only the most distinguished, proposed the expansion of trade, the development of industry and reform of taxation. All these writers, like the ministers themselves, built their plans more or less closely around the mercantilist principles which were evolving during the sixteenth century and were to influence France for more than another hundred years. Believing that France was rich in natural resources and potentially self-sufficient, they wished to keep gold and silver within the kingdom, to manufacture at home all those luxury goods which could be bought only at great expense from abroad, to expand industry, to employ the workless poor and to promulgate regulations for controlling every aspect of the economy. They particularly directed their propaganda at the Estates-General of 1614 and the Assembly of Notables of 1626, hoping that these bodies would pronounce in favour of the plans which the government had formulated. However, their assumption that France was a natural economic unit, whose frontiers could be clearly delineated by tariffs, was at variance with the provincialism of the country. Many provinces did not share these beliefs of the writers and ministers, certain of them feeling closer commercially to other countries than to some of their fellow Frenchmen.

Henri IV and Sully therefore concentrated on those of their reform plans which involved less of an attack on local privilege, namely the development of crafts and luxury goods, and of a share in the trade between Europe and the new colonial world. Trading companies were formed, and an attempt made at providing State protection for merchants. They did not feel strong enough to undertake the overhaul of the fiscal system, and France still lagged behind her competitors in consequence. Her fleet was poor, she lacked skilled workers, her industrial products were expensive and she was lying well back in the colonial race.

Not every example of opposition to royal economic and financial policy on the part of the office-holders can be explained simply by their corrupt natures. On some occasions the relevant officials could not raise the required revenues. But far too often they were disinclined to co-operate. It was impossible thoroughly to supervise whether royal orders were executed properly, and although Sully attacked a few flagrant instances of corruption or reluctance to obey the commands of the crown, the effort and expense involved prevented an investigation into all but this extreme fringe. Worst of all, by authorizing the establishment of the *Paulette* in 1604, he permitted, for the financial benefit of the treasury, the creation by royal edict of a hereditary bureaucracy, before which time venality had merely been permitted by custom alone.

During the ministry of Sully the sovereign courts – the *parlements*, *chambres des comptes*, *cours des aides* and *cour des monnaies* – began more and more systematically to put forward their own views, frequently in opposition to the wishes of the crown. The king in France was the unlimited author of law, but he relied on these courts to register his edicts and to dispense his justice. In return they were beginning first to be obstructive and soon to make positive demands on him. At the same time the central government was making irregular use of the *commissaire*, forerunner of the *intendant*, an official sent out by the king to investigate specific grievances and instances of maladministration, and reporting back to Paris. The *commissaires* were to become crucial targets of odium for the courts in their struggle with the royal ministers which culminated in the Fronde.

Sully fell from power soon after the assassination of Henri IV in 1610, and his successors quickly squandered the surplus funds he had left in the treasury. But the problems remained – the fear of Habsburg encirclement was growing, the nobility were still too dangerous, the finances were inadequate and the bureaucracy over-powerful, while the perils of a Protestant State within the realm seemed ever more alarming.

The Huguenots were a very difficult problem. With the memory of recent civil war in France, and the evidence of lasting religious conflict in other countries, few Frenchmen could regard the question of toleration objectively. The majority hoped for a more permanent solution than had been possible at the end of the sixteenth century. The *politique* party, mild Catholics who wished to put the peace of the kingdom before religion, had triumphed with the Edict of Nantes in 1598, which gave the Huguenots a considerable degree of security in political, administrative, financial, economic, military and religious matters. The Protestant nobles and their coreligionaries in the towns were prepared to defend these rights with vigour, but the slow attack on their religion began almost as soon as the Edict was signed and registered. Sully, himself a Protestant, was no advocate of them as candidates for high office. He, like any patriotic Frenchman, knew that a tolerant peace had been unavoidable, but that further integration of the faiths was unwise. As Henri IV showed increasing hostility towards his former religion, under the influence of his Jesuit confessor, the government began to exert pressure on this minority, offering every encouragement to converts and distributing no favour to those who remained staunchly Protestant. The Huguenots saw their numbers and their territory declining, but the wealth of their towns was sufficient to sustain their military strength. After Henri IV was killed in 1610, the kingdom was entrusted to the pro-Spanish and zealous Catholic Queen Mother, Marie de' Medici, and her favourites, which divided the Huguenot party. Their towns chose to remain loyal to the Regent, while their nobility joined forces with rebellious Catholic nobles. The Huguenot aristocracy supported any group which challenged the authority of the crown. Initially opposing the Queen Mother, they championed her cause after her disgrace and turned their hatred against the new minister, the Duc de Luynes. Louis XIII and Luynes were preparing for an attack on the Protestants, which they launched in 1620, and religious conflict raged during 1621 and 1622. The royal army was by no means the unqualified victor, especially as Luynes himself died during the campaign.

The leader of the revolt of the Catholic nobles, which the Huguenot nobility joined, was the Prince de Condé, son of the Condé who had featured prominently in the civil wars. Condé failed to win the important support of the *parlement* of Paris for his cause, because he had attacked the venal bureaucracy and demanded its destruction in an attempt to widen the ranks of his followers, and the movement failed. He was arrested in 1616, but in 1622 he and the disgraced Queen Mother were back in the circle of advisers around the king, which deprived them of some grounds for opposing royal policies. Only twice removed from succession to the throne of the childless king, Condé personified the power of a prince of the blood at its most dangerous. Moreover, during these disturbances the Thirty Years War was breaking out in Europe near every French frontier, and the strength of the French crown and that of the various anti-royalist parties was related to the complicated manœuvrings in European diplomacy. The Huguenots, fearing an alliance between France and their own most likely ally, England, even wooed their opposite number in religion, zealously Catholic Spain. The intertwining of national and international politics which had occurred during the later sixteenth century was again to be seen. After another Huguenot rising in 1625 the new minister, Richelieu, made a temporary peace with them in 1626, but the problem of religion remained unsolved.

1626 is a convenient moment to gauge the reactions of French society to the economic and religious policies of the preceding quarter century because in that year an Assembly of Notables was called which, like the Estates-General of 1614, revealed the attitudes of various social groups. At the Estates-General, meeting for the last time before 1789, a number of the problems confronting the crown were discussed. The Third Estate wanted peace through a strengthened central authority, a firmer attack on the Huguenots, the reform of military pay in order to prevent looting by the soldiery, the compelling of the able-bodied poor to work and the reduction of pensions paid to the nobility. The noble Estate deplored the increasing bureaucratic element within their class. All three Estates attacked luxury and the amount of money which left the kingdom to pay for luxury goods from abroad.

The Estates-General was not mourned when it lapsed in 1614. It had lost its powers of consenting to taxation, and its component Estates found it difficult to evolve opinions which were shared by all their members from the varied provinces of France. The surviving provincial Estates were more dynamic as they provided a forum in which the representatives of a more viable geographical unit could air their views and grievances, having also the right to vote certain taxes and to control much local administration and expenditure, which strengthened their hand in dealing with the central government. On the national level, the mood of the country was a little more clearly seen in the Assemblies of Notables, summoned for the last time in 1626 until 1788. After 1626, French kings relied for advice on royal councils and on personal friends.

The Assemblies were composed of specially invited nobles and clergy, who spoke as individuals and not on behalf of their order as was the case at the Estates-General, together with the *premiers présidents* and *procureurs-généraux* of the sovereign courts who did speak as representatives of their colleagues. Richelieu hoped that a decision by the Assembly would therefore bind the courts to act accordingly. The 1626 meeting expressed its belief in the economic strength of France, the need for a larger fleet and for the development of colonial companies, insisting however that the edicts establishing such companies be registered by the *parlements*, in the knowledge that those courts would use their right of remonstrance against them. Beyond that the nobles and officials each managed to nullify a number of proposals aimed at their own authority. The nobles complained again about the new nobility of office-holders, the officials insisted on the confirmation of all their past rights in administration and justice, the clergy clashed with the militant religious nationalism of the *parlements*. The overall effect was completely to wreck Richelieu's hopes for financial reform.

From this moment, the *parlements* and other members of the *robe* increased their opposition to the attempts of the royal ministers at relieving the ever worsening financial situation. Nor were other opponents silent. In 1626 Richelieu was the target of the conspiracy of Chalais, when a group of great nobles, including a number of princes of the blood, sought to dislodge him in answer to his efforts towards dismissing Montmorency from his position as Admiral of France, one of the high offices which gave powerful individuals an excessive degree of independent control over important aspects of government. The conspiracy failed, the post was abolished, and the corresponding rank in the army, the Constable, was suppressed in the same year on the death of its holder, the Duc de Lesdiguières.

Thus were the policies of Sully continued by Luynes and Richelieu. A last onslaught on the Huguenots, with the capture of their crucial port of La Rochelle, ended the conflict in 1629, and although many Protestants remained in France, their independent power was crushed. Further colonial ventures failed in seas now full of warships as well as pirates, and the struggle with the Habsburgs, so long awaited and prepared for, was imminent. The problem of financing it was a desperate one. The squandering of the surplus left by Sully and inadequate budgeting under the Regency had led to the raising of forced loans from royal officials, and in the 1620s to the creation of more offices for sale. Most of the resulting profits went on the army and on campaigns against the Huguenots, and a sizeable sum on pensions to the nobility. Already the government was anticipating the revenues of the following year, in order to balance its accounts.

During the minority the crown began to rely for revenue on a new social group, which also started to infiltrate into the bureaucracy – the financiers. These men had made their fortunes in the world of money and credit, and were often the tax-farmers who collected indirect taxation for the State, eventually buying themselves an office. Sully had obliged the tax-farmers to abandon their commercial interests, which conflicted with their priorities as collectors of revenue, and they therefore devoted themselves exclusively to finance. All indirect taxes were farmed out at public auctions to the highest bidder, who then appointed agents to collect the money for him to pay into the treasury. Even though the returns fluctuated with the economic state of the country, tax-farming was a profitable business at which men made quick fortunes, although until they purchased an office they lacked the security of tenure of the bureaucrat, which made it easier for the crown to obtain forced loans from them. If the system was unsatisfactory, it was beyond the power of ministers to change it, and at least the crown was borrowing from its own agents instead of from the independent and even foreign bankers on whom it had depended in the past.

Despite these problems, Richelieu was in a strong position. The year after the Protestant challenge had been finally repelled, the 'Day of Dupes' conspiracy removed the Queen Mother from her position of influence over her son. If there were further aristocratic attempts to unseat him, his survival in the king's favour was never really in doubt again. Until this moment he had not allowed France to enter the Thirty Years War, although he was subsidizing the Protestant Gustavus Adolphus of Sweden who was fighting to secure the same ends. Religious differences did not bother Richelieu greatly in choosing allies. When Sweden fared badly in 1634, Richelieu prepared for direct intervention and declared war in 1635, a conflict which was to last in Germany until 1648, and against Spain until 1659. The minister was left with little time to spare for the internal problems of France, and on his death in 1642 bequeathed them and the war to his successor as minister, Mazarin, a cardinal like himself, and to the five-year-old boy who in 1643 succeeded his father as Louis XIV.

One further aspect of life under the first two Bourbons must be mentioned – the development of the Catholic Church, apart from the Huguenot question. Protestantism was not the only religious issue during these years. The forces of Counter-Reformation Catholicism were active throughout Europe, and the memory of extreme Catholic partisans in the civil war was just as disquieting to the central government as their recollections of Calvinist dissidence. The king was effective head of the Church in France and divinely installed upon the throne, although royal and papal publicists argued passionately in the first years of the century about the theoretical basis of his sovereignty. So too the clergy at the Estates-General and at the Assembly of Notables preferred a less aggressive Gallicanism to that advocated by other groups, especially by the *parlements*. The *parlements* vigorously opposed the decision of Henri IV to readmit the Jesuits to France, but the king, with his influential Jesuit confessor, was now a true son of the Roman Church, working for ends of which the Pope himself approved. This co-operation became closer under the zealously Catholic regency of Marie de' Medici, when national policy was altered to suit the interests of the Church.

In the countryside the Church was playing a different role. The revived fervour of Catholicism was directed towards, among other things, the problem of the poor. Charitable associations were formed, such as the Companies of the Holy Sacrament, dedicated to creating poor-houses in which the needy could be imprisoned and compelled to work usefully, for this charity was not kindly and warm-hearted. Thus a potentially dangerous element on the urban scene was safely contained. People of all classes joined these charitable enterprises, working anonymously in order to appear more selfless. The government suspected such secret societies, just as it feared the purposes of the men, often of high *robe* nobility, who entered that other mysterious religious brotherhood – the Jansenists. Secrecy and extreme zeal, especially religious zeal, were all too frequently associated with treason.

Only a small percentage of the poor benefited from these charities during the reign of Louis XIII, and poverty was widespread all over France where it gave rise to frequent local revolts. The Fronde of 1648 was simply the culmination of a series of separate insurrections which had punctuated the preceding thirty years, and even earlier centuries, revolts which were often incited by privileged members of society but in which the hungry formed the bulk of the rebels. The peasant, torn between the fiscal demands made on him by the crown on the one hand and by his *seigneur* on the other, tended to support these local and more personally relevant forces against the agents from distant Paris. Sometimes it was the local courts or the municipal authorities who stirred up trouble – anyone in fact except the merchants, for whom revolt meant the disruption of business. Such insurrections were largely short-term attacks on specific grievances, usually fiscal. They had no genuinely revolutionary characteristics, and were quick to subside either when a royal army was said to be approaching or when the temporary distress of plague or a bad harvest had been followed by a more prosperous season in which the tax burden seemed a little less than unbearable. The Frenchman could sincerely cry 'Long live the King, but without taxation'.

Louis XIV

Mazarin, first minister from 1642 until his death in 1661, inherited formidable problems, though he might at least have derived some comfort from the defeat of the Spanish army at Rocroi when the new reign was but a few days old. In addition to the burden of war, the chaotic royal finances, the large venal bureaucracy and the stubborn opposition of privileged groups in society, he now had to defeat the reviving ambitions of the princes of the blood, for whom a long minority meant a chance to seize supreme authority. The Regent – the Queen Mother, Anne of Austria – and Mazarin found these challenges all-absorbing, and allowed commercial life to stagnate. The superintendent of finances, Nicolas Fouquet, gave some stimulus to commerce in the later 1650s, and was the moving spirit behind the improved poor-relief of that decade, but for Mazarin himself commerce was interesting only in so far as it brought in revenue. Therefore the cardinal was keen to raise tariffs but reluctant to spend money on the navy. One of the few signs that the traditional economic rules were being observed was the promulgation of laws against luxury, but this simply served to offend the growing ostentation of the bourgeoisie and nobility.

In 1648 Mazarin's foreign policy reached a high point with the ending of the Thirty Years War by the Peace of Westphalia, but that acted almost as a signal for a wave of fresh disturbances within the kingdom. There have been many conflicting interpretations of the Frondes, because the Frondeurs seem to have been composed of so many different groups, whose unity was short-lived and whose sole common emotion appears to have been their hatred for the Italian cardinal. He was now the target of an enormous number of satires and slanders which were being widely circulated – the 'Mazarinades'. It is true that the whole realm was affected by the war, the ruinous level of taxation, the extra subsidies and the passage of troops across the countryside, but beyond this point the complaints diverged. The greatest nobles hoped to replace Mazarin in the centre of power; the *seigneurs* found that the peasants could not afford to pay their feudal dues in addition to the royal taxes; those who had lent money to the State, especially the humbler townsmen who had invested in royal bonds (*rentes*), feared for their investments as the government became increasingly impoverished; the sovereign courts objected to the attempts by the cardinal to force them to register unpopular edicts, while the lesser office-holders were concerned for their offices; the peasants simply wished to avoid the starvation which followed from the coincidence of high taxes and bad harvests. The crown was in the hands of the financiers and could not free itself, and it needed only the Peace of Westphalia to release those criticisms which had been partly suppressed during the Thirty Years War, even though the Spanish war was still continuing.

The rallying cries of the Frondeurs did not correspond to all these grievances. The loudest claims were voiced by the *parlement* of Paris, which became a self-appointed tribune for other groups in society who would normally have regarded its friendship with suspicion. In particular the *parlement* championed the financial officials in their opposition to the royal *intendants* in the provinces, whose dismissal was one of the principal demands made by the Frondeurs. The *intendants* or *commissaires* had existed since the sixteenth century, though their irregular visits had lengthened over the years. Richelieu had used them, but not excessively. The royal officials therefore were complaining not so much that these agents of the central bureaucracy were undermining their powers at the moment, but rather that they feared the usurpation of their authority in the future. It was ironic, of course, that the post of *intendant* was now a recognized step in the hierarchy of promotion within the *noblesse de robe*, and that many who disliked this kind of official would have been willing to accept such a post for themselves.

The most remarkable manifestation of the newly found *robe* solidarity was the pact of union of 13 May 1648, when all the sovereign courts of Paris joined forces and met during the following month in the Chambre de Saint-Louis, to put forward their demands for the reform of abuses. At the same time, other levels of the bureaucracy were submitting their grievances too. The courts demanded that all administration be carried out by the proper permanent officials, that the *intendants* be withdrawn immediately and that the conditions of office-holding be confirmed and safeguarded. The *Paulette* had been suspended briefly on previous occasions since its establishment in 1604, and the office-holders perpetually feared that the crown might do so again, thereby abrogating their right to bequeath their offices to their heirs. Making the fatal mistake of arresting the popular *parlementaire* Broussel, the Regent saw the barricades rise in Paris. In the first days of 1649 she was forced to take the little king by night from his capital, where he could not be said to be safe in his own palace because of the menaces of his angry people, much as they loved him personally. Thus in January 1649 the Fronde began, the *parlementaires* being led by some of the greatest nobles who soon showed themselves unconcerned about the views of the courts and preoccupied instead with establishing their own authority which, needless to say, they claimed to exercise on behalf of a king who was evilly counselled by wicked ministers. As Condé and the royal troops advanced, the *parlement* decided that its princely allies were too unreliable and made peace at Rueil on 11 March 1649.

The parlementary Fronde was over, but the longer Fronde of the princes lay ahead. From 1650 until 1652 this conflict raged throughout France, usually stimulated by the highest aristocrats, and leaving misery in many areas which had experienced a bad harvest in 1649 and now suffered another in 1651. Mazarin found it expeditious to leave the country on two occasions, but still retained control of the government. Condé turned his allegiance to the princely side, the *parlement* again flirted with the princes and was again disillusioned, and the struggle ended with the arrest of the leading rebels who were members of the royal and other distinguished noble houses. The bourgeoisie in many towns remained loyal, if disgruntled, while the poorer townsmen often supported the risings. Mazarin had been compelled to recall the *intendants*, but he had no intention of respecting for one day longer than necessary the promises extracted from him by the *parlement*. Thus ended the Frondes, a series of protests by reactionary groups, each trying to safeguard its own position and lacking any kind of revolutionary or reforming policies. Unlike the disturbances in certain other European countries in the middle years of the seventeenth century, which some recent historians have tried to explain by a general theory,[1] the Frondes included no significant group which wanted to acquire powers it had never possessed. In France such groups were rather defending their existing powers, and traditional paths had already been created by which the ambitious could gain influence. There was no need or cause for revolution.

In the later 1650s the country was tired of civil and international war, and Mazarin wooed the *parlement* of Paris at the same time as he was putting his own trusted servants into important positions in the government – men like Colbert, the future chancellor Le Tellier, Lionne and Fouquet, the great ministerial names of the personal rule of Louis XIV. Mazarin was restored to full power under a king whose majority had been declared, so that a rebel could no longer claim that he was fighting for a minor king who was being misled by wicked ministers. Throughout the Frondes the Huguenots had remained firmly loyal, no doubt because many were traders who shared Catholic middle-class resentment at the disruption of commerce by war. Also they took great care to dissociate themselves from the behaviour of their coreligionaries in England, whose murder of their rightful and God-given king horrified Frenchmen.

Meanwhile the war with Spain dragged on and the royal finances were still in a deplorable state. When the Treaty of the Pyrenees ended the conflict in 1659, and friendship was cemented by the marriage of

[1] See the articles contained in T. Aston, op. cit.

Louis XIV to a Spanish bride in 1660, Mazarin could justly pride himself on concluding a war which had finally broken the threat of Habsburg encirclement of France on the Spanish and imperial frontiers; but the expenses of these campaigns had prevented him from attempting any major financial reforms, and the confusion which he bequeathed to his successors was serious indeed.

When in 1661 Louis XIV declared that he would rule without a first minister, there began a period for which a great deal of documentary evidence survives, far more than for preceding years. These rich funds of source material are vital for the historian, because they reveal the practical limitations on royal power which are not easily perceived from a study of the plans and pronouncements of the king and his ministers. The personal rule was a long struggle between reforming ministers and reactionary society.

How far can the government of Louis XIV be described as 'absolute'? As was said above, royal authority was widely thought to have a clearly defined sphere of influence, and within its bounds no one thought to challenge the king. The princes might try to displace a minister in order to surround the monarch with advisers of aristocratic outlook, although Louis was determined that they should not influence his personal rule, but not even they could seriously hope to limit the royal power of decision. Nor were there any bodies who could be said to speak on behalf of the nation. Yet the authority of the king was limited in fact. Although Louis XIV intended to govern without a minister to replace Mazarin, preferring instead to make decisions in small councils of highly favoured secretaries, and although these councils relied on the *intendants* for detailed information about the situation in the provinces, the policies evolved in the central councils and approved by the king had to be implemented by the monolithic venal bureaucracy. Here were ample opportunities for men to delay royal orders, especially as the *intendant*, who was supposed to supervise the work of the officials and report delinquents, was often too busy to watch closely over them. Many royal decisions were reiterated more than once over the years, because they were being only partially carried out in the localities. When the *intendants* came to be more widely used under Colbert, the government received more reliable information but without a corresponding improvement in the machinery by which policies were enacted. Moreover in the *pays d'états* the provincial Estates controlled much of the administration within the province as of right, while municipal authorities throughout France had a considerable degree of independence. The battle between central government and local privilege was far from being decided.

1661 brought little change to the upper levels of government. The new ministers – Le Tellier, Fouquet, Lionne and Colbert – were all trusted servants of the cardinal and came from *noblesse de robe* families of no great antiquity, often being decried as 'bourgeois' by their detractors. Every one of them was an expert administrator. Fouquet, the superintendent of finances, was soon removed from their ranks, being arrested in September 1661 and finally disgraced after a long trial in 1664, because the independent wealth he had acquired made him a positive threat to the king. Louis XIV intended that he himself should be seen to be sole master of his kingdom, the ruler whom the people were demanding in the 1650s as their saviour from ministerial tyranny and as the reincarnation of the great Henri IV. They did not realize at first that little had altered, and that the Le Tellier family and Colbert were nearly as hateful as Mazarin. Within the new councils Louis XIV personally made the decisions, but was of course dependent entirely on the material which his ministers put before him. This is not to say that they regularly tried to mislead him, but the increasing volume of routine state business was too vast for one person to supervise. A man of unremarkable intelligence, the king nevertheless laboured long hours with his ministers and secretaries of state at the ever more complicated tasks which lay in front of them, attempting to apply the principle that every important action of his administrators should have been approved first in these central councils.

Louis XIV still had close aristocratic friends whom he trusted and frequently asked for advice, particularly if they held that one important office which could be given only to a great noble who was also an intimate of the monarch – a provincial governorship. In those provinces that were far from Paris and had turbulent local Estates, a powerful aristocratic governor, usually with lands in the area and with effective influence through clientage, was an essential agent of the crown if royal policies were to be successfully accepted by the people. He might be aided by an *intendant*, about whose appointment he would often have been consulted. The difference between those provinces which were administered by an effective governor and those which were supervised solely by an *intendant* was that the former had a champion who, while he was devoted to executing the commands of the crown, would also defend their interests and plead on their behalf to the king. Louis XIV often listened sympathetically to these reports from his noble friends. The *intendant*, in contrast, tended to regard everything with the eye of the central government, and was not infrequently rebuked by the royal ministers for exceeding his authority and for disregarding the regulations which limited his own power and preserved the rights and powers of others.

Great claims have been made for the *intendants* as agents of so-called absolute monarchy, especially when Colbert made them into permanent and resident officials, drafted to an area in which they had no personal connections and therefore impervious to local interests and pressures. This is too simplified a picture. The *intendants* came from the ranks of the *robe* and hoped to return to a higher post within them. In an effort to accelerate their promotion and escape from virtual exile in a remote district, they sometimes distorted the situation in their province, telling the central government what it wished to hear and making their own administration seem more successful. As their tasks multiplied, they were forced to rely on the services of *sub-délégués*, helpers who were natives of the area in which they worked and involved in local affairs, and the *intendant* might himself decide to co-operate with local interests as well. Even if he were scrupulous, he could not hope to scrutinize all aspects of administration within his region every year, particularly as his only way of checking corruption in the fiscal system was to inspect all aspects of the process, from the interrogation of every humble taxpayer to the auditing of the accounts of the various strata of collectors. He did not replace existing officials, but simply observed their conduct and reported on it to Paris. Moreover the crown was reluctant to give him general powers, preferring to authorize him to take specific action against specific abuses on which he had reported to the royal council. It is true that the *intendant* made some improvement in the system of administration, but only by exposing and punishing the most flagrant examples of corruption in the hope that others, less corrupt, would take fright and behave a little more honourably. In a difficult situation and a hostile area, the sole means by which the *intendant* could enforce the orders of the king was by calling out the royal troops – and this itself had a disruptive effect on society because of the disorders which always attended the passage of the army, not to mention the fact that there were insufficient soldiers to permit regular administration by this method and that they and their officers could not always be wholly relied on.

There could be no question of replacing the venal bureaucracy by an alternative system. Colbert tried hard in the 1660s to reduce surplus offices, although his success in doing so was eventually undermined by the creation of further offices to help finance expensive wars. Yet the method of instilling fear into the many by punishment of the few worked satisfactorily within limits. The disgrace of Fouquet alarmed people, as did the occasional exile of members of sovereign courts who were being unusually obstreperous. In 1661 a *chambre de justice* was created to investigate all financial abuses, and terrified corrupt financiers and officials before it was abolished in 1669 on the grounds that it was causing more ill-feeling than it was producing benefits. Judicial officials were even more harassed by the special royal inquests in the provinces, the *Grands Jours*, that in the notoriously corrupt province of Auvergne in 1665 inspired terror among the privileged classes. Such demonstrations, because of their vigour and disruptive effect, could also be used only occasionally and to set an example. Longer-term reform of the system was needed.

Although Colbert tried to stamp out corruption in the bureaucracy, that did not solve one problem – namely that the jurisdictions of various officials overlapped, so that some might reverse the decisions of others, though all were acting legally and within their rights. The most serious clashes occurred between the *intendants* and certain of the law courts. For example the *intendants* acquired the right to adjust the allocation of taxes by on the spot impositions, but the taxpayer was then entitled to appeal against this new assessment to the *cour des aides*. All too often the court allowed the appeal.

The courts and officials were in a strong position. In France there had never been a distinction between the judiciary and the executive. Each branch of the administrative hierarchy dealt with infringements of its own regulations. It was therefore difficult to win a case against an official, as he was part of the system whose own court heard the charge. Because of the hierarchy of courts through which a case might travel, together with the slowness and the cost of litigation, many people never bothered to initiate legal proceedings. If the king was unlimited in his power to make law, he had to rely on these venal office-holders of the courts to administer it. Although in 1673 the *parlements* lost their right to remonstrate against edicts before they registered them, having henceforward to register them first and remonstrate afterwards, they still had considerable power to delay the execution of many royal decrees by allowing the appeals of litigants in cases which were brought to them for judgement. Colbert's reforms undoubtedly improved the situation, and made officials afraid of going too far in opposition to royal orders, but the reforms often seem more impressive on paper than they were in reality. Thus the great codification of French law – the Civil Ordinance of 1667, the Regulations for Waters and Forests of 1669, the Criminal Code of 1670, the Commercial Ordinance of 1673, the Naval Ordinance of 1681 and the Black Code on slavery and colonies in 1685 – did reduce the conflicts in jurisdictions and the variants in local practice, and some of these codes formed the basis of French law until the nineteenth century, but in the seventeenth century, from the moment these ordinances were promulgated, there were frequent complaints that some of their specific provisions were being habitually disregarded and infringements going unpunished. All these codes imposed heavier penalties for corruption and breaches of royal regulations than had been decreed in the past, but also removed the death penalty from those crimes which offended superstition rather than reason.

The burning problem for the French crown in 1661 was financial, and it was tackled rapidly and successfully by Colbert. This was doubly necessary because, no matter how meagre the resources in the treasury, Louis was always prepared to spend lavishly on his court and on the other physical manifestations of royal authority, expenditure which the loyal and patriotic Colbert was ever willing to condone. The 1660s saw a number of attempts to increase the revenue of the crown, and to tap other reservoirs of wealth in the realm which escaped the burden of taxation. Unfortunately, the years of financial exploitation under Richelieu and Mazarin had bred a strong mistrust of government intentions, and some schemes accordingly cancelled each other out. For example, Colbert investigated the legitimacy of noble titles, in order to prove who was not truly noble and therefore not eligible for tax exemption. On the other hand he annulled the laws forbidding nobles to enter seaborne trade, in the hope of persuading them to join his new colonial companies. Many aristocrats, apart from the disdain they felt for commerce, linked the two policies and feared they were being tricked into forfeiting their nobility by entering commerce and being declared commoners.

Colbert was very well aware of the massive fiscal burden which fell on the humbler subjects of Louis XIV. Accordingly his policy was to decrease direct taxes and increase indirect levies which fell on a wider range of people. Also he hoped that a much-publicized reduction in direct taxation would encourage foreign investment in a France which thus appeared to be in a stronger financial position. It should not be thought that the government was motivated by a genuine human concern for the peasant – it was simply that extreme action against them, like the seizure of their livestock as payment for outstanding taxes, deprived them of their livelihood and prevented them from paying taxes in subsequent years. So too Colbert sought to stop the widespread imprisonment of the local, elected collectors of the direct taxes for failing to extract these dues from a poor peasantry, as it deprived them of the opportunity to collect anything at all and was harmful to the interests of the state. At least the indirect taxes could be farmed out to financiers, whose fortunes could be unscrupulously exploited by the royal ministers without endangering their survival.

In the *pays d'états* the Estates had the right to dispute the exact amount of direct taxes to be levied within the province. This gave rise to lengthy bargaining in which the Estates demanded the preservation of provincial privileges as the price which the crown had to pay for much-needed revenues. Such methods were accepted practice, the king requesting too large a sum, the province offering too little, after which the noble governor and others used all their influence and patronage behind the scenes to bring about an eventual compromise. The Estates had sole responsibility for allocating the tax burden within that area and, ironically, based their assessment on fairer principles and more detailed information than was possible in the *pays d'élections*, for in the former the actual resources of the taxpayers were estimated whereas in the latter the allocation was on a *per capita* basis. Colbert tried to extend the more detailed method to the whole country, but it proved impossible to gather sufficient information to make it viable. The *pays d'états*, for all their opposition, privileges and pride, were in many senses more efficiently administered than the other provinces.

The expansion of commerce was the means by which Colbert hoped to bring about the greatest improvement in French finance, although these policies received only cursory support from a king who preferred to think of wars and glory. The problem was twofold. There was the need to increase the French share of trade between western Europe and the colonies, and there was the equally vital task of abolishing the numerous privileges and regulations which hampered trade within the kingdom. Even the colonial trade affected local rights, by giving monopolies to certain ports at the expense of others. Colbert was more successful than his predecessors in attracting investors to his colonial companies, but too many wealthy men still preferred to purchase office or, if they were noble already, to follow the traditional and extravagant life of the aristocrat. A few nobles were becoming involved in commerce, but they were outnumbered by commoners who abandoned their business interests on joining the bureaucracy. The obsession with social prestige still restricted economic advance.

Colbert followed the mercantilist principles which earlier ministers and their advisers had observed throughout the seventeenth century, but this too provoked hostility in the provinces. Because of internal customs barriers, especially the heavy duties on goods crossing the boundaries of the *cinq grosses fermes* (the customs area which comprised most of northern France), some provinces concentrated on trading with other countries, paying less dues than when they traded with their own capital. Although Colbert simplified the tariffs of the *cinq grosses fermes*, the problem remained, and when he began to wage a tariff war against the Dutch, he was attacking the regular commercial partner of a province like Brittany which was outside the *cinq grosses fermes*. Many other national policies conflicted with the interests of the varied and separate provinces in the further reaches of the kingdom, partly because the merchants were not always the most objective and far-sighted of traders. In Marseille their concern was always to keep control of all commerce which passed through the port, deliberately sabotaging attempts to attract the ships of other countries which would have benefited France as a whole. Despite constant encouragement of ship-building, in which there was admittedly an improvement, the French lagged far behind the Dutch and the English.

Louis approved Colbert's hatred of the Dutch, if for different reasons. To Colbert they had an unfair share of European trade, to the king they were Protestants and republicans. Their agreed solution was to destroy them. At other times during his ministry, Colbert found himself at loggerheads with the bellicose war minister Louvois, son of Le Tellier, resenting the drain imposed by such hostilities on the revenues he was painstakingly accumulating. But for the Dutch War he was eager. Had he known that it was to last from 1672 until 1678 and cause him to reintroduce short-term means of raising money which he had spent much of his first ten years in abolishing, he might have been less enthusiastic.

Although Colbert reorganized the customs dues of the *cinq grosses fermes*, he failed to reduce the many tariffs on road and river routes throughout the rest of France. He did sponsor schemes for new bridges and canals, notably that for the Canal du Languedoc which was to connect the Atlantic with the Mediterranean, but once again the royal administration proved inadequate to supervise such projects. They were therefore entrusted to private individuals, who were allowed to impose a new toll on the completed route to recompense themselves. In much of France the crown would make a grant towards the most important of these works, but in the *pays d'états*, which the king considered to be undertaxed, almost the whole financial burden was laid on the provincial Estates themselves.

Colbert also speeded industrial development, although he concentrated chiefly on producing within France industrial products which normally came from abroad. To this end he encouraged the immigration of foreign craftsmen, tried to mobilize the poor, established stern regulations about quality, attempted with little success to standardize weights and measures and advocated the expansion of mining. He was not alone in following this course, and it is interesting to note that he received relevant information about further opportunities for industrial growth not only from the *intendants*, but also from the aristocratic governors of Brittany, Boulogne and Burgundy. These great nobles, the last named being none other than the Prince de Condé, sent him detailed reports on existing manufactures and proposed new ventures, while the governor of Lyon introduced pilot schemes for foreign luxury goods on his own estates.[1] If many Frenchmen despised the world of commerce and industry, there were also influential supporters of an economic revival.

The municipalities were another serious problem. Elected councillors and mayors, although the latter were increasingly royal nominees, flagrancy abused their powers. Many towns had become heavily in debt and, despite Colbert's attempts to free them from this burden, continued to squander funds needlessly. As they were responsible for financing public works within their walls, for providing forces of law and order, and for sanitation and street-cleaning, such matters were often neglected. Town life could be filthy and dangerous. Many town councils were in the hands of established families who showed little concern for the interests of other citizens, especially for those of the merchants. Once again the *intendant* could recommend the punishment

[1] The governors illustrate admirably the dangers of studying only the pronouncements of the king and the ministers, without examining individual examples. The king decreed that governors should be appointed for only three years at a time, thereby giving him an opportunity to unseat those who proved unsatisfactory. Yet in a number of provinces, mostly *pays d'états*, great nobles who were trusted friends of the monarch, and often their descendants too, held a governorship for years and even for generations.

of a few, very corrupt councillors, but there was a limit to the number he could select and to the time he could spend in such investigations. Paris was better organized, and in 1667 was given a better police force, but this was especially necessary because it was a natural centre for vagabonds and harboured all the principal intellectuals, both groups featuring prominently in any seditious movements which might arise from time to time.

If Colbert was not wholly successful in his reforms, he at least improved the efficiency of the administration, reduced the differences in outlook and policy between the localities and the central government and extended the control of the royal ministers over the kingdom. Much remained as it was, however, and even his improvements were not achieved rapidly. They occupied every minute of his twenty-two years as minister, and there was much he was not able to attempt. A major cause of his partial failure was his rivalry with Louvois, and Louis XIV deliberately played off the two ministers against each other. Louvois was gaining supreme influence in the last years of Colbert's life, and Louis favoured his glorious military plans, even though they undermined the economic health of France. To the king no price was too high to pay for a prestigious victory.

All provinces of France and all levels of society suffered, in addition to their other miseries, from the regular presence of the soldiery, who were renowned for their lawlessness and riotous behaviour. The seventeenth century had seen the slow development of a standing army, to defend the kingdom and to protect the king from the rebellious ambitions of his greater subjects. Although Louvois continually tried to impose high standards of training and discipline on the troops, the burden of billeting and of providing supplies was a grievous one for many provinces. The first war of the personal rule had been short, lasting from 1667 until 1668 and bringing substantial territorial gains in the east and north-east. From this moment Europe became alarmed, and coalitions built up against France. The 1672–8 Dutch War brought favourable peace terms, albeit after a prolonged and exhausting struggle, and the next ten peaceful years saw Louis as the unchallenged master on the European scene. However, from 1680 the glory of Louis XIV began slowly to dim.

The greatest single expression of that monarch's glory was his enormous and elaborate court. Yet the permanent move to Versailles, to a fitting shrine for the cult of the Sun King, took place in 1682 when the apogee of the reign had passed. Even when the court was still itinerant, its splendour had become legendary. Learning and the arts were lavishly patronized, and rigorous censorship prevented any excessively outspoken criticism of the regime. All enterprises which might increase the reputation of France were given the royal blessing. The most important and potentially dangerous nobles were showered with honorary offices and kept firmly within sight of the throne, while a host of other aristocrats flocked to court in search of favour and patronage. Some of these men chose to stay within easy distance of the king and created a way of life for themselves out of what became a boring round of complicated and expensive etiquette, made tolerable only by the hope of catching a ministerial or royal eye. Others paid more fleeting visits in search of honours, and then returned to the provincial centres where they had estates, office and influence. Despite the crowds of aristocrats in the garden at Versailles, the nobles were still the powerful men in the provinces on whose co-operation royal ministers had to rely if their policies were to be successful.

When war subsided temporarily in the 1680s Louis XIV, while continuing to intimidate other, preferably smaller, European powers, turned his attention to another of his obsessions, which was second only to his quest for military glory – the imposition of religious uniformity throughout the realm. Although this had always been one of his most cherished dreams, he pursued it more vigorously during the late 1670s when a new wave of piety swept over him, stimulated by his Jesuit confessor and by the last of his many mistresses, the only one seriously to have influenced his policies, the devout Madame de Maintenon. The atmosphere of Versailles was filled with this new religious fervour, a marked contrast with the more frivolous splendours of the court as it travelled with the younger king. The religious problem was threefold – there were still the Huguenots to eliminate, the troublesome Jansenists to curb and the claims of Rome to reject. Before the end of the century there would also be the mystical Quietists to combat.

Richelieu and Mazarin had not liked the survival of a Huguenot party in France, but the need for alliances with Protestant powers abroad had tempered their desire to destroy it. Louis himself steadily imposed further restrictions on the Huguenots by twisting the clauses of the Edict of Nantes, and in 1679, with European peace assured and armed with his new religious zeal, he increased the rate of persecution. Moreover, Colbert was approaching his death and his influence was waning, so that his pleas on behalf of the industrious Protestant craftsmen and merchants went unheeded. Despite the minister's objections because of the loss of revenue, tax concessions were offered to converts from the heretic faith, while soldiers were cruelly billeted by Louvois on those who remained obdurate. In 1685 the Edict of Fontainebleau revoked the Edict of Nantes, and officially there were no longer any Protestants in France. Although the effects of the Revocation have been exaggerated, there is no doubt that the exodus of Huguenots from France did harm her economy, and enriched the talents of her competitors. In addition it aroused the hostility of many Protestant states and brought no compensating offers of friendship from Catholic rulers or from the Pope. Many Catholic Frenchmen applauded the Revocation itself, but condemned the cruelty with which it was implemented, while a large number of the Huguenots simply feigned conversion, thereby gaining exemption from taxes but remaining as a potentially subversive force within the kingdom.

Nor was the Jansenist problem finally solved in the 1680s. In the years before the Frondes, the Jansenists had acquired a number of adherents from the *noblesse de robe*, which increased the distrust felt for them by the royal ministers. Although many members of the sect condemned the parlementary Fronde, a number of important Frondeurs frequented their headquarters at Port-Royal, so that the government felt this group, with its rigorous and arid intellectual beliefs, to be a threat to the order of the state. In 1668, after lengthy disputes, the 'Peace of the Church' brought a temporary victory over the Jansenists who, it seemed, had acknowledged their theological errors. But Port-Royal remained a centre for important and pious visitors, and produced morally severe works which were widely circulated. In 1679 expulsions from Port-Royal were authorized, although the king had too many other preoccupations, particularly the Huguenots, to carry his policy to its conclusion. Another impediment was the antagonism between Louis and the Pope, which antedated the increased persecution of Jansenists and Huguenots. The Pope would have welcomed such an assault on heresy had not Louis offended Rome in 1673 by extending to the whole kingdom his right to receive the revenues of vacant sees. The militant Pope Innocent XI, who ascended the throne of St Peter in 1676, was not prepared to permit this initiative and in 1680 refused to accept some royal nominees for benefices. Although most of the French clergy, some with misgivings, loyally supported the Gallican position of the king, the Pope declined to give way, and it was only his death in 1689 which ended a position of stalemate.

From 1680 the monarchy slowly took a downward path and its opponents became more outspoken. There had been local revolts throughout the personal rule, but they were short-lived, and were prompted by specific taxes or attacks on privileges. Sometimes incited by local nobles, especially by the officials of the royal law courts, they differed little from the disturbances which frequently disrupted the reign of Louis XIII and the minority of Louis XIV himself. In the fifteen years after the Revocation more elaborate and sustained reform plans appeared, firstly from Huguenot writers and secondly from some of the aristocrats who gathered round the king's grandson, the Duc de Bourgogne, voicing a more general disquiet which many Frenchmen were feeling. The policies of the ministers did not seem to be bringing great benefits, and the old society and institutions which they were undermining seemed preferable. Not that these reformers were simply reactionaries. It is true that they were mostly aristocrats and did indeed seek to revive the role of the higher aristocracy as advisers of the crown, in place of those men of more recent origins who had failed to solve France's problems; but they also advocated some decentralization of power, which was not so unrealistic because local ties were strong, and men still felt a more real loyalty to their province than to the Paris government. Those provinces which were ruled for the king by aristocratic governors and administered by their local Estates seemed more efficient than the *pays d'élections*. The aristocrats could therefore quote much evidence in support of their beliefs and of their class, although none of them thought of limiting the royal power of decision. It was simply the advisers who needed to be changed, the familiar slogan of loyalty to the king but hatred of his ministers.

In fact the ministers like Colbert and Louvois were succeeded by inferior men from the same social background, and the financial situation worsened. Nevertheless Colbert's son, the Marquis de Seignelay, did make an effective attempt at continuing his father's policies, despite the influence at court of Louvois. The great war minister himself died in 1691, leaving France to fight the long war of the League of Augsburg in which, from 1688 to 1697, most of Europe demonstrated its hostility to Louis XIV. The Treaty of Rijswijk in 1697 contrasted sharply with the Nijmegen Treaty of 1678, because the king had to concede where before he had gained. Moreover this was but a pause in the conflict. The knotty question of the succession to the Spanish throne when its childless king should die, which finally occurred in 1700, affected every European country. When Louis decided to champion the claims of his grandson Philippe, another war was precipitated, which lasted from 1702 until peace was eventually made at Utrecht in 1713.

The long financial crisis of the later reign was not simply caused by the cost of the wars. There was the disruption of trade, but above all this was a period of severe economic depression. Riots were frequent, not least among the Huguenots who still survived despite cruel persecution. Peasants died of starvation and groups of unruly beggars increased. There was a sharp contrast between the lower levels of society and those financiers who were prospering by exploiting the urgent financial needs of the government. Many men realized that reform of the finances and the tax system was vital, but that could be attempted only in a time of peace and relative prosperity. The crown would dearly have loved to buy back surplus offices which wasted precious revenue, but instead had to create more of them. One of the ablest ministers, Pontchartrain, tried every method of solving the crisis, even listening to some of the aristocratic reformers and trying their plans for a new tax which fell on all classes – though this was imposed simply as an emergency and therefore temporary levy, known as the Capitation in 1695 and the Tenth in 1710. These taxes suffered the same fate as others, the wealthy escaping from payment of their full share and the peasantry bearing the extra load which resulted. A single bad harvest was enough to make conditions intolerable.

Although the personal rule of Louis XIV had begun with poor harvests, especially that of 1662, the ten years before the Dutch War were almost free from such disasters and from the plagues which usually accompanied them. Prices were low, and industry and commerce prospered. The years 1674–84 were in contrast very hard, conditions improving in 1685–8, but then the situation deteriorated until real disaster struck in 1693–4, when a terrible harvest caused numerous deaths, perhaps a tenth of the whole population dying within a few months. Whatever this meant in human terms, to the government it meant the loss of vital taxpayers at a crucial moment. Although the financiers could profit by financing the war and thus compensate for the decline in revenue from their tax farms, the merchants also found the 1690s a decade of hardship. Trade had prospered during the 1680s, but during the War of the League of Augsburg the ports declined considerably, and industry was affected by the return of foreign craftsmen to their native lands.

A brief period of improvement followed the Rijswijk Treaty of 1697. A few good harvests, a sudden increase in trade and reductions in taxation changed gloom to hope. But success still lay in the future, and the government needed stronger financial resources before it could reduce office-holding and abolish the temporary measures it had resorted to under pressure. Another great war ended such fantasies, and once again the crown used any means of raising money, however unfortunate. The finance ministers Chamillart and Desmarets simply could not solve the problem, and desperate remedies like the manipulation of the coinage greatly harmed the state's credit. In 1709 and 1710, when the war was going worse than ever, the climate again added its contribution to the worries of the ministers. At various times of the reign there had been reports of peasants living in caves and subsisting on roots, and in 1676 Locke had discovered Provençal peasants lunching on slices of congealed blood fried in oil, but the crisis of 1709 was far worse. Terrible reports reached Versailles of innumerable deaths from hunger, and even of cannibalism among starving children. If Louis saw an improvement in his military fortunes towards the end of the war, the harvests showed no inclination to follow suit, and 1715 found the country in the depths of poverty.

Tragedy rewarded the prayers of the king, his advisers and the aristocratic reformers that the next reign might see a turn for the better. The heir to the throne died in 1711, and in the following year the king's grandson, the Duc de Bourgogne, on whom the reformers had pinned their hopes, died within six days of his delightful wife, leaving a two-year-old as heir to his great-grandfather. Although there was barely a single Frenchman who could remember the days when Louis XIV had not ruled, the prospect of a long regency meant an opportunity for the ambitious to further their own careers, and the scheming began.

The one major attempt made by any French minister to reorganize the whole of the kingdom, that of Colbert, had been far from completely successful and had been virtually abandoned at his death. Many of the king's wisest advisers had died as well during the last fifteen years of the reign, and the old king was reluctant or unable to find adequate replacements. There was a dearth of talent for ruling France during the minority of Louis XV.

French Society in the Eighteenth Century

Eighteenth-century France witnessed an ever-increasing divergence in society, between the poor countryside with its depressed and backward peasantry and the rising, expanding populations of the towns whose leading citizens possessed great wealth. The peasants formed about four-fifths of the 20,000,000 Frenchmen alive in 1700. This figure remained quite constant, with temporary fluctuations, throughout the seventeenth and early eighteenth centuries, giving France a healthy lead over the populations of other European nations until they began to catch up rapidly in the eighteenth century. Although the French peasants were always poor, they recovered a little economic ground in the first few years of the Regency. Some good harvests, combined with the lessening pressure on land afforded by depopulation, compensated for the heavy burden of taxes and the reduction in the number of taxpayers. Still, there were plenty of taxpayers left, even if their ranks did not include the wealthiest fifth of the nation. The methods of agriculture and industry had not improved, but at least a large number of Frenchmen were at work again under peacetime conditions; the hinterlands of the ports were more prosperous, because overseas trade had been increasing steadily since just before 1700; the construction of more army barracks reduced the need for widespread billeting and made the presence of a nearby army a less terrifying fact. It is true that there were years of misery when some epidemic paid an irregular visit to a few provinces and carried off an extra large share of the inhabitants, but these crises never equalled those of 1693 and 1709. Although many small peasant proprietors lost their land and sought work as servants or as day labourers working for the increasing group of larger owners of land or industry, without which they had to join the roaming vagabonds, there was nevertheless a marginal improvement in the conditions of the humble townsman and peasant during the eighteenth century.

Not that this changed his suspicious attitude towards the government. Every new royal approach always seemed to herald an attack on local privileges or a novel tax. Change was always for the worse. Although the peasant had to pay the additional burden of seigneurial and ecclesiastical dues, it was those paid to distant and remote Paris which were most disliked and which, by their sheer magnitude, formed the really cruel burden upon him. If there were a few richer peasants in a village, they soon moved to the towns because they found that, if they stayed behind, they were required to pay an extra tax contribution in order that the sum demanded from the parish by the crown could be paid in full, despite the inability of some of their poorer neighbours to find the money for their own share. The localities continued to defend their still considerable rights with as much fervour as they had in the preceding century, more so perhaps as the attempts to undermine them became more regular. Such privileges frustrated the ministers of Louis XV and Louis XVI, just as they had in the personal rule of Louis XIV. The *intendant* remained the mouthpiece voicing the king's wishes throughout the countryside, but he was now listening more and more to local complaints and was often influenced by what he heard. An ever more busy man, he and his *sub-délégués* could do no more than tidy up the confused loose ends of provincial administration. Major reform was beyond their means and sometimes beyond their inclinations.

The provinces were administered as before, no matter how watchful the *intendant*, by the same profusion of officials, and by the tax-farmers who at least proved to be better at collecting taxes than the royal bureaucrats and made a profitable living for themselves at the same time. The familiar brakes on centralized power had largely survived – the local representative Estates or assemblies in Brittany, Languedoc, Burgundy and Provence, the *parlements* and other sovereign courts, the municipalities and the guilds. The crown never ceased to undermine these immunities and rights, but it ostentatiously respected them as long as they remained, knowing too well the tiresome disruption of provincial life which might follow from a disregard for them.

At the top of the social pyramid were the illustrious and privileged ranks of the nobility and higher clergy, although the composition of these groups had changed since 1600. Many wealthy bourgeois, investing in office and in land, had risen during the seventeenth century through the noble hierarchy until some of them were aristocrats of considerable prestige, and an increasing number of marriages between these more recently ennobled families and those of greater antiquity had welded them into a more unified class. The high clergy too drew its members almost exclusively from the aristocracy. After 1715 the nobility became particularly keen to defend their privileged and traditional aristocratic life, based on landed wealth, because a new figure of immense power was gaining access to their ranks – the financier. For these financiers, and for certain other bourgeois who were now becoming very rich, nobility of office or of the sword was still the ultimate social goal. The leading financiers, who built impressive town houses and country châteaux, often married their daughters into poor but distinguished aristocratic houses and purchased nobility for their sons. This élite, recently elevated from the middle classes, was received courteously by the king at Versailles, for these were the men on whom his policies depended. The old nobility hated to see this social outrage and sought to preserve the superiority of their order, voicing their grievances through the high *noblesse de robe* of the *parlements* who, throughout the century, became the spokesmen for the aristocracy and the defenders of their rights. In the second half of the eighteenth century they tried to exclude *parvenus* from their ranks by imposing strict regulations about the noble ancestry of applicants for high *robe* office, but the rules proved unenforceable and money remained a sufficient qualification for even the most important posts.

The alliance of *robe* and *épée* was a formidable one. It was still true that the officer of the sovereign court worked at his profession in a manner which the ancient noble, 'living nobly', did not, but many old aristocratic families now regarded the high *robe* as a desirable and profitable group to join. The senior *robins* enjoyed great prestige and were well placed in the social hierarchy; they frequented the most fashionable salons of Paris, contributed to the discussions there and acquired friends from distinguished houses; above all they were building their own families into veritable dynasties, not only by advantageous marriages, but by the inheritance of offices, by the purchase of further offices for relatives, by investment in land, and by placing their sons in the more traditional noble callings of army and Church, thereby widening their sphere of influence further. The families of the sword had no choice but to ally with these powerful defenders of their privileges.[1]

Defence was necessary primarily because of attempts by the central government to tap the wealth and reduce the independence of the aristocracy. Not until the years immediately preceding the Revolution was there any need to protect their order against attacks by other groups in society. The royal ministers knew that financial reform and solvency were virtually impossible while the nobility were exempt from direct taxation and had a stranglehold on the courts and provincial institutions. The people, on the other hand, did not resent these privileges, regarding them simply as unexceptionable legal rights enjoyed by their holders. They too considered the government to be the really serious threat, and the *parlements* encouraged them in this belief. To complicate the picture further, the nobles and clergy were themselves split, as was the Third Estate, by the line separating rich and

[1] It was also from the ranks of the *robe* that some of the royal ministers came, who were to scourge the class in which they had originated.

poor, some nobles, still denied the right to participate in retail trade and probably disinclined to do so, bearing more resemblance to peasants than to *grands seigneurs*.

One final privileged group, the urban patriciate whose members had not sought noble office but had remained in the world of business, sometimes made common cause with the nobility against the crown but had little in common with them. The great guilds of merchants and craftsmen had been given a new lease of life by Colbert, because it was they who had to supervise the new regulations for commerce and industry which he had promulgated, and they rose to an even higher position of influence in the eighteenth century as the fortunes of their members increased. In some important provincial centres, such as Bordeaux and Toulouse, the wealthy guilds allied with *robe* and with *épée*, holding among themselves all the offices of *parlement* and city, mixing in the same salons to which they also invited the principal tax farmers, and thus forming an unshakeable body of wealth, power and privilege. With so secure a position in their province, these men did not care if the nobles at court sneered at their society for being 'provincial' – it offered greater security and rewards than the precarious world of favouritism at Versailles.

The theory of aristocratic superiority remained, of course, even though the middle and upper classes were drawing somewhat closer together. But for all this increase in wealth, the society of France remained essentially static for much of the eighteenth century. Few went to the colonies. Few indeed changed their place of residence permanently, certainly not straying beyond the province which was the only large geographical unit they comprehended.

Louis XV

In 1715 the forces of discontent saw their chance. The aristocratic reformers and the *parlementaires* seized the opportunity to establish a monarchy which was counselled by its traditional advisers, although the two groups did not agree about the degree of pre-eminence that should be accorded to the peerage and to the *parlements*. The peers, that small number of most illustrious aristocratic families which included some of the reforming writers, but also contained powerful provincial governors, influential favourites and powerless reactionaries, was united by certain major grievances which all its members held against Louis XIV and his ministers. Firstly the king had given his illegitimate children precedence over them, with the consent of a reluctant *parlement* which now reversed its decision. Secondly they loathed the advisers on whom Louis had relied, because of their low social origins and because peers had always been royal counsellors by right of birth. The third complaint was voiced only by those who had never been favoured with an office which carried real civil or political authority – namely that the peerage had been deprived of all power, by which they really meant not just that the peers as a class were offered no important role in the running of the state such as they had the right to expect, but that, and this was more galling, certain individual peers did indeed wield extensive authority as governors, diplomats and high officials at court while others were kept in a position of complete impotence. Now was the moment for a reassertion of their status as an élite group, so that all of them might exercise this kind of sway. The reformers among the peers and nobles genuinely believed that an aristocratic conciliar system would pursue more enlightened courses, reversing destructive bourgeois policies like Colbertian mercantilism, but the motives of most nobles were more limited and selfish. While the enlightened few advocated the universal taxes which would have solved the government's problems, the majority clung tenaciously to their exemptions.

The peers, high aristocrats and *parlements* became the leading spokesmen during the first days of the Regency. Louis XIV had realized that his hated nephew, the Duc d'Orléans, would have to be Regent, but had placed his heir in the hands of his beloved natural sons and had prescribed the composition of the council with which Orléans would govern. The Regent found little difficulty in setting aside the king's will, relying as he could on the support firstly of the nobles, who detested the royal bastards and hoped that the power of the bureaucracy would be curbed; secondly the *parlements*, who sought to regain their lost influence; and thirdly the Jansenists and all who loathed Madame de Maintenon and the Jesuits. The *parlement* was given back its right to remonstrate before registering edicts, and it in return confirmed the full power of the Regent and excluded the bastards. Under the licentious leadership of Orléans, society abandoned the piety and moralizing which Madame de Maintenon had imposed on it. Now too the higher aristocracy was given its chance, as the Regent implemented some of the proposals of the reformers, notably by creating the series of councils known as the 'Polysynodie'. These noble bodies, composed of *robe* and *épée*, were inefficient and consequently short-lived, being suppressed in 1718, and the secretaries of state were left in sole charge of the central bureaucracy. The first noble reaction had failed and for the peers it was a permanent defeat. They had lost their opportunity of gaining a real position of pre-eminence, and their rivals as leaders of the nobility, the high *robe*, were to be the vocal champions of aristocracy from then on. The peers, by their arrogance, had alienated other members of the ancient nobility, who therefore welcomed the more reasonable counter-claims of the prestigious and respected members of the *parlement* of Paris. They, in all their elaborate panoply and ceremony, had little need to protest on behalf of the forces of reaction while Orléans was Regent, and rejoiced at their increased authority.

The principal task for the government was the reform of the crippled royal finances. If the Polysynodie was a failure, there had been a sufficient revival of noble influence to make inappropriate any talk of new taxes which all classes would pay. A *chambre de justice* was instituted to extract money from the financiers, but although it condemned many smaller ones, with scant regard for justice, the wealthy survived unscathed. The Regent pinned his hopes for financial reform on one man, the Scot John Law, whose great plans began to unfold in 1716. He acquired personal control of all tax collection, and tried to persuade everyone into trading with North America. Many speculators took the risk but the whole basis of the venture was unsound, and the scheme collapsed in 1720, leaving a few men with considerable fortunes but many more completely ruined. Although this stimulus to commerce did last, the disaster confirmed the already prejudiced views of the upper social levels that the world of trade and credit was dubious and unsafe.

In 1723 the Regent died, and the next senior prince of the blood, the Duc de Bourbon, took over the government until Fleury, the Bishop of Fréjus, engineered his downfall in 1726. Fleury then held office until 1743, so that once again a cardinal, which he became in 1726, had supreme ministerial power in France with the entire confidence of the king. After the long years of expensive war, Orléans' foreign minister, Dubois, and after that Fleury himself steered a peaceful but strong course in foreign affairs, so that one sizeable drain on revenues subsided and there was a chance for the royal finances to recover. The length of Fleury's ministry is remarkable because he was already seventy-three in 1726, and yet he was to create the most efficient team of ministers in the whole of eighteenth-century France, led by the great chancellor d'Aguesseau and containing some able secretaries of state. Despite all the skill of the cardinal as a master of diplomacy, pursuing peaceful policies, war could not for ever be avoided, but a short war from 1734 until 1736 led to a profitable peace with no real exhaustion for France. This long spell of calm on the international front gave the crown an opportunity to bring some order to its own affairs and into the country, in so far as this was ever possible.

One group of subjects whom Louis XIV had failed to bring to heel became a focal point for more general discontent in these early years of the new reign – the Jansenists. In 1713 the Bull *Unigenitus* marked the successful conclusion of lengthy negotiations between the king, strongly influenced by his Jesuit confessor, and Pope Clement XI. The bull, an attack on the writings of Pasquier Quesnel (1634–1719), was deliberately worded so as to avoid offending Gallicans, but bishops and *parlementaires* did not wholly approve of it and the *parlements* declined to register the edict enforcing its acceptance, demanding a number of modifications. When the Pope tried to insist on its observance by refusing to consecrate certain nominees for vacant sees, the *parlements* supported some bishops in protesting against it. The religious issue was of little concern to the sovereign courts, who were simply continuing their long fight to gain cognizance of all matters concerning ecclesiastical discipline, but whatever their reasons, these challengers of Rome were regarded sympathetically by the chief minister, Bourbon. When Fleury replaced him, policy changed. Fleury purged the episcopate of undesirables, and chose as bishops high aristocrats who were prepared to follow the lead of Versailles, which prompted the *parlements* to champion the lower clergy. Jansenism was becoming particularly dangerous because it was gaining a wider, popular appeal as a new miraculous element, totally foreign to the spirit of the founders of the movement, received superstitious acclaim from the lower classes. Although these manifestations of enthusiasm were controlled, the Jansenist dispute lasted into the middle years of the century.

Meanwhile the commercial revival of the last years of Louis XIV's reign was continuing. Colonial trade was increasing rapidly and in 1722 a *bureau de commerce* was created to assist overseas expansion. Prosperity came to Marseille, Dunkirk, Le Havre, La Rochelle, Nantes and above all to Bordeaux where merchants built themselves handsome houses and commissioned public buildings fitting for the centre of so great a city, and for the massive commercial transactions taking place within them. In other French towns beautiful schemes for rebuilding were devised, while Paris grew into new fashionable suburbs as well as reconstructing its centre.

Industry did not improve in the same way. For the first half of the century the regulations imposed during the ministry of Colbert were implemented quite rigidly, under the direction of the guilds and the royal officials who provided the link between them and the Paris government. But control and restriction tended to discourage innovations in method, and industry still relied on the labour of domestic workers using traditional means. In contrast to overseas trade, the internal commerce of France was still hampered by customs barriers, especially that between the *cinq grosses fermes* and the other provinces. Reform plans leading to a unified customs area were successfully opposed on many occasions by the principal tax farmers, and the dues which thus survived required a host of officials and collectors. There was an extensive scheme for building roads, but these routes corresponded more to the needs of the government than to those of commerce because they radiated from the capital. Not, of course, that the importance of good contacts between the central and provincial administrations should be decried, because one of the worst features of the French government was the time taken by Paris to communicate with its agents in the more distant regions of the kingdom. In Colbert's day, however, some commercial routes would have had higher priority.

Among the peasantry, little changed or improved. The population based on the land was now beginning to grow, and with it the number of vagabonds and bands of casual labourers. Poorly cultivated fields yielded increasingly meagre return for these rising numbers, and the poverty of the countryside began to contrast sharply with the wealth and therefore the attraction of the town.

Yet all was not peaceful in the France of Fleury. In 1737 he disgraced his foreign minister Chauvelin, who had been attempting to prosecute a more aggressive foreign policy and who had a faction of adherents behind him. Other factions were growing in Paris and at Versailles, and the secretaries of state themselves had united in opposition to the cardinal. Fleury's death in 1743 opened up new vistas for Chauvelin and other possible successors, but Louis XV followed his great-grandfather's example by refusing to replace Fleury with any comparably powerful minister. From then on he played off against each other ministers from the various factions who continued perpetually to intrigue at his court, where favourites and mistresses could hope to exercise stronger influence over the king than most of their predecessors had ever achieved over Louis XIV. For the secretaries of state, the refusal to appoint a first minister was a victory. But, whereas Louis XIV was a determined man who, having heard the advice of his secretaries, put forward his own decisive policies, Louis XV lacked confidence in his own powers of decision and failed to pursue consistent plans of action. More and more he preferred to hunt and to devote himself to his mistresses, and especially to the girl from a financier family who in 1745 became the official royal mistress with her title of Marquise de Pompadour. Now, under her supervision, the court began to be adorned in the best of taste, giving rise to complaints about extravagance and waste from the country. It is true that the sums spent were vast, but they were trifling compared to the cost of a full-scale war. The real financial problem had still not been faced – how to impose a universal tax to replace the existing revenues, which were derived from an inefficient system of farmed indirect taxes together with direct taxes which fell solely on the poorer elements in the state. Inadequate for running the administration and an expensive court, they would undoubtedly not permit a long period of war.

War, despite the efforts of Fleury, had begun before his death. The War of the Austrian Succession lasted from 1741 until 1748, and with it, from 1745 until 1754, came to power the controller-general of the finances, Machault d'Arnouville. Too often in the earlier years of the reign, the pressure from influential financiers had prevented a finance minister from gaining supremacy. The needs of war, which Machault managed to meet, gave him the opportunity for this kind of superiority and in 1749 he introduced a new direct tax, the Twentieth, to be levied on everybody, in the manner of the short-lived taxes of 1695 and 1710. Immediately the privileged classes took up an attacking position – the perpetual quarrel between centralized government and local liberties was as alive as ever. Involved in it were other disputes which had not been solved earlier in the century, notably that between Jansenists and Jesuits.

The *parlements* had not been completely docile since they regained their right to remonstrate before registering edicts in 1715. Although the provincial *parlements* usually gave way after repeated requests by the government, it was often only a personal appearance by the king which compelled the Paris *parlement* to obey the royal will. In 1717 it obtained the suppression of the new and hated tax on all classes, the Tenth. It tried unsuccessfully to oppose John Law more than once, and was exiled from Paris until after his fall and until it had moderated its opposition to the anti-Jansenist policies of the crown. It upset further plans for a small direct tax in 1725 and became deeply involved in the religious issue again in the 1730s, when it gained some ground for the Gallican and Jansenist side at the cost of the exile of certain *parlementaires.* Between 1733 and 1748 its role was more peaceful, though it still made efforts to limit the temporary imposition of new direct taxes, and this relative calm was brought about largely by the care of the ministers in not raising issues which might provoke it to react. Thus the *parlements* were by now clearly to be seen as the principal defenders of fiscal and provincial liberties, and of Gallican and Jansenist beliefs against the policies of ultramontanes like Fleury and the Jesuits, although in foreign affairs they offered no opinion. Similarly the king made it plain that he was not prepared to share one jot of his authority with them. The *parlements* still based their claims on the fact that they were defending French traditions against the evil acts of the royal ministers, and in addition, of course, they continued to carry out their extensive tasks in their capacity as the principal law courts of the realm. It was unfortunate that in this period of their great and increasing influence there was a decline in the general standard of professionalism among their members, with a few notable exceptions.

The opposition shown by the *parlements* to John Law and the new taxes began to gain them regular and reliable popular support, which they had not enjoyed in the past for any length of time, and their Gallican views brought them the staunch backing of the lower clergy as well. By 1748 the central government realized that the *parlements* could cause a general uprising if they were alienated, a threat as serious as the government's own ability to imprison or exile members of or even whole *parlements.* These sovereign courts were quick to sense any plot to erode privileges and change the almost mythical constitution and fundamental laws of France, the *intendant* being the royal official whom they most readily suspected of complicity in such scheming. Many ordinary subjects shared the *parlementaire* view that the king would act in his subjects' best interests if he were properly counselled, while theorists still distinguished between 'absolute' and 'arbitrary' monarchy, between monarchy and tyranny. If these were misguided beliefs, it was at least true that the decisions taken in Paris bore little resemblance to what was done by royal agents in the localities, and to what was desired by the people.

From the death of Fleury, whose influence had been waning since

1740, there was no supreme minister either to govern France or to become a focus for hatred. There were the Pompadour, the foreign minister d'Argenson and the controller-general Machault. With Machault's Twentieth of 1749, battle commenced. The *parlements* and the Estates had to be forced to register the edict instituting it; the nobles refused to pay and no tax-collector had the power to compel them to change their minds; and the clergy made the most vocal protests, supported by the Jesuits, by members of the royal family and by Machault's now powerless enemy, d'Argenson. Behind the controller-general was the full strength of the Pompadour. In 1751 the tax was suspended on clerical property, and Machault acknowledged that the finances could not be reformed in any drastic way.

Linked with this was a religious struggle. Although there were still conflicts between the crown and the Huguenots during the middle years of the eighteenth century, the crucial issue was now Jansenism. If the number of Jansenist bishops had declined under the Regency, the movement had continued to gain adherents among the lower clergy. Fleury had controlled the most extreme manifestations of their beliefs, but in 1750 a new outburst of fervour coincided with the disputes about the Twentieth. The upper clergy feared for their authority as the *curés*, supported by the *parlements*, claimed for the laity a greater share in the running of the Church. The king, influenced by the *dévots* at court, sided with the high clerics, even though this entailed the abandonment of Machault's financial proposals.

In 1753 the *parlement* of Paris strongly reasserted its right to defend the fundamental laws, assigning to itself as much authority as it dared without being plainly revolutionary. When Louis XV refused to receive these remonstrances, the *parlement* staged a judicial strike, and was promptly ordered into exile from the capital. When the legal profession refused to attend the new court which the king substituted for the *parlement*, compromise became unavoidable, and in 1754 the *parlementaires* returned to Paris in victorious mood. By this time, Jansenism was again receding from the scene, although the hostility of the lower clergy towards their superiors, and of the *parlements* towards the Jesuits, had not abated. If the king's affection for the Society of Jesus remained, he could no longer offer its members adequate protection.

Machault ceased to administer the finances in 1754 and two years later became chancellor, but, after further attempts to humiliate the *parlement* of Paris, he was disgraced in 1757. The king needed the support of the *parlementaires* in approving emergency measures for raising money to finance the Seven Years War, which began in 1756 and started badly for France, the situation improving only when Choiseul became foreign minister in 1758. Even so, the Peace of Paris, which ended the war in 1763, marked the virtual end of the French colonial empire. Thus in the difficult circumstances of war, a period of parlementary dominance began, and one in which the provincial courts drew closer and closer to their *confrères* in the capital. One merit of the parlementary case was that, although such steadfast opposition to fiscal innovation was not likely to solve the difficulties of the crown, it was at least consistent and was supported by sound legal precedent. The government, in contrast, continually resorted to hasty expedient and, when the opposing side gained too much ground, policies, revenues and ministers were sacrificed by the king as an offering to peace, co-operation and compromise. This was an age when royal advisers came and went with alarming rapidity, and factions rose and fell.

The Seven Years War over, the magistrates drastically curtailed plans to prolong new wartime taxes. At the same time they launched a further attack on the Jesuits, which led to the suppression of the Order in France by a reluctant Louis in November 1764. Disputes about the role of the *parlements* continued for the rest of the 1760s, and the king openly clashed with those of Paris and Brittany. By January 1771 they had created a state of near anarchy in the kingdom, and the crown could barely be said to be in control. Towards the end of that month, dramatic, swift and decisive action was taken – the chancellor Maupeou abolished the *parlement* of Paris!

Meanwhile Choiseul was trying to improve the quality of the armed forces, reducing the power of the greater officers and rebuilding the navy which the war had shown to be so vital. Yet his days of power were numbered, and once again, though for different reasons, the *parlement* of Paris and a royal mistress were involved. Choiseul had survived the death of his staunch advocate, Pompadour, in 1766, who had greatly influenced the fortunes of many individuals at court, and he had avoided becoming a victim of the customary parlementary hostility towards ministers because he gave way to the *parlements* whenever it was possible. They were not as upset by the loss of a colonial empire as they would have been by a new tax. Yet, although he successfully negotiated the marriage of the daughter of Empress Maria-Theresa, Marie-Antoinette, to the Dauphin in 1770, the king himself decided to disgrace him for showing considerable dislike for the new royal mistress, Madame du Barry, and for his subservience to the *parlements*, together with the evidence against him which had been collected by the anti-*parlementaire* Maupeou and controller-general Terray. In December 1770 Choiseul was stripped of all his powers and exiled, taking with him the support of the nobility, the sovereign courts and the general public, who designated the new mistress as the source of such intrigues. One positive result for France, however, was that this action averted the war which Choiseul had been planning.

The abolition of the *parlement* of Paris in the first month of the new year was a bold step, and was greeted with an outburst of protest from all privileged groups in society who had come to regard the courts as their defenders, even though differences remained between them. The king was thus shown to be in control after all, and men might well speculate as to where his power in fact ended. New courts were set up to fulfil the judicial role of the *parlement*, while opposition to the formulation of royal policy now ceased – though the problem of how these policies were to be implemented throughout the provinces was still very real.

At last Terray was able to propose financial reforms, unhampered by remonstrances. The long-cherished plans for a tax on all classes could be imposed. All that was needed was time – and with the sudden death of Louis XV in 1774, time began to run out.

Louis XVI

Under Maupeou and Terray it seemed that the monarchy had never been stronger, although it had seldom been less popular. The enlightened thinkers, who disliked the *parlements*, also opposed what they considered to be the unenlightened policies of these ministers, while the privileged orders loathed them for their dangerous radical nature. Not that the financial measures of Terray brought a great improvement in efficiency, and when Turgot took control of the finances in 1774 the crown was heavily overspending. Yet an annual deficit in 1774 of 37,000,000 *livres* was to rise to 112,000,000 by 1787, growing partly as a result of the cost of the heavy and itself ever-increasing public debt. War was the largest consumer of funds, and no financial expedient gave the monarch the means to meet these demands adequately. The king simply had to rely more and more heavily on the financiers, ironic in a country which was not denied some degree of prosperity in its commerce and industry. If ministers still dreamed, as Colbert had once done, of abolishing internal customs dues, the consequent loss of revenue ensured that such plans remained in the world of fantasy. Moreover there were limits beyond which one could not tax the peasantry – they had nothing further with which to pay. Turgot observed that the number of landless peasants and vagabonds was growing too, in a France which was considerably more densely populated than it had been fifty years before. Wealth was becoming more and more concentrated in fewer and fewer privileged hands.

Yet French society was fairly docile. There were spasmodic and localized disturbances in countryside and town, but no signs of grievances which might lead men to expect a revolution. It was higher in the social scale, among the upper bourgeoisie, that enlightened ideas were being discussed and resentment against the privileged orders was growing, but even here the concern was largely with the possible solution of practical problems, not with the underlying philosophical spirit.

The new king, grandson of Louis XV, did not receive equally wise counsel from all the ministers he chose to help him in his early years as king. Choiseul's hopes to reassert his influence were dashed by his enemies of the *dévot* party at court, who persuaded Louis XVI to look elsewhere, and Maurepas, a capricious intriguer, became his chief adviser. The unpopular ministers of his grandfather's last years were not long to survive and new names appeared – Vergennes in foreign affairs, Miromesnil as chancellor, and of course Turgot as controller-general of finances. With Turgot, who had already carried into effect a number of reforms as *intendant* of Limoges, the philosophers believed that a minister after their own heart had at last come to power. Turgot believed in complete freedom for commerce and industry, and in basing taxation not on those sectors of the economy but on landed wealth. However he realized that caution and gradual change were the only methods at his disposal. Although no lover of the *parlements*, he did feel it wise to restore the magistrates to a part of their former authority, in the hope of gaining some support for the new government and of avoiding further *dévot* influence. He confidently believed that his plans for enlightened reform would have sufficient appeal that the courts would never again have such widespread support from the country. He began, not by following Maupeou's method of attacking strong institutions, but by introducing moderate financial reforms during 1774 and 1775. One of them was the abolition of the practice by which the wealthier members of parishes had to pay the taxes which their poorer fellows had failed to produce, while innovations in 1776 included a tax on landowners to pay for road building and maintenance, which had formerly been carried out by conscripting free labour from the local peasantry. Another edict abolished most of the Paris guilds. These decrees were forced through an unwilling *parlement* and the peasantry rejoiced, but the complaints of the privileged orders prompted Maurepas to engineer the dismissal of Turgot. His successor, Clugny, quickly undid his work during a few brief months in office, and the king now began to consider an expensive war policy which Turgot had always rejected.

France was to be involved in the War of American Independence from 1778 until 1783 under the guidance of Vergennes, one of the longest-serving ministers of the reign, who steered foreign policy from 1774 until his death in 1787. To provide the necessary funds, the Swiss financier Necker was appointed as director of the state's finances and, although he believed in a partially restrictive commercial policy, basically continued Turgot's programme of piecemeal financial reform. He also kept the support of the privileged orders for some time, but he was never liked by Maurepas who became keener to replace him as the months went by. By 1781 the magistrates too were objecting, their grievance being his partly implemented scheme for setting up new provincial assemblies. Maurepas seized this chance to force Necker to resign but himself died before the year was out, leaving Vergennes as chief minister though without such supreme authority. The next two controllers-general, Joly de Fleury and d'Ormesson, soon provoked opposition and were removed, leaving the office vacant for Calonne.

Calonne spent lavishly on public works to restore confidence in the government, but began to plan reforms, especially a novel universal tax which was to be administered by new local assemblies, composed of men from all the social orders. Resorting to a device which had not been employed since the ministry of Richelieu, he suggested that the king should invite carefully selected men to an Assembly of Notables, in order that these plainly revolutionary proposals might be supported by this sample of the privileged orders, making it more difficult for the magistrature to stage a wholehearted attack on them. As Calonne had rejected piecemeal reform in favour of more massive changes, it was only through an Assembly of Notables or the Estates-General that he could hope to persuade the country to accept such innovations from the government. He considered the latter institution to be cumbersome and antiquated and that it would not serve his purpose, but, as it turned out, the Notables were far from amenable. Their hostility was vented upon the plans from the opening of the assembly in February 1787, and in April he was dismissed. His successor, Loménie de Brienne, was a stern critic of his policies and was accordingly more acceptable to the Notables, who became more co-operative. Yet the outcome was not a royal victory, for, against a background of numerous pamphlets, the Notables recommended and soon the *parlement* demanded the summoning of the Estates-General, as being the only body competent to discuss such matters. Judicial, clerical and public opinion joined in the clamour that it should assemble at once. Under Turgot, Necker and Calonne, hope of enlightened reform had begun to appear more feasible and an improvement seemed in sight, even if privilege always remained a barrier. Now privilege had triumphed.

The interminable disputes between the privileged orders and the royal ministers were not the only cause of contention during the last decades of the *ancien régime*. At the peak of the social pyramid there was the controversial figure of Marie-Antoinette, living her pleasurable life where the people of France never glimpsed her, and always suspect because of her Austrian birth. In fact she had tried hard to forget her fatherland and become truly French, but pamphleteers attributed every kind of scandalous behaviour to her and she was accused of many an intrigue. In 1785 the affair of the diamond necklace finally dragged her name through the worst kind of social mire.

The court nobility who plotted against ministers did not represent the interests of all nobles. The provincial aristocracy, whom the great courtiers ridiculed for their rusticity, disliked the court nobles as much as they hated the ministers, and were more concerned to revive the power of local assemblies and courts than to support the *parlement* of Paris. Further tension was growing in the provinces because, although some nobles were keen to farm their estates efficiently or participate in new industrial developments, many preferred to boost their income by exploiting their feudal dues and rights to the limit. Yet the peasantry reacted by opposing specific instances of such exploitation, still not condemning the whole concept of privilege.

Townsmen were in their perpetual state of ambivalence, castigating noble exemptions but keen to acquire nobility themselves. Equally they disliked the despotic aims of the crown, and it was difficult to do that without supporting the champions of privilege. Moreover there was as wide a gulf as ever between humble townsman and great bourgeois, and between peasant and lord, and between lowly *curé* and prince of the Church. Clerical taxation seemed to go into the pockets of remote ecclesiastical nobles, and was accordingly hated by the taxpayers, although once again the assault was on the specific burden, not the whole principle.

The eventful reign of Louis XVI took place against this general backcloth of discontent and poverty. Increased population led to high prices and a shortage of grain, which might be satisfactory for the peasant with produce to sell, but not for the labourer, the peasant who was not fully self-supporting, or the poorer townsman who had to pay the prices. Landowners were changing from arable to pasture, and the resulting unemployed joined the rootless men who swamped the small towns, for whom adequate poor relief could not be provided. No government could afford to give the necessary substantial aid, although an *intendant* could assist a little on occasions by some form of tax relief. Turgot tried to help the needy more effectively, but lack of funds curtailed his success and later ministers showed less willingness to continue his policy.

The poor at times were pushed to the point of revolt. A short but severe food crisis in 1775 prompted grain riots in Paris and the neighbouring provinces, aimed specifically against Turgot's policy of free trade in grain. The bourgeoisie, who stood to gain from this free trading and who approved of this enlightened minister, opposed these revolts while army and clergy helped the crown to suppress them. A rebellion by the lower orders alone could not hope to succeed. There were further spasmodic local riots between 1775 and 1786, and towards the end of this period there were disturbances in Paris in which the tax-farmers and the Church were the targets. These hostilities were still the work of disunited social groups, acting individually against the government and other tax-collecting bodies. Even at this late date they did not feel that their principal grievances could be blamed on whole classes in society.

In 1787 the political atmosphere began to undergo drastic change. The Paris *parlement* accepted the newly created provincial assemblies, but opposed innovations in taxation and was exiled. Strong protests from the other sovereign courts caused its reinstatement, and its return was signalled not only by popular acclaim but also by rioting among the clerks of the lower courts and among journeymen and apprentices in the luxury industries. The *parlement* loudly supported the clamouring for the Estates-General and the people of Paris were delighted, not yet being aware that their champions, although containing a group of reformers, were in reality the strongest bastion of privilege.[1] A further royal attack on the stubborn *parlementaires* in 1788 provoked such a violent outcry in the provinces, chiefly in those with *parlements* and those which still possessed, or had formerly possessed, Estates of their own, that again it was allowed to return to the capital, this time more triumphantly than ever, in September. The minister responsible was once more Necker, who had replaced Brienne in August. Then the *parlement* declared its true hand. Insisting that voting in the forthcoming Estates-General be based on the equal influence of each individual Estate, and opposing the Third Estate's demand for double representation, thereby ensuring that the privileged classes could always outvote the Third, they revealed their championship for the old order and much of their support vanished. The Third Estate now saw an enemy where a friend had stood.

Meanwhile, in the provinces, the new assemblies aroused the opposition of the nobility and clergy, who in the *pays d'états* petitioned the weak government successfully for the summoning of their old Estates, which met at various dates during 1787 and 1788. This aristocratic initiative was supported by riots of lawyers' clerks, aided by humble townsmen and peasants who had come to the towns, and directed against the increasingly impotent *intendant*, but the greater bourgeois were becoming unhappy with this leading role which the privileged accorded themselves. It was the process of electing deputies in early 1789 to the Estates-General which would really expose these differences. Thus in the winter of 1788–9 the crown could not rely on its officials, and it often dared not actively support the *intendant*, but at least it could take heart that the battlefield had shifted and now lay between the Third Estate and the privileged orders. In the elections of deputies it was not simply that the Third Estate rejected the leadership of the nobility. The provincial aristocrats rejected that of the high court nobles as well, and the composition of the Second Estate reflected this divergence. The upper clergy were less reactionary, but many higher churchmen deemed it wiser to join with the privileged orders, and the more lowly *curés* made common cause with the Third Estate so

[1] Although these reformers were to play a significant role in later years and were very different from the rest of the *parlementaires*, they shared their more reactionary colleagues' hearty disapproval of the ministers and their arbitrary methods. Therefore it suited them to agree to a united parlementary attack on the central government.

that it was their deputies who dominated their order when the assembly met.

Faced with the aggressive stance of the nobility, the government of Necker, harassed on all sides and in an impossible situation, decided to support the Third Estate in its demand for double representation and was suddenly popular in the towns again. If the privileged were to be defeated, the crown was to be the leader of the attacking forces. On 31 December 1788 the conflict was still basically between town and country. The peasantry, in despair after the two brutal harvests of 1787 and 1788, were not yet making a violent onslaught on their *seigneurs*, even though they might be hoping that the Estates-General would produce some improvement in their position. The more outspoken views of the Third Estate were those of townsmen, who had greater cause to loathe the nobility.

For all the tensions within it, French society had remained unchanged in all its essentials for the two hundred years before 1787. In two years a wholly new climate developed, grievances were being formulated in novel terms, and new ideas were emerging from drawing-room discussions and beginning to catch hold of men's minds throughout the country.

Bibliography

French historians and their publishers have a masterly knack of producing introductory books which are both concise and profound, outlining a subject clearly and at the same time summarizing the latest researches associated with it. The new student of early modern French history can therefore have no better guide than the slim volumes by Hubert Méthivier in the 'Que sais-je?' series: *L'Ancien Régime* (Paris, 1961); *Le Siècle de Louis XIII* (Paris, 1964); *Le Siècle de Louis XIV*, 2nd ed. (Paris, 1960); and *Le Siècle de Louis XV* (Paris, 1966) (numbered 925, 1138, 426 and 1229 respectively in the 'Que sais-je?' catalogue). A book which covers the same ground as M. Méthivier, but in more detail, is R. Mandrou, *La France aux XVIIe et XVIIIe siècles* (Paris, 1970), in another celebrated series, the 'Nouvelle Clio', and like its companion volumes discusses the state of each topic, describes research at present in progress and considers the lacunae which remain to be filled. He is particularly strong on the recent economic and demographic studies whose varied and complex conclusions are here reduced to manageable proportions. A similar blend of overall structure, recent scholarship and unsolved problems is produced by J. Ellul, *Histoire des institutions de l'époque franque à la révolution*, 5 vols (Paris, 1969–72). A more dramatic presentation of this kind, less thorough and satisfying than M. Mandrou but directing vivid shafts of light on to the social scene in eighteenth-century France, is the anthology of extracts from other historians collected and introduced at length by Pierre Goubert in *L'Ancien*

Régime, Vol. I (Paris, 1969), now translated into English. Also in English is a contribution to the *New Cambridge Modern History*, Vol. VI, by one of the most distinguished historians of our time, Jean Meuvret, on 'The Condition of France 1688–1715'.

In recent years an English school of French historians has come into considerable prominence, some of whose members have written introductory works as well as volumes of penetrating scholarship. From the former category a number can be selected whose authors really understand the atmosphere and preoccupations of *ancien régime* society. C. B. A. Behrens, *The Ancien Régime* (London, 1967), is an admirable guide to the period 1748–89; J. H. Shennan, in the introductory chapter to his collection of documents *Government and Society in France, 1461–1661*, presents a clear but brief survey of the presuppositions underlying ideas of sovereignty, government and society in the seventeenth century and before; J. S. Bromley in his chapter on 'The decline of absolute monarchy 1683–1774' from the volume edited by J. M. Wallace-Hadrill and J. McManners, *France: Government and Society*, 2nd ed. (London, 1970), evokes the social climate of eighteenth-century France with as much brilliance as the author of the preceding chapter shows ineptitude in understanding the age of Louis XIV; the contribution to the same collection by Professor McManners – 'The Revolution and its antecedents 1774–94' – is also valuable, but so indeed is everything which he has written on the *ancien régime* and its fall.

In turning to more substantial works on French society, it is therefore most appropriate to begin with J. McManners, *French Ecclesiastical Society under the Ancien Régime: a Study of Angers in the Eighteenth Century* (Manchester, 1960), because he is able to bring to life with great clarity an area of provincial France at a crucial period of French social history. This book is not only penetrating and informative but is also a delight to read. The only other work of this quality in English is Olwen Hufton, *Bayeux in the Late Eighteenth Century: a Social Study* (Oxford, 1967). In French the recent social, economic and demographic studies have tended to become more and more restricted in their geographical and chronological scope, and increasingly technical in their concepts and language. In an essay of this kind, it is wise to recommend only a selection of the very best. Outstanding are the article by J. Meuvret, 'Les Crises de subsistances et la démographie de la France d'ancien régime', *Population* (1947); and the weighty books of E. Le Roy-Ladurie, *Les Paysans du Languedoc* (Paris, 1966); Pierre Goubert, *Beauvais et le Beauvaisis de 1600 à 1730, contribution à l'histoire sociale de la France au XVIIe siècle* (Paris, 1960); Marc Venard, *Bourgeois et paysans au XVIIe siècle: recherches sur le rôle des bourgeois parisiens dans la vie agricole au sud de Paris au XVIIe siècle* (Paris, 1957); Jean Meyer, *La Noblesse bretonne au XVIIIe siècle* (Paris, 1966); and Gaston Roupnel, *La Ville et la campagne au XVIIe siècle: étude sur les populations du pays dijonnais*, 2nd ed. (Paris, 1955). This last work first appeared in 1922, when it was not recognized as the masterpiece of rural history which it is now considered to be.

Turning now to more specific historical situations and themes, the reader finds that the ground is covered very unevenly and that, because the preoccupations of historians have shifted strongly in recent years towards the realm of social history, there are few books printed before 1955 which are still relevant to current historical debates. A notable exception is the now classic work of C. W. Cole,

Colbert and a Century of French Mercantilism, 2 vols (New York, 1939), and happily reprinted in 1964, which devotes substantial chapters to the economic policies of each seventeenth-century minister before commencing its valuable and nearly exhaustive analysis of the attempts made by Colbert to revive and expand all aspects of French economic life. A later volume by the same author, *French Mercantilism 1683–1700* (New York, 1943), takes the story through the more difficult years of the personal rule of Louis XIV.

The ministry of Richelieu has unfortunately given occasion for a number of disappointing or biased books, whose omission here is intended to discourage their perusal. Of noticeably higher quality and especial interest is a work from one of the small group of distinguished historians of France who come from the Soviet Union, Mme A. Lublinskaya, *French Absolutism: the Crucial Phase 1620–9* (Cambridge, 1968). After a few paragraphs to placate the Russian censor, of which the Western reader need take little note, she embarks firstly on an analysis of the current historiographical controversy about the possibility of a 'general crisis' in the seventeenth century, after which she examines the changing social situation during a vital decade of the ministry of Richelieu when, she convincingly argues, the balance of social forces moved and there was a significant development in the confrontation between the crown and its opponents from the privileged ranks of society.

The middle years of the seventeenth century, on which any supposed 'general crisis' is centred, have produced a flood of conflicting books and pamphlets, ranging from wild polemic to meticulous archival scholarship. The possible ways in which the situation in France can be related to or distinguished from more general European trends are most conveniently found in the single volume containing reprints of the articles which began the whole debate, and edited now by T. Aston, *Crisis in Europe 1560–1660: Essays from 'Past and Present' 1952–62* (London, 1965). Further controversy centres around the nature of the revolutionary movements in France itself at this period, springing originally from the work of another Russian historian, Boris Porchnev, *Les Soulèvements populaires en France de 1623 à 1648*, first published in Russian in 1948, appearing in French in a Paris edition of 1963. This thesis was soundly criticized in a lengthy review article by Roland Mousnier, 'Recherches sur les soulèvements populaires en France avant la Fronde', *Revue d'histoire moderne et contemporaine* (1958), which M. Porchnev answered in the French edition of his book. Too many other writers have since joined the battle to be listed here, although the main arguments of the Porchnev–Mousnier debate have now been translated and edited, together with some other excellent articles, by P. J. Coveney, in *France in Crisis 1620–75* (London, 1977); and special mention must be made of R. Pillorget, *Les Mouvements insurrectionnels de Provence entre 1596 et 1715* (Paris, 1976), and Y.-M. Bercé, *Histoire des Croquants: études des soulèvements populaires au XVIIe siècle dans le sud-ouest de la France*, 2 vols (Geneva, 1974). If these writers have considered seventeenth-century French revolts in general, a large number of others have concentrated specifically on the civil disturbances which disrupted the ministry of Mazarin. Among the most stimulating are P. R. Doolin, *The Fronde* (Cambridge, Mass., 1935); E. H. Kossman, *La Fronde* (Leyden, 1954); A. Lloyd Moote, *The Revolt of the Judges: the Parlement of Paris and the Fronde 1643–52* (Princeton, 1971); and an article by Professor Moote, 'The Parlementary Fronde and Seventeenth-Century Robe Solidarity', *French Historical Studies*, II (1962).

The personal rule of Louis XIV has been less well served by recent historical scholarship. Too many historians have concentrated on the attempts to develop the central government machinery without adequately considering the way in which the royal administration worked in the localities. Exceptions to this are R. Mandrou, whose *Louis XIV en son temps* (Paris, 1973) is therefore the most complete history of the personal rule; R. Mettam, whose *Government and Society in Louis XIV's France* (London, 1977) is primarily concerned with the problem of whether the crown was able to exercise effective control in many fields of administration or whether it was deceived, obstructed and sometimes defeated by the forces of opposition in the provinces. These apart, the bulk of recent work on this theme has appeared in article form, although a number of excellent collections of these shorter pieces have recently appeared. In the volume edited by J. Rule, *Louis XIV and the Craft of Kingship* (Ohio, 1969), there is a useful introduction by the editor, another thought-provoking piece from Professor Moote on the bureaucracy, a brilliant and densely packed contribution to the debate about the motivation of the king's foreign policy by Professor R. M. Hatton, and a reprint of the excellent article by H. G. Judge, 'Church and State under Louis XIV', originally published in *History*, XLV (1960). Unfortunately many of the remaining contributors to Professor Rule's volume fall well below this high standard. The Hatton article is reprinted in the first of the volumes she has edited, *Louis XIV and Europe* (London, 1976), in which many contributors offer complementary interpretations of French foreign policy in different years and areas, building up a coherent picture which is very far removed from the old portrait of the glory-hunting monarch. Her second volume, *Louis XIV and Absolutism* (London, 1976), includes revisions of many former views on the internal administration, as does R. Kierstead's *State and Society in Seventeenth-Century France* (New York, 1975), although the articles he has collected range over the whole of the century. J. Wolf's biography, *Louis XIV* (London, 1968), is not as comprehensive as its size and title suggest, and has little on the internal side of the government, but it is the most detailed survey in English of the sun-king's foreign policy. Perhaps the most important religious issue during the personal rule was the persecution and expulsion of the Huguenots, which is discussed by W. C. Scoville, *The Persecution of Huguenots and French Economic Development 1685–1720* (Berkeley/Los Angeles, 1960), who wisely modifies some of the more extreme generalizations which were previously current. Most other aspects of the declining years of the *roi soleil* still await their modern historians.

The same is true of the reign of Louis XV, although certain themes have been selected for recent study. The most significant single trend in eighteenth-century society was the *rapprochement* of the *noblesse d'épée* and the *noblesse de robe*, which is admirably discussed by F. L. Ford, *Robe and Sword: the Regrouping of the French Aristocracy after Louis XIV* (Cambridge, Mass., 1953), although he makes some unwarranted assumptions about society in the preceding century. The whole question of a suggested aristocratic reaction in the last decades of the *ancien régime* has recently been examined and disputed more hotly, and the various positions have been clearly delineated and assessed by William Doyle, 'Was there an aristocratic reaction in pre-Revolutionary France?', *Past and Present*, LVII (1972). This eighteenth-century topic cannot be considered without reference to the preceding period, on which a significant light has been thrown by R. B. Grassby,

'Social Status and Commercial Enterprise under Louis XIV', *Economic History Review*, 2nd series, XIII (1960–1). On the aristocracy under Louis XV and Louis XVI there is the work of R. Forster, *The Nobility of Toulouse in the Eighteenth Century* (Baltimore, 1960); the chapter by J. McManners, 'France', in the collection edited by A. Goodwin, *The European Nobility in the Eighteenth Century* (London, 1953); the article by C. B. A. Behrens, 'Nobles, Privileges and Taxes in France at the End of the Ancien Régime', *Economic History Review*, 2nd series, XV (1962–3); and the more recent books by J. Egret, *Louis XV et l'opposition parlementaire 1715–74* (Paris, 1970), William Doyle, *The Parlement of Bordeaux and the End of the Old Régime 1771–90* (London, 1974), and S. Kaplan, *Bread, Politics and Political Economy in the Reign of Louis XV*, 2 vols (The Hague, 1976).

The historians of the Revolution itself – although that topic is outside the scope of this essay – have obviously posited ideas about the *ancien régime* in their introductory pages. Some have shown little understanding of its methods of working, tensions, strengths and weaknesses, but there are a number who have truly comprehended its nature. Perhaps the most masterly work is Alfred Cobban, *The Social Interpretation of the French Revolution* (Cambridge, 1964), whose pages contain the mature reflections of a distinguished historian who had examined and re-examined these issues over the years. A great teacher, it is not surprising therefore that the volume of essays in memory of his life and work should contain fascinating contributions by pupils whose own scholarship is now renowned. J. F. Bosher has edited this tribute, *French Government and Society 1500–1850: Essays in Memory of Alfred Cobban* (London, 1973).

With a companion chapter in this volume on French thought, it seems improper here to attempt a summary of the vast literature on political and philosophical ideas, at times so intimately bound up with social and political problems during the *ancien régime*. Finally, then, a work of reference must be listed: Marcel Marion, *Dictionnaire des institutions de la France aux XVIIe et XVIIIe siècles* (Paris, 1923; reprinted 1968), which, though biased at times in its historical interpretations, is largely correct in its factual information and is an indispensable guide to the complex institutional terminology and regional variations of *ancien régime* administration.

4 French History and Society from the Revolution to the Fifth Republic

DOUGLAS JOHNSON

The Revolution

Fortunate the historian who knows the starting-point of his subject. The French Revolution has been given various *points de départ*. Napoleon believed that it began with the affair of the queen's necklace (in 1785 the Cardinal de Rohan was arrested for having used the queen's name in order to procure a necklace without paying for it, a scandal which associated the queen's name with an unfortunate collection of crooks and intriguers). Others have suggested that French intervention in the War of American Independence, especially from 1780 onwards, was the principal cause of the French Government's amassing debts, and therefore perhaps represents most directly the beginning of the crisis. Certain modern historians tend to see the measures taken by the Government to meet the financial difficulties as creating the real conflict: thus Calonne, in August 1786, presented the king with important plans for the restoration of solvency and in February 1787 unsuccessfully confronted a special Assembly of Notables with his projects; Brienne, who succeeded Calonne, found himself in conflict with the *parlements*, and his attempt to create new assemblies led to aristocratic revolt in the provinces and to distinct signs of a breakdown of the Government's authority. These modern historians are joined by many contemporary observers in believing that the decision to summon the Estates-General (which had not met since 1614), the process of its election and its meeting on 5 May 1789, constituted a revolutionary situation. For everyone, the famous events of 14 July 1789 must be seen as the symptom of a long crisis, and not as its beginning.

But the difficulties of interpreting the beginning of the Revolution are not simply a matter of dates. For many historians the collapse of the *ancien régime* was a simple enough matter. They saw a system of government which had become impossible. Not only was it oppressive and corrupt, it was also overwhelmed by a variety of crises which it could not resolve. And traditionally, the greatest of these crises was a class struggle. A privileged feudal aristocracy found itself in conflict with a bourgeoisie, which was not privileged since it belonged to the Third Estate. The aristocracy was becoming more of a caste, and more exclusive in its privileges, whilst at the same time it was ruining itself by extravagance, by shutting itself off from the main process of money-making and, most serious of all, it was a class which was not renewing itself demographically. The bourgeoisie, on the other hand, was shown to be a class which was becoming more important within the State, which was continually growing in wealth as demand and production grew, which was naturally becoming more self-confident, and therefore more consciously resentful of its unprivileged status. Thus there was a clear and simple framework of generalization within which the Revolution was to be understood. But the work of modern scholars has made it increasingly difficult to accept this way of looking at things. It is impossible now to speak of either the aristocracy or the bourgeoisie in any meaningful way as a social class. The varieties of income and the diversities of ways of life both within the general category of aristocracy and within the general designation of bourgeoisie make it impossible to generalize about either. The nobility was sometimes becoming richer rather than poorer. The bourgeois, far from showing resentment against the noble, was sometimes able to emulate him, often by purchasing land and feudal rights, occasionally by purchasing a title. In these and other ways the suggestion that there was a fundamental struggle going on, between two social entities, becomes difficult to sustain. Historians are rather obliged to recognize a number of areas of social conflict and rivalry, a considerable complex of hostile and disparate interests, about which it is not easy to write in broad categories.

There is a tendency, therefore, to eschew generalizations, or to seek even wider ones, such as suggesting that the fundamental distinction in French society was that between rich and poor. But fortunately there do remain important elements of the crisis about which there is little or no disagreement among historians. It is clear that there were serious financial embarrassments. The general rise of prices which had taken place throughout the eighteenth century, the increase of Government expenditure (particularly on road works and on poor relief) and above all the cost of the four wars which France had waged between

1733 and 1783 had created a situation in 1788 whereby three-quarters of the State expenditure was being spent on servicing a huge national debt and on defence. A growing annual deficit threatened national bankruptcy. Yet what could be done? Expenditure could not be drastically reduced without touching the debt and thereby undermining public credit. The possibility of increasing indirect taxation was limited by the fact that indirect taxes were leased out to powerful financial agents, the farmers-general, in return for a fixed money payment which could only be increased once every six years. The possibility of increasing direct taxation implied the abolition of the fiscal exemptions enjoyed by the clergy, the nobility and middle-class office-holders and a radical reform of the machinery of tax collection. The whole financial question stressed the need to endow the Government with a proper budgetary system, that is to establish and define its powers. Thus any action which the Government might consider as a way of moving out of its financial difficulties would have meant administrative, social and political changes which were tantamount to revolution, and this was the experience of the reformers during the reign of Louis XVI.

In the light of this crisis and all that it involved, it is evident that there was a struggle for power. A set of choices was placed before all those who were politically conscious. For the first time it became necessary to define where power lay and to discuss who should rule. When the extent of the crisis was realized by 1787, then there was general talk of the need for reform, and there were hopes for national regeneration. It seemed that there had been both corruption and negligence at the centre of affairs. The rejection of the Government's plans for reform by the *parlements* and by the provincial Estates raised the question of privilege. It also underlined the confusions inherent in the organization of the *ancien régime*, which obstructed the tasks of administrators. It threw light on the belief, shared by all the *philosophes*, that the laws should rule, that they should be precisely formulated and that they should be interpreted by specialized judges.

The resistance of the *parlements* and the revolts of the nobility obliged the Government to announce that it was going to summon the Estates-General. And this news created a new aspect of the political struggle. The *parlements* and the provincial nobility had already amplified their protestations by deliberately stirring up popular riots and revolts. When the Parlement of Paris reassembled in September 1788 it did so amongst the cheering of the crowd and the ringing of church bells. But almost immediately the Government stated that when the Estates-General met, it should be constituted and should meet as on the occasion of its last meeting in 1614. This meant that the First Estate (the clergy) and the Second Estate (the nobility) could always outvote the Third Estate, by two to one. Immediately there was an intensification of the political debate. Week after week pamphlets were published, attacking the privileged orders and demanding that the numbers of the Third Estate should be doubled and that voting should be by head. But the political debate was also widened. It was asked at whose expense the financial problem was to be solved. It was asked whether or not commoners were to be excluded from the most important positions in the army, the judiciary, the clergy. It was claimed that the Third Estate formed the most important part of the realm. Thus apprehension went with ambition; the political education of the Third Estate made great progress; and something equivalent to a revolutionary mentality was created.

This was not all. This agitation took place within a particular economic situation about which historians are in general agreement. The great mass of the population was, of course, the peasantry. Most of the peasantry were personally free and were not serfs; many peasants were the owner-occupiers of the soil. But within the great diversity of their conditions their situation was often precarious. The great majority of peasant landowners, and the majority of tenant-farmers and share-croppers, possessed only small holdings. They had sometimes to work as agricultural labourers or they had to engage in some form of rural industry. In addition there were large numbers, in some areas they could even be the majority, who owned no land at all and who were dependent upon earning wages. The rise of the population during the eighteenth century meant that there was increasing pressure on land and a growing demand for food; the general rise of prices adversely affected those who had little to sell and who often had to buy; the introduction of agricultural reforms which attacked common rights, the tightening-up of leases and the revival of many feudal claims were all further characteristics of the second half of the eighteenth century which made life more precarious for the rural populations. The whole situation worsened with an economic depression which coincided with the reign of Louis XVI. But the real disaster was the catastrophic harvest of 1788. From August of that year until July 1789, prices did not cease to rise. The importance of grain was such that these high prices absorbed the purchasing power of the urban communities, and helped to create industrial crisis, since production closely followed consumption. Thus, in 1788 and in 1789, when the political debate was reaching its climax, economic difficulties were at a maximum. There were grain and bread riots, in the countryside and in the towns; there was unemployment in the towns; it was impossible to collect taxes. And just as the political controversy generated its own myths and slogans, so starvation and acute distress produced their legends and rumours. Invariably it was the aristocratic class which bore the brunt of all obloquy.

The election to the Estates-General took place from the end of January 1789. France was divided into electoral districts formed out of bailliwicks, the territorial divisions within which justice was traditionally administered. The deputies were elected in their separate orders. All bishops and parish priests could attend the electoral assembly of their order in the bailliwick and monks could send representatives. Lay nobles, aged twenty-five and over, could similarly attend their electoral assembly, either in person or by proxy. In both cases election was direct. Deputies of the Third Estate were chosen by a complicated system of indirect election. Except in Paris, where the vote was restricted to those who paid six *livres* in poll-tax, the franchise was almost universal, and those males aged twenty-five and over whose names were inscribed on the taxation lists were able to vote in their local assemblies. The election of their representatives then took place in two, three or four stages, according to the classification of the bailliwick. In December 1788 it had been finally decided that the Third Estate should have the same number of representatives as the clergy and nobility put together (but it was not settled how the orders should vote, whether by order or by head). Thus of the 1,165 deputies who were elected to the Estates-General nearly 600 composed the Third Estate.

The clergy had generally elected ordinary parish priests, only forty-six being bishops (and these including Talleyrand, who had recently been appointed Bishop of Autun, and Champion de Cicé, from Bordeaux, both reputed liberal). The majority of the nobility was made up of provincial aristocrats, but a group of about ninety (including Lafayette and Adrien Duport) were also liberal. In the Third Estate, lawyers and royal officials predominated, but their two most famous members were both men who had been elected out of their order, the Abbé Sieyes (who had published a highly successful pamphlet *Qu'est ce que le Tiers État?*) and the Comte de Mirabeau (also a pamphleteer, elected by Aix-en-Provence).

Louis XVI ceremonially received the three orders separately, at

Versailles on 2 May. He gave no indication of what decision he would take concerning the manner in which they would vote. But since he had been on the throne he had most distinguished himself by his uncertainty and his weakness. He had invariably given way to pressure and he had usually shown just sufficient obstinacy to offend all parties. On 4 May the Estates-General went in procession to the church of Saint-Louis. The deputies of the Third Estate were obliged to dress in plain black coats, whilst the clergy were in ceremonial robes and the nobles wore silk coats and plumed hats, and carried their swords. In the church the Bishop of Nancy presented the king with the homage of the clergy, the respects of the nobility and the most humble supplications of the Third Estate.

At last, the next day, the Estates-General began its work. After a vague and inconclusive address by the king, and an exhortatory (and largely inaudible) intervention by Barentin, the Garde des Sceaux, the longest and most important speech was made by Necker. This Swiss banker, who had been the Controller of Finance from 1777 to 1783 and who had presented a deliberately inaccurate account of the financial situation in 1781, had been recalled to power in August 1788. His reputation was considerable and Necker himself had always been at pains to encourage confidence in himself. But apart from announcing a reform of taxation, with the establishment of fiscal equality, and a few references to other areas in which there would be change, his speech was inconclusive. It made no mention of whether voting was to be by order or by head. Consequently, the next day, deputies from Brittany and from Dauphiné, areas where there had already been particularly lively refusals of royal authority and where political education must have been proceeding rapidly, took the lead in persuading the Third Estate that they should insist upon the Estates meeting in common. This attitude received the support of many of the clergy, but for about a month all the discussions had little effect other than maintaining excitement. It was not until 13 June that some members of the clergy joined the Third Estate, and not until 17 June that the Third Estate proclaimed itself the National Assembly. Then, the king having been greatly upset by the death of the Dauphin on 14 June and by the dynastic uncertainties which this had caused, it was decided to prevent the Assembly from meeting. The result was the Tennis Court oath, and some members of the nobility started to attend the Assembly. On 24 June the king gave way and invited the clergy and nobility to unite with the Third Estate. It seemed as if the Third Estate had gained a great victory.

All these events took place within the logic of their own development. Individuals were surprised by what was happening; no one had a clear-cut plan of reform any more than they had plans for revolution. But amongst the pressures which facilitated the victory of the Third Estate there was that of popular agitation. During April there had been an important riot in Paris when the house of a paper manufacturer called Réveillon had been sacked because he had been understood to suggest that wages should be reduced. Throughout May and June there had been widespread disturbances throughout the country and on 19 June the commander of the troops in the Paris region had stated that these incidents were unprecedented. Invariably, such manifestations encouraged the belief that there were many plots and conspiracies afoot. In the towns and in the countryside it was rumoured that the nobility was calling upon armies of brigands, foreigners and clerics, in order to maintain a shortage of grain and to crush the people. It was suggested that individuals such as the Duc d'Orléans, the king's rich cousin, were preparing to seize power. And it was inevitable that all these fantasies were linked to the inability of the Estates-General to start upon its reforming work. It was feared that the king and the nobility would seek to crush the Third Estate. A number of municipalities began to arm themselves; regular troops began to fraternize with the people.

It was therefore in the worst possible circumstances, after the National Assembly had turned itself into a Constituent Assembly, seeking to endow France with a constitution, that the king decided to restore his authority by force. He had been offended that Necker had not assisted him in his humiliating dispute with the Third Estate, but his dismissal of Necker on 11 July took place in an atmosphere of military indiscipline and bread queues in Paris. It seemed clear to the Paris population, when they learned of Necker's removal on Sunday, 12 July, that this would be followed by the dissolution of the Assembly. It was believed too that a further increase in the price of bread and national bankruptcy would necessarily accompany this event. There followed speech-making, demonstrations and insurrections. On 13 July customs barriers were burned, prisoners were set free, supposed stores of foodstuffs attacked, armourers' shops ransacked for arms and gunpowder. Drums were beaten, cannon were fired and the tocsin sounded as certain of those who had elected the members of the Third Estate sought to establish an organization which would control events. On Tuesday, 14 July, it was the prison of the Bastille which was attacked and captured, partly because it was hoped that arms would be found there, partly because this building seemed a sombre symbol of the authority which was now being contested. Several important officials were killed by the exultant crowd. As the news of the dismissal of Necker reached the provincial cities, such as Dijon, Rennes, Lyon, Nantes and Le Havre, there were similarly violent reactions.

Louis XVI then rejected the advice of those who told him to go to some garrison town. On 16 July he recalled Necker. The next day he went to Paris where the National Guard had been formed under the leadership of Lafayette and the astronomer Bailly (leader of the National Assembly). The king put the red and blue colours of the municipality of Paris next to the white cockade of the Bourbons. This *tricouleur*, and the fall of the Bastille, were to be the symbols of the Revolution. But a real revolution was taking place outside Paris. In the towns the municipal authorities either came to agreement with new revolutionary committees and their citizen guards, or were overthrown by them. In the countryside there were important risings which seemed to take on a certain unity in what has become known as 'The Great Fear'. The rumour of an aristocratic army or of brigands about to descend upon villages and destroy the corn which was ripening in the fields and the constant realization of peasant insecurity led to attacks on the châteaux, the burning of manorial rolls, the abolition of enclosures. If the professional men and the prosperous classes had seized power in the towns, there seemed to be a danger that rural France was falling into the anarchy of an enormous *jacquerie* which was a threat to all property. It was in order to meet the awkwardness of this situation that the deputies from Brittany, who used to concert policy together in the Breton Club (later to be called the Jacobin Club), decided that it would be politic to propose a voluntary renunciation of certain feudal privileges. On the night of 4–5 August, in an extraordinary session which got out of control, the privileges of nobles, tithe-holders and various institutions were abolished. It is true that subsequent sessions modified the decisions of this great occasion, and that, with the exception of personal services, the *status quo* remained in force until it could be decided which privileges had to be bought out and which were simply abolished. But no one can question the fact that 4 August represents a turning-point, since the social structure of the country was now being affected by a movement which had hitherto been political.

Thus it could be said that there were three revolutions in the course of 1789. That of the Third Estate which obliged the king to give way and which began the process of giving France a constitution; that of Paris and other French towns; and that of the countryside. The question has to be asked whether it is possible to see in any of these revolutions any sign of an organized conspiracy or plot, which would give some sort of overall explanation to events. Thus it was suggested by contemporaries, and the legend has not died, that the Duc d'Orléans was prominent in creating riots in the capital and tensions in Versailles. It has been claimed that the rising of 14 July was organized and paid for by bankers who feared a declaration of national bankruptcy on Necker's dismissal. Part of the *Grande Peur* is the repeated stories of horsemen riding into some village with stories of brigands and marauders being on their way and then riding off, presumably to spread the same panic elsewhere. But it is impossible to lend any credence to the idea of a vast conspiracy. It is true that the deputies of the Third Estate maintained political excitement high in Paris and other towns by their reports of the struggle of the Third Estate against the king and the privileged orders and that this was a new element in political life. It is true too that the Duc d'Orléans tried to profit from the situation and that the closing of banks and counting-houses made a number of individuals available for the happenings of 13 and 14 July. Within the Third Estate certain deputies, especially those from Brittany, guided their colleagues at certain crucial moments. But no one was in charge of events. Often, as in the case of Mirabeau, deputies appeared more daring in terms of language and tactics than they were in terms of ideas or intentions. The outstanding fact was that an original form of political crisis was working itself out against the background of a traditional form of agricultural crisis. It was easy to believe that there were aristocratic plots to get rid of the Third Estate and to starve the people into submission. Thus the isolated and sporadic urban and rural violence that had occurred throughout the spring took on a new dimension and was fanned into a movement of major revolt by the political crisis.

The revolutions of the Third Estate and of Paris and the major towns were extremely self-conscious. Perhaps it was the extraordinary procedure of summoning the Estates-General which caused those who were taking part in these dramas to feel that they were engaged in events of great historical significance. And a sign of this self-consciousness was the number of times that observers believed that the Revolution was over. When the king gave way and allowed the three orders to sit together on 27 June, Arthur Young wrote that the whole business was over and the Revolution was complete. After 14 July another English observer in Paris, Dr Rigby, spoke of the importance of what had happened 'with but a few days' interruption to the common business of the place', and at the end of the month Gouverneur Morris was also writing that the Revolution was complete. Such an impression was in no way surprising. For all the differences that separated the men of the Estates-General from one another it did seem that the victorious Third Estate was agreed upon its ultimate objectives. They wanted a government which would be rationally organized and which would not be arbitrary; they believed that those who were important in the community should have access to political power; they believed that what was good for one part of France should be good for another and they wanted government to be national rather than particular. In their attack upon ancient privileges they were self-interested and they were in no way democratic. But they were also moved by considerations of humanity and by their belief that they were accelerating the progress of mankind. The fact that the country was in the hands of these moderate, property-loving believers in a balanced constitution, like the fact that the harvest of 1789 was fair, seemed to suggest that the dangers were past. 1790 was to be called 'l'année heureuse'.

But, in fact, political stability was to prove elusive. Fundamental to any new system was the king. Distrust of him, of his queen Marie-Antoinette and of various other influences at Versailles was all the greater because his brother, the Comte d'Artois, and other nobles had emigrated from July onwards and were contributing to the suggestion that the French throne was only suffering a temporary embarrassment. In October certain military manifestations at Versailles created rumours of a royal coup. In reply, insurgents in Paris stormed the town hall (Hôtel de Ville) and then set out for Versailles. This uprising was mainly composed of women and it seems to have been organized. At all events it seems possible that neither Lafayette nor Bailly disapproved of the fact that both the royal family and the Assembly left Versailles for Paris. But from this time onwards the court was completely hostile to the Revolution, and its chief activity was to find some way of escaping from a situation which appeared to be intolerable. From this time onwards, too, the Revolution was to be dominated by Paris. Already political life in Paris had qualities of its own. The presence of a lively press and of influential orators, conflicts between Parisian workmen and their employers, the inexperience of the municipal authorities and the vital tradition of the Paris mob's power meant not only that both the enthusiasms and the suspicions that had been essential to the Revolution so far were sustained, but that there was a turning to new and more humble sections of the population.

Disturbances did not cease. There were continued movements in some towns against the high price of bread, some *parlements* challenged the power of the Assembly, there were parts of France where the peasantry continued to attack châteaux and to reclaim common land, there were serious conflicts between soldiers and their officers. To some extent the new system of local government increased the tension, since power was in the hands of an electorate based upon property qualifications. It elected officers (who were also eligible through their ownership of property), but they were without experience, there was no adequate machinery for linking their activities with the work of the central government, they had no financial resources, and they seemed to come into conflict with the poorer sections of the population.

However, the greatest cause of concern remained financial. The financial crisis which had been the basic reason for the summoning of the Estates-General in the first place still awaited solution, and had only been exacerbated by the breakdown in the collection of all taxes during the spring and the summer of 1789. The Assembly tried orthodox means, such as long-term and short-term loans, patriotic taxes and even the organization of gifts to the State. But when they had all failed they were forced to resort to a more dramatic act. It was claimed that the land and property of the Church belonged to the general community of believers, that is to the nation as a whole. If the State were to take over financial responsibility for the Church, then it could sell Church property, and this would not only solve its financial problems, it would also administer a great incentive to the economy since land would come on to the market and be available for new developments. The nationalization of Church lands was voted in December 1789, with little opposition, although there were those who declared that it was an attack on private property. The Civil Constitution of the Church whereby the State assumed responsibility for the clergy became law in July 1790, and in November the clergy were asked, as public servants, to take an oath of allegiance. These measures aroused violent resistance and more than half of the clergy refused to take the oath. Whilst awaiting the actual sale of the Church lands, negotiable bonds called *assignats* were issued, based upon these lands. For the time being these *assignats*, which were soon to be used as a form of paper money, maintained their value, but by the summer of 1791 the process of devaluation had begun.

Thus the measures concerning the Church were amongst the most important of the Revolution. Men went further than they had realized towards taking decisions in the name of the nation. A centre of opposition which included both the nobility and humble people was formed. A source of economic instability had been created. These factors have tended to outweigh the Declaration of the Rights of Man, voted in August 1791 (which guaranteed equal treatment before the law), the Constitution of 1791 (which gave greatest weight to an Assembly elected by the wealthiest citizens, probably well over four millions) and the thoroughgoing reform of the legal system which the Constituent Assembly began. Other reforms have also been overlooked such as the abolition of the venality of offices and a mild democratization of both the army and the navy.

The next phase of the Revolution was to bring France into closer contact with the rest of Europe and to destroy any belief that it was complete, or that the country could settle down. Whilst the Comte d'Artois and other émigrés openly urged a foreign invasion of France and worked for a civil war which would restore the old order (and maintained unrest in certain parts of France, especially in the south), the king decided to leave Paris and seek the protection of loyal troops in eastern regions. In June 1791 the king (and the royal family) were arrested at Varennes and brought back to Paris. It was impossible to go on as before. Whilst the moderates spread the fiction that the king had been 'kidnapped', a great impetus was given to the formation of popular societies and to more extremist clubs by their desire to dethrone and to try the king. It was at this time that those who were to be called *sans-culottes* first appeared. When the Constituent Assembly gave way, in October 1791, to the new Legislative Assembly, the problem that was most to the fore was still that of the dangers to France which resulted from émigrés and foreign courts. Although at the Jacobin Club Robespierre opposed the idea of solving this problem by starting a war, yet there were others led by Brissot who began to think that this was desirable. Other politicians believed that the political deadlock in which France had found herself would be resolved by a short and successful war, and that the crown would be able to resume its rightful place in the constitution. There were still others who looked forward to a French defeat and to the king being rescued. The result was the French declaration of war against Austria on 20 April 1792.

Almost immediately it was clear that the French army was not in a position to fight. An offensive misfired and Paris lay apparently open to the enemy (Austria and Prussia). The enemy was not only on the French frontiers; the enemy was also to be found in the counter-revolutionary forces which had come alive once war had been declared, particularly in the south. The decline in the value of the *assignat* led to the interruption of the normal processes of exchange, and many parts of France began to grow short of food. Once again there was suspicion that there had been a great betrayal of the Revolution and of the country. The forty-eight local constituency divisions of Paris, the sections, set up a revolutionary Government of Paris, the Commune. On 10 August 1792 they invaded the royal palace and imprisoned the king. The moderate Government found that it was obliged to summon a new Assembly, the National Convention, this time to be elected by universal suffrage. A Jacobin, Danton, who was working with the Commune, became Minister of Justice, the journalist Marat proclaimed that only through violence would the poor gain any benefits. But a few days later the Prussian army crossed the French frontier.

10 August 1792 was in many ways like 14 July 1789. But the French Revolution had changed in character. Up to 10 August the Revolution had been moderate and it had been legal. The people, whether in Paris and the towns or in the countryside, had played a vital part. But the representatives of the Third Estate had always been in charge. There had been little which was democratic or socialist; much of the work of the Third Estate had been to make a society where the economy would be free, where producers would be unhampered by tradition, privilege or arbitrary government. A law passed in 1791 protected these producers by forbidding all forms of association by capital or labour, thus attacking the guilds and preventing working-people from assembling together. But this liberal spirit could not survive the sort of crisis which the war was creating. French resources were scattered, so that an invading enemy did not have any easy target, but it was necessary for a French Government, organizing its defence, to mobilize the whole nation, its army, its supplies, its morale. It became necessary to control the movement of goods and to limit the rise of prices. Since the enemy was inside the frontiers of France as well as outside it was necessary to root out the enemy within, to find the traitors, to identify those whose opinions and interests seemed to clash with those of the nation as a whole. Because the Revolution had become popular it was

to take the form of endless meetings, demonstrations, debates, resolutions. In September 1792 there was the first manifestation of the Terror, when those suspected of having sympathy with the enemy received summary justice. From this time onwards the emphasis was on patriotism and the need to defend the Revolution by all means. Since the ordinary man was playing his part in all this, the ordinary things of life were changed too. People no longer addressed each other as 'Monsieur', they called themselves 'Citoyen', they addressed each other familiarly (*tutoiement*), they affected the careless dress of the *sans-culotte*, the names of the streets were changed into names showing the sovereignty of the people.

Thus the Revolution was no longer moderate, liberal and legal. The Revolution could be dictatorial, extreme, social and unpredictable. The change could be symbolized by the change in the role of Robespierre, the lawyer from Arras. As a deputy in the Third Estate he was distinguished by his humanity and his zeal for freedom. He wanted the under-privileged and the persecuted (such as actors and the Jews) to be protected; he wanted the death penalty to be abolished; he urged that justice should be reformed because it was better that a hundred guilty men should escape than that one innocent man should be condemned. But in this period of history Robespierre appears in a different light, as the most typical representative of a Government which was more powerful, more able to interfere in the private affairs of citizens, more organized in a great witch hunt so as to smell out the enemies of the Revolution, than any other Government in French history. This was not because Robespierre had changed in character. It was because the situation had changed.

And the crisis was prolonged. In September 1792 the French beat the Prussians at Valmy, in November they defeat the Austrians at Jemappes and their armies occupy Belgium, the left bank of the Rhine, Nice and Savoy. Danton proclaims a war of the peoples against the kings, and after the Republic has been proclaimed in France, Louis XVI is sentenced to death. 'You have not a sentence to give for or against a man', claims Robespierre, 'but a measure of public safety to take.' The king is executed in January 1793. But by February France is at war with a coalition that includes England, Prussia, Austria, Spain and Piedmont. The French armies are defeated in Holland and the French general goes over to the enemy. In the west of France there is an anti-Revolutionary rising in Anjou, which spreads to Brittany, Maine and Normandy. The rise in prices leads to insurrection in the towns. The Government attempts to maintain its hold on affairs; it establishes a revolutionary tribunal to try suspects ('soyons terribles, pour dispenser le peuple de l'être' is Danton's advice); it sends its representatives into the departments to organize the mobilization of an enormous army; it passes laws confiscating the property of aristocrats, fixing the value of the *assignat*, putting a ceiling on the price of corn and flour; it establishes a Committee of Public Safety. But it remains suspect, and after some initial failures on Sunday, 2 June 1793, yet another Parisian rising expels the Government from the Tuileries, and France finds itself in the grip of civil war.

The moderates who were evicted in this rising have commonly been called the Girondins, because Brissot and some of his followers came from the department of the Gironde, and it was they who largely dominated the Government since the meeting of the Legislative Assembly. However, it would be wrong to suppose that the Girondins formed a coherent or organized political party. They represented rather a group of individuals, romantic in their oratory, idealistic in their adherence to the principles of 1789, conceited in their conviction that they were destined to lead the country, who were fearful of carrying the Revolution forward. They suspected every increase in governmental power, they were reluctant to introduce further measures of reform, they feared as they deplored movements of the crowd. Behind the principle of this refusal to accept the creation of a Government which could be tyrannical, and sometimes more important than it, were questions of personality. The rivalry between Girondins and Jacobins was that of rival factions, but since the Jacobins were not in power they naturally became associated with the need for more effective action and therefore with the need for a strong Government which would save the Revolution. The Jacobins were prepared to work with the masses and with the *sans-culottes* of the Paris sections, and this was what was finally achieved on 2 June. But elsewhere in France, the moderates found support. There were movements in towns such as Lyon and Marseille which overthrew the Jacobin municipalities. After 2 June this movement was encouraged by Girondin fugitives and by a general refusal of provincial France to accept what had happened in Paris. Moderates who believed that the sovereignty of the nation had been violated joined with the royalists, the non-juring Catholics, the constitutional monarchists, in their opposition to Paris. Those who were wealthy and who had property to protect looked with apprehension at what was happening in Paris and with sympathy at the armies which were being raised, particularly in the south and in Normandy, to fight for this cause. The insurrectionaries in the west were being successful, they had captured Saumur on 9 June and they were reported ready to march on Paris. A French army was besieged in the Rhineland, and an allied army was advancing from the north of France.

Nor was the Government secure in Paris. The sections were disappointed that their demands for more direct control of government and for the creation of a more revolutionary army were not met. There was the danger of further insurrection. During this period the Committee of Public Safety was dominated by Danton, who in spite of his fiery oratory and massive appearance sought to meet all the dangers by a policy of compromise. He and his colleagues went particularly out of their way to reassure the peasantry, and abolished all remaining feudal dues without any compensation; the middle-class officials were placated by increases of salary; special representatives were sent to win over the provinces and to discredit the Girondins; a new democratic constitution was proclaimed. All these measures had some success. But they did not solve the problems created by high prices, shortage of food and a devalued money. Jacques Roux, a former constitutional cleric, denounced the laws which had been made by the rich and for the rich. It was pointed out that the constitution did not provide bread for those who had none and it was claimed that the Government had done nothing for the people. Bad news still came from the war and on 10 July Danton and his associates were not re-elected to the Committee of Public Safety. Three days later the dangers to the Revolution were emphasized by the murder of Marat, the journalist and orator and reputedly the friend of the people. Lyon was declared to be in a state of rebellion, certain Girondin and army leaders were accused of treason, measures against hoarders were announced, and it was thus in a tense and dangerous situation that Robespierre was called to become a member of the Committee of Public Safety.

It should not be thought that Robespierre was to dominate the Committee, any more than it should be thought that this Committee was the sole institution which governed France. There were other patriots and there were other revolutionary committees. But Robespierre had an influence which was particular. In so far as there were wide differences in ideas between the Jacobins and the *sans-culottes* it was necessary to find someone who would command respect amongst both. Robespierre seemed able to win the confidence of those who were attached to the Revolution as it had been conceived in 1789, and because of his undoubted patriotism, honesty and determination to save the Republic, he appealed to the *sans-culottes*. Since it was necessary to analyse and explain policy in the light of principles and ideas, then it was necessary to have someone in power who could express and define the philosophy of the Revolution. Robespierre was also by now experienced, and he had always been able.

In some ways the presence of Robespierre did not make any practical difference. Many of the important decisions had been taken before he became a member of the Committee (the decision to try Marie-Antoinette, for example). As before, some decisions were taken only reluctantly and as a result of *sans-culotte* pressure, such as that to enforce a *levée-en-masse* of all unmarried men between eighteen and twenty-five. But a new determination was apparent. The Terror became more effective in dealing with the supposed enemies of the State (both Marie-Antoinette and the Duc d'Orléans were executed). Churches were closed and a deliberate policy of dechristianization was launched. Prices were given a maximum, goods were requisitioned, wages were controlled. Festivities were organized to give the people confidence, and a Revolutionary calendar was adopted with the year One dating from 22 September 1792 so as to emphasize that a new era had dawned. What was perhaps more significant of Robespierre's power was that social reformers such as Roux (and the *enragés*) were imprisoned, and even the *sans-culotte* influence was reduced.

In practice the Committee of Public Safety had great success. By October Lyon was captured by the republican army and the important port of Toulon surrendered in December. The Vendéens suffered many reverses, and the Revolutionary generals won successes on all fronts. By 1794 there were nearly a million men under arms, and it was a member of the Committee of Public Safety, Lazare Carnot, who was known as the organizer of victory. In March and April 1794 Robespierre was able to send both Hébert and his left-wing followers and Danton and some of his friends who were financial speculators to the guillotine. In June the great battle of Fleurus opened Flanders to the French army and it was clear that the Republic was no longer fighting a defensive battle but had taken the offensive. The climax of the Revolution was over, yet Robespierre did not seem able to let up. In June and July there were 1,285 people condemned to death. He was associated with the Cult of the Supreme Being, a naturalistic, 'rational' religion which offended many of his followers. He had alienated many of his supporters among the people of Paris; there was jealousy and fear of the

Committee of Public Safety, and in the Convention there were many who regarded Robespierre with apprehension. He did little to defend himself and showed no sign of wanting to change his policies. It was simple to organize a conspiracy against him and on 26 July 1794 he was arrested and, later, executed.

The French statesman and historian Guizot was often to recall that he could remember seeing his mother kneel down and give thanks when she learned of the death of Robespierre. It was perhaps inevitable that he should have become the symbol of this period in Revolutionary history when the most extreme measures had to be taken in order to save the Republic. But the ease with which he was overthrown is also significant. It demonstrates how the Revolution was invariably controlled by those who were moderate, and most of whom were probably satisfied with a constitutional monarchy or with a bourgeois Republic. The ideals of the *sans-culottes*, who wanted each man to have his small piece of property, who wanted to control the politicians, who wanted goods to be plentiful and at a reasonable price, were irrelevant to the Revolution except in moments of unusual crisis. The *sans-culottes* represented an institutionalized popular movement, and since it was always possible that their sectionary societies could be stifled by the Jacobins, then there is something inevitable about their decline. And whilst it is true that the revolutionary crowds contained important elements of workshop masters, craftsmen, shop-keepers and small-traders who were able to formulate their ideas on the way in which society should be organized, it is impossible not to consider that the 'masses indigentes', the beggars, the unemployed and the ordinary workers played a most important part in the great days of the Revolution. At all events they were usually activated either by immediate needs or by particular hatreds and suspicions, such as the hatred of the aristocracy or the suspicion of betrayal. At moments, perhaps the real characteristic of the revolutionary crowd was exaltation; but by its very nature this could only be a transitory affair. The decrees of March 1794 which distributed property amongst the poor were directed at the property of those whose loyalty was suspect. It was an example of the importance of patriotism, not an example of belief in socialism.

With the overthrow of Robespierre, the Revolution began to back-pedal. Those who had succeeded in getting rid of important national figures, and who were not themselves famous in any way, encouraged a general hostility, both in Paris and in the provinces, against those who had been governing France. There was perhaps a general feeling of exhaustion, so that the people of Paris or groups in the provinces were without their natural leaders. Those who had been imprisoned by Robespierre formed such a heterogeneous group that it was not possible for them, on their release, to take up any organized policy other than that of revenge against those who had hitherto been in charge. Throughout the country there were those who took the opportunity to settle old scores, and in Paris a form of opulent and extravagant youth made its appearance. There were areas where a Counter-Terror was organized, and in many parts of the south the Jacobins were massacred. Elsewhere there were hesitations and intrigues, just as there continued to be popular demonstrations. But in November 1794 the Jacobin Club was closed down and preparations were under way to get rid of the assemblies of the sections. Most typical was the abolition of all price control, the abandonment of the attempt to stabilize the value of the *assignat* and the issue of more paper money. In April and May 1795 the *sans-culottes* rose against these conditions. It was to be their last rising and it was unsuccessful. Several thousands were imprisoned in the repression which followed, and it was clear that Paris could easily come under military control. However the real enemy, in 1795 as it had been for the Girondins, was strong central government. So when the Convention legislated to end its own existence by a new constitution, it established as its executive a five-man Directory. The franchise was limited to those who were wealthy, and there was a complicated system whereby there were annual elections and a constant apprehension that every year would bring about some important change in the political complexion of the State. The point really was that with the death of Robespierre and with the move towards the moderates and the persecution of Jacobin revolutionaries it seemed that the political options of the country remained open. It appeared possible that royalists would recover their position, and there were those who believed that the cause of social revolution was not irretrievably lost either. The closing stages of the Convention were marked by a rising of Parisian royalists in October 1795 (the rising of Vendémiaire) which was crushed by General Bonaparte; royalists were prominent and successful in electoral matters and they had an important and fashionable centre in the Rue de Clichy, so much so that in September 1797 General Augereau intervened and deported a number of deputies and journalists, whilst measures were taken against royalists and priests; in May 1796 'the conspiracy of equals' led by Babeuf attempted to put in practice a more thoroughgoing social revolution, based upon a redistribution of wealth, but the leaders were arrested before they could accomplish anything. Thus there were political oscillations and an atmosphere of plot and counter-plot. But the Directory survived. Too much attention has probably been placed upon the relaxation of morals and the search for pleasure which is to be found in Parisian society at this time. Barras (famous because of his friendship with Bonaparte) was exceptional as a Director who was cynical and corrupt; the other Directors were sincerely republican and devoted to the Revolution as it had existed in its earlier stages. They were opposed to the monarchy, the aristocracy and the Church, and they sought, through education and through a systematic cult of patriotic republicanism, to create a stable and humane society. Once again, power lay with those who were wealthy and was not affected by the fact that in the last five years of the century there were many *nouveaux riches*. As a historian has put it, the Directory represented an attempt to govern normally in abnormal circumstances.

What particularly marked the Directory was its foreign policy. Although by 1795 the Revolutionary wars against Prussia, Holland and Spain had been concluded satisfactorily for France (which had annexed Belgium), war continued against Austria, particularly seeking the conquest of northern Italy. This war, in which Bonaparte became the commander, was to be explained in many ways. For example the economic situation remained poor and there was still no satisfactory means of exchange. There were those who hoped that the plunder of Lombardy and Tuscany would solve the financial problems of the Government. But there was probably a more general consideration. Patriotism remained a great unifying factor; few Governments felt strong enough to make peace and to dispense with military victories. The result was Arcola (1796) and Rivoli (1797) and a peace treaty which gave France the left bank of the Rhine and which created the Cisalpine Republic out of the conquered lands of northern Italy. The expedition to Egypt followed, seeking to make Egypt into a French colony and to destroy British commerce. The result was the coalition of 1799, which brought England, Russia, Turkey and Austria against France, and which threatened a new invasion and a new crisis.

It was natural enough that this provoked a new wave of Jacobinism. The Directors (and by this time Sieyès was one of them, so that the Revolution seemed to have come full circle) declared that they were willing to take measures of public safety yet they did not wish to see a revival of the Revolutionary committees and the spirit of 1793. But patriotic Jacobins retorted that the Directors were afraid of using 'that omnipotent force' which was the people and that they feared the mass of republicans more than they feared the invaders. All sorts of accusations of treason were present and the situation was made more complicated by royalist risings, notably a serious affair in the south-west which began in August 1799, and by a revival of activity in Brittany. It was in this situation that Bonaparte decided to abandon his army in Egypt and return to France. It is true that by the time he reached Fréjus (9 October 1799) Masséna had won military victories in Switzerland and the immediate threat of invasion had disappeared. But the war would begin in the spring; the political predicament would return in some form or another; the economic crisis remained strident. The idea of 'arranging' for Bonaparte to seize power appealed to many politicians. A terrorist plot was invented and the stage was prepared, not without difficulty. Bonaparte played the part that had been assigned him, and on 10 November 1799 (18 Brumaire) he expelled the Assembly and took power into his own hands.

In December 1799 Bonaparte announced his new constitution. His language was curt, as he told his fellow citizens that the Revolution was over. But it is difficult to believe that the action of a number of bold republicans in bringing this general to the forefront had ended anything. Only if the Revolution is to be equated with certain days of excitement and popular action (usually in Paris) or if it is to be identified with the unusual circumstances and the fragile constructions of 1793 or 1794 can Bonapartist rule be seen as the definitive ending of the Revolution. Still less can Bonaparte rule be seen as the triumph of what has sometimes been called the Counter-Revolution. Much has been made recently of the forces within France which opposed the Revolution and which, at certain times, opposed the Revolution by force of arms (such as the four departments of Brittany, Lyon or the Vivarais). It has been suggested that whilst this Counter-Revolution appeared particularly dangerous because it was supported by foreign powers which were France's enemies, in reality the Counter-Revolution was largely a French phenomenon in which the main trends of the Revolution were opposed. It could take the form of a large peasant revolt or it could be urban, but it was invariably opposed to the centralization, rationalization and anti-clericalism which appeared to be the most important parts of the Revolution. There was bound to be an aggravation of all sorts of local issues when the Revolution introduced its governmental system; there were bound to be local resentments when the central government called for conscripts. It is difficult to make this into a movement having its own ideology and which saw with satisfaction the establishment of Bonaparte's anti-democratic regime. In terms of principles (though possibly not in terms of the individuals concerned), the Counter-Revolution saw that Bonapartism was a continuation of the Revolution and perhaps we would be well advised to see it in the same light.

The Empire

The Revolution had not produced men of outstanding quality. Mirabeau had not been trusted; Lafayette proved himself to be shallow; Danton's pre-eminence was probably more apparent than real; Robespierre had not been able to adapt himself to changing events. It is natural therefore that historians should see the arrival of Bonaparte on the scene as an event of particular significance. History is always more easily explained if it is seen in terms of an individual. And Bonaparte seemed to have considerable talent as well as considerable ambition. Not only did he seek to rule France himself but he seemed to have the ability to do so. He was energetic, he could work long hours without apparent signs of fatigue, he had a remarkable memory, he had a clear mind which could grasp what was essential in any discussion. Generally speaking too he was free from any ideology, and could approach affairs cynically and practically. It is not surprising that he can be quoted as saying many contradictory things at different times. But he had many limitations. He was over-loyal to his family (which was not always loyal to him) and the Bonapartist 'clan' was a source of weakness. He was too dominated by the Mediterranean and did not appreciate the importance of other seas, the Baltic and the Atlantic. He was too peremptory and did not always realize that his interventions in administrative matters often created confusion rather than efficiency. He was a gambler, invariably ready to risk everything on the outcome of a single battle. Above all, he was always in a hurry. He never had time to prepare a campaign, he seldom had the opportunity to reflect, he sometimes could do little more than initiate measures which he could not follow through, in spite of his passion for detail. In a sense the Empire was an improvisation and it is ironical that certain of its institutions proved to be particularly lasting. It hardly seems that Napoleon himself had much impression that his rule would be a long one. In his talkative self-centredness he often remarked that there were many generals who thought they had as good a claim to power as himself or that, unlike a king or an emperor, he had only to suffer a single defeat and all would be lost for him. Perhaps he was always essentially a soldier, and just as it was the speed of his troop movements which disconcerted his adversaries, so in politics it was his incessant and rapid activity which allowed him to keep the initiative.

At first it is the continuity with the preceding regime which is most obvious. Bonaparte was a republican and a patriot. Just as he had told the Austrians with whom he had negotiated in Italy that the French Republic existed like the sun in the heavens, so he extolled the principles of the Republic, and it was always recognized that his power had emerged out of the Revolution. The *coup d'état* with which he was associated, after all, had had its predecessors under the Directory. The constitutional arrangements (and Bonaparte maintained the Revolutionary calendar, speaking about the 'Constitution de l'An VIII') were as complicated as those of the Directory, with different assemblies and means of election. The desire for conciliation was even more marked than under the preceding regime, and Bonaparte took the initiative in granting individual pardons, revising the lists of those who had been exiled, encouraging both royalists and Jacobins to rally to him and to 'wear the uniform of Bonaparte', seeking a religious pacification. But there was also a new element: that of the State's authority as interpreted by Bonaparte. His most significant departure was from the role which some of those who had organized the *coup d'état* had thought of giving him, that of a presiding *roi fainéant*. Bonaparte became First Consul (with Cambacérès, a legal specialist, and Lebrun, a financial expert and formerly secretary to Chancellor Maupeou, as Second and Third Consuls) and alone had the power to appoint to the Council of State, nominate officials, propose and promulgate laws. Authority became concentrated in the one man, and as the constitution was frequently revised, so its revisions were always in the direction of reducing popular control over matters of State. His method of exercising this authority was also noticeable. He had always encouraged propaganda around his person and this was continued. In January 1800 the liberty of the press was abolished and all newspapers which could be classified as political were suppressed (so that whilst there had once been seventy-nine newspapers in Paris, eventually, as the Government became progressively more severe, there were only four). Censorship was extended to theatres. The administrative reform of 1800 established a rigid centralized system, with the departments presided over by the prefects, the *arrondissements* by the sub-prefects, the communes by the mayors. The judicial reforms of 1800 established a similar hierarchy for the administration of justice, presided over by the Minister of Justice, and the Code Civil (which was not completed until 1804) established authority as the legal principle of social life: the authority of the father over the children, of the husband over the wife, of the employer over the employees. And whilst Bonaparte showed his readiness to conciliate, he was prepared to oscillate between conciliation and repression, and in the west there were times when his forces showed a brutal determination in their suppression of dissident groups.

No one can believe that Bonaparte's success is to be explained only by his talents. It probably corresponded to a certain moment in the life of France when there was a need for the security of strong government and possibly even a turning against the parliamentary government of the Directory. Bonaparte guaranteed the conquests of the Revolution. Those who had bought the lands of the Church or who had acquired land taken from émigré noblemen were assured that they could keep this land. There was no possibility of restoring aristocratic rights or privileges, no question of reviving the ecclesiastical tithe. With the foundation of the Bank of France in 1800, Bonaparte conciliated a number of powerful private bankers and later endowed this institution with the right to issue paper money based upon gold deposits. Thus with an alliance between private capital and the Government and a reform of the tax-collecting system, the State's finances began to be healthy; with a reliable means of exchange economic life could become normal. When supplies of food ran short in 1800 Bonaparte organized the purchase of wheat abroad, whilst the Prefect of Police in Paris built up stocks, controlled prices, established a corporation of bakers; any rioters, whether in Paris or the provinces, were ruthlessly dealt with. Meanwhile abroad Bonaparte won the victory of Marengo in June 1800 and it seemed that there could be no foreign menace to France. It was therefore as if there was a wide vested interest in maintaining Bonaparte's rule. With customary shrewdness Bonaparte saw this and in September 1800 he at last replied to the exiled Louis XVIII (the brother of Louis XVI, Louis XVII the Dauphin having died in 1795) who had twice written in the hope of persuading him to become a royalist. A royalist restoration, he said, would mean 100,000 corpses. Louis XVIII, he suggested, could not hope to return to France in such conditions and he should sacrifice his interests to the repose and the welfare of France. Part of the essence of Bonapartist rule was the suggestion that a page had definitively been turned in the history of France.

With this there was propaganda. Bonaparte consolidated his position with military communiqués which surrounded his person with an aura of successful glory. And there was also patronage. Bonapartism meant official posts. The Senate, the Legislative Corps, the Tribunate, the Council of State, the Ministers, prefects, a growing administration – all meant vacancies right at the beginning of the regime. Bonaparte was able to conciliate a host of the most politically conscious classes, and this was a task for which his excellent memory, his cynicism and his desire both to be and to appear powerful constituted the perfect equipment. It should be noted that he did not favour those who were particularly humble. The best means of gaining employ from Bonaparte was to be serving the State already, or to have a father who was serving the State. In this way Bonaparte was able to make use of administrators who were experienced; but he was also able to reinforce his own position amongst the political élite. In addition Bonaparte used the immense resources of the State as a means of bribery. Diplomats, generals and statesmen throughout the period of the Consulate and Empire received huge gifts of money as well as honours. Thus the system whereby one man established an authority which was based upon the administration, the army, the notables and a vague general consent gradually established itself.

The Treaty of Lunéville in February 1801 brought peace between France and Austria and confirmed French possession of Belgium and the Rhine frontier, whilst Italy (except for Venetia) passed under French influence (in 1802 Bonaparte became President of the Italian Republic). In March 1802 the Peace of Amiens was signed with England. The year 1802 also saw some significant developments at home. An amnesty was accorded to the émigrés and such lands as had not been confiscated were given back to them. A new form of school, the lycée, was created; a new form of decoration, the Legion of Honour, was instituted; slavery which had been abolished by the Revolution was reinstated in the French colonies; the Concordat which had been signed with the Pope in 1801 (and in which the Pope had recognized the First Consul's right to appoint bishops and the First Consul recognized the bishops' rights to appoint priests) was followed by the Government's publication of the organic articles on the Catholic religion which controlled many of the external aspects of church life (ecclesiastical dress, the ringing of church bells, etc.). Most telling of all,

Bonaparte suggested that the French people should be consulted on whether or not he should become Consul for life. With three and a half millions voting in favour of this, over a period of three months, and with only a few more than 8,000 voting against, Bonaparte was proclaimed Consul for life in August 1802 with the right to appoint his successor. 15 August 1802, Napoleon's thirty-third birthday, was celebrated as a national holiday, and in 1803 his effigy appeared on the coins. France had become a monarchy again.

In May 1802 Bonaparte put a crippling duty on all British colonial goods and believing that England was vulnerable to this sort of economic warfare began to encourage French production and trade. He maintained his troops in Holland in spite of the Treaty of Amiens. He intervened in Switzerland to weaken the federal government. He sent missions to Egypt, Syria, Turkey and India. In Italy he annexed Elba, Piedmont and Parma. Finally he insisted that England should evacuate Malta and that, on the English refusal, it was England which was responsible for the outbreak of war. But the outbreak of war seemed to point to a crisis in the State. There were generals who were jealous of Bonaparte's power, notably Moreau; there were royalists in the west and in Paris who were in league with the British. The presence of the Bourbon prince the Duc d'Enghien in the neutral state of Baden seemed to be linked to these conspiracies about which there were many rumours. Bonaparte had him seized and shot in March 1804. In May it was declared that the Government of France was entrusted to an emperor. A plebiscite gave overwhelming support to this decision and in December, in the presence of the Pope, Napoleon crowned himself and the empress, Joséphine. The execution of the Duc d'Enghien meant that there was a definitive break between Napoleon and the royalists. Cynical royalists commented that they had hoped to have a king, but they had created an emperor.

If the Empire coincided with a European crisis, this crisis was to be prolonged. A new coalition was formed against the emperor and soon war was continuous. In Bavaria Napoleon won the battle of Ulm, in Moravia that of Austerlitz, in Saxony Jena, in eastern Prussia Eylau, in West Prussia Friedland. By 1807 Napoleon had come to an agreement with the Tsar at Tilsit, he had reorganized Germany into a confederation of the Rhine, the Grand Duchy of Warsaw was virtually governed by a French general, Switzerland and Italy were distributed to Napoleon's family and associates, and an economic blockade against England from Brest to the Elbe was being organized. 15 August 1807 was a great fête of the Empire. Napoleon was at the apogee of his power. From this time onwards it is possible to see a decline: after Portugal had refused to join in the blockade of English goods, Napoleon intervened unsuccessfully in Spain and Portugal; at home both Talleyrand and the Minister of Police, Fouché, considered replacing him by Murat; in 1808 Napoleon ordered the occupation of Rome and subsequently had the Pope arrested, thereby destroying the good relations with the Catholics; a fifth coalition was formed against France and with the sending of a British force to the Low Countries and with the British fleet in liaison with the royalists in the south of France, it looked as if there was an intrigue to replace Napoleon by another general, Bernadotte, which was only broken by Napoleon's victory against the Austrians at Wagram (1809). Conscious of the fragility of his system and desirous of having an heir, he divorced Joséphine and married Marie-Louise, the daughter of the Austrian emperor, in 1810.

Napoleon's heir, called the king of Rome, was born on 20 March 1811. He was heir to an enormous empire, comprising nearly 43 million people, stretching from Rome to Lubeck, administered in 130 departments. Beyond them stretched the vassal states which through military and fiscal means were regarded as simple prolongations of France. But it was widely recognized that all this was a precarious inheritance. As the emperor grew more authoritarian, then the opposition to him, whether of individuals, of Catholics, of different sorts of royalists, of liberals, Jacobins or intellectuals, grew more intense amongst a popular hostility to continued taxation and conscription. When Napoleon left for the Russian campaign in 1812, an obscure and discredited general called Malet declared in Paris that Napoleon had been killed and announced the formation of a new Government. His attempt only lasted for a few hours, but it was enough to show that no one thought that Napoleon II could succeed. The disastrous Russian campaign was followed by further reverses in Germany (Leipzig, October 1813) and Italy, the loss of Spain and Holland and by the invasion of France at the beginning of 1814. Napoleon's victories against the allied armies (Brienne, Champaubert, Montmirail, Vauchamps, Montereau) were useless. The opposition of the liberals to him became vocal, the British occupied Bordeaux, the royal family returned to France. On 31 March 1814 the Tsar, the king of Prussia and their troops entered Paris, a provisional government was established under Talleyrand, and, deserted by his marshals, Napoleon abdicated on 5 April. A few days later he was given a pension for life and the tiny island kingdom of Elba, and after having met with further humiliations and some public hostility, he arrived in his exile at the beginning of May. It was an inglorious ending to the Empire.

The decision to recall the Bourbons to the throne of France was in no way a national decision. There was no movement of opinion in favour of the royal family, there was simply a number of intrigues in Paris. In these intrigues it was Talleyrand and the personnel of the imperial administration who were able to impose their views on the foreign sovereigns, especially the Tsar, who seemed to have the destiny of France under their control. The idea of Talleyrand and his associates was to safeguard their own positions and to impose upon the Bourbons the condition of a form of constitutional government. This manoeuvre was largely unsuccessful in the sense that once Louis XVIII had been proclaimed king (6 April), the fact that conditions were attached to the proclamation appeared insignificant. Louis XVIII left England two weeks after the proclamation and journeyed towards Paris with agonizing slowness; the temptation to go and pay homage to him was irresistible and many of those who had been most insistent upon imposing conditions openly accepted him as king. But Talleyrand's manœuvre was successful since on 2 May, just prior to entering Paris, Louis XVIII deemed it prudent to announce that he would be drawing up a form of constitutional government, whilst maintaining that such an act was voluntary on his part.

Thus began the Restoration. But whilst the greater part of the *notables*, the aristocracy, the Church, the political class, the officials, bankers, businessmen and intellectuals, accepted the return of the Bourbons with remarkable ease, there was little enthusiasm amongst the ordinary people. Soldiers disobeyed their officers and deserted in large numbers; unemployed workers demonstrated beneath the windows of the Tuileries palace; elsewhere a general indifference was reported. The outstanding feature of this Restoration was that within a short time the goodwill had been destroyed and the hostility had been intensified. This was partly the fault of the royal family and its advisers. They were often ignorant of the nature of the administration which they had inherited ('What is a department? What is a prefect?' wrote the king's brother, the Comte d'Artois, to the Minister of the Interior); they were divided, the moderate royalists finding themselves countered by more intransigent figures who wished to mark the ending of the Revolution by a more decided return to the *ancien régime*. The Government gave way on many matters. Sundays were to be observed as rest days. It became obligatory for houses to be decorated on certain saint-days, for officials to take part in certain religious processions. The anniversaries of the executions of Louis XVI and Marie-Antoinette were to be regarded as days of penitence and expiation, and this was even extended to include the Vendéen leader Cadoudal. Because the Restoration had inherited many debts, a high level of taxation had to be maintained (although the earlier royalist propaganda had promised a reduction of indirect taxes), many officials were sacked, officers put on half-pay, soldiers dismissed from the service. The magistrature was purged and a form of censorship was re-established. And the discontent caused by all this was heightened by the insistence with which returned émigrés demanded offices and positions. (It was said that one nobleman claimed to be made a Rear-Admiral since, having been a naval cadet in 1789, this would have been his rank had the Revolution not intervened. The justice of his claim was officially admitted but he was told that unfortunately he had lost his life at Trafalgar in 1804.) Most serious of all, in the countryside, the nobility in some cases claimed the return of their lands which had been bought (usually many years previously), and in many cases both they and the clergy demanded the revival of former privileges. Royalist newspapers and pamphleteers joined in this counter-revolutionary activity and although the Government protested, there were many rumours about the return of feudal obligations and the tithe.

It was in these circumstances that Napoleon, on Elba, received an emissary from France who assured him 'as a positive and undeniable fact' that the existing Government had lost the support of the people. There was no agreement amongst the critics of the Bourbons as to what should replace them, and those (such as Fouché) who were most anxious to have regular constitutional government would have preferred the proclamation of Napoleon II and a Regency. But characteristically Napoleon took a rapid decision and without any preparations he left Elba on 26 February, accompanied by a thousand soldiers. Having won over the first detachment of soldiers that he met, he encountered no opposition and travelling with remarkable speed he entered the Tuileries on 20 March, shortly after Louis XVIII had fled to Ghent.

If this resurrection of the Empire had been apparently simple, and explicable essentially in terms of Napoleon's boldness and swiftness, it is essential to see it also as a political move. Proclamations, which had been drawn up at Elba or during the journey at sea, were printed at

Digne and at Gap in the south-east, and distributed in considerable quantities. They were addressed essentially to the revolutionary and democratic sentiments of the people. They claimed that the Bourbons had attempted to make the army dependent upon the aristocracy and to restore feudalism to French society. At Grenoble he claimed that he had come to deliver France from 'the insolence of the nobility, the pretensions of the priests, and the yoke of the foreign powers'. Later he was to say that nothing had surprised him more on his return to France than the hatred of priests and nobles. He claimed that it was as widespread and as violent as at the beginning of the Revolution, and he clearly aimed to profit from it. In addition to restoring the *tricouleur* flag and reinstating many dismissed officials, his first decrees promised a constitution which would be in the interests and according to the will of the nation. In a message to the Conseil d'État he stated that sovereignty resided in the people and that this was the only legitimate source of power. Nevertheless he was anxious that the continuity of the Empire should persist, and when the new constitution was drawn up it was given the significant title of Acte Additionnel. It was also disappointing since it did not institute parliamentary government, as expected, but left the initiative of proposing laws to the emperor. When it was submitted to the approval of a national plebiscite there were literally millions of abstentions. When the first elections were held in May, it was liberals rather than Bonapartists who triumphed.

Thus Napoleon's return had created great excitement and he had appeared as the saviour of the Revolution. But within a short space of time support had waned. Rival political groups discussed the need for important changes in the future. There was a general feeling that Napoleon's return could only be temporary. Certain of his Ministers were in touch with royalists, whilst the Government appeared slow and strangely inefficient in many ways. An economic depression affected industry and trade. There was general apprehension concerning the length of the war, which the allied sovereigns had immediately declared. But the Belgian campaign only lasted four days. Napoleon was defeated at Waterloo on 18 June 1815, he abdicated on 22 June, and Louis XVIII returned to Paris on 8 July.

This Second Restoration was also the result of intrigues (this time Wellington joined Fouché and Talleyrand) and it was accompanied by considerable violence and by a large army of occupation. In the south, sometimes as soon as the news of Waterloo was learned, there were attacks against the Bonapartist personnel which frequently took the form of a spontaneous Terror, 'the White Terror' as it has been called. In some areas it spread beyond the royalist–Bonapartist struggle and became a Catholic–Protestant confrontation, and although order was restored by the arrival of Austrian troops, in November 1815 the reopening of the Protestant church at Nîmes gave rise to further violence. The presence of 150,000 foreign troops also gave rise to a sporadic agitation, and a whole number of incidents took place in which foreign troops were accused of destruction and pillaging, whilst French individuals were guilty of assassination and violence. In all these ways Napoleon's adventure of the Hundred Days (for when the king returned to Paris he was welcomed with the words, 'it is but a hundred days since your Majesty left us') was to leave an impressive mark on French history. The impression was given of a Bonapartism which was revolutionary, popular and liberal. The association between the Bourbons and the foreign powers was enforced, and the peace treaty not only reduced France to the limits of 1792, but removed Sarrelouis, Savoy, Philippeville and Marienburg and imposed a massive indemnity. Thus foreign policy was to become an important issue and it became normal to attack the treaty arrangements of 1815. Finally, although it seemed that there was a great consensus of opinion in France which was in favour of some liberal, bourgeois and moderate constitutional government, the Hundred Days indicated yet again that there was a fragility about power in the French State, that it was there for the taking, and that there was an underlying current of violence in French society which could cause savage conflict.

The Restoration and the July Monarchy 1815–1848

The population of France in 1815 was probably just short of thirty millions. To some extent the high birth-rate, which had been a characteristic of the *ancien régime* and which had given France a large and young population, had been maintained, and the persistence of military conscription for bachelors had encouraged early marriages (in 1813, for example, there had been an unusually large number of marriages in order to escape military service, and the birth-rate in 1814 had been high). But there are some signs that the increase had been checked. The numbers killed in the wars (perhaps 900,000), the growth of practices of birth-control, the fact that 1812 was a year when food was short and the typhus epidemic of 1813 were amongst the principal causes of this check. The 1820s, however, were to see a considerable increase, and by 1831 the population was over thirty-two and a half millions. It was probable that something like one-seventh of this population lived in towns with a population of 20,000 or over. There were only three towns that had a population of over 100,000: Paris, which by the beginning of the Restoration period had a population of just over 700,000, but where the rate of expansion seemed to slow down at the beginning of these years; Marseille and Lyon which had about 115,000 each. Towns such as Bordeaux and Rouen had populations in the neighbourhood of 90,000. It has been calculated that there were some twenty departments that possessed no town of more than 10,000 inhabitants, and that there were nearly 500 towns that had a population of between 2,000 and 3,000. Thus France was essentially a country dominated by agriculture and by a rural population.

For a long time it was assumed that this rural population had been responsible for a steady improvement in agricultural conditions and productivity. It was believed that only in this way was it possible for the countryside to support the continual growth of population, and that the legal changes of the Revolution, by freeing the peasant from many irksome obligations, had placed him in a situation where he could respond to the challenges and the opportunities of the market. It does not, in fact, seem that this was always the case. The class of enlightened peasants, with their small and medium-sized landholdings, who were able to transform certain regions, such as the Nivernais, does not seem to have been general. Because a great quantity of land was made available, the Revolution often encouraged the peasant to extend the amount of land he possessed, rather than to increase his productivity by improving his method of farming. There could be some reluctance amongst landowners to see tenants introduce new methods, and old feudal dues were sometimes incorporated in the new leases. Then, whilst some agricultural workers saw their wages rise during the Revolutionary and Napoleonic periods, it is true to say that many, whether peasant landowners, tenant-farmers or labourers, saw their economic situation become more precarious. Historians now prefer to put an emphasis on the diversity of agricultural conditions and to point out that just as the different geographical regions introduce a considerable variety into French agricultural life so the position of the rural population was bound to change from one part of France to another. There were some agricultural communities which were largely self-sufficient (except for supplies of salt and luxuries); there were others which were closely integrated with the economy of neighbouring towns; there were some areas which regularly sent labourers to work in the towns during the winter months; there were regions where it was customary to live on a wide variety of different foods, others which were dominated by a single (and often inferior) type of corn. Perhaps the only safe generalization that one can make about the rural population as a whole is its poverty. As Stendhal's hero Julien Sorel observed, most men could come home to their cottages on a winter's evening and find neither bread nor chestnuts nor potatoes there.

The most common way of supplementing income for the rural population was through industry. Rural industry had become widespread during the eighteenth century. It had been encouraged by the Government, entrepreneurs had been attracted by the cheaper wages they had been able to offer, and the manufacturers of new cloths had sometimes thought that they would be more successful with the newly found workers in the countryside. So important had the spread of rural industry become that there are examples of authorities forbidding industrial work during the harvest period. This had continued throughout the Revolutionary and Napoleonic years. But by 1815 industrial production had taken on different aspects. France had become more industrialized during the Empire. The drop in industrial production which had coincided with the Revolution had been stopped and until there was an industrial crisis in 1810–11, French industry was producing more than at the end of the *ancien régime*. This includes the building industry which had been stimulated by Napoleon's interest in public works, as well as textile, metallurgical and chemical industries. Factories equipped with modern machinery had been installed at great expense, and the use of steam-engines to drive the machinery meant that work was more regular and more intense. In towns such as Rouen, Lille or Mulhouse there was demand for women and children to work the machines and there was the need for specialist mechanics (who often came from England) to install and service them. But the characteristic of French industry was the manner in which different forms of production existed side by side together, old and new. The cotton industry became largely mechanized by 1830, woollen much less so, linen and flax still less. The cost of products varied from one region to another, but they all feared English competition and demanded that there should be high protective tariffs.

French society of the Restoration was dominated by the political system. Louis XVIII had announced in 1814 that he would endow France with a constitution, and this royal concession, obviously granted by a monarch who was stressing his own benevolence and not admitting that his powers could be restricted or that sections of the population possessed rights, took on the medieval term of the Charter (*La Charte*). It created two houses of Parliament – the Peers who were created by the king and the lower house which was elected by a limited number of citizens. One's right to vote was judged by one's wealth, and in this calculation, by which less than 100,000 men were adjudged able to vote (and perhaps a tenth of these were eligible to be elected a deputy), the possession of land was more important than other forms of wealth. Thus the nobility tended to dominate the Chamber of Deputies and it was not uncommon for more than half of the deputies to be noble. The nobility had a dominant place in the administration and in the countryside, and the abolition of feudal rights and the confirmation of the sales of ecclesiastical and émigré lands during the Revolution did not remove their influence.

The political circumstances with which the Restoration began also emphasized the importance of the nobility. The first elections were held in the abnormal conditions of August 1815. About a third of those who had the right to vote abstained and there were considerable pressures on those who did vote. The result was the Chambre Introuvable, as it was called, in which an enormous majority of nobles and landowners expressed only one idea, their hatred of the Revolution and the Empire. They wished to punish those who had been prominent in support of the preceding regimes and they demanded indemnification for their property losses under the Revolution. It was as if they were returning to the aristocratic revolt of 1788 and seeking for a devolution of power towards the provinces in which they were the natural leaders. They found support for their ideas from the heir to the throne, the king's brother, the Comte d'Artois, who virtually set up an independent and parallel Government, and there were aristocratic and Catholic organizations throughout the country which sought to embody the ideals of this Counter-Revolution. Some 70,000 arrests were made, the administration was purged, more than 150 specially designated personalities were banished, and some generals who had gone over to Napoleon in 1815 were shot. Attempts were made to reconstitute the Church's wealth and it was suggested that the tithe should be reintroduced. Divorce was made illegal.

There was thus an atmosphere of conflict and repression which the king attempted to moderate. He dissolved the Chamber and a more moderate Parliament was re-elected in 1816. He matched plots with counter-plots, he chose as his Ministers those who were liberal and who were anxious to make the system work, he sought to place his government on a sound financial basis. Doubtless Louis had his reasons for this. He was shrewd; he did not want to be the prisoner of a rebellious aristocracy; he had a personal liking for the leading liberal of the time, Decazes; he was under pressure from foreign ambassadors. But in effect, he was appealing from the aristocracy to the section of the country which had profited from the Revolution, the bourgeoisie which was important in the central administration and the banking and financial groups which enabled the Government to pay off the indemnity and get rid of the occupying forces. These men had their connections with the *ancien régime*, and they had sometimes been important as moderate royalists under the Revolution or as officials under the Empire. They believed in national government, and they were opposed to the arbitrary, sectarian and violent measures which they saw advocated by the ultras. When the ultras, convinced that they represented popular opinion, became more democratic, then the moderates, who were far from believing in democracy, were all the more decided in their opposition to them. This was the time when politicians such as Royer-Collard and Guizot, trying to achieve a government of justice and reason, seeing the Parliament as a body which should define the interests of France rather than represent opinions, or intellectuals such as Madame de Staël and Benjamin Constant, trying to explain the significance of the French Revolution, became attached to the Charter as the salvation of the country.

But their position was necessarily weak. They could not call upon any great movement of opinion and they were dependent upon the Government and overwhelmingly on the position of the king. The fragility of their position was all the more evident since the constitution required the election of one-fifth of the Chamber annually, and the rising number of Bonapartists and ex-Revolutionaries began to cause fear and alarm. This was a movement of reaction against ultra excesses, but it could only arouse the hostility of the king and his supporters because it was essentially anti-Bourbon. The rise of these extremist groups illustrated the divisions amongst the constitutionalists. Royer-Collard and Guizot, for example, believed in the sovereignty of reason, but Benjamin Constant believed in the sovereignty of the people. There was therefore a gradual shift of political power which came to a climax in February 1820 when the Comte d'Artois's son, the Duc de Berry, who was known to be the only member of the royal family able to have children, was assassinated. It seemed that the Bourbon line might be made extinct by virtue of revolutionary action, and there was a complete change in royal policy. (In fact the Duchesse de Berry, who was pregnant at the time of the assassination, gave birth to a son.) Important Ministers such as Decazes, and influential and younger personalities such as Guizot, were dismissed. The electoral laws were revised so that the rural landowning aristocrats were given more favourable weighting as against the urban bourgeoisie. In 1821 it was a provincial nobleman, the Comte de Villèle, who became the Prime Minister. The newspapers were closely supervised; the University was put under the control of the clergy. Finally the triumph of this reaction seemed complete when on the death of Louis XVIII in September 1824 the Comte d'Artois succeeded as Charles X. He was anointed king in Reims cathedral; he announced his intentions of restoring the sacred interests of religion and of healing the last wounds of the Revolution. In practice this meant laws which would indemnify the émigrés for their loss of property during the Revolution and which would punish sacrilege with the death penalty.

It was not surprising that these policies created a reaction. When the law for giving indemnity to the émigrés came before the Chamber, it inspired a revealing debate about the Revolution. On the right it was claimed that such a law suggested that the Revolution had been legitimate and that, in fact, it was those who had acquired the lands who ought to be receiving an indemnity, since they had been duped into illegal acts. On the left it was claimed that this whole procedure was in itself illegal and, more important, that it was but a prelude to a series of other laws which would reconstitute an aristocracy and restore the Church to its old position. Thus Villèle found that he had critics everywhere. In addition there were Catholics who emphasized their Gallicanism and who found a dangerous ultramontanism in the religious ideas of the Government. The popular rumour that Charles X was a secret Jesuit gave a force to these resentments. But by the 1820s there was a new generation of electors, men who had been born after 1789 and who felt distant from the generation of the émigrés. In 1825 a funeral had provided the opportunity for the opposition which was excluded from political activity to manifest itself. General Foy's death inspired a great demonstration at his funeral and the organization of a national subscription for his children. A number of important personalities were in opposition to Villèle, Chateaubriand, for example, who had been badly treated by the Government, and Montlosier, who wrote effectively in favour of the Gallican Church. Many of the most interesting of the intellectuals were both young and associated with liberalism. Guizot (born in 1787) and Victor Cousin (born in 1792), who had lectured at the Sorbonne from 1820 to 1822; Thiers (born in 1797) who began to publish his *Histoire de la Révolution* from 1823 onwards; Charles de Rémusat (born in 1797), Jouffroy (born in 1796) and Sainte-Beuve (born in 1804) who began to publish articles in the newspaper *Le Globe*, founded in 1824. The liberals created societies and published pamphlets which not only denounced governmental manipulation of the elections, but explained how this interference could be countered. And in this atmosphere Villèle found that even the king was intriguing against him.

The elections of 1827 brought about a considerable increase in the liberal strength. Villèle found that he was outvoted by the combination of the left and right oppositions and he was replaced by a Government which had no official Prime Minister but in which the Minister of the Interior, Martignac, soon appeared as the leader. Charles X, however, regarded this as temporary and after many negotiations in August 1829 he formed a Government presided over by the Prince de Polignac, with La Bourdonnaye, who had been one of the most violent members of the Chambre Introuvable, as Minister of the Interior and General de Bourmont, who had gone over to the enemy on the eve of Waterloo, as Minister for War. The opposition newspapers denounced this Government as the Government of the Counter-Revolution, formed of Coblenz (the centre of the émigrés), Waterloo and 1815. 'On the one side,' wrote *Le Globe*, 'there is the Court, on the other side, there is the nation.' There was talk of refusing to pay taxes; there was a flurry of liberal organizations; there was talk of replacing an impossible king by his cousin, the Duc d'Orléans, and organizing a revolution similar to the English Revolution of 1688; there was a revival of republicanism and student groups got in touch with Lafayette. In March 1830 a majority of the Chamber voted an address which claimed that the views of the people were not being taken into account by the Government.

There was also an economic crisis. The harvest of 1828 had been bad and food prices had risen alarmingly. This had affected purchasing power and had probably helped to bring about a general recession of industry and trade. The banks had suffered from this recession and there was a general tendency to hold the Government responsible for all these economic difficulties. But Charles X was not prepared to give way. He was convinced that had his brother, Louis XVI, been firm and decisive, then the Revolution could have been arrested. He was convinced that he was popular, and that the opposition (which was divided) could not resist his power and authority. He believed that the expedition to conquer Algiers, which was announced in March and set sail in May, would bring a great popularity to his Government. He was confident that the support which the Church was prepared to pronounce for him, in every cathedral in the land, would render him invincible. Therefore he dissolved the Chamber and when in the election of July 1830 he still had no majority, he issued ordinances dissolving the Chamber which had never met, disqualifying many of those who had the vote, establishing a strict censorship of newspapers and periodicals, and fixing the date of new elections. The result was the *Trois Glorieuses* – 27, 28 and 29 July – in Paris. Manifestations led to the barricades going up; the king absent from Paris lost control of the situation; some of the troops fraternized with the rebels; a provisional Government was set up at the Hôtel de Ville and a vigorous campaign was organized in favour of the Duc d'Orléans. On 31 July the Duke accepted to be Lieutenant-Governor of the kingdom. On 2 August Charles X abdicated; a week later the Duke accepted the throne as Louis-Philippe I.

There are various attitudes which can be taken to the revolution of 1830. One is to suggest that there was no revolution at all. The system established in 1814 and re-established in 1815, whereby there was a monarch and two chambers (existing within a centralized administrative system) and a small wealthy electorate, persisted. It had worked regularly under Louis XVIII and Charles X until the crisis of 1830. Under Louis-Philippe it worked again. And the fact that it was Louis-Philippe emphasized the continuity. He, as Duc d'Orléans, son of the man who had been prominent in the earlier period, had received compensation from the Villèle Government in 1825, and he clearly represented the royal tradition. Nor is it true to say that there was any significant change in the personnel of those who governed France. It is true that there was a rush for new positions, and that the administration included many new faces, but there were few social implications in these changes. There were many individuals who had held public office under Napoleon. But there were no new categories of society that were suddenly brought to power and influence. In any case the revolution appeared to be essentially Parisian. The provinces had often learned of it many days after *les Trois Glorieuses*, and it could be said that the downfall of the Bourbons was as much caused by the inaction of provincial towns and the provincial nobility as by the activity of the population in Paris. This, again, is to treat the revolution of 1830 as a non-revolution, an accident of the Parisian streets which was sent to the rest of France as a sort of newsletter which required acknowledgement rather than action.

But it can be argued that the revolution of 1830 was a classical type of revolution. The ordinances appeared on Monday, 26 July, and although there were lots of people about in the streets there were few signs of excitement or interest. Yet by 29 July there had been a general movement of the population of Paris against the Government, and so many had died on the barricades that it was declared unthinkable that Charles X should rule again. Was it because there was economic crisis, because the price of food was high, because there were many unemployed? Was it because the population of Paris had been growing rapidly and there were many immigrants there who, uprooted from their normal social background, were prone to respond to crisis and unusual events with violence and aggression? It has been suggested that those most prominent in the revolution were the artisans and the skilled workers, who were responding to the fear of economic crisis and misery, and to the presence of despotism, rather than to their own particular sufferings and hardships. Those who had some organization and some self-consciousness took action, and it was these factors rather than any particular economic crisis that counted. It has also been suggested that there were particular happenings, such as the hoisting of the *tricouleur* flag over the towers of Notre-Dame, that really launched the movements of enthusiasm and violence, or that it was the presence of Bonapartists with military experience that enabled the barricades to be erected successfully. All these suggestions make this revolution an important source for the understanding of all modern revolutionary movements.

It should not be forgotten that the revolution of 1830 brought about some direct changes in the organization of political life. The age for the eligibility both of the deputies and of the electorate was lowered, and the tax qualification for voting was also reduced. Thus the number of those who had the vote grew to about 166,000 and never ceased to grow during the reign of Louis-Philippe, reaching nearly a quarter of a million by 1846. The press became more resolutely free, and a form of legitimate, normal political struggle became an accepted fact.

Organized political parties were still difficult to identify, and foreign affairs tended to play an unusually large part in public life, since those who had taken part in the revolution of 1830 thought that it could be overthrown by other European powers or that it could itself be overthrown by outside intervention. But perhaps the most important significance of the revolution was to emphasize the precariousness of power in France. Just as Napoleon could be overthrown and could return, just as Louis XVIII could return and be overthrown, so Charles X had disappeared (in fact he lingered in France for an awkwardly long time before going to exile in England), and it was striking how regimes could be overthrown with no one to defend them. The realization of this was to embarrass succeeding Governments.

Another embarrassment was the whole nature of Louis-Philippe's monarchy. From the start he emphasized to the foreign powers that he was a peace-loving ruler, who did not seek to disrupt the calm of Europe in any way. Yet he felt that France's importance in the world was linked to France's association with the principle and the idea of revolution. From the start too he emphasized that he was king because he was of the blood royal, a descendant of St Louis and a Bourbon. Yet he knew that he was king because of revolution. It could have been a revolution which, without his opportune arrival on the scene, would have led to a republic, so that it was, as Victor Hugo called it, a turned-in revolution ('une révolution rentrée') or a confiscated revolution. But it was a revolution none the less and although Louis-Philippe's insistence caused him to be recognized eventually by all the sovereigns of Europe as one of them, yet he remained a monarch whose position was ambiguous.

The revolutionary tradition was maintained right from the beginning of the reign. There was always the possibility of counter-revolution, of those who believed in the Bourbons taking action. They were particularly strong amongst the nobility, in Brittany and in the south. Worried prefects reported that there were whole regions where aristocrats, owning large areas of land, sometimes in isolated and backward parts of the country, maintained loyalty to the Bourbon family. In the west there was the tradition of Vendée and the Counter-Revolution; in the south, especially where there were Protestants, there was the tradition of the White Terror. In both regions the Church was opposed to the new regime and in 1832 the Duchesse de Berry tried to raise these two areas. There was also the possibility of social revolution. Those who were disappointed at the betrayal of the people's cause, since the people had risen in Paris and had fought and died on the barricades, organized themselves into clubs for the furtherance of revolution. In foreign countries such as Belgium and Poland they identified and supported the cause of freedom. For others, it was through assassinating Louis-Philippe that the needed changes would come, and that monarch's life was frequently in danger.

Yet revolution was not immediately successful. There were legitimist plots, scares, sulks and manifestations, but there was no legitimist uprising. It was as if the legitimist sentiments of the aristocracy and the clergy were not strong enough to force a real rupture with the bourgeoisie or to destroy their co-operation in business and officialdom. There was also the parade of socialism, and there were demonstrations of popular violence. Yet such movements were invariably linked to particular grievances, and once these were settled it was hard to see the workers as a real revolutionary force. It was all typified by the episode of Louis-Napoleon. Napoleon having died in 1820 and his son in 1830, it was his nephew who became the pretender to the imperial crown, and he attempted to seize power more than once. Under Louis-Philippe these attempts were fiascos, but his very presence and the fact that people were prepared to fear his success were examples of how power was fundamentally weak, although in practice convinced and resolute. It was as if power was always there for the taking. The unique position of Paris in the centralized administrative system meant that France was particularly vulnerable to revolution.

The men who ruled France after 1830 were all anti-revolutionary, although connected with the moderate and legal revolution which had been accomplished by the Third Estate. Louis-Philippe, the son of Philippe-Égalité, had fought at Valmy and Jemappes; Guizot, a Protestant, had a father who had been associated with the ideas of 1789 and with the Girondins; the Duc de Broglie was married to the daughter of Madame de Staël; the fathers of all three of them had been guillotined. Casimir Périer, the banker, was the son of Claude Périer who had led the revolt of the Estates in Dauphiné; Thiers had a father who had been ruined during the Revolution; Soult, Gérard, Mortier, Molé and others had all served under Napoleon. It was clear that there would be no going back to the principles of the *ancien régime* and this issue was definitively closed. On the other hand, beyond this restricted governmental personnel, there were those who believed that the revolution should go forward, and new generations and different social groups looked to further developments. One of the difficulties was that there was no agreed procedure whereby the system could either be stabilized or reformed. Parliament had worked reasonably well under the Restoration and a political tradition was growing up. But no political parties or organizations had taken shape. There had been groups that had been associated with particular ideas or with particular individuals, and it had been possible to speak in general terms about 'ultras' or about 'liberals', but there was no party organization as there were no traditional political parties. When men were elected to the Chamber it was often not known whether they would vote for the Government or against it, since it was customary in elections for candidates to make profession of their independence. Undoubtedly the fundamental reason for the failure of political parties to develop was that, although the electorate was a very small one, it was socially and ideologically very varied. In 1831 the revised Charter increased the number of electors to more than 160,000, and the normal process whereby wealth grew caused more men to qualify as electors, so that by 1846 there were nearly 250,000. But whereas in Paris there was a large number of electors and an election represented a struggle between political tendencies and an argument between ideas as well as interests, in some departments the elections concerned only a few hundred electors and hardly represented a political issue. It was an affair of local personalities, or of local matters, in which the prefect or sub-prefect could play an important role, as could all the notabilities of birth, wealth or profession. It was clearly impossible for such deputies to be welded into any national system of organized ideas and interests.

This incoherence of the Chamber of Deputies helped to create other forms of political instability. The Chamber of Deputies never lasted the full five years for which it had been elected. Apart from the partial elections held in October 1830 to fill vacancies, many of which had been caused by the revolution, there were six general elections held in less than eighteen years. More remarkable still was the ministerial instability of the first ten years of the reign. Up to October 1840 there were fifteen different Governments, some lasting for a few days only. After October 1840 there was virtually only the one Government, dominated by Guizot. It is clear that personal elements were important in creating these ministerial changes, and the fact that there was no obvious reason why one man should be Prime Minister rather than another must have exacerbated personal rivalries. But there were two other factors which helped to shape the nature of political life. There was the question of the monarch. What was the role of the king under the Charter? Since Louis-Philippe was king because he was of the blood royal it could be argued that his political role was fundamental and that he should be the dominant influence in government. But since he was also king as the result of revolution, and since the Charter was the basis of all political action, then it could also be argued that the royal role should be less decisive than that of the Ministers and legislators. In the circumstances Louis-Philippe was always determined to be an active and powerful king, but he preferred to act by stealth rather than by royal command, and it was clearly in his interests to be a permanent presence amongst the shifting, uncertain and shapeless political forces. Thus this astute political king contributed to the instability of the system.

There was also the question of foreign affairs. The July Monarchy was particularly conscious of the importance of what went on in neighbouring countries because it seemed that its whole destiny depended upon it. The revolution was a change in the Vienna settlement of 1815, and it was always possible that the other powers of Europe would intervene in order to restore the rightful royal family and to crush a dangerous revolution in its birthplace. Louis-Philippe was quick to send special emissaries to the important capitals of Europe in order to reassure his fellow monarchs and he was always anxious to present himself as a lover of peace and order. But July 1830 in Paris was not an isolated European revolution. The risings in Brussels and Warsaw were confirmation of the fact that revolution was a more general phenomenon, and there were those who believed that it was the opportunity for France to put herself at the head of a European movement. In this way the cause of liberty would be sustained, French power and influence would be increased and the humiliations of 1815 would be erased. There was another calculation. Just as the revolution had been impelled forward by the war of 1792, so the French involvement in the national movements of the 1830s would bring about further political and social changes within France. This calculation became more important when after 1834 there was a falling-off in the intensity of social movements. It seemed that the only way in which any form of domestic change could be accomplished would be by some involvement in foreign war. And even those who did not wish for considerable change at home thought that a successful war would consolidate the throne and believed that it was only in patriotism that a divided nation could find its unity. Thus the conduct of foreign affairs achieved an unusual importance and different views of what the Government should do helped to increase the instability of Governments and the complications of politics.

Yet France did not become involved in European war. In 1830 and 1831 Louis-Philippe rejected the opportunity of occupying Belgium or of seeing one of his sons become king of the Belgians. In 1836 he refused to allow Thiers to patronize an armed intervention in Spanish affairs. In 1840 when France had found herself diplomatically isolated because Mehemet Ali, the Pasha of Egypt and the ally of France, was threatening to attack the Ottoman Empire, he again dismissed Thiers rather than allow the affairs of the Middle East to involve him in a war on the Rhine and in the Alps. Only in Algeria was there constant warfare as the Government decided to maintain this last conquest of the Bourbons and found themselves obliged to extend their occupation to cover the whole coast-line and much of the interior. Just as there were many who criticized Louis-Philippe and his Ministers for their alleged timidity in Europe, so there were those who were quick to point to the expenditure of men and money in order to hold on to a territory that appeared to have little value and few possibilities.

Yet all this political discussion, or the debate on foreign affairs, concerned only a relatively few people. It was true that there were moments of excitement, as in 1840, when certain issues appeared to be of vital importance, and Paris was the scene of endless debate and discussion. But there was a vital difference between the small number of those who had political rights (the *pays légal*) and the very large number that could neither vote nor become a deputy (the *pays réel*). Newspapers were important, and the number of regular readers increased (especially after the foundation of *La Presse* in 1836, a cheap newspaper which carried many advertisements and serialized novels), but they only reached a small minority of the population. This was a moment too when the publication of certain books had a remarkable impact upon the public, and when literature and politics were closely allied, yet even writers such as Hugo or Lamartine cannot be thought of as reaching the masses of the population. News-sheets, popular songs (especially those written by Béranger), almanacs, printed illustrations and various sorts of devotional works must have reached a much wider public and inculcated it with stories of famous crimes, a constant anticlericalism, a nostalgia for Napoleon and a belief in miracles.

The population as a whole was most concerned with three areas of activity. One was local government, especially municipal government since the law of 1831 gave the right to elect a municipal council to more than a million Frenchmen. These councils had a relatively restricted importance since it was the Government that nominated (and could dismiss) the mayors, and the centralized administrative system gave little opportunity for municipalities to influence their decisions. But local politics could arouse excitements and it could create a consciousness of political issues that was important for the future.

A second subject of activity and interest (and one which directly affected municipal government) was education. In 1833 Guizot, as Minister for Public Instruction, formulated his law on primary education. This stated that every commune was obliged to have a school and a school-teacher, whilst every department would eventually have an institution for training teachers (an *École Normale*). Education was neither made free nor compulsory, although it was theoretically possible for the children of the indigent poor to go to school without paying. The municipal authorities, who were responsible for the supervision of the school, were sometimes hostile to the idea of education, and parents could often see no reason why their children should learn to read and write. But the number of those who attended school began to rise, the number of those that could neither read nor write began to decline. Within the villages the presence of a schoolmaster (the *instituteur*) and his relations with the priest was often the subject of controversy and invariably the source of debate and discussion. This debate was not as acrimonious nor as considerable as the debate on secondary education which brought about a confrontation between 'the sons of Saint-Louis and the sons of Voltaire', in which the Catholics claimed the right to send their children to secondary schools, run by those that they knew to be Catholics, and the supporters of the existing system believed that the maintenance of some sort of State control over secondary schools and teachers was essential to the unity of France. But it meant that there was a strong movement of opinion amongst Catholics, stretching over classes, that there was no reason why they should support the regime, whilst *instituteurs* in their conflicts with the priest and the municipal authorities wanted to see a Government which would help them more decisively.

The third activity which concerned the mass of the population was obviously their work. Under the July Monarchy the progress of industrialization continued and there was also a necessary progress in agriculture to keep pace with the steady rise of the population. More land was cultivated, new crops were introduced and the peasantry as a whole profited from the remarkable progress in communications (canals, roads, railways) which was the most dramatic economic change of the period. Thus the statistical record in both industrial and agricultural production was favourable, but within this general picture there were important items of hardship and crisis. Thus, in agricultural terms, there were conflicts in the countryside as the wealthy landowners and peasants tried to take over common land, as the administration tried to plant trees, as the development of towns brought about a decline of rural industry, as the small peasantry determinedly tried to acquire more land and ran into debt, as a large population meant an unsafe dependence upon food harvests. In industrial terms there remained the three types of workers, the artisans (who were by far the most numerous), the factory workers (usually in a few towns) and the domestic workers either in the countryside or the towns. As always their conditions varied, living conditions in Paris or in Lille, for example, being worse than in Alsace or in the south where the progress of industrialization was much slower and where the workers' links with the countryside remained much more meaningful. But since industrial production of all sorts tended to be closely tied to the market, there was an insecurity in the life of all workers. There were always those that were unemployed, and their numbers could rise alarmingly given any form of economic crisis. If these working populations appear to have faced the prospect of a life of terrible hardship and the possibility of an early death (since the working-class areas of some towns were known to have a much higher mortality rate than the areas inhabited by the more comfortably off) with a certain fatalism, they could not but be conscious of the nature of the economic situation and the terms of their employment.

Between the peasantry and the workers, and the controlling political élites, there lay a number of social categories. There were doctors, lawyers, veterinary surgeons, journalists, schoolteachers and students; there were all sorts of officials or *fonctionnaires*; there were shopkeepers, artisans (such as coopers or smiths), merchants, café proprietors and many others. These were to be distinguished from the working population often because they had access to wealth, because they had power through their functions or because they had been educated, but they could often have been only recently removed from these working classes. They were sufficiently near to them to know their bad conditions, and whether through sympathy or through fear, they believed that the Government should do something about them. They were usually excluded from political power. Sometimes, as with the financing of railway construction, the wealthier amongst them, in the provinces for example, found themselves excluded from the opportunities of investment. For all of them the development of financial concentration, the increasing importance of mechanization, the need for higher standards of education than hitherto, meant that social mobility was becoming more difficult. All the indications show that whilst in an expanding economy there were always new opportunities being created, it was increasingly necessary to have some sort of capital to begin with.

Thus a firm impression is created that in the July Monarchy there was a small élite that had achieved the monopoly of all power, whether economic or political, and that beyond it lay the great mass of the population, in which a middle bourgeoisie was forcibly allied with peasants and workers since they were all excluded from power. This suggestion that there was such a polarization of social groups was made by Marx, and by certain of his contemporaries. It has to be modified in many ways. Many of the political élite were the old political élite, that is to say the landowners often noble or having pretensions to nobility, who still dominated the electoral circumscriptions. In 1840 137 deputies out of 459 gave their profession simply as 'landowner' (without any other profession being mentioned, although most of them must have had other interests). The administrative and official class remained vitally important and had its own professional interests and cohesion. The wealth of France remained remarkably scattered throughout the country and it is simply not true to say that it was being seized by a relatively small number of men. But under the July Monarchy it seemed as if the process whereby the government of the country would come into the hands of such an élite had begun. In a country where suspicion and exaggeration were part of the political tradition, it was not surprising that it was widely believed that government was conducted in the interests of a small group of men. It was not only Stendhal who, travelling between Dol-de-Bretagne and Saint-Malo, felt depressed as he encountered the rich bourgeois of the July Monarchy triumphant. Exclusion could take place on many levels and as one famous deputy, Alphonse de Lamartine, saw himself always excluded from office, in 1843 he entered the opposition 'pour toujours'. But for him, this was the opposition to the whole system. Like those who had remained loyal to the Bourbons, or like those who dreamed of a Jacobin republic, he did not want to reform the system but to change it. 'Guizot, Thiers, Molé, Passy, Dufaure,' he said, naming the most prominent members of the political spectrum. 'Five ways of saying the same thing.' Thus the system of the July Monarchy had its enemies both within and without.

In the summer of 1846 the Government, which was presided over by Marshal Soult, but which was effectively directed by Guizot, won a considerable electoral victory. It had been in power since October 1840 and Guizot felt entitled to boast that France had the most stable Government in Europe. Perhaps it was this victory that began the crisis. It seemed as if the Government was immovable, that it was permanently blocking the way to change and progress, that the 'outs' were always to be 'out'. The moderate opposition decided to press for parliamentary and electoral reform as a means of dislodging the Government; allegations that the Government had won its majority by means of corruption became frequent (and they were usually exaggerated); those whose attitude towards power had always been more violent were confirmed in their view that it would only be by some violent shock that they would get rid of the existing regime.

But the real crisis was economic, and it took place in various phases. The first was traditional, that is to say that it began with a bad harvest in 1846, leading to exceptionally high prices for bread in the spring of 1847. It must be noted, however, that it did not affect the whole of France, that in certain places it was caused as much by fear as by an actual shortage, and that it did not last long. Well before the harvest of 1847, food prices were falling. The second was an industrial crisis and was less traditional. To some extent the high price of food affected purchasing power and thereby caused industrial production to be reduced, but essentially the crisis was one of credit and it had preceded the bad harvest of 1846. The economic developments of the 1840s, particularly the construction of railways, had absorbed vast quantities of capital. Suddenly it appeared that there was no capital available, and that the intense activity of 1845 had overstrained the resources of the money market. The railway promoters found that they had underestimated their costs, many businesses and enterprises became particularly conscious of the strains of progress. Throughout 1847 there was a shortage of credit and a consequent slump in business activity. The third phase of the economic crisis coincided with this slump and it was based upon the fear that the Government would be unable to meet its financial obligations. The State had greatly increased its commitments (over education, communications and Algeria, for example) and yet it existed on a small budget with the manipulation of various funds and with a policy of loans. All this led to some alarmist comments which weakened the Government's position. Once again, the extent of these crises should not be exaggerated. There were areas and industries which did not suffer from a regression; there were those who were claiming that the worst of the crisis was over by the end of 1847; many were reassured by the Minister of Finance who said that the Government would be able to meet its obligations.

But the situation was gloomy. The agricultural crisis had led to various movements in the countryside, markets had sometimes been pillaged and the movement of grain had been interfered with. The recession had led to a high rate of unemployment, particularly in coal-mining, textile production and railway construction. The money market was jumpy and was anxious about any form of political crisis, so that the Government felt unable to take any initiative and its majority began to drift away. Opinion was affected too by foreign affairs and by a number of domestic scandals. Both Louis-Philippe and Guizot had always wanted to have a special understanding with England, but this was broken in 1846 when the British Government reacted strongly to the son of the French king marrying a Spanish princess and creating the possibility of a French succession to the Spanish throne, so that it was said that the British alliance had been sacrificed to purely dynastic interests. Subsequently Guizot collaborated with Metternich and with the Continental powers, a collaboration which was not only unpopular but which was also unsuccessful (their support for the Swiss Catholics, for example, did not prevent them from being defeated). Even the final defeat of the Algerian nationalist leader, Abd-el-Kader, in 1847, gave rise to bitter dispute since it was claimed that the king's son, the Duc d'Aumale, had mishandled the terms of surrender. At home it was revealed that former Ministers had been guilty of corruption; a prominent member of the Chamber of Peers murdered his wife and then committed suicide (it was widely rumoured that he had been allowed to escape); a minor scandal concerning the Government's use of patronage affected one of Guizot's closest collaborators and therefore was said to implicate even him.

Naturally none of this created a revolutionary situation. If the widespread discontent with the Government and the general pessimism about the situation can be analysed in terms of long-standing grievances, and if one can point out that the easy violence with which orators such as Lamartine had been speaking about revolution was bound to have had some effect, it remains true that the events of

February 1848 were largely accidental. A demonstration organized against the Government's refusal to allow a reform banquet to be held in Paris convinced the king that he should dismiss Guizot, which he did on 23 February. Later that evening troops fired on the crowds in a moment of panic and fifty-two people were killed. Some of these corpses were piled on to a cart which was taken on a torch-lit procession of the city. This inflamed the population which put up more barricades; columns of troops had to be withdrawn; a small resolute group of republicans demanded the proclamation of the republic and began to circulate the names of a provisional Government. Finally, just after noon on 24 February, Louis-Philippe, by now elderly and apprehensive, abdicated in favour of his nine-year-old grandson. But the crowds invaded the Chamber of Deputies, all the members of the royal family fled or went into hiding, and a Government was chosen by insurgents and groups of republicans.

Thus after a few confused hours the July Monarchy had been brought down. As in 1830, the rest of France was faced by a Parisian *fait accompli* and there was no movement anywhere to support the disappearing dynasty. But there were important differences between 1830 and 1848. In 1848 all organized and official power disappeared. The royal family had gone and there was no younger branch which could take over; the Chambers had been dispersed; no one was prepared to uphold the Charter; the provisional Government of eleven men included eight who had been republicans at a time when it is thought that there were less than 5,000 republicans in Paris. And very rapidly the demands of the revolutionary crowds made themselves felt. On the morning of 25 February armed workmen interrupted the deliberations of the new Government and demanded that the right to work should be guaranteed. In consequence such a decree was drawn up, the National Workshops were eventually created and a Special Commission for workers was set up to look after the interests of working men and to foster their organizations. The impression was created that the revolution of 1848 was a revolution which sought to make life better for all the population. It was a revolution which looked back to the days of hope in the great Revolution, which it still saw as a model, but it also looked forward to a future of change. It was believed that things would never be the same again. 1848 was socialist, romantic, utopian, and even when this created more apprehension than enthusiasm, the revolution was accepted everywhere, supporters both of the Bourbons and of Louis-Philippe declared that they were republicans, priests blessed the trees of liberty which were planted throughout the country, bourgeois and *notables* of all sorts fraternized with the workers in great demonstrations. Exactly one week after Louis-Philippe's abdication the provisional Government declared that universal manhood suffrage existed in France, a form of voting which few had believed in and which existed nowhere else in Europe. When the elections took place in April, something like 97 per cent of those who voted had never voted before and the electorate leapt from 250,000 to 9,000,000. In a fever of discussion, it seemed that France was undergoing a rapid and complete revolution.

But the election revealed that the clubs and the newspapers of Paris were not representative of the whole of France. There was a general rejection of those who had ruled under the July Monarchy (Thiers, for example, was defeated) but the majority of the Assembly should be classed as moderate, drawn mainly from the provincial bourgeoisie, including more than seventy nobles and not a single peasant. Probably most of the Chamber had been monarchists before 1848 (including a fair number of Legitimists). In some parts of France there were worker demonstrations in protest against these results and there was a serious demonstration in Paris on 15 May when the Assembly eliminated the socialist Left from the provisional Government. People such as Barbès, Blanqui and Raspail, who were appearing as the leaders of the extremist groups in Paris, were imprisoned, and both Marx and Tocqueville described the situation as being one of class warfare. Once again it was the artisans in the traditional crafts and the recent immigrants into Paris who were providing the shock troops for the expected, final showdown, and once again it was in conditions of considerable economic distress that the insurrection took place. When the Government decided to send men from the National Workshops into the provinces, organized groups of workmen protested on 22 June. Believing that the Republic was in danger, that the rising was socialist and was aimed at the destruction of property and that rival political groups (including Legitimists, Orleanists and Bonapartists) were fomenting insurrection, the Government decided on a brutal repression. The army and the National Guard, both from Paris and the provinces, killed some thousands of the insurgents and more than 11,000 were imprisoned.

From June onwards the Government, under General Cavaignac who had been the man primarily responsible for the repression, attempted to consolidate the existing institutions and introduced a number of moderate reforms. But its main preoccupation was with drawing up a new constitution. The most notable feature of this constitution was that the executive was to consist of a President elected for four years by universal manhood suffrage. It was true that this President had many checks on his powe , and a single Chamber, also elected by universal male suffrage, was given the exclusive right to make the laws and to decide upon war and peace. But the position of the President was clearly to be vital to the constitution and there were many republicans who had doubts about the wisdom of giving such power to one man, and who wondered whether such a President were compatible with the principle of the Republic. But a powerful speech by Lamartine in favour of direct popular sovereignty won the day and it was arranged that there would be a presidential election in December 1848.

A number of candidates were announced well in advance of this date. The last was that of Louis-Napoleon Bonaparte, the nephew of the emperor. He had not been well known before 1848 and he had not returned to France from his English exile until September. But he had been elected in by-elections by a number of different departments as well as in Paris and he had entered into negotiations with the different political groups that used to meet in the Rue de Poitiers, where Legitimists, Orleanists (including Thiers) and Catholics had weekly discussions. Partly because they had no agreed candidate of their own, partly because it seemed that the name of Bonaparte was being successful, and possibly because they thought they could dominate a man who seemed inexperienced and unimpressive, they decided to support him. Louis-Napoleon was elected by almost 75 per cent of those that voted.

The Second Republic and the Second Empire

It is not as easy as some historians have thought to explain Louis-Napoleon's success. It is not enough to suggest that it was simply his name that served him ('his candidature dates from Austerlitz,' Victor Hugo had remarked when he had first been mentioned as a possible deputy). Nor is it enough to suggest that since the first need of a saviour of society is to have something to save society from, it was the fear of further social movements and insurrections that incited people to vote for him. In spite of the understanding between Thiers and Louis-Napoleon many of the notables, some of the bishops and conservative newspapers supported Cavaignac who always presented himself as a man of order. Nor can one say that Louis-Napoleon was elected by the peasantry, and that the election was the '*coup d'état* of the peasants' as

Marx put it. His votes were consistently in the majority in most of the large towns. One is therefore forced to the conclusion that Louis-Napoleon won votes from all sections of the population, partly because of the ambiguity of his position, since few people knew him and since he encouraged everyone to expect things from him; and partly because to vote for him was to protest against all the things that had gone before, whether it was economic distress, disorder, the conservatism of the republican Government, Catholic discontent with the educational system, the continued supremacy of the *notables* or the feelings of uncertainty which had both preceded and followed February 1848. It was as if it were Louis-Napoleon who divided Frenchmen the least. His situation was strong, but part of his strength lay in the very ambiguity that surrounded him, and he was to remain a puzzling and unpredictable ruler. His situation was also weak since he did not know France, he had no experience of Government, he had no organized political support and his constitutional powers were surrounded by complicated restrictions.

He was known as the Prince-President and he began his functions by showing considerable political skill. The press was subsidized, different parts of the country were visited, the Catholics were pleased by being allowed to establish primary and secondary schools, conservatives were impressed by his dismantling of radical organizations. The sending of a French army to Rome to destroy the recently created Roman Republic and to restore papal authority was satisfying to Catholic opinion and was an assertion of the importance of France in the world. But Napoleon had also to appear as the hero of the liberals and democrats. He did this by criticizing Pope Pius IX, who was following a policy of reaction, and by saying that he had not sent an army to Rome to stifle Italian liberty. But above all he was enabled to do this by the action of the Assembly (dated in 1849) which sought to remove the vote from some three million Frenchmen; he appeared as the opponent of these reactionaries and frequently pointed to his own position as the representative of the people. Thus when on 2 December 1851 a carefully planned and neatly executed *coup d'état* arrested the leaders of the opposition and dissolved the Assembly it was possible for this to be presented as a democratic measure. It was announced that universal suffrage was restored and that the people would be asked to accept or reject what had happened by plebiscite. There were armed movements against this, especially in the south, and the repression involved the imprisonment of some 30,000. In Paris 80,000 troops were deployed against a few hundred workers (although a contemporary observer spoke of 2,000 insurgents being killed). But the plebiscite gave an overwhelming approval to Louis-Napoleon's overthrow of the Assembly. On 2 December 1852, the anniversary of the *coup d'état* (2 December was also the anniversary of Austerlitz), Louis-Napoleon made his formal entry into Paris as the Emperor Napoleon III.

It was strange that Napoleon III was so frequently to cast himself as the successor to his uncle, to revive the imperial emblems, to make 15 August (Napoleon's birthday) a national festival, even to consider bringing the Pope to Paris in order to crown him. Napoleon III was very unlike Napoleon I. Whilst his ancestor had been decisive, energetic, talkative and daring, Napoleon III was uncertain, lazy, silent and cautious. Napoleon I was a gambler; Napoleon III tried to keep all his options open for as long as possible. Napoleon I was a soldier; Napoleon III was more of an intellectual, a connoisseur of ideas. But where they did resemble each other was in a shrewd and cynical detachment, which caused them both to realize that there were different elements in Bonapartism and which led them to try and keep the initiative, always to be one step in advance of their opponents. Napoleon III tried to show that he was both an authoritarian ruler and a liberal, that he was a defender of property and a friend of the worker, that he believed in peace but that France could embark on an adventurous policy abroad. In political terms the 1850s were characterized by the emperor's control of executive and legislative power, with the Senate nominated by him, a Legislative Assembly which could not initiate legislation and which was packed by governmental interference, with a press and a theatre that were strictly controlled, and an administration that had extensive police powers. All political opposition seemed to have disappeared and the official opposition in the Legislative Assembly could be counted on the fingers of one hand.

But this personal supremacy was never so evident as in the series of measures by which the emperor decided to liberalize his regime. In 1859 there was an amnesty; in 1860 both the Senate and the Legislative Assembly were given the right to frame, discuss and vote an annual address; in 1861 the right was given to the press to publish the debates; in 1863 a Minister was given the function of defending Government policy in the Assembly; 1867 and 1868 saw the Chamber given the right to ask Ministers questions, newspapers benefited from a slight relaxation of their control and public meetings became easier to organize.

The result of all these reforms was that in the elections of 1863 and 1869 the opposition grew considerably. But Napoleon III regarded this as an incentive to further change. In September 1869 the Chambers were given more freedom over their own affairs and control over business. The move towards a form of parliamentary government reached completion when in January 1870 Émile Ollivier was invited to lead the Government and to regard himself as the leader of a parliamentary majority. But in May 1870 the emperor revealed the complexity of his thought by submitting his reforms to a plebiscite. More than 80 per cent of those who had voted approved, so that it was as if the Empire had been founded for the second time. Two powers existed: the power of the emperor, approved by the population as a whole, and the power of the Assembly and of the Chief Minister. It was a curious situation.

Doubtless none of this political evolution would have been possible without two other features of the Second Empire. The one was that this was an era of business confidence and industrial prosperity. There was considerable industrial growth, mechanization spread, railway construction was important, Paris was replanned and there was a large extension in the credit facilities available (as in the amount of capital exported). In 1860 an economic agreement with England reduced the amount of protection available for French industries and this caused some firms to reduce the number of workers employed or to try to reduce their wages. It also aroused much discontent amongst the employers. From this time onwards Napoleon found himself opposed and criticized both by the employers and by the workers. His attempts to create some sort of labour legislation for the latter seemed inadequate to the workers, whilst they appeared to be a betrayal to those who were employers. The other feature of the Second Empire was its active foreign policy. In 1854 Napoleon associated himself with the British in the Near East, and fought in the Crimean war with Britain and Turkey. The peace conference at the end of this war was held in Paris in 1856, and Napoleon was sometimes called 'the emperor of Europe'. In 1859 he made war on Austria in support of Italian unification, but after some victories he suddenly deserted his ally and made peace (it was then that Nice and Savoy were annexed to France). He intervened in Indo-China (making Cochin-China a colony and Cambodia a protectorate), Syria, Mexico and West Africa. But every one of his successes was double-edged, as other powers were both impressed and suspicious of this activity. At home the Catholics resented his support for the nationalists, liberals regretted that he had not gone further, and the conservative-minded wondered about the wisdom of these adventures.

There are those who have claimed that there was an inevitability about the decline of the Second Empire. From the 1850s onwards, it is suggested that the emperor was simply alienating one element of French opinion after another. Bonapartism was meant to be a consensus, a bringing-together of different parts of society; since it was no longer doing this then it was no longer fulfilling its function, and however much the emperor tried to share his authority, there was no getting away from failure. Yet it is difficult to accept this point of view. As has been shown here, there was always a deliberate ambiguity in Napoleon's position and there is no evidence that he was forced into making concessions. He showed his force by retaining the initiative, and there was a general agreement that the liberal Empire of 1870 was a strong regime. Some of the opposition had been won over, however reluctantly, and the remaining opposition was discouraged. It was true that the emperor was no longer in good health and that he had lost much of his vigour. The empress (Eugénie de Montijo, who had become empress in 1853 and who gave birth to a male heir in 1856) was critical of the reforms, and the court was a great centre of intrigue. In January 1871 Prince Pierre Bonaparte had shot a journalist, Victor Noir, this giving rise to a ferociously hostile outcry. But when war eventually came, the opponents of the Government were saddened because they thought that it would strengthen the Empire. No one saw it as a means of facilitating the destruction of a doomed regime.

The belief that the succession of a Hohenzollern to the Spanish throne was a form of Prussian encirclement of France was a curious exaggeration, and the French insistence that the Prussian king should renounce in perpetuity any Hohenzollern claim to the Spanish throne was a petulant foolishness. From this came the impression that both the French and the Germans had been insulted and Napoleon responded to the excitement by declaring war in July 1870. He was to find that France was diplomatically isolated; that earlier military reforms were incomplete since they had come up against so much opposition; that the officers in charge were incompetent, often having been chosen for reasons of favouritism or political preference. The emperor himself put the seal on a confused mobilization by himself taking command when he was physically unable to do so. The result was that with one French army encircled at Metz, the emperor was forced to surrender at Sedan on 2 September 1870. The principal part of the constitution was thus removed. The Prince Impérial was too young and no one had any confidence in the empress. Fearful of a more radical riposte, since the war continued and since the road to Paris lay open, a group of moderate republicans proclaimed the Republic on 4 September 1870.

The Third Republic to 1914

There was nothing new in a French regime collapsing and in there being no support for it. But the situation in 1870 was spectacular in its uncertainty. The Republic had been proclaimed. But the republicans were conscious of the fact that they were a minority in the country; they were divided amongst themselves, since a new generation had grown up, which had little in common with the persistent utopianism of the 1848 generation, and since there was a great variety of opinions sheltering under the name of republican, stretching from a simple resentment of Napoleon III to more ambitious plans for a social and democratic organization; the differences amongst republicans were also regional. In these circumstances how could a group of inexperienced men hope to face up to the crisis of a continued German advance and the absence of any settled Government? For the war, they prepared themselves for a long siege in Paris, and a prominent young republican, Gambetta, left Paris by balloon in order to raise troops and to direct provisional Governments, first at Tours, then at Bordeaux. So far as the settling of the institutions of the country was concerned, they were not agreed. There were those republicans who claimed that the Republic existed and that no one could abolish it, even by virtue of universal suffrage (here there was the fear that the peasantry, the majority of the population, would continue to vote Bonapartist, so that the republicans saw themselves in opposition to the *campagnocratie*). But other republicans thought that it was necessary to consult the population. There were many moderates who felt that the situation was disturbing: within a besieged Paris the attempts at breaking out had been accompanied by flurries of social movements, and on the Loire Gambetta's raising of armies had also given rise to a violent patriotism which promised to be uncontrollable. There seemed to be a connection between continuing the war and accepting forms of political radicalism which would destroy the social organization of the country. It was in these circumstances that the opinion of the moderates prevailed and with German consent to an armistice elections were held in February. The circumstances of the electoral campaign were strikingly unusual, and perhaps too much should not be made of the fact that an overwhelmingly large majority of the country voted conservative and monarchist, that is to say, voted for peace. There had never been an elected assembly that had had so many aristocrats. The supporters of Gambetta were a mere handful. In the light of this result the Government was able to ask for peace terms, and at the beginning of March preliminary terms were drawn up by which the Germans annexed all of Alsace and part of Lorraine, whilst imposing a heavy indemnity and the right to occupy certain areas. It was to the elder statesman Thiers that the Assembly had turned and who seemed to represent the hope of returning to a more stable situation.

But not everyone was in full agreement with this policy. In Paris particularly, after a long siege, it seemed that the Government had not done everything which was necessary to protect it. When the Government decided to leave Bordeaux and to return, not to Paris, but to Versailles, it seemed that an unpatriotic Government was seeking to downgrade the city. When the Government decided to disband the National Guard, thus ending the only regular wage which many Parisians had, and to render all Parisians liable to pay bills and debts again (a liability which had been suspended during the siege), then it seemed that there was being made a deliberate attack on Parisians. Consequently when the Government attempted to remove cannon from Montmartre on the night of 17–18 March 1871, there was an insurrection, probably caused by a mixture of panic as well as resentment. It was true that this accident became graver as the crowds killed two generals, but the real gravity developed as the rising began to appear in the perspective of a wider meaning. The Paris insurrectionaries were patriots, fighting against the Government in Versailles and the provincial bourgeoisie, just as an earlier revolutionary Government had fought against the court and the provinces. Thiers, perhaps profiting from his experience of 1830 and 1848, withdrew all his forces from the capital, and the insurrectionaries found themselves in charge of the city. They therefore organized elections and in April a municipal Government, the Commune, was set up. In France there were therefore two Governments.

The Paris Commune of 1871 is a complicated subject. It has rightly been said that it is one of those incidents where the legend is more vital than the fact. One of the legends was that Paris fell under the rule of a mob, in which foreigners were prominent, and that this mob, putting forward the heady and dangerous principles of socialism, mixed with atheism, immorality and drunkenness, held the population in terror. Hence, in expiation, the Basilica of the Sacré Cœur was subsequently built at Montmartre. The other legend was that the rising of the Commune was the first worker rising in world history, and that it was here that the practice of a Marxist socialism was tried. Consequently there has been a cult of the *communards*, especially in revolutionary or left-wing political parties. Modern historians tend to be more sympathetic to the second view than to the first, but tend to emphasize certain features. As with all French revolutions there are different perspectives through which the Commune can be viewed. It is true that from the 1860s onwards there was an increase in worker organizations. The emperor himself had helped to sponsor co-operative and mutual credit societies, but under the influence of Proudhon's ideas, there were organizations which sought to further worker power and to reduce government centralization. Amongst the new radical organizations too there was a demand for endowing Paris with municipal liberties, such as the right to elect a mayor. During the war and the siege, the people of Paris had found themselves in an unusual position. They had suffered great hardships and they had been extensively organized in order to fight, as they saw it, for the defence of the nation and of the Republic. They were suspicious of being betrayed, whether by officers or by politicians. Perhaps they had become accustomed to violence: at all events the attempt to remove the cannon from Montmartre appeared as an assault upon them and when they set up a rival Government then they had committed themselves. Thiers and the Versailles Government did not attempt to negotiate. Within this impasse, and in an atmosphere of freedom and exaltation, the leaders of Paris began to discuss the future. They had plans for the establishment of liberty, the organization of the municipalities of France, the spread of education and the emancipation of the proletariat. There was a great variety of ideas, but obviously those who were familiar with socialist or Marxist doctrines expressed themselves most forcibly, and attacks on the Church and on those who exploited their workers became frequent. A number of the ideas put forward, such as that for the emancipation of women, were very advanced, and the persistence of such discussions suggests that many of the *communards* were conscious of the uniqueness of their position. Meanwhile Paris was governed in a moderate, efficient way (one English commentator noted that the streets of Paris were kept clean) and whilst the Commune adopted some socialist or semi-socialist measures, such as fixing minimum wages in a number of workshops, and exploring the possibility of reopening abandoned workshops under worker co-operatives, it was in practice timid and cautious.

In the organization of its own defence it was also ineffective. In 1871 the troops of the Versailles Government stormed and took the city. In the final week of May (21–28 May) there was an onslaught on the forces of the Commune which far outdid the repression of June 1848. Perhaps 20,000 were killed in the fighting, some 50,000 were arrested and there were many thousands who fled. Since the *communards* had largely been men from the artisan and working class, this meant that the working population of Paris was decimated. The Versailles Government was triumphant and secure, and when partial elections were held in July 1871 in order to fill a large number of seats (143) which were vacant because a deputy could be elected to more than one circumscription, the republicans were overwhelmingly successful.

Thus within a relatively short time there had been a number of political experiences in France. France had voted imperialist, then monarchist, then republican. There had also been the experience of the Commune which, although it was essentially a Parisian manifestation, had led to similar, short-lived manifestations in other cities. There was no certainty that July 1871 was the end of a period of change and uncertainty. All parties and groups showed similar uncertainties. The royalists were split into those who supported the descendant of Charles X (the Comte de Chambord, son of the Duchesse de Berry), who made matters difficult by refusing to accept the three-coloured flag, and those who supported the descendant of Louis-Philippe, the Comte de Paris. The Bonapartists, who were beginning to make their return to the political arena, hardly mentioned the name of Bonaparte (except in Corsica) but pushed the idea of popular sovereignty. The republicans were distrustful of Thiers and sometimes voted radical in order to make sure that the idea of the Republic should be more clearly affirmed. As Thiers was at his most successful, since the country was subscribing to pay for the indemnity and to get rid of the German occupation, he was deserted by the Chambers and forced to resign. He was succeeded by Marshal MacMahon, who was thought to be arranging for the transition to a king. But in 1875, when a former monarchist, Wallon, proposed an amendment which would give the Republic a legal permanency, the Orleanists decided to vote for it. They preferred such a Republic to a more radical version or to a revival of Bonapartism. The

Republic was conservative, therefore it had to be supported. But Wallon's amendment passed by only one vote.

It is customary to emphasize the instability of the Third Republic. It is easy to show this in terms of the difficulty with which Governments were formed and their usual lack of success in staying in power, so that in the years up to 1914 there were more than fifty, with an average life of less than nine months each. This has been given various explanations. The fragmentation and multiplicity of political parties (possibly a reflection of the varied social and ideological state of France) made every Government a coalition Government which could easily break up. There was a decline in Presidential power, particularly after Marshal MacMahon had unsuccessfully tried to impose himself on the Chamber in 1877, and although the constitution gave an important role to the Presidents of the Republic, they tended to become ceremonial figures who did not use their powers (such as dissolving the Chamber of Deputies). There was no corresponding rise in the power of the Prime Minister who remained entirely dependent upon the Chamber and who was therefore forced to play the political game as dictated by the deputies. Thus ministerial instability seemed inseparable from parliamentary government. But there was a deeper form of instability. It often appeared that the regime itself was in danger and that it could easily be transformed into something entirely different. In 1877 when MacMahon attempted to force his views on a staunchly republican Chamber and then dissolved the Chamber (this was the last time a President of the Republic was to do this until 1955), it seemed that there was a possibility of France being dominated by monarchists, aristocrats and army officers. In 1888 and 1889 it seemed as if the Republic might fall under the control of General Boulanger, whose temporary popularity implied a return to strong executive government, but the Government weathered the storm and Boulangism collapsed as rapidly as it had grown. In 1892 the affairs of the Panama Canal Company attracted attention, when it appeared that many officials of the Republic (including deputies) had been bribed into silence concerning the company's bankruptcy. The Dreyfus affair, which began in 1894 with the arrest of a Jewish officer on the charge of selling secrets to the Germans and which became a resounding affair when it appeared that Dreyfus's conviction was unjust, highlighted the differences that existed amongst Frenchmen. In both cases it appeared that the Republic was in the hands of unworthy men and that there were others, often monarchists, Catholics, nationalists, officers, who were ready to take it over. Thus France seemed divided, even decadent.

But behind the political factors there were other elements that showed a much greater stability. There was, for example, the movement of the French population. Whilst the populations of countries such as England and Germany rose rapidly in the years between 1870 and 1914, the French hardly increased in numbers, progressing from 36 million in 1870 to less than 40 million in 1914. In these circumstances it was possible to see the perpetuation of many French conditions and values rather than their transformation. France tended to remain a country with small-scale enterprise, with small towns, small factories, small farms, small commercial establishments. There was neither the vast labour resources, nor the large market for the mass-produced goods that existed everywhere else. Whilst all types of industrial production increased, these increases were in no way comparable to those of countries such as England or Germany, and whilst French inventors and designers were successful in many fields, there was little move to mass-produce their prototypes. In a similar way, whilst French agriculture felt the impact of American, Russian and Australian competition, and incidentally suffered in wine and silk production from the accidents of disease, nevertheless by 1914 about a half of the French population was still engaged in agriculture, and France did not join those countries where agriculture almost perished.

In foreign policy there was also stability. It is true that the acquisition of colonies was not a subject of general agreement, and the formation of the Indo-Chinese Union, the establishment of French protectorates over Tunisia and Morocco, and the acquisition of colonies in West and Equatorial Africa and Madagascar led to many disagreements. But once this colonial expansion had been accomplished it was generally seen as an extension of French power and prestige at a time when the defeat by Prussia and the loss of Alsace-Lorraine had reduced her strength and diminished her position. It was Germany, and the considerations attached to German actions, which dominated French foreign policy and caused French diplomats to break out from the isolation into which Bismarck had attempted to confine them. In 1894 the French signed an agreement with Russia which gave France greater security against German aggression, although it increased France's commitments in eastern Europe. In 1904 the Entente Cordiale between France and England put an end to Anglo-French colonial rivalries and, whilst it made no mention of military agreement, it nevertheless paved the way for military and naval discussions and co-operation. Relations improved between France and Italy. So that although there could be many disagreements about the details of French policy, and although the dangers of allying with Russia or the humiliation of giving way to England could be stressed by this or that group, there was a general agreement that France had to face up to the existence and threat of a united, powerful Germany. Even the socialists agreed that the nation should be protected against aggression, however deep their anti-militarism or their conviction that the German workers were their brothers.

Within politics too there was the basis of agreement which could modify division. In order to face up to the Catholic Church's hostility to the Republic and its attachment to the monarchist cause in the 1870s, the republicans had launched an important educational programme. In fact an insistence upon education was to be the main ideology of the Third Republic. In 1879, 1882 and 1886 education was reformed. It was necessary for religious teaching orders to receive authorization from the State; primary education was made free, compulsory and secular for all children aged between six and thirteen; the State imposed its standards upon all teachers in the public educational system. Education and educational methods became uniform; the lingering belief that it was because of their superior educational system that the Prussians had won the war of 1870 caused it to become patriotic in France; the old ideal remained that French unity could be attained through a State system. The number of primary teachers had more than doubled by 1914, more than 85 per cent of children attended school, and they were all taught about the growth of French national unity as they were taught to respect and to appreciate the geographical diversity of their country. Although relations between Church and State fluctuated, and became bad after the Dreyfus affair, with the 1905 law separating Church and State, yet it is possible to see a decline in anti-clericalism. Once it seemed that the State educational system had been fully created, and once it was apparent that there were Catholics who were supporting the Republic, then it was not so necessary to be anti-clerical. The Republic was supported in every village by the schoolmaster. The schoolmaster became a notable and by virtue of his position in society he was the equal of the priest. No one feared any real resuscitation of ecclesiastical rights or tithes. Even such a convinced anti-clerical as Clemenceau who became Prime Minister between 1906 and 1909 declined to enforce all the provisions of the 1905 law which called for the inventory of the Church's property and for its transfer to lay associations. The Republic was prudent.

Another factor that promoted unity was that all the attacks on the Republic seemed to come from the Right. Since the downfall of the Commune it had been the army, the Catholic Church, the monarchists which had attacked, or had threatened to attack, the regime. The result of this was that the Republic began increasingly to appear as something which was worth saving. Perhaps the real significance of the Dreyfus affair was not that it divided Frenchmen but that it brought many together to fight for the cause of justice and truth, and when it was over, whilst there were supporters of Dreyfus, such as Péguy, who suffered from disillusionment, there were many others who were confirmed in their belief that the Republic was something that had to be defended. Those who had been cynical about the Republic and its chances of survival looked back to the affair, and they saw that the Republic had a past and a future. Recalling the affair, at Zola's funeral, Anatole France exclaimed, 'There is only one country in the world where such things could be accomplished. How great is the genius of our country!' A republican ideology emphasized that the Republic was inclusive and that all categories of society were acceptable to it. Even those who believed in future revolution accepted the Republic as the inheritance of anterior revolution.

Prominent amongst those who accepted the Republic, and who had been moved by the Dreyfus affair to proclaim his preoccupation with the welfare of all humanity, was Jean Jaurès. It was only in 1901 that the French socialists had established themselves in two parties, the one led by Jaurès, and in 1905 unity was attained. By 1914 the socialists had a million and a half voters and more than a hundred deputies. But this political movement had little connection with the French trade-union movement. From 1884, when freedom of association was granted (under certain conditions of registration, which were deeply resented and not always followed), and 1895, when the Confédération Générale du Travail brought the unions together, there was a quickening of trade-union activity. But as a movement it was dominated by the doctrines of anarcho-syndicalism, which rejected co-operation with political parties or action within the political system, and looked to direct worker action as the means of replacing the existing state by social and economic arrangements that would create conditions of justice and equality. By 1914 only about 9 per cent of French workers were in trade unions (as compared, say, to 28 per cent in Germany).

In the violent clashes which occurred between workers and their employers, it was always possible for the State to intervene and to crush the workers.

It was true that the social climate deteriorated on the eve of the 1914 war. As with the July Monarchy, there were scandals which suggested that all was not well with the governing élites. The second wife of a prominent statesman and Prime Minister, Joseph Caillaux, shot and killed the editor of the newspaper *Le Figaro* in the spring of 1914. Socialists and trade-unionists insisted that were there a war they would not fight. There were many fears and apprehensions. But the State was strong, with half a million officials employed by it. There was a general prosperity; many classes were experiencing a sense of well-being; there was the comfort of believing that social ascension was to be attained through the republican institution of the school. France was not alone in Europe, as in 1870, and any comparison with that unfortunate year seemed quite irrelevant.

The War 1914–1918

The 1914 war arose out of the affairs of eastern Europe. France was involved in any possible conflict between Russia and Austria-Hungary because Russia was France's ally, and the President of the Republic, Raymond Poincaré, was on a visit to Russia in the crucial month of July 1914, assuring the Russian Government of French support. But France was more immediately involved because of the nature of German war plans. Unwilling to envisage a war against both Russia and France in which two fronts would be active, the Germans had prepared to send an army wheeling through Belgium which would move rapidly and eventually encircle the French army in eastern France. In this way the French would be disposed of militarily and it would be possible for the Germans to concentrate on the more difficult task of defeating the Russians. It did not suit the Germans that France should consider neutrality, since the presence of a French army on Germany's western front would necessitate the keeping of large German forces in the west and would hamper the Russian campaign. In this sense France was condemned to a war and it is interesting to reflect on how little diplomatic opportunity was available to her.

At all events the war was greeted with apparent enthusiasm by many Frenchmen. It was true that socialists and trade-union leaders had been pressing for strike action as a means of preventing their Government, and, they hoped, the Governments of other states, from going to war. Many politicians and observers had protested about the prolonged absence of the President of the Republic, who was accompanied by the Prime Minister, Viviani (they returned on 29 July). But the assassination of Jaurès on 31 July, by an isolated young man who believed that the socialist leader was betraying France, met with universal reprobation. The next day came the news of the German declaration of war on Russia; on 2 August the Germans addressed an ultimatum to Belgium. It seemed clear that Germany was the aggressor. 'They have assassinated Jaurès, we will not assassinate France.' 'The country of the French Revolution is in danger.' 'The France of Voltaire, Diderot, Zola and Jaurès is in danger.' It was with such words that the socialists abandoned all idea of resisting the war. The crowds in the streets shouted 'À Berlin!' and the President of the Republic called for 'l'union sacrée'. The Germans declared war on France on 3 August.

The French army, after a smooth mobilization, numbered some 3,700,000 men. Its commander-in-chief, General Joffre, had presided over the careful elaboration of Plan XVII, which prepared for a French attack in the east, and it was in accordance with this plan that Mulhouse was occupied by forces under General Pau. But immediately things went wrong. The French were forced to withdraw under heavy German fire and it became clear that the German offensive in Belgium was heralding a much more important movement than Joffre had anticipated. By the end of August the French, British and Belgian forces were falling back and the Germans were moving rapidly in the direction of Paris. On 1 September the Government decided to leave Paris and went to Bordeaux; the official communiqués could not conceal the gravity of the situation. But Joffre succeeded in strengthening his forces so as to face the advancing enemy, and when the Germans had shown themselves to be imprudent in their organization, he gave the order to counter-attack on 6 September. After three days of fighting the Germans were in retreat, the immediate danger to Paris was over. What was perhaps more important, the German plan for a quick defeat of France had failed and the Germans were faced with the necessity of fighting a war on two fronts. There was no question but that the allied troops, mainly French, who had been in full retreat for a fortnight, had fought heroically, and that the Battle of the Marne had been a great victory.

Yet the war was not over. The German troops re-established themselves on the Aisne, and before the end of 1914 a continuous front was established from Switzerland to the North Sea. Ten French departments were occupied, including those departments which provided France with most coal, and this occupation, together with destruction and the number of peasants who had been mobilized, meant a substantial drop in French food production. Furthermore, French losses had been very heavy, and by the end of 1914 there were 300,000 French dead, and nearly 600,000 wounded, prisoner or missing. As it became obvious that it was going to be increasingly difficult to relaunch a war of movement, it was clear that such a situation was very unsatisfactory for France. The French army had had to abandon its plans for attacking in the east. France's ally Russia had been heavily defeated (and the French command said, somewhat unjustly, that whilst the French had held five-sixths of the German army, the Russians had allowed themselves to be defeated by the remaining one-sixth). The war, which had generally been thought of as being short, was becoming a long war. In 1915 the French endeavoured to take the offensive in Champagne and in the region of Arras. In February 1916 the Germans started a battle of attrition by attacking Verdun, where General Pétain was placed in command. In July 1916 the British and the French attacked on the Somme. In April 1917 a new general, Nivelle, launched an offensive in Champagne. Not one of these operations had any real effect on the situation; not one of them was successful; every one of them was enormously costly in men's lives.

Since France had traditionally been thought of as a country that was divided, it might have been thought that such a strain as this would have a most disrupting effect. It is true that 'l'union sacrée' was not always effective. The Viviani Government more or less disintegrated in October 1915 and was replaced by one led by Aristide Briand. There were continued disagreements amongst the politicians and the military leaders. French socialists and union-leaders rediscovered their vocations, and in 1915 there were strikes in many of the main industries. By 1917 strikes were much more important and a number of French leaders, such as Caillaux, were flirting with the idea of peace and creating an atmosphere of fear and suspicion. The rumour, in May 1917, that certain French units had mutinied and had refused to take up their positions in the line, seemed destined to cause considerable upset, and a socialist spokesman, Pierre Laval, in a secret session in the Chamber, was quick to denounce the military leaders whose incompetence had led the troops to despair. But in reality French unity persisted, as did the determination to continue the war. The administrative system at the disposal of the Government enabled it to control opinion; the educational system had succeeded in creating a general patriotism. The mutinies were, in fact, both limited and localized, and they had no political content. When the Bolshevik revolution and the Italian defeat at Caporetto seemed to form the climax of a disastrous year, the effect in France was that Clemenceau took power on 16 November 1917. The suggestion that a Clemenceau Government could cause the workers to revolt and result in civil war (since he had brutally broken a whole wave of strikes between 1906 and 1908) was discounted. From that time onwards there was never any doubt that France would fight to the end. Attacking those who were supposedly guilty of treason, Clemenceau created a nervy atmosphere, but it helped him to reinvigorate the nation. Thus when in March 1918 the Germans took the offensive, nearly succeeded in separating the allied armies, once again reached the Marne and were within 75 kilometres of Paris, the French not only held on but on 18 July they counter-attacked. At the beginning of October 1918 the Germans asked the Americans for an armistice. It was eventually signed on 11 November and, since it was a long time before peace negotiations got under way, periodically renewed.

France had lost over 1,300,000 killed (about 16 per cent of those mobilized). For every ten men aged between twenty and forty-five, two had been killed. This was a terrible blow to a country which had experienced a relative decline of population, and even with the recovery of Alsace-Lorraine, the population figures for the 90 departments of 1921 were half a million less than for the 87 departments of 1913. This demographic consequence of the war was of outstanding importance. Compared to it, the wholesale destruction of farms, houses, industries and cattle was a series of minor tragedies. But the financial effects of the war were also devastating. Up to 1914 the franc, which was based on gold, had been one of the most secure currencies in Europe. But the suspension of convertibility, the rise of wartime expenditure, the reluctance to proceed to new taxes, meant that the war had been financed by loans and by an increase in the number of bank-notes in circulation. The consequential rise in prices was considerable, and all those who were dependent upon fixed incomes suffered. France was undoubtedly a poorer country by the end of the war. But in the euphoria of victory such considerations did not seem to matter. With an election expected in 1919 it was only natural that the politicians should join with public opinion in stating that the Germans would pay for everything.

But one thing appeared clear to most Frenchmen. France had won the war, but only at the cost of an enormous sacrifice, and only because, at various moments, France had had as allies England, Russia and the United States. Therefore France had to have security against Germany so that there would be no possible repetition of this catastrophe. From the very start of peace negotiations the French placed the greatest importance in seeking this security. There were those who thought that it would be necessary for Germany to be divided, and that one convenient way of doing this would be by encouraging separatist movements. Then there was the possibility of reducing German strength, both by refusing the Germans the right to have an army and by imposing a crippling economic fine on the German people. There was the suggestion that France should have alliances with Britain and America, and perhaps at the same time with some of the new states of eastern Europe. There were those who thought that if the League of Nations could become an organization with real power, then it could be a means of preserving the peace in Europe and of protecting France. But as the negotiations proceeded the real position of France in Europe became more evident. For economic reasons, there were those countries which did not want to see Germany ruined or divided. Many Frenchmen shared the fear that Germany could become Communist. Neither Great Britain nor America were prepared to commit themselves by treaty to guaranteeing France's frontiers. Other countries saw the League as an eventual means of changing treaty arrangements rather than as a means of maintaining them. The economic difficulties inherent in making Germany pay an indemnity (or reparations) were such that complicated and acrimonious discussions were to continue well into the 1920s and the amount expected was steadily whittled down. The chief French negotiator, Clemenceau, was always conscious of the danger that France would be isolated. France had to be satisfied with an arrangement whereby there was a temporary army of occupation, the Germans agreed to demilitarize the Rhineland area, and France could come to agreements with some of the smaller states of eastern Europe. Such diplomatic achievements hardly seemed fitting after four long years of warfare.

The Inter-War Years 1919–1939

The history of France between the wars is filled with paradox. In the elections of November 1919 a large coalition stretching from the radical to the moderate right wing formed a Bloc National and won nearly three-quarters of the seats, thus preserving the impression of national unity; but within two months a series of intrigues united Catholics and socialists in a successful manœuvre to prevent Clemenceau from becoming President of the Republic in succession to Poincaré. The reconstruction of the devastated areas was carried out swiftly and efficiently, and the 1920s appear as years of considerable progress, with the pre-war production rates easily overtaken by 1925 and with the rapid development of new industries. But these were also years when the Government had great budgetary difficulties, was dependent upon loans, often from quite small investors, and was most insistent upon gaining reparations from Germany. Indeed, more attention was paid to the question of reparations than to the failure of the American Senate to ratify the Treaty of Versailles. It was in December 1920 that the socialist congress at Tours voted for the formation of the Communist party. This party, which attracted an increasing number of supporters during the 1920s, so that in 1928 it received a million votes, declared itself a revolutionary party, believing in the class struggle, affirming its loyalty to Soviet Russia and its opposition to social democracy. But in spite of an important strike movement during 1919 and 1920, the trade-union movement remained weak, was divided into Communists and non-Communists and appeared ineffective. France took part in a considerable number of international conferences in the post-war years, both to discuss reparations and to settle the details of peacemaking. From 1921 onwards it was Aristide Briand who appeared as one of the chief French negotiators, a man whose thought was very European and who started the process of effecting a reconciliation with Germany and a general *détente* in Europe. Yet in 1920 Millerand pursued a policy independent of England over Poland, and sent General Weygand to assist the Poles in their war against the Russians, and more spectacularly Poincaré, who had become Prime Minister in 1922, sent French troops to occupy the Ruhr in January 1923 in order to guarantee the full German payment of reparations. Thus France appeared both as a conciliatory power and as a domineering, nationalist state with the strongest army in Europe.

The sort of difficulty experienced by France is well illustrated by the formation of the Cartel des Gauches and by their electoral victory in May 1924. There was a wide discontent both with and within the Bloc National. There had been a misunderstanding over Poincaré's occupation of the Ruhr. Some had seen in it a deliberate attempt to reduce German power, possibly to dismember united Germany. Those who had followed Poincaré's carefully chosen and legalistic statements were well aware of the fact that his action was to be seen as a means of exacting the terms of the treaty. As the French occupation led to a crisis in the German economy there were those who claimed that even this limited objective was not being attained. The danger of straining both the German political situation and the French financial situation (since the occupation was a costly operation) was pointed out. Internationally the argument was that if Germany was ever to pay reparations, then the allies must first seek to make Germany prosperous. In these circumstances there seemed to be a case for resorting to some new form of foreign policy, and since the movement of an army had not succeeded, then the more idealistic talk of international co-operation was attractive. In addition Poincaré was increasing taxation. In these circumstances the claim of the Cartel des Gauches to represent the republican tradition and to attack the clerical policies of Governments that had sent an ambassador to the Vatican seemed to have a certain resonance.

The premiership of Édouard Herriot was the triumph of the Radical party. This party could look back to Gambetta and could claim to represent the republic in a modern form. Radicals believed in the French State, its centralization and administration, since they believed that what was good for one Frenchman was good for another. They believed that the task of government was to create a better world, and that the principal method of doing this was through an educational system which would emphasize French unity and which would give equality of opportunity. But at the same time the Radicals believed in the individual. Life had to be lived by the individual, he had to make his existence by his own efforts, and not by the intervention of the State. The Radicals believed, with their philosopher who wrote under the name of Alain, that the State should not enrich them, all the more that the State should not impoverish them. They had a vision of a nation of small shopkeepers, peasants and artisans. They saw them as independent, rational, progressive. At times the State was their enemy, when it tried to tax them or inquire into their private lives; but the State was their friend when it came to organize education and to protect them from the aristocracy, the Church, big business, the prejudices of the few or the many. Édouard Herriot appeared as the ideal Frenchman, who had made his way to the Premiership from humble origins because of his scholastic attainments, who was firmly anchored in provincial France through his attachment to Lyon (where he was mayor) and who represented all the aspirations of the ordinary man for peace. It was true that the Left had been united in the elections only, and that the Socialists had refused to share power with the Radicals. This possibly explains a renewal of anti-clericalism which aroused the inevitable riposte of Catholic organizations. It was also true that the Right found itself particularly critical of Herriot's determination to come to agreement with England, since this seemed to imply the abandonment of certain French positions. But the real stumbling block of the Government was the financial crisis. There was disagreement as to how the question of France's finances was to be handled technically, and neither the political leaders nor public opinion seemed to understand the nature of the problem. Essentially the French Government, heavily in debt, was dependent upon public confidence and the willingness of the public to invest in Government bonds. For political reasons, that is to say his need to secure socialist support, Herriot spoke vaguely about taxes on capital, and as the value of the franc declined on the international money market, the possibility of the State being unable to meet its obligations appeared more likely. In these circumstances Herriot was defeated in the Senate and resigned in April 1925, accepting the end of a period of left-wing government by taking office in the succeeding Government which was orientated more to the Right. After considerable confusion and the rapid succession of five Governments in ten months, Poincaré returned to power with a Government that laid claim to be a Government of national unity. This restored confidence, so that capital began to return to France. In June 1928 he stabilized the franc, rendering it convertible but at one-fifth of its pre-war value. From a vague aspiration for reform and progress, France had returned to a traditional leader, who was conservative, moderate and cautious. It was during this same period that Aristide Briand, replacing Herriot at the Quai d'Orsay, established his ascendancy in foreign affairs and claimed to have found security for France in the Locarno agreements, which gave an international guarantee for the French frontiers, and in the Kellogg pact, whereby a number of states renounced force as a method of procedure. When Poincaré retired in July 1929 it could be claimed that up till then, the post-war years had been successful for France. Although it had appeared, during the Herriot Government, that an anti-militarist policy had been temporarily pursued, there had been a general agreement on defence, and plans had been laid for a massive defence construction, the Maginot Line (named after a Minister) in the east. The Battle of Verdun had taught the lesson that a properly fortified defence line could withstand almost any amount of attack. If the French frontiers were protected, then France could be secure.

But succeeding years suggested that France was in no way secure. After a brief post-war increase, the French population continued to decline and it was evident to all that France was a country with an ageing population. By about 1930 for the first time the urban population of France exceeded the rural population. This disturbed those who believed that a large rural population was necessary for stability, and since France's demographic situation as an industrial state coincided with the great international crisis which began on Wall Street in 1929, this too was inauspicious. Both French industry and agriculture as small, self-financing enterprises, were reasonably well cushioned from the outside world, but from 1931 onwards French trade began to fall back, and the luxury items which formed an important part of the French economy suffered. Unemployment was less serious in France than in other countries but it was all the more dramatic in France because it was less well known. By 1932 production had dropped by a quarter and there were more than 260,000 unemployed. It was particularly tragic that this economic crisis should coincide both with the coming to power of Hitler in Germany (1933) and with the realization of political deadlock at home. The international crisis wiped out all hopes of reparations and one theme of French policy came to a dead end. The resignation of Poincaré removed all idea of consensus, no man and no party succeeded in imposing itself. It was at this time that various groups of extremists began to emerge, sometimes representing those classes in society that were suffering from particular hardship and could identify themselves with a tightly knit organization, such as the ex-servicemen; sometimes representing admiration for the apparently strong Fascist doctrines of other states and expressing common feelings of frustration and apprehension.

In February 1934 the inevitable happened. A scandal surrounding a fairly minor crook called Stavisky suggested that there was corruption in high places, especially amongst the Radicals. A demonstration organized by right-wing groups in Paris led to the deaths of sixteen people and to the resignation of the Government although it still had a parliamentary majority. Was 6 February 1934 another French revolution? It seemed not, since the demonstrating groups seemed to have no rational hope of seizing power. But the sense of crisis was so great, the fear of a French Fascism so real, that a remarkable change took place amongst the rank and file of the left-wing organizations. Communists turned to co-operate with the Socialists and Radicals. Possibly they thought that they were making progress and that they could afford to work with bourgeois parties (the number of party members was on the increase); possibly the Soviet Union encouraged this move. At all events a Popular Front emerged and in May 1936 it was this electoral alliance that won the elections. For the first time a left-wing coalition which included the Communists was successful. For the first time too a Government came to power in a movement of popular enthusiasm, with an agreed programme of reforms, and under the leadership of an entirely new man, Léon Blum. The Government of the Popular Front should have marked a turning-point in the history of the Third Republic.

But Léon Blum, whilst remarkably honest and sincere, was also timid and probably lacking in self-confidence. The Communists refused to participate in the actual government, and their presence outside the Ministry was an embarrassment. The electoral victory had been far from complete, the parties of the Popular Front gaining only 55 per cent of the vote and the Radicals being somewhat disgruntled since they actually lost seats. Before the Government could be formed there was an unprecedented wave of strikes which took the unions and political parties entirely by surprise, and whilst this movement probably enabled the Government to push various items of social legislation through (holidays with pay, the forty-hour week, full recognition of collective bargaining), there was the fear in some quarters that violent revolution was just round the corner, whilst in others there was the regret that revolution had been betrayed. Finally there was the outbreak of the Spanish Civil War, which became a subject of tremendous bitterness as the left wing attacked Blum for abandoning his comrades in Spain and the centre urged that France should not get mixed up with things that did not concern her.

By 1937 there was disillusionment with the Popular Front. Blum had devalued the franc, which the Communists regarded as a sell-out and the petit-bourgeois regarded as a tragedy. The cost of living had increased and had absorbed the wage increases of 1936. The movement for reform seemed to have run out of steam. In short, the sense of crisis which had brought the Popular Front together seemed to have passed, in spite of the bad economic and diplomatic situation. From now onwards the Chamber which had elected the Popular Front Government tried to find another Government which was more to the centre. It was these Governments that tried to deal with the international crisis created by Hitler as he extended German power by the absorption of Austria and Czechoslovakia. It was these Governments too that endeavoured to undo some of the work of the Popular Front and encountered in consequence a general strike (in November 1938). The paradox of the inter-war years persisted. The Popular Front Government had created the greatest enthusiasm; but it had also created bitterness, division and disillusionment.

The War 1939–1945

The French Government was linked to Poland in various ways. A convention had been signed in 1921, a treaty in 1925, a military agreement in 1939. The French Committee of National Defence had met on 23 August to decide what it would do if Poland were attacked. It had decided that France had no alternative but to keep her engagements and when on 1 September 1939 German troops crossed the Polish frontier, the French Government ordered a general mobilization. The next day in the Chamber of Deputies the President of the Assembly read a statement condemning the German–Soviet pact which had preceded it. It was noted that the Communists joined in this applause. A message from the President of the Republic recalled Poincaré's call for unity in 1914, a speech by the Prime Minister, Édouard Daladier, recalled that of Viviani at the same time. But the session ended on an ominous note of uncertitude, probably caused by Daladier's belief that a final attempt at some sort of diplomatic settlement of the conflict was in the process of developing. The declaration of war was handed to the German chargé d'affaires on 3 September, but in spite of certain expectations, there was no formation of a Government of *l'union nationale.* The Communist party had had its newspaper seized in August, in September it was dissolved and afterwards a number of Communists, acting in a newly named political group, made suggestions that appeared to be in favour of a negotiated peace. Consequently the immunity of Communist deputies was lifted and a number of Communists (including their leader, Thorez) went into hiding. The Government had difficulty in getting a special powers bill through the Chamber in November and it was widely expected that there would be a number of Cabinet changes. When these did not take place, and when it was suggested that the Government had not done everything in its power to support Finland in its war against Soviet Russia, the majority of the Chamber abstained on a vote of confidence. On 22 March 1940 Paul

Reynaud obtained a vote of confidence for a new Government, in which Daladier remained as Minister for Defence. But if one counts the number of abstentions as well as those who voted against him, his majority was of one vote only (and there was considerable discussion as to whether the counting had been correct). After calling his Ministers together in order to decide whether to continue or not, Reynaud decided to go on.

Thus the war was starting in an atmosphere of confused division for France. Newspapers were always commenting that it was 'just like peacetime'; it was the *drôle de guerre* ('the phoney war'). Apart from a small movement of French troops towards the Saarland, there had been no military action. Five million Frenchmen had been mobilized, but with none of the enthusiasm of 1914. There was no Alsace-Lorraine to recapture, and since there had not been a war over the German occupation of Czechoslovakia it hardly seemed appropriate that there should be a war over Poland. They had spent a cold and inactive winter. Public opinion was either too confident, thinking that the war would be won without a battle and by means of an economic blockade, or too pessimistic, believing that the Germans could never be defeated and that France was engaged in a war which had no hope of military success. French propaganda was put in charge of Jean Giraudoux, the writer and, symbolically perhaps, author of *La Guerre de Troie n'aura pas lieu* (being preferred to another writer Jules Romains, author of *Verdun*); but it had little effect and hardly competed with German propaganda.

It was this atmosphere that many people believe was responsible for the French defeat. It has been suggested that long before the German offensive (which began in Norway and Denmark in April, and attacked Holland, Belgium and Luxemburg on 10 May 1940) the French had no will to fight and no unity in favour of fighting. However, it is hard to explain a military defeat purely in such moral terms. The defeat of the French army requires a military explanation. Nor is it correct to say, as has often been said, that the French army was overwhelmed by superior German equipment. It does seem as if there was a greater parity of force than has often been assumed. It is probably wiser to look at a number of vital factors. Firstly, the French command had prepared for a German move through Holland and Belgium, similar to the Schlieffen Plan. When the Germans attacked the Low Countries they therefore moved their armies to the north (along with the British Expeditionary Force). In fact the main German offensive came through the Ardennes, between Namur and Sedan, and even when the German troops had reached the Meuse, on 12 May, and had started to cross it on the next day, the French command was slow to realize the importance of this. Secondly, there was the fact that the Germans crossed the Meuse, which was a difficult operation, and that they then proceeded to divide the allied armies by moving towards the Channel ports. This meant, as observers such as the British Prime Minister Winston Churchill pointed out during his consultations with the French Government, that the Germans were extending their lines of communication, facing great difficulties of supply and generally speaking they were exposing themselves to counter-attack. Yet the French were never able to mount a successful counter-attack. Whether it was because their commanders were over-trained and over-orthodox, whether it was because they were demoralized by the speed of the German advances and by the impact of weapons such as dive-bombers, the opportunities of taking the offensive were lost. Thirdly, it was in the light of these disasters that Reynaud made a fairly lengthy change in his governmental organization: he replaced the exisiting Commander-in-Chief General Gamelin by the ageing General Weygand who had to be recalled from Syria, the legendary figure of Marshal Pétain became a deputy Prime Minister, and a young officer, General de Gaulle, who had been associated with Reynaud for some time, took a junior post at the War Ministry. Doubtless these changes were inevitable and Reynaud had been anxious to get rid of Gamelin for some time. But precious time was wasted as the new Commander-in-Chief had to familiarize himself with the situation; the fact that he was called in to organize a battle which was already lost caused Weygand to be pessimistic. Thus after the Belgians had capitulated on 27 May, after the British (and some French units) had been evacuated from Dunkirk to England between 27 May and 4 June, when the Germans broke through the defence line which had been organized along the Somme and the Aisne, from Arras to the Maginot Line, then Weygand began to talk of the need to make peace. It was on the 12 June, in one of the châteaux which the fugitive French Government was using as it made its way south, that the question of an armistice was clearly posed for the first time. Two days before this Italy had declared war.

It is inevitable that there should be a great deal of confusion about all these events. A nineteenth-century French writer, Gobineau, has claimed that it is a French characteristic to believe not that they have been defeated but that they have been betrayed. There was much talk of betrayal, and Paul Reynaud had added to this by a broadcast in which he claimed that the bridges over the Meuse which ought to have been blown up had been left intact for the Germans to use (which was, in fact, not true). Equally there were allegations that the French had been let down by the British, especially by British air power. There were fears that a continuation of the war would lead to disturbances amongst the civilian population, even to Communist revolution and to civil war, and these rumours were given a certain credibility by the large number of civilian refugees that were then on the roads fleeing from the German armies and dive-bombers and hampering all forms of military action. Under enormous pressure, and feeling that he could not continue the war if both Weygand and Pétain resigned, as they were threatening to do, Reynaud himself resigned on 16 June. Immediately Marshal Pétain was invited to form a Government which he did very rapidly. He then officially requested an armistice, which was signed on the 25 June.

The speed with which Pétain formed his Government has suggested to some observers that there was a deep-laid plot to end the war and to abolish the Republic. It was certainly true that when the Government and the two Chambers were installed in Bordeaux there was a great deal of intrigue and pressure was brought to bear on many individuals in order that they should accept a Pétain Government. Pierre Laval who had left the Socialists long ago and who had always shown a certain hostility to the war, was prominent amongst them. It is also true that many of those who had always been hostile to the Republic, who had been most cynical about its politicians, and who were Catholics, monarchists, Fascists or various forms of extremist, rallied to the Government of Pétain. The idea was present that everything had gone wrong in France since 1789, and that now was the moment for the 'counter-revolution' to put things right. But none of this adds up to a plot. There was so much confusion in France during 1940 that all one can see is the traditional French approach of personalizing the crisis and confiding the nation to the one elderly (he was eighty-three) soldier whose heroic defence of Verdun in the First World War was the guarantee of his patriotism.

The starting-point of 'Pétainism' was the armistice. By this the Germans occupied about three-fifths of France, the area north of the Loire and the Channel and Atlantic coasts. In the unoccupied zone there was to be a French Government (which eventually settled in Vichy) which would have control of the French colonies, the fleet and a small security force. Thus the first justification was that France had escaped the direct rule which the Germans had inflicted on other defeated territories, such as Poland. To Pétain, as to Pierre Laval, it seemed that with the advantages of this position, they should be able to negotiate and bargain with the Germans on many matters, including the fate of the French prisoners of war and the general economic situation. The better thereby to engage in this negotiation, and with the clear conviction that the war would soon end and that British resistance would collapse, a joint session of those members of the two Chambers voted to empower Pétain to be the Head of State and to promulgate a new constitution.

It is a subject of great controversy whether the Vichy regime was legal or not. General de Gaulle, who had established himself in London on 17 June, and who had on the next day broadcast an appeal to all Frenchmen and women to join him in order to continue the war, maintained that it was illegal, although whilst he was making this claim the British Government was accepting the legality of Vichy. The most telling legal argument against Marshal Pétain is that he did not proceed to any consultation of the French people, a measure which would admittedly have been difficult in the circumstances. But in a sense this argument illustrates the strange position of the Vichy regime. It was a half-way house and it was necessarily a regime that was waiting on events, that is to say, the end of the war. As the war did not end but spread, with the British attacking the French fleet in the summer of 1940 in order to prevent it from falling under German control, with some of the French colonies entering into dissidence with Vichy and eventually with America's entry into the war and the landing of Allied troops in French North Africa in November 1942, the role of Vichy became more uncertain.

It was in any case a very varied regime. It contained its idealists, some of whom believed that a Nazi victory was necessary to preserve the world from Communism, and some of whom believed that it was necessary to organize the renaissance of France by attacking foreign elements within the country (notably the Jews) and by restoring the full powers of the Catholic Church. Then, also idealistic but more technical, were those who believed that there should be a fundamental reorganization of the State, which would be based upon corporations representing occupations and interests rather than democratic principles, and which would bring together and reconcile the forces of capital and labour. This group hoped to see a France which would be dynamic and modern, and for whom the episode of Vichy was the opportunity of getting away from the politicians. They had little in common with their colleagues who emphasized the importance of agriculture and believed in an old, rural France where the traditional values would be revived. Surrounding all these men were the politicians, who simply sought to defend national interests by a continued bargaining with the Germans, and the individual adventurers, in Vichy and in Paris, who profited from the circumstances to further their own interests. At the centre of affairs was Marshal Pétain. His unexpected coming to power had delighted him and with great skill and not a little cunning he endeavoured to steer his way through these difficult waters. Deliberately enigmatic, often silent, sometimes tired and senile, he tried to keep his options open. But as the German chances of victory receded, the usefulness of his position declined. His prestige remained and a visit to Paris at the beginning of 1944 confirmed his popularity. But when the Allies landed troops on the coast of Normandy on 6 June 1944 and as the success of the landings grew, then the Vichy regime crumbled. Eventually he was taken to Germany against his will and when he returned to France it was to be arrested and tried for treason.

The Liberation and the Fourth Republic 1944–1958

Whilst the greater part of France was occupied by the Germans (and the Germans had ended the distinction between occupied and unoccupied France with the landings in North Africa) and the Vichy regime was struggling to assert and to define itself, there were two other forms of French government developing, both of which were original in French history. The one was the Government of Free France, subsequently called Fighting France, which General de Gaulle had established in London and, later, in Algiers. This was a movement which cannot be considered apart from the personality of its founder since it was he who largely imposed a unity upon it and whose persistence made it a successful movement. De Gaulle claimed that the Vichy Government did not represent the sovereignty of France because it was dominated by the Germans. He saw his task as being that of saving the national identity of France and of seeing to it that it was not absorbed either by her enemies or by her allies. He claimed to represent France and he promised that when France was liberated, then there would be a great revolution. Justice would be done and the existing French 'establishment', those responsible for the defeats and the betrayal of 1940, would be removed from affairs. This preoccupation with politics and this egocentric approach to the problems of France irritated many people and alarmed others. But de Gaulle's importance was secured by the fact that he succeeded in gaining some sort of control over the other form of activity, which was the Resistance movement on French soil. At first the resistance to the Germans had been a matter for individuals, or at most for fairly small groups. But as time went by the Resistance grew considerably in numbers. The German invasion of Russia in 1941 meant that all Communist organizations turned to Resistance, whereas before this date those Communists in the Resistance had been organized locally rather than nationally. The Vichy persecution of the Jews and of foreigners caused many refugees to become *résistants*, and the decision to send young Frenchmen to work in German factories and the invasion of the unoccupied zone forced many into the movement. It was in 1942 that General de Gaulle's representative Jean Moulin succeeded in creating the National Council of the Resistance before he was tortured to death by the Germans, and although there were very many difficulties between de Gaulle and the National Council, de Gaulle's leadership was accepted.

It was on 6 June 1944 that the Allies invaded Normandy with the intention of establishing a provisional military government until a more regular French administration could be formed. In this they showed their suspicions of de Gaulle and their fear of Communist influence in the Resistance movement. But when on 13 June General de Gaulle was allowed to go to France, and when he went to the town of Bayeux, he was everywhere acclaimed as the leader of France. He appointed his own representatives and before this silent *coup d'état* the Allied military officials melted away. During June and July Allied progress was slow but from 25 July the breakthrough occurred and the process of liberation became rapid. It became all the more rapid because the Resistance movements in all parts of France either hampered the movement of German divisions or themselves successfully liberated whole regions. Typical of these movements was the insurrection of Paris on 19 August which preceded by many hours the arrival of Allied forces (including notably an armoured division of the Fighting French forces under General Leclerc). It was not till 25 August that de Gaulle entered Paris. On 26 August, with the Germans still within striking distance and with enemy snipers still within the city, de Gaulle organized a triumphal parade down the Champs-Élysées to Notre-Dame. It was one of the great moments in the history of France. De Gaulle was universally acclaimed, he was compared to St Louis, it was claimed that the great days of the Revolution were being lived again.

But the liberation of Paris did not mean the end of the war and it was many months before the whole of French territory was freed. The armistice with Germany was signed on 8 May 1945. All this period was a time of violence and bitterness in French life, since not only was there an acute shortage of all the necessities such as food, clothing, fuel and housing, but the Liberation meant the *épuration*, the meting out of justice which both the Gaullists and the Resistance had promised. Those who had collaborated with the Germans were to be punished. This meant that in some areas a sort of reign of terror was established. But although it is difficult to agree on figures and although it is not always easy to distinguish between those who were killed in actual fighting and those who were shot as a punishment for alleged treason, the highest accepted figure is 40,000 and there are those who maintain that it should be as low as 10,000. Both de Gaulle and the Communist party were anxious to avoid any indiscriminate blood-letting. The Communists abandoned any idea of treating the Liberation as the opportunity for a social revolution and the machinery of State was restored. The first Government, formed in September 1944, brought together the personnel of Gaullism, of the Resistance and of certain respectable elements who had been in power before 1940. De Gaulle was thus attempting to group together a large consensus of opinion, and whilst he carried out many of the promises for reform, nationalizing the coal-mines, the Renault motor-works, air-transport, and establishing a social security system, he was clearly anxious that he should appear as the leader of the nation rather than as the leader of any party or group. De Gaulle was also intensely preoccupied with the position of France in the world. He asserted this position in February 1945 by signing a treaty with Soviet Russia and by endeavouring to restore French rule in Indo-China.

It was in October 1945 that having consulted the electorate (including Frenchwomen) by referendum, General de Gaulle received an overwhelming vote to draw up a new constitution. Consequently a Constituent Assembly was elected in which the Communists, Socialists and a new political grouping, the Social Catholics or Mouvement Républicain Populaire, gained an overwhelming majority. Although its main task was to elaborate the constitution, this Assembly was also able to elect the Government, and although it never voted against General de

Gaulle, he began to find himself ill at ease before it. Possibly he considered that by retiring he would be able to return and impose himself on the Assembly. At all events, after some days of reflection, de Gaulle announced his resignation on 20 January 1946. If he had expected a popular movement in his favour he must have been disappointed. His resignation was accepted with a certain indifference. It marks the end of the period of provisional government.

With the Fourth Republic, as with the Third, it has become customary to stress weakness rather than strength. This was all the more apparent under the Fourth Republic because its birth was difficult and laborious. It was said that before he resigned General de Gaulle was only too conscious of the difficulties of governing since the political parties, which had made no secret of their hostility to him, an outsider who had come on the political scene by dramatically unorthodox means, had rediscovered all their old strength and vivacity. The left-wing majority which dominated the Assembly were agreed on very little and they were not always in touch with the country. Thus the first constitution to be elaborated was rejected by a national referendum. In the new elections which followed the Socialists saw their vote begin to decline and they regarded this as a warning that they should not be too close to the Communists. The second constitution to be drawn up was approved by the country, but with seven million abstentions. Thus there was little enthusiasm for a constitution which reproduced most of the characteristics of the constitution of the Third Republic except limiting still further the powers of the President with regard to dissolving the Chamber of Deputies. The constitution had only one advantage: it existed on paper. But after fresh elections in November 1946, in which the Communists maintained their strong position, it was impossible to find a Government which could command a majority in the Chamber. Therefore, there was a turning towards Léon Blum who accepted to become, in spite of age and fatigue, a temporary Prime Minister until the first President of the Fourth Republic could be elected. Thus it was that when, in January 1947, the former Finance Minister of the Popular Front, Vincent Auriol, was elected President by the two Chambers sitting together, the Fourth Republic resembled nothing so much as the Third.

Yet the crisis of November 1946 was in no way the sort of crisis that the Third Republic had experienced. It was a crisis that was to be typical of the Fourth Republic. At a time of severe economic crisis, with an acute shortage of goods and with a severe inflationary pressure, there seemed to be two sorts of political danger. The one came from the Communists. They had gained an immediate advantage over other left-wing parties because they had shown themselves to be patriotic, particularly after 1941. Their leader Maurice Thorez, when arguing with de Gaulle about the ministerial posts which his party could legitimately claim, had spoken of 75,000 Communists who had died for France. But there is reason to believe that the rise of the Communist party pre-dates the war, and that prior to 1939 there were signs that the Communists were becoming the principal left-wing party. At all events the Communists by 1946 could claim to have either the largest or the second largest party in France (by the elections of 1946 the MRP momentarily outvoted them) and they controlled the largest of the trade unions, the CGT. In this sense there was always a Communist danger. But ever since the Liberation the Communists had collaborated with the Governments. Those Communists (probably few in number) who had thought a Communist revolution possible in 1944 and 1945 had been overruled. There seemed little real danger of a Communist *coup*. On the other hand many, especially the Socialists, were fearful of what de Gaulle would do. Since his resignation he had not retired. In June 1946 he had spoken at Bayeux and had proposed a constitution built around a powerful, active President. At the end of 1946 and the beginning of 1947 the influence of his associates seemed to be considerable, and there were few politicians who were prepared to discount the possibility of a Gaullist *coup*. Finally, in April 1947 de Gaulle founded the rally of the French people (Rassemblement du Peuple Français, or RPF). In May, the Communist Ministers refused their confidence to the Government on the question of wages, and the Socialist Prime Minister, Paul Ramadier, then excluded them from his Government. From this time onwards the two enemies of the Fourth Republic, Communists or Gaullists, were outside the system. The fact that in 1947 and 1948 both these parties were extremely well supported, could only weaken the Republic.

Naturally these movements cannot be explained in terms of what was happening in France alone. The onset of the cold war, typified by the breakdown of the Moscow conference in May 1947, found the French Government essentially on the American side. It was argued that the Russian army was within striking distance of Paris, and it was pointed out that the economic situation in France was such that it was essential to have American aid. But overseas problems were of particular importance. Indo-China had been divided into two, North Vietnam (Viet-Minh) which was independent and Communist, and the south where the emperor Boa Dai was regarded as a French puppet. The outbreak of the Indo-China war, dating from 1947, was to weigh heavily from this time onwards. A rising in Madagascar and nationalist movements in North Africa emphasized the vulnerability of the French colonial system which the Fourth Republic was trying to fit in to a new and more liberal concept of the French Union. At all events, 1947 and 1948 were 'les années terribles'. France had to fit in to the cold war with social conflicts, political instability, economic crisis and colonial difficulties rendering the country weak and, in the eyes of some foreign powers, dispensable.

Yet the Fourth Republic continued. From September 1948 to October 1949 the Prime Minister was Henri Queuille, who had held office under the Third Republic and whose country-doctor approach to matters reduced the tempo of both political and social disputation. In preparation for the elections of 1951, several Governments were concerned with a device (the *loi d'apparentement*) whereby all those parties which were prepared to declare that they were allied together (and this excluded the Communist party) could gain the totality of the seats provided that together they gained 51 per cent of the votes cast. This law was also aimed at the Gaullists who experienced some difficulty in making alliances with centre groups, although there were examples of Gaullists taking part in *apparentements*. The result was that the centre parties gained considerably in seats (if not in votes) with the exception of the MRP. The Communist deputies declined in number and the Gaullists, whilst becoming the largest single party in the Chamber, failed to achieve the massive success that they had expected. The strong position of the centre parties was underlined by the unexpected election of Antoine Pinay as Prime Minister in March 1952. A number of Gaullists broke from their group and voted for him. The next year the Gaullists voted officially for a Prime Minister who was not in their party and they seemed to be less intransigent. In the meantime the Communists, whilst abandoning none of their principles, seemed to becoming a largely ritualistic party.

From June 1954 to February 1955 the Fourth Republic had a particularly dynamic and original Government, headed by Pierre Mendès-France, a member of the Radical party who had been a junior Minister with the Popular Front and who had served with de Gaulle both in Algiers and in the provisional Government from 1944 to 1945. Mendès-France shocked the National Assembly into giving him a majority by promising to end the Indo-Chinese war. This he did by negotiating the Geneva agreements establishing North and South Vietnam as independent states, whilst the French withdrew. He also negotiated an agreement whereby Tunisia became fully independent and no longer a French protectorate. He sought to direct the economy towards greater growth and vitality and he showed a new consciousness of the problems of youth. In European matters France had already taken certain initiatives (the Schuman plan of May 1950, announced by Robert Schuman, then Minister of Foreign Affairs) by putting French and German coal and steel production under joint control. A European Defence Community treaty had also been elaborated which had aroused the opposition both of Communists and Gaullists, whilst splitting the Socialists. Mendès-France undertook a cleaning-up operation and in October 1954 the London agreements allowed for the creation of a German army and for its entry into the North Atlantic Treaty Organization.

It could be argued that the moment was favourable for a Mendèsiste version of the New Deal. The period of reconstruction was largely over by 1951, the deflationist policies followed by Monsieur Pinay in 1952 had held production back, but from 1954 onwards production was increasing and it is possible to speak of an economic growth of about 5 per cent a year. The French economy had been dominated by a regular series of plans, and whilst the first of these plans (1947–53) had been directed essentially towards equipment, the second plan (1954–7) had been more concerned with the consumer. The popularity of Monsieur Mendès-France was associated with the idea that the war in Indo-China had to be ended, that other old quarrels had to be liquidated and that France should be on the move again. Yet this was not to be. A triple opposition was formed against the Prime Minister. The Communists opposed him because he was allowing Germany to rearm, the MRP could not forgive him his failure to support the European Defence Community; and a new subject of alarm grew with the appearance, in November 1954, of an important nationalist revolt in Algeria. It was argued that the man who had made peace in Indo-China might well sign away Algeria. In February 1955 Mendès-France was defeated. His final protest in the Chamber, that the national necessities which he had recognized continued to exist, was seen as an appeal beyond Parliament to the nation, and it aroused great resentment.

Throughout 1955 the divisions amongst the central parties hampered political action. In November the Government was defeated, and the fact that two constitutional crises (that is to say two Governments defeated by an absolute majority) had occurred in a period of less than eighteen months meant that Parliament could be dissolved. A hastily formed Front Républicain of Socialists (led by Guy Mollet), Radicals (led by Mendès-France), ex-Gaullists (led by Chaban-Delmas) and Democratic Republicans (led by François Mitterand) hoped to dominate the elections. But two and a half million voted for a Monsieur Pierre Poujade, almost an unknown, whose party was essentially a party of protest, bringing small farmers, shopkeepers and artisans together through nationalism, anti-parliamentarianism and anti-capitalism. The ex-Gaullists saw their votes slump, whilst the Communists maintained their position (25 per cent of those who voted) and their isolation. Although the Front Républicain formed the Government, Monsieur Mendès-France soon found himself in disaccord with his colleagues and he resigned.

Nevertheless, the Government led by Guy Mollet was the longest of the Fourth Republic. It carried out certain social reforms, such as increasing the length of holidays with pay to three weeks and increasing old age pensions. It began the process of decolonization in Africa south of the Sahara, by laws which gave the direction of domestic affairs to elected African Governments. It bargained hard as the negotiations for a European Economic Community took shape. And it indulged in an adventurous policy when it took part in (and to some extent initiated) the attack on Suez in October–November 1956, an Anglo-French venture, the failure of which caused great resentment in the French armed forces. But, throughout its period in office, Monsieur Mollet's Government was dominated by the Algerian affair. In spite of a considerable military effort and many local successes, the revolution spread. With one million non-Moslems claiming to be French, it had been taken for granted that Algeria was French and was, in fact, a prolongation of metropolitan France. Powerful economic interests, both in France and Algeria, urged that there could be no fundamental change in the nature of the two countries' relations. But it was not merely a question of sentiment or a question of economic pressures. It was precisely a question of power. Given the power of the Europeans in towns such as Algiers, given the power of the armed units in Algeria, and given the existence in Paris of a powerful Algerian lobby, it was never clear that Monsieur Mollet could have any independent policy. His weak political position was worsened by the growth of a budgetary crisis. The high level of consumer demand (which his Government had encouraged) and the high public expenditure, especially on the Algerian war, created difficulties which led to his resignation in May 1957 and the refusal of the Socialists to participate in the formation of another Government.

From then onwards the situation disintegrated. It was clear that the Governments formed had no real solidity. In spite of assurances, the war seemed no nearer to a successful conclusion. Amongst certain of the officers serving in Algeria there grew up the idea that France had become decadent and that the politicians would betray the soldiers. There was, therefore, an atmosphere of conspiracy, made all the more poignant by the suspicion that past Governments had been negotiating secretly with rebel leaders. When Pierre Pflimlin, an MRP leader from Strasbourg, attempted in May 1958 to form the twenty-fourth Government since the de Gaulle Government of November 1945, it appeared to some that Paris was near to abandoning Algeria. On 13 May a Committee of Public Safety, consisting mainly of settlers and students, but effectively controlled by the army, was set up in Algiers.

The crisis that followed was complicated. There were those in Algiers who hoped simply to frighten the Government in Paris. There were those in Paris who sought to impress the rebels in Algiers with their firmness. But there was an undercurrent of implication. The rebellion in Algiers was incomplete. Should it not be extended to metropolitan territory? There were those in the army who thought so and who prepared for such an eventuality. But there were those who were apprehensive of civil war in France and who thought that this would create a Popular Front Government. In these circumstances there was a search for some middle way and there was a turning towards General de Gaulle who had been in virtual retirement since he had allowed the Gaullists in Parliament to vote and act as they wished. That there should have been a turning to de Gaulle was far from being accidental. Without being directly responsible for what had happened, his supporters and agents were deeply involved and were determined that the crisis should end with de Gaulle in power. By and large it would be true to say that many of the instigators of the revolt were only too pleased to get rid of the responsibility for what had happened. And it must be added that de Gaulle showed remarkable political skill as he sought by carefully timed utterances both to reassure and to terrify the political world. But he never lost one thing from sight: that his return to power should be accompanied by a fundamental constitutional revision. Only in this way could he move from the constitution of the Fourth Republic, of which he had always disapproved, to a new and more solid Republic.

The Fifth Republic

There are many ways of approaching the Fifth Republic. The first is through the person of General de Gaulle. It was ironical that de Gaulle, who had restored the Republic with the Liberation, should have been voted into power as the last Prime Minister of the Fourth Republic on 1 June 1958, and should have presided over the creation of the new constitution. The accident of the Algerian crisis gave him the belated opportunity of putting into practice the ideas which he had expressed in 1946, and which essentially consisted of a strong presidential power and a limited role for the Assembly. Thus the Fifth Republic is to be seen as a development which suited de Gaulle and which was a testimony to his skill and to his prestige. After the many frustrations of the Fourth Republic, the patriotism and the devotion of the now elderly (he was sixty-eight) hero of 1940 and 1944 were impressive. But it is also possible to take a more analytical approach. It could be argued that profound changes were taking place in France. As the French population grew and as the economy underwent an increasing number of changes, it seeemed as if the whole structure of French society was on the move. The large number of agricultural workers who were leaving the countryside, the growth of new industries, the spreading of modern means of communication, all meant that France was no longer the country of small towns and small enterprises. The political system which had been based upon this was necessarily doomed. France had to move towards a more modern system and the real irony was that the man who was destined to introduce these changes was essentially a man whose ideology was that of the pre-1914 period. For all that he was haughty, de Gaulle was not a charismatic leader. He was rather an adroit politician, who surrounded himself with competent advisers and who cultivated the art of dramatizing and personalizing affairs. He saw to it that no one forgot the difficult situation of May 1958 when a catastrophic civil war had appeared imminent.

De Gaulle's Government can best be described in several phases, although it must be remembered that he was adept at dealing with different topics at the same time. The first phase concerned institutions.

A new constitution was drawn up and was approved by a considerable majority in a referendum. The point of this constitution was that the powers of Parliament were reduced, and that a President, who appointed a Prime Minister, was the dominant figure in the Government. Elections were held in November and since they were organized on the double-ballot system instead of the proportional representational system which had been used since the Liberation, there were many changes. Although the Communist vote remained steady, Communist representation fell dramatically, and a new Gaullist party, the Union pour la Nouvelle République, gained more votes than anyone. Finally in December a specially designated electoral college, made up of the two Chambers and a number of mayors and municipal councillors, to the number of some 80,000, elected General de Gaulle President of the Republic by an overwhelming majority. The fifth Republic was thus installed, with Michel Debré as Prime Minister.

The next phase was clearly that of Algeria. From the start it had been obvious that the strength of de Gaulle's position in France was the conviction that he and he alone could solve the Algerian problem. Since he had had no direct hand in governmental affairs since the Algerian revolt of 1954, no one had any idea of what his policies were. He deliberately prolonged this uncertainty by the ambiguity of his public speeches, secure in the knowledge of there being no other politician or party in France that was prepared to define a policy. The settlers in Algeria, and some of their supporters in France, including some prominent Gaullists, believed in the complete integration of Algeria with France, and throughout 1959 the idea persisted that de Gaulle would finally come out with this policy. In reality it seems as if de Gaulle was feeling his way, hoping to smash the rebels by a vigorous military campaign and hoping to rally the bulk of the Moslems to him by his personal prestige and a policy of massive investments. By the beginning of 1960, however, some of the extremists in Algiers were convinced that integration was being dropped and they tried to organize another rising, on the model of 13 May. But this time the army remained loyal, and the failure of this revolt strengthened de Gaulle. He was able to reveal that he foresaw the creation of 'une Algérie algérienne'. In April 1961 four generals attempted to seize power in Algiers, in opposition to de Gaulle. It was even rumoured that parachutists would drop on Paris and de Gaulle invoked his emergency powers. But this revolution also petered out. The proof was given that the bulk of the French population did not wish to fight for the maintenance of a French

Algeria, and the Government was able to devote all its energies to negotiations with the rebels (which had already started). Although de Gaulle for a time hoped to preserve French rights in the Sahara, the Évian agreements of March 1962 brought about a cease-fire and implied the complete independence of Algeria. In April a national referendum approved of this policy, 65 per cent of those participating voting in favour. The supporters of French Algeria were reduced to acts of terrorism and the majority of the settlers returned to France.

The third phase of the Fifth Republic began in difficult conditions. General de Gaulle was no longer an indispensable figure since the Algerian war was over. All that persisted was a certain bitterness. Faced with the possibility that the Republic, once its crisis was over, might fall apart, de Gaulle took a number of initiatives. He replaced Michel Debré by Georges Pompidou; in a press conference he deliberately broke with those centre groups who hoped that the European Economic Community would develop into European political unity by insisting on a Europe of independent sovereign states; at the end of the summer, after an unsuccessful attempt had been made to assassinate him, he announced his attention of changing the constitution by referendum. His proposal was that the President of the Republic should be elected by universal suffrage. In response the National Assembly passed a censure motion against the Government. The result was the dissolution of the Assembly, a referendum which approved de Gaulle's proposal, and a general election in November 1962 which increased the majority of the UNR whilst reducing the number of deputies from the centre. The fact that in January 1963 General de Gaulle publicly rejected British entry into the European Economic Community, that in January 1964 he stated that only the President could hold or delegate the authority of the State, that in April 1964 he called attention to France's prosperity, gives the tone to the remainder of this period. National independence, influence in the world, stability and prosperity at home, these were the tenets of triumphant Gaullism. De Gaulle's energy and vision were such that France seemed to dominate Europe and to challenge any idea of an American–Soviet hegemony in world affairs.

But the fourth phase was one of decline. When the first presidential elections, under the new law, were held in December 1965, de Gaulle only gained 43 per cent of the metropolitan votes. In the second ballot he was re-elected with 54·5 per cent of the votes as against his single opponent, François Mitterrand, who had 45·4 per cent. But the fact remained that at the first ballot more than half of the country were against de Gaulle and, even for the second ballot, de Gaulle's majority was far from massive. Then, in spite of careful preparation, the elections of March 1967 were a relative failure for the Gaullists. The UNR retained the majority, but by such a small margin that it was dependent upon the votes of certain deputies representing overseas departments. The Left, both Communist and non-Communist, had made progress, and Pierre Mendès-France, who had always opposed the Fifth Republic and who now appeared as a principal spokesman for the opposition, spoke of the possibility of taking power.

Much of the discontent was explicable. The economic boom had been slowing down; the Government had opted for a stable franc rather than for expansion; there were many sectors of French society which claimed that they were being badly treated. And whilst de Gaulle's foreign policies remained dramatic (in February 1966 he had announced that he would begin to withdraw from NATO since France was an independent nuclear power) there was a certain unease about his activities. His intervention in Canadian affairs ('Vive le Québec libre') and his criticisms of Israel after the Middle East war, were highly controversial.

Yet whilst it was clear that Gaullism was going through a difficult period, the crisis of May 1968 took everyone by surprise. It began with a student revolt, which was nothing very new. The number of students in France had doubled over a period of five years and the protests of this politically conscious group against the inadequacy of university organization had become frequent. But the violence of the pitched battles with the police, particularly in the Latin Quarter on 10 May 1968, was remarkable. Monsieur Pompidou thought it wise to be conciliatory. But within a few days the revolt had spread to industry. Within a week more than nine million people were on strike, the unions had lost control of their members and the political parties did not know what to make of events. Everywhere there was talk of the need for a fundamental change in society.

Whilst Georges Pompidou worked to establish an agreement over wages and working conditions, General de Gaulle seems to have been uncertain as to what to do. His announcement that a referendum would be held concerning profit-sharing and co-management of affairs was hardly taken seriously. Student demonstrations continued, the rank and file of the strikers refused to accept the agreements and it began to appear that the power of the State was disappearing.

Then on 30 May, de Gaulle announced that the Chamber was dissolved and that elections would be held. He claimed, strangely enough, that France was faced with the danger of international Communism. This announcement was all the more dramatic because it had been widely assumed that he would announce his resignation. At all events, the announcement was carefully timed. It coincided with a movement of opinion against the violence and the anarchy which had been so prominent. It provided the opportunity for ending the crisis, and the result was a sweeping UNR victory. This party gained the absolute majority by some fifty-one seats and those (such as Mendès-France) who had been associated with the student revolutionaries were defeated. General de Gaulle chose a new Prime Minister in the person of Monsieur Couve de Murville, and it seemed that yet another phase of Gaullism was about to begin.

But it was not to be. It had been demonstrated only too clearly that Gaullist power could be as fragile as any power. Even within the UNR it was asked whether de Gaulle (now approaching his seventy-eighth birthday) were not a handicap to them. The fact that Georges Pompidou was no longer Prime Minister suggested that an obvious successor was present. An international monetary crisis, the Soviet invasion of Czechoslovakia in August 1968, a feeling of stagnation in European affairs, obliged de Gaulle to look more favourably towards the United States of America and to revise some of his policies. But he insisted upon the administrative reform which he had announced in May 1968. In April 1969 a somewhat clumsily worded referendum was submitted to the electorate. This proposal was for decentralization and for transforming the Senate into a council for the discussion of economic affairs. It aroused the hostility of all the main political parties and little enthusiasm amongst the Gaullists. When it was defeated by a narrow majority General de Gaulle, on 28 April 1969, resigned.

Looking back one is struck by the fact that the proposed reform was defeated by a million votes only, out of nearly thirty million registered voters. But it is also clear that the tendency of policies under the Fifth Republic had been to turn away from personal power. General de Gaulle's popularity, whether measured by referenda, public opinion polls or the presidential election of 1965, had been steadily declining since 1958. On the other hand the so-called Gaullist political party, the UNR, had grown in strength since 1958 and, even allowing for the check of 1967, it had extended its hold throughout the country and was making inroads into regions of France where other political parties traditionally expected support. This original factor in modern French history, together with the customary division of the Left (in 1969 there were Communists, Socialists, Independent Socialists and Trotskyists, all seeking to demonstrate their strength as the true representatives of the Left), explains the comparative ease with which Georges Pompidou was elected President of the Republic, on the second ballot, in June 1969.

It was not easy to succeed to General de Gaulle. Georges Pompidou always said that he would be a President with a style of his own, but that he would adhere to the principles of Gaullism: national independence, the importance of the French role in the world, the unity of the French people. Both Pompidou, who, until 1968 at least, could claim to have been a trusted adviser of the General, and his first Prime Minister, Jacques Chaban-Delmas, asserted that they were in the true tradition of Gaullism. It became almost a customary Presidential riposte to state that he had no need for lessons in Gaullism. But in spite of de Gaulle's discretion and refusal to make any political statements after his resignation, most political observers thought that President Pompidou only showed complete self-assurance after de Gaulle's sudden death in November 1970. This did not prevent the development of certain resentments within the Gaullist group, which were made all the more noticeable because, whilst the President introduced a greater suppleness into the conduct of foreign affairs, and whilst the Prime Minister, proclaiming the need to create a new society, announced a programme of liberal reforms at home, there were indications that the constitutional uncertainties concerning the respective powers of the President and the Prime Minister were helping to create difficulties between the two men. It seemed that the work done in the Prime Minister's office was increasing; at the same time the President's activity was more widespread under Pompidou than it had been under de Gaulle.

Whilst Pompidou showed considerable diplomatic activity throughout the world, especially in the Mediterranean where he tried to establish particular protection for French interests, the principal European problem was that of the European Economic Community. The French Government had shown typical intransigence in the 1970 negotiations to establish economic and monetary co-operation, and had seemed most interested in the common agricultural policy which was beneficial to French farmers; but in May 1971 a meeting between President Pompidou and the British Prime Minister, Edward Heath, provided the Anglo-French agreement which would permit the enlargement of the Community by the admission of Great Britain, Ireland and Denmark (to date officially from 1 January 1973). This change of French policy was explained in various ways. Some saw it as a development which de Gaulle had already envisaged in his closing months of power; some suggested that President Pompidou was anxious to make an Anglo-French understanding the basis of his policy rather than an Anglo-German one, since West Germany, under the Social Democratic Chancellor Brandt, was taking many new initiatives; others preferred to see a French recognition of the permanence of the Community, since the French could no longer threaten to abandon it and, if they were to continue to appear as the dominant power, had to take the initiative in forging new agreements.

At home, after the slow dying down of agitation in the universities and lycées, attention was concentrated on the elections of 1973. They seemed to be particularly significant, since they would be the first elections since the war in which General de Gaulle would not be present as a living influence. Some divisions, and a number of scandals, within Gaullism, and the emergence of a Communist-Socialist-left-wing Radical agreement under the overall leadership of François Mitterrand (Socialist) suggested that the long predominance of Gaullism would be seriously challenged. Foreign policy and domestic affairs were made to come together when the President of the Republic, desirous of using the Gaullist weapon of the referendum, decided to ask the country to approve or disapprove the widening of the European Economic Community. In April 1972 the referendum showed a majority in favour, but the number of abstentions (nearly 25 per cent) was a record and the whole operation appeared to be a governmental failure. Consequently and in spite of a recent vote of confidence in the Chamber, President Pompidou replaced Jacques Chaban-Delmas by Pierre Messmer in July 1972. This was a return to a more rigid, and a purer, Gaullism, since Pierre Messmer, who had served for many years as Minister responsible for the army under de Gaulle, had the reputation of being a Gaullist without any liberal tinge. It was a preparation for the elections. It was a reaffirmation of Presidential power (and was followed by a decline in the activities and influence of the Prime Minister's office).

The general election of March 1973 had intrigued and baffled the experts. Communists, Socialists and left-wing Radicals adopted a common programme of sweeping reforms; the Gaullists and their allies ridiculed this programme as impractical and stressed the dangers of Communism; the name of General de Gaulle was hardly mentioned. The result was that the Gaullist majority lost nearly one hundred seats to the left-wing coalition, but, helped by the distribution of electoral boundaries in the country, they retained the majority in the Chamber; the pure Gaullists became more dependent upon the conservative Independent Republican group under its leader, Valéry Giscard d'Estaing, the Minister for Finance; the President of the Republic appointed a non-political personality from his own entourage, Michel Jobert, to be Minister for Foreign Affairs and continued to emphasize the importance of foreign policy and the need to defend French interests before all others. This attitude meant that the French Government had less difficulty than others in adapting itself to the changed circumstances which followed upon the outbreak of the Arab–Israeli war on 8 October 1973. French policy had always been critical of Israel and largely pro-Arab. Changes of French policy within the European Community, such as the floating of the franc in January 1974 and the attempt to make separate agreements to ensure the supply of oil, were regarded as traditional Gaullist attitudes, as was the French insistence on carrying out nuclear tests in the summer of 1973. But dissent amongst Gaullists on a variety of social and political problems preceded the sudden death of President Pompidou in April 1974. The presidential elections which followed found a surprising agreement amongst the Left, where Communists and Socialists agreed to support François Mitterrand, and only two Trotskyists and an ecologist attempted to continue the tradition of 1968, and a surprising disagreement amongst the majority, where the Prime Minister, Messmer, the former Prime Minister, Chaban-Delmas, and the Independent Republican, Valéry Giscard d'Estaing, disputed the succession. Eventually, Jacques Chirac, a young Gaullist who was known to be well thought of by the late President, at the head of some forty-three Gaullist Ministers and deputies, proclaimed his support for Giscard d'Estaing. The first ballot confirmed both the increasing popularity of the Left, with Mitterrand gaining more votes than anyone else (43.4 per cent), and the importance of the split within the Gaullists, with Chaban-Delmas receiving only 14.6 per cent of the votes cast. On 19 May 1974 Giscard d'Estaing was elected by the narrow margin of 350,000 votes (or 50.7 per cent) out of an electorate of nearly 26 million.

It seemed that France was clearly and evenly divided into two. On the one hand, Communists, Socialists and other supporters of the Left believed in the need for a fundamental change in the organization of French society; on the other hand, a rather vague and indeterminate Centre and Right remained conservative and anxious to avoid the adventures of any collectivist programme. Behind this division lay the international economic recession with its twin dangers of inflation and unemployment. But this was a division which the new President declared that he would not accept as a permanent feature of French society, and, although he made Jacques Chirac his Prime Minister and affirmed the continuity of Gaullist policy (especially in matters of national defence), he announced his determination to inaugurate liberal policies.

The vote was given to those who were eighteen; the television and radio organization, which had been completely controlled by the State, was divided into seven, supposedly autonomous, sections; abortion was legalized (with the help of opposition votes); certain forms of profit were taxed under a new law; divorce procedures were rendered easier; syllabuses in schools were revised. Everywhere the emphasis was on the 'quality of life', and the President himself sought to appear as an unpretentious and approachable man, in touch with the ordinary people of France.

But these reforms did not seem adequate to those who believed that there was growing social injustice and inequality within the country. The economic crisis continued and whilst in June 1975 the President had reassured the people of France that they could go on holiday confident that all was well, within a few months there was talk on the need to stimulate the economy while maintaining austerity in terms of wages. The Left made progress in by-elections and, although there were obvious difficulties between the Communists and the Socialists, the prospect of effective co-operation between them became more real.

It was with the prospect of a Communist–Socialist victory in the elections of 1978 that a very sharp disagreement took place between the President and his Prime Minister. In August 1976 Jacques Chirac resigned dramatically, claiming that he had not been given the means of governing the country effectively and suggesting that unless the elections were brought forward there was a danger of governmental defeat. This disagreement, and this prospect, seemed to threaten the nature of the Fifth Republic, since the respective constitutional positions of the President and the Prime Minister had never been clear. Chirac was claiming a greater say in the direction of affairs; the possibility of a Socialist becoming Prime Minister underlined the uncertainties of what would happen if the President and the Prime Minister were in disagreement. The President appointed Raymond Barre, a Professor of Economics, to be Prime Minister, who placed the emphasis of his government on maintaining economic stability.

By this time the election campaign was already open. In the municipal elections of 1977 Communists and Socialists made substantial progress and captured control of many large towns. Chirac responded by making the Gaullists a well-organized party under his personal control, and the split within the majority parties became more intense. On the Left, the Communists became increasingly wary of Socialist success, all the more so as the Socialists (supported by opinion polls) became confident that they had become the largest party in France and that they were far more important than any other left-wing or centre organization. The split between Socialists and Communists became most apparent in the summer of 1977, and was made official by the breakdown of negotiations in September 1977.

The elections, which were held in March 1978, presented French society in a most paradoxical light. The campaign was lengthy, and it was said that people had become bored; yet when it came to voting the turnout was extremely high. Everyone agreed that these particular elections were of outstanding importance; yet many of the most important issues were hardly raised (energy, education, violence, defence, foreign policy). For the first time there was a large section of voters aged between eighteen and twenty-one; yet they did not have any remarkable effect on the voting pattern. The divisions within the Left (Socialists and Communists) were reflected by divisions within the Right (Giscardiens and Gaullists).

By 19 March, France seemed divided into four large political families. The Communist and Socialist parties made some slight progress, each winning a few seats. The Giscardiens won a number of seats, and the Gaullists, though they lost some twenty-three seats, remained the largest party in the Assembly. The only clear victor of the contest was the President of the Republic who, whilst announcing his intention of proceeding to further reforms and changes, asserted continuity by inviting Raymond Barre to remain as his Prime Minister. The majority thus continued in power.

But the opposition remains considerable. Divisions between groups and parties are important. There are those who believe that as France continues to face the economic, social and international problems of the day, these divisions will make for instability. Others believe that the apparent divisions reveal an essential consensus. The policies of Valéry Giscard d'Estaing seek to emphasize this consensus and in that sense they are in a long tradition of French history.

Bibliography

Discussion surrounding the French Revolution has always been considerable. Some idea of the controversies concerning its origins and development will be found in the short books by Alice Gérard, *La Révolution française: mythes et interprétations 1789–1790* (Paris, 1970) (No. 21 in the series 'Questions d'histoire', Flammarion) and by Jacques Godechot, *Les Révolutions 1770–1799* (Paris, 1965) (No. 36 in the series 'Nouvelle Clio', Presses Universitaires). Particularly interesting contributions to the debate are made by Alfred Cobban, *The Social Interpretation of the French Revolution* (Cambridge, 1964) and *Aspects of the French Revolution* (London, 1968), who questions some of the assumptions on which many of the most widely accepted accounts of the Revolution have been based, and which are to be found expressed with learning and wisdom in Georges Lefebvre, *La Révolution française* (Paris, 1963; English translation *The French Revolution*, 2 vols, London, 1962 and 1964), and Albert Soboul, *Précis d'histoire de la Révolution française* (Paris, 1962). C. Mazauric, *Sur la Révolution française* (Paris, 1970), defends a Marxist stand-point. In English the most scrupulous general account is probably to be found in N. Hampson, *A Social History of the French Revolution* (London, 1963). Two splendidly illustrated volumes by F. Furet and D. Richet, *La Révolution française 1965–1966* (English ed. London, 1969), present the Revolution as an amalgam of several revolutions (juridical, urban and peasant) which 'skidded' into a popular and violent revolution, whilst the first three volumes (all of them short) in *La Nouvelle Histoire de la France contemporaine*, published by the Éditions du Seuil in 1972, cover the whole of the period up to Bonaparte's seizure of power and give full bibliographical references. These are Michel Vovelle, *La Chute de la Monarchie 1787–1792*; Marc Bouloiseau, *La République jacobine 1792–1794*; Denis Woronoff, *La République bourgeoise, 1794–1799*.

There are a number of studies of particular subjects which are important. The essays by Richard Cobb, *The Police and the People* (Oxford, 1970), *Reactions to the French Revolution* (Oxford, 1972) and *Paris and its Provinces 1792–1802* (Oxford, 1975), are always stimulating; the silent world of the peasantry and its links with the Counter-Revolution are analysed by the American sociologist Charles Tilly, *The Vendée* (London, 1964), and by two French historians, P. Bois, *Les Paysans de l'ouest* (1960), and M. Faucheux, *L'Insurrection vendéen de 1793* (1964); contacts between revolutionary and counter-revolutionary France and the outside world are described in Jacques Godechot, *La Grande Nation: l'expansion révolutionnaire de la France dans le monde 1789–1799* (Paris, 1956; English translation 1972); one of the great personalities of the revolution, Robespierre, is discussed in a special number of the *Annales historiques de la Révolution Française* (1958). As an example of the way in which local studies are vital for the general understanding of important periods of the Revolution see Colin Lucas, *The Structure of the Terror* (Oxford, 1973), which is a study of the Loiret departement, and J. R. Suratteau, *Le Département de Mont-Terrible sous le régime du Directoire* (Paris, 1964). Douglas Johnson (ed.) *French Society and the Revolution* (London, 1977), consists of a number of essays by various experts on the Revolution; Norman Hampson, *Robespierre* (London, 1975), is an original contribution to the study of this most important personality; and Martin Lyons, *France Under the Directory* (London, 1975), is to be recommended.

Biographies of Napoleon are endless. One which outlines his career with remarkable brevity and clarity is Felix Markham, *Napoleon* (London, 1963), while Vincent Cronin, *Napoleon* (London, 1971), is concerned more with his private life. Many important aspects of Napoleonic France are discussed in a special number of the *Revue d'histoire moderne et contemporaine* (July–September 1970), entitled 'La France à l'époque napoléonienne', whilst G. Lefebvre, *Napoléon* (Paris, 1965), is a survey of both France and Europe during the period. Volumes 4 and 5 of the *Nouvelle Histoire de la France contemporaine* (1972, see above) are short but extremely informative: Louis Bergeron, *L'Épisode napoléonien 1799–1815: aspects intérieurs;* Jacques Lovie and André Palluel, *L'Épisode napoléonien 1799–1815: aspects extérieurs.* They both contain bibliographies. Corelli Barnett, *Bonaparte* (London, 1978), is one of the most critical biographies to appear for some time.

Traditionally, the downfall of Napoleon and the restoration of the Bourbons was considered by historians as forming a new period in French history which was studied constitutionally in such a work as P. Bastid, *Les Institutions politiques de la monarchie parlementaire 1814–1848* (Paris, 1954), or as economic history in A. L. Dunham, *The Industrial Revolution in France 1815–1848* (New York, 1955). But more recently historians have tended to consider French social history over wider periods. One example is Georges Dupeux, *La Société française 1789–1960* (Paris, 1964), whilst Maurice Agulhon, *La République au village* (Paris, 1970), considers the populations of the Var department from the Revolution to the Second Republic. Two considerable histories, covering a wide time span and delving deeply into social and cultural aspects are by Pierre Sorlin, *La Société française*, Vol. 1, 1840–1914 (Paris, 1969), Vol. 2, 1914–1968 (Paris, 1971), and by Theodore Zeldin, *France 1848–1945*, The Oxford History of Modern Europe, 2 vols (1973 and 1977). R. D. Anderson, *France 1870–1914* (London, 1977), is a short and judicious survey which contains an excellent bibliography.

The problem of revolutions in France has received a great deal of attention. A theory of revolutions has been put forward by E. Labrousse and has been published in Crouzet, Chaloner and Stern, *Essays in European Economic History 1789–1914* (London, 1970), and one can also consult D. Pinkney, *The French Revolution of 1830* (Princeton, 1972), and G. Duveau, *1848 en France* (Paris, 1948). A remarkable pioneering work on Paris and its population in this period is G. Chevalier, *Classes laborieuses et classes dangereuses à Paris* (Paris, 1958; English translation 1973). Louis Girard, *La IIe République* (Paris, 1968), is a neat account of a short, but rich episode. Individuals are examined in order that a period of history can be the better understood in Douglas Johnson, *Guizot: Aspects of French History 1787–1874* (London, 1963), and F. De Luna, *The French Republic under Cavaignac* (Princeton, 1969). There are excellent essays in Roger Price, *Revolution and Reaction: 1848 and the Second French Republic* (London, 1976), and

Maurice Aguilhon, *Les Quarante-Huitards* (Paris, 1976), is a useful short survey. The Second Empire obviously gives good opportunity for the same treatment as shown in J. P. T. Bury, *Napoleon III and the Second Empire* (Paris, 1964), and W. H. C. Smith, *Napoleon III* (1972). Theodore Zeldin (ed.), *Conflicts in French Society* (London, 1972), consists of a number of excellent essays on various aspects of French life during the Second Empire. The war which ended Napoleon III's rule is the subject of a magnificent work by Michael Howard, *The Franco-Prussian War* (London, 1961).

The Third Republic, from the defeat of 1870 to the defeat of 1940, is outlined in J.-P. Azéma and M. Winock, *La Troisième République* (Paris, 1969), but anyone interested in its beginnings should consult the contributions to the colloquium organized by Jacques Viard, *L'Esprit républicain* (Paris, 1972), and to the colloquium organized for the centenary of the Commune, *La Commune de 1871* (Paris, 1972). S. Edwards, *The Paris Commune 1871* (London, 1971), and J. Rougerie, *Paris libre 1871* (Paris, 1971), are also valuable. The political history of the Third Republic is discussed in F. Goguel, *La Politique des partis sous la Troisième République* (Paris, 1958), is analysed in R. Rémond, *La Droite en France*, 2 vols (Paris, 1968), English translation of 1st ed. (Oxford, 1966), and is vividly narrated in Sir Denis Brogan, *The Development of Modern France* (London, 1967). Certain particular aspects have been studied in detail. The role of Gambetta in the first years of the Third Republic by J. P. T. Bury, *Gambetta and the Making of the Third Republic* (1973) (another volume is to follow); the inescapable *affaire* is discussed in M. Thomas, *L'Affaire sans Dreyfus* (Paris 1961), and in Douglas Johnson, *France and the Dreyfus Affair* (London, 1967); some sidelights of the 1914–18 war are illuminated in J.-J. Becker, *Le Carnet B* (Paris, 1917), and in G. Pedroncini, *Les Mutineries de 1917* (Paris, 1967), whilst the effects of that war and the general economic history of France between the two wars are considered in some detail by A. Sauvy, *Histoire économique de la France entre les deux guerres*, 2 vols (Paris, 1965 and 1967). One of the last great episodes before 1939, the Popular Front, was the subject of a colloquium, *Léon Blum, chef du gouvernement 1936–1937* (Paris, 1967), and is recounted in G. Lefranc, *Histoire du Front Populaire* (Paris, 1965). See too D. R. Watson, *Clemenceau: A Political Biography* (London, 1974). Jean Lacouture, *Léon Blum* (Paris, 1977), is a major political biography, while Tony Judt, *La Reconstitution du parti socialiste 1921–1926* (Paris, 1976), and René Rémond and Janine Bourdin, *Édouard Daladier chef du gouvernement* (Paris, 1977), are detailed examinations of special aspects of the period.

The war, and the national disaster of 1940, has inevitably created many controversies and an enormous literature. Perhaps A. Horne, *To Lose a Battle: France 1940* (London, 1969), and Henri Michel, *Vichy: Année 40* (Paris, 1966), provide the soundest descriptions of the military defeat and the emergence of the 'État Français'. An American historian has studied the Vichy government, R. O. Paxton, *Vichy France* (New York, 1973), and another American has explored Vichy, the Resistance and Gaullism, P. Novick, *The Resistance versus Vichy* (London, 1968). R. Aron, *Histoire de la Libération*, 2 vols (Paris, 1959), and *Histoire de l'Épuration*, 2 vols (Paris, 1967 and 1969), are not accepted in all their details by some historians, but they remain the most graphic accounts of these remarkable moments in French history. Marcel Baudot, *L'Opinion publique sous l'occupation* (Paris, 1960) (in the series 'Esprit de la Résistance', published by the

Presses Universitaires), and Henri Michel, *Les Courants de pensée de la Résistance* (Paris, 1963), are both standard works and likely to remain so, although research is modifying their conclusions as can be seen in H. R. Kedward, *Resistance in Vichy France* (1978).

After the Liberation there came the constitution-making which can be followed in such works as G. Elgey, *La République des illusions* (Paris, 1965), Dorothy Pickles, *The First Years of the Fourth Republic* (London, 1953), and M. Duverger, *Manuel de droit constitutionnel et de science politique* (Paris, 1948, and many further editions). The relations of France with her colonies and other overseas possessions, which was to be crucial for the Fourth Republic, has been examined with great care for this initial period by an American political scientist, D. Bruce Marshall, *The French Colonial Myth and Constitution-making in the Fourth Republic* (Yale, 1973). The political history of the Fourth and Fifth Republics is neatly outlined, with many references, in J. Chapsal, *La Vie politique en France depuis 1940* (Paris, 1969), whilst good accounts of the Fourth Republic are to be found in J. Fauvet, *La Quatrième République* (Paris, 1959), J. Julliard, *La Quatrième République* (Paris, 1968), Philip Williams, *Politics in Post-War France* (London, 1954). Special aspects of the Fourth Republic have been studied in S. Hoffman and others, *In Search of France* (1963), P. Rouanet, *Mendès-France au pouvoir 1954–1955* (Paris, 1965), Alfred Grosser, *La IVe République et sa politique étrangère* (Paris, 1961), J.-M. Jeanneney, *Forces et faiblesses de l'économie française* (Paris, 1959), and P. Bauchet, *L'Expérience française de planification* (Paris, 1958). Events in Indo-China can be studied in P. Devillers, *Histoire de Vietnam de 1940 à 1952* (Paris, 1952), or in D. Lancaster, *The Emancipation of Indo-China* (1961), but when one tries to get to grips with the war in Algeria, whether in a short pamphlet, such as Raymond Aron, *La Tragédie algérienne* (Paris, 1957), a documentary approach like T. Oppermann, *La Question algérienne* (Paris, 1961), or a broad sociological survey, as is W. B. Quandt, *Revolution and Political leadership 1954–1968* (Cambridge, Mass., 1969), one is inevitably involved in the Fifth Republic. The rising in Algeria, the threat of civil war in France and the problem of de Gaulle's involvement in the various conspiracies that were abroad, have given rise to a great many publications, many of them necessarily polemical or political or both. Perhaps they are best digested in the early pages of a two-volume study by P. Viansson-Ponté, *Histoire de la République gaullienne* (Paris, 1970 and 1971), or in one of the essays in P. Williams, *Wars, Plots and Scandals in Post-War France* (Cambridge, 1970). The subject of the origins of the Fifth Republic is looked at from different angles in R. Girardet, *La Crise militaire française 1945–1962* (Paris, 1964), and in A. Debatty, *Le 13 mai et la presse* (Paris, 1960).

On the constitution of the Fifth Republic there are good accounts in M. Duverger, *La Ve République* (Paris, 1963), and later editions, and in P. Avril, *Le Régime politique de la Cinquième République* (Paris, 1967). Institutions and politics are discussed in C. Debbasch, *L'Administration au pouvoir, fonctionnaires et politiques sous la Ve République* (Paris, 1969), and by two British experts on French government, Dorothy Pickles, *The Government and Politics of France*, 2 vols (London, 1971 and 1973), and J. Hayward, *The One and Indivisible French Republic* (1973). These last carry their discussions well beyond the resignation of de Gaulle in 1969; they contain bibliographies. J. Charlot, *L'U.N.R.: étude du pouvoir au sein d'un parti politique* (Paris, 1967), and *Le Phénomène Gaulliste* (Paris, 1970; English translation 1971), and Annie Kriegel, *Les Communistes français* (Paris, 1968; Chicago ed. 1972), examine the principal opposing parties. For foreign policy there is A. Grosser, *La Politique extérieure de la Ve République* (Paris, 1965; rev. English ed. Toronto, 1967), and Edward L. Morse, *Foreign Policy and Interdependence in Gaullist France* (Princeton, 1973); relevant to the Fifth Republic and Europe, there is J. Newhouse, *De Gaulle and the Anglo-Saxons* (London, 1970), and U. Kitzinger, *Diplomacy and Persuasion* (1973); Wolf Mendl, *Deterrence and Persuasion: French Nuclear Armament in the Context of National Policy 1945–1969*, deals with a fundamental aspect of Gaullist France; on the economy, Andrew Shonfield, *Modern Capitalism* (1965), contains a classical appraisal of what was happening in France, which can be read with the symposium published under the name Atreize, *La Planification française en pratique* (Paris, 1971).

There remains General de Gaulle himself. Out of many, four books can be particularly recommended. Paul-Marie de la Gorce, *De Gaulle entre deux mondes* (Paris, 1964), is a full account but uncritical: Jean Lacouture, *De Gaulle* (1969; English translation 1970), is penetrating; A. Hartley, *Gaullism: the Rise and Fall of a Political Movement* (London, 1972), discusses the General's writings and his actions and provides an acute analysis of both; Brian Crozier has written *De Gaulle: The Warrior* (London, 1971) and *De Gaulle: The Statesman* (London, 1973). In addition, Robert Aron, *An Explanation of de Gaulle* (New York, 1966), is short and stimulating. For the events of 1968 there is J. Gretton, *Students and Workers* (London, 1969), which was written close to the crisis, but takes a fairly broad view; for the events of 1969 and what followed, Jean Mauriac, *Mort du Général de Gaulle* (Paris, 1972).

On de Gaulle's successor there is a biography, P. Rouanet, *Pompidou* (Paris, 1969). On President Pompidou's first Prime Minister, Jacques Chaban-Delmas, it was his downfall which attracted the attention of P. Alexandre, *Exécution d'un homme politique* (Paris, 1973). The major political event of the first four years of M. Pompidou's Presidency, the general election of 1973, can be studied in Un Dossier du Monde, *Les Forces politiques et les élections de mars 1973* (Paris, 1973). See too Charles Debbasch, *La France de Pompidou* (Paris, 1974).

For a general assessment of the state of France there are three thought-provoking books: Michel Crozier, *La Société bloquée* (Paris, 1970); John Ardagh, *The New France* (1970); Pierre George, *France* (1967; English translation 1973). For recent events *L'Année politique* and the *Revue française de science politique* are regular publications which should be consulted. On the elections of 1978 the first serious study is *Le Monde: Les Élections législatives de mars 1978* (Paris, 1978). Most recently, one should consult Vincent Wright, *The Government and Politics of France* (1978), and Pierre Daix, *La Crise du PCF* (1978).

5 French Thought in the Seventeenth and Eighteenth Centuries

D. C. POTTS

The Seventeenth Century

If one were required to sum up the history of French thought in the seventeenth and eighteenth centuries in a single statement, it would be that this was the epoch which saw the rise of rationalist philosophy and liberal ideology. In the movement to free the human mind from the tyranny of traditional authority which characterizes this period in European thought as a whole, French thinkers played a prominent part, and by the end of the eighteenth century they were the intellectual leaders of Europe, having upheld the ideals of democratic government, humanitarian ethics and religious toleration, and having adumbrated in their philosophical thought the evolutionary materialism of the nineteenth century. The task was more difficult in France than was the case elsewhere. Religious opposition to new ideas was stiffer, and the application of censorship more rigorous, while the Roman Catholic Church, whose theology was the bulwark of the divine-right monarchy, occupied a dominant position in social and political life. However, the conflict between new and established ideas developed only gradually, and the issues were never as sharply drawn as is sometimes assumed. For one thing, words changed their meanings slowly, so that a subversive intention might sometimes lurk only half-perceived under an apparently orthodox form of expression. Hence censorship was not always sure of its ground; in any case, it was often evaded, notably by the circulation of clandestine manuscripts and the importation of banned French books from abroad. Nor were Church and State monolithic institutions completely devoted to opposing new ideas. Despite its claim to possess the only means of salvation, the Roman Church did not have a monopoly of Christian belief. Calvinism continued to be a live intellectual force, even after 1685 when the revocation of the Edict of Nantes drove most of its adherents out of France and its leading thinkers had to continue their work in Holland or England. Within Catholicism, Jesuits contended with Jansenists, while within Calvinism a 'liberal' wing developed in opposition to 'orthodox' Calvinist thought. At the extremes of the two faiths, Quietism represented a highly mystical, and controversial, development of Catholicism, while Socinianism (pervasive in France towards the end of the seventeenth century in nature if not in name, as Bayle pointed out) can be seen as Protestantism at its most rationalistic. This wide diversity of Christian thought meant that it could accommodate tendencies which were favourable as well as hostile to the spread of new ideas. Again, the authority of the monarch, although absolute in theory, was at various times challenged by the efforts of the aristocracy of birth to defend or reclaim its traditional privileges, and of the bourgeois magistrates to exercise their right to be the 'eyes and conscience' of the king. Within this framework there was already scope for the elaboration of political ideas critical of, or contrary to, absolutism.

The history of French thought in these two centuries is as much one of shifts of emphasis as of sudden upheavals, so that any purely chronological divisions are bound to be arbitrary. For expository purposes, however, it is convenient to see it as falling into three parts. The mechanistic view of the world which is the main feature of seventeenth-century thought had effectively supplanted traditional scholastic philosophy (though this continued to be taught in schools and universities) by the 1670s; on the other hand, the evolutionary materialism which is the most striking feature in the eighteenth century did not achieve coherent expression until the 1750s. This leaves us with an intermediate period, between 1670 and 1750, in which scientific and metaphysical issues, although still important, take second place to the use of reason as a weapon of criticism aimed not only at ideas but at religious, moral and political institutions, which constitutes what is perhaps the best-known aspect of the eighteenth-century 'Enlightenment'.

It is in the first half of the seventeenth century that reason (which on close inspection turns out to be a protean term) ceases to be subordinated to the authority of tradition, and comes to replace tradition as a means of knowledge and a guide to life. Rationalism in this sense is particularly associated with the rise of modern science. Galileo and Kepler, basing themselves on Copernicus's heliocentric theory, described the universe as a machine, operating according to laws which could be expressed as mathematical formulae. Mechanism was taken up in France by the philosophers and scientists (the seventeenth and eighteenth centuries recognized no real distinction between the two categories) in the circle of the Minorite Father Marin Mersenne (1588–1648). Mersenne's circle set an early example of co-operative scientific endeavour, which eventually gave rise to the founding of the officially sponsored Académie des Sciences in 1669. Among the best-known members of Mersenne's original group were Pierre Gassendi[1] (1592–1655) and René Descartes (1596–1650). The chief obstacles to their attempts to establish the mechanistic interpretation of nature in France were the widespread diffusion of scepticism and the authority of Aristotelianism. Scepticism had been given a powerful impetus towards the end of the sixteenth century by Montaigne's *Apologie de Raimond de Sebond*: Montaigne's contention that the mind is inherently incapable of attaining truth because of its dependence on the senses was extremely influential in the early part of the seventeenth century, partly (as will be seen) on account of the support it was believed to give to a certain type of religious apologetics. Mersenne and Gassendi countered this with what has been termed a 'mitigated scepticism': Mersenne, in particular, argued that men possess a principle of reflection which is independent of the senses.

Scepticism threatened the belief that *any* valid science could be established. Aristotelianism, on the other hand, placed barriers in the way of the establishment of the new science of Galileo and Kepler. Aristotle's philosophy had given rise to two quite different scientific doctrines. The scholastic science taught in France was an amalgam of Christian theology with Aristotle's physics. It taught that the earth was immobile at the centre of the universe, and that round it moved the spheres which carried the sun, the moon and the remaining planets. Although the privileged position, occupied by the earth showed that man was a unique creature, destined by God for salvation, man's fall from grace, recorded in the Bible, had made the region 'below' the moon into one of change and decay, whereas that 'above' the moon was unchanging and the abode of the angels. Everything in nature had its proper 'place', assigned to it by God, to which it tended to move. Beyond what was immediately explicable in terms of the 'qualities' (hot, dry, moist, cold)

[1] Gassendi's influence was restricted by the fact that he wrote only in Latin. A French digest of his philosophy began to appear only in the 1670s.

apprehended by the senses, movement took place as the result of an 'occult' (or secret) quality placed in objects by God – thus the lodestone was held to attract by virtue of an inherent 'attractive quality'. One of the major achievements of the new science was to get rid of such purely verbal explanations by substituting considerations of quantity for those of quality: it dealt only with the objectively measurable features of the shape, mass and displacement of objects, thus enabling movement to be expressed in mathematical terms. The French mechanists had also to contend with a different development of Aristotelianism, arising out of Aristotle's biology rather than his physics, and developed independently of theology. This was naturalism, which originated in Italy at the University of Padua. It was diffused in seventeenth-century France by Italian visitors, notably Vanini and Campanella, and by the French writers Théophile de Viau (1590–1626) and Cyrano de Bergerac (1619–55). The latter's science-fiction stories of imaginary voyages to the sun and the moon are particularly interesting examples of the influence of Italian naturalist ideas in French thought of the time. Naturalism differed from scholastic Aristotelianism in an important respect. For the scholastics, God was the Prime Mover who had set a universe of inert matter in motion; for the naturalists, God was the source of a force or vital principle diffused throughout and animating all matter, and known as 'nature' or the 'world soul'. Naturalism, like scholasticism though for different reasons, could not accommodate the new mechanistic explanation of the workings of nature. Between 1620 and 1640, Aristotelianism came under heavy fire in France, notably in the writings of Gassendi and Descartes. Gassendi's *Exercitationes paradoxicae* (1624) are a sceptical attack. His positive contribution, in his *Syntagma philosophicum* (1658), was to replace the Aristotelian scheme of qualities by a revival of classical Epicurean science, taking as the elementary data of physics the 'atoms' (the smallest units of matter) which constantly separate and combine to form the phenomena we observe, and which, possessing inertia and moving in a vacuum, can be made the foundation of a mechanical representation of nature.

The most influential of these thinkers was Descartes. Although on some points (notably concerning the elementary units of matter) practising scientists did not see much difference between his view and Gassendi's, the gulf between them is in fact immense. Gassendi (like Mersenne) based his scientific theories on observation and claimed only conjectural status for them. Descartes took an entirely different view. He turned his back on empiricism and claimed to have discovered the metaphysical basis on which scientific certainty could be founded. Although his arguments were at first sharply criticized, not least by his immediate colleagues, and although nearly every one of his conclusions was subsequently shown to be wrong, the way in which he seemed to have disposed once and for all of both scepticism and scholasticism, together with the broad sweep of his philosophy, in which he proposed to extend the mechanistic approach to all branches of knowledge, made a profound impression on his contemporaries and left a mark which is still visible in the philosophical discussions of our own day. An attractive account of his highly individual quest for truth, and of the outlines of his philosophy, is to be found in the *Discours de la méthode* (1637), but for a fuller understanding of his thought, and the problems to which it gave rise, it is necessary to go to his other works and especially to the *Méditations métaphysiques* (in Latin, 1642; in French, 1644). Rigorously exercising 'methodic doubt', Descartes turned the sceptics' own weapon against them, and showed that if one doubted all one could, a single irreducible certainty remained: 'Je pense, donc je suis.' On this, Descartes claimed, given a criterion for telling true from false, a whole system of universal knowledge could be erected. Descartes discovered his criterion in mathematics, where truth is perceived as a clear and distinct idea, is independent of the senses, and leads to other truths by deduction. It was confirmed in his apprehension of the *cogito* itself, which is a clear and distinct idea. Extending the deductive process to all branches of knowledge, Descartes was able to take scientific thought well beyond the stage of the collection of *ad hoc* findings, based on the provisional acceptance of sense data, at which Mersenne and Gassendi were prepared to leave it, but in doing so he raised difficulties which were to have far-reaching implications for the next two centuries, and which have continued to provoke controversy right up to the present day, when we are quite likely to find Descartes being praised for the incomparable way in which he posed fundamental problems, or accused of being responsible for all the errors of modern philosophy.

The central problem arose out of the radical way in which Descartes distinguished between the activity of the mind, including thinking, feeling and willing, which takes place in a realm of immaterial spirit, and the mechanically determined world of material objects (including the human body) perceived by the senses. This distinction, which scholastic philosophy had mitigated by speaking of a threefold soul in man, part 'vegetative' (which man shared with the plants), part 'sensitive' (shared with the animals), and part 'rational' (unique in man among the creatures of nature), the lower parts being included in the higher, raised two difficulties in particular. In the first place, Descartes claimed that all knowledge is innate, our ideas being somehow latent in the mind, so that sense experience merely triggers them off. Although Descartes seems at first to have wanted to restrict this to the claim that certain operations of the mind are innate, he was led into the position of asserting that the ideas of God, the soul, the extended universe of matter, and many others, were present in the mind at birth. In the second place, Descartes found it difficult to account for the interaction, an undeniable fact of experience, of immaterial mind and material body. His solution was to represent the mind as what Ryle has called 'a ghost in the machine', situated according to Descartes in the pineal gland, which lies at the base of the brain. Descartes explained bodily movement as the result of the displacement of small particles of matter (traditionally, but from Descartes's point of view, misleadingly known as 'animal spirits') along the nerves, which he thought of as being like hollow tubes, in such a way as to provoke muscular reactions. Similarly, the 'passions of the soul' were dependent on the effects of physical stimulation on the pineal gland. It will be evident from this that Descartes equated 'mind' with 'soul'. Animals, not having souls according to Catholic theology, were simply machines, a proposition which almost immediately gave rise to impassioned controversy, in which men of letters such as La Fontaine joined as well as professional philosophers.

It is characteristic of Descartes's reliance on the operations of his own mind to reach the truth about the physical world that he made no observations to verify his theory concerning the pineal gland or the structure of the nerves. He used experiment only to give the mind something to explain, or at the most to illustrate a theory, but not to corroborate or invalidate it. Even mathematics, the basis of his philosophy, provided him with no more than a criterion of metaphysical truth and a model of logical method. Although Descartes had invented analytical or 'Cartesian' geometry, which makes it possible to express a multitude of instances of the behaviour of a physical object by a single mathematical formula – thus giving science the mathematical tool which, as Mersenne had seen, was necessary if the chaos of appearances was to be given a rational interpretation, he rarely made use of it in his own scientific thinking, preferring to deduce the structure of reality from a primary intuition.

The bias of the mechanists' efforts was utilitarian, and they concentrated on the operations of nature rather than on its ultimate cause in God. As a result, some modern critics have accused them of holding views or harbouring intentions incompatible with their professions of Christian belief. But the impact of mechanistic science on religious thought was insidious rather than dramatic. Although the new cosmology shattered the scholastic distinction between the supralunary and the sublunary regions, and displaced man from his special position at the centre of the universe to set him wandering amongst the stars in the infinity of space, this seems to have served more as a lesson of Christian humility than as a sign that God had retreated from His creation. Mechanism could conflict with the letter of Scripture, as Galileo discovered, but the French mechanists did not press the point. The empiricists amongst them were fideists: that is to say, they held that scepticism had shown up the inadequacy of all proofs of natural theology (principally the existence of God and the immortality of the soul), and that all the doctrines of Christianity should therefore be accepted on the authority of revelation alone. Although a significant departure from the doctrine of Aquinas, fideism had, since the end of the sixteenth century, been looked on with favour by Catholic theologians who regarded it as a bulwark against both Protestant and freethinking rationalism. While it went out of favour when Cartesian rationalism gained ground in the second half of the century, fideism was not officially condemned by the Vatican until 1870. Although Descartes distinguished between the doctrines of Christianity, which are 'above reason', and the certainties of science, which are discoverable by reason, in a quasi-fideistic manner, his position was rather different from that of Mersenne or Gassendi, in that his proofs of God and the soul provided apologists with new arguments and were used to promote a revival of natural theology. The empiricists saw in the order and harmony of the universal machine support for the 'moral' proof of God's existence known as the argument from design. Descartes, by arguing from the concept of existence to the existence of an infinite and perfect Being, produced a proof which did not depend, like the argument from design, on the fallible evidence of the senses. On the question of the soul, Descartes claimed only to know that it is immaterial, but the apologists who followed in his traces found it a short step to assert its immortality. Descartes's somewhat off-handed attitude towards revealed theology, and the single-mindedness with which he applied himself to the discovery of rational certitudes and the promotion of the utilitarian aim of his philosophy, have caused doubts to be cast on his sincerity. It is clear, however, from the *Méditations* that the existence of God was vitally necessary to him. That God exists and does not deceive us (the hypothesis of the 'malin génie' which Descartes raises and refutes) is the corner-stone of his entire philosophy: without it, human certainty would be impossible.

The group of thinkers more legitimately suspect of using fideism as a cover for unbelief are the *libertins*. The French word means a free-thinker, but not necessarily a person of loose morals, as does its English equivalent. A *libertin* might be an atheist, a deist, or a heterodox Christian. The most notable seventeenth-century *libertins* are those who have been called 'libertins érudits' because they believed that in so far as truth was to be found at all, it would be through learning and not through speculation. They include François La Mothe le Vayer (1588–1672), Gabriel Naudé (1600–53) and Gui Patin (1601–72), all of whom were friends of Gassendi, who shared some of their views. They were sceptics, but they were influenced by Italian rationalism as well as by Montaigne. Following the Paduan philosopher Pomponazzi, they did not look upon faith and reason as two ways to religious truth, but as attitudes attributable to two classes of men, the philosophers who use reason to become 'déniaisés' and to lead a moral life in which virtue is practised for its own sake and not out of fear of hell-fire or hope of future rewards; and the masses, the slaves of ignorance and passions, who need religious belief and institutions to provide them with laws of conduct. They did not believe in enlightening the masses, and so conformed outwardly to established beliefs and customs while reserving the right to draw their own private conclusions. These were often provocative, even though habitually approached through the study of pagan religion, the inference being left open that Christianity did not constitute a special case. They propagated the view that religious institutions are not divine in origin, but are 'useful inventions' of politicians for their own ends. They were inclined to regard these ends as good and believed that religious uniformity was a prerequisite of political stability; as a result, they were unsympathetic to the idea of religious toleration. The same theory could, however, be developed into a denunciation of religions as 'impostures', and the legend that the world's great religions had been founded by three impostors, Moses, Christ and Mahomet, goes back to this period, although it reached the height of its diffusion in the clandestine manuscript literature of the early eighteenth century. The *libertins* expressed other views which tended to conflict with contemporary Christianity. If Patin stopped short at a vociferous anticlericalism, La Mothe le Vayer formulated a catalogue of doubts so universal as to undermine the current fideistic doctrine (which he claimed to espouse) that scepticism was essentially a Christian philosophy, while Naudé used doubt more systematically to criticize the content of the classical myths in a way which also seemed to call belief in the Christian supernatural into question.

The *libertin* belief that, for the enlightened élite, virtue is its own reward, is an indication that an element of rationalism is to be found in seventeenth-century ethical thought independently of the impact of science which, in this field, directly influenced only the moral ideas of Descartes (who linked morality with an understanding of the body as a machine) and perhaps of Gassendi (since Epicurean ethics was based on the physics). It is essentially a Stoic notion, and both Stoic and Epicurean ideas appealed to contemporary Frenchmen, many of whom saw moral problems in terms of the capriciousness of fortune in the uncertain times leading up to the civil war of the Frondes (1649–53). Seventeenth-century 'Stoicism' and 'Epicureanism' are overlapping categories. Few adepts of the former preached the full rigour of the doctrine that the sage must be impassive, while few of Epicurus' seventeenth-century disciples gave themselves up wholly to sensual debauchery: the serious moralists of both persuasions took the view that, as one writer has put it, virtue ought not to be deficient in pleasure, nor pleasure in virtue. Nevertheless, the distinction between them is a useful one, particularly when we consider the relationship of pagan moral ideas to Christianity in this period. Gassendi, who rehabilitated Epicurus' physics, also rehabilitated his ethics, the basis of which is the empirical observation that it is a law of nature that we should seek pleasure and avoid pain. But Epicurus specified as the major obstacle to pleasure our fear that the gods may harm us, in this world or in an after-life. He therefore set out to prove scientifically that the gods have no interest in human affairs, and that the soul does not survive the death of the body. Gassendi, on the other hand, performed the *tour de force* of reversing Epicurus' argument and claiming that it is Christianity, with its assurance of a benevolent God and its promise of eternal bliss, that is the best remover of fear. Gassendi thus provided those of his contemporaries, who were otherwise indifferent to religion, with an ulterior motive for seeking to be convinced of its truth. A case in point is that of Saint-Évremond (1614–1703), whom we shall meet again in another connection; Saint-Évremond was a disciple of Gassendi who for a time looked for religious certainty in fideistic acceptance and in Cartesian demonstrations, but he also differed significantly from his master in stressing the importance of the passions as a principle of action, and his own brand of Epicureanism comes as close as any French thinker's to that of Hobbes, whose definition of life as a 'continual process of striving and desiring' Saint-Évremond seems to echo.

The accommodation of Stoic ideas to Christian moral teaching had taken place long before the seventeenth century. Theologians had incorporated into the Christian doctrine of the Fall, as a result of which reason became a source of error and the passions, attracting the will, a cause of sin, the Stoic notion that a principle of 'right reason' and a knowledge of natural law have been implanted in all men, thus making virtuous action possible despite the ravages of original sin. In this perspective, Jesuit writers in particular had argued for the salvation of virtuous pagans, such as the great moral teachers of classical antiquity, even though they had not had the benefit of the Christian revelation. A similar point of view dominates the many moral treatises of the first part of the seventeenth century which it is convenient to range under the banner of 'Christian Stoicism', the most noteworthy example being the Oratorian Senault's *De l'usage des passions* (1641). But Anthony Levi, in an essential book, has shown that 'right reason', which originally included both intuitive intellect and moral will, and enabled a man to control his passions in accordance with God's purposes, had already been split up into 'reason', narrowed down to its analytical and critical functions, and will, considered as an autonomous faculty which puts the promptings of reason into action. Reason thus becomes the faculty which makes calculations of self-interest rather than the faculty (akin to conscience) which has an intuitive apprehension of God's will. This development reached its culmination in Descartes's *Les Passions de l'âme* (1649), a work which gives us a sufficient clue to the nature of the definitive ethical treatise which Descartes projected as the crown of his philosophy, but did not live to write. It is clear that Descartes considered ethics to depend on scientific knowledge of the union of the spiritual soul with the mechanism of the body. His ideal is the *généreux* who resolves to use rational judgement and autonomous will to manipulate his passions in such a way as to exercise complete control over his actions. For the passions are neither good nor bad in themselves, but are disturbances of the soul caused by the displacement of the animal spirits as the result of some external stimulus, which we can counter by switching the spirits in the pineal gland into some other part of the body. Descartes's theory of the passions is an outstanding example of the extreme point reached by optimistic ethical humanism in the seventeenth century. His moral ideal bears a superficial resemblance to that of Corneille's stage heroes, but in the cult of glory which affected large numbers of the French nobility in life as well as on the stage, passion is a manifestation of personal energy and an exigence of personal development, and the pursuit of glory is motivated by irrational drives which, as contemporary moralists recognized, go beyond the norms of reason. After the setback suffered by the aristocracy at the time of the Fronde, which was followed by their domestication to the absolute authority of Louis XIV, the ethic of glory was supplanted by the ethic of *honnêteté*, an ideal of civilized living aspired to by leisured bourgeois and nobleman alike. In the writings of its chief theorists, the Chevalier de Méré (1609–84) and Damien Miton, it emerges as an ethic of enlightened self-interest, such as Philinte urges on Alceste in Molière's *Misanthrope*, the end of which is the achievement of a harmonious society composed of people of cultivated good manners who find their own happiness in the happiness of others.

Blaise Pascal (1623–62) is outstanding among seventeenth-century authors as the acutest critic of the rationalistic tendencies we have so far described, and (in the opinion of many) the profoundest thinker of the entire century. He was a mathematician of genius and a scientist whose experimental practice was far in advance of his time, as well as an inventor, and a man who, at one time, frequented the company of the spokesmen of *honnêteté*, Méré and Miton. He was therefore well placed to judge both the deeper implications of mechanism and the tendencies of ethical thought in his day. Pascal wrote from a religious standpoint which was both intensely personal and in close sympathy with the views of the Jansenists of Port-Royal, who published the posthumous fragments of Pascal's projected defence of Christianity, known as the *Pensées*, in 1670. It was for a long time thought that Pascal's notes were in too much disarray for it to be possible to reconstruct the plan of his intended *Apologie*, but modern scholarship has shown that we can at least recover the provisional order in which the author had classified his material at the time of his death. Pascal put his finger on the weakness of Descartes's apparently orthodox separation of the domains of faith and reason which, given the philosopher's emphasis on the certainties to be attained by deductive reasoning, could only push revealed religion further and further into the margin of life. Although he failed to do justice to Descartes's reasons for introducing God into his system – he needed God, Pascal claimed, only in order to give the universe an initial push to set it in motion – he accurately foresaw that by reducing the universe to matter and movement, Cartesianism would be held to render revealed religion unnecessary and lead simply to deism. Pascal himself was convinced that the Christian revelation alone could make coherent sense of the human experience, and this is the central theme of the *Pensées*. He was writing for the intelligent agnostic of his day, someone influenced by Montaigne while in touch with the main developments in scientific thought, and he drew heavily on both Montaigne and science for persuasive imagery. He credits man with a desire for truth and happiness which, since it is beyond unregenerate human nature, causes him to relapse into scepticism and the pursuit of distracting activities ('le divertissement') which represent an unconscious attempt to escape from the anxiety inseparable from a true knowledge of the human condition. Only the Christian doctrine of the Fall and Redemption can make sense of the human dilemma, and only the grace mediated by the Roman Catholic religion, which alone has the truth, can offer an escape from it. Pascal's argument is impressive even to those who accept neither the diagnosis nor the cure. In particular, it contrasts advantageously with the moral and demonstrative proofs of natural theology offered by the overwhelming majority of seventeenth-century apologists. Pascal eschews such proofs. Even the notorious argument of the Wager, in which he attempts to persuade the reader, on the basis of an application of the calculus of probabilities, of the advantage of believing that God exists, is not presented as a proof, but as a means of encouraging the reader to commit his entire personality, and not simply his intellect, to the search for belief. In this as in his exploitation of the theme of anxiety, Pascal anticipates modern existentialism. Despite his attitude to proofs, Pascal is not an anti-rationalist, as the Romantics chose to think, largely on the basis of their misinterpretation of the term 'le cœur' and their disregard for the fact that 'la raison' is one of Pascal's 'trois moyens de croire'. He deliberately cites 'proofs' drawn from scriptural evidence of the fulfilment of prophecies, which illustrate the continuity of the Old and New Testaments and provide a figurative expression of the universality of Christian doctrine, because they are not demonstrative: if therefore the reader is convinced by them, it must be because his intellect has been illuminated by divine grace.

Pascal here writes not as a fideist (as it might seem) but as an Augustinian Christian, prepared to admit the possibility of rational demonstrations of natural theology, but denying that they are of any value in bringing a man to faith. Pascal's criticisms of the self-regarding nature of all contemporary ethical doctrines – he includes Stoicism, Epicureanism, the ethic of glory, and *honnêteté* in his condemnation – are made from the same standpoint, as are his views on the social order which he represents as the result of original sin and a necessary punishment imposed by God, thus precluding any serious possibility of reform. Augustinianism is an important factor in seventeenth-century French thought. Its most influential representatives (though far from the only ones) were the small group of clerics and laymen known as the Jansenists because they were followers of the Belgian bishop Jansenius, who died in 1638, two years before the publication of his commentary on St Augustine's theology, the *Augustinus*. While Augustinianism itself can be broadly distinguished from the mainstream of modern Catholic theology, by its strong emphasis on the infirmity of human nature as a result of the Fall, and on the inscrutability of God's plans for the salvation of the individual, Jansenism eludes close definition, since it was an intellectual tendency rather than a specific doctrine, despite the points on which the Pope condemned the *Augustinus* in 1649, but which the Jansenists never admitted they held. Jansenism is often equated with Calvinism, but the leading Jansenist theologians, Antoine Arnauld and Pierre Nicole, were among the most effective of the contemporary controversialists who undertook to write against Calvinism. The stress laid by the Jansenists on a personal experience of conversion (such as Pascal himself underwent) and on rigorous moral standards is not after all the sole prerogative of Protestantism, while the Jansenists consistently gave proof of their orthodoxy in upholding the specifically Catholic doctrine of the Church as the visible communion of the faithful and the essential source of grace through the sacraments.

The Jansenists were at the forefront of a reaction against the aristocratic, optimistic and humanistic tendencies in contemporary ethical thought, which set in during the middle years of the seventeenth century. They particularly denounced the dominance of the self-regarding motive of *amour-propre* and the absence of the theological virtue of charity or *amour de Dieu*. *Amour-propre* was also treated in the *Maximes* (1664) of La Rochefoucauld, who combined acute insight into subconscious motivation with a positive belief in the moral values associated with the ethic of *honnêteté*. Although La Rochefoucauld frequented Jansenist circles, the context of the *Maximes* is a secular one, and their bearing is quite different from that of the *Essais de morale* (1671–80) of the Jansenist Nicole, whose view of the subconscious workings of *amour-propre* led him to the extreme conclusion that we have no way of distinguishing objectively between virtuous and sinful acts. Against this, their bitterest enemies the Jesuits (already accused by Pascal, in his *Lettres provinciales* (1656–7) of condoning lax standards of morality) stressed man's natural capacity to know and do God's will, and counted as sinful only acts done in conscious awareness that a moral law was being broken.

Pascal's critique of both Cartesian rationalism and mundane ethics proved ineffectual so far as the next generation was concerned. His 'proofs' of Christianity, relying as they did in contemporary eyes on an orthodox (i.e. literal) as well as a figurative interpretation of the biblical text, were undermined by the modern techniques of biblical criticism initiated by Spinoza who treated the Bible as a work of Jewish history in his *Tractatus theologico-politicus* (1670) and employed by the Oratorian priest Richard Simon in his *Histoire critique du Vieux Testament* (1677). The Port-Royal editors of the *Pensées* had been won over to Cartesianism, and interfered with Pascal's text in order to accommodate the author's thought to their own ideas. Proofs of natural theology borrowed from or modelled on Descartes were used to revive rationalist apologetics. Bossuet (1627–1704), the most impressive and intelligent orthodox defender of Christianity in the seventeenth century, invoked the Cartesian criterion of clearness and distinctness in his *Traité du libre arbitre* (1677) and based the contemporary *Traité de la connaissance de Dieu et de soi-même* (published posthumously) on *Les Passions de l'âme*. Bossuet did, it is true, incorporate Cartesian ideas and demonstrations into the perspective of Augustinian Christianity, and eventually denounced Cartesianism as a threat to religion because it subordinated revelation to reason; moreover, he prolonged in his writings and preaching the moral rigorism of the Jansenists and Pascal. Fénelon (1651–1715) was Bossuet's adversary in a fierce controversy over the mystical doctrine of Quietism, but like Bossuet he used Cartesian ideas in his apologetics, and similarly inveighed against the increasing tendency of his contemporaries to value worldly goods above personal salvation (a major theme of moralist literature, as the expansion of trade and the development of luxury industries altered the nature of the economy) and associated mundane civilization with moral decadence much as Rousseau was to do half a century later. But the tide was running against such austerity, as a single example shows. Whereas in the *Pensées* the argument that Christianity is relevant to human experience is used to show the urgent need for grace and salvation, Christian moralists of the eighteenth century begin to present Christianity as 'relevant' in a different sense: Christianity is the best religion, it is claimed, because it is the best suited to procure personal happiness and social harmony. The Christian and the *honnête homme*, far from being incompatible as Boussuet preached, thus become almost indistinguishable.

'La Crise de la Conscience'

The last quarter of the seventeenth century and the first half of the eighteenth was first and foremost an age of criticism and reconstruction in which rationalism was used not only to undermine traditional authority, but also as a means of discovering man's basic needs and aspirations and the institutions which would enable him to satisfy them. This is the period of the 'crisis of the European mind', and subsequently of the emergence of the *philosophe*, a man who was not only a philosopher, but a critic and a social reformer. The 'Crise de la conscience' was perhaps not so much a crisis as a growing awareness of the corrosive powers of reason when applied to the dead wood of tradition. The motives of those who used reason critically were by no means clear-cut, and some of them continued to respect the framework of Christian belief within which their targets fell. But the *philosophes* themselves deliberately used reason to undermine established authority, fostering the movement of the Enlightenment, in which the purpose of knowledge was to liberate men's minds in order that they should enjoy happiness in the here and now: this meant open opposition to the exclusive Roman Catholic Church and the despotic outlook of the absolute monarchy. This period also germinated the concept of *sensibilité* which flowered, often over-luxuriantly, throughout the eighteenth century. To be a true human being no longer meant that a man successfully exercised reason and will in the pursuit of God's truth and the imitation of His goodness, but that he responded emotionally to the sufferings of others and was thereby moved to acts of charity towards his fellow-men. There was not yet, however, any question of preferring the promptings of the heart to the demands of reason, as was to be the case with the Romantics. Sentiment reinforced reason, restoring something of what reason had lost when its meaning was reduced from 'right reason' which embraced feeling as well as intellect, to its analytical and critical functions. Only later, when reason was further reduced to a mere reflection of sensation, did the cult of *sensibilité* begin to develop into a justification of man's instinctive drives and eventually come to be at odds with normative reason.

When particular cases are considered, it is not easy to draw a firm line between the *philosophes* and their precursors, between freethinking within a Christian context and that which carries its authors (whether consciously or not it is often hard to say) into direct opposition to the Christian basis of the social order. The plans of Vauban (*La Dîme royale*, 1707) for fiscal reform and those of Fénelon, tutor to successive heirs to the throne, for administrative reform and a relaxation of absolutism (*Tables de Chaulnes*, written in 1711), are attempts to reform the regime from within. Similarly, the celebrated *Caractères, ou les mœurs de ce siècle*, by La Bruyère (1645–96), published between 1688 and 1696, are the work of a man who, while acutely critical of particular abuses, remains a supporter of the divine right of monarchs and the Roman Catholic Church to the extent of vituperating against the Protestant usurper of the English throne, William of Orange, and approving Louis XIV's revocation of the Edict of Nantes in 1685 which resulted in the persecution and flight into exile of his Protestant subjects. Saint-Évremond, on the other hand, comes close to the outlook of the *philosophes* when he speaks of William of Orange as the example of an enlightened monarch and of the Revocation as an offence against humanity. Even so, he writes from within a Christian context, envisaging toleration as a stage on the way to Christian reunion. We are reminded of Erasmus more than of Voltaire.

The case of Pierre Bayle (1647–1706) is more complex. In his early *Pensées diverses sur la comète* (1682–3) he methodically exposed (in a manner which owes something to the example of Cartesian logic) the irrationality of the popular, and pious, superstition that comets are divinely inspired phenomena which presage or cause changes in human affairs. He then digressed on to the thesis that a society of atheists, supposing one to exist, would be as virtuous as a society of Christians. The *philosophes* thought that Bayle was claiming that morality is independent of belief, and were shocked or delighted according to their particular tendencies, but modern scholars argue that in order to understand Bayle's point we should replace his thought in the context of contemporary Calvinist polemics in which, as a French Calvinist who had fled into exile in Holland, he was personally involved. The digression can then be read as an attack on Roman Catholics, who are lumped together with pagan idolators as an inferior category to both Calvinists and atheists. Bayle's greatest work is his *Dictionnaire historique et critique* (1697; 2nd edition, 1702). With its anodyne text and provocative, immensely learned footnotes in which every opinion on the subject in hand is cited and shown to conflict, it becomes more intelligible if it is interpreted in a similar way. However, Bayle was a shrewd observer of the contemporary scene, who saw how far Christians had become disaffected from their traditional doctrines and institutions, rather than the apologist for Calvinism that some scholars have claimed. Contemporary Calvinists divided into two camps, orthodox and 'liberal'. The former believed in blind faith and coercion, the latter in a rational search for truth and in religious toleration. Bayle offended both parties by defending blind faith while championing toleration. His dialectic technique seems to have been aimed at driving the orthodox, convinced of their election, back within the retrenchments of their faith, thus preventing them from harming their liberal opponents, whom Bayle in turn requires to abandon the use of reason in theology because it is inevitably corrosive of faith. Religious toleration, which Bayle regarded as the highest requirement of Christian morality, is the real beneficiary of this strategy.

With Fontenelle (1657–1757) we are much closer to the *philosophes*. Fontenelle's *Histoire des oracles* (1686), like Bayle's work on comets, debunks a popular superstition, namely the belief that the pagan oracles were inspired by demons, supernatural beings whose voice was miraculously silenced by the birth of Christ. Fontenelle shows the influence of Cartesian logic when he takes the documentary evidence in the case, reconstitutes it into the chains of reasoning which are supposed to support the belief, and shows that these fall apart when rigorous standards of proof are applied. His conclusion that the oracles were 'worked' by their priests gave fresh life to the *libertin* thesis that religious institutions are man-made. Although Fontenelle was able to claim that leading ecclesiastics, and not simply *libertins*, were in favour of stripping Christian teaching of such superstitious accretions. His own view of religion seems detached and analytical. A noteworthy example is his *De l'origine des fables* (written in the 1690s, published 1724) where he puts forward the thesis that men have created divinities in their own image as a result of a fundamental disposition of the human mind to explain the unknown by the known. This psychological analysis of the origins of religious belief was taken further by the eighteenth-century materialists, notably Helvétius who was a great admirer of Fontenelle. Fontenelle's *Entretiens sur la pluralité des mondes* (1686) is noteworthy, despite factual errors, as a delightful popularization of the Copernican system and Cartesian physics, but perhaps the feature in it most indicative of the author's mentality is the way he substitutes the sentiment of joy in scientific discovery for the anguish and religious awe with which Pascal believed man should react to 'le silence de ces espaces infinis'.

Montesquieu (1689–1755) is the first author to whom historians normally accord the title of *philosophe*. His *Lettres persanes* (1721) is a brilliant example of the way the confrontation of two cultures was used not only to inculcate a lesson of relativism – and thus dislodge from the French reader's mind the conviction that only French ideas and institutions are valid – but also to point to the universality of deistic belief and the idea of natural justice. Deism may be defined as belief in a God who is the creator of the world, and whose existence is known by reason without the need for revelation. The deists accept the complete adequacy of the moral law laid down in the Gospels, which reduces to the requirement to practise justice and charity. This is the only divine command, and there is no need for priests, dogmas or ceremonies. The seeds of deism were sown in the seventeenth century, in the philosophers' proofs of God as the efficient cause of the universe rather than the final cause to which all human endeavour should be directed, in the use of reason to criticize revealed doctrine and especially miracles and, perhaps above all else, in the revulsion felt by many Christians at the intolerant acts committed in the name of a God of love, a revulsion which led them to subordinate doctrine to ethics, and to advocate toleration. Deism was also fostered by the discovery of foreign cultures, notably in the East, which showed that men could be devout believers in God and lead moral lives without the benefit of the Christian revelation and its dogmas. The same sources helped to foster a similar, if more discreet, lesson of social criticism, showing that stable government and the happiness and prosperity of the individual could be achieved without despotic rule, and with a minimum of imposed authority. When the foreign culture was not authentically discovered, it was invented, hence the popular stories concerning the voyages of Frenchmen to fictitious Utopias, such as Gabriel de Foigny's *La Terre australe connue* (1676) and Denis Veiras's *Histoire des Sévarambes* (1677). Like his precursor Marana, the author of *L'Espion dans les cours* (1684),

Montesquieu scored by bringing his foreign travellers to France, and by thorough documentation of the visitors' background.

Montesquieu's greatest contribution to French thought was in the field of political ideas. In *Lettres persanes* his characters discuss seriously the problem of the best form of government, and look in particular to England where monarchs who rule arbitrarily are deposed or executed, but the monarchy remains a respected institution. Bossuet had seen in this a sign of the inherent political instability of the English nation, but for Montesquieu the English have an enviable secret. The clue was later given him by Bolingbroke, who assured him that the basis of the English monarchy was the separation of powers and division of sovereignty among the legislative, executive and judiciary bodies. Montesquieu incorporated this factually erroneous notion into his major work, *De l'esprit des lois* (1748), whence it passed into the American Constitution. Both in *Lettres persanes* and in *De l'esprit des lois*, however, Montesquieu also harks back to the myth of the 'good old days' when the French king supposedly shared his power and responsibilities with the nobility in an ideal feudal society. The feudal myth had already inspired other discontented aristocrats, including Fénelon and the memoralist Saint-Simon, who published his *Histoire de l'ancien gouvernement de France* in 1727. In the main, however, *De l'esprit des lois* strikes a remarkable balance between the idea of a rational, universal principle of justice providing a yardstick with which to judge the positive laws by which a nation is governed, and recognition of the multifarious causes which make positive legislation evolve. Montesquieu showed himself in this to be one of the first thinkers of his day to recognize that the world in which he lived was not a static but a developing one.

Voltaire (1694–1778) dominates the entire *philosophe* movement, but it is not wholly arbitrary to see his career as dividing into two periods, one before and one after 1750. His fervent commitment to the righting of particular wrongs, and his battle against the Infamous Beast of clerical and political tyranny, date from after 1750. Before that date he was the pungent satirist of *Lettres philosophiques* (1734) and the somewhat complacent moralist of *Le Mondain* (1736) as well as, as will be seen, the French champion of Locke and Newton. *Lettres philosophiques*, in its critical aspects, inculcates the lesson of deism as *Lettres persanes* had done. It also offers the French reader object lessons, drawn from the example of his nearest neighbour, of how intellectual, religious and political affairs should be conducted. The boldest section of the work is probably that in which the author shows that the price of liberty, if reform is not put in hand from within, may be civil war and even regicide. This is the most inflammatory passage in any published work of the period, although similar sentiments had been expressed in the *Mémoire* or *Testament* of the atheist parish priest Jean Meslier (1678–1733), copies of which were in circulation in the late 1720s. Voltaire later edited and published Meslier's work in a somewhat watered-down form.

All the authors we have been considering were critical of metaphysical speculation, which they regarded as useless, and none more so than Voltaire who never tired of condemning the bogus profundity and obscure jargon, as he saw it, of the professional philosophers. Nevertheless, the period was rich in speculative philosophy, which influenced even those who appeared most scornful of it. Cartesian rationalism received an original development in the work of Malebranche and Leibniz: the latter, although not a Frenchman, wrote some of his works in French and soon became influential in France. English thought, represented by Locke and later by Newton, constituted another important foreign influence. Finally, there was a remarkable revival of naturalism, which seemed at first to have been eclipsed by the success of mechanism.

Nicolas Malebranche (1638–1715) was an Oratorian priest whose main work is the *Recherche de la vérité* (1675–6). Instead of simply drawing on Cartesianism for apologetic purposes as Bossuet and Fénelon had done, he set out to make it into a religious philosophy. The greatest difficulty he, along with other late seventeenth-century rationalists, found in Cartesianism was the distinction of the two 'substances', thought and matter, and more particularly the problem of their interaction. Malebranche replaced Descartes's solution by the doctrine of 'occasionalism' which had been put forward by a Belgian Cartesian, Arnold Guelincx (1625–69). Occasionalism states that our decision to act is not the real cause of the action: the decision and the action are simultaneously caused by a decision by God to put His laws of motion into operation. Although this apparently required God to perform a continual series of miracles, Malebranche saw it as a better solution than going back to the naturalist concept of an inherent 'vital force' which is responsible for the movement of physical objects. Malebranche also criticized Descartes's theory of innate ideas. It was implausible of Descartes to suggest that the mind could contain every conceivable idea it might ever have, and illogical of him to claim that the presence of an object could be the cause of an idea, even in the limited sense of triggering off one that was already in the mind. Only God can be the real source of our ideas, giving us a mental picture of the object on each 'occasion' on which our senses are confronted with it. In Malebranche's phrase, we 'see everything in God', who alone has true knowledge of things. God, for Malebranche, was above all the source of order in the universe. The concept of order as the ground of all truth and wisdom dominates his thought. The religious application of his philosophy is based on a clear distinction between the realms of nature and grace, a subject treated in his *Traité de la nature et de la grâce* (1680). The fact that we do not always have clear and distinct ideas, or make decisions and have desires which are in harmony with the ideal of order God has set before us in the physical universe, is due to the corruption of reason and will and the confusion of the senses, as a result of the Fall, and points to the need for salvation which can only be gained through recourse to God's revealed word in Scripture and the traditions of the Church.

Malebranche's is the most successful attempt to harmonize revealed Christianity and mechanistic science, and was more effective than Descartes's own philosophy in presenting the universe of the mechanists as an object of devout contemplation. Malebranche's influence has never been fully documented, but it was clearly immense. His theory of the origins of error is echoed in Fontenelle's *De l'origine des fables*; his theism impressed Bayle and saved him from complete scepticism; Voltaire ridiculed his doctrine of 'seeing things in God', but found that he was hard put to it to improve on it when he came to write the article 'Idée' in his own *Dictionnaire philosophique*. It was Malebranche, as much as the natural law jurists of the seventeenth century, who influenced Montesquieu's belief that the unvarying operations of nature revealed by science should constitute a model for human affairs. Like Malebranche, Montesquieu acknowledges that it is human infirmity which stands in the way of this ideal; where he differs is in turning to science rather than to religion for a remedy, for in *De l'esprit des lois* Montesquieu adopts towards society the same standpoint as the physical scientist with his knowledge of the workings of cause and effect.

Leibniz (1646–1716) took much the same starting-point for his philosophy as Malebranche had done, but against Malebranche he held that the synchronism of mind and body is pre-established. God has fixed once and for all the laws which govern movement in the physical universe, and relate thought and action, and so does not need to perform a continual series of miracles. But his greatest influence on French thought in the first part of the eighteenth century came through his *Essais de Théodicée*, written in French and published in 1710, which promulgated the doctrine known as philosophical optimism. Leibniz's work was a reply to Bayle's pessimistic contention that evil is inherent in nature, and only intelligible if we accept the heretical Manichean view that the fate of mankind is the subject of a perpetual tug of war between the equal and opposing forces of God and the Devil. Leibniz argued that in order not to simply reduplicate Himself, God had necessarily to create a finite world which fell short of perfection in every one of its parts; nevertheless, each part belongs to a harmonious plan, and we only see evil because we cannot grasp the contribution of the part to the general good. Leibniz's solution to the problem of reconciling the existence of a just God with the fact of evil and suffering in the world was popularized by Pope in his *Essay on Man*. In this form it influenced Voltaire whose earlier works, notably the last of the *Lettres philosophiques* where he attacks Pascal's view of the human condition, and the poem *Le Mondain* where he gives voice to a somewhat complacent view of the pleasures of existence, express a point of view against which he later reacted. Other aspects of Leibniz's thought, especially those concerned with the sensitivity of matter, and his profound understanding of movement as a process of organic change rather than mechanical displacement, were not taken up by French thinkers until the second half of the eighteenth century.

Voltaire regarded Malebranche, and later came to regard Leibniz, as the epitome of the professional philosopher who dresses up useless abstractions in pretentious jargon. His own sympathies went to the more down-to-earth English philosophers who restricted themselves to what could be verified by observation, Locke and Newton. Locke's work, the *Essay on Human Understanding* (1690), was in fact well known in France long before Voltaire praised it. It had been publicized in a long article in the *Bibliothèque universelle* two years before it appeared in print, and had inspired a systematic work of philosophy, the Jesuit Father Buffier's *Traité des premières vérités* (1724), which Voltaire himself admired. Locke's theory of knowledge, which made thought dependent on material supplied by the senses, the senses being the source and not simply the occasion of our ideas, was widely held to have refuted Descartes's doctrine of innate ideas. Locke's sensationalism also reinforced the empirical scientific method of Newton, whose *Principia* (1687) completely contradicted the premisses and conclusions of Cartesian physics, notably in the case of the movement of the heavenly bodies, which Newton ascribed to gravitational attraction across empty space. Here the English influence was markedly less successful. Cartesian physics had, it is true, moved some way towards empiricism. Whereas Descartes made reason alone the means of scientific discovery, his disciples referred to experience. But experience meant to them common-sense observations rather than controlled experiment. In his *Traité de physique* (1671), the most representative work of post-Cartesian physics, Jacques Rohault defended Descartes's theory that all movement in the universe is that of particles of matter impelling one another in a series of whirlpools, but instead of using the philosopher's own argument, namely that since extension is identical with matter, any other form of movement is metaphysically inconceivable, Rohault appealed to common-sense observation which appears to show that objects only do in fact move when something is impelling them. This same point of view was adopted by Fontenelle who, in the influential post of permanent secretary of the Académie des Sciences, effectively prevented the discussion of Newton's theories in scientific circles. Newton's idea of gravitational attraction seemed to Fontenelle to be a mere name for something that could not be explained mechanically, a throwback to the 'occult causes' of the scholastics. This view prevailed until Voltaire, prompted by Maupertuis, one of the few Newtonians in the Académie, successfully argued that a concept which could be expressed in a mathematical formula of such complete generality, and from which the correct results always followed, must represent a 'real' phenomenon in nature, and that it was the Cartesians, with their vortices and *matière subtile*, who had recourse to 'occult causes'. Voltaire thus made sure that the phenomenon of attraction would at least be seriously investigated by French scientists.

Voltaire was aware that the ideas of both Locke and Newton could be given a materialist interpretation. He flirted with materialism when discussing these thinkers in *Lettres philosophiques* and in his unpublished *Traité de métaphysique* (written 1734), before coming out against it in *Éléments de la philosophie de Newton* (1737). Materialism did not attain the status of a coherent philosophy until after 1750 when, as we shall see, French thinkers achieved a remarkable adumbration of the modern idea of evolution. The concept was, however, as old as antiquity, and the Epicurean philosophy which Gassendi revived and made respectable in the seventeenth century was originally a materialist system. In the last years of the century, materialism was given a new impetus by a development of Cartesianism which led it away from the direction originally given to it by its founder. Descartes had set side by side, as it were, a universe of matter in motion, and an immaterial realm of thought. It was clearly possible to reject this stark dualism, and to regard matter as a subjective perception of the mind (idealism) or thought as an aspect of matter (materialism). Berkeley (1685–1753) in England took the former course, but he was much less influential in France than those thinkers who turned Cartesianism into a materialist philosophy, representing the universe as a self-sustaining system of matter in motion which does not require the idea of God to support it. This version of Cartesianism, found particularly in Meslier's manuscript *Testament*, became confused with the philosophy of Spinoza. In his *Ethics*, posthumously published in 1677, Spinoza held that there are not two substances, as Descartes had claimed, but one; that God cannot be a cause outside nature, but must be immanent in nature; that nature, in all its aspects, is the manifestation of God. Spinoza's philosophy, though extremely influential, was almost wholly misunderstood until the very end of the eighteenth century. It was identified by some with the views of the *nouveaux cartésiens* who had eliminated God from nature, but others believed that by affirming God's immanence in nature Spinoza had revived the essentially un-Cartesian doctrine of the world soul which had come down from Italian naturalism. Naturalist ideas had indeed been kept alive in France despite Cartesian opposition, by Gassendi (in spite of his mechanistic astronomy), by Cyrano de Bergerac, and in the *Essais de physique* (1677) of Gassendi's disciple Gilles de Launay. After 1680, they were reinforced by accounts of oriental religions in which a concept similar to that of the world soul was said to be found; in the eighteenth century naturalism was further propagated through the influence of the English writer John Toland, whose *Letters to Serena* (1704) and *Pantheisticon* (1720) were known in France, and through the works of the Italian Francesco Colonna (1644–1726) who spent most of his life in France. According to Colonna there are two kinds of matter, one insensible, and the other capable of motion and feeling. He distinguished between plants, animals and men solely in terms of their capacity for feeling. Both naturalist and Cartesian varieties of 'Spinozism' were propagated above all in the numerous treatises which, throughout the early part of the eighteenth century, circulated clandestinely in manuscript copies: more than a hundred of these are extant, in over four hundred copies.

The ideas of Locke and Newton were indirectly drawn into this movement towards materialism. In a digressive passage of his *Essay on Human Understanding* Locke had raised the question whether matter can think and had concluded that God could, if he wished, 'super-add' thought to matter. Voltaire used this in *Lettres philosophiques* merely to embarrass the theologians, but in the clandestine *Mémoire* of Jean Meslier it was given a 'Spinozist' bias. In similar vein, Newton spoke of gravity as a property not inherent in matter, which God had nevertheless given to matter. This raised the question: why should it not be inherent in matter? What the orthodox Cartesian scientists denounced as a regression to the 'occult causes' of scholastic philosophy began to be regarded by others as 'occult' in a different sense – one of nature's secrets, not God's. The only way to solve the mystery was to 'approfondir l'idée que nous avons de la matière'. These words of d'Alembert constitute the whole basis of the new journey of intellectual discovery on which the *philosophes* embarked in the 1740s and 1750s.

The *Philosophe* Movement

By 1750 the *philosophe* movement could be said to have come of age. There are early signs of this in the essay *Le Philosophe*, published in 1743, which gives us the first formal definition of the new type of thinker and human being. The essay was written by Dumarsais, one of the contributors to the great *Encyclopédie ou dictionnaire raisonné des sciences et des arts* (Vols 1–7, 1751–7; Vols 8–17, 1765), which has been called the epitome of the Enlightenment, and it was the need to band together to defend the enterprise against the hostile criticism of the authorities which from 1752, for a time at least, welded the *philosophes* into a coherent group. The avowed aim of the editors, Diderot and d'Alembert, was to 'changer la manière *commune* de penser', and this meant to a large extent consolidating existing gains rather than opening up new horizons. Montesquieu's views find a large place in the political articles mostly contributed by his disciple Jaucourt, while the work as a whole assumes that Voltaire's deism, with its emphasis on toleration and reason and its satire of revelation, priestly cults and unnecessary dogmas, is the norm among 'reasonable men'. Occasionally, however, its pages reflect the bolder views which found full expression in the remarkable crop of publications, beginning in the 1740s, in which authors such as Maupertuis, La Mettrie, Robinet, Buffon, D'Holbach, Helvétius and, above all, Diderot, adumbrated a materialist philosophy which eventually split the *philosophe* movement, alienating two of its most outstanding figures, Voltaire himself and Rousseau. Setting aside the hesitations in their views and the divergences of detail between the different authors, the materialists can be seen to share a common conviction: that while Locke and Newton have laid the foundations of a true theory of knowledge and an accurate scientific method, they have not (as Voltaire believed) said the last word on all that men need to know; that the search for truth can only proceed by setting aside the metaphysical concepts of God and the spiritual soul; that reason and observation make us conclude that the universe is not a static mechanism created by a purposive deity, but a self-sustaining system of matter in perpetual transformation, in which man himself is, like all other forms of life, an evolutionary product of his material environment.

The materialists reached this conclusion through brilliant conjecture based on the growing body of knowledge concerning the life sciences, notably geology, botany and biology. Geological research pointed to the great changes which had taken place in the earth's crust, and indicated that the fossils found in rock strata were evidence that the forms of life had evolved over an immense period of time; Linnaeus's classification of plants by their distinguishing features also showed the difficulty of drawing firm boundaries between the species, while geneticists proposed that all species could in fact be derived by differentiation from a common pair of ancestors; practical observations and experiments showed that the animal and vegetable realms were continuous, and also that some species were self-regenerating. The mechanical model which had served so well in astronomy and physics now appeared inadequate to deal with this evidence of the inner dynamism of organic life, and to answer the fundamental questions which the life sciences raised concerning the origins of life, the variety of species, the principle of their reproduction and growth, and even the question of the connection between inert and living matter. The French materialists made an important break with the mechanism of their predecessors. Although explanations of a mechanical type loom large in Maupertuis's ideas on natural selection, in La Mettrie's physiology, and in D'Holbach's biology, these writers knew that before they could give a satisfactory account of the phenomena which they were trying to interpret, it was first necessary to discover the primary qualities of matter, so as to know what it was that had to be measured. Thus they allowed themselves to be stimulated by the naturalist tradition, opposed to mechanism: this had kept alive the notions of the universal sensitivity of matter and the diffusion throughout nature of an animating principle, which Diderot was eventually to reinterpret in a more truly scientific manner.

The French materialists provoked much the same kind of opposition from the Church as Darwin's documentation of the evolutionary theory in the *Origin of Species* was to do in England a century later. There is of course no reason of principle why a materialistic, evolutionary science should not coexist, as it often does today, with religious faith. The *philosophes* themselves did not become materialists in order to advance the cause of atheism, as is sometimes said; they attacked religion because the religious account of the universe was in conflict with the facts as they observed them, and incompatible with the further progress of scientific knowledge. They were not in fact all atheists. If the position of Buffon in his great *Histoire naturelle* (1749–88) or of Robinet in *De la nature* (1761) is equivocal, Charles Bonnet's *La palingénésie philosophique* (1770) reads like something by Teilhard de Chardin in its rhapsodic description of man's advance up the evolutionary ladder to ultimate union with God. Nor were leading ecclesiastics always happy about the repression of truth to which the Church committed itself when it had Diderot imprisoned, subjected Montesquieu's *De l'esprit des lois* to censure on the grounds of 'Spinozism', condemned Helvétius's *De l'esprit*, and held up the publication of the *Encyclopédie* for seven years, or with the obscurantist insistence by religious apologists that the whole history of creation, and of the origins of life, all the truths of geology, biology and even astronomy (Copernicus's works were still on the Roman Catholic Index of prohibited books) were literally recorded in the Bible. Yet all this is understandable when we recall that the materialist *philosophes*, in contradicting the literal account of the creation in the first chapter of *Genesis*, were removing at one blow the whole basis of the Church's authority over men's lives, and the very foundations of the faith that still sustained the majority of Frenchmen even if it had become largely meaningless to the educated élite.

In their doctrine of man, the materialist *philosophes* stressed the dependence of the mind on physical causes and held that all actions are physically determined. They were disciples of Locke, but whereas Locke had maintained that some operations of the mind are innate, his French followers believed that ideas are only a reflection of objects perceived by the senses. In his *Traité des sensations* (1754), Condillac denied that the mind contains any principle of rationality which interprets the evidence of the senses, and he defined the mind as an agglomeration of ideas which were once sense impressions. Helvétius went further, in defining man, in *De l'esprit* (1758), as a pleasure-seeking and pain-avoiding animal whose ideas are the result of his environment. The materialists further rejected in the name of the laws of mechanical causality the Christian idea of free will, which presupposes a spiritual soul free, under grace (and to an extent dependent on one's particular theological views), to accept or refuse God's commands independently of material contingency. Once the theological notion of free will was discarded, the concepts of 'virtue' and 'vice' as normally understood could be said to be meaningless: men, according to Diderot, are not virtuous or vicious, but fortunately or unfortunately born. The materialists' determinism did not, however, make them into fatalists. True devotees of Enlightenment, they held that knowledge of the causes which determined human thought and action should be employed to the end of personal happiness and the social good. This brings us to one of the most interesting aspects of the thought of this period – the tension between the determinism of the *philosophes* and their reforming ideals.

Although sometimes obscured by the ambiguity of the term 'nature', which could refer either to a system of material causes or to a moral norm, this tension came increasingly to the fore as time went on. It faced the *philosophes* with an ethical dilemma: how to reconcile the social end they believed to be appropriate to man, with their equally convinced belief in the natural right of the individual to give free play to his instinctive energies. On the one hand, they stressed the role of social engineering, the possibility of using education, public opinion, the laws and punishments to 'modify' the man who was unfortunately born in order to coerce him into becoming a useful member of society. On the other hand, they rehabilitated the passions, protesting against Christian asceticism and the miseries to which its inhibitions gave rise, and representing the passions not simply as the motive force of acts of benevolence, but as the sign of a healthy material organism. La Mettrie in his *Traité du bonheur* (1748) and much later in the century the Marquis de Sade (1740–1814) in his novels *Justine* (1795) and *La Nouvelle Juliette* (1797), pointed up the difficulty: since man is a part of nature ('un être formé par la nature et circonscrit par elle', as D'Holbach wrote), then everything he does must be natural; why then, if a man is so constituted as to find pleasure in crime, should he be punished? Sade's provocative depiction of the trials of virtue and the triumphs of vice may not be sufficient to make him the representative figure some scholars claim, but his work provides a valuable counter to the complacency of those authors who, ignoring the realities of life around them, declared that man was steadily and inevitably progressing towards perfect happiness and social harmony, a view nobly expressed under the shadow of the guillotine by Condorcet in his *Esquisse d'un tableau historique des progrès de l'esprit humain* (posth. 1795).

La Mettrie (1709–51) was a consistent materialist in all his writings, notably *L'Homme machine* (1747) which, despite its title, owes much more to its author's interest in the life sciences than to Cartesianism. But the most doctrinaire statement of materialism is the atheist D'Holbach's *Système de la nature* (1770). D'Holbach (1723–89), an Alsatian nobleman, is important for his translations of foreign scientific publications, for his numerous scientific contributions to the *Encyclopédie*, for the violent diatribes which he wrote in support of Voltaire's campaign against the Infamous Beast of clerical oppression and despotism, for his part in the publication of the clandestine manuscripts which had circulated earlier in the century, and in particular for grouping round him most of the major thinkers of his day in what became known as the 'côterie holbachienne'. The most outstanding figure, however, was Denis Diderot (1713–84), who was more tentative but also more open-minded than D'Holbach, and who ranks with Voltaire and Rousseau as one of the three great figures in eighteenth-century thought. It was he who gave the most boldly imaginative and the most prophetic account of the evolutionary theory. Diderot speculatively located the principle of organic change in the structure of matter itself, and also defined the true experimental method. He was able, while being inspired by the vitalist concept in naturalism, to purge naturalism of its pre-scientific and magical associations. He never ceased to develop intellectually, as can be seen if we trace his ideas through from the *Pensées philosophiques* (1746) and *Lettre sur les aveugles* (1749) via the *Pensées sur l'interprétation de la nature* (1754) and his contributions to the *Encyclopédie*, to the fascinating set of dialogues known as the *Rêve de d'Alembert* (written 1769, publ. posth.). In these works, Diderot anticipated not only the Mendelian theory of genetic inheritance and the Darwinian doctrine of natural selection (in both of which he had Maupertuis as a precursor), but also much of the modern theory of matter, including the notions of potential and kinetic energy, the atom and the cell. In the *Pensées sur l'interprétation de la nature* he gave a classic definition of the experimental method, stressing the need for imaginative hypotheses as well as well-devised experiments tested by accurate observations, in a way that avoids the pitfalls of a narrow 'Baconian' kind of empiricism, and the temptations of the Cartesian 'esprit de système'. Even so, his keenest concern was with moral problems, and he pondered more deeply than any of his contemporaries the eighteenth-century dilemma of the individual and the social. He agreed with his fellow materialists on the need for social engineering, but was distressed by the tendency of some of them to depersonalize human beings. He particularly objected to Helvétius's claim that since the differences between individuals are entirely due to environment, they can be levelled out by education: Diderot stressed instead the inherited nature of mental and moral characteristics. He showed an unusual awareness of the role of unconscious mentality, and was particularly sensitive to the moral problems posed by the presence of physically or psychologically abnormal individuals in society, and especially by the genius who might have to be considered to be above the law if he were not to be deprived of his special qualities. Diderot further objected to Helvétius that the doctrine that everything in nature is a sensitive organism does not imply that the needs of a man are the same as those of an oyster or a plant: 'Je suis homme, et il me faut des causes propres à l'homme.' Man is a complex organism, whose consciousness is not simply a bundle of sensations. He differs from the machine or the animal in possessing reason, and reason is more than a highly evolved form of instinct. In the *Rêve* Diderot drew on recent discoveries of brain surgery to affirm that man is a psycho-physiological unity. He did not try to reduce consciousness to physical changes in the brain, and came close to the modern view that the mind, while it depends on the mechanisms of the brain, harnesses them and is not determined by them.

It is the image of the social reformer, the campaigner against social prejudice, miscarriages of justice, religious intolerance and political tyranny, which is responsible for Voltaire's reputation as the dominant figure among the *philosophes*. The wit and verve of his *contes*, the eloquence of his *Traité sur la tolérance* (1763), the vituperative satire of the *Sermon des cinquante* (1762) and other works aimed at the Infamous Beast, in short the passion with which, from 1749 onwards, Voltaire pursued the practical ends of the Enlightenment, almost persuade one that he deserves it. But his thought is by no means the equal of Diderot's or Rousseau's. Instead of looking upon scepticism, like Diderot, as 'le premier pas vers la vérité', Voltaire was too fond of invoking it as a means of closing the door on further argument. The very title of *Le Philosophe ignorant* (1766) betrays this characteristic tendency. Although he enlisted the materialist *philosophes* in his campaign against *l'Infâme*, he was bitterly opposed to their ideas, which he contested point by point, denying that the senses and experience can ever tell us what matter is; that the human mind can penetrate to the causes of phenomena; and that the way in which we interpret nature can affect our knowledge of our moral duties, which comes from God.

Voltaire's positive ideas at this period are best gathered from the *Poème sur la loi naturelle* (1752), the *Dictionnaire philosophique* (1764–5) and the *Histoire de Jenni* (1775), one of his last *contes*, which he wrote with the specific intention of refuting atheism. In these works, Voltaire maintains that everything in nature displays art and purpose, and is the work of a 'divin fabricateur', gives voice to fluctuating opinions on the soul and on free will, first shelves the problem of theodicy in favour of positive action to reduce the amount of suffering in the world, at the time of *Candide* (1759), then finds himself forced to reconsider it when faced with the arguments of D'Holbach's *Système de la nature*. To D'Holbach's contention that Christianity, including its moral teaching, has been the cause of human suffering and crimes, and that man must build his moral code on the basis of observation and experience, Voltaire opposed his deep-rooted conviction that the highest ideas and most authentic motives of morality cannot subsist without belief in God, and that the Christian ethic is the supreme expression of the moral law. In reply to the atheists' argument that the existence of evil and suffering is incompatible with belief in God, Voltaire came close to using the kind of arguments he had derided when satirizing Leibnizian optimism in *Candide*. But the weight of his argument falls on the necessity of belief, not simply in God, but in a God who punishes and rewards in an after-life, if human existence is not to relapse into a state of moral and social anarchy. While his premiss is open to question (though it seemed much less so at a time when all but the most advanced thinkers rejected Bayle's 'paradox' concerning a society of virtuous atheists, than it does today), the genuineness of Voltaire's conviction is undeniable. His is an authentic pragmatism, the only philosophical position, perhaps, logically compatible with the scepticism which remained with him throughout his long career.

Despite his bitter anti-clericalism (which, for a short period in the 1760s, became a violent attack on Christianity and even on the person of Christ), Voltaire thus maintained belief in God and a universal morality against the atheist materialists. The same was true of the third great figure in the *philosophe* movement, Jean-Jacques Rousseau (1712–78). He shared many of the views that the *philosophes* had in common, and he contributed to the *Encyclopédie*, but his relationship with the *philosophes* was uneasy and he finally became convinced that they, as well as the common enemy, the Church, were persecuting him. Attacking Voltaire's deism as an intellectual abstraction and not a lived experience, Rousseau stressed (notably in the *Profession de foi du vicaire savoyard*, 1762) the primacy of inner conviction, and the personal relationship of the individual mind to God over rational argument, although he concurred with the deists' reasons. Like Voltaire, he believed in man's need to act by the inner light of conscience, but he thought of conscience as a God-given principle in the individual rather than as a sense of what is universal in human experience. In all this, he was just as much opposed to the materialists who subjected man to the determinism of physical forces, and the *Profession de foi* is in part a refutation of Helvétius. Rousseau's enthusiastic language and his rehabilitation of religious sentiment do not, as was once believed, make him an anti-rationalist. Reason, conscience and free will are seen by him as a triad of faculties with which God has endowed man so that he can attain perfection. Man's failure to achieve perfection Rousseau blamed on man himself and not, as the *philosophes* tended to do, on the machinations of a self-interested élite of priests and despots.

The central theme of many of his works is the problem of how man, having been thus endowed, has fallen into his present state of subjection to tyranny – in the *Discours sur les sciences et les arts* (1750), to the tyranny of false values nurtured by the kind of technologically orientated civilization which alienates man from his true nature; in the *Discours sur l'origine de l'inégalité* (1755) the tyranny of institutions founded on, and which perpetuate, social inequalities. Although Rousseau's is ultimately a political solution, he approaches it from the standpoint of a moralist. His account of man's degeneration from a hypothetical state of nature in which he was happy and independent, into his present unhappy condition, parallels the biblical account of the Fall and Redemption, but without the doctrine of original sin or the need for a Redeemer other than man himself. Rousseau imagines man as an animal capable of satisfying his instinctive needs so long as external nature does not prevent him, but gifted with the potential for reason which, while it differentiates him from the other animals, cannot be developed until he forms societies. Life in society, however, also develops his passions, and faces him with the problem of translating his original innocence into morality and his independence into the kind of freedom which is compatible with the freedom of others.

In *Du contrat social* (1762), Rousseau goes on to imagine the kind of State men would have set up had they, so to speak, taken the right turning instead of creating, as the second *Discours* describes, the institutions which have enslaved them. The fundamental principle is that of a pact which both seals association and places government in the hands of the entire community – earlier contract theorists had distinguished between a pact of association and one in which the community as a whole gives authority over into the hands of a few of its members. Sovereignty in Rousseau's conception is exercised through a Government which is only an executive agency. The community legislates in the interest of the General Will, a difficult concept which appears to represent a norm of 'rightfulness' inferred from the goodwill which the members of the community ought always to bear to one another. The institutions of Rousseau's ideal State are framed so as to give 'men as they are' the laws they need in order to develop their potential as rational, moral and social beings in accordance with their true nature. Rousseau thus transcends the *philosophes*' dilemma concerning the conflicting claims of social engineering and the free play of personal desires, by calling on men to submit voluntarily to the common rule of the kind of community which will enable them to realize their full potential of virtue. The institutions of his ideal State have been seen by many historians as totalitarian, but Rousseau's conception was not a totalitarian one. If his State is vested with a strong authority over its members it is because, like all the *philosophes*, Rousseau believed that a strong framework of law was necessary to protect individual liberty against the capricious rule of despots: only in comparatively recent times has it been at all widely asserted that liberty is incompatible with authority, or that it can only flourish in a state of anarchy.

Du contrat social (little read, incidentally, before the Revolution) was described by one contemporary reader as both useless and dangerous. Useless as a blueprint for practical politics (it requires a community small enough for all the citizens to be able to meet at any time in order to pass legislation – Rousseau's model here was the Swiss cantons rather than his native Geneva), its major premiss that popular sovereignty is the only legitimate basis of government was highly provocative. Other examples of the political thought of the *philosophes* tend to be either more practical or more utopian than Rousseau's conception of the State. In *Lettres philosophiques* Voltaire drew attention to the broad social basis of parliamentary representation in England (which he exaggerated) and to the more equitable system of taxation compared with the French, while Diderot called for a widely based suffrage, to include shopkeepers and farmworkers, together with a form of government which, while exercising strong authority, would protect 'the sacred right of opposition'. Diderot, apart from treating political matters in articles for the *Encyclopédie*, also made extensive contributions to Raynal's *Histoire des deux Indes* (especially to the third edition in 1780) which strongly attacks tyranny. Voltaire, on the other hand, having hinted in *Lettres philosophiques* that regicide and rebellion on the English model might be the only alternative to the reform of French political life by its leaders, soon became the advocate of enlightened absolutism, the monarch being, like Frederick II of Prussia, surrounded by *philosophe* advisers. Montesquieu, for his part, wanted to restore the power of former institutions: the ideas of *De l'esprit des lois* tend to support the alliance between the nobility and the magistrates who composed the *parlements* and considered themselves 'the eyes and conscience of the king', which came into being in the course of the eighteenth century. There was not a great deal here which represented a call for radical change and much that positively opposed it. The 'revolutionaries' among the *philosophes* were those like Jean Meslier in his *Mémoire* and Morelly in his *Code de la nature* (1755). The thesis of these works is that men have the choice between slavery and the abolition of private property. This was not a notion likely to carry much practical weight. The major *philosophes*, including even Rousseau, defended the institution of private property, and it has indeed been argued that only the man of property, for which he was unbeholden to a capricious monarch or a feudal overlord, had any chance of initiating the reforms which, rather than a revolutionary upheaval, it was the aim of the movement to bring about.

The *philosophes* were in any case restrained from advocating direct action by their belief (realistic or pessimistic according to one's point of view) that a great many people were, and were bound to remain, ignorant and the slaves of their passions. Some, notably Voltaire, also feared the social consequences of the diminution of the pool of unskilled labour through education. Enlightenment, however far it might or might not be desirable to take it, required in the long run something more than a campaign of pamphlets: it needed a total overhaul of the system of public education, and no Government was likely to initiate sweeping educational reforms which would undermine its own basis. Even after the expulsion of the Jesuit Order from France in 1762, public education remained a mainly clerical monopoly.

The responsibility of the *philosophes* for the Revolution, then, was probably restricted to creating the climate of opinion which made revolution possible. But for many Frenchmen at the time (and for many historians since) the Revolution exemplified the evils of Enlightenment. Paradoxically, their views were not very different from those of Robespierre, who denounced the materialist *philosophes* in the language of Rousseau's Savoyard curate. Both Rousseauism and materialism exerted an influence beyond the Revolution and into the nineteenth century. Rousseau's political writings were, indeed, pillaged to serve the purposes of revolutionary orators and counter-revolutionary polemicists alike. His greatest influence, however, came through his personal writings, the *Lettres à Malesherbes* (1762), *Rêveries du promeneur solitaire* (1776–8) and *Confessions* (posth. 1781–8). In contrast to Diderot's scientific approach to the problem of personality, Rousseau studied the nature of the self in his own acts of experience, as had Montaigne; but seeing life exclusively as it was mirrored in his own self-consciousness, he paved the way for Romantic subjectivism, even more than through his sensitivity to the beauties of nature and his morbid enjoyment of emotional and spiritual dissatisfaction, which anticipates the *mal du siècle*.

Romanticism also drew on the materialist tradition to which Rousseau was opposed. The last years of the eighteenth century witnessed a revival of personal magic and occult philosophy which looks like a throwback to the Renaissance but which was in fact indirectly fostered by the interest the materialists showed in naturalism. Diderot and Swedenborg, different as they were in almost every other respect, both saw nature as a unity, the spiritual being for Swedenborg an extraordinary manifestation of the material, perceptible only to an exceptionally endowed individual. Swedenborg's influence on the Romantics is well known. Authentic scientific materialism continued to flourish: here, Diderot's heirs are Jean-Baptiste Monet (known as Lamarck) whose works straddle the period before and after the Revolution, and who bears the greatest name in the history of evolutionary theory before Darwin, and Pierre-Jean-Georges Cabanis (1757–1808) whose *Rapports du physique et du moral de l'homme* (1802) is one of the classic documents of materialist thought. Cabanis carried on Diderot's interest in the problem of personality, ascribing consciousness to a central ego, identified with the brain which he called 'an organ whose peculiar function is to produce thought'. Cabanis is one of the founders of modern medical psychology; he was also one of the group known as the *idéologues*, who held that social organization can be studied scientifically in terms of the natural laws governing human relationships. In the nineteenth century the *idéologues* influenced the socialist thinker Henri de Saint-Simon and the philosopher Maine de Biran. Thus the impetus given to French thought by the *philosophes* was by no means abruptly arrested by the Revolution and the reaction against the Enlightenment which followed it.

Bibliography

In reading further about the topics treated in the foregoing pages, it will be helpful to have at hand a good general history of philosophy, e.g. F. Copleston, *A History of Philosophy*, Vol. 4: *Modern Philosophy from Descartes to Leibniz* (New York, 1963), which is both lucid and comprehensive. The importance of scientific thought in the period makes H. Butterfield, *The Origins of Modern Science*, new ed. (London, 1957), essential reading.

There is regrettably no general work on seventeenth-century French thought comparable in quality to those which will be mentioned on the eighteenth century. The symposium on 'La Philosophie au XVIIe siècle' in the periodical *Dix-septième siècle*, nos. 54–5 (Paris, 1962), can, however, be recommended as a helpful introduction. The position for the eighteenth century is very different. The relevant chapters of R. Niklaus, *A Literary History of France: The 18th Century* (London, 1970), constitute an excellent initial guide. Then French thought is brilliantly situated in the context of the general movement of European thought by N. Hampson, *The Enlightenment*, Pelican History of European Thought (Harmondsworth, 1968), as well as studied at closer range in J. H. Brumfitt, *The French Enlightenment* (London, 1972). These books would form a good approach to J. Ehrard, *L'Idée de nature en France dans la première moitié du 18e siècle* (Paris, 1963; republished in an abridged form, 1970), a masterly and original treatment of a whole range of problems extending well beyond both the strict subject of the book and its implied chronological limits. In comparison, E. Cassirer's *The Philosophy of the Enlightenment* (Princeton, 1951; orig. German ed. 1932), though much praised, treats ideas too schematically, and without adequate reference to context or chronology. On a larger scale, P. Gay, *The Enlightenment: An Interpretation*, 2 vols (London, 1966–9), is a rich source of bibliographical information about the period, as well as in part a reply to L. G. Crocker, *The Age of Crisis*, 2 vols (Baltimore, 1959–63), which has been criticized for dwelling too much on the negative aspects of eighteenth-century thought, but nevertheless points up well the period's fundamental dilemmas.

In default of a good general work on seventeenth-century thought, there is much to be said for beginning by reading Aldous Huxley, *The Devils of Loudun* (London, 1952), both as a reminder that not everything in the intellectual history of the period is to be accounted for in terms of the rise of scientific rationalism, and for its penetrating insight into what the author rightly calls 'that strange agglomeration of incongruities, the seventeenth-century mind'. Following this, there are various ways of investigating the changing attitudes which led to the eventual dominance of rationalism. Chronologically, one would begin with the sixteenth-century Italian sources whose background is well explained by P. O. Kristeller, *Renaissance Thought: the Classic, Scholastic, and Humanistic Strains* (New York, 1961), and then go on to the influences that undermined traditional modes of thought, discussed by R. H. Popkin, *A History of Scepticism from Erasmus to Descartes*, rev. ed. (The Hague, 1964), before coming to J. S. Spink, *French Free-Thought from Gassendi to Voltaire* (London, 1960), an altogether indispensable account of the development of naturalism and rationalism in the period. Among the major authors met with in Spink's earlier pages, Cyrano de Bergerac should be read in H. Weber's edition of *L'Autre Monde* (Paris, 1958), because of its excellent introduction. R. Lenoble, *Mersenne ou la naissance du mécanisme* (Paris, 1943), analyses many relatively inaccessible texts, while the symposium *Pierre Gassendi, sa vie et son œuvre* (Paris, 1955) is a good way of approaching another author whose actual works are hard to come by. There is also a specialist study, O. R. Bloch, *La Philosophie de Gassendi* (The Hague, 1971). The culminating point of Popkin's book, and the nodal point of Spink's, is Descartes. L. Roth, *Descartes' Discourse on Method* (Oxford, 1937), can still be read with profit, but the best introduction is A. Kenny, *Descartes, a Study of his Philosophy* (New York, 1968), and the best short account in French is F. Alquié, *Descartes, l'homme et l'œuvre* (Paris, 1956).

A lively introduction to the writings of the *libertins* is to be had from A. Adam, *Les Libertins* (Paris, 1964), an anthology of extracts. The relationships between the 'libertins érudits', as well as their ideas, are exhaustively studied by R. Pintard, *Le Libertinage érudit pendant la première moitié du dix-septième siècle* (Paris, 1943). Like H. Busson in his wider-ranging but more discursive *La Pensée religieuse française de Charron à Pascal* (Paris, 1933) and *La Religion des classiques* (Paris, 1948), Pintard sees these authors as deliberately bent on the subversion of religious faith. The same tendency marks the celebrated work of P. Hazard, *La Crise de la conscience européenne*, 3 vols (Paris, 1934; subsequently publ. in one vol. without notes and references), an extremely readable but, in the light of later work (much of it inspired by Hazard himself), somewhat superficial account of the mutation of the religious values of the seventeenth century into the secular humanism of the eighteenth. The reaction, in which the thinkers in question are seen as authentic if heterodox Christians, has probably gone too far, for the issues were in fact never so sharply drawn between genuine belief and subversive intent. It has, however, brought important gains, particularly in the case of Bayle. E. Labrousse, *Pierre Bayle* (The Hague, 1963–4), is a monumental work; the second volume, *Hétérodoxie et rigorisme*, convincingly rescues Bayle from the charge of complete scepticism and stresses the positive aspects of his thought, while W. Rex, *Pierre Bayle and Religious Controversy* (The Hague, 1965), puts beyond doubt the importance of Bayle's Calvinist background for a true understanding of his ideas. Another important work is C. B. Brush, *Montaigne and Bayle: Variations on the Theme of Scepticism* (The Hague, 1966), which also usefully complements Popkin's *History of Scepticism* already cited. There are two useful volumes of selections from Bayle's massive writings: *Œuvres diverses* (Paris, 1971) and the *Dictionnaire historique et critique* (Paris, 1974), both ed. A. Niderst. With the other major thinker of the 'crise', Fontenelle, the problem concerns not so much his religious position as his scientific stance. There is an excellent short introduction to his ideas in M. Bouchard, L'*'Histoire des Oracles' de Fontenelle* (Paris, 1947), which goes well beyond the promise of its title. J. R. Carré, *La Philosophie de Fontenelle, ou le sourire de la raison* (Paris, 1932), is a work by a philosopher which takes no account of (indeed it denies) any development in Fontenelle's thought. It should be complemented and where necessary corrected by A. Niderst, *Fontenelle à la recherche de lui-même (1657–1702)* (Paris, 1972), which adopts the historical method (and is of interest beyond the terminal date indicated in its title). On the problematical issue of Fontenelle's position in the dispute between Cartesians and Newtonians, on which Niderst has some good pages, there is a valuable and original discussion in L. Marsak, *Fontenelle and the idea of science in the French Enlightenment* (Philadelphia, 1959), and many important references in Ehrard's *L'Idée de nature* praised at the beginning of this bibliography.

On the ethical thought of the period under review, there is no lack of books describing the attitudes of the more celebrated 'moralistes' of the seventeenth century. The two most stimulating are P. Bénichou, *Morales du grand siècle* (Paris, 1948), and A. J. Krailsheimer, *Studies in Self-Interest from Descartes to La Bruyère* (Oxford, 1962). The 'moralistes' were largely concerned with contemporary life styles, but there was also an abundant literature which dealt with moral philosophy of a more technical kind. Here, the book by A. Levi, *French Moralists and Theories of the Passions, 1585–1649* (Oxford, 1964), is fundamental, but those who find it hard going might do well to seek out the long article by J. E. D'Angers, 'Le Renouveau du stoïcisme au XVIe et au XVIIe siècles' in the proceedings of the Seventh International Congress of the Association Guillaume Budé published at Paris in 1964, which will help to break the back of the subject.

The origins of Jansenism are steadily being laid bare in a series of monographs under the direction of J. Orcibal. Meanwhile L. Cognet, *Le Jansénisme* (Paris, 1961), gives a succinct account of its history, and C. Delassault, *La Pensée janséniste en dehors de Pascal* (Paris, 1963), a useful introduction to some of its less well-known figures. The interpretation of Jansenism continues to be controversial, the more so since the Jansenists differed widely amongst themselves on many points. An excellent comparison of the Jansenist and Jesuit standpoints is to be found in R. R. Palmer, *Catholics and Unbelievers in 18th Century France* (New York, 1961). See also W. E. Rex, *Pascal's Provincial Letters* (London, 1977), for a succinct and up-to-date discussion of the matter. In the eighteenth century itself, Jansenism was more important from a political than from a doctrinal point of view, as can be seen from L. Taveneaux (ed.), *Jansénisme et politique* (Paris, 1965), which includes an anthology of texts. The (somewhat paradoxical) relationship between some Jansenist ideas and those of the Enlightenment is among the topics investigated by E. D. James, *Pierre Nicole, Jansenist and Humanist* (The Hague, 1972).

Work on Pascal, of course, often casts light on Jansenism. Here J. Miel, *Pascal and Theology* (Baltimore, 1969), and P. Sellier, *Pascal et Saint Augustin* (Paris, 1970), are noteworthy. Both books also give the lie to those who have held that Pascal was not competent to write on theological matters. The principal authority on Pascal is J. Mesnard, whose pioneering *Pascal, l'homme et l'œuvre* (Paris, 1951) and

Les Pensées de Pascal (Paris, 1957) are both excellent. The symposium *Pascal présent* (Clermont-Ferrand, 1962) contains valuable articles by R. Pintard and H. Gouhier exploring the relationship between Pascal's ideas and contemporary free-thought. The historically important text of the Port-Royal edition of the *Pensées* has been republished in a critical edition by G. Couton and J. Jehasse (Paris, 1971). Its influence is the subject of a valuable study by M. Vamos, *Pascal's 'Pensées' and the Enlightenment: The Roots of a Misunderstanding*, Studies on Voltaire and the Eighteenth Century, Vol. XCVII (Banbury, 1972). In general, however, the student should use the text established by L. Lafuma, which supplants all previous versions; it is most conveniently to be found, along with Pascal's *Lettres provinciales* and other major writings, in the 'Intégrale' edition (Paris, 1963).

The transformation of moral ideas at the end of the seventeenth century and the beginning of the eighteenth is studied by R. Mauzi, *L'Idée du bonheur au 18e siècle* (Paris, 1960). The same work also underlines the shift from an other-worldly to a this-worldly attitude to human existence, which caused many Catholic apologists of the period to give hostages to secularism. The orthodoxy of Bossuet and the conflicts into which it led him is illuminated by T. Goyet, *L'Humanisme de Bossuet* (Paris, 1965), and by J. Truchet, *La Prédication de Bossuet*, 2 vols (Paris, 1960). On his political ideas, J. Truchet, *Politique de Bossuet* (Paris, 1966), is a useful commentated anthology. For Fénelon's political ideas, see C. Urbain's edition of *Écrits et lettres politiques* (Paris, 1920). Fénelon's clash with Bossuet over quietism, and his political views, make him one of the most interesting figures of his period, but there is no good short introduction to his thought. J. L. Goré, *L'Itinéraire de Fénelon* (Paris, 1957), is excellent but very long. Nor is there yet a reliable monograph on Saint-Évremond.

The influence of Descartes pervades the latter part of the seventeenth century, as that of the rationalist thinkers whom he influenced does the beginning of the eighteenth. F. Bouillier, *Histoire de la philosophie cartésienne*, 2 vols (Paris, 1868), is still useful, although it has been superseded on many points, notably by Spink in his chapter 'The Fortunes of Descartes'. An important Cartesian topic has been investigated by L. C. Rosenfield, *From Beast-Machine to Man-Machine* (New York, 1941), and H. Kirkinen, *Les Origines de la conception moderne de l'homme machine* (Helsinki, 1960). That Cartesianism was not identical with the philosophy of Descartes is one of the points well made by G. Rodis-Lewis, *Descartes et le rationalisme*, 'Que sais-je?' series (Paris, 1966). Mme Rodis-Lewis discusses Malebranche, Spinoza and Leibniz, all of whom were highly influential in France. She has edited the *Recherche de la vérité*, 3 vols (Paris, 1946–67). F. Alquié, *Le Cartésianisme de Malebranche* (Paris, 1974) is important, and his *Malebranche* (Paris, 1977) an ideal introduction. The extent of Spinoza's influence is shown by P. Vernière, *Spinoza et la pensée française avant la Révolution*, 2 vols (Paris, 1954) (cf. also J. Moreau, *Spinoza et le spinozisme*, 'Que sais-je?' series (Paris, 1971)), and that of Leibniz by W. H. Barber, *Leibniz in France from Arnauld to Voltaire* (Oxford, 1955).

The influence of thinkers who were mainly outside the Cartesian orbit is also important when we come to assess the ideas of the early *philosophes*. Fénelon's influence is considered by A. Chérel, *Fénelon en France au 18e siècle* (Paris, 1917), and Bayle's by P. Retat, *Le Dictionnaire de Bayle et la lutte philosophique au 18e siècle* (Paris, 1971), and by H. T. Mason, *Pierre Bayle and Voltaire* (Oxford, 1963).

Foreign influences are treated by N. L. Torrey, *Voltaire and the English Deists* (New Haven, 1930), and by D. Schlegel, *Shaftesbury and the French Deists* (Chapel Hill, 1956). A thorough study of Locke's influence in France remains to be written. A useful summary, noting the comparative lack of French interest in Hume as well as Berkeley, can be found in J. A. Perkins, *The Concept of the Self in the French Enlightenment* (Geneva, 1969). On the *philosophes* themselves, an excellent introduction is provided by A. Adam, *Le Mouvement philosophique dans la première moitié du 18e siècle* (Paris, 1967), which includes a concise survey of social and political conditions, and of major philosophical themes. On Montesquieu, R. Shackleton, *Montesquieu, a Critical Biography* (Oxford, 1961), is the authoritative work but see also L. Althusser, *Montesquieu, la politique et l'histoire* (Paris, 1959). G. Lanson, *Voltaire* (Paris, 1906), and R. Naves, *Voltaire, l'homme et l'œuvre* (Paris, 1942), have held their value, but the essential study is R. Pomeau, *La Religion de Voltaire* (Paris, 1956), which traces Voltaire's intellectual development in masterly fashion and brings out clearly the extent and depth of his fundamental deism.

Pomeau has an excellent chapter on Voltaire and the materialists, whose thought is now being given something like its due by scholars. Here the most important books are that by Ehrard already praised, and J. Roger, *Les Sciences de la vie dans la pensée française du 18e siècle* (Paris, 1963), which between them have revolutionized scholarly perspectives on eighteenth-century French thought. Also stimulating is A. Vartanian, *Diderot and Descartes* (Princeton, 1953), although it overstresses the role of Cartesianism in the formation of late eighteenth-century materialism, and a more apt title for it would have been 'From Descartes to Diderot'. A. C. Kors, *D'Holbach's Coterie: An Enlightenment in Paris* (Princeton, N.J., 1976), situates the materialists in their social context and illuminates their ideas and beliefs. One way of gaining access to the ideas of the materialists is to read the remarkable introduction by J. Varloot to his edition of Diderot, *Le Rêve de d'Alembert* (Paris, 1971), followed by the texts and introduction in R. Desné, *Les Matérialistes français de 1750 à 1800* (Paris, 1965). A good range of materialist texts (often, however, in the form of excerpts) is published by Les Éditions Sociales of Paris. These include writings of La Mettrie, Helvétius and D'Holbach as well as Diderot. Other important editions include La Mettrie's *L'Homme machine* by Vartanian (Princeton, N.J., 1960) and his *Traité du bonheur*, ed. Falvey (Banbury, 1975), D. Holbach's *Le Bon Sens*, ed. Deprun (Paris, 1971), and especially Meslier, *Œuvres*, ed. Deprun and others, 3 vols (Paris, 1970). In addition, there are modern editions of the most important clandestine manuscripts of the period, *L'Âme matérielle, Traité des trois imposteurs* and *Le Militaire Philosophe*.

Diderot's capital place in the development of materialist thought is well appreciated by Varloot in the introduction just mentioned. Intimations of materialism in his contributions to the *Encyclopédie* are highlighted by J. Proust not only in *Diderot et l'Encyclopédie* (Paris, 1962), but also in the shorter *L'Encyclopédie* (Paris, 1965) which stands with J. Lough, *The Encyclopédie* (London, 1971), as the best account of the whole undertaking. Diderot's own thought is best approached by way of J. Thomas, *L'Humanisme de Diderot*, 2nd ed. (Paris, 1938), which has stood the test of time well despite the subsequent discovery of important new material; H. Dieckmann, *Cinq leçons sur Diderot* (Geneva, 1959); the valuable chapters in J. Fabre, *Lumières et romantisme* (Paris, 1963), and A. M. Wilson, *Diderot* (New York, 1972).

The best approach to Rousseau is through the Pléiade edition of his *Œuvres complètes* (Paris, 1959–69); among the excellent introductions by well-known scholars, that by M. Raymond to the *Rêveries* is outstanding. There are very useful editions of *Du contrat social* and *Rousseau's Religious Writings* by R. Grimsley (Oxford, 1968 and 1970). Rousseau has been called an individualist and a collectivist, a rationalist and a man of feeling. These to some degree unavoidable dichotomies are well dealt with by E. Cassirer, *The Question of Jean-Jacques Rousseau*, trans. P. Gay (New York, 1954; original German ed. 1932), by P. Gay, *The Party of Humanity* (London, 1964), and especially by J. McManners, *The Social Contract and Rousseau's Revolt against Society* (Leicester, 1968). J. Plamenaz has an excellent chapter on Rousseau in his *Man and Society*, Vol. I (London, 1963). A fuller, more expository guide is to be found in J. H. Broome, *Rousseau, a Study of his Thought* (London, 1963). R. Derathé, *Jean-Jacques Rousseau et la science politique de son temps* (Paris, 1950), is fundamental. P. M. Masson, *La Religion de Rousseau*, 3 vols (Paris, 1916), contains much that is valuable but badly overstresses Rousseau's 'emotionalism'. R. Grimsley, *Rousseau and the Religious Quest* (Oxford, 1968), is excellent. The best examination of Rousseau's philosophy as an expression of his personality is P. Burgelin, *La Philosophie de l'existence de Jean-Jacques Rousseau* (Paris, 1952). The vagaries of some Rousseau criticism show how much work still needs to be done on the notion of 'sensibilité' in the eighteenth century. R. Mortier, *Clartés et ombres du siècle des lumières* (Paris, 1969), argues cogently against splitting the period chronologically into an 'age of reason' followed by an 'age of sensibility', as also does Gay in *The Party of Humanity*. Mortier's book also contains a fascinating account of the history of the idea of 'les lumières' in the period.

With the approach of the Revolution, French eighteenth-century thought begins to resemble that 'agglomeration of incongruities' which Huxley found at the beginning of the previous century. Evidence of this is to be found in R. Darnton, *Mesmerism and the End of the Enlightenment in France* (New York, 1969), and in the classic work of A. Viatte, *Les Sources occultes du romantisme français*, 2 vols (Paris, 1928). The contribution of the *philosophes* to the Revolution is still controversial. On the role of the *idéologues*, there is a book by C. H. Van Duzer, *The Contribution of the Idéologues to the French Revolution* (Baltimore, 1933), but their actual ideas are perhaps best approached through the now rather old book by R. Picavet, *Les Idéologues* (Paris, 1891), and the writings of Cabanis, whose *Rapports* . . . is included in Vol. 1 of the edition of his *Œuvres philosophiques* by C. Lehec and J. Cazeneuve (Paris, 1956).

In addition to the works mentioned in this essay, many valuable contributions are to be found in the specialist periodicals and series of monographs in which work on the subject is constantly being brought up to date. Mention may be made in particular of *Dix-septième siècle*, *Dix-huitième siècle* and the volumes of *Studies on Voltaire and the 18th Century*, *Diderot Studies* and *Annales de la Société Jean-Jacques Rousseau*.

6 French Thought in the Nineteenth and Twentieth Centuries

D. G. CHARLTON

Introduction – the Intellectual Context

French thought in the nineteenth century was marked first and foremost by intensified complexity and conflict. Certainly the preoccupations of the pre-revolutionary period persisted into the new age. On the one hand, the conservative orthodoxy of Catholicism continued to be defended and was restated even more firmly by such Traditionalist thinkers as Joseph de Maistre, Bonald and Lamennais (and, more lyrically, in Chateaubriand's *Le Génie du christianisme*). On the other hand, the empirically minded, agnostic, reforming tradition of Voltaire and the *philosophes* was maintained by *idéologues* like Destutt de Tracy and Cabanis and was extended – dramatically so – by the positivists from Henri de Saint-Simon and Auguste Comte to Littré, Renan, Taine and others in the later years of the century, and by socialistic reformers such as the Saint-Simonians, Fourier, Étienne Cabet, Pierre Leroux, Proudhon and Louis Blanc. Even the Eclectic group of thinkers, led by Victor Cousin and including Laromiguière, Royer-Collard and Jouffroy, was continuing the eighteenth-century search for a natural religion and a natural ethic, as it elaborated a middle way between the religious approach of the Catholics and the scientific and reforming approach of the *idéologues*, positivists and socialists. Yet the undeniable continuities were all but submerged by the changes – social and economic, educational and institutional, amongst others – ushered in by the Revolution and its aftermath. Thus, for example, the horrors of the Terror appeared to many observers in the new century to have stemmed from unbelief in France – 'Société sans dieu, qui par Dieu fus frappée', as Hugo was typical in asserting. Both conservatives and reformers assumed that ideas govern history, that political order can only be built upon philosophical order, and consequently the yearning for a more stable society transmitted to philosophical dispute a sense of urgent, practical significance. Moreover the harsh economic and social consequences of the industrial revolution in France reinforced the sense of crisis, for society as well as for the individual, attached to debates that were in part old and yet were now renewed by the differences of context and historical moment. Furthermore, the issues were intrinsically major and far-reaching – science and religion, free will and determinism, history and progress, economic *laissez-faire* and the new socialism, social conservation and social revolution – and it is thus no wonder that this generation should have felt it lived at a turning-point in history and ideas alike, in an age of revolutions that were intellectual no less than political and economic. In this situation some felt saddened by uncertainty and doubt – like the deeply liberal Quinet when he declared that 'aujourd'hui le monde entier est le grand sépulcre où toutes les croyances, comme toutes les espérances, semblent pour jamais ensevelies' (or like Stendhal's Bishop of Besançon in *Le Rouge et le noir* as he evokes 'cet état d'inquiétude et de doute qui, au dix-neuvième siècle, désole des esprits tristes et ennuyés'). Others were daunted and yet more hopeful – like such Romantics as Hugo and George Sand or Lamennais in his later years when he observed:

> Le vieux monde se dissout, les vieilles doctrines s'éteignent; mais, au milieu d'un travail confus, d'un désordre apparent, on voit poindre des doctrines nouvelles, s'organiser un monde nouveau . . .

Yet others such as Saint-Simon and Comte were transparently confident, sure that their own doctrine had arrived on its crucial historical cue and was uniquely fitted to rise to the level of the times.

The expansion and reform of higher education under Napoleon and the Restoration monarchy added to the argumentative confusion. The number of academic posts in philosophy, history, science and other disciplines was steadily increasing; unlike almost every major French thinker prior to 1789, their nineteenth-century successors commonly held university chairs. As to philosophy itself, under measures taken from the 1830s onwards by a philosopher-administrator like Victor Cousin, it almost pre-empted the role in the French educational curriculum that had belonged to religion. Effectively, society was subsidizing intellectual controversy, and consequently philosophical activity both increased and became far more professional – perhaps not with wholly beneficial results, for many nineteenth-century works of philosophy lack lucidity in both content and style. And another important factor that encouraged franker debate was the gradual extension of intellectual freedom; though there were certainly moments of panic-stricken repression, toleration was much increased over the century, and freedom to publish led naturally to a still larger diversity of ideas.

The nineteenth century was also a time – throughout Europe – of rapidly widening knowledge, and philosophical, religious and social thought was immensely affected by new facts, arguments and theories drawn from the natural sciences, from historical and philological studies and (by the mid-century) from the new 'human sciences' of sociology and psychology. A first example is offered by the renewal of studies in the history of philosophy. The ideas of earlier and of contemporary foreign thinkers were perhaps more widely diffused than at any time since the Renaissance – first by Madame de Staël and Constant, then Cousin and his Eclectic group, Quinet and Michelet (both much affected by current German learning), and many others throughout the century. Spinoza, Kant, Herder, Hegel, Schopenhauer, Feuerbach, Hartmann; Mill, Carlyle, Spencer, Darwin: these are only the most influential of the foreign writers who were admired, attacked and invoked, often in somewhat partial interpretations, and whose thought served to renew old arguments and to prompt new syntheses.

Even more decisive in some ways was the expansion of the natural sciences. From the creation of the École Polytechnique in 1794 and the re-establishment of the Académie des Sciences in 1795 onwards French science gained an international authority with physicists like Ampère and Sadi Carnot, chemists like Gay-Lussac, and biologists such as Lamarck, Geoffroy Saint-Hilaire and Cuvier, and the second half of the century saw Berthelot's creation of thermochemistry, Pasteur's foundation of bacteriology and fermentation science, Claude Bernard's pioneering studies on the liver and autonomic nervous system, and Henri Becquerel's work on the radioactivity of uranium. Moreover, whereas eighteenth-century science was only familiar to an educated minority, in the new era the power of science was clear to everyone through its everyday applications – in much improved surgery and medicine, in gas lighting, in industrialization and the railways.

This 'scientific revolution', as it has been fairly described, had vast intellectual repercussions, and so also did the concurrent expansion of historical and philological studies that was encouraged by both

Napoleon and later Governments, which created chairs of history in every university and in a variety of practical ways promoted scholarly research. Renan rightly refers to the 'revolution' (the same recurrent word) 'qui depuis 1820 a changé complètement la face des études historiques'. Some scholars were above all narrative historians – Thierry and Fustel de Coulanges, for example; others, such as Guizot, Michelet and Tocqueville, had a more theoretical interest in French or European history and studied historical developments in order to discern their underlying causes and phases; yet others, like Quinet, were above all philosophers of history, deriving from the examination of man's past a variety of theories concerning human progress and decadence. And not least important (and intellectually disruptive in their quiet, erudite way) were the *philologues*, probing into the remoter past, discovering more of the civilizations of Greece, Rome, India, China and elsewhere and of Nordic, Celtic and Romance folklore. Fostered by the foundation in 1795 of the École des Langues Orientales Vivantes and inspired by the example of distinguished German scholars such as Creuzer and Görres, French philology – by which was meant not only the mainly linguistic study of our own time but a much wider study of the history of the human spirit over the ages, centred in particular on the history of religions – made striking advances over the century. Through the many translations of ancient texts and the studies of ancient cultures by orientalists like Eugène Burnouf (a major mediator of Buddhist thought) and of hellenists like Louis Ménard, friend of Leconte de Lisle, French thought and literature alike were enriched by what Quinet called '[une] Renaissance orientale'. And as with the sciences and the history of philosophy, so too this influx of new ideas about history deeply affected the thinkers of the day. Some found in history a new creed based on the idea of progress, whilst others tried to rejuvenate the religions of antiquity and the alleged insights of primitive mythologies. Yet others attempted to denigrate Christianity by comparing it with other faiths, either to show that all share the same superstitions or that earlier ethics are superior to Christian morality, and still others were to draw from their survey of the history of civilizations a pessimistic doctrine of the inevitable decline and fall of all human societies. And – perhaps the most explosive of the *philologues*' contentions – Christianity was challenged to withstand the same dispassionate historical scrutiny as was applied to other creeds.

For all these reasons therefore, and for others, this chapter concerns a period of marked intellectual upheaval no less than of political, economic and social upheaval, a time of fierce ideological conflict leading to an ever extremer polarization of attitudes as between Catholics and freethinkers, spiritualists and materialists, right-wing conservatives and left-wing reformers and socialists. Any selective survey will thus inevitably oversimplify; it can at best seek to sketch certain major trends and isolate – even if misleadingly at times – some salient areas of controversy. The bibliography indicates guides to the history of philosophy in the more technical, professional sense; this chapter itself attempts to evoke the intellectual history of the time in more general terms, as it impinged upon a far wider public than the philosophers themselves.

It is rash to indicate any single theme underlying this survey: for the reasons suggested above all is complexity. But if such a theme can be found, it perhaps lies in the continuing tension between the scientific humanism of *idéologues*, positivists and others and the spiritualistic and often explicitly religious humanism of Catholics, idealist philosophers and others. In the earlier part of our period the initiative seemed to lie above all with the former outlook: Christianity was under attack; the scientific method was triumphantly extended to include the 'human sciences'; this was an 'age of systems', a time when new creeds in place of the old were widely propounded. The later years of the period, from around 1870 onwards, witnessed a strong critical reaction to these systems and creeds, a striking revival of Catholic thought, and – through the impact of Bergson in particular – a broadly diffused renewal of the idealist tradition in French philosophy. Clearly, such a schema greatly simplifies: in the earlier years, for example, Catholics, Eclectics and a philosopher like Maine de Biran were fighting against the new positivism; in the later years positivists like Durkheim and Lévy-Bruhl were still more influential than their predecessors, and Marxism, belonging to the same general tradition, has remained a major protagonist in present-day conflicts. Yet – treated with every caution – it may provide a preliminary orientation.

Science and the Rise of Positivism

The nineteenth century was pre-eminently the time when scientific humanism came of age as a fully argued philosophy – thanks, first, to the *idéologue* group, but more emphatically to the positivists who continued and extended its scientific approach.

The rise of positivism had two sources above all. The first was the 'scientific revolution' already outlined: its immense achievements naturally fostered an enthusiastic confidence in science and even a belief that scientific knowledge alone is reliable. Some – including such scientists as Cuvier, Ampère and Pasteur – might protest that there are moral and spiritual truths beyond the reach of the scientific method, but far more – including such men of letters as Hugo and Zola – were persuaded that science held out an unlimited future of material progress and human happiness. Secondly, the positivist philosophers inherited the empiricist tradition of the eighteenth century and earlier. From Bacon in England and Gassendi in France onwards an increasing number of thinkers had argued that knowledge is most reliably – or, indeed, uniquely – to be gained by deduction from what we observe. Descartes and other rationalist philosophers had contended, on the other hand, that we can attain *a priori* knowledge, prior to sense-experience; for Descartes the model was mathematics, and just as one can progress from the axioms of Euclid to other truths in geometry, so in other areas, he argued, reason can work from 'innate ideas' or from allegedly self-evident truths such as the existence of the self to arrive at other truths, especially in the realm of metaphysics. By contrast, the empiricists – Locke, Hume and others in England, and Fontenelle, *philosophes* like Condillac, Helvétius and others in France – took as their model branch of knowledge the science of physics, impressed above all by the discoveries of Newton. Man is born without 'innate ideas', a blank sheet, and all he can know must be *a posteriori*, after sense-experience (with the sole exceptions of the tautologous truths of mathematical and logical systems). 'Nothing in the mind which was not first in the senses'; 'nous n'avons point d'idées qui ne nous viennent des sens', in Condillac's words – such is the empiricist view and the basis of positivism, the theory of knowledge which the nineteenth-century positivists explored and expanded.

The first to do so was Henri de Saint-Simon (1760–1825). After a career as a soldier fighting with the Americans in the War of Independence and as a financial speculator, he became persuaded in middle age that his true mission was as an intellectual called to establish a new philosophy as the essential foundation for a new social reconstruction. Though influenced strongly by the *philosophes*, he claimed that their work was largely critical and that a positive system must be created in place of the Christian creed they had destroyed. And from his early writings – such as the *Introduction aux travaux scientifiques du dix-neuvième siècle* (1807–8) and his *Mémoire sur la science de l'homme* (1813) – onwards he asserted, as these titles imply, that the future lies with the sciences. Not only must they be unified and given a systematic theoretical basis; above all, the scientific method must be extended to man and human society, and this new 'science de l'homme' will rapidly lead to a scientific reorganization of society, to be hastened by giving far greater political authority to scientists and especially to the new 'social scientists'. In economic affairs likewise power should be given to the well-informed; he anticipated both socialism and a belief in what has since been called 'the managerial revolution' and urged that the workers and the managers – industrialists, bankers and the like – should unite (against such parasites as kings, aristocrats and soldiers, who draw on a wealth they do nothing to create) to enforce a more just and effective system of production and distribution – views which led Marx and Engels to praise him as 'with Hegel, the most encyclopedic mind of his age'. He differed from the socialists later in that he denied that there is any necessary clash of interests between the capitalists and the workers and he also defended the right to private property where it is used for the benefit of society as a whole, but he can rightly be seen as a major precursor of socialism in his demand that social and economic affairs should be planned by the State for the physical, mental and moral well-being of 'la classe la plus nombreuse et la plus pauvre'. Nor did Saint-Simon neglect the importance of religion as a moral spur and a unifying 'spiritual power', and he therefore sketched a new creed to replace Christianity and what he believed its socially reactionary and other-worldly attitudes. This was originally to have been a purely scientific and even materialistic system, enshrining Newton as religious prophet, but in his final years he developed the ideas of his *Nouveau Christianisme* (1825). Here he strongly criticized both Catholics and Protestants and claimed that Christ's own essential teaching is a gospel of charity and fraternity:

> Dieu a dit: *Les hommes doivent se conduire en frères à l'égard les uns des autres;* ce principe sublime renferme tout ce qu'il y a de divin dans la religion chrétienne.

The 'golden age', he asserted, does not lie in the past, in the Garden of Eden, or in a future life in heaven, but in an imminent earthly future when social order and fraternity have been established. Saint-Simon did not live to elaborate the teaching, worship and organization of the new Christian Church, and it was thus left to such disciples as Enfantin and Bazard to start churches and even a religious community and to develop the doctrines of the Saint-Simonian religion in the form which was to attract, amongst many others, the writers of the *Jung Deutschland* movement and several of the French Romantics. Indeed, the very varied theories of this warm-hearted and almost too fertile social thinker were to be widely influential – in the development of socialist ideas; in economic action under Louis-Napoléon; even in the building of the Suez and Panama Canals. And in philosophy likewise he provided the general ideas that others would restate in a more detailed and forceful way.

Chief amongst these thinkers was Auguste Comte (1798–1857), who began his career as secretary to Saint-Simon, and whilst the extent of his own originality can be debated, it is hard to deny that Comte gave the positivist philosophy its fullest exposition – to the point that he is commonly considered its intellectual 'father'.

Comte's work, pursued with relentless devotion from the age of nineteen, when he joined Saint-Simon, until his death, can be divided into two parts. In the first, best represented by his *Cours de philosophie positive* (1830–42), his concerns were with philosophy and the establishment of social science: this was the work which affected Littré and John Stuart Mill so profoundly and, after Harriet Martineau's abridged translation of the *Cours* in 1853, English writers such as Frederic Harrison, G. H. Lewes and George Eliot. In later life, after a short but intense relation with Clotilde de Vaux, he turned much more to social ethics and especially the creation of a new 'religion of humanity', which he expounded in works like his *Système de politique positive* (1851–4) and *Le Catéchisme positiviste* (1852). Now, he claimed, having already transformed science into philosophy, he would – a new St Paul – transform philosophy into religion. We shall observe this attempt later; here we are concerned with his earlier expression of his 'positive philosophy'.

Comte's central purpose was to establish a philosophy of science that would provide the basis for a scientific reordering of society. In the very first *leçon* of the *Cours* he announced his discovery of 'une grande loi fondamentale' governing the development of the human mind throughout history – his famous 'loi des trois états'. In every department of thought and life man moves in turn from the 'theological' to the 'metaphysical' and finally to the 'scientific, or positive' state. The theological mode of thinking assumes that we can attain an 'absolute' knowledge of the first or ultimate causes of events. In particular it attributes final causal power to one or more 'supernatural agents' whose intervention explains many of the occurrences within the natural order – thunder, for instance, being the expression of the anger of the gods and plague a divine punishment for sin. This 'state' also determines men's thought about their own life and society; thus, for example, the ruler within society and the husband within the family are conceived of as godlike, authoritarian figures. The second, metaphysical, state – which supervened in Europe from the time of the Renaissance – is a modification of the first. Men still believe they can know first causes and attain an absolute knowledge of ultimate reality, but now causal explanations are in terms of 'abstract forces' instead of 'supernatural agents'. The special error of this phase, Comte argues, is to attribute independent existence and power to our own abstractions, whether notions in science like 'the ether' or metaphysical concepts like 'nature'. Gradually, however, in at least some areas men's minds have advanced to the third state, 'l'état positif'. Men now recognize the impossibility of absolute knowledge, of the search for first and final causes, and by relying on observation combined with reasoning they concentrate on discovering the 'effective laws' determining the world of phenomena. This scientific approach, renouncing all theological or metaphysical explanations, has largely triumphed in the natural sciences, Comte continues: thus, astrology has given way to astronomy, alchemy to chemistry, and so on. But it must now be extended to the study of man and society – through the progress of physiology and above all through a new science – sociology – 'la physique sociale'. To establish this one missing science is, he says in the *Cours*, 'le plus grand et le plus pressant besoin de notre intelligence' and 'le premier but de ce cours, son but spécial'. Only by becoming fully scientific will the study of society be able to predict future phenomena, like the other sciences do, and thereafter adopt suitable social policies. 'Science, d'où prévoyance; prévoyance, d'où action': this was his motto from the start and remained his dominant concern as in turn he provided an allegedly historical demonstration of the truth of the 'loi des trois états', as he examined the methods of the various sciences in order to identify the theological and metaphysical errors still persisting in them, as he classified the sciences in their proper order, moving from the most simple to the most complex (and most useful to man) – mathematics, astronomy, physics, chemistry, biology, sociology – and as, above all, he discussed the methodology of social science. Observation is its basic method, though he fears this may be mere sterile 'empiricism' unless directed by some hypothesis one wishes to verify; experimentation is also possible in so far as we can note what happens in a society when some special factor, like a revolution, interferes with its normal functioning; and comparison is another fruitful method – between human and animal societies and between coexisting human societies. But above all he looks to a new method, peculiar to sociology: the historical method. By studying the history of societies up to the present we can verify the laws of 'social statics', of the factors that keep societies relatively stable, and discover the laws of 'social dynamics' – the factors producing change, the tendencies that have grown stronger and will become dominant in the future.

Such were the main ideas that earned him the status of a 'founder' of sociology and which led Mill and others to describe him as 'one of the principal thinkers of the age'. Yet it is not only his later religious teachings which may be thought to go beyond the limits of the positivist theory of knowledge from which he began. In his haste to reorder society and because of his rather dogmatic *esprit de système* he tends in this direction even in the *Cours*. In the first place, one may suggest, he was all too often uncritical and unscientific in his attitude to facts and has fairly been accused of selecting the facts which supported his generalizations and ignoring those which did not, especially in his treatment of history. Secondly, his theories rested upon certain assumptions which he failed to justify – that ideas determine history, for example, or that each stage in the evolution of mankind is rigidly determined and inevitable – and he never demonstrated that his laws were more than a pattern he was imposing on history or, alternatively, that they were validated by their predictive success. And above all perhaps he took it for granted that sociology can in fact be fully scientific. Early in the *Cours* his claims for it were relatively modest and he admitted that its methods were imperfect, but by the end he was attributing to it 'autant de positivité et plus de rationnalité qu'aucune des sciences antérieures déjà jugées par ce Traité'. His reduction of historical change to a few dominant laws, the dogmatism of his social theories, and the authoritarian organization he later devised for his religion – which he claimed to be no less scientific – were all symptoms of his 'scientism' – an exaggeration of the positivist position that greatly overrates both the potential range of science and the degree of certainty to which its conclusions can lay claim. Thereby he illustrates one of the most significant developments in nineteenth-century French thought – the move, in positivistic thinkers, towards an extreme confidence that science can solve all mysteries and answer all questions with assured authority.

Other positivists illustrated the same tendency, but directed to different ends, and none more so than Taine during the later part of the century. Hippolyte Taine (1828–93) lost his Christian faith as a youth and rapidly moved to a positivist outlook under the influence of the *idéologues*. He achieved repute in a surprisingly broad range of subjects – in literary history with his studies of La Fontaine (1853), Livy (1856) and his celebrated *Histoire de la littérature anglaise* (1864); in philosophical polemics with *Les Philosophes classiques du dix-neuvième siècle en France* (1857), an attack upon the unscientific philosophy of the Eclectics; in art history, in which he was professor at the École des Beaux-Arts from 1864; in psychology with *De l'intelligence* (1870); and in history with his vast and controversial work on *Les Origines de la France contemporaine* (1875–93). But underlying this diversity there was a unity of aim – to explore human psychology, either directly or as expressed in literature, art and historical action – and a unity of method, for in all these areas he sought to justify and apply a single, universal approach based in the first place on the positivist theory. He appeared to many of his contemporaries as the embodiment of scientific humanism in its most high-minded and uncompromising form. Thus, for example, he stood alongside Théodule Ribot and Pierre Janet as a champion of scientific psychology, and even if much of *De l'intelligence* may now be outdated, it helped to replace the previous reliance on mere introspection (as exemplified by the Eclectics) by an emphasis on experiment, the search for causes, the physiological basis of personality and the study of pathological cases – though this attitude not surprisingly intensified his opponents' accusations of materialistic determinism. Even literature, and especially the novel, he urged, should be a 'collection of experiments', a contribution to a scientific understanding of human nature, revealing the physical and psychological determinants of man's behaviour – a view accepted by literary admirers like Flaubert, Zola and Maupassant. 'Toute réalité est perçue expérimentalement par l'homme', he asserted – a view which led him to reject the ideas of God, the supernatural, the soul, and its immortality. He even contended, most notoriously, that our moral decisions are as causally determined as any other natural event: 'le vice et la vertu sont des produits comme le vitriol et le sucre' – albeit he argued that moral responsibility remained compatible with determinism as he conceived it. He brought a similar attitude to his study of literature and art, and his method was well stated in the celebrated Introduction to his *Histoire de la littérature anglaise* in which he gave his ambitious and stimulating ideas for the future of a 'scientific' cultural history, a study which he believed could lead us to discern the great causal factors operating in history as a whole. Examination of the literary 'documents' will lead us to a deeper understanding of their author's psychology, and this, complemented by scrutiny of the facts of his life and personality, will in turn permit us to grasp the 'faculté-maîtresse' – the disposition of thought and feeling – which determines his work. And we can then go further still and 'explain' this by reference to three great 'causal facts', the author's 'race', 'milieu' and 'moment' – that is, in brief, his inherited personality, the social, political and geographical background, and the historical context in which he was writing. Even now, however, Taine's ambitions are not exhausted, for he maintains that the same three factors underlie all historical phenomena and that the historian can thus discover the laws of history and observe their operation in the main provinces of human civilization – religion, art, philosophy, government, the family and industry. His bold claim here is thus that a literary document, scientifically studied, can reveal to us 'la psychologie d'une âme, souvent celle d'un siècle, et parfois celle d'une race'.

This example reveals Taine's fondness for generalization and wide-ranging explanation, and he always loved, he tells us, 'sinon la métaphysique proprement dite, du moins la philosophie, c'est-à-dire les vues sur l'ensemble et sur le fond des choses', and we must now note that beyond even his claims to establish a scientific literary study, psychology and history he aspired, throughout his career, to find a method for nothing less than a scientific metaphysics. The positivist approach, he believed, gives us certainty – a view which is itself indicative of his over-confidence – but it cannot at present yield completeness of knowledge, a synthetic explanation of the whole of life and the universe. He found such an all-inclusiveness in the philosophies of Spinoza and Hegel, who influenced him from an early stage, but without certainty. He asserted that his own method of 'abstraction' could fuse the merits of their idealism and of positivism and lead us to 'l'absolue, l'indubitable, l'éternelle, l'universelle vérité'. By a process of successively repeated abstractions and verifications we can move from the causes of particular phenomena to the causes of those causes and ultimately grasp the supreme causes of universal life: at the summit of the pyramid of knowledge, he claimed, 'nous découvrons l'unité de l'univers'; we achieve the goal of metaphysics – by a method Taine asserts is scientific at every stage.

Not surprisingly, perhaps, even positivists like Mill rejected these views and thought he was ignoring 'the inherent limitations of human experience'. Taine's method may be modelled on that of the sciences, but since a Hegelian meaning is given to such notions as 'fact', 'law' and 'cause', it is certainly not, as he alleged, the scientific method itself. But Taine's confidence faded only in his final years; earlier he foresaw no limits to the scope and reliability of his approach and declared:

> Dans cet emploi de la science et dans cette conception des choses il y a un art, une morale, une politique, une religion nouvelles, et c'est notre affaire aujourd'hui de les chercher.

This famous assertion reveals that like Comte he trusted that science could surmount its own boundaries and confirms that the real conclusion of his thought was a scientism of an even more audacious kind.

A similar judgement may fairly be passed upon others in the same positivist tradition – the famous chemist Berthelot, claiming that 'le triomphe universel de la science arrivera à assurer aux hommes le maximum possible de bonheur et de moralité'; in literature Zola, in *Le Roman expérimental* and *Le Docteur Pascal*; in sociology Espinas, Izoulet and Durkheim; and, in particular, Renan (1823–92), whose book on *L'Avenir de la science* (published in 1890 but written within four years of his break with the Roman Church in 1845) is the most exalted expression in the whole century of optimistic confidence in science – by which he especially meant the history of the human spirit, the 'science' of *philologie*. He ardently believed that this could save men from the 'shipwreck of scepticism' on moral and metaphysical questions which positivism might seem to have produced, that science could replace religion as a guide for mankind, and we shall later note his own version of its teaching.

> La science est donc une religion [he proclaims]; la science seule fera désormais les symboles; la science seule peut résoudre à l'homme les éternels problèmes dont sa nature exige impérieusement la solution.

These thinkers claimed too much for the scientific method, one may well think, as regards both the potential area of its application and the certainty of its conclusions. Reality was exclusively equated with what is scientifically knowable, and the provisional, working determinism of the sciences was replaced by a form of fatalist determinism. Their excesses would soon provoke, as we shall see, a critical reaction that grew in strength in the final years of the century. Meanwhile, we must turn to the debates around a second major area of concern: religion.

Religious Orthodoxy, Doubt and Aspiration

'La religion naît de toutes parts', observed Bonald in 1796, and Napoleon's Concordat with the Pope in 1802 seemed to seal the official restoration of Catholic Christianity after the suppressions of the Revolution. A retreat from Voltairian irreligion marked the opening decades of the century, and a variety of factors conspired to strengthen the Church's position: social conservatism allied with fear of a return to revolutionary anarchy, Romantic religious feeling, the natural self-interest of priest and aristocrat, and from 1815 the restoration of the Bourbon monarchy. On the intellectual plane too the Catholic 'Traditionalists' were active and influential. Already in 1802 Chateaubriand's *Le Génie du christianisme* was contending that the truth of the Christian faith is shown by its unique ability to satisfy our inmost needs, by its beneficent and stabilizing impact on society, and by the rich aesthetic heritage it has inspired. Even his short novel *René*, he claimed, proves 'la puissance d'une religion qui peut seule fermer des plaies que tous les baumes de la terre ne sauraient guérir'. Louis de Bonald (1754–1840) and Joseph de Maistre (1753–1821) took an even more firmly orthodox stance, the former in works like his *Théorie du pouvoir politique et religieux dans la société civile* (1796) and the latter, most readably, in *Les Soirées de Saint-Pétersbourg* (1821). Their position is in strong reaction against the *philosophes* and the scientific attitude and expresses in its most forceful and uncompromising form the outlook of the so-called ultras. Society can only find a stable foundation in the authority of the Roman Church to curb human sin and pride and in the authority of a strong monarchy, which they believed to be the divinely ordained form of government. Lamennais, in his earlier work, supported the same views. His *Essai sur l'indifférence en matière de religion* (1817–23) attacked the principle of free examination and linked social dissolution with sceptical 'indifference' to the revealed moral truths of the Church. Individual reason, inner experience and the senses are alike distorted by illusion and error, and we should thus subordinate our personal judgement to the 'general reason' of mankind as a whole as enshrined in the values of 'tradition'.

A very different approach to Catholic faith is found in Maine de Biran (1766–1824). He began as a sensationalist, an admirer of Condillac and a member of the *idéologue* group, but the deeply introspective meditations described in his *Journal intime* (published in 1927) finally led him to replace his earlier scepticism by religious conviction. Whereas empiricism has normally regarded sense-experience – observation of the external world – as the main criterion of knowledge, Biran argues that our inner experience and reflection upon it are even more rewarding. Our immediate awareness of the reality in ourselves of conscious effort shows us that the self is primarily will (even more so than it is reason) and that, despite some physical determinism, it is ultimately free. We do not always utilize this freedom, for we tend to passivity as well as to action – as his treatise on *L'Influence de l'habitude sur la faculté de penser* (1803) examines – but in our 'vie active', and beyond that in our 'vie divine', the essential self finds its true expression. In his own day Biran was an original but little-appreciated philosopher in the tradition of French introspective writing, but later spiritualist thinkers – notably Bergson – were to draw upon his insights, and he has perhaps never been more highly respected than at the present day.

Other Catholics in the earlier nineteenth century were more socially involved. This is true to some extent of 'liberal Catholics' like Lacordaire and Montalembert during the 1830s and 1840s. They adopted a more moderate, less reactionary approach than Bonald and Maistre, and their influential journal, *Le Correspondant*, contributed to an undoubted resurgence of belief, amongst the bourgeoisie and upper classes at least, during the Second Empire period. And yet other Catholics went still further and, like Buchez and Ballanche, for example, propounded varieties of Christian socialism – and so, most famously, did Lamennais.

Lamennais (1782–1854) had become a priest in his mid-thirties and in his earlier work, we have noted, was a leading advocate for a conservative monarchy and for an ultramontane belief in the supreme authority of the Pope. No change of allegiance in the whole century, therefore, is more dramatic and arresting than Lamennais's conversion to a doctrine of democratic Christian socialism and his defiance of the papal censure of his views in 1832. In 1834 he published his most celebrated work, *Paroles d'un croyant*, written in high-flown biblical verses, a moving apologia for a Christianity of charity and brotherhood which has even been described as 'a lyrical version of the Communist

Manifesto'. To a present-day reader its ideas may seem too imprecise, dithyrambic and utopian, even though so deeply humane.

> Dans la cité de Dieu, tous sont égaux, aucun ne domine, car la justice seule y règne avec l'amour . . .
>
> Dans la cité de Dieu, nul ne sacrifie les autres à soi, mais chacun est prêt à se sacrifier pour les autres . . .
>
> Quand vous aurez rebâti la cité de Dieu, la terre refleurira, et les peuples refleuriront, parce que vous aurez vaincu les fils de Satan qui oppriment les peuples et désolent la terre, les hommes d'orgueil, les hommes de rapine, les hommes de meurtre et les hommes de peur.

Yet such poetic apostrophes, in chapter after chapter, spoke to the hearts of numerous radicals who, like him, were greatly disturbed by the poverty and inequalities of the newly industrialized conurbations. And the Pope's renewed condemnation of his views, which led him to break with the Church, seemed to his many admirers – including George Sand, Sainte-Beuve and other Romantics – to confirm that the Church was incompatible with the modern age. For them Lamennais and his book were important above all for what they symbolized – the idealistic integrity of the social prophet rejected by a reactionary priesthood. For the rest of his life Lamennais sided with the republican socialists of his day in such works as *Le Livre du peuple* (1837) and *De l'esclavage moderne* (1840). He retained a religious belief, expressed in his *Esquisse d'une philosophie* (1841–6), but died, somewhat embittered, without being reconciled with Rome. And indeed it is the case that the Church's general response, until almost the end of the century, to the scientific, intellectual, democratic and industrial challenges it encountered took the form of an ever firmer assertion of its authority – culminating in the *Syllabus of Errors* of 1864 and the proclamation in 1870 of papal infallibility in matters of faith and morals. And hence, whereas in England and Germany one finds many religious doubters who sought to adapt and to compromise with Protestant Christianity, in France most freethinkers felt compelled to oppose and to replace Catholic Christianity.

The state of the Roman Church at this time was, however, very far from being the sole factor which separated men from the Christian doctrines, and we must now survey the reasons underlying one of the most significant developments in nineteenth-century thought in France as elsewhere – namely, the widespread loss of belief in Christianity.

Unbelief in the late-seventeenth and eighteenth centuries had in general been aggressive and primarily rationalistic, confident that all religion is superstitious and reactionary. For the nineteenth century unbelief was far more often reluctant and even anguished – since both society and individual man were now felt to have need of religious faith – and was also and above all based on empirical and scientific grounds rather than on the sometimes callow rationalism of earlier sceptics. The rationalist contentions of the *philosophes* were certainly reiterated, however, and indeed strengthened by a still more confident appeal to the authority of science and the positivist philosophy: the so-called metaphysical proofs of God's existence are unsound; there is no place for supernatural intervention in a world ruled by natural laws; true knowledge derives from observation, whereas religion makes assertions about a realm that is in principle 'unknowable'. As to the alleged miracles of the Christian Gospels, they can be explained in naturalistic terms – as illusions, deceits or myths – an approach notoriously illustrated first in D. F. Strauss's *Life of Jesus* (1835, translated into French by Littré) and, no less controversially a little later, in Renan's *Vie de Jésus* (1863).

But in addition to these arguments nineteenth-century unbelievers were affected by much of the new scientific and historical knowledge of the day. It led them, first, to reject the doctrine of the literal infallibility of the Bible, at that time accepted by Catholics and Protestants alike. Geology reveals the world to be far older than the Bible narrative suggests. Zoology and biology, and especially the work of Lamarck and, later, Darwin, show man to have evolved from the animals, and if so the Creation story of the Book of Genesis must be historically false – not to add that it becomes harder to attribute to man a special, God-designed role in the world. Again, biblical scholars, applying the ordinary criteria of philological study, allege that there are inaccuracies and contradictions in the Scriptures and they are even led to question the doctrine of Christ's 'inerrancy'. Other historians contend that there is inadequate independent evidence to confirm the Gospel stories – nor, some add, is there any sign of God's providence at work in human history. Yet again, comparative philologists note the frequency in other ancient religions of allegedly miraculous events similar to those in the Bible and ask whether all the stories of virgin births, resurrections and ascensions may not stem from a common myth-making tendency in primitive man. Considerations such as these seemed decisive even to some practising Christians. The young Ernest Renan, for example, in training for holy orders at Saint-Sulpice, abandoned his faith in 1845 after a mere two years of philological study. His *Souvenirs d'enfance et de jeunesse* vividly describe the crisis he underwent and his central difficulty: if the Bible is proved to be fallible but the Roman Church proclaims it to be infallible, then the Church itself is in error and its claims to total authority are destroyed.

Physiological and psychological studies prompted another line of questioning: mind and body are so intimately linked that it is difficult to believe man has a soul (which has, in any case, never been observed) or that the soul could survive bodily death. And, more generally, both the Lamarckian and the Darwinian theories of evolution seemed able to give an account of the world and life in wholly naturalistic terms: thus, for example, the many signs of human and animal adaptation to environment do not oblige us to postulate a Divine Designer but can be explained as the outcome of an age-long, ruthless process of the survival of the best adapted. Well might Sainte-Beuve's Amaury, in *Volupté*, sum up the Lamarckian view in the words:

> La nature, à ses yeux, c'était la pierre et la cendre, le granit de la tombe, la mort! La vie n'y intervenait que comme un accident étrange . . .

These arguments that Christianity is unscientific and is contradicted by modern knowledge affected many anxious intellectuals, but no less widespread in their effects were various ethical contentions. First, it was alleged, certain Christian doctrines are immoral – notably the idea of eternal punishment in Hell for the unredeemed and also the substitutionary view of the Atonement, which holds that Christ died to satisfy God's demand that human sin be paid for, even if by an innocent substitute. Both rested upon a retributive theory of punishment that was being increasingly questioned, and both thus presupposed a morally repugnant idea of God. Poets like Vigny (in 'Le Mont des Oliviers'), Musset (in 'L'Espoir en Dieu') and Leconte de Lisle (in 'La Vision de Snorr' and 'Le Nazaréen') were particularly repelled, and the problem was made the more acute by the assertions of psychologists and sociologists that man's actions are determined by forces outside his control such as heredity and environment. And some even added that the Church's very doctrine of the Fall of Man diminishes the individual's responsibility for his sin – for which, all the same, it teaches that he may be eternally damned. Secondly, it was argued, the world itself is far from evidencing the alleged goodness of its

Creator; the cruelty and impassivity of nature, the ruthless struggle for survival highlighted by Lamarck and Darwin, the sufferings of disease and death, these seem rather to suggest a God who cannot be both morally perfect and omnipotent. And thirdly, it was contended, the moral and political attitudes of the Churches are often as immoral as their doctrines, marked by intolerant absolutism, worldly corruption and social apathy.

Forceful Christian replies to all these objections have not been lacking, and especially in the twentieth century, and it could well be argued that in response to them Christian teaching has now achieved greater clarity and hence force, has been purified of inessential accretions. In nineteenth-century France, however, the situation was still one of increasing conflict and polarization of beliefs, marked by ever more intransigent opposition between the adherents of Catholicism and *la libre pensée.*

Yet the unbelievers were in general far from being irreligious materialists. Regret for lost faith and the barrenness of religious scepticism became virtual commonplaces of French thought and literature at this time. 'J'étais incrédule, mais je détestais l'incredulité', wrote one Eclectic philosopher, and this reaction is typical of a time which Gérard de Nerval once called 'un siècle sceptique plutôt qu'incrédule'. Religion was prized as a basis for political stability, we saw, as a barrier against moral indifference, as an essential means to spur the masses to ethical action – and as much so by anti-Christian reformers like Comte and many of the socialistic reformers as by the Traditionalists. Furthermore, many of them recognized man's personal need for belief and expressed repeatedly their respect for his 'religious sentiment' – 'universal', 'indestructible', 'a fundamental law of his nature', as Constant's great work *De la religion* (1824–31) declared – for his sense of awed reverence as he surveys 'the starry heavens without and the moral law within'. Thus, for example, Michelet, following Constant and numerous other disciples of Kant and of Rousseau's Vicaire Savoyard, could say that religion is born 'presque toujours d'un vrai besoin du cœur', and a scientist like Claude Bernard declared: 'Il ne faut . . . pas chercher à éteindre la métaphysique ou le sentiment religieux de l'homme, mais l'éclairer et le faire monter plus haut.' And Renan could maintain – *after* his loss of Catholic faith: 'Ce qui est de l'humanité, ce qui par conséquent sera éternel comme elle, c'est le besoin religieux, la faculté religieuse.' These and many others could agree with Musset when he attacked Voltairian scepticism and spoke with dismay of 'le lait stérile de l'impiété'.

Consequently, whether for social or for personal reasons, the conviction spread that either the old religion must be restored or a new synthesis must replace it. Ballanche was typical when he reported in the early years of the century: 'Une nouvelle ère se prépare; le monde est en travail, les esprits sont attentifs.' These expectations were not to be disappointed, and it must be emphasized that the nineteenth century was not only critical in its intellectual life – critical of Christianity, critical of paternalistic government and *laissez-faire* economics – but was also a period of remarkable constructive enterprise and not only in the scientific realm. For all its scepticism this was an age that longed for infallibility – and found it, whether in the papal infallibility proclaimed first by the Traditionalists and later by the Church, or in the infallibility of science announced, as we saw, by Comte and other *scientistes*, or in the metaphysical infallibility claimed for Hegelian absolutism, or in the infallibility of progress as expounded by Marx and many other believers in a theoretical philosophy of history. Again and again any mood of scientific caution gave way to messianic hope and prophetic fervour, to the creation of new systems – new religions, indeed – to replace the discarded creeds of the past. It is arresting to note that this 'age of science' was also a time which rediscovered the fascination of magic and *spiritisme* (for Hugo was not the only one by a long way to be obsessed by 'les tables tournantes') and of occultism and illuminism – so influential as to leave their mark on literature from the Romantics and Baudelaire to Rimbaud, Huysmans and Villiers de l'Isle-Adam. Freemasonry became increasingly popular, and so did numerous minor religious sects, ranging from the Swedenborgians to such 'rational religions' as Victor Charbonnel's humanitarian cult in the 1850s, complete with its 'Human Christmas' and 'Festivals of Reason'.

New Creeds for Old

Of the many non-Christian creeds devised in the middle years of the century some merely borrowed the terminology of religion to lend an aroma of the infinite to purely ethical doctrines. Thus Vigny, writing at the conclusion of his *Servitude et grandeur militaires* (1835) about 'le naufrage universel des croyances', finds only one faith still intact – 'une dernière lampe dans un temple dévasté' – and without any sign of linguistic strain he goes on to describe his own stoic ethic as 'la religion de l'honneur' – 'une Religion mâle, sans symbole et sans images, sans dogme et sans cérémonies' – without the alleged accretions, that is, which alienated him from Christianity! And likewise Michelet, in *Le Peuple* (1846), described his ethic of French patriotism as a religion of fraternity: we should embrace 'la France, comme foi et comme religion'.

But many other thinkers went further and offered for men's worship a new deity, with new forms of religious service and new doctrines, even of immortality. Some proposed a primarily social religion, concerned to inspire man in his role as citizen: the 'new Christianity' of Saint-Simon and his disciples, Comte's 'religion of humanity', the creeds of Pierre Leroux (so enthusiastically admired by George Sand), Fourier, Cabet and his 'Icarians'. Others suggested primarily metaphysical religions which deified an explicitly metaphysical concept, such as Cousin's 'natural religion', based on reverence for 'the true, the beautiful and the good', and the religions of the 'Ideal' embraced by Renan and Vacherot. Yet others turned back to the non-Christian world-religions and mythologies popularized, we saw, by contemporary *philologues* and also by the many epic poems – from Hugo, Quinet, Ménard, Laprade and others – which reviewed the range of past religions in search amongst 'cette poussière divine' (in Quinet's words) for 'quelque débris de vérité, de révélation universelle'. Of these 'neo-pagan' creeds, as we may term them, some admired a single doctrine, and in particular Buddhism – as witness Senancour, Lamartine at certain moments, Vigny towards the end of his life, Leconte de Lisle, Brunetière, Amiel and others – whilst some hoped for a more comprehensive and eclectic faith, for some form of religious syncretism – as did Ménard and Ravaisson, Musset and Gérard de Nerval.

Even so brief an outline may suggest something of the profusion and diversity of these systems, but the great majority of them divinized either humanity or nature. In the former category, one of the most characteristic religious substitutes and the most successful in terms of durability proved to be Comte's positivist religion, to which he devoted much of his later career and which found adherents in England, North America, Brazil, Sweden and elsewhere as well as France.

Comte's first aim was to replace the unobservable deity of supernatural religion by a god that verifiably exists: he therefore proposed the new deity of 'Humanity', renamed 'le Grand Être', and if anyone protests that humanity is merely an abstract noun, his claim, like

Saint-Simon before him and Marx after him, was that on the contrary individual men exist only in and through mankind, the one true human reality. Secondly, he wished to avoid what he thought of as the other-worldliness and mysticism of supernatural faiths and to harmonize the everyday and religious lives. He believed this new worship would achieve this end, since the very preservation and development of the new deity become dependent upon our loving service. In future, he affirms, science, poetry and morality will be consecrated to the study, praise and love of humanity and our life will thus become a continuous act of worship. Comte acknowledges that men are at present self-centred, but he claims that his religious ethic based on love of mankind will cure this – especially with the help of a didactic art and literature, the beneficent moral influence of women, a political reorganization in which duties will take the place of rights, and above all the impact of a newly organized Church of Humanity. There is to be a hierarchy of priests – under Comte as high priest – and, like the Roman Church, holy festivals will be held – to celebrate now the basic social relations (marital, paternal, filial, and so on), now the earlier stages of man's religious development such as fetichism, and now various social groups – like womanhood (for which Comte had a particular veneration following his love for Clotilde de Vaux), the priesthood, the proletariat and even the capitalists. Again, there will be 'social sacraments' – beginning with 'presentation' (the equivalent of baptism) and ending with 'transformation' (burial) and, seven years after death, 'incorporation' into the great family of past humanity. So thorough was Comte that he even replaced the Christian calendar with months and saints' days named after great men like Aristotle and Archimedes and starting from 1789. As to immortality, he rejected the occultist notions which appealed to many of the utopian socialists of his day – ideas of metempsychosis, interstellar migration and the like; we live on after our death only by virtue of our thoughts and actions and their influence upon those who succeed us, but he believes that this 'subjective' existence is a 'noble immortality' and that extra moral impetus will stem from our desire to be counted and, in special festivals, commemorated as 'true servants of humanity', what his English followers somewhat humourlessly called 'the *holy* dead'.

This creed embodies a common and far from ignoble ambition in nineteenth-century secular thought: to satisfy religious aspiration by redirecting men's hopes and devotion towards the creation of a happier and more moral society on earth, and to do this by stressing practical service in this world instead of a more mystical worship of a transcendental Being. Yet one may fairly wonder whether this faith can inspire what for many people is the essence of religion – the sense of the holy, awe before the infinitely perfect – and also note that Comte's confidence in the potential goodness of man seems to be belied by the authoritarianism of his religious and political proposals. And some admirers of his earlier thought rejected these ideas: Littré suspected he was insane and Mill was tempted to 'weep at this melancholy decadence of a great intellect'. But others, no less idealistic, preserved the 'Église Positiviste' into our own century, and, for example, the last English 'Church', in Liverpool, only closed in the 1940s.

Probably the most popular substitute deity of the century was not humanity, however, but nature, and in one guise or another many of these new creeds were variants of the age-old doctrine of pantheism – of the belief, essentially, that God is everything and everything is God. Several different tendencies in the century's thought led to pantheism. Even in Christian circles a marked emphasis was laid upon God's immanence, His presence active in this world. But the Christians also held fast to the counterbalancing doctrine of God's transcendence, His existence in a transcendental realm: not so many unbelievers who doubted precisely the reality of such a realm. Hence in Christian circles, as the century advanced, there was a mounting – and fully warranted – concern about the spread of pantheism. Romanticism, German idealism (diffused in France by the Eclectics and others), occultism, the 'neo-pagan' creeds already mentioned – all of these, or rather certain elements within them, converged on the same position. This is apparent, first, in certain of the French Romantics, with their belief in the goodness of nature and their concept of 'Dieu en nous'. 'O nature! ô mère éternelle!' declaimed Gérard de Nerval, linking nature-worship with the cult of Isis. But in him and other poets like Lamartine and Hugo we find only a vague, diffuse pantheism, not unlike that of Wordsworth. It became far more emphatic in philosophical circles under the influence of Spinoza and especially Hegel. The world and in particular human history are conceived to be a vast, implacably determined unity moving towards the realization of an absolute of consciousness. Moreover, the criterion of historical necessity gives a criterion of moral value: whatever is (in the long-term trends of history) is right. History is seen as the working-out of a single design, as the product of a motive-force that impels (it is often claimed) not only mankind but the whole of nature. One good example amongst others is offered by the system

Renan devised after losing his Christian faith, his 'religion of the Ideal' as expressed in *L'Avenir de la science* and his *Dialogues philosophiques* (1876). He claims that a scientific study of universal history reveals a gradual but inevitable progression towards complete mental consciousness. This final goal he terms the Absolute, or the Ideal, or – just as readily – God. For the present 'God' exists in an 'ideal' state, but our moral duty is to work to bring 'God' into full reality, to fulfil the final end to which all history is moving. Such were the rudiments of the 'religion' which Renan then movingly embroidered with equivalents – non-supernatural equivalents – of the principal notions of Christianity: prayer as self-examination and meditation, a 'priesthood' of scholars, philosophers and poets, a form of immortality 'dans le souvenir de Dieu', and a future 'paradise' on earth. And this creed rested, as Renan himself made clear, upon a pantheistic belief that nature is good: 'Le mal, c'est de se révolter contre la nature . . . Son but est bon; veuillons ce qu'elle veut.'

Other thinkers began not from Romantic sensibility or Germanic intellection but from science – from its postulation of the unity and determined interrelationship of the natural order. They then overlooked that this is merely a working hypothesis for the true scientist and claimed it to be a certainly known and supreme truth about the world. One need only add the further belief that nature is good, and one possesses the main elements of Saint-Simonian pantheism, which affirmed both the 'infinite unity' and the 'infinite, universal love' of the universe, and also of the ethic of stoical pantheism developed later by Taine. We saw that Taine's method for a 'scientific metaphysics' claims to lead us to the 'supreme cause' of nature: 'nous découvrons l'unité de l'univers et nous comprenons ce qui la produit'. And as we contemplate the beauties of nature, Taine affirmed, we feel that 'les choses sont divines' and experience 'la sublimité et l'éternité des choses'; this in turn inspires a serene confidence in the harmony of nature, fortitude in bearing our own sufferings, and a willingness to subordinate ourselves to the purposes of '[ce] Dieu universel dont je suis un des membres' – attitudes he believed were enshrined in the outlook of Marcus Aurelius and in the teaching of Hinduism and Greek polytheism. And, summing up his ethic, Taine arrestingly declares:

> Il n'y a qu'un être parfait, la Nature; il n'y a qu'une idée parfaite, celle de la Nature; il n'y a qu'une vie parfaite, celle où la volonté de la Nature devient notre volonté.

One may feel that these pantheistic systems movingly revive man's age-old awe before the vastness and beauty of the universe. Yet it is also hard not to think that pantheism deifies merely what is biggest – 'le Grand Tout' so often hymned by these thinkers – and that scientific scrutiny may lead away from any belief in the universal moral goodness of nature or human history or individual human nature. We may sympathize with the dream, entertained by many ardent idealists like Cabet, Fourier and the Saint-Simonians, of a 'natural life', without vice or frustration, away from the corruptions of urban, capitalist society, a life in which virtue would become (in Taine's words) 'le fruit de l'instinct libre'. But the new model communities founded, in North America in particular, on the basis of this faith all too swiftly broke down, and if the Darwinian evidence of the cruelty of nature posed problems for the Christian, these were no less severe for the pantheist. Furthermore, as nineteenth-century critics like Renouvier stressed, pantheism rests upon a doctrine of universal determinism – a fatalism which tends to deny the reality of the individual.

More generally, it has to be conceded that little or nothing survived into the twentieth century of these religious substitutes – and of the others, syncretist, Buddhist and illuminist, that have been omitted here; even Comtism only remained alive in our own time with a much-diminished following. These creeds failed in part, one may suggest, because certain of them were authoritarian in an age of increasing liberalism: they offered (as T. H. Huxley said of Comte) 'Catholicism minus Christianity'; in part they failed because they lacked the efficient organization of an established Church and the inevitable vested interests which help to give it stability; in part because they lacked the emotional appeal of distant origins and an ancient tradition; in part because they tended to compete so publicly and stridently with each other. But above all perhaps they failed, for all their idealism, because what they were attempting was, if not impossible, harder than they appreciated. For many of these thinkers the very starting-point of their religious search was the assumption that there is no supernatural God, that any acceptable creed must be rational and scientifically based. But if religion is to be more than just (as Matthew Arnold held) 'morality touched with emotion', if its heart and its appeal to most men lie in a 'sense of the holy', of a 'mystery' beyond man's grasping, then we may wonder whether any effective religion can be confined within the rational and scientifically observable.

These difficulties may perhaps have weighed with other thinkers who were no less impelled to offer a new creed equal to the needs of the time – and who did indeed invoke sometimes the support of a new religion, like Cabet with his 'vrai christianisme' or Leroux with his 'religion métaphysique de l'humanité'. Yet in general, though tempted to imitate Saint-Simon's 'nouveau christianisme' or Lamennais's linking of Christianity and socialism, the many social reformers of the age – Charles Fourier, Étienne Cabet, Pierre Leroux, Proudhon, Louis Blanc and others – sought to give their ideas a quasi-religious appeal through a cult of history and progress.[1] Their individual systems naturally differed, but the cumulative impact of their writings – Fourier's *Le Nouveau Monde industriel* (1829–30), Cabet's romantic *Voyage en Icarie* (1842), Leroux's *De l'égalité* (1838) and *De l'humanité* (1840), Proudhon's celebrated *Qu'est-ce que la propriété?* (1840) (with its answer: 'La propriété, c'est le vol'), and Blanc's *L'Organisation du travail* (1839), amongst many others – was to provide a social and political rather than a religious solution for contemporary problems but to do so in messianic terms derived from an optimistic theory of historical inevitability. For most of them contended that history's age-long advance has brought us to the very threshold of a golden era in which will be vindicated the principle they themselves are advocating – social harmony for Fourier, fraternity for Blanc, equality for Leroux and also (though with a more ambivalent view of history) for Proudhon, liberty for yet others. By their critiques of industrial capitalism and their sometimes utopian plans for economic reorganization and social renewal – commonly through new model societies based on a communistic system of work and ownership – these thinkers have a major place in the early history of European socialism and helped to give it the optimism and prophetic idealism it still retains; the confidence they based on their faith in history would mark French socialism into our own age, as with socialists like Jean Jaurès and Léon Blum and Marxists like Jules Guesde.

Nor was the idealization of history and progress confined to social reformers; it is found in a very different form, usually with a Hegelian starting-point, in more metaphysical thinkers – notably Eclectics like

[1] On the social reformers and the historians of this period, cf. Chapter 8 below. The fortunes of the ideas of progress and history are complex; for a fuller survey, cf. J. B. Bury, *The Idea of Progress*, 2nd ed. (New York: Dover, 1955), and D. G. Charlton, *Secular Religions in France (1815–1870)* (London: Oxford University Press, 1963), chs vii and viii.

Victor Cousin and Jouffroy and even certain Christian believers in divine providence. They were as convinced as the socialists that history is a unity, manifesting a single great design, motivated by a force transcending human control, moving beneficently towards (in the view of Cousin and his disciples) the realization of the absolute. The natural religion of the Eclectics was otherwise abstractly bare, based on worship of the metaphysical notions of the true, the beautiful and the good; it came nearest to gaining messianic appeal in its philosophy of history. (In Karl Marx, it may be added, one finds a fusion of the social and metaphysical theories, of socialism and Hegel, that helps to explain why his has proved the most formidable of all these deifications of historical inevitability.)

A host of other writers shared the mood of confident hope – whether derived from trust in scientific advance, from socialist progressivism, from Hegelian-type metaphysics, or from Christian belief in God. Hugo was characteristic when he declared in *Les Misérables*: 'L'éclosion future, l'éclosion prochaine du bien-être universel, est un phénomène divinement fatal . . . Le progrès marche; il fait le grand voyage humain et terrestre vers le céleste et le divin.'

Yet if a belief in progress encouraged many of the thinkers we have so far considered, it was to be increasingly challenged – already before the 1850s by such 'liberal' thinkers as Michelet and Quinet and historians like Guizot and De Tocqueville; later under the influence of political disillusionment following, first, the *coup d'état* of Louis-Napoléon and, in 1870–1, French defeat in the war with Prussia. One even finds growing evidence of what one scholar calls a 'sense of decadence' – after 1848 and still more after 1870.[1] And more generally too the intellectual tide was turning and slowly ebbing from the cults of science and history and the other 'secular religions' we have surveyed.

The Critical Reaction

In the first part of our period intellectual initiative has seemed to lie above all with thinkers who, having rejected Christianity, developed alternative philosophies based on science or progress, on socialism, a cult of humanity or a secularized pantheism, and marked by optimism about man and the power of human intelligence, by confidence in

[1] Cf. K. W. Swart, *The Sense of Decadence in Nineteenth-Century France* (The Hague: Nijhoff, 1964).

scientific method and informed social planning. This has rightly been described as 'l'époque des systèmes' – systems, in general, that purport to establish in one form or another a scientific humanism.

Gradually, however, from 1860 or 1870 onwards, the mood was modified. In some ways, certainly, the Third Republic was to be the very incarnation of reformist secularism and the universities seemed strongholds of anti-clerical and scientific thought, dominated by rationalists like Léon Brunschvicg (1869–1944) and such positivist sociologists as Émile Durkheim (1858–1917) and Lucien Lévy-Bruhl (1857–1939), who adopted a rigorously scientific approach both to sociology and to religion and ethics, which they considered to be useful products of social evolution now needing to be purged of their unscientific elements. Yet the final decades of the century appear in retrospect as a time of critical reaction against many of the ideas we have surveyed, as a time also when the outlooks of spiritualist philosophy and Catholic belief were reasserted more vigorously. This is not to imply that these outlooks had ever lacked strong advocates or that opposition to scientism had ever disappeared. On the contrary, scientists like Ampère (*Essai sur la philosophie des sciences*, 1834–43), Claude Bernard (*Introduction à l'étude de la médecine expérimentale*, 1865) and Théodule Ribot (*La Psychologie anglaise contemporaine*, 1870) all rejected the extravagant claims for science advanced by Saint-Simon, Comte and others and dissociated the true scientific attitude from belief in fatalism and materialism. Philosophers like Maine de Biran and the Eclectics led by Victor Cousin had argued during the earlier part of the century for a spiritualist and libertarian position. Philosophers of history like Quinet and Michelet had defended the reality and rights of individual liberty against authoritarian and determinist theories of inevitable progress. And in literature too concern for the 'ideal' was as strong in the Romantics as in Baudelaire and his fellow symbolists.

Yet only from the end of the Second Empire did the philosophical resistance to scientific humanism achieve a certain coherence and impact and the reaction against the positivists' dogmatic dismissal of the mysterious and spiritual in human life find wider diffusion in literature as well: in symbolist poetry; in the later plays of Dumas *fils* and the theatre of Maeterlinck, Villiers de l'Isle-Adam and others; in the Catholic literary revival of the late nineteenth century illustrated in Huysmans, Bloy, Jammes, Bourget and Claudel; in the naturalists' own rejection from around 1885 of Zola's preoccupation with material reality; in the literary criticism of Brunetière and others. Even the foreign authors who were most acclaimed in France at this time were interpreted as idealists who offered arms against the *scientistes* – Tennyson, Carlyle and Ruskin; Wagner, Schopenhauer and Hartmann amongst the Germans; Russian novelists like Tolstoy.

In philosophy this critical reaction was expressed above all in the work of the neo-criticist and idealist groups. The earliest of the neo-criticists was Cournot (1801–77), a difficult but penetrating thinker who was no less original in political economy than as an analytical philosopher. Philosophy for him was first and foremost a critique of the sciences; deeply influenced by Kant, like all the neo-criticists, his central concern was with the nature of knowledge, especially scientific knowledge. He claimed that Kant's notion of a scientific law was too rigid – for he had equated all science with mathematics and physics – and that the development of biology and sociology since Kant had shown that laws can attain no more than probability. To aspire to complete certainty, as Kant did in his *Critique of Pure Reason*, is to end with utter scepticism. Cournot, who began his career with work on mathematical theories of chance and probability, himself sought a middle way between Humean agnosticism and over-confident dogmatism; he conceived of a critique, he says, 'qui procéderait par voie d'induction probable, et non de démonstration positive'. Hence the essential problem of all knowledge, from the moment it passes from observations to generalizations and inductions, lies in the evaluation of probabilities. We must accept that 'l'absolu nous échappe', that we can never 'pénétrer l'essence des choses et en assigner les premiers principes'. But if we do acknowledge these limitations on our knowledge, then the way is open for us to affirm conclusions even in metaphysics, albeit they will never be more than tentative probabilities.

Contentions like these are plainly critical of the dogmatic assurance we have noted in the *scientistes*. They were to be reinforced, we shall see, by Lachelier and Boutroux and also by the works of Bernard and Ribot already mentioned, and similar views were to be authoritatively expressed a little later by the celebrated mathematician, Henri Poincaré, who in *La Science et l'hypothèse* (1902) and other books underlined that science, far from giving certain knowledge, can in principle offer no more than useful hypotheses of greater or lesser probability and subject to constant revision.

In addition to this epistemological argument the neo-criticists also stressed the problem of freedom and moral responsibility. Jules Lequier (1814–62), largely unknown in his day and influential only through his impact on Renouvier, has been hailed in our own time as a precursor of existentialism. His chief concern was with this problem, and his *Recherche d'une première vérité* (published by Renouvier in 1865) vividly describes his attempt to think his way through it without any appeal to his Catholic beliefs. He concludes that there is no compelling empirical evidence or rational argument that we are either free or determined; we are thus obliged to adopt a belief, to opt for or against free will, since knowledge is impossible. Determinism, he argues, destroys both moral responsibility and also the very possibility of an impartial search for truth (since, on that hypothesis, our statements are the products of extraneous factors), and he therefore urges, in a manner reminiscent of the argument of Pascal's 'wager', that we should choose to believe in the reality of our liberty. As he declares, in distinctly 'existentialist' terms,

> Je préfère affirmer la liberté, et affirmer que je l'affirme au moyen de la liberté. Mon affirmation me sauve, m'affranchit. . . . C'est un acte de la liberté qui affirme la liberté.

Charles Renouvier (1815–1903), the leading neo-criticist and important both for his books and as editor of two important reviews, *La Critique philosophique* and *La Critique religieuse*, began from these notions of choice, belief and liberty but greatly widened their application. He agreed with the positivists that we only know phenomena but stressed against them that even this knowledge is incomplete and relative: we are never passive in the act of perception, our personality and especially our will are inevitably involved, and our knowledge thus always includes a 'personal' as well as an 'external' element. It follows for him that any certainty must be based on an act of will to believe, and he interprets the main problems of philosophy as a series of dilemmas on which a choice must be made. He himself opts for belief in free will, in an ethic which takes as its supreme value the fulfilment of individual personality, and in a pluralist notion of the world in which God exists but has only finite power, and he also emphasizes that if the individual is free, then progress is not inevitable and we are not subservient to historical necessity.

The neo-criticists may appear modest and unemphatic compared with the dogmatism they opposed, but to accept their arguments is to reject the claims to scientific certainty made by Comte, Taine and others as well as the assertions of metaphysical or theological certainty made by the Hegelians and the Roman Church, and it is also to dismiss materialism, fatalism, pantheism and the cult of history as mere metaphysical conjectures. These thinkers worked, in short, to undermine all the principal systems earlier in the century that we have surveyed, whilst at the same time, on the positive side, insisting on the free creativity of the individual and thus of society as a whole.

The idealist group of philosophers pursued similar lines of argument. Jules Lachelier (1832–1918) was particularly influential, partly through his teaching – his pupils included Bergson, Brunschvicg and Blondel, not to add Jaurès – and partly through his major book, *Du fondement de l'induction* (1871). Here he challenged the status of scientific laws by demanding how we can ever induce a law of allegedly infinite and permanent applicability from a finite number of previous observations. We can do so, he submits, only by virtue of two principles (the mechanist and the finalist) which our reason 'projects' on to the external world – principles, that is, which are not derived from sense-experience. It follows that we do not know the world as it is (as Comte and other 'realists' had asserted) but only as seen through the categories of our own mind.

Émile Boutroux (1845–1921) opposed scientism from a different standpoint. In his thesis, *De la contingence des lois de la nature* (1874), and later works he challenged the assumption – without which scientific laws cannot claim universal reliability – that a strict determinism rules in the natural order. Examining the actual workings of scientific study as well as its results, he contended that as we move from the physical to the biological sciences and on to the 'human sciences' we encounter an increasing area of 'contingency', of indeterminacy, and, at the human level, of liberty – a notion he sought to elaborate in his later ethical and religious thought.[1]

In retrospect the importance of these thinkers appears twofold. In the first place they initiated some of the principal tendencies of philosophy in the twentieth century – the movement towards a new spiritualism and a preoccupation with the themes of liberty, choice and personal creativity, for example. In the second place, by virtue of what they attacked they cleared the ground, as it were, for later French philosophy. By the mid-1880s the more confident forms of scientific humanism increasingly appeared as fallen idols. Some writers in their disillusionment relapsed into scepticism and pessimism or into a *fin de*

[1] Other idealist philosophers at this period are F. Ravaisson (1813–1900), É. Vacherot (1809–97) and A. Fouillée (1838–1912), in addition to late disciples of Eclecticism like Jules Simon and Paul Janet.

siècle cult of the self – like the young Anatole France, who had earlier revered Taine, or the Maurice Barrès of the trilogy of novels called *Le Culte du moi*, or Huysmans – earlier a disciple of Zola – at the stage he portrays under the guise of Des Esseintes in *A rebours*. Some returned to the Catholic Church, as did Huysmans and Barrès a little later, in common with Bourget, Claudel and others. Yet others moved from a philosophical to a political creed and, preserving something of their scientific humanism, embraced socialism in one guise or another – as, for example, did Anatole France. And still others were drawn by the ideas of new philosophers – and above all Henri Bergson, who both summed up in their most effective form the critical arguments just outlined and also presented the spiritualist philosophy in a way that was to appeal to some of the leading writers of the new generation – Péguy, Proust, Valéry, Gabriel Marcel and Louis Lavelle amongst others – and to prove a salient feature of the French intellectual scene in the twentieth century.

Henri Bergson

Henri Bergson (1859–1941) represented the culmination of the tradition of French spiritualism from Maine de Biran onwards and of opposition to nineteenth-century materialism and scientism, and at the same time he anticipated and indeed inspired some of the most significant developments in later French thought. He first won acclaim with his thesis in 1889, his *Essai sur les données immédiates de la conscience*, and after a period in schoolteaching, mainly in Paris, during which he published *Matière et mémoire* (1896), he became a lecturer at the École Normale in 1898 and, in 1900, professor of philosophy at the Collège de France. His other major works include *L'Évolution créatrice* (1907) and *Les Deux Sources de la morale et de la religion* (1932), and he also published an interesting study on *Le Rire* (1900) and a number of short but illuminating essays, of which *Introduction à la métaphysique* (1903) provides an especially useful summary of his philosophical attitude.

Bergson's achievement was both critical and constructive. The principal targets of his criticism were the positivist notion of determinism (in his *Essai*), materialism (in *Matière et mémoire*), mechanical concepts of evolution (in *L'Évolution créatrice*), and any primarily sociological interpretation of religion of the kind offered by Durkheim (in *Les Deux Sources*). And out of his attacks on these positions there emerged the positive themes of his own philosophy, as we shall see.

He contended that many nineteenth-century philosophers had equated science too narrowly with mathematics and physics – whence the deterministic, materialist and mechanistic notions he rejected. He himself, having acquired a detailed knowledge of biology, physiology and psychology, sought to derive from these more recent sciences a fresh approach to philosophy.

He began from the 'immediate data of consciousness' and observed a distinction he regarded as crucial between time as it is artificially measured for the ends of practical life and scientific experiment (by clocks, etc.) and time as 'la durée', time as I experience it – in which a few minutes of boredom may seem an hour or an hour of happiness may appear to pass in a few minutes. This in turn led him to distinguish between knowledge acquired by the intelligence – a faculty which has evolved for the purposes of action in the practical world, he believed – and inner experience or, as he termed it, 'intellectual intuition'. The intelligence is obliged, given its everyday goals, to split up the stream of time into separate 'moments', to divide an essentially continuous activity into separate stages. But this (as the paradoxes of Achilles and the tortoise and of Zeno's arrow illustrate) is to falsify the reality of things – a reality, he contended, that is ceaseless movement and change. The universe and everything in it is in a condition of unending 'flow', whereas the static 'snapshots' of life which we find useful in daily life or in scientific inquiries inevitably omit its essential elements of movement and duration. Only through the process of sympathetic self-immersion in duration which Bergson called 'intuition', 'a kind of intellectual sympathy', can we 'enter into' the reality of life. A symphony, for example, can be analysed intellectually into a succession of separate notes, but the essential nature of the symphony can be understood only if we experience it as a totality.

Two important examples of the intellect's distortion of reality are seen in the doctrines of determinism and materialism, Bergson believed. Our psychical life as we constantly know it contains an element of spontaneity, of freedom, manifested in action; it can only be reduced to a rigid causal chain of events if each event or act is taken in isolation – an approach which is falsifying. Taken as a whole the individual's mental life is free and creative. Similarly, he contends, our mental life cannot be reduced to purely material, cerebral events. He invokes physiological and psychological facts to show that the mind's activity conditions and overflows the activity of the brain: for instance, the psychopathological phenomenon of dual personality is independent of physiological change, he claims, and so also is our subconscious dream life. The brain is not consciousness itself but the organ of consciousness, through which consciousness enters into or affects matter. The phenomena of memories illustrate and confirm this analysis. Habit-memory – remembering how to walk or facts needed for daily life – is dependent on the brain, on 'physical traces' in the brain. But (as Proust's celebrated description of the working of 'involuntary memory' also reminds us) we possess as well a faculty of 'pure memory', through which we can gain a 'total recall' of past experiences that cannot be voluntarily remembered. Whereas the brain retains only the memories that are useful for life and dismisses, as it were, those other experiences which would otherwise overburden our consciousness, the mind retains all our past life (hence the feasibility of Proust's 'recherche du temps perdu') – and indeed gives us some assurance as to the permanence of the self, a self which is in other ways constantly changing.

Bergson also drew on biological science when he sought to provide an explanation of the facts of evolution. He criticized the two dominant theories provided by Lamarck and Darwin, both of which postulated a mechanical process without the intervention of mind or conscious purposes. He lists occurrences in the animal, vegetable and insect world which he claims cannot be accounted for in this way, and he also asks why, if the determining factor in evolution is no more than adaptation to environment, evolution did not cease many millennia ago. A very simple organism like the amoeba is very well adapted to survival; why, on this criterion, has life developed ever more complicated and hence endangered organisms? Bergson asserts that in reality there is an impulse driving life to take ever greater risks towards the goal of an ever higher efficiency, and this impulse he names 'l'élan vital' – a vital, creative surge, a psychological factor which pervades and drives on whatever is alive. This is the great force behind evolution. The factors isolated by the mechanists, such as the notion of adaptation, can explain the inner windings of evolutionary progress but cannot account for the general direction of its movement, still less the movement itself. And Bergson adds that the stream of change, of 'becoming', which is everywhere evident in organic life, is nothing other than this movement, this 'évolution créatrice', animated by 'l'élan vital', striving upwards, contending against the resistance of merely inert matter (whose existence, one may think, Bergson did not wholly explain), of the purely mechanical. (His criticism of mechanism is also reflected, one may add, in *Le Rire*, where he interprets laughter as a means – produced by evolution – whereby society seeks to discourage mechanical, inadaptable and thus ultimately antisocial behaviour by mocking those who are guilty of it.)

In his later career Bergson turned to a more serious consideration of religion and morality. He had earlier argued that metaphysical speculation by the traditional intellectual means must be misleading (since intellect has evolved for the ends of utility) and that some of the traditional metaphysical problems are in fact false dilemmas (like the so-called problem of free-will, as we noted). In *Les Deux Sources de la morale et de la religion* he advanced a more positive view that expanded the doctrines already seen of 'intellectual intuition' and of the individual's free creativity. He attacks the attempt, by Durkheim and others, to explain all religion and morality as the expression of social constraints or of psychological conditioning. Such 'static religion' and 'closed morality' do indeed exist, but Bergson urges us to study the religious and moral in their highest forms – as shown by such mystics as St John of the Cross, St Francis of Assisi and St Joan of Arc. In them we see religion linked with authentic spiritual experience, with an admirable balance of personality and with outflowing, creative love in action: they exemplify at their best 'la religion dynamique' and 'la morale ouverte'. Where 'closed morality' is the conventional ethic which society tries to impose on individuals to defend itself from chaos, 'open' or 'expanding' morality springs from the individual himself and his aspiration to a higher and more authentic level of moral goodness: it is essentially a personal invention.

Bergson's thought was expressed in a vivid, apparently lucid and even poetical style: it has even been suggested that this may have won some readers' assent to 'propositions which would hardly carry conviction if expressed in plain and sober prose'! Some critics have argued in particular that the insights of intuition are unverifiable and that Bergsonism thus condones irrationalism and subjective assertion, and they have also queried his account of material objects and his postulation of 'l'élan vital'. But however that may be, the effect of his ideas was refreshing and liberating, and by his positive assertions he also undoubtedly heralded some of the principal themes of existentialist philosophy. Both turn away from abstract intellection and closed dogmatics; both give primary emphasis to man's freedom and creativity and erect a vitalist form of humanism; both interpret moral values far less as standards outside ourselves, passively accepted by us, than as our own freely adopted inventions. Before turning to existentialism, however, we must now consider a second major manifestation of the spiritualist reaction in the twentieth century against the positivistic ideas of the nineteenth – namely, the renewal of Catholic thought.

The Catholic Revival

It is not surprising if to many observers around 1875 the Roman Church seemed to be in decline – assaulted by the arguments surveyed earlier in this chapter, dismissed by scientific humanists as irrelevant to the modern age, shorn of its territorial possessions and political power. The *Syllabus* of 1864, condemning such modern 'errors' as democracy, and the proclamation of papal infallibility at the Vatican Council of 1870 appeared to be rather desperate last-ditch attempts to reinforce a waning authority. But the outcome has been quite different – to the point that the renaissance of Catholic thought has proved one of the dominant features of the French intellectual scene in the twentieth century, matched only by the impact of Marxism, of Bergsonian philosophy, and of existentialism.

The Catholic revival was most evident in the later nineteenth century amongst literary writers – Barbey D'Aurevilly, Francis Jammes, and – more dramatically – other authors who were converted, within only a few years, from scientific naturalism or a sceptical cult of the self to Christian conviction. A novelist like Huysmans, earlier a naturalist admirer of Zola, evokes in *A rebours* (1884) the emptiness of an Epicurean search for novel sensations and in *En route* (1895) the motives which thereafter led him back to the Church, and in his later works he elaborates on the primarily personal and aesthetic reasons underlying his conversion. Bourget and Brunetière – having earlier been disciples of Taine – moved in the same direction, albeit more slowly and hesitantly, for primarily social and pragmatic motives: they prized Christian faith above all as a bulwark of moral and political order. Further illustrations are provided by Verlaine, by the young Paul Claudel, converted by a sudden experience in Notre-Dame-de-Paris in 1886, by Léon Bloy, Maurice Barrès and Charles Péguy, writers who created a tradition of Catholic literature that has been continued in more recent years by François Mauriac, Georges Bernanos, Gabriel Marcel and others.

In the realm of philosophy and theology this revival has been no less significant. The first and most orthodox group of French Catholic intellectuals who call for note are the Thomists – adherents of the thought of St Thomas Aquinas (1227–74), which had been proclaimed in 1879 as the official philosophy of the Roman Church, and closely linked with an international group of theological scholars (notably, Cardinal Mercier in Belgium). Jacques Maritain began as a Protestant admirer of Bergson, but after his conversion to Rome became a major Catholic thinker, influential both by his restatement of scholastic ideas in such works as *Saint Thomas d'Aquin apôtre des temps modernes* (1923) and *Primauté du spirituel* (1927) and by his attacks on post-medieval individualism and irrationalism. Amongst contemporary thinkers he particularly attacked Bergson – notably in *La Philosophie bergsonienne* (1914), the more striking since written by an erstwhile disciple. He can praise Bergson for his attacks on materialism, scientism and Kantian relativism but condemns him for his anti-intellectualist standpoint. Bergson's denial that our intellect can know reality opens the way to a new phenomenalism, a subjectivism that is inevitably in conflict with Thomist 'realism'. Similarly and more widely, Maritain contends, the Renaissance, the Reformation and Cartesianism represented in their break with scholastic orthodoxy an assertion of individualistic pride and error – a judgement expanded in *Antimoderne* (1922) and in his studies of Luther, Descartes and Rousseau in *Trois Réformateurs* (1925). Étienne Gilson has been equally forceful in expounding medieval philosophy – in studies like *La Philosophie au moyen âge* (1922; revised ed. 1944) and *L'Esprit de la philosophie médiévale* (1931–2) and also through his teaching at the Collège de France and the University of Toronto – and the reaffirmation of the scholastic outlook has been strengthened also by reviews like the *Annales de philosophie chrétienne*, the *Revue néo-scolastique* and the *Revue thomiste*. The achievement of these thinkers has been above all to re-examine and restate the Thomist teaching, to extend it by reference to modern knowledge, and to argue its relevance to the present age – a tendency seen also in the Dominican scholar A. D. Sertillanges. His expository works on *Saint Thomas d'Aquin* (1910) and *Les Grandes Thèses de la philosophie thomiste* (1928) stressed the need to 'nourrir par le dedans ce vivant qu'est le système en lui faisant assimiler toute la substance nutritive que les siècles ont depuis élaborée', and in his work on *Le Christianisme et les philosophies* (1941) he described 'le travail de rénovation' Thomism must undergo, in his view, in order to be fully revivified.

The Thomists represent the most traditionalist aspect of the Catholic renaissance. Other thinkers have moved in more 'modernist' directions; they offer new variations on the permanent themes of Catholic doctrine. They have sought to reinterpret the old faith in the light of modern ideas, whether Bergsonism (as with Édouard Le Roy) or existentialism (as with Gabriel Marcel). This is not to imply that most of them strayed into the full modernist 'heresy' which was condemned by Rome in 1907. Alfred Loisy (1857–1940) was almost alone in doing so (though Loyson went still further). Loisy was on the staff of the Institut Catholique in Paris, until he was dismissed in 1894 on account of his unorthodox ideas, and later became professor of the history of religions, from 1909 to 1932, at the Collège de France. His views are well indicated by his controversial book on *L'Évangile et l'église* (1902). His work on biblical criticism led him, first, to follow in the steps of Renan by denying the Church's doctrine on biblical infallibility: the Pentateuch (for instance) cannot be considered the work of Moses but is the product of successive generations, and the Gospels were probably compiled in a similar manner. He also interpreted Christ's teaching in primarily moral terms and denied that the Church was explicitly established by Christ or had any consequent right to impose its dogmas on the individual Christian.

Less unorthodox and in the long term more influential was the development of a Catholic 'philosophy of action'. This found its basis in the thought of Léon Ollé-Laprune (1830–99) and was developed more fully by Maurice Blondel (1861–1949) and the Abbé Laberthonnière (1860–1932). Ollé-Laprune rejected a merely abstract or intellectual concept of knowledge so far as moral truths are concerned. He stressed the primacy of practical reason, the role and dynamism of the will and the importance of creative action. 'Les vérités morales, règle pour la volonté en même temps que lumière pour l'esprit [he declares in his first major book, *De la certitude morale* (1880)], exigent un acte moral, un acte conforme à leur nature même, pour être pleinement reconnues et acceptées.' This approach was adopted by Blondel – as is indicated by the title of his doctoral thesis and best-known work, *L'Action: Essai d'une critique de la vie et d'une science de la pratique* (1893). Our life is above all a life of action, and philosophy should thus deal with this rather than with merely theoretical speculations. Action transcends the grasp of intellect (a view parallel to Bergson's) and is above all an expression of the will. In words that clearly anticipate the existentialist attitude Blondel proclaims: 'Nous sommes engagés et nous agissons, nous optons, que nous le voulions ou que nous ne le voulions pas. Ne pas faire, c'est encore se décider. Un enfant se noie; ne pas se décider à aller porter secours, c'est se décider contre.' Hence his opposition to dilettantism of the kind adopted by the young Maurice Barrès, for this fails to take seriously the consequences of our acts, and also to pessimism which preaches their ultimate pointlessness. On the contrary, Blondel believes, since action strives to attain some end beyond itself it presupposes a reality superior to action – a reality he claims to be divine and both immanent in man and also transcendent. For him, therefore, our actions are 'sacramental' – the manifestation of the divine that is both within us and beyond us – and to examine the life of action is to be led to a religious faith in God and in love as the ultimate good.

Another illustration of a Catholic modernism that opposes Thomism is offered by Édouard Le Roy (1870–1954), who was deeply influenced by Bergson. His primary aim was to reconcile Christian faith with science and philosophy. He continued his master's attack on the dogmas of scientism by maintaining that scientific laws, far from corresponding with reality, are artificial, even arbitrary, although useful constructs. The regularity and determinism which Taine and others attributed to the natural order are in fact the creation of the scientists themselves. But Le Roy also attacked the dogmatism of theology and particularly of the Thomists, notably in his *Dogme et critique* (1907) and *Le Problème de Dieu* (1929). Religious doctrines, like scientific laws, are useful and practical: they serve to exclude errors and guide us as to how we should act, but they cannot circumscribe ultimate truth or reduce it to a set of formulae. His more positive ideas, in such works as *Les Origines humaines et l'évolution de l'intelligence* (1930), developed the Bergsonian notion of creative evolution but have proved less durable, other than his stress on a practical and open moral idealism.

Other modernists active at this period included the Abbé Laberthonnière, who expanded Blondel's ideas, and Jacques Chevalier, who sought to link Bergson's thought with earlier philosophy, and one may sum up the main concerns of all these thinkers as being to fuse the old doctrines with new knowledge and preoccupations, to emphasize a vitalist and creative notion of man, and to oppose abstract philosophical and theological intellection. From the standpoint of the Roman Church certain of them fell into heresy: Loisy was excommunicated in 1908, and works by others were placed on the Index. None the less their thought has remained active and did in fact prefigure several contemporary trends within Catholicism – the 'personalism' of Emmanuel Mounier, the movement of 'la Philosophie de l'esprit' led by René Le Senne and Louis Lavelle, the ideas of Teilhard de Chardin, and, even earlier, Gabriel Marcel's Christian version of existentialism – the third dominant development in French thought in our century which we must now outline.

Existentialism

Existentialism tends to be considered a distinctively contemporary intellectual movement, stimulated by French experience under Nazi occupation and expressed in the works of wartime and post-war writers. Yet the first clearly existentialist thinker lived well over a hundred years ago – Sören Kierkegaard (1813–55), a deeply anguished Danish Christian – and in our own age German philosophy was much affected by such thinkers as Karl Jaspers and Martin Heidegger well before the rise of Hitler. In France Gabriel Marcel (1889–1973) was writing existentialist plays and essays from the 1920s onwards and Louis Lavelle's first two books appeared in 1921. The authors we most often connect with this movement – Sartre (b. 1905), Simone de Beauvoir (b. 1908), Maurice Merleau-Ponty (1906–61) and, to some degree, Camus and others – are in fact expanding and popularizing an already well-founded philosophy. If their thought has had a wider impact than their predecessors', this is because most of them have succeeded in conveying its ideas in the vivid and concrete modes of imaginative literature as well as in speculative writings. Comparatively few readers have studied (say) Sartre's *L'Être et le néant* (1943), his major and lengthy philosophical essay in 'phenomenological ontology', but his plays and novels have directly expressed its main themes to countless readers and spectators. Indeed, related to this fact, contemporary existentialism has almost certainly had less effect on professional philosophy than it has exerted on a wider audience as a body of general attitudes and ideas – and it is on this aspect that (for lack of space) we shall concentrate here.

It is arresting – at first sight at least – to note that the existentialist position has been expounded by both Christians such as Marcel and atheists like Sartre. What are the ideas which all of them hold in common? In the first place, they are all in reaction against abstract, intellectualist philosophy. Just as Kierkegaard began by opposing the rationalist metaphysics of Hegel, so his modern successors contend that most academic philosophers have been less concerned with the imperative problems posed by man's personal situation than with largely unreal or trivial questions. They have also thought primarily in terms of essences and universals – as when Plato describes the world as a mere reflection of the world of abstract ideas or Aristotle and many others seek to derive an ethic from a notion of 'universal human nature' to which each individual should seek to conform. The existentialists, on the contrary, assert the priority of existence over essence (an affirmation we shall return to) and press us to think in concrete terms about the actual problems of our existence. The 'essentialist' thinkers, moreover, emphasize rationality and objectivity as the prime desiderata of philosophy; the existentialists, on the other hand, are avowedly subjective. They are so, first, in that their concern is with the individual and his predicament – caught up in the dilemmas and sufferings of life and confronting his own inevitable death: hence in part their fondness for diary and meditation forms of writing – as illustrated by Antoine's diary in *La Nausée*, Rieux's diary in *La Peste*, or Marcel's *Journal métaphysique*, for instance. And they are so, secondly, in that their purpose is to appeal not only to their reader's intellect but to 'the whole man', man as subject: hence their belief that literary forms may offer more adequate means of communication than philosophical prose, that (in Simone de Beauvoir's characteristic words) 'seul le roman permettra d'évoquer dans sa réalité complète, singulière, temporelle, le jaillissement originel de l'existence'.

These attitudes stem from a preoccupation with existence, and these thinkers are all urging us to become more fully aware of the fact and implications of our existing. Many people pass their life in a dream, as it were, in a state of non-reflexion and habit, searching only for a passive state of satisfaction, without ever considering their true situation – the chanciness of the very existence of the world and themselves, the moral choices which life challenges them to make, the inevitability of their death. Pascal (often invoked as a precursor of existentialism) could declare: 'Je m'effraie et m'étonne de me voir ici plutôt que là, car il n'y a point de raison pourquoi ici plutôt que là, pourquoi à présent plutôt que lors.' So, likewise, the existentialists feel (in Marcel's words) that 'l'existence n'est pas séparable de l'étonnement'. Furthermore, we neglect all too often the existence of others as well as of ourselves – as when we treat them as mere objects which are useful or injurious to us – in the manner, at worst, of Nazism, but no less commonly in our daily lives where we only rarely achieve what Marcel terms 'true intersubjectivity' and meet other people 'in openness'.

But existence is a highly ambiguous term. These writers distinguish three kinds of existence in particular – for which a German terminology developed by Heidegger and others is most helpful. 'Vorhandensein' indicates the existence of inanimate objects. 'Dasein' indicates the existence of animals – and of humans in so far as they exist for (say) government officials. 'Existenz', in contrast, may be translated as 'full existence' – 'really living' as opposed to 'merely existing'; it involves an active 'engagement' in life as opposed to the passive engagement of 'Dasein'. It fundamentally implies developing oneself and realizing one's potentialities; it presupposes constant change – and not the passive change undergone (say) by heated metal or freezing water, but an active, conscious, willed change that derives from choice and freedom. And since only man has freedom to choose in this way, it follows that 'Existenz' is the special, distinguishing prerogative of man.

Yet many people do not utilize their freedom; they accept society's conventional values and share its mass reactions. And hence the existentialists seek to insist that one must choose one's own values, utilize one's freedom in an authentic way, create one's own essential self – and here is another way in which existence precedes essence, for what I essentially have been will only be finally fixed when I no longer exist. They do of course accept that we are all determined to some extent by external factors – society, class, education, heredity, and so on – but they assert that we still retain freedom as to the ways in which we react to these conditioning factors.

To choose implies motives and standards for choice, however. Yet these are not evident, they believe, do not obviously inhere in the objective world. Even the Christian existentialists are conscious of a metaphysical darkness, an apparent irrationality, in the world. Pascal urged man in this situation to 'wager', and Kierkegaard postulated the need for a 'leap of faith'. The modern existentialists agree that each man must adopt his own values, but atheists and Christians differ as to the values they support, as we must now see – just as, indeed, their statements of even this common outlook naturally reveal somewhat differing emphases.

The first distinctive stress of atheists like Sartre is upon the experience of 'absurdity', of (in the title of Sartre's first novel) 'la nausée'. This sense of the meaninglessness of life and of revulsion from it and from other people seems to have four principal sources. First, since God does not exist in their view it follows that there is no objective, 'God-given', purpose in human life. Like Nietzsche and Malraux before them, Sartre and Camus (who shared some existentialist notions whilst rejecting others) realize the vast moral consequences of 'the death of God'. Whereas earlier atheist humanists asserted that accepted moral values remain no less imperative even without a deity to validate them, the existentialist, Sartre tells us, 'pense qu'il est très gênant que Dieu n'existe pas, car avec lui disparaît toute possibilité de trouver des valeurs dans un ciel intelligible'. The feeling of absurdity derives, secondly, from the inevitability of our death: given this final end (for it is assumed by these thinkers that we enter no after-life), no value or purpose can have any ultimate status for us. Thirdly, we observe that the world and all within it are contingent, fortuitous, finally inexplicable. Nothing is 'necessary', and at times, therefore, the existentialist feels disgust at the sight of objects (such as the chestnut tree described in *La Nausée*), of other people, and even of himself. And this feeling of the pointlessness, the superfluous quality of people is heightened as we observe them (and ourselves) leading a life of habit, of passive conventionality.

Yet fully to realize our absurd situation need not be depressing; on the contrary, we are liberated to live our own existence untrammelled by fear of divine punishment, moral conventions, or hope and concern for the future. At times, certainly, our total freedom will weigh upon us: we are (Sartre notes) 'condemned' to be free, and though each of us is 'un projet', 'une liberté pure', we have no obvious criteria to guide our choices. But even this can be reinvigorating and challenging – as Hugo in Sartre's *Les Mains sales* finds when he finally affirms his justification for killing Hoederer. Furthermore, these thinkers do suggest that there are at least some signposts as to how we should live – and here one may discern indications of the old humanist values they began by rejecting! Thus Sartre contends that, since all that is 'given' is man's liberty, we should embrace that liberty as a supreme value; we should be constrained in our choices by a sense of responsibility to others and by the imperative of freedom – for others as well as ourselves. He also urges that we should seek to live 'authentically', without falling into that deception of others and of ourselves which marks 'la mauvaise foi', and he adds that only by living in this wholly honest way can we establish fruitful and genuine relations with other people. At first sight others appear to menace and delimit our own freedom, and in the face of their challenge we may be tempted either to surrender to them – to conform to what they want us to be (the reaction Hugo finally rejects at the conclusion of *Les Mains sales*) – or to fight against them (the reaction of the characters in *Huis-clos*, a play ending with the words: 'L'enfer, c'est les autres.'). But either response brings frustration, deceit, hypocrisy, and makes men into enemies; by contrast, 'authenticity' allows us to achieve a new relation of equality and friendship with others.

Sartre has turned increasingly to the political arena since he first expounded these ideas, but the leading French representative of existentialist *Christianity*, Gabriel Marcel, remained concerned above all with the individual person and his relations with other individuals.

It may first be noted that Christianity is in several ways an existentialist religion *avant la lettre*. It has always stressed the existential reality of God Himself – a personal Being, not a mere First Cause or abstract principle, a God 'who was made flesh and dwelt amongst us', a God with whom men can achieve a personal link – and equally of each human individual, eternally himself. The Christian faith also emphasizes each person's moral freedom and responsibility and the imperative of choice. In addition, some Christians have experienced a deep sense of anguish before life's irrationality – a tradition illustrated, for example, by Tertullien, Augustine and Pascal, underlying also the theology of predestination, and most clearly related to existentialist themes by Kierkegaard.

Marcel is less anguished than they, however, and manifests greater confidence in divine justice than at least Kierkegaard. He was converted to Catholicism in 1929, but well before that he was keeping his *Journal métaphysique (1913–1923)* (published 1928) and writing his first plays. Yet his major philosophical essays come later – notably *Être et avoir* (1935), *Homo Viator* (1945) and *Le Mystère de l'être* (1949–50) – the last consisting of particularly probing lectures – and his mature thought is basically Christian as well as existentialist.

Marcel is deliberately unsystematic in his thinking: to summarize his outlook is to risk reducing it to a quite misleading orderliness. His aims are to stimulate awareness and contemplation about man's situation and, in a discursive manner, to explore certain experiences and aspects of life which seem to him significant. He does not wish to impose a philosophy upon his readers, to compel their assent, but rather to solicit them to find a philosophy of their own, to achieve a belief that must be personal and involve personal commitment. This attitude follows from certain of the principal themes of his own meditations. He is first and above all aware of the 'mystery of being' – the mysterious in life itself and the universe, in the religious order, and especially in the individual. The question: 'Who am I?' dominates an early play like *Un Homme de Dieu* (1925) and is reiterated throughout his work, both essays and plays, many of whose characters are seeking to 'know themselves'. To plumb this realm of the mysterious cannot be achieved by a reasoning that is abstract, mathematical, systematic, he contends; the kind of reason apt for this task must be concrete, intuitive, contemplative – what he terms 'la réflexion' – and hence he defines metaphysics as 'la réflexion braquée sur un mystère'. He also stresses that this contemplative process of inquiry should begin not from abstractions or *a priori* notions but from experience – from one's personal experience in particular, for Marcel is less interested in sensory observations than in man's inner, spiritual life. Thus he declares: 'L'expérience s'intimise pour ainsi dire et s'exerce à reconnaître ses implications.' Moreover, he points out, my basic experience of myself is less of an object than of a subject: whereas we observe an object from without, we identify ourselves with a subject, and Marcel argues that a particularly significant kind of knowledge comes from such 'participation', especially as found in our acquaintance with other people. Indeed, he claims that love is the only starting-point for a complete understanding of persons and the 'mysteries' of interpersonal existence.

The distinction of subject and object is linked for him with other, parallel distinctions. Thus he juxtaposes the realms of 'being' and of 'having': 'l'avoir est tout ce qui peut être aliéné; l'être, c'est l'inaliénable, l'intransmissible'. And whilst the world of 'having', of objects and of persons treated as objects, presents 'problems' which can be solved by reason and calculation, the world of 'being', of subjects, confronts us with 'mysteries' with which we are personally 'engaged' and which are not amenable to 'solutions'. Regrettably, the modern technological world treats people as mere 'fonctionnaires', that is as objects, reduces life to a series of 'problems' to be solved, evaluates it in terms of 'having', of profitability and possessions, and increasingly deprives men of their privacy – and thereby of the inwardness, imagination and creativity that go with it. We live in a 'broken world', Marcel asserts – of the kind portrayed in his play of 1933, *Le Monde cassé*: 'Chacun a son coin, sa petite affaire, ses petits intérêts. On se rencontre, on s'entrechoque . . . Mais il n'y a plus de centre, plus de vie, nulle part.'

The link between these themes and Christianity is evident, and in addition Marcel stresses our experience of a 'transcendental' dimension and interprets Christian belief as centred on belief in a person, Christ, and on achieving full 'intersubjectivity' between man and man and

God and man. In 1950 existentialism was the object of papal condemnation – for its irrationalism, individualism, subjectivism and pessimism, amongst other reasons. But these charges would seem to leave almost wholly unscathed Marcel's contemplative, human and – in his own word – 'neo-Socratic' Catholicism.

More generally, however, Marcel illustrated one of the ways in which even Catholic thought has moved, in some of its exponents, in the same directions as have been discerned in Bergsonism and the atheist existentialists. Amongst other Catholic examples we can only note, for lack of space, the 'personalism' of Emmanuel Mounier (1905–50), best expressed in the pages of his review *Esprit* and in such books as *Le Personnalisme* (1949), and the movement of 'la Philosophie de l'esprit' founded by René Le Senne and Louis Lavelle (1883–1951) and most fully developed in Lavelle's philosophical works, notably *La Dialectique de l'éternel présent* (4 vols, 1928–51). What are these common tendencies – which can also be discerned in literary writers from Péguy and Gide to Malraux and Saint-Exupéry? We may summarize them, all too briefly, as a movement away from traditional philosophy and towards a more undogmatic and personal commitment; towards a primary emphasis on man's freedom and creativity and on a vitalist humanism; towards a conception of moral values less as rules accepted from outside ourselves than as our own personally adopted inventions. Important differences naturally persist, but underlying them one finds affinities both in what is rejected – the authoritarianism of those earlier nineteenth-century attitudes which this chapter began by surveying in positivists and Catholics alike – and in what these thinkers have aspired to achieve: a largely undogmatic adumbration of a humane, creative personalism.

Structuralism

If existentialism was the dominant intellectual movement in Paris from around the Second World War to at least the mid-1960s, since then a comparable influence has been gained by structuralism. It is easy to be alienated by some of its features as a reigning 'fashion', in America especially as well as France: an apparent cult of jargon and stylistic mystification; a sometimes strident intolerance of other views; tendencies to collective self-promotion and to academic camp-following, not least in literary criticism. But these, even if irritating, are perhaps typical of every new movement seeking acceptance; structuralism should be seen as a longer-term, not merely fashionable phenomenon and be judged by its leaders rather than its more inadequate disciples and epigones and the younger scholars they tend to dominate. Even so, however, it is rash to attempt a brief summary of a movement still in contentious development, which ranges so widely, and whose full implications cannot yet be clear – and the more so as some of its leading exponents have sometimes denied belonging to any group at all.

Structuralism may be defined in a broad sense – likely to prove to have been the more significant over both past and future decades – and in a narrower sense which is more dominant at present. In its broader meaning it expresses a general tendency of thought or, better still, a method of approach – or 'activity', as Barthes puts it – that has been influential in physics, mathematics, biology, anthropology, psychology, history and sociology as well as cultural studies, linguistics and philosophy. All individual facts or phenomena are to be understood not in themselves but as the elements of an organized whole or 'structure', a 'structure' being not the sum of its separate parts but essentially an 'organism' whose parts have value only as they function within the totality and are interrelated with its other parts (like, for example, the separate parts of a human body). One can indeed see structuralism as a culmination of the move from the *atomism* of Cartesian or Newtonian physics to the *organicism* introduced by biological studies from the later eighteenth century onwards (and it is perhaps no coincidence that some structuralists and scholars of the history of linguistics have been particularly interested in that chronological period), even though many structuralists invoke less the notion of 'organisms' than that of more abstract, conceptual 'models', as increasingly utilized by the natural sciences.

But the structuralists go distinctly further than this: they argue that the 'structures' which can explain surface phenomena are deep below that surface; they are not explicit in the data studied but can only be discerned by sensitive analysis of what is implicit and underlying – though, when that is achieved, we shall see that these underlying factors largely determine and account for the explicit phenomena. This determinism is not total: an individual or social group may, as it were, 'play variations upon a theme', but the 'theme' itself – notwithstanding such idiosyncrasies – derives from fundamental structural realities that are common (it is asserted in principle by many structuralists) to all mankind, not merely to just one social group or even collection of similar societies. Hence, for instance, Lévi-Strauss can write of primitive mythologies: 'Nous ne prétendons pas montrer comment les hommes pensent dans les mythes, mais comment les mythes se pensent dans les hommes et *à leur insu*' – without men being conscious of them or the ways their myths derive from and illustrate a universal 'structure'. It follows that for him and other structuralists little or nothing in our life is gratuitous ('absurd' in the existentialist sense); there is a coherent totality which decides (contrary to Sartre's postulation of our free will) the basic features of human activity. Such views have led to the claim that structuralism is a reaction against existentialism or even its very antithesis – though here one can note the influence on structuralists like Lévi-Strauss of the existentialist philosopher Merleau-Ponty (whose first major work was on *La Structure du comportement*), and also that some structuralists – Chomsky in America, for example – do emphasize human creativity.

Structuralism in this wider meaning has found precursors in earlier periods: for example, in *Gestalt* psychology (which stresses, for instance, that what we perceive are 'meaningful wholes') and in the sociology of Durkheim and Mauss (who see a society as an articulated system existing independently of the individuals within it), but especially in Marx and Freud, whose systems have been reinterpreted in structuralist terms by, in particular, Louis Althusser (b. 1918) and Jacques Lacan (b. 1901) respectively. For Marx a society's laws, institutions, thought, morality, literature, and so on, form a 'superstructure' that is ultimately determined by its economic 'infrastructure'; more broadly, he claims that 'life is not determined by consciousness, but consciousness by life' – a view that seems basic to structuralism too. For Freud our actions and mental life are analogously determined – less by our conscious thoughts and decisions than by subconscious forces – forces, moreover, wider than the individual alone; and he adds that the study of dreams, for instance, can lead us to discern 'the structure and functions of the psychic apparatus'.

Naturally, not all Marxists or Freudians accept the interpretation given by Althusser or Lacan of their master, and parallel disagreements exist as to the utility of structuralist notions in other subjects – in mathematics, for example, where a group of French scientists using the pseudonym of N. Bourbaki have developed notions of mathematical structure derived from the work earlier of Cantor, Frege, Russell and others. Yet it is clear that, first, structuralism existed to a significant extent *avant la lettre* (much as, say, existentialism has been discovered in Socrates, St Augustine or Pascal) and, second, that it has a wide-ranging interdisciplinary significance. This has been stressed especially by Jean Piaget (b. 1896) in his book on *Le Structuralisme* (1968). Zoologist, psychologist, philosopher and historian of science, Piaget – though perhaps too neglected by structuralists elsewhere – is the most senior and distinguished thinker amongst a number of Genevan intellectuals whose role has been distinct from the Parisian developments. For him structuralism is a method of analysis applicable to numerous disciplines, both scientific and humanist, and he also affirms that every 'structure', in whatever area, has the same basic characteristics of *totalité* (to be understood only as a whole), *transformations* (never static, constantly self-developing) and *autoréglage* (self-regulating and understandable wholly from within itself). A similarly comprehensive view has been taken by others – by Ernst Cassirer in America from the pre-war period on, for example, and notably by N. Trubetzkoy in the 1930s who noted 'the tendency of all scientific disciplines to replace atomism with structuralism'. He was a leading member of the Prague Linguistic Circle in the inter-war years and, perhaps ironically, it was this group, influenced by the Russian formalists of the 1920s, which first developed structuralism in its narrower sense. (Trubetzkoy would certainly regret that structuralist analyses have now become as limiting as, in earlier decades, the philological study of literature or the slavish practice of *explication de texte*.)

In its more limited but currently influential meaning, structuralism claims that the theories and methods of structural linguistics first formulated by Ferdinand de Saussure (1857–1913; *Cours de linguistique générale*, 1916) are valuable and even indispensable for the analysis of all aspects of human culture. Saussure's teaching, at Paris and then Geneva (even now the two principal European centres of structuralist work), established the approach and the distinctions still dominant today. He claimed that every distinct language is a functional structure of relationships between its many units, each of whose significance lies solely in those relationships, and he also emphasized certain distinctions necessary, in his view, to study language on this basis – notably, between *le signifiant* and *le signifié*; *langage*, *langue* and *parole*; and the synchronic and diachronic approaches to any language, the former studying language as a state at a point in time, the latter as a succession of states through time. Moreover, he thought that language is only one 'system of signs' amongst others within a society and thus argued that linguistics is only one branch of a much wider 'science of signs' (semiology or semiotics) – a notion that had already been sketched by the contemporary American philosopher Charles S. Peirce. It follows for him that his methods for linguistics can be no less fruitfully applied to other socio-cultural systems of signs – myths, customs and so on.

Saussure's pioneering ideas on linguistic methodology were developed above all by Trubetzkoy and R. Jakobson and, later, by scholars in America (where the latter moved early in the Second World War) like N. Chomsky. By contrast (though this is to overgeneralize), the actual applications of the methods to other cultural areas have been attempted above all in Paris and notably at the École Pratique des Hautes Études, of which Lévi-Strauss was appointed Directeur in 1950, of whose 6ᵉ section Barthes later became Directeur d'Études, and to which Lacan went in 1963. In Paris (one should also note) commitment to 'total history', *histoire intégrale*, had already been illustrated by Lucien Febvre, Fernand Braudel and other contributors to the journal *Annales* (in which, incidentally, Barthes published at least one early article and which shares the structuralists' interest in Michelet – on whom Barthes has published a book – as historian of 'la résurrection intégrale du passé').

The most seminal Parisian structuralist is Claude Lévi-Strauss (b. 1908). He began his career as professor of anthropology in Brazil; his most accessible book, *Tristes Tropiques* (1955), draws on his expeditions there and indicates the structural approach to primitive myths and social anthropology (in which he became professor at the Collège de France in 1959) that is expanded in *Anthropologie structurale* (1958), *La Pensée sauvage* (1962) and *Le Cru et le cuit* (1964). (Merleau-Ponty was a fellow passenger on his return sea-voyage from Brazil, as it chanced, and *La Pensée sauvage* is dedicated, appropriately, to him.) It is presumptuous to summarize a highly significant life's work, but much of it follows from Lévi-Strauss's belief that linguistics is 'la science sociale la plus développée'. Underlying a wide variety of Brazilian, Red Indian and other myths, and apparently different social customs and attitudes – about dress, or raw as opposed to cooked food, for instance – he finds a common structure that expresses the structure of human nature itself. The separate activities of a given society relate to its basic deep structure, but, beyond even that, there are fundamental similarities between the activities of different societies – as will emerge when we study their art, kinship systems, myths, cooking customs, etc. Each of these is a system of signs, exactly as a language was for Saussure, and Saussure's distinctions are equally essential for their understanding. Even those who allege that Lévi-Strauss may sometimes force the evidence to fit his hypotheses would not deny the greatly extended understanding of communication and cultural expression which his major achievements have inspired.

A younger but, in literary-critical circles, even more currently influential structuralist is Roland Barthes (b. 1915), who has worked in two main areas. His work and impact in literary criticism are outside the scope of this chapter,[1] but one can just note that it is characteristic of his basic attitude (an attitude more broadly based in Marxism, Freud, existentialism and structural linguistics than that of his numerous imitators) that in studying (say) Michelet he seeks for 'une thématique . . .; ou mieux encore: un réseau organisé d'obsessions'. His approach could be simply put as: 'Analyse from within; the author's life and society or literary and intellectual history are secondary' – an approach which some of his disciples have amply utilized to justify their ignorance or distortions of such matters. More significant in the longer term, it may prove, is Barthes's work in wider cultural studies – in books like *Mythologies* (1957), *Éléments de sémiologie* (1965) and *Système de la mode* (1967). This last work applies to clothing fashions the Saussurean distinctions mentioned earlier: Saussure's *le langage* = *le vêtement, la langue* = *le costume, la parole* = *l'habillement*. Dress is treated as a typical cultural expression amongst many others, as another system of signs. The phenomena of our clothing (mini-skirt or deliberately frayed jeans for some; bespoke suit, striped shirt and silk tie for others, to give random recent examples) pose, for Barthes, 'les problèmes essentiels de toute analyse culturelle'. In basic terms, we communicate information to others not only through what we say and write but also through the way we dress, the sort of house we live in, the kind of food we choose to eat (breakfast *croissants* and coffee for citizens of Calais; eggs, bacon and tea for people twenty miles away in Dover), and the kind of analysis rewarding for one means of communication (language) is no less applicable to others: all cultural 'indicators', in his view, 'sont signifiants dans la mesure seulement où ils sont liés par un ensemble de normes collectives'.

Numerous other scholars have exemplified the structuralist approach to their various disciplines, in literary criticism and elsewhere. One example is seen in the work in the history of science and of ideas of Michel Foucault (b. 1926), since 1970 professor at the Collège de France. Whilst he has rejected the structuralist label, his works on

[1] Cf. Chapter 9, pp. 472–5, for an outline of structuralist literary criticism.

Histoire de la folie (1961), *Les Mots et les choses* (1966) and *L'Archéologie du savoir* (1969), and more recent studies, are seeking for 'les codes fondamentaux d'une culture', alleging (amongst much else) that the possible sciences of a given period derive from factors that are 'structurally' determined.

Instant judgements about structuralism would be foolish (though they have already been plentiful). One may readily assent to the 'structured' model mentioned earlier; one may, justifiably and with academic and self-protecting gravity, find the structuralists to be 'stimulating' or 'suggestive'. The fundamental question – it seems to one reader – concerns their theory of knowledge: how, precisely, can we verify or, alternatively, falsify structuralist analyses? Are structuralists too subjective and too selective as to evidence? This has certainly been alleged, and Lévi-Strauss himself stresses that 'structure' is not of the order of observable fact. Marx's allegedly scientific theories, Freud's psychoanalytical interpretations, the analyses of Lévi-Strauss or Barthes, such literary-critical assertions (to cite just one instance) as that Michelet's 'underlying desire' is to be 'a sacrificial mother' – all of these pose the same epistemological problems about verification and meaning. Leading structuralists are well aware of such questions and claim answers to them (unlike certain of their followers who seem to make anti-empiricist appeals to 'insights' hidden from more humdrum minds), and Lévi-Strauss, for example, is rigorously empirical in gathering anthropological data. Yet the methodology of interpretation of data may at the present still seem – at least to those reared in the empiricist tradition – to be inadequately established.

Bibliography

GENERAL

Less attention has been given to nineteenth- than to twentieth-century French thought in recent decades, even in France itself, social and political ideas alone excepted, and even major texts by nineteenth-century philosophers are not always easy to find in print. However, there is a recent, comprehensive and major survey by Frederick Copleston, *A History of Philosophy*, Vol. IX, *Maine de Biran to Sartre* (London, 1975), which may help to reverse that tendency; it also contains a most useful bibliography, to which students of detailed subjects and of many individual thinkers must refer. Standard French histories of philosophy are É. Bréhier, *Histoire de la philosophie: La Philosophe moderne*, Vols III and IV (Paris, 1932; English translation, Chicago, 1968–9); J. Chevalier, *Histoire de la pensée*, Vol. IV: *La Pensée moderne* (Paris, 1966); L. Lévy-Bruhl, *History of Modern Philosophy in France* (London, 1899); V. Delbos, *La Philosophie française* (Paris, 1919); and, for the period since *c.* 1870, I. Benrubi, *Les Sources et les courants de la philosophie contemporaine en France*, 2 vols (Paris, 1933); J. Guitton, *Regards sur la pensée française, 1870–1940* (Paris, 1968); L. Lavelle, *La Philosophie française entre les deux guerres* (Paris, 1942); and D. Parodi, *La Philosophie contemporaine en France* (Paris, 1919). Briefer studies in French, providing a more rapid survey, are A. Cresson, *Les Courants de la pensée philosophique française*, 2nd ed., Vol. II (Paris, 1931); J. Lacroix, *Marxisme, existentialisme, personnalisme* (Paris, 1951); and J. Wahl, *Tableau de la philosophie française* (Paris, 1962). In English, three lucid but now somewhat dated works are G. Boas, *French Philosophies of the Romantic Period*, 2nd ed. (New York, 1964); A. L. Guérard, *French Prophets of Yesterday* (London, 1913); and J. A. Gunn, *Modern French Philosophy (1851–1921)* (London, 1922). A more recent survey of nineteenth-century thought is given by D. G. Charlton, *Secular Religions in France (1815–1870)* (London, 1963), and on twentieth-century thinkers there are M. Farber (ed.), *Philosophic Thought in France and the United States* (New York, 1950), and C. Smith, *Contemporary French Philosophy* (London, 1964) – both of them offering useful studies in English.

CATHOLICS

A long-standing and still illuminating study of one strand in Catholic thought is G. Weill, *Histoire du catholicisme libéral en France (1828–1908)* (Paris, 1909), whilst wider and authoritative studies are A. Dansette, *Histoire religieuse de la France contemporaine*, 2 vols (Paris, 1951–2), and L. Foucher, *La Philosophie catholique en France au dix-neuvième siècle* (Paris, 1955). Briefer studies, which also discuss literary writers, are provided by J. Calvet, *Le Renouveau catholique dans la littérature contemporaine* (Paris, 1931); H. Guillemin, *Histoire des catholiques français (1815–1905)* (Paris, 1947); and V. Giraud, *De Chateaubriand à Brunetière: Essai sur le mouvement catholique en France au dix-neuvième siècle* (Paris, 1938). On one important development there is the major work of J. B. Duroselle, *Les Débuts du catholicisme social en France (1822–1870)* (Paris, 1951), and on modernism two books by E. Poulat, *Histoire, dogme et critique dans la crise moderniste* (Paris, 1962), and *Alfred Loisy: sa vie, son œuvre* (Paris, 1960). On the 'philosophy of action' there are H. Duméry, *La Philosophie de l'action* (Paris, 1948), and J. Paliard, *Maurice Blondel ou le dépassement chrétien* (Paris, 1950). A helpful study of its subject in English is B. Menczer, *Catholic Political Thought, 1789–1848* (London, 1952). On recent Catholics like Maritain, Gilson, Teilhard de Chardin and Marcel, the bibliographies in Copleston (cited above) are especially helpful.

POSITIVISTS

In French there is a long-standing major study of one aspect of the positivist movement by S. Charléty, *Histoire du saint-simonisme*, 2nd ed. (Paris, 1931), but more of the general surveys, surprisingly, are in English: D. G. Charlton, *Positivist Thought in France (1852–1870)* (Oxford, 1959); F. A. Hayek, *The Counter-Revolution of Science* (Glencoe, Ill., 1942) (written, however, from a particular critical viewpoint); and chapters in F. E. Manuel, *The Prophets of Paris* (Cambridge, Mass., 1962). On individual thinkers most studies are naturally in French. On Comte, two difficult but major works are J. Delvolvé, *Réflexions sur la pensée comtienne* (Paris, 1932), and P. Ducassé, *Méthode et intuition chez A. Comte*

(Paris, 1939), to which one may add an older but still valuable study in G. Dumas, *Psychologie de deux messies positivistes: Saint-Simon et A. Comte* (Paris, 1905), and an authoritative historical survey in H. Gouhier, *La Jeunesse d'A. Comte et la formation du positivisme*, 3 vols (Paris, 1933–41). Useful short expositions are G. Cantecor, *Comte* (Paris, n.d.); A. Cresson, *Comte* (Paris, 1941); and (from a somewhat uncritical admirer) P. Arnaud, *Pour connaître la pensée d'A. Comte* (Paris, 1969). Two most interesting and, at their time, influential analyses by philosophers who were themselves much affected by Comte's earlier thought (but rejected his later religious ideas) are É. Littré, *A. Comte et la philosophie positive*, 2nd ed. (Paris, 1864), and J. S. Mill, *A. Comte and Positivism*, 2nd ed. (London, 1866). On Taine, the major studies in French are still G. Barzellotti, *La Philosophie de Taine* (Paris, 1900), and A. Chevrillon, *Taine: Formation de sa pensée* (Paris, 1932) to which can also be added a detailed study of Taine's intellectual duality in C. Evans, *Taine: Essai de biographie intérieure* (Paris, 1975); good shorter treatment is found in M. Leroy, *Taine* (Paris, 1933), and P. V. Rubov, *Taine: Étapes de son œuvre* (Paris, 1930). In English there is little – a chapter in Charlton, op. cit., and (on his thought as a would-be scientific cultural historian) S. J. Kahn, *Science and Aesthetic Judgment* (London, 1953); L. Weinstein, *Hippolyte Taine* (New York, 1972), is a recent survey but deals mainly with the literary and art criticism to the neglect of his philosophy. On Renan as a thinker the works of J. Pommier are authoritative: *Renan* (Paris, 1923); *La Pensée religieuse de Renan* (Paris, 1925); and *La Jeunesse cléricale de Renan* (Paris, 1933). The best short surveys are P. Van Tieghem, *Renan* (Paris, 1948), and M. Weiler, *La Pensée de Renan* (Grenoble, 1945).

ECLECTICS AND LIBERALS

These thinkers have been too little examined in recent decades; the best studies are mainly in French. J. M. Carré, *Michelet et son temps* (Paris, 1926), and G. Monod, *La Vie et la pensée de Michelet*, 2 vols (Paris, 1923), both remain important, and more recent studies include O. A. Haac, *Les Principes inspirateurs de Michelet* (New Haven, 1951), and J. L. Cornuz, *Jules Michelet* (Geneva and Paris, 1955). On the Eclectics there is little other than P. Dubois, *Cousin, Jouffroy, Damiron* (Paris, 1902), and P. Janet, *Victor Cousin et son œuvre*, 3rd ed. (Paris, 1893), though much useful material is contained in J. Barthélemy-Saint Hilaire, *V. Cousin, sa vie et sa correspondance*, 3 vols (Paris, 1895). On Quinet, one may consult R. H. Powers, *Edgar Quinet: A Study in French Patriotism* (Dallas, 1957), and H. Tronchon, *Le Jeune Edgar Quinet* (Paris, 1937), in particular. On Jouffroy, interesting but incomplete studies are Dubois, op. cit.; M. Salomon, *Jouffroy* (Paris, 1907); and (authoritative but on limited subjects) J. Pommier, *Deux études sur Jouffroy et son temps* (Paris, 1930).

HISTORY, PROGRESS AND POLITICAL THOUGHT

These subjects are treated mainly in Chapter 8. On the many 'secular' creeds of the nineteenth century there is a select bibliography as well as a survey in D. G. Charlton, *Secular Religions in France (1815–1870)* (London, 1963), pp. 217 ff. Certain of them are discussed more fully in P. Bénichou, *Le Temps des prophètes* (Paris, 1977). Considerable attention has been given to the social and political thinkers of the period – more so than to its philosophers, one may think. Amongst many studies, the following are good general surveys: R. Aron, *Main Currents in Sociological Thought*, 2 vols (London, 1968–70); C. C. A. Bouglé, *Socialismes français*, 2nd ed. (Paris, 1933); J. B. Bury, *The Idea of Progress*, 2nd ed. (New York, 1955); A. Gray, *The Socialist Tradition* (London, 1946); L. Halphen, *L'Histoire en France depuis cent ans* (Paris, 1914); M. Leroy, *Histoire des idées sociales en France*, Vols II and III (Paris, 1950–4); J. P. Mayer, *Political Thought in France from Sieyès to Sorel*, 3rd ed. (London, 1961); P. Moreau, *L'Histoire en France au XIXe siècle* (Paris, 1935); R. Pierce, *Contemporary French Political Thought* (Oxford, 1966); R. Soltau, *French Political Thought in the Nineteenth Century* (London, 1931); and J. L. Talmon, *Political Messianism: The Romantic Phase* (London, 1952) (though this may be thought a somewhat tendentious study). On individual writers there are likewise numerous works, of which one may note in particular: D. W. Brogan, *Proudhon* (London, 1934); J. Lively, *The Social and Political Thought of Alexis de Tocqueville* (Oxford, 1962); A. Pinloche, *Fourier et le socialisme* (Paris, 1933); G. Woodcock, *P. J. Proudhon* (London, 1956); *Revue internationale de philosophie*, LX (1962), fasc. 2, *Charles Fourier*; and F. E. Manuel, *The New World of Henri Saint-Simon* (Cambridge, Mass., 1956) – a particularly full study in English – to which one can add a good selection in translation and an introduction in F. M. H. Markham, *Saint-Simon: Selected Writings* (Oxford, 1952).

THE CRITICAL REACTION

This major development in later nineteenth century French thought warrants renewed examination. The principal studies remain A. Aliotta, *The Idealistic Reaction against Science* (London, 1914); G. Fonsegrive, *L'Évolution des idées dans la France contemporaine* (Paris, 1920) (concerned more with literary than philosophical writers); two important volumes by D. Parodi, *Du positivisme à l'idéalisme*, 2 vols (Paris, 1930); and an incisive, lucid thesis by L. S. Stebbing, *Pragmatism and French Voluntarism* (Cambridge, 1914). Richard Griffiths, *The Reactionary Revolution* (London, 1966), has numerous useful insights but does not seek to explore the philosophical reaction itself. On individuals the most useful studies are S. W. Floss, *Outline of the Philosophy of Cournot* (Philadelphia, 1941); J. Grenier, *La Philosophie de Jules Lequier* (Paris, 1936); L. Prat, *Charles Renouvier, philosophe* (Ariège, 1973); and G. Milhaud, *La Philosophie de Renouvier* (Paris, 1927); but the entire movement in which 'idealism' (in its differing senses) was opposed to 'positivism' and 'scientism' requires fresh scrutiny. Two difficult but major works on its most philosophically outstanding thinker are O. Hamelin, *Le Système de Renouvier* (Paris, 1927), and R. Verneaux, *L'Idéalisme de Renouvier* (Paris, 1945).

BERGSON AND THE NEO-SPIRITUALISTS

New general surveys are needed to supplement A. Etcheverry, *L'Idéalisme français contemporain* (Paris, 1934), and A. Thibaudet, *Le Bergsonisme*, 2 vols (Paris, 1924). Very helpful studies of individuals are provided by I. W. Alexander, *Bergson* (London, 1957); J. Chevalier, *Bergson* (Paris, 1926); G. Mauchaussat, *L'Idéalisme de Lachelier* (Paris, 1961); and G. Séailles, *La Philosophie de J. Lachelier* (Paris, 1921). A. D. Lindsay, *The Philosophy of Bergson* (London, 1911), provides an earlier but still useful English assessment of its subject, whilst more recent Anglo-Saxon views are found in *The Bergsonian Heritage*, ed. T. Hanna (New York and London, 1962).

EXISTENTIALISTS

There are numerous works of which the best general examinations are P. Foulquié, *L'Existentialisme* (Paris, 1949); R. Grimsley, *Existentialist Thought* (Cardiff, 1955); and E. Mounier, *Introduction aux existentialismes* (Paris, 1947). On individuals, likewise, there are many studies; perhaps the most helpful for English readers are S. Cain, *Gabriel Marcel* (London, 1963); N. N. Greene, *J.-P. Sartre: The Existentialist Ethic* (Ann Arbor, Michigan, 1960); I. Murdoch, *Sartre* (London, 1953); A. R. Manser, *Sartre: a Philosophic Study* (London, 1966); M. Cranston, *Sartre* (London, 1962); M. Warnock, *The Philosophy of Sartre* (London, 1965); and G. Sennari, *Simone de Beauvoir* (Paris, 1959). In addition, a vivid evocation of existentialist debates is provided by Simone de Beauvoir, *Les Mandarins* (Paris, 1954). For Merleau-Ponty see below.

STRUCTURALISTS

Surveys proliferate, of which the most useful in French are probably J. Piaget, *Le Structuralisme* (Paris, 1968), *Qu'est-ce que le structuralisme?* (Paris, 1968), and chapters in E. Morot-Sîr, *La Pensée française d'aujourd'hui* (Paris, 1971). A useful English account is *Structuralism: An Introduction*, Wolfson College Lectures (Oxford, 1973), and equally interesting is *The Structuralist Controversy*, ed. R. Macksey and E. Donato (London, 1972). Translated extracts from structuralist writers are, as a first introduction, given in R. T. and F. M. de George, *The Structuralists: From Marx to Lévi-Strauss* (New York, 1972), and *Structuralism: A Reader*, ed. M. Lane (London, 1970). J. Culler, *Structuralist Poetics* (London, 1973), has an extensive bibliography, as well as being perhaps the best discussion of structuralism's application to literature study. English accounts of individual structuralists include E. Leach, *Lévi-Strauss* (London, 1970), and, more critical, P. Thody, *Roland Barthes* (London, 1977), and B. Rotman, *Jean Piaget: Psychologist of the Real* (London, 1978). Readers interested in questions of meaning and methodology could well start from the existentialist philosopher Merleau-Ponty, on whom A. Robinet, *Merleau-Ponty* (Paris, 1963), and A. De Waehlens, *Une Philosophie de l'ambiguité: l'existentialisme de Merleau-Ponty* (Louvain, 1951), are perhaps the best of several guides. A very recent and lucid introduction, stressing the linguistic and literary aspects of structuralism, is T. Hawkes, *Structuralism and Semiotics* (London, 1977).

7 French Literature from 1600 to 1750

W. D. HOWARTH

Introduction

This period may be said to be the beginning of the modern era. It saw none of the great technological innovations which, from the early nineteenth century onwards, have accelerated the pace of human progress; and, sandwiched between the last of the great dynastic civil wars of Europe and the first of the great revolutions based on political ideologies, it brought about no violent social upheaval in France. Yet it was during this period, nevertheless, that the most decisive political and social changes came about in the development from feudalism to bureaucracy, from the medieval to the modern way of life. For between 1600 and 1680, as a result of the deliberate policies of Richelieu and other statesmen, the great feudal families were deprived of their effective political power. This was a relatively painless process, in spite of such outbreaks of resistance as the Frondes; and although France was still far from an egalitarian society based on constitutional monarchy and parliamentary democracy, the unity of the State was consolidated in the person of the monarch, the foundations were laid for an efficient internal administration, and the seventeenth and eighteenth centuries were a period of relative social stability for France.

One way in which this stability was reflected was in the encouragement it gave to a more active cultural life. Whereas the unsettled climate of the Wars of Religion had been unfavourable to learning, culture and refinement, particularly in Paris and at court, the first half of the seventeenth century saw the beginnings of the *salons* as focal points of the social and intellectual life of the capital, the foundation of the Académie Française, and the establishing of the first permanent theatres in Paris. Similarly, at court, the rough military type gradually disappeared, to be replaced by something more nearly resembling

Castiglione's ideal courtier, versed in the social graces and able to take an intelligent interest in literature and the arts.

In these favourable conditions, French classical literature took shape and grew to maturity in a brief half-century or so of creative activity which still today, in the eyes of the most iconoclastic modernist, represents the finest flowering of the native French literary genius. The qualification 'native' is important, because this was a remarkably self-contained phenomenon, produced at a time when French cultural and intellectual life was probably more insular than at any other period in its history. The literature of this age forms in this respect a complete contrast with a truly European movement such as Romanticism: it was hardly fed at all by other contemporary cultures, and while it did depend heavily on links with the literature of antiquity, this influence was so blended with other local and contemporary stimuli as to make of French 'classicism' something unique in modern literature.[1] That this creative achievement should so soon be followed in certain genres by a falling-off into imitative mediocrity was no doubt due as much to the continued stability of social conditions, and to reluctance on the part of over-cautious writers to question the basic structure of society,[2] as it was to a complacent refusal to vary the formulae which had produced the masterpieces of the 1660s and 1670s. At any rate it is easy to see that the authors who counted in the decades leading up to 1750 were those who were willing to look abroad for new ideas and styles, and who were in the vanguard of the new cosmopolitanism which characterizes the literature of the mid-eighteenth century.

The Baroque Age 1600–1640

At the beginning of the seventeenth century, the full flowering of the classical manner was still far off; but before the century is very old, it is possible to see various indications of the new tendency towards order, stability and refinement. First, as regards the preparation of the reading

[1] As Professor Peyre has remarked, it would be easy to write a history of other modern literatures, Italian, Spanish, German or English, without ever using the word 'classical'; '. . . mais on ne peut concevoir une histoire de la littérature française où ce mot commode ne désigne les grands écrivains du XVIIe siècle' ('Le Mot *classicisme*', in J. Brody (ed.), *French Classicism: A Critical Miscellany* (Englewood Cliffs, N.J., 1966), pp. 104–13).

[2] As La Bruyère points out (*Caractères*, XIV, 65), it was not a question of there being no 'grands sujets', but of these being 'défendus'.

public: the widespread desire for self-improvement, for refinement and culture, is reflected in the numerous manuals of 'politesse' which appeared throughout the first half of the century, the most celebrated of which was *L'Honnête Homme, ou l'Art de plaire à la Cour* (1630) by Nicolas Faret (*c.* 1600–46). More important, from the point of view of strictly literary culture, the celebrated 'chambre bleue' of Madame de Rambouillet (?1588–1665) went a long way towards bridging the gap between men of letters, mostly of bourgeois origin, and the nobility and leaders of fashionable society. Here, writers and noblemen seem to have mixed in an easy relationship, without pedantry or affectation, enjoying the pleasures of the mind in the widest, freest sense. Other *salons* may have been more exclusively literary, more highbrow in tone; none had the reputation of the Hôtel de Rambouillet. These regular gatherings of like minds did much to refine the literary language, and to focus the attention of writers on the study of real human relationships; more generally, they helped to prepare a cultured public for the serious analysis of moral and psychological problems.

The earliest imaginative literature which catered for – and at the same time stimulated – this new taste was that written in imitation of the pastoral literature of Italy and Spain. The masterpiece of this genre, and a favourite with readers throughout the century, was *L'Astrée* by Honoré d'Urfé (1567–1625), of which three parts appeared in 1607, 1610 and 1619, parts IV and V being published in 1627 by his secretary. Manners are stylized and settings conventional; the plot is full of complicated contrivances; and the ideal of courtly love assumes the character of a quasi-religious ritual. But when the author analyses the sufferings of the shepherd Céladon, separated by misfortunes and misunderstandings from his beloved Astrée, there is genuine psychological realism.

While this is the primary interest of *L'Astrée*, it also shares the tendency, notable in almost all genres, towards a more polished and harmonious form of expression. Other prose-writers who catered for this new public of cultured readers, though in very different ways, were François de Sales (1567–1622), whose style, harmonious and full of agreeable imagery, not of pedantic abstractions, matched his purpose: to persuade his reader to adopt a 'dévotion' purged of its more extreme austerity and asceticism; and Guez de Balzac (1597–1654), who acquired tremendous fame as a letter-writer and moralist. Balzac made of the epistolary art not the spontaneous expression of the writer's personality, but a self-conscious exercise in literary style: his skilful combination of prose rhythms, oratorical periods and contrived rhetorical effects likewise aimed at clarity, harmony and *agrément*; and his collections of letters, published from 1624 onwards, became veritable best-sellers.

Refinement of the language of poetry was the self-imposed task of François de Malherbe (1555–1628). He was as resolutely opposed to the exalted conception held by the Pléiade of the poet as an inspired favourite of the Muses, as he was critical of the actual poetic works of Ronsard and his followers. His place in literary history is due not so much to his own creative writing, which was rarely distinguished, as to his critical doctrine; principally embodied in his *Commentaire sur Desportes*, and in his friend Racan's *Mémoires pour la vie de M. de Malherbe*, this was imposed on his fellow poets by word of mouth and by force of personal example. Malherbe called for a simple, harmonious metre, in which the grammatical unit of the phrase or sentence should coincide with the metrical unit of the line of verse, and a sober, almost prosaic vocabulary, pruned of the extravagances and idiosyncrasies of imaginative flights of poetic fancy. His own practice was less extreme than his precept; cf. for instance his use of metaphor, not only in his early 'Larmes de Saint-Pierre', but also in his later occasional poems: love poetry (written on his own behalf, or on behalf of Henri IV), 'consolations' or other *vers de commande* written for various patrons and protectors. However, even in practice, he was seldom more than a conscientious craftsman. His influence was to help to make of French lyric verse, for nearly two centuries, something elegant and harmonious, but lacking the imaginative inspiration of true poetry; though on the credit side it is only fair to recognize that the alexandrine as he envisaged it – clear, measured, energetic – was a metre marvellously suited to be a vehicle for Corneille's dramatic dialogue.

While certain prominent poets of the time such as Honorat de Bueil, Seigneur de Racan (1589–1670) or François Maynard (1582–1646), who can be counted as disciples of Malherbe, wrote occasional odes and conventional love poetry illustrative of that doctrine which, at any rate in its broad lines, was to find most favour with following generations, the opening decades of the century witnessed a great variety of poetic activity on the part of other, more independent writers, some of whom have only recently begun to emerge from a long period of unjustified neglect. Jean de La Ceppède (1548–1623) wrote a long sonnet-sequence on Christ's Passion (*Théorèmes sur le sacré mystère de notre Rédemption*,

1613 and 1622), whose religious symbolism, biblical erudition and intellectual conceits make him the French poet most nearly comparable to the metaphysical tradition represented by Donne and his contemporaries in England. Mathurin Régnier (1573–1613), a nephew of Desportes and a determined champion of the old order against Malherbe's restrictive innovations, confined himself almost entirely to the writing of satire. Colourful, vigorous and realist, his verse gives a caustic picture of the society of his times, in the manner of a modern Juvenal; his portrait of Macette, the hypocritical bawd, in Satire XII, has always been an anthology piece. But the most distinguished of these 'independent' poets was Théophile de Viau (1590–1626), who not only represents opposition to Malherbe in matters of style and technique, but also exemplifies, as regards subject-matter and intellectual content, that *libertin* current of thought which continued the materialism of the Italian Renaissance. His verse, which has an engaging flavour of spontaneity and sincerity, is marked by a materialist's delight in physical sensation and the world of natural phenomena. The expression of his ideas may not seem unduly provocative to the modern reader; and indeed when he was brought to trial by the Jesuits for impiety, it was largely on the basis of anonymous poems of which it is doubtful whether he was the author. But Théophile's whole way of life was a provocation to the *bien-pensants* of his time: he was at the centre of a freethinking bohemia of young noblemen and men of letters, completely emancipated from the hypocrisy and intolerance of orthodox religion, and practising a new social ethic based on an Epicurean philosophy of nature. The poet's persecution, imprisonment and early death put an end to all this: *libertinage* went underground, and repressive orthodoxy was solidly entrenched for another century or more. Several surviving members of the *libertin* group judged it prudent to make public profession of orthodoxy; the conformist supporters of the establishment centred round Richelieu had their hand strengthened; while Théophile's former patron, the Duc de Montmorency, was to be one of the most notable victims of the Cardinal's desire to curb the power and privilege of the great noblemen.

From a purely literary point of view, the poetry of Théophile and others who resisted Malherbe's influence provides one of the principal manifestations of that manner to which modern criticism has given the name 'baroque'. Definitions of this term, as applied to the literature of the period in France, vary considerably in the emphasis given to different characteristics: style, structure, subject-matter, moral purpose; perhaps one of the most helpful (particularly if one is considering lyric poetry) is the following:

> poetry in which, although the problems of the age are reflected, the perfect poise between intelligence and sensibility is either destroyed or not achieved or not attempted, with the result that the poet has a distorted vision of life, distorted through imagination and sensibility, without any apparent care for proportions or balance.[1]

Thus, while in the case of a Malherbe, sensibility is strictly controlled by reason, and imagery submitted to the test of common sense, Théophile and other baroque poets, such as Antoine de Saint-Amant (1594–1661), embellish their nature descriptions by vivid, spontaneous imagery, or indulge in subjective flights of fancy which may even in some cases assume an absurd or surrealist flavour. The picture they offer of the world may be either serious and visionary, or imaginative and playful; but it is an intensely personal one, far removed from Malherbe's cliché-like generalizations.

Drama in the latter half of the sixteenth century had remained a bookish affair. Such plays as were acted were performed in the colleges or in private houses; it is probable that many were not performed at all; and the divorce between the humanist playwrights and the professional theatre was almost complete.

Alexandre Hardy (*c.* 1572–1632) was nothing if not a man of the theatre. He was the first professional dramatist, *poète à gages* to the Comédiens du Roi; he wrote several hundred plays, of which thirty-four were published (1623–8). As well as writing tragedies on traditional themes (e.g. *Didon se sacrifiant, Mariamne, Coriolan*), Hardy was instrumental in developing the tragi-comedy and the pastoral which were to become the most popular genres throughout the first three decades of the century. Generally speaking, his tragedies, as well as the plays belonging to other genres, fully exploit the possibilities of contemporary stage practice (the *décor simultané*, symbolic rather than representative, which involved the use of separate compartments, like medieval 'mansions'): structure is episodic, there is little unity of time or place, and the interest is focused on striking – often sensational – events (cf. *Scédase*, a 'free' tragedy showing rape and murder on stage; or *La Force du sang*, a tragi-comedy whose heroine is miraculously able to

[1] O. de Mourgues, *Metaphysical, Baroque and Précieux Poetry* (Oxford, 1953), p. 74.

identify, and marry, her repentant ravisher and father of her seven-year-old child).

But though Hardy's plays have something of the vigour and colour of English Elizabethan and Jacobean drama, his style is extremely uncouth and unattractive; and in the theatre as elsewhere, the pastoral was to be one of the chief refining influences, developing dramatic language as a vehicle for the subtle analysis of feeling, without bombast or crudity. This was the achievement of Racan in his *Bergeries* (1625) and of Jean Mairet (1604–86) in his *Silvie* (1628), two very successful adaptations to stage requirements of the style and subject-matter of *L'Astrée*. What stands out in both plays, in spite of the conventional artifices of plot, is the delicate portrayal of natural feelings, aided by an appeal to the notion of a sympathetic nature. However, the most attractive play of the 1620s is not a pastoral but a tragedy, although Théophile's *Pyrame et Thisbé* (1623) does share certain features with the plays of Racan and Mairet, particularly their fresh, lyrical charm. If it is hardly a tragedy in the Aristotelian sense, lacking both inevitability of outcome and tragic guilt (it presents the pathetic fate of two innocent lovers, victims of a family feud, and the 'catastrophe' is brought about by the untimely arrival of a lion), it has a poetic intensity and imaginative force lacking in the pastoral. Indeed, this imaginative quality led to the unjust depreciation of the play for centuries, following an egregious example of 'common sense' criticism on the part of Boileau.

While the highly personal imagery of Théophile's tragedy represents one baroque feature of the theatre of this period, it is generally agreed that it is tragi-comedy that is the baroque form *par excellence*. Here, the favourite themes of disguise, mistaken identity and false appearances, the ubiquitous figure of the magician, the disjointed, episodic structure and such devices as the 'play within the play' all reflect the essential characteristics of baroque art: instability, impermanence, superficial brilliance and ostentation, lack of aesthetic unity.[1] Whereas tragicomedies still outnumbered other types of play in the 1630s, this was the decade in which the real struggle was taking place between the adherents of the freer, irregular type of drama which can conveniently be called 'baroque', and those who were already turning to a more refined, more disciplined and simpler alternative. The choice crystallized, in theoretical discussion, round the 'rules' – the three unities of

[1] The subtitle given by J. Rousset to his *Littérature de l'âge baroque en France* (Paris, 1954) is 'Circé et le paon': the sorceress represents themes of magic and metamorphosis, the peacock ostentation and display.

time, place and action which modern theorists mistakenly claimed to derive from Aristotle – but the *bienséances* (conventions regarding subject-matter and style) were as important as the 'rules' themselves in settling the form and the linguistic idiom that the mature classical theatre was to adopt. The view once held of playwrights unwillingly forced into obedience to pedantic theorists and critics has now been thoroughly exploded: to begin with, at any rate, the unities were eagerly accepted by a group of young avant-garde writers as a means of appealing to the *cognoscenti*. The first play written consciously and deliberately in observance of the rules was Mairet's *Sylvanire*, composed to please his patron in 1631. This was a tragi-comedy; but in general, when writing tragi-comedies dramatists preferred not to be hampered by such restrictions, and it was in tragedy and comedy that the unities and other conventions became established.

Comedy suffered something of an eclipse at the beginning of this period; but the genre was given a new lease of life around 1630, and here again, the influence of the pastoral was of the greatest importance: indeed, it could be said that these new comedies are no more than the transposition of *Les Bergeries* into an urban setting. The definition of comedy by Pierre Corneille (1606–84) as 'une peinture de la conversation des honnêtes gens' is illustrated by his first play *Mélite* (1629), a genteel imitation of the speech and manners of ordinary men and women, with a complicated plot concerning the traditional obstacle to the happiness of a pair of lovers. This was a style sharply distinguished from that of popular farce with its extravagant characterization; and indeed, after *Mélite*, Corneille wrote a series of comedies in which there is no 'comic' writing at all. Other dramatists followed suit, and *la comédie littéraire* was rapidly consolidated along these lines. But at the same time, these ambitious young playwrights, competing for public favour and the patronage of the two Paris theatre companies at the Hôtel de Bourgogne and the Marais, did not neglect other genres. Regular tragedy was inaugurated, Mairet's *Sophonisbe* (1634) being outstandingly successful and influential, along with *Hercule mourant* (1634) by Jean de Rotrou (1609–50), *La Mariane* (1636) by Tristan l'Hermite (1602–55), and Corneille's *Médée* (1635). The first three of these plays could be called backward-looking, in that there is little dramatic conflict, and the tragic, or pathetic, event is predetermined – though *Sophonisbe* is a particularly poetic evocation of the fate of two lovers, crushed by the power of Rome; but Corneille's first tragedy, adapted, like Rotrou's, from Seneca, not only appeals to the lingering taste for the spectacular, but also foreshadows in the character of the legendary sorceress the poet's later preoccupation with strong-willed individualists.

However, it was some time before Corneille, any more than his competitors, was to profess an exclusive allegiance to regular tragedy, and the eclecticism of his early years is further illustrated by *Clitandre* (1632), a vintage tragi-comedy of episodic construction, crowded with action, and *L'Illusion comique* (1635), which the author himself described as 'un étrange monstre'. Although labelled 'comédie', it has much in common with the tragi-comedies of the time, and perhaps more than any other play epitomizes the spirit of the baroque theatre: it is one of the most successful examples of the 'play within a play', and illustrates on several levels, from the hollow boasting of Matamore, the braggart soldier, to the portrayal of theatrical illusion which gives the play its title, that preoccupation with the interplay between truth and fiction, reality and illusion, which characterizes much of baroque art.

The point at which these two trends come together in Corneille's theatre is *Le Cid* (1637). Often described as the first classical tragedy in France, it is in fact less regular in form, and less 'classical' in spirit, than for instance *Sophonisbe*. It was labelled a tragi-comedy when first published, and although the way in which the dramatist has chosen to develop the principal dramatic conflict in the minds of Rodrigue and Chimène, whose love is threatened by the claims of family loyalties, suggests the concentration and psychological exploration in depth proper to tragedy, nevertheless the profusion of external events, the superfluous role of the Infanta, and the happy ending, all indicate the affinities of *Le Cid* with the freer, less disciplined genre. But if *Le Cid* is a tragi-comedy, it represents a very considerable development since *Clitandre*. The emotional range that Corneille achieves with his verse, from the poignant expression of Rodrigue's dilemma in the *stances* of Act I to the jubilant self-congratulation of the conquering hero, and from Chimène's energetic cry of vengeance for her father's death to the tenderness and spontaneity of the lovers' duet in Act III – this is something unmatched in any previous play, whether tragedy or tragi-comedy. No wonder that 'beau comme *Le Cid*' became a proverbial expression: contemporary audiences at once recognized the play as a masterpiece, and Corneille's fellow authors did him the honour of a critical attack such as no other play had ever faced.

Much of what passed for comment in the 'Querelle du *Cid*' was spiteful and petty; but the controversy caused such a stir in the world of letters that it led to the intervention of Richelieu. The Cardinal had a genuine interest in the theatre (he built the first theatre in Paris specifically designed as such, for premises used as theatres were usually converted tennis courts) and serious ambitions as a dramatist: he engaged a team of writers, the 'Compagnie des cinq auteurs', to which Corneille, Mairet and Rotrou all belonged, and legend has it that Corneille's restiveness in this role earned him Richelieu's disapproval. It seems more likely, however, that Richelieu intervened as a mediator rather than as a partisan, and it was possibly with largely disinterested motives that the play was submitted on his orders to the newly created Académie Française as an opportunity to exercise its judgement.

Classicism: the Formative Years 1640–1660

The formation of the Academy, the earliest of the moves to place cultural activities under State patronage, occurred in 1635 when the private gatherings of a small group of individuals with literary interests gave way to the more formal meetings of an officially constituted body of forty members. The examination of *Le Cid* on the Cardinal's orders was in one sense an exception to the normal functions of the Academy, which was from the beginning primarily concerned with the standardizing of the French language. The major fruit of this work was to be the Academy's own *Dictionnaire* of 1694, though the search for clarity and regularity had by this date also produced rival dictionaries: in 1680 by César-Pierre Richelet (1631–98), and in 1690 by Antoine Furetière (1619–88) – the latter being expelled from the Academy for his show of independence. A similar desire for codification and standardizing of linguistic usage animated Claude Favre de Vaugelas (1585–1650), also an academician, whose *Remarques sur la langue française* (1647) provide an analytical record of 'la façon de parler de la plus saine partie de la Cour, conformément à la façon d'écrire de la plus saine partie des auteurs du temps'. And in the field of poetic and dramatic theory the same kind of methodical application of reason and *bon sens* produced the *Poétique* (1639) of Hippolyte-Jules de La Mesnardière and *La Pratique du théâtre* by François Hédelin, Abbé d'Aubignac (*c.* 1604–*c.* 1673), both of these treatises, which played an influential part in the establishment of 'classical' doctrine, being due to the personal patronage of Richelieu (the *Pratique*, though not published until 1657, was begun in 1640). Meanwhile, another protégé of Richelieu, Jean Chapelain (1595–1674), was already beginning in the 1630s to exert an influence not unlike that of Malherbe a generation earlier. Chapelain resembles Malherbe in that his reputation did not depend on any important doctrinal work: instead, he made his mark in the salons, in his correspondence and in sundry occasional writings. Destined to be a prominent butt of Boileau's satire on account of his epic poem *La Pucelle*, and to be discredited by later generations because of the pedantic critical attitudes he was thought to have represented, Chapelain nevertheless counts as one of the most important architects of French classicism. And as recent scholarship has acknowledged,[1] his attitude to poetry was much more liberal than that of Malherbe: he made full allowance for that intangible element that no rules can produce, and that he knew his own verse did not possess.

It was to Chapelain that the Academy entrusted the task of adjudicating between Corneille's play and Scudéry's hostile *Observations sur le Cid*: an invidious task, given the enormous popular acclaim for the play on the one hand, and the interest shown by the Cardinal on the other. The *Sentiments de l'Académie* represent a prudent compromise; but it is possible to discern beneath the pedantry and triviality of some of the comment a genuine feeling for that harmony between simplicity of subject, regularity of form and purity of diction which classical tragedy was about to achieve.

The result of the *Querelle* on Corneille's development as a dramatist is unmistakable. While he remained to the end of his career remarkably flexible and adaptable in his attempt to please the public, there were to be no further examples of the irregular, episodic construction of tragi-comedy, and all his experimentation was henceforward to be carried out within the stricter classical formula. After a gap of three years, *Horace* (1640), *Cinna* (1640) and *Polyeucte* (1641) followed in quick succession. These three plays, together with *Le Cid*, have always been considered the high peak of Corneille's achievement, but *Pompée* (1642), *Rodogune* (1644) and *Nicomède* (1650) do not fall far short. This remarkable spell of creative activity constitutes a triumphant justification of the formula which Mairet and others had helped to develop, but which Corneille himself, responding to the stimulus of the 'Querelle du *Cid*', perfected. The essence of classical tragedy is a single action, seized at crisis-point: this is what distinguishes the new genre from the concentrated, but static, tragedy of the previous century on the one hand, and from the complex interrelations of plot and sub-plot which characterize tragi-comedy on the other. Despite the prominence always

[1] See in particular E. B. O. Borgerhoff, *The Freedom of French Classicism* (Princeton, 1950), pp. 31–46.

given by literary historians to the unities of time and place, it is the unity of action that gives the essential character to classical tragedy: the others merely help to make unity of action more effective. Unity of action – or, as Corneille calls it, 'unité de péril' – means that the plot must contain nothing to distract the spectator from the central tragic issue, which yet remains in suspense until the end because of the balance of opposing forces. *Horace*, indeed, was later criticized by Corneille himself, because the hero escapes from one *péril* – death at the hands of the enemy, when the Horatii fight the Curiatii – only to fall into another, when he is arraigned for the killing of his sister, who has insulted the name of Rome. *Cinna* and *Polyeucte*, however, leave nothing to criticize in this respect, and by the middle of the 1640s Corneille's own brand of classical tragedy, in which sublime effects are created by the confrontation of attitudes subtly analysed or heroically proclaimed, was firmly established.

This move towards a highly intellectualized form of drama was not followed by all playwrights, of course. While regular tragedies on subjects from mythology or ancient history become more and more numerous, tragi-comedy continues to provide a popular alternative; though of the most talented writers, only Rotrou still shows in the 1640s the eclecticism which Corneille and others had shown in the previous decade. Rotrou's *Le Véritable Saint-Genest* (1647) makes an interesting contrast with Corneille's *Polyeucte*: both are religious tragedies, but whereas Corneille takes the baptism of his hero as his starting-point, and shows the effect of divine grace by a clash of intellectual attitudes presented with a high degree of abstraction, Rotrou on the other hand, as a baroque artist, prefers to portray a visual enactment of a conversion as the climax of his play, when the actor Genest, taking the part of a Christian martyr, is himself visited by divine grace: pretence becomes reality, and he is led away to his own martyrdom. The play on the theme of reality and illusion, the richness of the imagery and the structural feature of the 'play within a play' combine to make *Saint-Genest* the last, and perhaps the most noteworthy, example of the French baroque drama – a kind of dramatic writing which has more real affinity with our own Elizabethan drama, or with the drama of the Golden Age in Spain, than with the classical forms that were to supplant it.

Rotrou, however, is something of an *attardé*, or at least an independent; he was much less susceptible than many of his contemporaries to those standardizing influences in the social and intellectual life of the country which brought about the change from a baroque to a classical literature. For a variety of reasons, from about 1640 onwards, writers seem to have become more and more responsive to these influences, and the results of this can be seen in several ways. Descartes's *Discours de la méthode* (1637), with its opening sentence, 'Le bon sens est la chose du monde la mieux partagée', is firmly based on the assumption that the mental processes of all men, if properly conducted, will lead to identical conclusions; and a similar assumption is implicit, as regards the psychology of the passions, in the same author's *Traité des passions* (1649). Much the same appeal to universal reason can be seen in the poetic treatises of La Mesnardière and D'Aubignac, as the foundation on which the *bienséances* as well as the 'rules' were based; while as regards creative writing, the poets of the mid-century come to distrust the promptings of the individual sensibility, and prefer to mould their imagination to the common denominator of a social group. So that whereas the typical baroque writer, however close his involvement with the society in which he lived, had been an individualist with regard to his artistic inspiration and his creative manner, the mid-century writer tends more and more to be a representative member of a social group, his own habits of thought and forms of expression corresponding closely to those of his readers.

The most striking example of this is to be found in the field of lyric poetry, where the linguistic and stylistic tendencies crystallized by the 'reforms' of Malherbe and Vaugelas combined with the favourite preoccupations of the habitués of the *salons* to produce a kind of writing that was often no more than intricate and mannered word-play. The principal theme of this poetry was love; but in the voluminous *poésie galante* of the period, sensuous imagery has given way to witty conceits, and the poet uses his imagination to appeal, not to the individual reader's senses, but to a much more universal intelligence. Content, although sophisticated, was frequently trivial; and the interest lay more often in the ingenious use of set forms such as the sonnet or the *rondeau*, than in genuine originality of theme or treatment.

Vincent Voiture (1598–1648), the 'court poet' of the Hôtel de Rambouillet, was one of the most successful exponents of this agreeable, but essentially minor, form of poetry. Every poet had his partisans, and literary controversies in the salons (e.g. the one over the respective merits of Voiture's 'Sonnet à Uranie' and Benserade's 'Sonnet sur Job') were frequent and lively. Among the collections of *petits vers*, the most celebrated was the *Guirlande de Julie* (1641), presented to Madame de

Rambouillet's daughter, Julie d'Angennes; the work of a score of habitués of the Hôtel, it contained ninety-odd 'floral tributes' in madrigal form. Altogether, this *poésie galante* was a most fitting expression of a refined, leisured society, which sought its amusements in parlour-games and practical jokes as well as cultivating more serious literary pursuits.

Generally speaking, these tendencies away from baroque individualism towards a literature more expressive of the cultural and social values of a homogeneous society made their mark earlier with regard to form than in respect of content. For the self-centred aristocratic idealism which inspired the protagonists of the Frondes also finds expression in the literature of the period – and nowhere more clearly than in Corneille's tragedies. His self-reliant heroes, capable of meeting every challenge and of overcoming all obstacles, are motivated by the same *éthique de la gloire*, that highly self-conscious moral code peculiar to a princely élite, which animated the Cardinal de Retz, Madame de Longueville, and other real-life leaders of the heroic but futile resistance to Mazarin's policies. In neither case is devotion to a cause free from the impulse to self-glorification; in both, there is an ever-present regard for the approbation of others, the desire to leave a striking example for posterity. The subtitle of *Cinna* is *La Clémence d'Auguste*, and the emperor's true greatness asserts itself as he pardons the conspirators instead of punishing them:

> Je suis maître de moi, comme de l'univers;
> Je le suis; je veux l'être. Ô siècles, ô mémoire,
> Conservez à jamais ma dernière victoire.

In *Horace*, the hero, having surpassed all expectations in the service of the state, asserts that

> pour laisser une illustre mémoire
> La mort seule aujourd'hui peut conserver ma gloire

– and even the martyrdom of Polyeucte is strongly marked by a similar urge:

> J'ai de l'ambition, mais plus noble et plus belle:
> Cette grandeur périt, j'en veux une immortelle,
> Un bonheur assuré, sans mesure et sans fin,
> Au-dessus de l'envie, au-dessus de destin.

The success of Corneille's plays, up to his withdrawal from the theatre in 1652, was due, as a recent writer has said, 'to the fact that the audience was prepared to share the same heroic assumption as the author';[1] his public held the same optimistic view of the individual's place in the universe, the same feeling for the sublime, idealized Roman virtues as portrayed in Plutarch.

It may be felt that these heroic, optimistic attitudes are unsuited to a tragic view of the world; and indeed, many critics find it impossible to accept the typical Cornelian plays of this period as tragedies. At best, this is a highly idiosyncratic kind of tragedy; and Corneille himself provided the key to its originality in the *Examen* to *Nicomède*, by substituting for the traditional Aristotelian tragic emotions of pity and fear the goal of *l'admiration*. The 'admiration' that we are intended to feel for Corneille's heroes has very much the sense of the Latin *admirari*: it implies 'awe' and 'astonishment' rather than moral approval;[2] and though most of his heroes do earn approval – for instance Nicomède, in whom contemporaries saw a portrait of Le Grand Condé – it is difficult not to feel a certain alienation from some of them. What we are asked to 'admire' in Corneille is something larger than life, out of the ordinary; this is very much what his tragedies are about, and the best of them, such as *Polyeucte* or *Pompée*, are still capable of arousing such a response.

In a much less intense, less dramatic, and altogether more *romanesque* way, the same appetite for idealized, heroic subject-matter, and the same optimistic belief in the individual's power to mould his own fortune, are reflected in the novels which were popular in the middle years of the century. These 'heroic' novels resembled *L'Astrée* in that they were longwinded, multi-volume adventure stories with incredible complications of plot, but they have shifted from D'Urfé's pastoral setting to the world of acient history; the two most celebrated examples of the genre, *Le Grand Cyrus* (1649–53) and *Clélie* (1654–60), both by Madeleine de Scudéry (1607–1701), being set in Persia and Rome respectively. Mademoiselle de Scudéry was a distinguished bluestocking and salon hostess, whose ideas – and those of her milieu – on the place of women in society, education and the relations between the sexes occupy a prominent place, in the form of discussions, in her novels; *Clélie* contains the famous 'Carte de Tendre', or allegorical map of the passions, which charts the traveller's way from Nouvelle Amitié to the cities of

[1] A. J. Krailsheimer, *Studies in Self-Interest* (Oxford, 1962), p. 78.

[2] Just as, to take two key-words from the vocabulary of Corneille's tragedies, *vertu* has very much the force of Lat. *virtus*, Ital. *virtú*, 'courage'; and *générosité*, closely connected with Lat. *gens*, denotes the values of a social caste.

Tendre sur Inclination, Tendre sur Estime and Tendre sur Reconnaissance, avoiding the Lac d'Indifférence and the Mer d'Inimitié. Mademoiselle de Scudéry's novels also reflect the developing *salon* fashion for the literary 'portrait': set-pieces combining a physical and moral description of a well-known individual. They are *romans à clef*, which offered the initiated reader the satisfaction of recognizing the originals (Condé as Cyrus, Madame de Longueville as Mandane, etc.). As in Corneille's heroic tragedies, the courage, magnanimity and perseverance of these idealized characters are finally rewarded, and it is easy to see how the element of wish-fulfilment added to the pleasure of Mademoiselle de Scudéry's readers.

Such novels may be virtually unreadable nowadays, but they are of considerable interest as a reflection of the society of the time. And they do help to show how the public of the classical age was formed: for if the involved plots, depending so heavily on disguise and mistaken identity, are a mark of the second-rate in literature (though it is worth noting the similarity of the plots of some of Corneille's own plays, such as *Pertharite* or *Héraclius*), the minute and searching analysis of the passions, when divorced from this superficial *romanesque*, can be seen to look forward to the greater psychological subtlety of Racine.

There were other writers at the same period, however, who made a more individual use of the novel form. Cyrano de Bergerac (1619–55), for instance, harks back to the Renaissance tradition of fictional voyages as a framework for social and political satire, and indeed may be regarded as an early exponent of science fiction. But so bold and provocative were the social ideas expressed in his *États et empires de la lune* and *États et empires du soleil* – based on the new Copernican system, they constitute an attack on the Aristotelian explanation of the universe – that neither work was published until after his death (in 1657 and 1661 respectively, the former in much expurgated form). Paul Scarron (1610–60) is much more down-to-earth as regards both his purpose and his literary manner: in his *Roman comique* (1651–7) he sets out to parody the heroic novel. Charles Sorel's *Francion* (1622) is Scarron's most obvious model in what is often called the 'realist' tradition in the seventeenth-century novel; but we are a long way here from the techniques of nineteenth-century realism, and in any case the contrived nature of the plot, with its sequence of brawls, fights, abductions and rescues, makes it clear that the author's prime purpose was to transpose the fictional structure of the heroic novel into a comic key. As the title indicates, this is a novel about the theatre: the reader follows the fortunes of an itinerant troupe of actors in 'la basse Normandie'. From this point of view, it has some real documentary value, but in his portrayal of provincial society Scarron yields to his penchant for good-humoured burlesque; and for an example of a novelist whose manner really does approach the documentary realism of the modern novel, we must turn to Furetière's *Roman bourgeois* (1668). Here, plot is minimal, and though Furetière also had a comic and satirical purpose, this does not prevent him from creating a convincingly authentic record of the day-to-day life of the Parisian bourgeoisie.

Scarron's gifts as a comic writer were not confined to the novel. There was quite a flowering of burlesque verse around 1650, of which his *Virgile travesti* (1648–52) is the best-known example. Charles Perrault was later to distinguish two ways of writing in burlesque style: 'L'une en parlant bassement des choses les plus relevées, et l'autre en parlant magnifiquement des choses les plus basses.' The latter, which we normally call the mock-heroic style (*l'héroï-comique*), is that of *Le Roman comique* (and later of Boileau's *Lutrin*); whereas in the true 'burlesque' of *Virgile travesti* the gods, goddesses and heroes of tragedy and the *romans héroïques* talk like market-porters and fishwives. It was not a very subtle form of entertainment, but it had its own sophistication, and was a cultured way of not taking one's culture too seriously.

Classicism: the Creative Years 1660–1680

Partly owing to the influence of the *salons*, and partly to the spread of those other civilizing forces which had been at work in society since the beginning of the century; also no doubt partly as a result of the failure of the Frondes and the collapse of so many heroic illusions, the *éthique de la gloire* was gradually replaced as a social ideal between about 1650 and 1660 by the concept of the *honnête homme*. The *honnête homme*, unlike the aspirant after *la gloire*, cultivated the social graces, and valued above all the pleasures of conversation and social intercourse. He was a cultured amateur, modest and self-effacing: 'Le vrai honnête homme est celui qui ne se pique de rien', to quote La Rochefoucauld's well-known *maxime*. Yet this was no pedestrian ideal. It was as demanding in its way as the Renaissance concept of the *uomo universale*, and the true *honnête homme* was a complete all-rounder: 'Cette science est proprement celle de l'homme, parce qu'elle consiste à vivre et à se communiquer d'une manière humaine et raisonnable', in Méré's words.

The day of the Hôtel de Rambouillet was now over, but other

salons, notably those of Mademoiselle de Scudéry and of Madeleine, Marquise de Sablé (*c.* 1599–1678), had taken its place. And under the personal rule of the young king the capital became, from 1660 onwards, more than ever the focal point of the cultural life of the country. The policy of attracting the nobility to court, and keeping them there to fulfil purely nominal ceremonial functions, created and maintained a large social group with few other interests but hunting, intrigue and the pleasures of the mind. The transfer of the court to Versailles in the early years of Louis XIV's reign gave a new precision to the formula 'la Cour et la Ville': here were the two milieux, not mutually exclusive but overlapping and interlocking, which were to provide the public for the new generation of writers, themselves for the most part courtiers and *honnêtes gens*.

François de La Rochefoucauld (1613–80) provides an interesting illustration of the transition between the two ages. An aristocrat who had played a leading part in the Frondes, he had been motivated in his early years by ambition and family pride – in other words by the quest for *la gloire*; but after the Frondes, defeated and badly wounded, as well as older and more experienced, he retired to private life, began a new career as a man of letters, and confessed, in a self-portrait, to 'une si forte envie d'être tout à fait honnête homme que mes amis ne me sauraient faire un plus grand plaisir que de m'avertir sincèrement de mes défauts'. The *Maximes* (1665), his principal literary achievement, owed a great deal both in form and content to critical analysis and discussion in Madame de Sablé's *salon*. They are a collection of 500 highly polished reflections on human behaviour, expressed in the most universal terms ('Le refus des louanges est un désir d'être loué deux fois'); the general tone is cynical, and self-interest is presented as the mainspring of all our actions ('Les vertus se perdent dans l'intérêt comme les fleuves se perdent dans la mer'). If there is a more positive message to be read into the work, it is the recognition of *l'honnêteté* as a code which preserves society as a viable institution ('S'il y a beaucoup d'art à savoir parler à propos, il n'y en a pas moins à savoir se taire'). Even *honnêteté*, however, is touched with cynicism in the *Maximes*; La Rochefoucauld's view of it is a pragmatic one, falling a long way short of the ideal defined by Antoine de Gombaud, Chevalier de Méré (1610–85), in his *Discours de la vraie honnêteté* and other essays, where it is presented as a real *art de vivre*.

The Frenchman who by the common consent of his contemporaries most nearly lived up to such an ideal was Charles de Saint-Denis, Sieur de Saint-Évremond (*c.* 1616–1703), who, after being active in politics and the army, was exiled and spent the last forty years of his life in England. Here he cultivated the pleasures of the mind, while not neglecting those of the senses: he was a true Epicurean, rejecting excess in all things, but believing, as he wrote, that 'nous avons plus d'intérêt à jouir du monde qu'à le connaître'. One of the most independent thinkers of his time, Saint-Évremond was also one of the most versatile writers; he wrote satire, comedy, philosophical verse, and above all was known as a letter-writer and essayist. He took a stand against religious intolerance, anticipating the deists of the following century; his exile from France gave him a valuable detachment as a commentator on public affairs; and, above all, his taste and discernment in literary matters make him, as has been said, 'probably the most interesting literary critic of the seventeenth century . . . we are not far from the later conception of criticism as the criticism of beauties, not faults'.[1]

Few *honnêtes gens* had the culture, the taste and the temperament to practise the art of living in such an exemplary way as Saint-Évremond; but it was this same ideal of tolerant, cultured Epicureanism which, whatever its limitations as a source of spiritual inspiration, for a spell of twenty years or so set the tone of the social life of the capital.

If this period saw the perfecting of the masculine ideal of *honnêteté*, it also saw the fullest development of the predominantly feminine cult of *préciosité*. The two phenomena are often regarded as opposites, and to the extent that *honnêteté* stands for moderation in all things, and preciosity for affectation and extravagance, this is obviously the case. However, it should be remembered that the 'précieuses ridicules' satirized by Molière and others were far from representing the whole picture, and that while the term *précieuse* itself may have been used as a pejorative label, the women to whom it was applied (Mademoiselle de Scudéry was the most celebrated, and the most influential, of the *précieuses*) were responsible for introducing a new subtlety and precision into the language, for establishing exacting standards of delicacy and refinement in matters of taste, and for propagating advanced social ideas about the equality of the sexes in marriage. In all these things, the aims of the *précieuses* ran parallel to those of the *honnête homme*, and the ideal of the educated, emancipated woman was very like a female counterpart of the masculine ideal defined above. But the natural desire of these early feminists to assert themselves meant that their ideas were often taken to

[1] P. J. Yarrow, *A Literary History of France, Vol. II: The Seventeenth century* (London, 1967), p. 333.

extremes, so that in practice the educated all-rounder tended to become a pedantic bluestocking, the civilized notion of 'honnête amitié' between the sexes sometimes became a prudish revulsion from the facts of life, and the *précieux* style in language and literature too easily degenerated into the affected jargon of a coterie.

The most complete representation of the *honnête homme* in the imaginative literature of the period is without a doubt to be found in the theatre of Jean-Baptiste Poquelin (1622–73), known as Molière. It was for a long time a commonplace of Molière criticism to identify him with the Cléantes, the Philintes and the Clitandres of his theatrical world, and to see such characters as representing his own philosophy of life. However, recent criticism has tended to emphasize the fact that as well as being a bourgeois by birth and upbringing, a courtier and an *honnête homme*, Molière was also an actor-manager and an entertainer. More completely a man of the theatre than any dramatist since Hardy, he was brought up on the *farceurs* of the Hôtel de Bourgogne, the leading comic actors of his youth, and the improvised acting of the Italian players in Paris. Departing to tour the provinces with his troupe in the mid-forties because of financial difficulties, he returned in 1658, and soon succeeded in imposing on audiences a completely new brand of comedy. While his early plays may be divided into full-length *comédies littéraires* in verse (e.g. *L'Étourdi*, 1658; *Dom Garcie de Navarre*, 1661) and one-act farces (e.g. *Les Précieuses ridicules*, 1659), from *L'École des maris* (1661) and particularly *L'École des femmes* (1662) onwards these two strains are fused. Molière's originality is thus to have created a formula which combined the 'classical' structure, the linguistic refinement and the portrayal of manners belonging to the accepted conventions of 'comedy', with the heightened, even caricatural, characterization proper to farce. Even in polished verse comedies, therefore, such as *L'École des femmes*, *Le Misanthrope* (1666), *Tartuffe* (1669) or *Les Femmes savantes* (1672), the comedy of manners – that is, the realistic representation of certain features of contemporary society – merely provides a framework for a comic portrayal of a central character or characters, in which exaggeration and fantasy play a considerable part. This mixture was hardly to the taste of highbrows and traditionalists; but Molière's spokesman Dorante in the *Critique de l'École des femmes* (1663) explicitly reconciles the two styles of comic writing in his defence of the new formula: 'Il n'est pas incompatible qu'une personne soit ridicule en de certaines choses et honnête homme en d'autres.' And indeed, Molière's comic characters, as well as being the object of our critical laughter, are also rounded personalities: we can accept them as plausible, representative members of society even though each is endowed with a particular obsession or *idée fixe* which renders him vulnerable to the comic process. An extreme case is that of Alceste in *Le Misanthrope*, in whom sympathetic and comic traits are so delicately balanced that they have provided a perennial subject for differences of interpretation, both inside and outside the theatre.

Le Misanthrope is the only play set in aristocratic circles; other plays mentioned, as well as prose comedies such as *L'Avare* (1668), *Le Bourgeois Gentilhomme* (1670) and *Le Malade imaginaire* (1673), portray the comfortable bourgeois milieu that was Molière's own. The central figures represent a variety of comic obsessions, some of universal relevance (miserliness, hypochondria), others of specifically contemporary significance (women's emancipation, social climbing, religious bigotry); but however topical the subject, and however prominent the satirical content, Molière's characters always possess a common denominator of humanity which makes them permanently acceptable as being like ourselves. Most plays contain, alongside the comic character, one or more examples of the *honnête homme*, either as active protagonists or as lay figures; whether or not we choose to identify the author himself with these 'raisonneurs' (and it would certainly be wrong to place too much emphasis on the didactic element in his plays), in a more general sense we can easily recognize the social norm against which his comic characters offend as that of a tolerant, humane exponent of *honnêteté*.

In *Tartuffe*, and in *Dom Juan* (1665), topical references and satirical implications were so provocative, since both plays dealt with the delicate subject of religious belief and feigned *dévotion*, that there were strong reactions from ecclesiastical quarters; while even *L'École des femmes* had given rise to a vigorous and sustained controversy with rival actors and men of letters. But from an early stage in his Paris career Molière could count on the support of the king, who became an active patron of his troupe. A number of plays were in fact written for performance at Versailles or other courts; and besides his *hautes comédies* and more traditional farces, both in the French and the Italian manner (e.g. *Le Médecin malgré lui* (1666) and *Les Fourberies de Scapin* (1671), both still highly popular), Molière also wrote several *comédies-ballets*, and collaborated in other *divertissements* which brought together the arts of poetry, music and dance in something not unlike the English court masque.

Such mixed entertainments – including the new genre of opera, and the *pièces à machines* with spectacular scenic effects due to the expertise of the Italian designer Torelli – were always favourites with the public. The biggest 'box-office' success of the century, however, judged by length of first run, was the *Timocrate* (1656) of Pierre Corneille's younger brother Thomas (1625–1709), a prolific playwright who was adept at gauging the public taste. *Timocrate* was exactly contemporary with the *précieux* novels of Mademoiselle de Scudéry; and like Philippe Quinault (1635–88) in his *tragédies galantes*, the author reproduced those *romanesque* features of disguise and amorous intrigue which the habitués of the *salons* so much admired.

However, the 1660s were to see the rivalry between the century's two acknowledged masters of serious drama. Corneille, returning to the theatre in 1659, wrote ten more plays in the next fifteen years; but though certain of these – *Sertorius* (1662), or his last play *Suréna* (1674) – will bear comparison with the plays of his middle period, the heroic idealism has now almost completely lost its conviction. His heroes have become much more materialistic and self-seeking in their aspirations; or else, like both Sertorius and Suréna, tragically aware that ideals are doomed to defeat. While Corneille retained his partisans among play-goers of an older generation, it was Jean Racine (1639–99) who appealed to the new audiences of the 1660s, for they were no longer so idealistically minded in their attitude to psychology; there was a new realism, in tune with La Rochefoucauld's *Maximes* rather than with Descartes's *Traité des passions*. Of all the numerous 'parallèles' between the two great dramatists, none expresses this difference better than that written by Fontenelle, Corneille's nephew, with its cynical implication:

> Quand on a le cœur noble, on voudrait ressembler aux héros de Corneille; et quand on a le cœur petit, on est bien aise que les héros de Racine nous ressemblent.[1]

Whether, as has often been maintained, Racine's Jansenist upbringing was responsible for his view of human nature as perverse and wilful, controlled by the passions, or whether his knowledge of Greek tragedy, and the choice of Sophocles and Euripides as models, is sufficient to account for the fatalism of his own tragedies, it is certain that the imaginary world inhabited by his heroes is very different from that which we have analysed in the case of Corneille. Tragedy is for Racine

[1] Quoted in R. J. Nelson (ed.), *Corneille and Racine: Parallels and Contrasts* (Englewood Cliffs, N.J., 1966), p. 23.

the working-out of an inexorable series of events leading to a foreseeable catastrophe; plot is of the simplest: the action is already at crisis point when the play opens; and once the inexorable first step is taken, tension mounts between the incompatible protagonists until one or more of them is destroyed. Racine's career began in 1664 with *La Thébaïde*, a grim study of the mutual hatred of Oedipus' sons; this was followed by *Alexandre le grand* (1665), his only attempt at the manner of Thomas Corneille and Quinault. His masterpieces date from the highly successful *Andromaque* (1667), another tragedy based on Greek legend; after which, for *Britannicus* (1669) and *Bérénice* (1670), he turned to subjects from Roman history. *Bajazet* (1672) is based on an episode from modern Turkish history; *Mithridate* (1673) has as its hero the legendary enemy of Rome; and finally there followed two plays based on Greek mythological subjects: *Iphigénie* (1674) and *Phèdre* (1677), before Racine renounced the theatre, becoming reconciled with Port-Royal, marrying, and accepting a court office as *historiographe du Roi*. Even leaving aside his two later biblical plays, therefore, those based on Greek sources form a minority among his tragedies; if, nevertheless, one thinks of Racine as 'Greek' in comparison with the 'Roman' Corneille, this is because he endows the historical themes, like the legendary ones, with the same tragic fatalism: the downfall of Mithridate, or the shaping of the career of Néron, the 'monstre naissant' of *Britannicus*, are due not so much to some combination of historical contingencies, as to the corrupt human nature that these characters embody.

But dramatically powerful as his Roman plays are (even *Bérénice*, a tragedy with no bloodshed, and almost no action – merely the parting of a pair of lovers, in obedience to a 'raison d'État'), it is in his Greek plays that Racine reaches his greatest heights; and for many readers and playgoers, *Phèdre* in particular is one of the greatest tragedies of any literature. Construction of the play is exemplary: the unities are faultlessly, yet unobtrusively, observed, and each stage of the action accelerates the downfall of this perfect Aristotelian heroine, whom her creator saw as 'ni tout à fait coupable, ni tout à fait innocente, . . . engagée par sa destinée, et par la colère des Dieux, dans une passion illégitime dont elle a horreur toute la première'. Mythological allusions are aided by powerfully evocative imagery; and Racine makes of the classical alexandrine, and of the restricted vocabulary of *le style noble*, a medium so flexible in its range, and so marvellously expressive of tragic emotion that the 'poésie tragique' of *Phèdre* has never been equalled. Altogether, this play is the perfect example of that 'creative imitation' which was central to the theory of seventeenth-century classicism: Euripides' *Hippolytus*, and the versions of Seneca and other imitators, are left far behind, and from the moment of Racine's creation onwards, *Phèdre* stands as a truly French masterpiece.

In addition to comedy and tragedy, other poetic genres still enjoyed a traditional prestige – as can be seen from *L'Art poétique* (1674) of Nicolas Boileau-Despréaux (1636–1711), where the genres most highly regarded are the epic (ironically, since no epic of distinction was written during the whole classical period in France), the ode (of which Boileau himself, Racine and others wrote rather formal examples to commemorate official occasions) and satire. It was in his own *Satires* (1660 onwards) that Boileau had made his mark with contemporaries, using the form principally as a vehicle for literary criticism. As in the *Art poétique* (modelled on Horace's *Ars poetica*) and his *Épîtres* (1674 onwards), Boileau took his stand on formal perfection, and on the paramount importance of *la raison, le bon sens* in matters of literary taste. However, he recognized the inability of 'rules' on their own to produce poetry; and though he was himself a clever versifier rather than an inspired poet, what he looked for in the works of other poets was that intangible element of *le sublime* which defies definition – indeed, which perceptive critics throughout the century had referred to as *le je ne sais quoi*. The most attractive side of Boileau's talents as an original writer is shown in *Le Lutrin* (1674–83), the mock-heroic poem in six cantos based on personal rivalries in clerical circles in Paris, which provided a model for Pope's *Rape of the Lock*. Wit, fantasy, satirical purpose are all controlled by an urbane sense of form and style, which make of *Le Lutrin* a masterpiece of comic writing in the classical manner.

The other major non-dramatic poet of the classical age, Jean de La Fontaine (1621–95), surely suffers from the fact that the fable is usually associated with didactic writing for juvenile readers. However, in his *Fables* (1668; 1678; 1694), La Fontaine completely transcends the limitations of his chosen form; and though an earlier critical tradition concentrated excessively on the ethical teaching to be derived from them, we are perhaps better able today to appreciate, beneath the apparent naïvety of these traditional tales about animals, or these simple parables about stylized allegorical figures, the mature literary skills of a highly imaginative writer. The mock-heroic is one of the many elements which go towards making up La Fontaine's inimitable manner; but though he is often thought of primarily as a comic poet, deflating the vain and the pretentious, his range also includes the tender and the intimate, as well as the lyrical expression of a feeling for nature rare among his contemporaries. His vocabulary breaks the confines of *le style noble* – indeed, he derives great effect from the humorous juxtaposition of the stylized and stately with the homely, the concrete and the picturesque – and as regards metre, while he can handle the noble alexandrine very impressively, his most characteristic manner depends on the virtuosity with which he manipulates the irregular rhythms of his favourite *vers libres*.

The novel was meanwhile being adapted to suit a new generation of readers; and although contemporaries still regarded it as a secondary genre, it produced at least one masterpiece which is an excellent embodiment of the essential classical manner. This is *La Princesse de Clèves* (1678) by Marie-Madeleine de La Fayette (1634–93), which may have owed something to collaboration with La Rochefoucauld and others, and certainly reflects ways of thinking, as well as linguistic habits, current in the *salons*. The novel has now turned its back on the fanciful *romanesque* settings of its pastoral and heroic predecessors, in order to explore the relationship between various kinds of love and the demands of society, in a sober, realistic context. (Indeed, the first novel to demonstrate such acute perception in a similarly realistic setting, *Les Lettres portugaises* (1669), was so convincing that for generations this remarkable little work – a collection of five letters written by a nun to her faithless lover – was thought to be authentic; its attribution, as a work of fiction, to Gabriel-Joseph de Guilleragues (1628–85), is now generally accepted.) Although Madame de La Fayette's novel is set in the French court of the sixteenth century, this is a transparent disguise for the manners and preoccupations of her own times; and her heroine, who rejects the chance of an apparently 'happy' marriage, because she is aware that few men are capable of preserving their love after marriage, and fears to sacrifice her own peace of mind, represents a mature blend of 'Cornelian' idealism with 'Racinian' realism. The language of the novel is very much of its time, achieving its effects by understatement and subtle nuance rather than by rhetorical flourish; and it is entirely fitting that a woman novelist should have created the most distinguished literary monument to that feminine influence which, in the *salons*, was largely responsible for making of the French classical language such an expressive medium for the lucid analysis of the affairs of the heart.

When we turn to Marie de Rabutin-Chantal, Marquise de Sévigné (1626–96), the other outstanding woman writer of this generation, we find someone who though very much of her time, is – not unlike La

Fontaine – too idiosyncratic in her manner to be truly representative. Her correspondence (published in the eighteenth century) gives a marvellously rich picture of the social scene, at court and in private, as well as a charmingly intimate portrait of the writer herself. Yet even when her letters are humorous, inconsequential and informal, they are written with a careful eye to literary effect, products of that art which consists in concealing artifice. Madame de Sévigné is not only an admirable example of the cultured, educated, critical reader for whom the *grands classiques* themselves wrote, but one of the most skilful – and one of the most engaging – prose-writers of her day.

But perhaps the most distinguished prose-writer of the period was a man who stood completely apart, and who, if he does reflect the society in which he lived, reflects it in a highly critical light. The *Pensées* of Blaise Pascal (1623–62) represent an uncompromising reminder of the spiritual values of the Christian faith. This work remained incomplete at Pascal's death, so that in place of the dialectical cogency of the *Lettres provinciales* (1656–7), his masterly satire directed against the casuistry and the 'morale relâchée' of the Jesuits, the *Pensées* possess a certain enigmatic quality and lack of structural coherence, in spite of the aphoristic brilliance of many individual fragments. However, the central theme – human weakness, and the futility of worldly life – is clear enough: Pascal's view of human nature has much in common with that of La Rochefoucauld or Madame de La Fayette, but in his case 'la misère de l'homme sans Dieu' is contrasted with man's potential greatness, which can be achieved through divine grace. It seems reasonably certain that the structure of the completed work would have focused on a persuasive appeal to the *honnête homme* to forgo the transitory delights and *divertissements* of this world, staking everything on winning the more lasting rewards of an after-life.[1]

Pascal is the first master of a really modern prose style, and a comparison with a writer like Descartes is most revealing in this respect. While Descartes's prose is full of tortuous Latinisms, Pascal uses a short sentence, and is sparing with subordinate clauses; and the ease, clarity and precision which result are equally appropriate to the penetrating analysis of human nature in the *Pensées* and to the irony and comic force of the *Provinciales*.

[1] Pascal's celebrated 'wager' is formulated in *pensée* no. 343 (ed. L. Lafuma, Paris, 1960).

Classicism: the Imitative Years 1680–1715

Something of what Pascal had hoped to effect with the *Pensées* was brought about by other means after his death. The example of the *solitaires* at Port-Royal, and the influence of Jansenist teaching generally; the pulpit oratory of Bossuet and others; the widespread work of lay *directeurs de conscience* in aristocratic and bourgeois households; and at court the personal example of Madame de Maintenon: through a combination of these factors, a new climate of *dévotion* begins to become apparent towards 1680 throughout French intellectual and cultural life. The consequences are numerous and varied. A new premium on orthodoxy led to a wave of 'conversions' among notabilities, some certainly genuine, many no doubt feigned – for to quote La Bruyère, 'un dévot est celui qui, sous un roi athée, serait athée'; renewed clerical opposition to the theatre led to persecution of actors (who were not to enjoy full civil rights in France until the Revolution); while at Versailles there was a new moral earnestness, even austerity, which contrasted oddly with the elaborate pomp and ceremony.

However outspoken some of his criticisms of the king, as well as of his subjects, for their falling-off from religious duties, it is impossible not to see in Jacques-Bénigne Bossuet (1627–1704) one of the principal pillars of the regime of 'le Roi Soleil'. For Bossuet, Louis represented the ideal of kingship, as God's representative on earth, the divinely ordained head of a society in which he saw the culmination of a providential historical process leading from the beginnings of Judaeo-Christian civilization to this magnificent climax. This theory of history, and of the Divine Right of Kings, was set out in the *Discours sur l'histoire universelle* (1681) and the *Politique tirée de l'Écriture sainte* (published posthumously in 1709), both written in Bossuet's capacity as tutor to the dauphin. But influential though this office was, he exerted a much wider influence through his sermons (up to 1669) and more particularly his funeral orations (up to 1687), which represent probably the highest level of classical oratory known in modern times. Bossuet, like Pascal, uses simple constructions; he makes little use of affective vocabulary, and his appeal is to the rational faculty of his hearers; but his sober, intellectual vocabulary is powerfully aided by rhetorical rhythms and patterns. For example, see how compellingly, in the *Oraison funèbre d'Henriette d'Angleterre* (1670), his message – a simplified version of Pascal's theme of the duality of man, the *grandeur* alongside the *misère* – is reinforced by an oratory whose power stands out even on the printed page.

Another royal preceptor (to the Duc de Bourgogne, the king's grandson) was François de Salignac de la Mothe-Fénelon (1651–1715). Fénelon was cast in a different mould from Bossuet: gentler and more inclined to mysticism in religion (his involvement with quietism, the doctrine of passive submission to the divine will, caused him to fall foul of Bossuet), yet readier to see faults in the system of absolute monarchy. The political reforms advocated by Fénelon and other liberals grouped round the Duke were principally expressed in a series of pamphlets and treatises; but the Archbishop also used fictional narrative as a vehicle for moral instruction to a young prince, in the allegorical novel *Télémaque* (1699). This purports to be a continuation of the fourth book of the *Odyssey*, and tells of Telemachus' wanderings in search of his father; instruction is chiefly provided by the goddess Minerva, in the guise of his wise companion Mentor, while the episodic structure permits of frequent portraits, exemplary or cautionary, of good and bad kings. *Télémaque* is more dated than most works of its time; but obeying, as it did, the precept of *instruire et plaire*, and combining pagan mythology with Christian ethical teaching, it is an excellent embodiment of the classical aesthetic. Rather marginal to the main development of the modern novel, it nevertheless represents a link between such seventeenth-century novels as those of Mademoiselle de Scudéry and the use of the novel form, for didactic purposes, by Voltaire and others a generation or two later.

Like Fénelon with Homer (and we may compare Boileau's relationship with Horace, Racine's with Sophocles and Euripides, and La Fontaine's with Phaedrus or Aesop), Jean de La Bruyère (1645–96) showed himself to be thoroughly 'classical' in placing himself under the patronage of a writer of antiquity; indeed, his *Caractères* (1688) began modestly as a translation of Theophrastus' *Characters*, amplified with some original 'portraits' of his own. However, compared with his Greek original (and with La Rochefoucauld, with whom he is often coupled), La Bruyère is less interested in generalized psychological abstractions common to all ages than in the specific follies and failings of seventeenth-century France (as the full title of the work, *Caractères de Théophraste traduits du grec, avec les Caractères ou les Mœurs de ce siècle*, indicates). Successive editions, up to 1694, added more material, and a very personal point of view emerges, critical of the king's warmongering and of extravagance at Versailles, and scornful of the vanities and pretensions of a status-conscious society. The final impression is of a humane, ironical view of mankind, sharpened in places into a trenchant criticism of his own age. If at times La Bruyère can write like La Rochefoucauld, and at others like Theophrastus, his more characteristic manner is one of graphic description; as has been said, he had the makings of a naturalist novelist.

A gift for description, allied to a very personal critical view of the court of the Sun King, also characterizes the *Mémoires* (covering the period from 1692 onwards, published in the nineteenth century) of Louis de Rouvroy, Duc de Saint-Simon (1675–1755). The approach is a somewhat jaundiced one: Saint-Simon shows the haughty prejudice of a *duc et pair* against what he calls a 'règne de vile bourgeoisie' (in other words, one in which administrative power had passed from the hereditary nobility into the hands of Louis's Ministers); but here is an enormously rich canvas, painted with a remarkable eye for detail.

Concentration on significant differences between individuals (as opposed to the preference for generalized abstractions about human behaviour, shown by Pascal, La Rochefoucauld, Madame de La Fayette – or even Racine) was still rare in imaginative literature; but such an approach is, of course, very much that of comedy. In prose comedy, writers like Edmé Boursault (1638–1701), Molière's colleague Michel Baron (1653–1729), Charles Dufresny (1648–1724) and Florent Carton Dancourt (1666–1725) developed a profitable vein of social satire. Baron's *Homme à bonnes fortunes* (1686) and Dancourt's *Chevalier à la mode* (1687) focus on the same social type, the *petit-maître*, while a number of Dancourt's other plays deal with the phenomenon of social climbing among wealthy *bourgeoises*, female counterparts of Molière's Monsieur Jourdain. The masterpiece of the genre is *Turcaret* (1709) by Alain-René Lesage (1668–1747), in which the central comic figure is a rich tax-farmer whose social climbing leads to his undoing. Lesage's view of society is thoroughly cynical, and the plot produces a 'ricochet de fourberies', as each confidence-trickster is in turn duped by another.

However, pride of place was still claimed, in the hierarchy of comic genres, by five-act verse comedy, and for another century playwrights were to continue composing very derivative *comédies de caractère* in this medium, in imitation of Molière; though one author to impose his own characteristic formula was Jean-François Regnard (1655–1709), who introduced into *haute comédie* destined for the Théâtre-Français the comic devices he had learned in writing for the less hidebound 'Italiens'.

His plays, of which *Le Légataire universel* (1708) is the best, contain a large measure of gay fantasy and literary parody; like the Italian actors, Regnard exploits theatrical illusion instead of trying to conceal it, and he is completely lacking in the sententious moralizing that was to affect his successors.

Otherwise, the general impression is of a period in which 'pure' literature remains derivative and uninspired. Exception must be made in tragedy for Racine's own last plays, *Esther* (1689) and *Athalie* (1691), in which creative dramatic writing was skilfully reconciled with the new climate of puritanical *dévotion* at Versailles; both plays were written, not for the professional theatre, but for the young ladies of a college at Saint-Cyr. Returning to the biblical subjects popular in the previous century, Racine also introduces a chorus of young women; in both plays, the choral passages were set to music. *Esther* hardly transcends the range of elegiac oratorio, but in *Athalie* the powerful characterization of the Queen of Judah, and the savage revenge executed by the prophet Joad in Jehovah's name, have caused many connoisseurs to see this as the peak of Racinian tragedy. Other writers of tragedy were as much overawed by the reputation of Corneille and Racine as comic playwrights were by that of Molière. Racine's outstanding successor was Prosper Jolyot de Crébillon (1674–1762), who in the early years of the century wrote a series of tragedies (e.g. *Atrée et Thyeste*, 1707; *Rhadamiste et Zénobie*, 1711), in which the subtler emotions of pity and fear are replaced by the pathetic and the terrifying. Crébillon is said to have declared: 'Corneille avait pris le ciel, Racine la terre; il ne me restait que l'enfer'; the spectator's sensibility is assaulted by scenes intended to shock, and by an abuse of emotive vocabulary.

Perhaps one sign of the lack of inventiveness in imaginative literature is the amount of attention given to theory and criticism: this period saw the outbreak of the 'Querelle des Anciens et des Modernes', in which the perennial controversy about the possibility of 'progress' in the arts came to a head in the Academy and elsewhere. While Boileau and others saw the best literature of antiquity as embodying permanent standards of excellence (and advocated imitation of such models as the means of attaining similar excellence), the 'Modernes' such as Charles Perrault (1628–1703) in his *Parallèle des anciens et des modernes* (1688–97) and Bernard Le Bovier de Fontenelle (1657–1757) in his *Digression sur les anciens et les modernes* (1688) claimed that the best of contemporary literature was inevitably superior, because of the greater maturity of the human mind. It was a sterile and inconclusive debate – paradoxically, the 'Modernes' illustrated their case by pointing to the excellence as creative writers of those who, as theorists, championed the superiority of ancient literature – but the underlying issue was a most important one. For the 'Modernes' indirectly, if not explicitly, anticipated those eighteenth-century thinkers whose rejection of the notion of a single universal aesthetic, valid for all time and place, in favour of a relativist approach, was to bring about the end of the neo-classical age.

For the time being, however, such ideas lay dormant, and creative writing remains largely derivative. If we turn to the literature of ideas, however, we find Pierre Bayle (1647–1706) and Fontenelle much more forward-looking. Besides his *Digressions . . .*, Fontenelle wrote an important work popularizing science in his *Entretiens sur la pluralité des mondes* (1686), an exposé of the Copernican system in the form of an urbane dialogue between the author and an intelligent, but uninformed, noblewoman; and in the *Histoire des oracles* (1687) he surveys pagan belief in oracular prediction in the spirit of Cartesian rationalism. Bayle, whose life-work was to be the erudite *Dictionnaire historique et critique* (first edition 1697), showed himself equally sceptical towards religious superstitions in his *Pensées diverses sur la comète* (1682). The seeds are here of that rationalist critique of tradition and authority in all spheres of intellectual activity, which was to characterize eighteenth-century thought. But if such signs of what was to come are already visible in the period which has been given the label of *la crise de la conscience*,[1] French culture still remained too insular for the crisis to become a general one; in particular, it lacked that contact with the outside world which was to prove the necessary catalyst.

The Age of Reason 1715–1750

After Louis XIV's death, the relaxed atmosphere of the Regency brought about certain tangible changes (for instance, the return of the Italian players who had been expelled in 1697 for a satire on Madame de Maintenon). There was a gradual increase in foreign contacts, and as the century progressed, intellectual life became more and more cosmopolitan. English influences became particularly important – it is common, indeed, to speak of eighteenth-century 'anglomania' – though in the first half of the century, such influences chiefly concern the literature of ideas rather than imaginative writing. The rapid growth of periodical literature produced many new journals which both reflected

[1] Cf. P. Hazard, *La Crise de la conscience européenne (1680–1715)* (Paris, 1935).

English influence – e.g. the *Spectateur français*, launched by Marivaux in 1722 in imitation of Addison's *Spectator* – and disseminated knowledge about England, e.g. Prévost's *Le Pour et contre*, begun in 1733. In Prévost's case this followed a visit to England, and other major writers who visited this country at a decisive point in their careers were Montesquieu and Voltaire.

Charles Secondat, Baron de Montesquieu (1689–1755), owed to the example of English life and letters several important features of his major work, *L'Esprit des lois* (1748): the notion of the separation of the three powers (executive, legislative and judiciary), and the ideal of a 'mixed', or constitutional, monarchy. But however widely read, and however influential (e.g. on the shaping of the American constitution), this was a work for specialists, which lies outside the province of imaginative literature – as does Montesquieu's historical work *Considérations sur les causes de la grandeur des Romains et de leur décadence* (1734). The work which best illustrates the spirit of the age, *Lettres persanes* (1721), was written before Montesquieu's English visit. Purporting to be a collection of letters written by two Persian travellers in Europe, with enough replies from the seraglio to sustain a flimsy plot, this volume appeals to the Regency taste for the licentious in literature, and also to the vogue for the exotic, which had been stimulated by the translation of the *Arabian Nights* (1704) and the publication of several authentic travellers' tales. But more important, its *romanesque* framework and episodic structure allow the author to cover a very wide range of social, economic, political and religious practices; the naïve reactions of the Oriental travellers provide a means of submitting the customs of Western civilization to the critique of Cartesian rationalism; and Montesquieu is able, under a fictional cloak, to preach a message of tolerance, deism and social justice.

François-Marie Arouet (1694–1778), known as Voltaire, made direct use of his stay in England from 1726 to 1729 to compose an even more striking indictment of French society; indeed, his *Lettres philosophiques* (1734) were seized by order of the Parlement de Paris and publicly burnt. The *Lettres* contain a comprehensive survey of English political, religious, intellectual and cultural life; at each stage there is an implied comparison with France, almost everywhere to the advantage of the English. What Voltaire admires in English life is the evidence of a pragmatic, empirical outlook, resulting in religious tolerance, a constitutional monarchy, respect for the individual, and social and economic progress. The *Lettres* are most agreeably written: Voltaire covers his tracks by the use of irony, and by feigning to criticize English 'abuses' (as in the opening letters on the Quakers); though hardly subtle, this approach is very effective, and Voltaire's allusive, ironical manner is the one the *philosophes* were to favour throughout the century.

But we must remember that although to us Voltaire is principally remembered as a *conteur*, a *philosophe* and a campaigner for justice and truth, to his contemporaries – at least up to 1750 – he was first and foremost a writer of tragedy, to be spoken of in the same terms as Corneille and Racine. And if he was a 'Moderne' in intellectual matters generally, Voltaire was the most reactionary of 'Anciens' in matters of taste, never swerving from an uncompromising belief in a universally applicable aesthetic. His attitude to Shakespeare illustrates this. In the *Lettres philosophiques* he finds it possible to praise the English dramatist as a creator of 'belles scènes'; but judged as a whole, he finds him 'sans la moindre étincelle de bon goût et sans la moindre connaissance des règles'. And though on his return from England he appears not unwilling to commend certain features of Shakespearian tragedy to his readers, towards the end of his life (by which time other, much more sympathetic, interpreters were at work) he dismisses him scornfully as 'un sauvage ivre'. Other dramatists, even at the beginning of our period, were more openminded; for instance, Voltaire carried on a controversy with Antoine Houdar de la Motte (1672–1731), a friend of Fontenelle and champion of the Moderns, who argued for the use of prose as a medium for tragedy. However, in practice even La Motte lacked the courage of his convictions, and the real originality of his highly successful *Inès de Castro* (1723) was that it catered so well for the new wave of sensibility, concentrating on the pathetic sufferings of an innocent victim. Inès is persecuted because she has contracted a morganatic marriage with the Infante of Portugal, and the appearance of their young children on stage represents a *locus classicus* of that *pathétique moralisateur* which is found in so much of the imaginative writing of the century, based on the belief that display of the emotions must be salutary, and that readiness to be moved is proof of moral worth.

Even Voltaire himself made concessions to the *sensibilité* he affected to scorn. For instance, a completely inappropriate love plot is introduced into his first tragedy *Oedipe* (1718); and in *Zaïre* (1732), his finest play, the 'Aristotelian' tragic hero Orosmane takes second place to the pathetic heroine, killed as a result of her jealous lover's unfounded suspicion. But this updating of the Othello theme is only one aspect of *Zaïre*: the play is also an excellent example of the way in which Voltaire introduced ideological issues into tragedy, for Orosmane is a Moslem prince, and Zaïre a Christian; and the catastrophe is at least partly due to the fanatical zealotry of the Crusaders. In other early tragedies Voltaire introduced borrowings from Shakespeare: a crowd-scene in *La Mort de César* (1731), Hamlet's ghost into *Ériphile* (1732) and *Sémiramis* (1748); but the essential formula remains derivative and uninspired. If anything, there is a tendency for tragedy to degenerate into melodrama; and the only redeeming feature is the vigorous portrayal of a thesis, when Voltaire uses the theatre to preach his gospel of humanitarian tolerance (e.g. in *Alzire* (1736), which portrays the inhuman Spanish conquest of Peru in the name of Christianity; or in *Mahomet* (1742), in which the unscrupulous tyrant stands for all political oppression practised under cover of religion).

It was not only in tragedy that *le pathétique* made its appeal to theatre audiences. Among the ouststanding *hautes comédies* of the period, there are few which are frankly comic: *La Métromanie* (1738) by Alexis Piron (1689–1773) is a refreshing exception. More typical are the heavily moralizing comedies of Philippe Néricault Destouches (1680–1754) such as *Le Curieux impertinent* (1709) or *Le Glorieux* (1732), and *Le Méchant* (1745) by Jean-Baptiste-Louis Gresset (1709–77). But Pierre-Claude Nivelle de La Chaussée (1692–1754) went much further, and created a new genre, *la comédie larmoyante*, which achieved its edifying effect above all by a pathetic appeal to the spectator's sensibility. *Le Préjugé à la mode* (1735) portrays the plight of a wife, unjustly neglected by her husband in obedience to the fashionable idea that to love one's wife is old-fashioned; but more typical is *Mélanide* (1741), in which the central character is a long-suffering unmarried mother (for the 'mariage secret' which was such a cliché of the sentimental literature of the age was merely a euphemism for a liaison). Virtue inevitably triumphs, but not before every pathetic possibility has been exploited, including the recognition-scene, the *scène à faire* of all these tearful dramas. Although Voltaire dismissed *comédie larmoyante* as 'la tragédie des femmes de chambre' he himself wrote one or two examples, his *Nanine* (1749) being inspired, like La Chaussée's *Paméla* (1743), by Richardson's novel.

An altogether subtler form of comedy had in the meantime been developed by Pierre Carlet de Chamblain de Marivaux (1688–1763). Marivaux began writing for the Italians, and although he never reproduced the stereotype 'Italian' comedy with its buffoonery and slapstick, he did take over stock characters such as the colourless lovers and the stylized valets. Freed from the need to develop 'character', he could exploit to the full his talent for light, graceful, inconsequential dialogue; similarly, his plots are of the simplest, and the conventional parents, guardians and rivals are never important in Marivaux's comedy: indeed, they are often dispensed with altogether, and what matters is the psychological 'obstacle' in the characters' minds. So, in the most characteristic of his plays, *La Surprise de l'amour* (1722), *La Double Inconstance* (1723), *Le Jeu de l'amour et du hasard* (1730) – generally considered his masterpiece – or *Les Fausses Confidences* (1737), dialogue acquires a real autonomy. It is from the very fact of two persons being together and conversing that the significant developments in his plots come about: they meet, each wishes to attract the other, but neither wishes to be caught; they fall in love; they become aware of their feelings; they resist; they yield. This sort of dramatic writing has been given the name *marivaudage*; the term is often used pejoratively of other writers, but applied to Marivaux himself it denotes a style which may be mannered and affected, but is full of psychological penetration. Marivaux is, with Beaumarchais, one of the two really original dramatic writers of the century; his plays have lasted better than most of the imaginative writing of the time, and have had a remarkable success in the theatre in our own day.

Something of the same delicacy of touch, particularly in the exploration of the feminine mind, marks Marivaux's two novels, *La Vie de Marianne* (1731–41) and *Le Paysan parvenu* (1735–6). These are both 'memoir-novels', written in the first person; and rather than a 'realist' picture of a social scene, they provide a very personal record of the reactions of an individual temperament to the places and persons surrounding the writer. The particular contribution of Marivaux to the novel is his sensitivity to nuances of behaviour and especially speech, as indices of character; but like most of his contemporaries, he paid little attention to form and structure in the novel, and both *Marianne* and *Le Paysan* are unfinished.

It was still common at this time to draw a distinction between a *roman* (a self-confessed work of fiction) and an *histoire* (a short story or 'memoir' which at least claimed to be authentic).[1] Marivaux may be said to represent a fusion of these two traditions; the other two major novelists of the time can be situated more easily with regard to existing categories. Lesage wrote two novels, *Le Diable boiteux* (1707), a fantasy in which a friendly demon lifts the roofs of houses in Madrid and reveals life as it is lived; and *Gil Blas* (1715–35), which adopts the

[1] Cf. F. Deloffre, *La Nouvelle en France à l'âge classique* (Paris, 1967).

episodic form of the Spanish picaresque novel. Both contain a series of good-humoured satirical sketches: though more down-to-earth than the *romans héroïques* of the previous century, they are less earthy than for example Scarron, and Lesage represents the equivalent in the novel of an urbane *comédie de mœurs*. Antoine-François Prévost (1687–1763) adopts a different sort of framework for his *Mémoires d'un homme de qualité* (1728–31) and *Le Philosophe anglais, ou les Mémoires de Cleveland* (1732–9): a first-person narrative, into which can be interpolated shorter autobiographical 'memoirs'. One of these, 'L'Histoire du chevalier des Grieux et de Manon Lescaut' (originally forming volume VII of the *Homme de qualité*), so transcends the limitations of its framework, and of the tradition to which this belongs, that it stands as a self-contained masterpiece among the great French novels. In view of Prévost's habitual prolixity, *Manon Lescaut* possesses a truly remarkable economy; the 'confessional' first-person narrative makes the idealization of the faithless Manon by her lover completely plausible, and the account of Des Grieux's degradation as a result of his passion for her has such a compelling fatalism and mythic power that the novel has understandably been called both 'Jansenist' and 'Racinian'.

The two kinds of novel – the autobiographical 'memoir' and the 'romance' – are further represented by Claude-Prosper Jolyot de Crébillon *fils* (1707–77) in *Les Égarements du cœur et de l'esprit* (1736) and *Le Sopha* (1745), the one catering for contemporary taste by offering the exemplary lesson of a 'case-history', the other by titillating the imagination. Prévost's later novels (e.g. *L'Histoire d'une Grecque moderne*, 1740) fulfil both aims; they are very much of their time, and have not survived the age in which they were written. Only in *Manon Lescaut* did Prévost capture a more universal appeal; with *La Princesse de Clèves*, *Manon* represents the expression of the French classical ideal in novel form.

Manon Lescaut is often compared with Defoe's *Moll Flanders*. Almost contemporary, and dealing with similar milieux, the two novels are nevertheless totally unlike in literary flavour. While Defoe the realist offers at every point material proof of Moll's poverty, Prévost is content to establish credibility by the autobiographical memoir form, and otherwise makes few concessions to 'realism'. In fact, he uses the same elevated, highly abstract *style noble* as usage decreed for poetic genres, and this is the key to the essential literary quality of his novel: Des Grieux's lament over the body of his dead mistress, for instance, constitutes an elegiac prose-poem. But however successful in such rare instances in raising the prosaic to the level of the sublime, *le style noble* was to cripple poetic expression, and inhibit imagination, throughout the century.

The most celebrated poet of this generation, Jean-Baptiste Rousseau (1671–1741), remained derivative as regards form and subject-matter, as well as expression; and perhaps the genre which best suited the stylized poetic diction, with its limited vocabulary, its abstractions, its colourless epithets and its heritage of clichés, was the philosophical ode developed by Voltaire. Voltaire's poetic output was considerable, one of his first literary achievements being the epic *La Henriade* (1723); but neither this nor his mock-epic *La Pucelle* (1755) equals poems such as his *Discours sur l'homme* (1738), modelled on Pope, *Le Mondain* (1736), a panegyric of modern civilization and a vindication of luxury, or the eloquent and moving *Poème sur le désastre de Lisbonne* (1756). In tragedy, the limitations of the impoverished vocabulary become more apparent as Voltaire and other playwrights turn from ancient history and mythology to modern subjects; cf. Voltaire's tragedies based on medieval French history (e.g. *Adélaïde du Guesclin*, 1734; *Tancrède*, 1760) and on Oriental civilizations (*Mahomet; L'Orphelin de la Chine*, 1755). Although the emphasis in such tragedies remains ideological, and local colour is not stressed, the shortcomings of *le style noble* are revealed when cannon and firearms have to be called 'foudres mugissantes' or 'longs tubes d'airain'.

Among prose-writers, the classical style continued to serve those who were concerned to generalize about human behaviour, such as Montesquieu in *L'Esprit des lois*, or Luc de Clapiers, Marquis de Vauvenargues (1715–47), whose *Introduction à la connaissance de l'esprit humain, suivie de réflexions et maximes* (1746) continues the manner of La Rochefoucauld, though without the latter's characteristic cynicism. It was not so suitable to the purpose of those – novelists, psychologists, lyric poets – who were less concerned with such general truths than with the exploration of the individual personality in relation to its surroundings. Such writers needed a more varied, concrete, colourful vocabulary, and the enrichment of the affective resources of the language; this is a development that we associate above all with the generation of 1830, but it was a continuous process, and the language of Diderot and Rousseau is no longer that of Montesquieu and Voltaire. In this sense, if in no other, there is some truth in Goethe's remark, 'One world finishes with Voltaire, another begins with Rousseau'.

In spite of his conservatism in literary matters, Voltaire created, or at least made his own, the genre which best represents the spirit of the closing decades of our period. *Gulliver's Travels* is perhaps the nearest antecedent to Voltaire's *contes philosophiques*; indeed, *Micromégas* (1752), in which the Earth is visited by giants from Sirius and Saturn, clearly owes a good deal to Swift. More characteristic, however, are those *contes* in which the central character is a human traveller whose reactions to the vicissitudes of life make him wiser and if not happier, at least more resigned to his lot. Social satire abounds – from passing digs at rival philosophers or men of letters, and caricatural portraits of priests or politicians, to a much more sustained attack on various aspects of French life in *L'Ingénu* (1767). But Voltaire's chief subject in the *contes* is metaphysical speculation, and he uses this narrative form for the imaginative treatment of those philosophical issues which concerned him all his life: the question of a benevolent Providence (*Zadig*, 1747); the problem of evil (*Candide*, 1759; *Le Blanc et le noir*, 1764). Characterization remains rudimentary: the 'rounded' characters of the novel would not have suited the author's purpose, and Voltaire's ideal traveller is a simple, passive figure – the names Candide and l'Ingénu are indicative of the quality shared by most of his heroes – surrounded by caricatural puppets who respond in a predictable way to every new experience. In fact, this is the world of the comic strip cartoon – or would be, were it not for Voltaire's mastery of the literary language; for here we have the supreme example of classical French as the language of reason: crisp, economical sentences constructed with an eye to balance and antithesis, and gaining the maximum effect from irony and understatement.

Candide is the richest of the *contes*, and one of the acknowledged masterpieces of eighteenth-century literature. This is a devastating attack on the optimism professed by Leibniz and Pope, sparked off by the facile religious and philosophical explanations of the Lisbon earthquake. As one nightmarish experience succeeds another, Candide progresses from parrot-like repetition of Pangloss's 'Tout est au mieux' to a reasoned acceptance of the message of the wise old Turk, 'Il faut cultiver notre jardin'. An avoidance of futile speculation; the acceptance of life as it is; a practical endeavour to improve one's lot and that of others: such is the positive conclusion offered in *Candide* by one who was to write as his own epitaph:

> J'ai fait un peu de bien; c'est mon meilleur ouvrage.

Bibliography

GENERAL STUDIES

As regards comprehensive literary histories of the period, A. Adam, *Histoire de la littérature française au XVIIe siècle*, 5 vols (Paris, 1948–56), is in a class by itself, combining as it does detailed information over a very wide range with an individual (and often original) point of view. This period is also covered in such single volumes as J. Vier, *Histoire de la littérature française, XVIe–XVIIe siècles* (Paris, 1959), and P. J. Yarrow, *A Literary History of France, II: Seventeenth Century* (London, 1967), as well as in a volume of essays by several hands, J. Cruickshank (ed.), *French Literature and its Background, II: Seventeenth Century* (London, 1969). An excellent series of volumes by various authors, still in course of publication (*Littérature française*, published by Arthaud), includes J. Morel, *La Renaissance, III: 1570–1624* (Paris, 1973), A. Adam, *L'Âge classique, I: 1624–1660* (Paris, 1968), P. Clarac, *L'Âge classique, II: 1660–1680* (Paris, 1969), R. Pomeau, *L'Âge classique, III: 1680–1720* (Paris, 1971), and J. Ehrard, *Le XVIIIe Siècle, I: 1720–1750* (Paris, 1974). The eighteenth century has also been treated in J. Vier, *Histoire de la littérature française, XVIIIe siècle*, 2 vols (Paris, 1971), R. Niklaus, *A Literary History of France, III: Eighteenth Century* (London, 1970), and J. Cruickshank (ed.), *French Literature and its Background, III: Eighteenth Century* (London, 1970).

Two volumes by J. Lough, *An Introduction to Seventeenth-Century France* (London, 1954) and *An Introduction to Eighteenth-Century France* (London, 1960), survey the historical and social background against which the literature of the respective periods was written; while a rather more specialized background is treated in each of two works by G. Mongrédien, *La Vie de société aux XVIIe et XVIIIe siècles* (Paris, 1950), and *La Vie littéraire au XVIIe siècle* (Paris, 1947). The two volumes by W. D. Howarth, *Life and Letters in France, I: The Seventeenth Century* (London, 1965), and R. Fargher, *Life and Letters in France, II: The Eighteenth Century* (London, 1970), portray the social and intellectual world of selected authors of these two centuries and of the public for whom they wrote. G. Reynier, *La Femme au XVIIe siècle* (Paris, 1929); M. Magendie, *La Politesse mondaine et les théories de l'honnêteté en France de 1600 à 1660* (Paris, 1925); A. Adam (ed.), *Les Libertins au XVIIe siècle* (Paris, 1964); R. Lathuillière, *La Préciosité*, vol. 1 (Geneva, 1966); and G. Mongrédien (ed.), *Les Précieux et les précieuses* (Paris, 1963), between them give a very informative account of various social movements which were intimately connected with the literature of the century. For the detailed picture of an immensely wide range of the intellectual life of the seventeenth century, there is no modern work to equal C. A. Sainte-Beuve, *Port-Royal*, 3 vols (Paris, 1953–5; first published 1840–59); though J. C. Tournand, *Introduction à la vie littéraire du XVIIe siècle* (Paris, 1970), offers a brief but helpful survey of the intellectual and moral climate of the time. Stimulating interpretative studies of the moral climate of the seventeenth century from a personal point of view are offered by P. Bénichou, *Morales du Grand Siècle* (Paris, 1948), and A. J. Krailsheimer, *Studies in Self-Interest* (Oxford, 1962). The first two volumes of P. Trahard, *Les Maîtres de la sensibilité française au XVIIIe siècle*, 4 vols (Paris, 1931), deal with the moral and intellectual atmosphere of the period 1700–50.

Within the seventeenth century, there was until quite recently a tendency to concentrate excessively on the generation of 1660–85 (together with such other 'classical' phenomena as the early tragedies of Corneille). However, the post-war years have seen a remarkable widening of this interest, with the development of an important new focus of critical attention in the literature of the 'preclassical' or 'baroque' generation, and in the contrast between this and classical literature itself. Among critical works reflecting this new orientation are R. Morçay and P. Sage, *Le Préclassicisme* (Paris, 1962); J. Rousset, *La Littérature de l'âge baroque en France* (Paris, 1954); M. Raymond, *Baroque et renaissance poétique* (Paris, 1955); I. Buffum, *Studies in the Baroque from Montaigne to Rotrou* (Yale, 1957). G. de Reynold, *Synthèse du XVIIe siècle: France classique et Europe baroque* (Paris, 1962), and V. L. Tapié, *Baroque et classicisme* (Paris, 1957), explore the relationship between the two critical concepts, relating the literary context to the intellectual background and the context of the visual arts respectively.

Among the wealth of secondary literature devoted to French classicism, the following will be found particularly useful. R. Bray, *La Formation de la doctrine classique en France* (Lausanne, 1931), deals with the background of theory, while G. Highet, *The Classical Tradition* (Oxford, 1949), relates French (and European) neo-classicism to the literature of classical antiquity. D. Mornet, *Histoire de la littérature française classique, 1660–1700* (Paris, 1947), studies the relationship between the masterpieces of the 'grands classiques' and the more general development of the genres within which they worked; and H. Busson, *La Religion des classiques* (Paris, 1948), investigates the religious beliefs reflected in the works of the major writers of the period 1660–85. W. G. Moore, *French Classical Literature: An Essay* (Oxford, 1962), and P. H. Nurse, *Classical Voices* (London, 1971), present critical studies of the acknowledged masterpieces of the period; while M. Turnell, *The Classical Moment: Studies of Corneille, Molière and Racine* (London, 1947), studies the three major representatives of classicism in the theatre. J. Brody (ed.), *French Classicism: A Critical Miscellany* (Englewood Cliffs, N.J., 1966), is an anthology of critical views on the subject from the seventeenth century to the present day; and among the most important interpretative essays published in recent years are H. Peyre, *Qu'est-ce que le classicisme? Essai de mise au point* (Paris, 1942), and E. B. O. Borgerhoff, *The Freedom of French Classicism* (Princeton, 1950).

Turning to works dealing with the post-classical generations, we find fewer general studies. A. Tilley, *The Decline of the Age of Louis XIV* (Cambridge, 1929), treats the literature of the period 1687–1715, while G. Atkinson and A. C. Keller, *Prelude to the Enlightenment* (London, 1971), choose for their survey the period 1690–1740. F. C. Green, *Minuet* (London, 1935), approaches the imaginative literature of the eighteenth century by means of a comparison with its English counterpart.

DRAMA

Modern historical scholarship has produced an invaluable reference-work in H. C. Lancaster, *A Study of French Dramatic Literature in the Seventeenth Century*, 9 vols (vol. 9 *Recapitulation*) (Baltimore, 1929–42): while offering little critical evaluation, this gives exhaustive information about troupes, stage conditions, authors and plays. For material conditions in the theatre, the acting profession, etc., W. L. Wiley, *The Early Public Theater in France* (Cambridge, Mass., 1960), constitutes an excellent introduction; this can be supplemented by more specialist works such as S. W. Deierkauf-Holsboer, *L'Histoire de la mise en scène dans le théâtre français à Paris de 1600 à 1673* (Paris, 1960); T. E. Lawrenson, *The French Stage in the Seventeenth Century* (Manchester, 1957); J. Lough, *Paris Theatre Audiences in the Seventeenth and Eighteenth Centuries* (London, 1957); G. Mongrédien, *La Vie quotidienne des comédiens au temps de Molière* (Paris, 1966). J. Scherer, *La Dramaturgie classique en France* (Paris, 1950), is an important work analysing the conventions within which the seventeenth-century dramatist worked.

The dramatic literature of the seventeenth century is surveyed, briefly and in a highly personal manner, by W. G. Moore in *The Classical Drama of France* (Oxford, 1971); and that of the later period, unimaginatively but quite informatively, in E. F. Jourdain, *Dramatic Theory and Practice in France, 1690–1808* (London, 1921).

Tragedy is dealt with, economically but suggestively, in G. Lanson, *Esquisse d'une histoire de la tragédie française* (New York, 1920), and in J. Morel, *La Tragédie* (Paris, 1969). Its more detailed history during various parts of our period is covered in E. Forsyth, *La Tragédie française de Jodelle à Corneille (1553–1640)* (Paris, 1962); G. Brereton, *French Tragic Drama in the Sixteenth and Seventeenth Centuries* (London, 1973); and H. C. Lancaster, *French Tragedy in the Time of Louis XV and Voltaire* (Baltimore, 1950). As regards tragicomedy, the standard work is H. C. Lancaster, *The French Tragicomedy; its Origin and Development from 1552 to 1628* (Baltimore, 1907), while the other popular dramatic form of the early seventeenth century is dealt with in J. Marsan, *La Pastorale dramatique en France à la fin du XVIe et au commencement du XVIIe siècle* (Paris, 1905). The hybrid sentimental comedy which flourished in the 1730s is the subject of G. Lanson, *Nivelle de La Chaussée et la comédie larmoyante* (Paris, rev. ed. 1903). General works on comedy during the period include E. Lintilhac, *Histoire générale du théâtre, III: La Comédie, XVIIe siècle* (Paris, 1908); *IV: La Comédie, XVIIIe siècle* (Paris, 1909); R. Guichemerre, *La Comédie avant Molière, 1640–1660* (Paris, 1972); P. Kohler, *L'Esprit classique et la comédie* (Paris, 1925); J. Lemaître, *La Comédie après Molière et le théâtre de Dancourt* (Paris, 1882); P. Voltz, *La Comédie* (Paris, 1964); and most recently G. Brereton, *French Comic Drama from the Sixteenth to the Eighteenth Century* (London, 1977).

However, most of the critical writing on classical drama has been concerned, not with the development of genres, but with the work of particular authors; and the volume of writing devoted to Corneille, Molière and Racine bears abundant witness to their pre-eminence.

Corneille criticism has taken on a new character since the war. G. Lanson, *Corneille* (Paris, 1898), is the most valuable early study; but a new approach may already be seen in V. Vedel, *Deux classiques français vus par un étranger* (Paris, 1935), while O. Nadal, *Le Sentiment de l'amour dans l'œuvre de P. Corneille* (Paris, 1948), remains the most influential revaluation. L. Rivaille, *Les Débuts de P. Corneille* (Paris, 1936), and G. Couton, *La Vieillesse de Corneille* (Paris, 1949), helped to turn critical attention away from a handful of 'major' plays by focusing on the beginning and end of the playwright's career respectively. G. Couton, *Corneille* (Paris,

1958), is a workmanlike general introduction, while other recent studies of value include S. Doubrovsky, *Corneille et la dialectique du héros* (Paris, 1963); R. J. Nelson, *Corneille, His Heroes and their Worlds* (Philadelphia, 1963); P. J. Yarrow, *Corneille* (London, 1963); and J. Maurens, *La Tragédie sans tragique: le néo-stoïcisme dans l'œuvre de P. Corneille* (Paris, 1966).

The long-standing critical comparison between Corneille and Racine, which forms the subject of an anthology, R. J. Nelson (ed.), *Corneille and Racine: Parallels and Contrasts* (Englewood Cliffs, N. J., 1966), has been brought up to date by G. May, *Tragédie cornélienne, tragédie racinienne* (Urbana, 1948), and G. Pocock, *Corneille and Racine: Problems of Tragic Form* (Cambridge, 1973); while the contrast between Racinian and Shakespearian tragedy has perhaps nowhere been better handled than in L. Strachey, *Landmarks in French Literature* (London, 1912). Among recent critical works on Racine, an excellent introduction would be J. C. Lapp, *Aspects of Racinian Tragedy* (Toronto, 1955), or O. de Mourgues's sound and balanced *Racine, or the Triumph of Relevance* (Cambridge, 1967). T. Maulnier, *Racine* (Paris, 1935), still offers a very stimulating interpretation. P. France, *Racine's Rhetoric* (Oxford, 1965), and G. Cahen, *Le Vocabulaire de Racine* (Paris, 1946), provide the best guide to a critical assessment of Racine's literary technique; and E. Vinaver, *Racine et la poésie tragique* (Paris, 1951), stresses the part played by the poetry in the make-up of Racinian tragedy. The sociological interpretation of L. Goldmann, *Le Dieu caché* (Paris, 1955), has been influential, as has the structuralist interpretation of R. Barthes, *Sur Racine* (Paris, 1963). In the 1960s Racine became the subject of a sharp critical controversy between the 'nouveaux critiques' represented by Barthes and others, and their more conservative opponents led by R. Picard, whose *La Carrière de J. Racine* (Paris, 1956), is a valuable source of detailed documentation. A. Bonzon, *La Nouvelle Critique et Racine* (Paris, 1970), gives an account of this controversy; while R. C. Knight (ed.), *Racine (Modern Judgements)* (London, 1969), provides a more general selection of modern critical views.

In Molière's case, post-war criticism shows a turning away from earlier preoccupation with the 'meaning' of the plays towards a more objective aesthetic approach. Two works in particular stimulated this change: W. G. Moore, *Molière: A New Criticism* (Oxford, 1949), and R. Bray, *Molière, homme de théâtre* (Paris, 1954). The best recent interpretations include D. Romano, *Essai sur le comique de Molière* (Berne, 1950); J. Guicharnaud, *Molière, une aventure théâtrale* (Paris, 1963); J. D. Hubert, *Molière and the Comedy of Intellect* (Berkeley and Los Angeles, 1962); and M. Gutwirth, *Molière ou l'Invention comique* (Paris, 1966); while H. Bergson, *Le Rire* (Paris, 1900), still remains one of the most stimulating brief introductions to the essential character of Molière's comedy. R. McBride, *The Sceptical Vision of Molière* (London, 1977), makes an interesting attempt to relate comic form to moral viewpoint. A conspectus of modern critical views is presented in J. Guicharnaud (ed.), *Molière (Twentieth-Century Views)* (Englewood Cliffs, N.J., 1964). Readers interested in the interpretation of classical drama in the theatre by various actors should consult M. Descotes, *Les Grands Rôles du théâtre de Molière* (Paris, 1960) (cf. Descotes's companion volumes on *Racine* and *Corneille*, published in 1957 and 1962 respectively).

Turning to the post-classical period, Regnard's comedy is dealt with in A. Calame, *Regnard, sa vie et son œuvre* (Paris, 1960); Marivaux's dramatic writings are the subject of K. N. McKee, *The Theater of Marivaux* (New York, 1958), and are also dealt with at length in E. J. H. Greene, *Marivaux* (Toronto, 1965), and P. Gazagne, *Marivaux par lui-même* (Paris, 1954); and Voltaire's tragedy is studied in H. Lion, *Les Tragédies et les théories dramatiques de Voltaire* (Paris, 1896), and R. S. Ridgway, *La Propagande philosophique dans les tragédies de Voltaire* (Geneva, 1961).

Texts of the major dramatists are readily available in a variety of editions, both of collected works and of single plays. Useful anthologies of the works of minor playwrights are: *Théâtre du XVIIe siècle*, ed. J. Scherer, Vol. I (Paris, 1975) (Vol. II to follow); *Théâtre du XVIIIe siècle*, ed. J. Truchet, Vol. I (Paris, 1972), Vol. II (Paris, 1974).

POETRY

The works indicated above as dealing with baroque literature nearly all pay considerable attention to the poetry of the early seventeenth century. These should be supplemented by R. Winegarten, *French Lyric Poetry in the Age of Malherbe* (Manchester, 1954); J. Rousset, *L'Intérieur et l'extérieur* (Paris, 1968); and O. de Mourgues, *Metaphysical, Baroque and Précieux Poetry* (Oxford, 1953). For the second half of the century, J. Brody, *Boileau and Longinus* (Geneva, 1958), provides an important revaluation; while with regard to La Fontaine, O. de Mourgues, *La Fontaine: Fables* (London, 1960), is the best short introduction; H. Taine, *La Fontaine et ses fables* (Paris, 1853), is still useful despite a rather old-fashioned approach; and J. D. Biard, *The Style of La Fontaine's Fables* (Oxford, 1966), presents a detailed analysis of the poet's technique. For a recent work treating the whole period, see R. Sabatier, *Histoire de la poésie française*, Vol. II (*XVIIe siècle*) and Vol. III (*XVIIIe siècle*) (Paris, 1975).

Anthologies of verse covering the period under review include A. J. Steele (ed.), *Three Centuries of French Verse, 1511–1819* (Edinburgh, rev. ed. 1961); J. Rousset (ed.), *Anthologie de la poésie baroque française*, 2 vols (Paris, 1961); O. de Mourgues, *An Anthology of French Seventeenth-Century Lyric Poetry* (Oxford, 1966); and M. Raymond and A. J. Steele (eds), *La Poésie française et le maniérisme, 1546–1610* (Geneva, 1971).

PROSE FICTION

The standard account of the novel in the early and middle years of the seventeenth century is M. Magendie, *Le Roman français au XVIIe siècle, de l'Astrée au Grand Cyrus* (Paris, 1932); E. Showalter, *The Evolution of the French Novel, 1641–1782* (Princeton, 1972), deals competently with the development of this genre over the remainder of the period under review; A. Le Breton, *Le Roman au dix-septième siècle* (Paris, 1890), is workmanlike but old-fashioned. F. Deloffre, *La Nouvelle en France à l'âge classique* (Paris, 1967), surveys the short story throughout the seventeenth century and up to 1735.

M. Magendie, *L'Astrée d'Honoré d'Urfé* (Paris, 1929), situates this novel in its period and assesses its influence; and Mme de La Fayette's work is studied by H. Ashton, *Mme de La Fayette, sa vie et ses œuvres* (Cambridge, 1922); C. Dédéyan, *Mme de La Fayette* (Paris, 1956); and J. Raitt, *Mme de La Fayette and 'La Princesse de Clèves'* (London, 1971).

For the period 1700–50, A. Le Breton, *Le Roman français au XVIIIe siècle* (Paris, 1898), has been superseded by V. G. Mylne, *The Eighteenth-Century French Novel*

(Manchester, 1965), and G. May, *Le Dilemme du roman au XVIIIe siècle* (Paris, 1963). Individual novelists of this period are studied in H. Roddier, *L'Abbé Prévost, l'homme et l'œuvre* (Paris, 1955); P. Brooks, *The Novel of Worldliness: Crébillon, Marivaux, Laclos, Stendhal* (Princeton, 1969); and in the works on Marivaux by Greene and Gazagne referred to above.

For the philosophical *conte* as created by Voltaire, see J. Van den Heuvel, *Voltaire dans ses contes* (Paris, 1967), and V. Schick, *Zur Erzähltechnik in Voltaires 'Contes'* (Munich, 1968).

NON-FICTIONAL PROSE

From the profuse Pascal bibliography, J. Mesnard, *Pascal, l'homme et l'œuvre* (Paris, 1951), stands out as a useful brief introduction. Another general study is J. H. Broome, *Pascal* (London, 1965); while Pascal is treated in a stimulating but idiosyncratic way in L. Goldmann, *Le Dieu caché* (see above). On Pascal's style, see P. Topliss, *The Rhetoric of Pascal* (Leicester, 1966). La Rochefoucauld is presented succinctly in W. G. Moore, *La Rochefoucauld, his Mind and Art* (Oxford, 1969); Saint-Évremond is treated in Q. M. Hope, *Saint-Évremond, the 'honnête homme' as Critic* (Bloomington, Ind., 1962); and La Bruyère in the very compact P. Richard, *La Bruyère et ses 'Caractères'* (Paris, 1946). Mme de Sévigné may best be approached through A. Tilley, *Mme de Sévigné, Some Aspects of her Life and Character* (Cambridge, 1936), or A. Bailly, *Mme de Sévigné* (Paris, 1955); and E. Carcassonne, *Fénelon, l'homme et l'œuvre* (Paris, 1946), and J. Calvet, *Bossuet, l'homme et l'œuvre* (Paris, 1941), provide good introductory guides to their respective subjects.

For the literary aspect of the 'ancient *v.* modern' controversy, the comprehensive studies of H. Rigault, *Histoire de la querelle des anciens et des modernes* (Paris, 1856), and H. Gillot, *La Querelle des anciens et des modernes en France* (Paris, 1914), may be supplemented by T. A. Litman, *Le Sublime en France (1660–1714)* (Paris, 1971). For the literature of ideas at the turn of the century, P. Hazard, *La Crise de la conscience européenne (1680–1715)*, provides a most valuable introduction.

A suitable brief guide to Montesquieu is J. Dedieu, *Montesquieu, l'homme et l'œuvre* (Paris, 1943); and R. Naves, *Voltaire, l'homme et l'œuvre* (Paris, 1942), N. Torrey, *The Spirit of Voltaire* (New York, 1938) and H. T. Mason, *Voltaire* (London, 1975), provide a sound general introduction to Voltaire as a thinker and as a writer. A. Noyes, *Voltaire* (London, 1936), is readable but controversial.

THE CLASSICAL LANGUAGE

The language of the period 1600–1750 is often deceptive in its resemblance to twentieth-century French. Where texts cannot be read in scholarly editions which provide linguistic assistance, it may be useful to refer to specialist dictionaries such as the *Dictionnaire de l'Académie française* (facsimile reprint of the 1694 edition) (Lille, 1901); G. Cayrou, *Le Français classique* (Paris, 1924); or J. Dubois and R. Lagane, *Dictionnaire de la langue française classique* (Paris, 1960). A. Haase, *Syntaxe française du XVIIe siècle* (Paris, 1914), gives an authoritative account of the linguistic usage of the period; and F. Brunot, *Histoire de la langue française des origines à 1900*, vols 3–6 (Paris, 1909–33), provides a thorough analysis of all aspects of the classical language.

BIBLIOGRAPHICAL AIDS

Suggestions for further reading may be found in A. Cioranescu, *Bibliographie de la littérature française du XVIIe siècle*, 3 vols (Paris, 1965–6); *Bibliographie de la littérature française du XVIIIe siècle*, 3 vols (Paris, 1969); and in *A Critical Bibliography of French Literature, III: Seventeenth Century*, ed. N. Edelman (Syracuse, N.Y., 1961); *IV: Eighteenth Century*, ed. G. R. Havens and D. F. Bond (Syracuse, 1951); *IVA: Eighteenth Century, Supplement*, ed. R. A. Brooks (Syracuse, 1968). O. Klapp, *Bibliographie d'histoire littéraire française* (Frankfurt-am-Main, 1956–), continues as an annual publication.

8 French Literature from 1750 to 1870

HENRI M. PEYRE

General Characteristics of the New Age

No century in the history or in the literature of France constitutes a harmonious whole, and the eighteenth century least of all. By 1750 or thereabouts, some profound changes had occurred. The literary prestige of the age of Louis XIV had declined. Even in the theatre, where Voltaire continued to proclaim his admiration for Racine, a new trend was leading away from classical tragedy toward bourgeois drama and toward plays with the political and ideological bias. Comedy was no longer following in the wake of Molière. The novel of manners was becoming the true heir to the moralists of the seventeenth century who had satirically portrayed the ridicules and the types of 'la cour et la ville'. The heroic fiction of the age of *préciosité* and the conventional idealization of love were making way for the search for sensations and for a strange combination of eroticism and of sentimentality. The philosophical spirit which Bayle, Montesquieu and the early Voltaire had done much to foster grew more bellicose after 1750: it had become clear that, in France at least, improving things through despotism was a forlorn hope. Louis XV was not to be converted to reforms and would not heed the advice proffered by philosophers. The cultural prestige of France throughout continental Europe had never been greater; but neither the diplomacy nor the armies of the French king deserved much admiration. In France itself, the fashionable society and the men of letters were more and more sensitive to the novelties imported from Great Britain. Voltaire might recant his youthful enthusiasm for Shakespeare; but Shakespeare, dressed up in French garb, Milton, Richardson, Sterne, the English constitution as presented (and often distorted) by Montesquieu provided new models for Diderot and

Rousseau; and the *Encyclopédie* itself originated from a British forerunner, Chambers's *Cyclopedia.*

Montesquieu had published his great work, *L'Esprit des lois,* in 1748 and was to die seven years after. The novelist Lesage disappeared before the middle of the century, in 1747. Fontenelle survived to reach in 1757 the age of a hundred years; Marivaux, no longer active as a playwright or as a novelist, died in 1763. The new spirit of the age was asserting itself as Buffon, in 1749, brought out the beginning of his *Histoire naturelle*, Diderot, also in 1749, his *Lettre sur les aveugles,* to be followed in 1751 by his *Lettre sur les sourds et les muets,* Rousseau his first *Discours sur les sciences et les arts* and Turgot the second of his *Discours sur le développement de l'esprit humain* in 1750, exactly a century after Descartes's death. In 1750 also, Voltaire left for the court of Frederick II of Prussia, convinced that the reign of the Enlightenment would be ushered in by his stay in Berlin, where he would bask in the admiration of a liberal and philosophical king. His *Siècle de Louis XIV* (1751) reflected his glowing optimism. His illusion was short-lived; two years later he left, embittered, to exercise his sovereignty over literature closer to France, in his residence near Geneva. In 1751, the first volume of the *Encyclopédie,* of which Diderot was the indefatigable master mind, started the organized campaign of the *philosophes* for the ideas of freedom, toleration, progress, applied science bringing greater happiness to the masses and helping to vanquish the age-old control of the Church over the minds of men.

Several works of lasting beauty appeared during the second half of the century; but the aim of most men of letters then was no longer to produce carefully elaborated, sedulously polished works of art. They were determined to act upon their countrymen, and their fellow beings in other lands, 'here and now'. Hence the multiplicity of short pamphlets, of aggressive and satirical pieces touching on religion, philosophy, politics. New ideas were sprouting everywhere. The style aimed at alertness, often at levity, and was used to arouse the readers from their complacency and to impel them to action. At no time probably had literature thus strained every nerve to change man through changing institutions and redressing the wrongs caused by superstition, ignorance and passivity. If De Quincey's famous distinction between the literature of knowledge and the literature of power may be resorted to, the immense and varied knowledge of the French thinkers of the Age of Reason was of the kind which also brings power. The studies on the eighteenth century initiated by Gustave Lanson in a memorable series of Sorbonne lectures (1907–10), followed up by his disciples in France and elsewhere, have altogether routed the previous assertions of historians like Tocqueville and Taine who had declared the *philosophes* to be but dreamers building a heavenly city and reasoning on man in the abstract. On the contrary, they were persons who travelled outside their own country; who observed all kinds of men under all social conditions; who devised empirical remedies for specific woes which aroused their pity and shocked their reason. Several of them had attempted administrative tasks and had been confronted by prejudices and selfishness. Rousseau himself, as self-centred as any sensitive, suffering Romantic ever was to be, informed himself carefully on local conditions and moods in Poland or in Corsica, before he agreed to offer projects of constitutions for those countries. Religious polemics, philosophical speculation and theology had, during the previous two centuries, been treated by, and as, literature. The second half of the eighteenth century did not deem it unworthy of literature to deal with constitutional and administrative questions, with inequities, privileges, social misery, and to offer new hopes for improvement of their fates to suffering creatures. The social sciences, as we have come to call them, were the creation of the Encyclopedists and of their friends. Ethics was by them divorced from any revealed religion and linked with reason. A writer of small talent, Toussaint, proclaimed the total severance of ethics from religion in a book, *Des mœurs* (1748), which was condemned to be burned, but widely read throughout the second half of the century. La Mettrie and d'Holbach warmly argued that the atheist can be the most moral of creatures.

At the same time as the thought of the age was directed to devising empirical solutions for problems which should no longer be tolerated in their present state, outrageous to reason and goodwill, it also rose above the immediacy of the practical. The decades which preceded, and to some extent prepared, the French Revolution offered to men throughout Europe the lineaments of a new faith. If Christianity was indeed on its decline, new myths, that is to say, great visionary concepts presented as passionately desirable because opening the gates of a new Garden of Eden, had to be forged, from which the religion of humanity would evolve. They were chiefly the myth of progress; the notion of the unity of mankind, resting on mutual toleration and peace, substituted for fanaticism and national hatreds; the search for happiness in this world, 'a new idea in Europe', announced triumphantly the revolutionary Saint-Just; the innate goodness of nature and the rightful claims of instinctive forces; and the reliance upon sensibility and upon the dynamic power which accrues to ideas when they are felt and lived as well as thought. Most socialist and communist movements of the nineteenth and twentieth centuries, most revolutionary trends and reforms stressing more well-being for men of all conditions have looked back to that nursery of ideas and of myths which the second half of the eighteenth century was in Britain, Germany, Italy and, above all, France.

Voltaire, Diderot and the Encyclopedists

The concentration on a better future to be prepared for mankind in no way precluded a clearer vision of the past. History, as distinct from chronicles and memoirs, had reappeared, after a long eclipse, with the new sense of relativism which accompanied the breakdown of dogmatist complacency around 1700. Voltaire had a vivid imagination which enabled him to conjure up figures of individuals, details of daily life, the concerns of the men who had lived in bygone eras. He was not altogether impartial and avoided above all else being lifeless. He realized, as many of his successors in our midst have acknowledged, that ultimately all history is contemporary history, that is to say, written from the vantage point of a present to which the historian cannot help being committed. And he also realized the immense power of history, which can be a dynamite, exploding prejudices, overturning mental habits of inertia and even institutions, impelling men to evolve from the contemplation of the past the guidelines towards a better future.

The earliest attempt at historical writing by Voltaire was his lively narrative of the meteoric rise and of the tragic fall of a contemporary king, Charles XII of Sweden. *L'Histoire de Charles XII* had appeared in 1731, thirteen years after the actual death of a king who had been an adventurer and a warrior of genius. Voltaire's analytical clarity and the sprightliness of his narrative style endowed that early volume with all the attractions of a novel, and few novels then existing could be compared with it. Soon after, Voltaire set to accumulating notes, ransacking documents, questioning older people in preparation for *Le Siècle de Louis XIV*, published in 1751 and corrected and revised until 1768 when it received its final form. It is a work of dazzling intelligence and of very thorough and rich documentation. Voltaire condemned the greatest errors of the long reign during which he himself had been born: Louis XIV's bungling of religious affairs, his blindness in expelling from his kingdom the Protestants who would not be converted to Catholicism when he revoked the Edict of Nantes in 1685, his lack of tolerance. He did not condone the follies of endless and fruitless wars which ruined the country. But he was rightly fascinated by the excellence of Colbert's administration, by the dignity and the achievements of the monarch, and especially by the flowering of letters, arts and the adornments of life under the reign of Louis XIV. That volume imposed for over a century on posterity the image which it was to retain of the so-called 'classical' age of France.

At the same time, however, impatient to overturn the narrow philosophy of history proposed by theological historians like Bossuet, who saw in world history the unfolding of a providential plan and the Judaeo-Christian tradition as alone concerning modern men, Voltaire had undertaken a radically new attempt: a history of civilization. Kings, great personages, warriors, would be relegated to a secondary place. History would cease being a dismal record of fights, banditries, love affairs or greedy rapines of sovereigns; it would tumble down from their pedestals those who had passed for traditional heroes and often were mere plunderers. True great men would be those who have served civilization and contributed to the increase of human happiness. The title of the new work, a milestone in the writing of history, first published in 1756, then in its definitive shape in 1769, is *Essai sur les mœurs et l'esprit des nations*. It surveyed some eight centuries of world history with brilliance. The implicit assumption was that the Jewish and Christian nations and those of Graeco-Roman antiquity should cease to be central in world history. Peoples of Africa, America and Asia in particular, and above all the Chinese dear to Voltaire, had counted also in the development of manners, commerce, art; the concept of a chosen people or of a superior race was derided. The progress of reason had been halting and difficult; but it offered mankind the one glimmer of hope for the future. From that book dates the modern conception of history.

Voltaire's activity during the last twenty-five years of his life was prodigious. His light verse would be enough to win immortality for any poet, in playful genres, neither lyrical nor epic, which are the most difficult of all to practice. His *Mélanges*, some personal memoirs on his ill-starred sojourn at the court of Frederick II of Prussia, other scathing expositions of the gross improbabilities in the Old Testament and sarcasms at the claims of the Scriptures to be God's revealed word, stand among the most entertaining as well as the most impudent pieces of literature. Voltaire's huge correspondence is generally regarded as his masterpiece, and the greatest ensemble of letters in the whole range of world literature. There are treasures of mordant wit, of raillery against superstition and fanaticism in many of the articles of the *Dictionnaire philosophique* (1764), but also much solid information and not a little deep as well as courageous philosophical speculation on religion, ethics, laws, politics, tolerance. At the same time, Voltaire ceaselessly indulged in polemics against institutions and men that denied equality and toleration to those individuals who suffered in a society founded upon privileges. He proved to be a man of action, taking risks, pleading earnestly for freedom of conscience, for freedom of speech, for individual liberty and for a minimum of economic security. Some high-brow historians of philosophy have denied him the title of philosopher, because he never attempted to erect a comprehensive system and to imprison himself in it. On the essential articles of his generous humanitarian faith, however, Voltaire never wavered. He would not accept Christianity, on account of the monstrous crimes committed by the Churches which called themselves Christian; but was always a deist, fairly close to pantheism, believing in a deity that was the guarantor of justice and charity but who could not work miracles or be moved by prayers. There was much in the world, in Voltaire's eyes, which displayed fanaticism, cruelty, hatred; but through work, hope, generosity to others, the burden of those evils might some day be lightened for Voltaire's successors.

Voltaire's glory eclipsed that of many of his contemporaries. Yet Diderot (1713–84) was at least as great as he as an initiator of new ideas, as a bold philosophical speculator, and as a practitioner of genres of writing (the modern novel, the drama, art criticism) which were to develop and to endure, while the epic, tragedy and even the philosophical tale were to die with Voltaire. But Diderot published only a portion of his multifarious writings in his lifetime. He disseminated paradoxes, brilliant considerations on nature, on evolution, on language, psychology, the techniques of arts and crafts throughout ephemeral articles or in the pages of the *Encyclopédie*. He suffered in the eyes of posterity from not having summed himself up in two or three masterpieces or in systematic treatises which could be quoted conveniently in anthologies. The middle of the twentieth century has fully rehabilitated him. With his unevenness, the swiftness of his touch, his impatience and his versatility, he is, of all the eighteenth-century authors, the one who most completely gives the impression of a genius: of achieving with ease what the most assiduous talent can never hope to accomplish.

Diderot's intuitive and impatient manner of thinking did not allow him to compose an elaborate novel with a contrived structure and characters depicted as independent from the author. He accumulated anecdotes, intervened with philosophical digressions, favoured an oral style which mirrored the verve and the ebullient richness of his own conversation. Yet *La Religieuse*, an epistolary novel portraying the torments of a nun in an eighteenth-century convent, and *Le Neveu de Rameau*, a superbly animated dialogue and the portrayal of a Bohemian individualist, count among the best novels of the age; both were published long after Diderot's death. Diderot's dramas, substituting the portrayal of social conditions for the analysis of characters and sentimental middle-class families for princely or aristocratic heroes, are too didactic; they lack the imaginative grip on the audience (*Le Père de famille*, published in 1758; *Le Fils naturel*, 1757). But Diderot's fertile mind teemed with brilliant ideas on the drama, which were to influence much of the French mid-nineteenth-century un-Romantic comedies. His *Paradoxe sur le comédien* (published only in 1830), contending that self-mastery and deliberate histrionics, not sincere and overpowering emotion, should hold the key to the actor's success, is a brilliant and provoking piece of sophistry. In his *Salons*, and in a number of occasional writings on aesthetics and on ancient and modern literature, Diderot poured out penetrating remarks: he wanted to be the advocate of truth, naturalness, balance, wisdom and moderation. But there were always two men in him, waging an intestine struggle. He confessed his rage at being shackled by a philosophy of which his mind could not but approve, but which his heart belied. More even than Montaigne or Gide, he always was to remain a creature of dialogue. He never reached a harmonious system of serene conclusions on any great issue, aesthetic, ethical, political or philosophical. He oscillated, threw illuminating flashes, fighting tirelessly as a committed man who ran risks and persecution, and anticipating the future.

His letters to his mistress, Sophie Volland, are less witty and acrid than Voltaire's, but more passionate and, along with some of Rousseau's, the most exaltedly lyrical in French. Almost alone, he inspired, directed, stubbornly defended the gigantic undertaking of the *Encyclopédie*, a systematic dictionary of ideas, arts, techniques, in thirty-three volumes. The great mathematician d'Alembert wrote the preliminary

Discourse which, in 1751, expounded the philosophy underlying the work. The Catholic parties and the royal authority did all they could to have the work condemned and came near to success more than once. For the whole enterprise was to be a tribute to reason, hence also to toleration, to science helping mould a new ethic; tradition was disregarded and, in spite of many precautions and shows of submission to the ecclesiastical authorities, religion was ridiculed and attacked.

Diderot was not alone in that labour of fifteen years. He drew little effective assistance from Voltaire, from Rousseau who soon broke away from the group of Encyclopedists. He had secretaries, polygraphists who borrowed second-hand information here and there. Among his friends were a dozen great and active minds, who, each in his own right, some retaining an allegiance to traditional religion, others assaulting it frontally, fought for the victory of knowledge, science, toleration, enlightenment through education, over the forces of darkness. None had the profundity and the originality of touch of Diderot; several wrote a turgid prose and had little sense of form. But they helped spread abroad the new ideas. Helvétius (1715–71), with whom Diderot often disagreed, upheld a materialistic doctrine in his book *De l'esprit* (1758) which the censors had burned; he negated innate ideas and set much store by education. D'Holbach (1723–89), a German baron and, like Helvétius, a man of immense wealth, although verbose and repetitious, expounded a consistent materialistic view of the universe in his *Système de la nature* (1770), borrowing some of Diderot's views. Condillac (1714–80), an *abbé* and apparently a man of faith to the end, is one of the earliest original speculators on language and an empiricist, explaining all of the child's development through sensations and denying, with Locke, that any innate ideas could exist which did not spring from sense-experience. D'Alembert (1717–83), a mathematician of genius, lent his prestige to the Encyclopedists. Several other priests, Abbé Morellet (1727–1819), a skilled polemicist, Abbé Raynal (1713–96), who indicted the behaviour of Western Europeans in their colonies of Asia and of America and a bitter foe of the Church, drew suggestions from Diderot's universally curious mind. Less well-known polemicists went over to atheism and even to advocating a form of communism in politics. La Mettrie (1709–51), a medical man and a scientist of note, attempted to dissect and to study man as a pure mechanism. Diderot, who stood in need of a more imaginative and more human view of things, balked at the mechanistic materialism of his friends.

He might have felt closer to Buffon (1707–88), whose vision of the early ages of the earth and of the slow development of man was both poetical and philosophical. He observed facts, studied first-hand reports of explorers; but his bent was toward systematization and broad and bold generalizations. He wrote with great care, with an excessive and starched dignity. But he married literature and science, as was the wish of his century, and he opened up majestic vistas on the origins of the world and of man.

Diderot's imagination was even bolder: it was fired by the study of medicine and of biology. It was attracted by a materialism which was then a more poetical, and even a more spiritual and organic explanation of natural phenomena, than the desiccated orthodoxy of the traditionalists. To the moderns, the most prophetic intuitions of Diderot are to be found in a very few booklets published in his lifetime (*Pensées sur l'interprétation de la nature*, 1754; *Entretien d'un philosophe avec la maréchale de . . .*, 1776) and in others which only appeared posthumously (*Dialogue avec d'Alembert, Rêve de d'Alembert*). Diderot dauntlessly came to grips with the problem of how matter can become life and eventually spirit. He introduced into philosophical thinking, before Hegel, the momentous notion of development, and he stands as the direct forerunner of Lamarck's transformism and even of Darwinian evolutionism. God (on whom Diderot never quite made up his mind in order flatly to deny His existence or to consider it as a possibility) is not, for him, the creator of the universe. Rather is He an ideal notion, created by man, which will assume more reality as man acquires more consciousness and a more generous sense of his solidarity with other men. 'Élargissez Dieu!' exclaimed Diderot to his contemporaries, if you wish me to believe in Him. 'Tout ce qui blesse l'espèce humaine me blesse,' he added, in sentences which anticipate Hegel, Marx and even the twentieth-century existentialists. The quest for happiness is legitimate; but happiness is most securely reached if, through education and through altruism, we also work for the general happiness of our fellow beings.

Jean-Jacques Rousseau

There was a fundamental contradiction in Diderot's thought governed by his sensibility, as there was in much of the second half of the eighteenth century, torn between negativism and the wish to propose a new faith, between the cold data of modern science making it well nigh impossible to believe in the soul and in an immortal life, and the desire to salvage the best which religion had once embodied for man. Diderot admitted those contradictions with honesty. Jean-Jacques Rousseau (1712–78), under an appearance of more implacable logic, was no less of a Proteus and lived his ideas passionately not mistaking consistency for truth. Hence unresolved contradictions and a tension in his writings which have constantly puzzled and moved the generations which came after him. Hence also the secret of his enormous influence on the world, on ideas, on sensibility, on the manner in which men have looked into their inner selves, on politics, on ethics and on religion. The British historian Lord Acton asserted one day that Rousseau had achieved more with his pen than perhaps any man who ever wrote.

He was an outsider to the French, having been born in Geneva of Swiss parents, and he understood the French all the more acutely from feeling both as an alienated man among them and yet as one of them. He hardly knew his mother, who died soon after his birth; his father took little care of his education. He was for all practical purposes a self-made man who wandered across Savoy, then on the roads of France until, in 1742, at the age of thirty, he reached Paris. The varied incidents of his youth, and even more the impressions left in him by that strange and hardly regular life, are well known to us through the *Confessions* which he wrote late in his life. That self-taught man succeeded in acquiring a vast knowledge and in developing a style remarkable for its terse rigour, its cogent rhetoric and, often, its poetical beauty. He was perhaps a sick man, afflicted with nervous troubles and probably also with physical ills which made him very shy with women. He had known poverty, years of anxious wandering in solitude, the humiliation of living as a servant scorned by persons whose intellect and taste he could not esteem. He was ready to turn into a rebel against much that struck him as unjust and corrupt in the existing order. His capacity for enthusiasm, his warmth, his concern with his own ego which he cherished as unspoiled by intellectual disquisitions and by the quibblings of sophists, were soon to oppose him also to the *philosophes* of his day. He found a congenial spirit in Diderot and was dazzled by the fireworks of his intuitions. They later diverged in their views and their temperaments clashed. Rousseau's extreme touchiness doomed him to solitude and even to the self-inflicted torment of anxiety. He held little hope in the ability of reason to improve man's fate or even to discover a truth which might satisfy him. 'Si c'est la raison qui fait l'homme, c'est le sentiment qui le conduit.' All his assertions were to be passionate denials of the claim that knowledge truly coincides with life. Kierkegaard, Nietzsche, Tolstoy and a great number of Romantic poets of Germany, Britain and France were to be, in that respect, Rousseau's spiritual heirs.

Rousseau leapt into the limelight in 1750 with his first *Discours*, probably set in motion by a brilliant flash of Diderot's conversation, in which he contended that no moral or social improvement had resulted from the progress of the arts and the sciences. There is rhetorical declamation in the development, but there is also an ardent conviction that society life and the cultivation of letters and arts carry with them the seeds of corruption. In 1754, an even more thundering 'Second Discours', *Sur l'origine et les fondements de l'inégalité parmi les hommes*, denounced inequality, and men's passive acceptance of it, as an unmitigated evil: it attacked property, which until then had been treated by Locke and other political thinkers as a sacrosanct right. Wealth was regarded by him as being almost synonymous with evil and with the exploitation of others. Rousseau reasoned in the abstract: so little was then known about primitive men that all that could be done was to imagine what may reasonably have happened in the beginnings of human history. Rousseau's thought was later distorted and caricatured; he was depicted as advocating a return to primitivism and even to savagery. He always knew better, and that his *Discours* was a Utopia: human nature, he repeated, does not retrace its steps backward. But he introduced into modern sensibility a very powerful feeling of nostalgia for the past and the no less epoch-making theme of Western man's profound dissatisfaction with modern civilization.

Rousseau had suddenly become one of the most famous men in Europe: the upstart that he had been and the former lackey had turned into a haughty moralist who advised and chided mundane Parisians. He indicted the theatre in an eloquent *Lettre à d'Alembert sur les spectacles* in 1758, contending that the portrayal of passions, often of crimes, in tragedy and the laughter at the expense of innocuous fools in comedy are incompatible with morality. Far from acting as a purgation of passions, literature, and especially dramatic literature, envenoms them and instils them into audiences.

Soon after, in a feverish crisis of creativity, Rousseau composed, between 1756 and 1762, three works of great length and weight: a novel, *La Nouvelle Héloïse*, which appeared in 1761, a treatise on education which is also a novel in its own way and the embodiment of a myth like those of Plato, *Émile, ou De l'éducation* (1762), then the most momentous work of political philosophy in the French language, *Le Contrat social* (1762). Soon after, from 1764 on, in a state of nervous upset and of exasperated sensibility, Rousseau began his *Confessions*, to be published posthumously.

La Nouvelle Héloïse, composed feverishly while Rousseau was in love with Madame d'Houdetot, seduced by her coquettish charm but warned beforehand that his exalted desire of her would never be rewarded, is a great love novel; when all is said and in spite of much didacticism in it and of many artful digressions, one of the greatest love novels in literature. Rousseau portrayed in it the dissociation between desire and possession, the lover's attempt to reach the whole being, or the soul, of his partner through the senses, the ecstasies of imagination transfiguring the loved one and far preferable to the cold and cerebral calculations through which Laclos or Sade then reviled love. In several respects, Stendhal's idealization of women and Proust's delineation of love as created by imagination are prefigured in the novel. Julie, clear-headed, naïvely calculating, evolving from the temptations of the flesh to the placid happiness of married life but tempted again when her elaborately acquired wisdom is near collapse, is a very real and appealing woman: she has few equals in the whole range of nineteenth-century French fiction.

Émile is by definition more didactic and more schematic. Rousseau, having shown in his novel how, through repentance and acceptance of one's fate, adults can again become natural and true beings, wished to provide an ideal model of a child preserved from the evils of bookish conventional education and from the corrupting influence of society. To this very day, some of the lessons offered in that fictional treatise have inspired reformers of education in several countries. The book is instinct with nostalgia and warmth, for Émile is the child that Rousseau would have wished to be. The latter sections of *Émile* illustrate Rousseau's view of religion. They were condemned by the authorities, the book was banned and the author persecuted. For it founded religion solely on the heart and its immediate certainty. The divinity of Christ and the authority of the Scriptures were left out of Rousseau's theology. Still, more than in the writings of the *philosophes*, Rousseau's treatise, like his moving letters to Monsieur de Malesherbes, breathed a need for the divine and conveyed a direct religious experience. Some of its exclamations are unforgettable: 'J'étouffe dans l'univers' or 'Que d'hommes entre Dieu et moi!'

The *Contrat social*, strangely, failed to impress and to disturb the contemporaries. It only came into its own with the French Revolution, and through its influence over Robespierre and Saint-Just. It proposed an ambitious reorganization of society, founded upon the consent of the governed who alienate part of their autonomy in order to strengthen the State. The scheme is ingenious, delicately balanced, unworkable in practice. But Rousseau acutely perceived the vices of political society as it existed in his time: built-in privileges and inequality; the artificial arousing of new needs which end in enslaving us; the stifling of the personality under the weight of selfishness. To Rousseau, happiness should lie in the art of concentrating one's feelings around one's heart and in the preservation of freedom. Might can never establish right. Inequality cannot be complacently tolerated. Through Rousseau's ideal contract, natural inequality is corrected through civic equality; men, born unequal in strength and talent, become equals in their rights. Political science had been chiefly descriptive with Locke and Montesquieu; with Rousseau it became normative. What exists in no way stands justified because it does exist. Society must be reformed just as man can be made better.

The *Confessions*, then the *Rêveries du promeneur solitaire* composed in part in 1776 and left unfinished at Rousseau's death in July 1778, are his masterpieces as a writer of prose, not yet musical and colourful, but delicately sensuous, vibrating with warmth and sincerity. Those volumes opened up the sluices of romantic confessional literature (in Goethe, Wordsworth, Hazlitt, Stendhal, Nerval). The cult of Rousseau began soon after his death. Kant, Hölderlin, Fichte, Hegel and Schiller celebrated him in Germany. Shelley excepted Rousseau alone from his condemnation of most French authors and appealed to him as his guide, as Dante had done Virgil, in his last poem, *The Triumph of Life*. Tolstoy venerated Rousseau as a saint all his life. The threefold stages of Rousseauistic philosophy, pristine innocence of man in the instinctive state, fall through greed and selfishness, redemption through repentance and spiritual rebirth, parallel to Christian theology, have since been found to haunt many a utopian and socialist system. The spirit of revolt which animated the Genevan reformer lies at the source of the many movements of discontent which, in the twentieth and twenty-first centuries, are likely to impel several continents to seek for more justice, for a greater harmony with nature, a closer communion with our environment and more fraternity. Whether Rousseau, or any eighteenth-century thinker, would have welcomed the Revolution is doubtful. To some extent at least, Rousseau and others inspired it, through suggesting to the people that things should and might be better and that society as it existed then was rotten at the core. Their influence in that sense has been a revolutionary and a constructive one.

Literature from the Later Eighteenth Century to Chateaubriand

There was a rich fictional production throughout the second half of the eighteenth century – probably not quite equal in works of towering eminence to what it had been in the England of Richardson, Fielding, Sterne and Goldsmith, but extraordinarily varied. The novel of feeling, often preposterously sentimental, lachrymose, mawkish, replete with complaints about the inanity of life and about *ennui*, paved the way for the romantic outbursts of the succeeding eras. Its best work is *Paul et Virginie* (1785) by a strange neurotic adventurer, Bernardin de Saint-Pierre (1737–1814), who was endowed with a powerful descriptive talent and introduced a new sense of colour in literature. The story, on the innocent and touching loves of two children grown up on a French island off the coast of eastern Africa, enjoyed a world-wide fame. It is told with delicacy and with no fear of ridicule. But the novel of sensuousness and of eroticism, which also appeared in the same era, is the one in which the sophisticated modern readers delight. Restif de la Bretonne (1734–1806) is both an eroticist, multiplying imaginary love adventures, and a sentimentalist; he wrote as many novels as he had, or so would he want us to believe, love affairs: close to 250. The best owe their value to his acute gift of realistic observation of farmers and artisans (*La Vie de mon père, Monsieur Nicholas*) and to his visionary evocation of Paris as the city of feminine adventures and of vice. Choderlos de Laclos (1741–1803), an army officer, intent on being a moralist and in truth a fervent admirer of Rousseau's sentimentality, composed one of the most astonishing volumes in the whole range of French fiction: *Les Liaisons dangereuses* (1782). It is an epistolary novel, like *La Nouvelle Héloïse*, but in no way one of confession or of respect for the eternal or for the ephemeral feminine. Valmont, a calculating seducer, undertakes to win the physical love of a girl just out of her convent education; then, through appealing to her pity, to her wish to reform a corrupt man, through surrounding her with insidious attacks like a fortress to be stormed, he convinces a respectable and pious woman to yield to him. He conspires all the while with another woman, bent like him upon destroying virtuous and chaste people. The plotting seducers are punished in the end, as in a good moral tale. But few delineations of pure evil, set free in a society where moral values had broken down, can match that cerebral, pitiless, powerfully and tersely written masterpiece. The Marquis de Sade (1740–1814) in comparison seems coarse in his devices and effects, repetitious, verbose and unreal in his naïve invention of impossible cruelty. He enjoyed a secret popularity with a few throughout the nineteenth century, when it was hardly possible to read him openly. Ever since the middle of the twentieth century, when all censorship of his tedious stories was given up, the fame of Sade as a novelist, as distinct from the curiosity which may go to a pathological case, is in danger of being exploded. His talent is mediocre.

The Parisian stage during the reign of Louis XVI was lively; translations (or more properly adaptations) of Shakespeare suddenly caught the imagination of the public; the melodrama tended to replace moribund tragedy, and did so almost completely during the Revolutionary years. Pastoral comedies flourished, often interspersed with pretty musical pieces. The one important writer for the stage, who impressed his contemporaries and has lost none of his vitality and forcefulness to this day, is the strange, self-taught adventurer Beaumarchais (1732–99). His life was incredibly full of dubious undertakings, speculations, histrionism. With *Le Barbier de Séville* (1775) and even more *Le Mariage de Figaro* (1784), he wrote plays which are neither profoundly analytical nor didactic, but which carry the audience along through their verve, their inventiveness and their gift of life. Insolently, Beaumarchais attacked the inequalities in society and the greed of courtiers. The character of Figaro, which soon became an immortal type, raised to an even more poetical plane by Mozart's opera (1786), stands among the unforgettable creations of universal drama.

Poetic diction, the lack of boldness in breaking away from old-fashioned moulds and discredited formal conventions, had hampered the renewal of poetry in France, while Blake, Cowper, then Wordsworth and Coleridge in England, Goethe and Schiller in Germany were already treating renewed themes in a fresh language and asserting the rights of imagination. A great deal of verse was written in the eighteenth century in France, but the only poet who survives today is André Chénier (1762–96). He had a keen sense for the beauty and simplicity of ancient Greek poetry. He imitated with rare felicitousness the poets of the Palatine anthology and Theocritus. He also composed tender elegies, and ranks among the most delicately sensuous poets in the French language. He attempted scientific poetry and he had the courage to break the rigid mould of French versification. When his poems were made accessible to the general public in 1819, the Romantics at once hailed him as a renovator of verse. There is however nothing Romantic about him, no passionate nostalgia for Greece as in Hölderlin or Keats, no reliving of the myths and symbols of Hellas; but he is an exemplary artist. And the verse which he composed, in a vengeful mood when imprisoned by the Revolution or in a tender note of protest attributed to a woman prisoner against an untimely death ('La Jeune Captive') reaches an intensity of emotion unmatched by the poetry of his age. He was guillotined under the Terror, two days before the fall of Robespierre which would have brought him his release from prison.

Literature has often flourished in the midst of social and political unrest and lagged in periods of prosperity and peace. The age of Euripides and of Aristophanes, that of Lucretius and Cicero, the blossoming of poetry and philosophy in Germany when she was oppressed by foreign conquerors testify that violence and uncertainty as to the future can foster original creation. But the era of the French Revolution (1789–99) and of the Napoleonic wars which followed until 1815 stand as an exception. Too many of the potential talents were drawn to political action, to military campaigns and to administering conquered territories all over Europe. The public which might have welcomed literary innovations in the wake of Diderot and Rousseau was scattered by emigration, threatened by the guillotine or engrossed in revolutionary eloquence when clubs and groups multiplied in Paris; journalism, aiming at immediate and often brutal effects, prospered at the expense of finished novels and of elaborate moralists' essays. Melodrama appealed to an enlarged and less fastidious public and helped relegate to a bygone era many of the classical theatrical conventions. Patriotic odes and military songs were more in honour than polished madrigals and sentimental elegies. Philosophy continued to be cultivated, chiefly in a dry, analytical vein, by a group of theoreticians called the *idéologues*, much admired later by Stendhal. Science knew an extraordinary development, with Monge, Lamarck, Bichat, Lagrange, Laplace and Ampère, but left no enduring literary monument; it did impress the literary imagination of the Romantics.

The outstanding writers of the first fifteen years of the nineteenth century lived in majority outside France: Madame de Staël (1766–1817) suffered much when, exiled by Napoleon, she had to remain near

Geneva; she was Swiss, but Parisian at heart. Her tumultuous love affairs and her imperious character brought her rich material for fiction or even for the probing analysis of herself. But her two novels (*Delphine*, 1802; *Corinne*, 1807) are cold and unimaginative. She was at her best in manipulating ideas, often borrowed from others, at times original with her. *De la littérature* (1800) and even more *De l'Allemagne* (composed in 1810, published in London in 1813) offer confused but occasionally illuminating views on the relations between letters and society and on the need to create a renovated and 'Romantic' literature, answering the needs of the moderns. Unlike other émigrés, she understood and praised the positive legacy of the French Revolution.

One of her intimate friends, Swiss also and even more cosmopolitan than her, was Benjamin Constant (1767–1830). He wrote some powerful pamphlets on politics and philosophy of history, assailing Napoleon's thirst for conquest and advocating liberal causes. But his chief claim to fame is his contradictory, vacillating, often pathetically abject but lucid *Journal intime*, which displayed his lack of will, and his novel *Adolphe* (1816). In *Adolphe*, in a splendidly economic style, he told of his romantic longings, soon followed, once they have reached their object, by pitiless cruelty. It is a masterpiece in cerebral dissection and in exposing the stages of slow *désamour*, or falling out of love; long before Proust, the lovers may be said to discover there that love is a mutually inflicted torture, but the woman is the pathetic, sorrowful victim. Another Swiss, Senancour (1770–1846), published in 1804 a touching series of imaginary letters, *Obermann*, displaying the same inflexible gift for searching analysis of oneself as does Constant, but a more poetical leaning to reverie and a voluptuous enjoyment of melancholy. The French Romantics after 1833 when they rediscovered *Obermann*, and Matthew Arnold in Britain, were to hail the book as a mirror to their own disenchantment.

Napoleon was himself one of the great writers of his time, in the burning love letters of his youth, in his proclamations to his soldiers, in the hundreds of articles which he dictated to sway the public opinion of his subjects. His early interest lay in literature and he had nurtured the ambition to be a writer. Indeed, without the *Mémorial de Sainte-Hélène* written by his companion Las Cases, his figure and his thought would not have dominated nineteenth-century history as they came to do. Literature made and perpetuated his legend. Chateaubriand (1768–1848), born one year before him, first praised by the emperor when he attempted to bring the French back to the Christian fold, then

Napoleon's political opponent, never ceased being fascinated by him. He is the one supreme French writer between Rousseau and Hugo. After a brief trip to America in 1791, from which he derived images and reminiscences which enriched all his work, then a stay with the émigrés fighting the French Revolution, and years of poverty as a teacher in England, he became famous with a short novel, *Atala* (1801), with a long, uneven, chaotic praise of Christianity as providing writers and artists with original themes and feelings, *Le Génie du christianisme* (1802), and an autobiographical and sombre *récit*, *René* (1802). His thought lacked consistency, his information was chiefly acquired at second hand; his favourite theme of the religious faith of two lovers (one Christian, the other pagan or Moorish), impeding their happiness, became a trite cliché. But he had an unequalled gift as a writer of musical, voluptuous prose. His arguments in defence of religion are often childish; he hardly lived a life of piety himself, he was an indefatigable lover of married women, and loved by them even more ardently than he could love. He did not succeed in politics when, after the fall of Napoleon, he became Ambassador to London and Minister of Foreign Affairs. He was aghast at the young Romantics who looked up to him as a revolutionary, while he always remained faithful to the 'glory that was Greece'. But he had, in *René*, then in his *Mémoires*, offered a poetical analysis of the *mal du siècle* with which most of his followers were afflicted: the realization of the gap between man's yearnings and his possibilities, between idealized woman and real ones, and a gloomy obsession with *ennui*. Musset and Baudelaire were to echo his plaintive moan. His masterpiece, one of the great works in French literature, is his *Mémoires d'outre-tombe*, composed over forty years and published, as the title stipulated, after his death. The book is as filled with his dominating personality as Rousseau's *Confessions*; the portrait he draws of himself is not accurate in many details; facts are transposed or transfigured; the fear of old age and of death echoes through it like an obsessive anthem. But the splendour of the prose, seldom purely decorative, more often terse, evocative and always unerringly felicitous, never ceases to hold the reader under its spell.

Romanticism

The Romantic movement, which Diderot and Rousseau had heralded as early as 1760, and which had permeated the sensibility of the young in France under the reign of Louis XVI, was then delayed in its full outburst through a number of causes, some historical and the product of chance, others deep-seated. Its true flowering is often assigned, for French literature, to the years 1818–22, when at last poetry seemed to shake itself free from classical trappings and to express personal moods in more musical verse. By 1818–22, the German Romantic movement, in poetry and in philosophy, had spent itself: Goethe alone survived and stood serenely above all literary controversies, contemptuous of the eccentricities and follies of the young Romantics who had not learned, as he had, the lesson of wise resignation and replaced the Wertherian longing for suicide with acceptance of one's fate and the consolation to be found in beauty. The first great generation of English Romantics, that of Wordsworth and Coleridge, had by 1820 spent its inspiration and certainly its spirit of rebellion. Their successors, Keats, Shelley and Byron, were all cut off in their prime between 1821 and 1824. Walter Scott's novels of chivalry had already become more popular on the Continent than they were in Britain, where a new mood of realistic portrayal of society was dawning. As Romanticism seemed to be waning elsewhere, it stormed literature, the arts, even society in France. It had grown slowly and against many odds; but it also had struck sturdier roots. In spite of appearances to the contrary and of glib assertions in manuals of literary history, Romanticism refused to bury itself after its glorious outburst of 1820–45. It revived, often with more impetuous, more morbid vigour; first with the generation of Flaubert, Leconte de Lisle and Baudelaire, then with Taine, Zola, Verlaine and Rimbaud; then again with the symbolists, with the surrealists. It is hard to mention a writer of the twentieth century who has not relived Romanticism in one or other of its facets, be it Huysmans, Apollinaire, Claudel, Aragon, Bernanos, Mauriac, Giono, Cocteau or Céline. In technique, in style, in restraint, those modern Romantics differ from Balzac, Michelet and Hugo. Their blend of pose and of sincerity is more expertly contrived. But their discontent with the present and with the human condition, their spirit of revolt, their concern with their own ego reconstructing the world from the microcosm of the self, their poetical vision of life – these are the expressions of a deep Romantic sensibility.

Romanticism in France, more so than in other Western countries, affected, and even invaded, fiction, drama, the writing of history and of criticism, philosophical speculation, political theorizing, the fine arts and, naturally, poetry. It long was the custom to stress the theories, manifestos and doctrines which accompanied, and occasionally preceded, the appearance of the works themselves. Literary debates have indeed always been a favourite pastime of the French writers, who are fond of elaborating theories in order to justify their practice and to convert followers. In truth, the discussions around Romanticism, which ranged from Madame de Staël's writings to the final victory of the new school or group, after 1830, were confused, contradictory, chaotic. Magazines were founded which soon perished. Newcomers to the world of letters shifted from one circle or *cénacle* to another. As always in France, politics and religion intruded into the literary feuds: most of the young Romantic poets, including Lamartine, Vigny and Hugo, began by being royalist and Catholic. But the political regime which followed the fall of Napoleon and the clerical reaction which so angered the hero of Stendhal's *Le Rouge et le noir* soon disappointed them. In poetry, they wanted to suggest rather than to state, to appeal to the reader's imagination and not so much to his rational intellect, and to rival the soft and languorous effects of music.

As elsewhere in Europe, the Romantic mood in France was an assertion of the rights of imagination against the primarily analytical function assigned to the intellect in some aspects of eighteenth-century thought. It stressed each individual's uniqueness, as manifested in his sensibility and in the cherished treasure of childhood memories; the self, in its originality and even in its idiosyncrasies, counted for more than man envisaged in his generality and in attempting to reach truths valid for all men in general. The social and political upheavals of the Revolutionary and Napoleonic period had left young people frustrated, ill-adapted to a reality which suddenly appeared prosaic and inglorious to them. Their discontent expressed itself in politics; in literature, against the constricting theories inherited from arid neoclassical legislators; it spread to the whole of life and lamented the finiteness of man's fate and the impossibility of reality ever to come up to the desires or the dreams of those sons of the new century. *Le mal du siècle* is the name they gave to their grief and to the enjoyment of that anxious sorrow paraded as a badge of superiority. Werther, René, Byron's mysterious criminals, Musset's characters were in part literary types and soon degenerated into conventional ones. But many of the young, in books and in life, modelled themselves on those heroes. Classicism had seldom been lived in actual daily existence, or been an ideal of conduct mirrored in the letters and memoirs of seventeenth-century people; Romanticism was. Neurotics, insane artists, suicides, hunted men pursued by their own passions or yearnings abound in the literary works, but also among the men and women who actually lived in the years 1820–60.

A peculiar feature of French Romanticism is that the innovators encountered a revered and built-in classicism, taught in the schools and established officially in the salons, the academies, the State-subsidized theatres, such as no other country in Europe had. That classical tradition, once inspired by the examples of Greece and Rome, had come to be regarded by the French as having sprung from their soil and as somehow in harmony with the land and the character of the country. It stressed the values of order, of restraint, of clarity, and the Romantics soon realized that they could only win against the classical forces by borrowing much from them. More important still, along with an elaborate concern with form and recourse to rhetoric, the French classical writers (from Montaigne to Pascal and Bossuet, from Corneille to Racine and Madame de la Fayette) had displayed a rare insight into the inner life of man. The Romantics who first assumed an attitude of opposition to the partisans of the classics had resorted to vituperation and insult; but they soon realized that ultimately they would have to be judged according to their success in probing the innermost secrets of men (in their moments of passion, ambition and tragic stress, or in their lyrical and elegiac moods) as penetratingly as the classical moralists and dramatists had done. Hence a considerable element of what may be called 'classicism', or 'le classicisme des romantiques', in Stendhal, Mérimée, Lamartine, Hugo, Musset and Nerval.

Finally, literature has long been far more institutionalized in France than in other countries. It enters into the daily lives of people, occupies a prominent place in their conversations and in the daily press and is a means of acceding to honours and even to political power. The stakes in literary controversies are therefore high. The more resistant to change the literary institutions are (academies, universities, Ministries of Education), the more exacerbated and violent their young opponents become; hence the violence of the struggles around questions of versification, matters of style, the dramatic unities, mixing the tragic and the comic genres or, as Hugo advocated, the grotesque and the sublime. The Romantics had to wage far more stubborn fights in Paris than in London, Milan, Jena or Weimar; but their victory, when at last it came, proved also more lasting. French Romanticism was no longer a small clique of innovators grouped around a banner and a manifesto; it incorporated into itself the best of the legacy of classicism. It became the lasting new French tradition.

Romantic Poetry

Poetry was the literary genre that had lagged behind for decades, and it was in the realm of lyrical poetry that the renovators were most eagerly awaited and could achieve most. Romanticism has often, in consequence, been equated with lyricism and with a new freedom in the treatment of diction and verse. For a long time, literary historians traditionally singled out Lamartine, Vigny, Hugo and Musset as the giants of Romanticism. Our perspective is different today. Hugo may well be regarded as the Romantic poet *par excellence*, although he really came into his own as an original visionary and symbolic genius long after the heat of the Romantic debates had cooled off. But the other giants of French Romanticism were not poets in verse: rather Delacroix the painter, Berlioz the musician, Balzac the novelist and Michelet the historian.

Lamartine (1790–1869) had immense natural gifts as a poet: a rich, responsive sensibility, a unique, if perilous, facility, the talent of a soft, melodious musician in verse. His *Méditations poétiques*, in 1820, filled the public with rapture. In truth, many of the poems were rhetorical developments on immortality or on man seeking consolation for his love sorrows or his oppressive solitude in a divine presence; the nature poems and the elegies expressed in verse what Rousseau and others had earlier expressed in prose. But they included at least one poem, 'Le Lac', which has lost none of its freshness and cogency as a masterpiece. There are love poems even more feverish, such as 'Ischia', in the *Nouvelles Méditations* (1823); or longer, more ambitious hymns to nature, love and death in the *Harmonies poétiques et religieuses* (1830), the poet's greatest lyrical achievement. Then, having reflected deeply and with much vigour on politics and society, having revolted bitterly against religion after his daughter died in the East, Lamartine composed some of the bitterest and most virile poems in the French language: 'Les Révolutions', 'Gethsémani ou la mort de Julia'. In 1835, he published a strange, modern, profoundly moving epic, set in a rustic background, *Jocelyn*, perhaps the most successful long poem in French. Politics, fiction, history and essays then attracted him and he only rarely returned to his poetical inspiration.

Alfred de Vigny (1797–1863) came, like Lamartine, from an aristocratic and royalist family, but his imagination always bore the imprint of the Napoleonic influence and suffered from the mediocrity of French army life (he was an army officer for fourteen years) and of the materialistic ambitions of the middle class during the Romantic era. He wrote only two slim volumes of verse, *Poèmes antiques et modernes* (1826), of which 'Moïse', on the theme of the solitude to which genius is doomed, is unforgettable, and *Les Destinées* (1864, but published in reviews twenty years earlier). Vigny also wrote plays and novels of merit, if not of the very first order, and left some of the most pregnant reflections of a philosophical moralist since Pascal. His poetry was long and profoundly thought, it is expressed with condensation and at times illuminated, especially in 'La Maison du berger', with the most grandiose and evocative images in French poetry before Baudelaire. It is an indirect lyricism; the poet seldom says 'I'; he prefers to impersonate himself as Moses, Samson cursing womanhood because he has been betrayed by Delilah, or Christ on the Mount of Olives urging God to enlighten and guide the forlorn world of men.

Hugo had all the talents and he attempted all the genres of poetry. Born in 1802, he survived until 1885 and composed verse almost to the very end. His very early verse is picturesque, scintillating, rich in metrical experiments; with *Les Orientales* (1829), he displayed the dazzling gifts of a virtuoso and flooded French poetry with colour. Between 1831 and 1840, having lost some of his early royalist fervour and while uninterruptedly composing plays and novels, he published four volumes of poetry: *Les Feuilles d'automne* (1831), tinged with melancholy and already tempted by the invisible lurking behind the visible tapestry of shapes and colours; *Les Chants du crépuscule* (1835); *Les Voix intérieures* (1837); *Les Rayons et les ombres* (1840), in which nature, reverie, love, Napoleon's epic figure haunting the poet, politics, social pity and art serve as themes for Hugo's extraordinary facility. Political ambitions, an active and complicated series of affairs of the heart, the overwhelming grief caused in 1843 by the accidental drowning of his daughter and of her young husband at Villequier and then the revolution of 1848 brought a respite to Hugo's production. Only in 1853 did he come out with the most impassioned and vengeful satirical poetry written in French since Agrippa d'Aubigné: *Les Châtiments*. Some pieces are still splendidly lyrical, but less personal: they herald the ultimate triumph of justice and of democracy over the tyranny of Napoleon III, whom Hugo hated all the more for having himself through his verse contributed to spreading the Napoleonic legend which was to help elect the 'petit Napoléon' as a caricature of the great one. Hugo condemned himself to exile in Jersey, then in Guernsey, in the Channel Islands: for eighteen years, he lived in that gloomy, tempestuous landscape, meditating on the watery abysses which had engulfed his daughter, on death, on the meaning with which life should be endowed in order to be livable, on mystical philosophies and strange religions. The great volumes of poetry composed by Hugo, often in a state of trance, appeared in 1856 and in 1859 (for the first series): *Les Contemplations* and *La Légende des siècles*. None, not even *Les Fleurs du mal*, equals them in variety, depth and forcefulness. Romantic they are, in so far as they are passionate, personal, anguished by all the questions asked by a religious sensibility which came near to identifying itself with the divine. Lyrical they are also, through the exaltation of their impassioned tone, the musical riches of the verse and the prominence of the poet's personality questioning the cosmos in order to unravel the secrets of life after death. But in the long metaphysical developments of 'Ce que dit la bouche d'ombre', more concisely in 'Paroles sur la dune', in the sublime evocation of Adam and Eve mourning, in the early days of creation, the death of Abel and the fate of Cain ('Les Malheureux'), finally in the grandiose epic fragments of *La Légende des siècles*, reaching its most grandiose and wildest beauty in 'Le Satyre', Hugo pushed back the limits which had until then circumscribed French poetry. Later still, in grave hymns collected in *Toute la lyre* (published only in 1888), in the one French epic which can be compared to Milton's *Paradise Lost*, *La Fin de Satan* (published in 1886), Hugo showed that he was far more than a virtuoso of metrics and an orator in verse: an original thinker and a decipherer of the unknown.

It had been fashionable for a time, after Hugo's death and as a petty revenge against the enormous place he had occupied in his century, to belittle his dramas, his novels and his essays. Twentieth-century critical opinion has reversed that verdict. The psychology of Hugo's dramas is rudimentary; the dramatic devices used are crude. But, in the best of them (*Hernani*, 1830; *Ruy Blas*, 1838) the bold marriage of comic and melodramatic elements and the splendour of the lyrical passages carry audiences along. Neither Vigny (in his more austere but also tense and unconvincing play with a purpose, *Chatterton*, in 1835), nor Alexandre Dumas the elder in his hastily contrived plots, came so near as Hugo to creating the theatre of the new era. Hugo had reflected with independence on the means by which the drama of the moderns might be less stylized, less pure and also less aloof from ever diverse and chaotic life, of wider appeal to the masses, than the classical theatre of old. He illuminatingly envisaged the grotesque (in his eyes as necessary as the sublime *élans* of lyricism in the drama) as a moment of pause, a springboard from which to leap towards the beautiful with a fresher and intenser perceptiveness. His many novels, likewise, cannot be set beside those of Stendhal for psychological acuteness or discreet poetry or beside those of Balzac for convincing creation of characters. But their merits lie elsewhere. *Notre-Dame de Paris* (1831) is one of the powerful historical novels in the world; *Les Misérables* (1862) combines sentimental idylls, mystery thrillers, vivid evocations of Paris and pictures of social evils and of misery which are to this day much admired by social historians. In 1866 and in 1868, during his exile, Hugo completed two of the most powerful visionary novels, as hallucinating as anything in Dostoevsky, Emily Brontë or Melville, *Les Travailleurs de la mer* and *L'Homme qui rit*. Even when he stood at the peak of his popularity and revered by the masses as no poet had ever been in France, Hugo continued experimenting with new forms, striking new paths, taking immense risks. He filled his volumes of prose essays, such as *William Shakespeare* (1864) and *Post-Scriptum de ma vie* (posthumously published in 1901) alternately with declamatory platitudes and with lucid insights. 'Poètes!' he exclaimed, 'voilà la loi mystérieuse: aller au delà.'

Alfred de Musset (1810–57) was ten or twenty years younger than the three poets who ruled over the poetical domain between 1820 and 1835, when Romanticism was triumphant. He had neither the powerful creative imagination of his elders nor their concern with expressing philosophical or cosmological thoughts in his verse. Like other poets who were almost exactly his contemporaries, Aloysius Bertrand, Gérard de Nerval, Maurice de Guérin and Théophile Gautier, all born between 1807 and 1811, he felt frustrated at reaching the literary stage too late. 'Je suis venu trop tard dans un monde trop vieux,' he lamented in one of his oft-quoted lines. It was necessary for these men to strike new paths. They attempted the poem in prose: Aloysius Bertrand (1807–41) in the vivid, colourful and quaint descriptions of *Gaspard de la nuit*, which Baudelaire considered as the inspiration for the new language of his own prose vignettes; Maurice de Guérin (1810–39) with more passionate pantheistic warmth and a pagan fervour which he blended strangely with his Christian faith, in 'Le Centaure' and 'La Bacchante'. Théophile Gautier (1811–72) became, later, a respected literary figure and the champion of art for art's sake. His lifelong fight for the purity of literature and his passionate acts of faith in art as alone deserving and bestowing immortality, while gods and men, philosophies and political regimes come and go, won him the admiring friendship of Flaubert, Baudelaire and Mallarmé. His place in French poetry, however, rests on his much earlier, and far from impassive and serene achievement. *Albertus* (1833), *La Comédie de la mort* (1838) and even *España* (1845) are obsessed by religious symbols and the melancholy regret of lost faith, and even more by death in its most macabre shapes. Hugo later, and Baudelaire in particular, who both admired Gautier, were impressed by that vision of skeletons, of corruption of the flesh, worms gnawing at vigour and beauty. Gautier's stress on artistry and his insistence upon finding in the cult of art a substitute for all the other lost absolutes have left a deep imprint upon the poets of other nations, among them Ezra Pound.

The two poets from that second Romantic generation who appear most significant to us after a century and a half are Musset and Nerval. Musset's nature was highly nervous, indeed almost morbidly so, capricious, eager for pleasure and doomed to fits of despair: he was, as much as Baudelaire, Nerval or Verlaine, one of the 'accursed poets' of the last century. Success had very early hailed his dazzling talent and his insolent *joie de vivre*. He made fun of the Romantics' poses and of their sentimental affectations with wit and a cheerful, well-meant irony. He had a rare gift for dividing himself into dual personalities and for dramatic dialogue. He needed passion, however, and the understanding of patient, loving women who would nurse his whimsical moods and perhaps hold him on the slope which ultimately led him to drinking and to the drying-up of his talent. His Venetian adventure with the novelist George Sand, a few years older than he, in 1833, is famous. He emerged from it embittered, tortured by jealousy, prone to cursing womankind as a whole, but also a more sincere poet of love. Four lyrical dialogues between his muse and himself, and in truth between the two facets of his nature, his *Nuits*, are his supreme poetical achievement. The tone of anger, the unrestrained display of sentiment, the rhetoric of those *Nuits* have been criticized by the poets succeeding Musset who had more sanity and more self-control than he. But there is another side to Musset's poetry: a concrete, humorous, lucid and intelligent form of lyricism, the original charm of which has not vanished. Musset is moreover a master of vivid, witty prose, reminiscent of the eighteenth century in its economy and swiftness. He is the author of stories and tales scarcely less effective than those of Mérimée, and of the best plays left by the nineteenth-century theatre: *Les Caprices de Marianne* (1833), *On ne badine pas avec l'amour* (1834) and the enigmatic and tragic *Lorenzaccio* (1834) were not acted when they appeared; but they have held the stage ever since. The marriage of Romantic passion and of classical insight into the secrets of the human heart, of the instinct for self-destruction and of the Hamlet-like analysis of that destruction by its very victim, is most felicitously concluded in Musset's plays.

Gérard de Nerval also attempted the dramatic genre, but he could not dramatize his own inner conflicts to carry an audience along with him. He lived, miserably, by his pen and he had to write much ephemeral criticism, like his friend Gautier. But he revealed in some delicate, dreamy tales, the best-known of which is *Sylvie* (1854), the talent of a deft, poetical story-teller, and a vision of life which melts reality into dreams and symbols. The symbolists and the surrealists alike, Alain-Fournier, Marcel Proust and Jean Giraudoux have sensed, and proclaimed, their affinities with that writer of the purest prose of any Romantic who, although he went through four crises of insanity and probably hanged himself in a wretched alley in Paris in 1855, never forsook his attachment to a classical clarity. His most vibrating prose, tormented, discontinuous, mysteriously moving, is in an unfinished half-mystical record of one of his descents into the inferno of madness, *Aurélia* (1855), probably the most faithfully poetical document on the state of dream which Nerval calls 'a second existence'. In the last ten years of his brief life, Nerval also composed some six or eight very mysterious sonnets, alluding to his very personal experiences as a worshipper of women, as a religious seeker who tried to marry paganism and Christianity, as a dreamer of dreams formerly dreamt and as an explorer of the realm which lies beneath and beyond reason: 'El Desdichado' (the disconsolate one), 'Delfica' and 'Artémis' are the finest of them. Their very obscurity, which defies all explanation, and their allusiveness, as well as their weird evocative power, have immortalized Nerval among the French poets.

Romantic Theatre and Fiction

The Romantic age, intent upon the liberation from all artistic constraints, had expanded the drama beyond all formal limits. In its rejection of the unities of time and place, which in truth had long degenerated into mere superstitions, Romantic drama also disregarded the need for concentration and for some unity of interest.

Yet the limitations in any audience's capacity for attention are not easily cast aside, and the drama stands in need of tension and of confrontation of adverse forces or individuals. Hugo's *Cromwell*, Goethe's *Faust*, the poetic dramas of several English Romantics, later those of several symbolists are too ambitious, too all-encompassing, too diverse to be brought down to the humble necessities of staging, interpretation and performance. The novel, on the contrary, lay open for the Romantics to experiment with to their hearts' content. It had inherited a relatively short tradition, scarcely two centuries old, and not yet venerable. It offered no models which might be called perfect, as drama and, to a lesser extent, poetry did. It was meant to reach new layers of the reading public, to whom powerful effects, even if crude, ebullient vitality, suspense and a reflection of the surrounding society mattered more than analytical subtlety. The eighteenth-century French fiction, with its stress upon aristocratic life and prejudices of class, on cerebral eroticism and on escape into lachrymose sensibility, no longer seemed attuned to the society which emerged from the Revolution and the Empire. Even when set beside the reforming zeal of the *philosophes* and their audacity as thinkers, that novel had appeared anachronistic or puny. The novel, after 1820 or so, underwent a rebirth in France, Britain and Russia. It caught up with the moods and the problems of the new age.

One of its aspects was the personal novel, which Chateaubriand, Constant, Nerval and several lesser Romantics renovated. It is one of the original creations of modern literature and, under diverse forms, it was to be attempted by Flaubert (in *Novembre* and others of his early works), Loti, Gide and Proust in France. The German Romantics had been fond of the *Bildungsroman*, or novel in which the old-fashioned and somewhat disconnected picaresque adventures were presented as moulding the personality of the young man and serving as his education, sentimental and intellectual. Thackeray's *Henry Esmond*, Meredith's *Harry Richmond* and subsequent portraits of the artist as a young man in the twentieth century are personal novels after a fashion. The genre is close to, yet different from, the autobiography or the memoirs, for the novelist does not survey his past experience from the vantage-point of the present and he does not attempt to vindicate his actions or to endow his existence with a meaning. The work remains a fiction, in no way enslaved to reality as it may have been lived or remembered. The novelist is all the freer to create half-imaginary characters with his own experience as he is aware of reaching thereby a higher or deeper truth. He endeavours to convey the feeling of time passing and slowly corroding adolescent dreams. Balzac's *Le Lys dans la vallée* (1835) and *Louis Lambert* (1833), even Stendhal's *Le Rouge et le noir* (1831) and most of the early novels of George Sand could be termed personal novels and owe much of their intensity to the close links between the author and the protagonist who is also the narrator.

A second characteristic innovation achieved by the Romantics in the realm of fiction was the blossoming of the historical novel. The new era had witnessed the introduction of the great concept of relativism in all branches of human thinking. Remote people, chronologically five, ten or more centuries distant (the Crusaders, the early French kings, the early Germanic or old Scottish heroes), geographically thousand of miles away (Orientals, Egyptians, African blacks, New World Indians) fascinated the once self-contained Western nations. Walter Scott enjoyed an immense fame in France and gave an impetus to the historical novel. Picturesque details, vivid descriptions, at times an excess of local colour marked those novels; the psychological delineation of characters was often sacrificed to this affluence of exterior details. Still Balzac, in *Les Chouans* (1829), an evocation of the Vendean wars, and in many other stories set in the Napoleonic past or earlier, Hugo in *Notre-Dame de Paris* (1831), Mérimée in his *Chronique du règne de Charles IX* (1829) and, in a more superficial way but with a fertility of imagination seldom equalled, Alexandre Dumas (1802–70), lover of the intricate conspiracies of the French court under Charles IX, Henri III and Louis XIII, remain as the chief representatives of that form of fiction.

The enormous importance of political and social factors, which had escaped the eighteenth-century novelists, had been projected forward by the Revolution and by the upheavals in French society. It could not be ignored by the fiction writers of the Romantic age. George Sand for several years wrote socialist and reformist novels; Balzac aimed at no less than depicting the whole social scene of Paris and the provinces; Stendhal's *Lucien Leuwen* (posthumously published) is, among several things, a novel on politics, and so is, in one at least of its facets, Flaubert's *L'Éducation sentimentale* (1869). The theme of the decadence of a society, and of the corresponding ascent of the speculators and upstarts and of the greedy and selfish middle class, was to be treated many times by the novelists of several countries after Balzac. Even more than the tragedy of old, the novel was to feed on the collapse of the great under the blows of fate and, like comedy, on the triumph of the mediocre ones.

The term Romantic often connotes an excess of the imaginative faculty and a concentration on the self which would seem to preclude the cool, realistic observation of things as they are. Flights of visionary imagination, metaphysical ambitions and the desire to reach the invisible behind the concrete characterize the fiction of Balzac, Hugo and even that of George Sand. Baudelaire did not err when, in a lucid passage in prose, he hailed Balzac, not as a realist, but as a rival of reality and as a visionary. Still there is a passionate view of the real which, instead of leading a novelist or a historian to copy it, to draw an enumerative catalogue of its parts, to analyse it scientifically, brings reality back to an intenser life. That imaginative realism (it has also been called 'magic realism' when its power of transforming and of purifying the real is granted free rein, or 'symbolic realism') is that of Dickens, of Gogol and, naturally and primarily, of Balzac. The Paris of *La Fille aux yeux d'or* (1835) or of *Le Père Goriot* (1834), the Touraine of *Eugénie Grandet* (1833) or the Normandy of *La Vieille Fille* (1837) are more mysterious, more hauntingly alive and, in a word, truer than truth. The vision of a passionate man, who identifies himself with what he perceives or contemplates, is often more acute than that of a detached and cool observer. There is a realism of the Romantics, to which Zola was to be the heir, far truer because it is selective and alive, than that of the few novelists of scant talent who brandished the banner of realism in France around 1855–65.

George Sand (1804–76) lived even more novels than she wrote. The story of her loves has delighted many a biographer. Great men (and not a few small ones) were drawn to her, as lovers (Mérimée, Musset, Chopin) or as friends (Delacroix, Sainte-Beuve). She failed to find much lasting happiness in those liaisons, and she had been wretchedly deprived of it in her unfortunate marriage. Her most moving, and weirdest, novel, *Lélia* (1833), hinted at some of the frustrations, physiological or psychological, to which her love life was doomed. It is doubtless the most high-pitched as well as the most declamatory of the French personal novels, and it offers the most clear-sighted analysis of the sexual, sentimental and social problems faced by woman in a society which does not grant her her due. After a number of social novels, vindicating the rights of the industrial workmen and of the economically oppressed in modern society against the conservative establishment, George Sand reached a vast audience through her stories of agrarian, and idealized and idyllic, life in the country: *La Mare au diable* (1846) and *François le Champi* (1850), eagerly read by Proust's Marcel and by many a French child. Their poeticization of country life strikes us today as artificial and insipid: the French peasantry has ceased to be lauded as pure, healthy and moral by French writers. However, the author's love for nature is genuine. In other respects, and while not one of her novels remains as a masterpiece of fiction, George Sand must be considered as one of the five or six great women writers of France. Like Lamartine, she did not learn how not to yield to her natural facility. She attempted almost every subject in the novel, including religious mysticism in her strange story of monastic life, *Spiridion* (1839).

Stendhal (1783–1842), fond of irony as he was, obsessively introspective but much too discreet to flaunt his ego unrestrainedly, compulsively fond of hiding under assumed names and of putting on sneering masks, stands at the opposite pole from George Sand. He studied mathematics with zeal, then the severe analytical methods of logicians and materialistic thinkers of the Napoleonic age; he served in the emperor's armies, adored Italy, while missing Paris as soon as he had crossed the Alps and well aware that his beloved Italy was a figment of his imagination crystallizing youthful memories. He wrote a great deal, borrowing unashamedly here and there; he launched into Romantic controversies in his very disappointing *Racine et Shakespeare* (1823–5), proved far more acute in his small and disconnected treatise *De l'amour* (1822), which was neglected by his contemporaries. He filled out pages with private jottings or heterogeneous fragments of a desultory, at times very perspicacious, diary. Almost as an amateur, he wrote a very curious novel, *Armance* (1827), on a theme then seldom broached in literature. The delineation of feelings has rare charm and mystery and the technique is ingenious in its lack of self-consciousness. He then published two of the most admired novels in the whole range of literature, but which it took Europe fifty years to assess with justice: *Le Rouge et le noir* (1831) and *La Chartreuse de Parme* (1839). *Lamiel*, left unfinished at the author's death, with a young woman as the heroine, almost deserves to be set beside those masterpieces and is less artificial and less incredible than *Lucien Leuwen* (also posthumous and unfinished), in which the woman adored by Lucien lacks all convincingness.

Stendhal's creation, like his personality, is replete with contradictions, and that complexity, which at times is merely a pose to cover the author's ingenuous naïvety, that apparent disregard, or unawareness, of rules of composition, recipes, structural devices, accounts for much of the originality of the Stendhalian fiction. Julien Sorel (in *Le Rouge et le Noir*), the son of a poor carpenter who dreams of the warrior's glory, attempts to make his way in a hypocritical society by turning into a Tartuffe; he appears at first to be a cold, calculating character. He analyses the mechanics of post-Napoleonic society and hopes to assert his intellectual's superiority over the selfish and narrow-minded nobles who too long had stifled talent. But his romantic sentimentality, his shyness and his impulsiveness give the lie to Julien's will to remain cool and calculating. He triumphs momentarily over his shyness to win the love, tender and half-maternal, of Madame de Rênal. He moves to Paris, trains himself to appear energetic and cold, succeeds in several diplomatic missions and in elaborate schemes to seduce highly placed ladies. The proud daughter of his aristocratic employer, Monsieur de la Mole, falls in love with him; he is just as wildly in love with her, but both play a game of haughty indifference in order the better to insure the slow crystallization of feelings into passion, dear to Stendhal. An amazing marriage is planned between the humiliated aristocrat and the carpenter's son; but Julien is still in love with Madame de Rênal. He shoots her in church, without killing her, with no apparent or logical motive, and is condemned to death. Mademoiselle de la Mole, his frustrated bride, will gruesomely treasure the head of her guillotined husband-to-be, which she is allowed to carry away, in the proud manner of her sixteenth-century ancestors. The delineation of a society torn between the heirs to privilege and the men from the masses who wish to unleash further the revolutionary forces makes the novel a dramatic comment on the society of 1830: 'Chronique de 1830' was the novel's subtitle. But the creation of characters, impossibly heroic and capricious in their contradictory moods, like that of Mademoiselle de la Mole, whose passion is chiefly what Stendhal had classified as 'amour de tête', maternally tender like Madame de Rênal, of half a dozen secondary figures all sharply drawn and full of life, is what gives its greatest price to the novel. The ambivalence of love and hatred, of scorn and remorseful humility, is superbly depicted. The dénouement is illogical, as life often is; but it is in harmony with the character of the hero, and of Stendhal's own romantic view that to be condemned to death is the only thing which cannot be bought and which ennobles a man. The style is swift; it eschews pompous romantic descriptions and lyrical élans. Yet, in a few evocations, the whole poetry of sentiment surges forth, suggested with a superb economy of words: Julien 'brûlant d'amour, mais la tête dominant le cœur', asks himself in the second part of the novel: 'Qui jamais m'aurait dit que je ressentirais de telles délices à pleurer?' or, listening to the sound of the vain words uttered by his own lips, Mademoiselle de la Mole's lover dreamingly remarks: 'Ah! . . . si je pouvais couvrir de baisers ces joues si pâles, et que tu ne le sentisses pas!'

The secret of Stendhal's appeal to the century which followed his own lies primarily in the poetical suggestiveness of his novels. An amateur among novelists, he confessed to Balzac, who had the generosity and the vision to hail him in 1839 in a fine article, that it had never occurred to him that there could exist laws for the art of fiction or rules how to fabricate a novel. He observed none. Physical description bored him; so did any realistic portrayal of the setting of his scenes, or of his characters. He did not build up his stories around a climax or a dramatic crisis. He followed his own rhythm, now nonchalant, now hurried. He smiled at his own heroes, Julien, Fabrice, Lucien, Lamiel, in part through shyness and for fear the reader would recognize too much of himself in them, in part through kindly irony. His love affairs are astonishingly pure; not a trace of eroticism in them, and even less of a stress upon crude physical contacts. In daily life, Stendhal's avowed purpose was to set out every morning on a hunt for happiness, and he would have liked to be a conqueror of beautiful ladies: he was ugly, shy, too imaginative and hence conscious in advance of the poor showing he would probably make. But he presented himself in Lucien Leuwen, understood and loved by an intelligent father (as Stendhal had not been), and especially in Fabrice, the hero of *La Chartreuse de Parme*, who is present at the Battle of Waterloo without realizing that a great battle is being fought, as radiant with charm, seductiveness and an insolent independence from all social shackles. That projection of what Stendhal would have wished to be is perhaps the most beloved by the moderns of all the heroes in French fiction; and the woman who loves Fabrice with devotion and intelligence, in an affair which remains platonic, may well be, along with one or two heroines of Tolstoy, the most attractive woman in the whole range of the European novel.

Mérimée (1803–70), more versatile and more expert in social life and in literary strategy, was a close friend of Stendhal, twenty years his elder; but he treated him somewhat condescendingly, as did Sainte-Beuve and many of his contemporaries. Mérimée enjoyed a greater fame much earlier; he has paid for it, rather unjustly, by being less eagerly read in our own time. His prose is more direct, slightly dry in its stress upon irony and in its affectation of remoteness from the reader. His art of story telling is more self-conscious, skilful at working up to a dramatic climax, fond of surprising and of slightly upsetting the public. In fact, there was much sentiment and tenderness also in Mérimée, and a profoundly romantic longing for all that is primitive, violent, even cruel. He had a keen eye for local colour, for spontaneous and unrestrained characters (the gypsy Carmen, the Corsican woman Colomba), for all that seemed to jolt the complacency of refined, worldly culture. There is much in common between Ernest Hemingway and him; but Mérimée's knowledge of literature, of art, of sophisticated people extended much further. In many fields he was a pioneer: as an archaeologist and art critic, who rediscovered romanesque architecture and frescoes and helped preserve them; as a specialist of Russian literature (Pushkin, Gogol), which he read in the original and translated; as the author of *récits* or long short-stories of which he left exquisite models to Flaubert, Maupassant and his other successors in English and American letters. *Carmen*, his most celebrated novel, appeared in 1845 and struck the Romantic public with its restraint, its hardness and its vitality. Bizet's opera (1875), which itself took several years to be accepted by the musical audiences, has popularized its theme but not matched the force of the original. *Le Vase étrusque, La Double méprise, La Vénus d'Ille* and *Tamango* (a heart-rending story on the slave trade from Africa to the New World) are masterpieces of economy and of vividness as well as of half-repressed pity for the follies and self-inflicted miseries of passionate creatures.

The range of Honoré de Balzac (1799–1850) is immeasurably wider. He has often been said to be the most prolific and powerful giver of life to other creatures, next to God and next to Shakespeare. Most critics would readily declare that he is second to none among the novelists of the world, except perhaps Tolstoy and Dostoevsky; and for the latter, Balzac's work served as a point of departure. He wrote incessantly, harassed by debts, by business undertakings which ruined him, by time- and energy-consuming love affairs. His first novels, of scant literary merit, appeared under pseudonyms. From 1830 on, Balzac became aware of his extraordinary powers of observation and imagination. Both faculties had in him a similar source: the memories of an unhappy youth and a prickly and vulnerable sensibility. 'Il n'y a que les âmes méconnues et les pauvres qui sachent observer, parce que tout les froisse et que l'observation résulte d'une souffrance. La mémoire n'enregistre bien que ce qui est douleur.' That avowal in one of his early letters to Madame Hanska, in 1833, is revealing. He pierced through objects, landscapes and people with a searching glance, plumbed them to their depths, and he at once reconstructed the inner life of the characters, or even the houses and towns thus seized by his lucid and intuitive sympathy. In 1833, he hit upon a new concept of creation which filled him with joy: to have the many characters of his series of varied novels reappear from one book to another. Thus they had a past, a well-rounded personality, more density than fictional creatures who briefly go across a story and vanish before the reader has been able to identify with them. Some monotony also is entailed by that device, which has probably been praised to an excess, and there is artificiality in linking those men and women from the four corners of France, all meeting in the slums or the salons of the metropolis. In 1842, boldly rivalling Dante, Balzac defined his aims in a preface to the *Comédie humaine*, which claimed to be nothing less than the huge fresco of a whole society in a state of flux, with a bulging inferno abandoned to greed and vice, and a shrunken paradise.

All aspects of life in France (Balzac who had travelled across Europe for his love encounters gave only scant place, and only in his short stories, to countries other than his own) are portrayed and generalized upon in Balzac's fiction: for he was determined to establish laws of society and even laws governing human passions. He insisted that it is not enough to be a man: one must be a system. Provincial life, army life and the Napoleonic epic in particular; the peasantry, to which he was not partial; shopkeepers and tradesmen; courtesans, convicts, lesbians, inverts; married couples, dissolute wives, husbands addicted to debauchery; philosophers, inventors, artists, monomaniacs of all sorts. The greatest of Balzac's novels are not those which are traditionally read by schoolchildren and students, but *Béatrix* (1839), *Les Illusions perdues* (1837–43), *Le Curé de village* (1839), *La Rabouilleuse* (1842). His short stories at their best cannot be matched in the French language: *L'Auberge rouge*, *Le Réquisitionnaire*, *El Verdugo*, *Le Chef-d'œuvre inconnu*. Faults abound in works which were hastily written, often to pay off urgent debts: lengthy descriptions which always play a function in the novel but which strike some readers as too slow-moving, an obsession with money, budgets, sordid calculations and generally an abundance which overwhelms the average reader. Henry James commented upon that virtue of saturation in Balzac, which is perhaps inseparable from genius at its most restlessly inventive. Many of the world's greatest novels are indeed long novels, through which we thread our way as through a confusing but tantalizing labyrinthine universe.

His grip upon reality is one of Balzac's outstanding gifts. But he never submits to things as they are. To him, as later for Balzac's admirer, Marcel Proust, reality truly begins in the mind of the artist who selects scattered and unconnected elements in nature and recomposes them into a living whole. Balzac unashamedly alluded to his gift of second sight and compared his glance into others' secrets to that of God: nothing remained hidden from him. Since Baudelaire first called him a visionary, the word has been used to designate him. He had been impressed by, even converted to, the mystical doctrines of Swedenborg. Man, he repeated, is capable of reaching the infinite. 'Nous sommes nés pour tendre au ciel', Balzac asserted in his strange Swedenborgian novel *Séraphita* (1835). Energy and will-power, the qualities which had been displayed to an unheard-of degree by the great men of the Revolution and by Napoleon, could, in his view, be multiplied in man by systematic cultivation. Such was the dream of *Louis Lambert* (1833), who died from an excess of happiness after attempting to multiply his, and man's, will-power. Balzac's characters are often criminals or half-insane individuals devoured by the evil forces in them. But the greatest of them are perhaps those who rashly leap forward to wrestle with fate: the inventor (in *La Recherche de l'absolu*, 1834), the gambler (in *La Peau de chagrin*, 1831), the artist redoing the work of God or forcing God to surrender some of his secrets (*Le Chef-d'œuvre inconnu*, *Gambara*, *Facino Cane*). 'Il s'agit', declared that supremely Romantic novelist eager to help man transcend himself, 'de donner des ailes pour pénétrer dans le sanctuaire où Dieu se cache à nos regards.' (*Les Proscrits*, 1831.) Romantic characters in drama and fiction had Cain, Lucifer himself, Mephistopheles and other adversaries of God as their prototypes or else, in their yearning to expand man's powers, they aimed at nothing less than becoming gods themselves.

Historians, Reformers and Critics

If the nineteenth century was in Western Europe the supreme age of fiction, it was also, and chiefly in France, the age of history. Dissatisfaction with the present was part of the Romantic mood: their dreams were too lofty, and too utopian, for them to be prosaically content with the *hic et nunc.* They either wanted to rush the oncoming of a better future by changing social and political conditions, or else they felt nostalgic for the past ages in which they wished they could have lived: primitive times, Greece, India, the Middle Ages, the times of the troubadours and of the cathedrals. The relativist trend already conspicuous in eighteenth-century thought afforded the Romantics a clearer perspective on manners, customs and outlooks on life other than their own. Unlike periods of contentment with the prevailing regime and way of life, the decades that followed the French Revolution, aghast at some of the upheavals through which their country had just gone, lavishly bestowed their sympathy on past ages. Few of the historians then aimed at an objectivity which, to them, would have been tantamount to indifference and coldness. It was an anguishing concern for the men of 1820–50 to attempt to explain to themselves why and how the Revolution had had to heap up ruins and to erect a new order by breaking away with much of the past. Were the Terror and the massacres of 1794, were the dead and wounded of the Napoleonic wars, necessary to a Providential scheme? Or were they an act of evil forces which God would not curb? Were they essential to the progress of enlightened society of which the eighteenth century had dreamt? The new age was haunted by the ambition to elicit, from the contemplation of the past, the probable course of the future and perhaps the over-reaching laws of history. In its imaginative *élan*, it also endeavoured to reduce multifarious, irrational events to one great underlying force: conflict of races, nationalism, the spread of humanitarian socialism, revolutionary urges blindly sweeping man along. Moreover, and the secret of the momentous importance of history for the nineteenth century lies primarily here, history was conceived as literature and even as poetry. Its appeal was taken to be imaginative and sentimental. Nations would discover in their history an exciting source of poetry and a spur to greatness. 'Every nation's true Bible is its history,' Carlyle was to declare. Michelet, Renan, Taine and others were all convinced that we can only understand, and perhaps control, the present if we know how that present has come to be what it is: in other words, its genesis and the rationale underlying its development.

The impact of that history which was also an integral part of literature was enormous, and has remained so to this day; because it contained vivid scenes, easily detached from their context and read in anthologies, and because, as elementary education spread, every child in France was exposed to extracts from French historians, on the Gauls, on Joan of Arc, on the splendour of the Renaissance, on the growth and spread of civilization, on the achievement of the Revolution. The epic of Napoleon, related by historians and conjured up in Balzac or Hugo's novels, spread a screen of glory between the feudal and monarchical past of France and the present. The clock would never again be moved back. Michelet, in that respect, is not only one of the two or three supreme prose writers of France; he has also been the architect of democratic France.

He had predecessors: austere, professorial Guizot (1787–1874) and clear, didactic, logical Thiers (1797–1877), both of them statesmen whom their historical talent catapulted to political power, as has often been the case in France. Augustin Thierry (1795–1856) had a more vivid power of recreative sympathy with the past and a more brilliant talent as a writer. He upheld theoretical views on race which are no longer considered as valid, but which dramatized his perspective on the past. In his *Histoire de la conquête de l'Angleterre par les Normands* (1825), he sided with the conquered Saxons, whose rights he vindicated, against the invaders from France. In French history, he likewise read a justification of the former serfs and oppressed classes revolting, thanks to the French Revolution, against the conquering 'race' of Germanic oppressors. He gave arguments for the resolute ascent of the Third Estate against the privileged aristocracy.

Michelet (1798–1874) is a more feverish and passionate temperament, along with Balzac and Hugo one of the three great visionaries of French literature. He had grown up in poverty and he always remained close to the poor, refusing to become the favourite and thereby the prisoner of the official circles or of the salons. His was a tense, neurotic temperament, obsessed by death, dramatically in need of feminine love and even prone, as his *Journal*, published only in 1965, has revealed, to idolizing the other sex. He felt with an almost morbid intensity, suffered with those whom history had crushed, passionately hated the oppressors. His sensations, when recalling or reimagining past events and reconstructing figures of history, were acute and intense. They were immediately rendered into images and magnified into symbols. His style is the most naturally, overpoweringly metaphorical of any prose writer. The past, studied in archives and old prints, sprang to life for him; and, like Homer's Ulysses visiting the nether world, he poured out his own life blood over heroes and forces of old to resurrect them. His definition of history has remained famous: 'la résurrection intégrale du passé'.

Michelet, after being tempted by Thierry's utilization of the concept of race, rejected it as a deterministic explanation of history. Instead, he stressed geography, as moulding some of the factors on which history depends, the relations between men and their environment (including the food they grow, the land and the stones among which they develop), and mostly man's unconquerable will, as Wordsworth had called it, 'le travail de soi sur soi'. For man is his own Prometheus and he makes history with his own free will and his intellectual energy. It is clear that history thus understood can be neither dispassionate nor impartial. Michelet's imagination is dramatic and antithetic, like that of Hugo. It reaches piercing intuitions when the historian describes and interprets the French provinces, when he relates the life of the masses in the age of Gothic cathedrals and of Joan of Arc, the daughter of the poor, and in Michelet's grandiose narrative of the French Revolution. It is closed to the greatness of France's classical age and absolute monarchy, hostile to Britain, attracted to the vertiginous chaos which Michelet saw in Germany, until the war of 1870–1 grievously shattered his dreams.

Michelet's *Histoire de la révolution française* (1847–53) and his sentimental, patriotic volume in praise of the workmen and peasants of France, *Le Peuple* (1846), were the highest mark of his historian's career. Deprived of his teaching position by the Government of Napoleon III, no longer allowed to work freely in the National Archives, he wrote books of another kind, in which he gave free rein to the sentimental and tender side of his nature: *L'Oiseau* (1856), *L'Insecte* (1857), *La Mer* (1861) and two other visionary masterpieces: *La Sorcière* (1862), in which he pictured some of the dark forces which give the lie to optimistic rationalism in history, and a splendid spiritual history of the great religions and cultures of the world, *La Bible de l'humanité* (1864). Just as fully as Hugo in his *Légende des siècles*, Michelet had composed what Taine called 'l'épopée lyrique de la France', and even that of mankind from the Greeks to the abortive revolution of 1848.

Tocqueville (1805–59) is the other great historian of the first half of the nineteenth century. An aristocrat by temperament, resigned with some regret to the eventual victory of democracy, a cool and analytical philosopher, curbing his own passions and attempting to observe and to explain instead of feeling, he stands at the other extreme from Thierry and Michelet. For a long time, he was much less read and influential than they. His haughty maxims, his incisive pronouncements on American democracy, on French institutions, occasionally on

Britain or Russia, seemed too dogmatically imperious and to lack any vibration of sympathy with the ordinary men and women who live and make history. Posterity, however, has raised him to a respected position among the very few great philosophers of history and the even fewer prophets whose views have almost all been confirmed by events. At the age of thirty-one, he visited the United States of America, convinced that the march of that young democracy toward equality anticipated the future development of France. He observed, quickly but penetratingly. He was not blind to the faults of a regime and of a country where egalitarian passion, the greed for materialistic enjoyment of goods, the pursuit of money, the trend toward conformity and intellectual monotony offered grave threats. He did not foresee the extent of the industrial and technological revolution which has since altered the country, but he wrote incisive remarks on the issues posed by slavery and the cohabitation of several races in America. That analysis of the spirit of American democracy, presented in 1836 and 1841 in *De la démocratie en Amérique*, remains valid to this day. Tocqueville then undertook a painstaking inquiry into what the French Revolution had actually done to the division of property in France. In *L'Ancien Régime et la révolution* (1856), a volume even more solid and acute than his study of America, Tocqueville showed that the regimes of 1789–99 had not really broken extensively with the past; that much had already been done away with before 1789, and many French peasants had already become the owners of their land. In other words, with coolness and wisdom, he proved that the margin for innovation left to any revolutionary regime, to any Government faced with fulfilling the high-sounding electoral promises it has made, is a very narrow margin indeed. In France, as later in Russia and elsewhere, the forces or the conditions inherited from the past soon temper, if they do not stifle, the innovations attempted in the flush of ideological victory.

Literature has never held up a faithful mirror to the society in the midst of which it emerges and which, in its more sophisticated layers at least, delights in it. More often it offers an escape, or a picture of what should exist and does not, or a sarcastic criticism of the selfish philistinism of that society. Such was the case during the years 1830–48, and again later, when the bourgeoisie grew rich and powerful and often bought the very etchings and paintings by Daumier, the very novels which satirized it mercilessly. In those very same years, France had a surprising number of social reformers who do not rank among the writers of great talent, but who profoundly impressed the men of letters. Some of the latter were, at least for a time, converted to their doctrines, which promised the poet and the artist a significant function in the society of the future; others, reluctant to subscribe to socialist schemes in which every citizen would become an anonymous spring in a huge piece of machinery, turned away from politics and proclaimed the purity and the sanctity of art, cultivated for its own sake. The literature of those years, directly or indirectly, owed much to Saint-Simonism which came near to being a new religion as well as a far-sighted fusion of capitalism and socialism; to Fourier and his more utopian cult of the pleasure principle as the basis of social organization; to other semi-socialist or idealistically communist systems which, after the middle of the century, came to be displaced by the more scientific and practical political philosophy of the German Karl Marx. None of the French writers of that era, except Musset, Mérimée and Gautier, remained untouched by political speculations. During the latter part of the reign of the most bourgeois of French kings, Louis-Philippe, France appeared to be weary of some of the declamations and sentimental exaggerations of the Romantic writers and of the socialist reformers. She tried, weakly, to advocate common sense, middle-of-the-road wisdom, acceptance of reality at its most prosaic, as virtues worthy of literary eulogy. The attempt soon foundered with the sudden upheaval of 1848, which at first seemed to make Romanticism come true and be lived.

A further eminent Romantic, who searched for a faith with the Saint-Simonians, then with Lamennais, and who had appeared at first as the champion of the aesthetics of the new literature, is Sainte-Beuve (1804–69). He yearned for a creed or for a doctrine which might afford him some stability in a world where all is in flux and our judgement incessantly fallible. He failed as a poet, in spite of three or four quaint pieces which Baudelaire appreciated; he failed as a novelist, and never forgave Stendhal or Balzac their superiority as imaginative creators; but he could be, at his best, a superior critic. At first he served the new group of poets, encouraged them in their innovations, revealed them to themselves. Soon, however, out of pettiness, out of conservatism, he lost his taste for the experimental element in modern literature. He failed to appreciate with any justice Vigny, Hugo, Stendhal, Balzac, Michelet and later Baudelaire and Flaubert. But he acquired an enormous and an almost infallible erudition, ransacking unknown documents, memoirs, minor pamphlets; on the memorialists and men of action of the eighteenth century, on the dramatists and the moralists of the seventeenth, Sainte-Beuve's subtle intellect, resting on his precise knowledge of texts and on his talent for confessing souls posthumously, succeeded in being as definitive as any critic can ever hope to be. *Port-Royal* (1840–59), while magnifying the originality of the Jansenists and belittling other religious circles and figures of the seventeenth century, is an imposing and still valid seven-volume achievement. After 1848, Sainte-Beuve, while still delighting in displaying the pettiness and the pose of Chateaubriand and while erring grossly on poetry, proved more just and more lucid to the younger talents then asserting themselves in the realms of criticism, history and thought detached from orthodoxy, such as those of Renan and Taine.

Literature During the Second Empire

The Revolution of February 1848, striking France like a bolt from the blue, and the bloody insurrection of the following June which frightened provincial France, divided the country as it had not been for decades. The middle class, which had reaped the profits from the first Revolution of 1789 and even more from that of 1830 felt suddenly threatened by the social claims put forward by the industrial workers and by their socialist inspirers. Riots and near-revolutions, soon harshly repressed, broke out elsewhere on continental Europe, and Britain felt torn asunder by the Chartist movement. In history, and as a consequence in literature, the date was to mark a pivot in European evolution. Immense, chimerical hopes had been aroused for years; they were crushed and a mood of gloom ensued. In France as elsewhere, disappointment and pessimism invaded thinkers, writers and artists. Those who reached the age of twenty-five to thirty when 1848 shattered their illusions had been nurtured on Romantic dreams and on Romantic literature. In their provinces, Leconte de Lisle, Baudelaire (first a schoolboy at Lyon), Fromentin, Renan, Flaubert and several Norman friends of his had taken Hugo, Michelet, Balzac and Delacroix as their heroes. While their great Romantic predecessors had found an outlet in action or had cured themselves of their melancholy through creation, the new generation, disgusted with the reactionary politics of the Second Empire and by the industrial revolution which France was then energetically effecting, felt its wings clipped. Its illusory hopes for changing the world had been shattered. Embittered, unable or unwilling to find much comfort in traditional Christian faith, they took refuge in art as the only enduring value and a substitute for religion. Less concerned with their own individual, puny sufferings than the earlier Romantics had been, they were more objective and cooler in the sarcasms which they heaped on the conditions imposed by fate. They no longer moaned 'I suffer', but rather 'man suffers'; the circumstances meted out to him in the modern world render happiness an utter impossibility.

Matthew Arnold, the Tennyson of *In Memoriam*, Swinburne and others in Britain in prose and verse expressed that mood of discouragement. So did Heine, Wagner and several philosophers in Germany. In French poetry, the greatest of the poets who have been called Parnassians – for having collected samples of their verse in *Le Parnasse contemporain* (the first collection published in 1866) – Leconte de Lisle (1818–94), found fault with the sentimentality and the verbal facility of some at least of the Romantics, including Lamartine and Musset. Yet his condemnation of life recalls Vigny and his passion for colourful landscapes, for animals, heroes of primitive violence, reveals his affinities with Hugo, whom he succeeded in 1886 at the French Academy. In 1852, after several curious pieces inspired by Fourier's socialist utopias, Leconte de Lisle published his *Poèmes antiques* with a manifesto advocating more knowledge, more thought in poetry and a return to the vigour of the early ages of man's cultural history, those of ancient India and of Greece. He varied his inspiration further and perfected his form in his *Poèmes barbares* (1862), the theme and the scene of which are often in the tropics or in strange mythologies of northern Europe or of the New World. The poetry is haughty and, on first appearance, may seem impersonal and forbiddingly pedantic. The author sums up defunct cultures in their religion, their mythology and their artistic achievement. The form is monotonous: few rare images, many vague, abstract epithets. The descriptions of animals, attentive and evocative, have become popular more easily than the epic fragments which conjure up the sumptuous mythologies of remote lands. Yet, in his poems on the gods and heroes of Greece ('Khirôn'), on 'Hypatie', the priestess of pagan philosophy murdered by Christian fanatics, and even more in his evocations of his own romantic childhood ('Ultra Coelos', 'La Fontaine aux lianes', 'Le Manchy'), in his invectives against the materialistic ugliness of the modern world ('Dies irae', 'Solvet saeclum') and in a few graceful and musical pieces on young women ('La Fille aux cheveux de lin', 'Épiphanie'), Leconte de Lisle composed several of the noblest and richest pieces in the French language. His friend and disciple, the Cuban Heredia (1842–1905), collected his sonnets later in the century; but he had published some of the most majestic ones, like 'Les Conquérants', as early as 1869. Mallarmé, Verlaine, even the young Rimbaud, before 1870, looked up to the group of the Parnasse, in which Gautier and the fanciful, more humorous Banville (1823–91) were held in honour, as the fountainhead of poetical innovations in the years 1866–70.

The other great poet of that generation, Baudelaire (1821–67), belonged to no group. He did not look back to the past like the Parnassians or profess the cult of plastic, impassible beauty. He deliberately wanted to be modern and to elicit and convey the poetry of urban life. A very original section of his *Fleurs du mal*, his poems in prose curiously entitled *Le Spleen de Paris* and brilliant aesthetic essays in his *Curiosités esthétiques* (1868) are a plea for modernity in art and letters. Manet, Degas, Monet, Toulouse-Lautrec, and Daumier before them, were to reorient French painting away from mythological and historical subjects and towards the epic beauty of life around us. Baudelaire, unafraid of prosaism and eschewing the grandiloquence of some Romantics, brought poetry down to the evocation of silent, intimate tragedies of everyday life: 'Le Cygne', 'Les Petites Vieilles', the dramatic and mysterious sonnet 'A une passante', opened up a vein of poetry altogether different from the Parnassian stress upon remote and majestic beauty. They constituted an attempt to achieve in verse, much more tersely, what Balzac had accomplished in prose: to introduce the beauty and the mystery of modern urban life into literature.

Baudelaire had received other legacies from the Romantic movement, in which he saw the latest embodiment of beauty: the stress upon acute, rare, even morbid sensations; the substitution of strangeness (which he had especially admired in the stories of Edgar Allan Poe), of ugliness, of fear and even of hysteria, for the former aesthetic ideal placed in harmony, idealization and serenity; the exploration of the subconscious, erotic, at times sickly layers of our own beings, in which the flowers of evil are rooted. Some of his most original poems jolted the readers of 1857 and of 1861 (the dates of the first two editions of *Les Fleurs du mal*) who wanted security and prudent normalcy in literature: six pieces were condemned in court and had to be omitted from the volume. In truth, however, there is nothing obscene or even deliberately erotic in Baudelaire's poetry. Physical desire is always softened or offset either by tenderness and the treatment of the woman as a kind sister or motherly soothing presence or by spiritualization. 'Une Charogne', 'Une Martyre', even the long 'Femmes damnées' on the theme of lesbian women which had fascinated Baudelaire, end in Platonic exaltation of the spirit above and behind the flesh or in austere moral lessons. Elsewhere, as a remnant of an exasperated Romanticism, Baudelaire treats the loved and hated woman as a vampire or as an agent of the devil sent to torture the lover: there are banalities in *Les Fleurs du mal*, and there are artistic flaws also (excessive generality, monotony of the adjectives, halting inspiration and consequently poor endings of sonnets, the quatrains of which had opened triumphantly). When all is said, however, Baudelaire remains the greatest love-poet in the French language and (in 'L'Héautontimoroumenos', 'L'Irrémédiable', 'Spleen') the most relentless psychological and moral analyst of guilt, dread and remorse in poetry.

All other poets of the generations that grew to manhood in 1845–60 pale into insignificance when set beside Baudelaire, Leconte de Lisle and Hugo who was still in those years the chief poetical force. The newcomers, all impressed by the *Fleurs du mal*, Verlaine, Mallarmé, Corbière and Rimbaud, composed their greatest work after 1870. Lautréamont (1846–70), also an heir to the morbidly weird and, regrettably, to the declamatory rhetoric of the strangest of the Romantics, remained unknown to his contemporaries. The drama of the Second Empire era enjoyed great vogue as comedy, musical comedy, operetta and moral plays with a purpose (the latter chiefly attempted by Alexandre Dumas *fils*, 1824–95); but it had scant originality and hardly counts as literature. The novel and the philosophical, moral and critical essay are the two vital branches of literature, along with poetry. The age was one of startling prosperity, of material progress, of modernization of the houses, the cities, the countryside; but its literature, as often is the case in eras of prosperity (in America in 1920–30 or in 1960–70, and in France after World War II) turned its back against that reign of comfort and security. It criticized the society and portrayed the frustrations and failures of individuals.

A good many of the novels published between 1850 (when Balzac died) and 1870 (when the Goncourts, Daudet and Zola brought about the renewal of fiction through a more systematic realism) were platitudinous stories which, under the banner of realism brandished by Champfleury (1821–89), undertook to observe and to copy reality at its most commonplace. Most of that realism was woefully deficient in style, in power of organization and even in the gift of personality which alone can endow observation with significance and with life. Others were well-meant moral portrayals of the aristocratic and middle classes, insipid and timorous, which, for several decades, made up the reading allowed to French 'jeunes filles de bonne famille', until the emancipation or the revelation of marriage opened up to them tales of adultery. Fromentin (1820–76), a painter and an art critic of note, published in 1862 a personal novel, *Dominique*, which, while still lacking in boldness and recoiling before a silent tragedy of a young man's controlled passion for a married woman, was impregnated with the charm of rare delicacy in the analysis of feelings and in the rendering of nature poetry in the country of La Rochelle. Barbey d'Aurevilly (1808–89) was a more impetuous personality, fanatically Catholic and furiously romantic, who lived and wrote in solitude, convinced that his age had passed him by. He made himself famous through his original critical judgements, often altogether erratic, at times surprisingly discerning. He is also the author of novels in which his Catholic inspiration and his nostalgia for the past do not hamper the delineation of violent passion: *L'Ensorcelée* (1854), *Un Prêtre marié* (1865), *Les Diaboliques* (1874). Huysmans, Bourget himself and Bernanos belong to the same spiritual family.

The truly great novelist between Balzac and Zola, a Norman like Barbey d'Aurevilly, less of a visionary than he, but the supreme technician of the art of fiction and a powerful influence on the literatures of English-speaking countries, is Gustave Flaubert (1821–80). His early novels, the most revealing of which is *Novembre* (1842), and even the first version of *L'Éducation sentimentale* (1845) reveal the intensity with which he felt and lived all the excesses of romantic sensibility. There was a morbid strain in him as much as in Baudelaire, youthful dreams of suicide, a constant meditation on death. With rare determination, young Flaubert resolved to silence the almost hysterical romantic in him, to reserve his dreams of violence and of monstrous excesses for his historical fiction: *Salammbô* (1862) and the long, tedious series of apparitions which tempt, metaphysically and sensually, the saint in *La Tentation de Saint Antoine* (1874). These are such richly documented books, such pedantic reconstitutions of the ancient world in which Flaubert wished he had lived, that the virtue of life, of chance or passion upsetting the elaborately contrived structure, has been banished from them.

There lingers some coldness and probably an excess of self-awareness on the part of the novelist, too relentless a control of his inspiration in *Madame Bovary* (1857). 'Toute maîtrise jette le froid,' remarked Mallarmé, who was even more of a calculating artist, athirst for the perfection of an absolute, than Flaubert. Flaubert's supreme mastery over every episode, every page of his novel, every pronouncement, every gesture of his characters, does not actually throw a shiver down our spine. But at times, and the novelist was aware of it, his quest for a gradual progression from incident to incident, for the elimination of chance or the emergence of the unforeseen, satisfied the reader's intellect more than his urge to be moved or to dream. Flaubert wrote a revealing sentence in the notes of his trip to Carthage in 1858, as he realized that Parnassian beauty can mean the elimination of life and of the involuntary, unforeseen, destructive intrusion of truth in a work of art: 'Il faut faire, à travers le Beau, vivant et vrai quand même.' Still for the student and for the technician of fiction, no novel is more superb than *Madame Bovary* with its blend of pathos and of irony, of carefully observed country life and of all the chaotic impulses of average creatures in revolt against surrounding mediocrity but unable to escape from their own harassed selves.

Many devotees of Flaubert have preferred his next masterpiece *L'Éducation sentimentale* (1869). There is indeed even more of Flaubert himself in the dreams, the romantic idealization of woman, the melancholy resignation of the protagonist, an average man 'without qualities' and without serious faults, too weak either for crime or for heroism. But the book is more than a *Bildungsroman*: it is the portrayal of a whole generation, for which 1848 was the dividing line between illusions and reality, the idealists bent on reforming society and the shrewd pragmatic ones who knew how to profit from the collapse of many hopes and how to adapt themselves. The bankruptcy of a whole generation and of a chimerical romantic love is the subject of that slow-moving fresco. *Bouvard et Pécuchet* (published posthumously in 1881), left unfinished by the author, is an epic of human stupidity, sarcastic yet kindly; Flaubert's universal pessimism gave itself free play there. *Un Cœur simple* is a short masterpiece of tender irony, less tense than Flaubert's novels, and in his other *contes* (*Saint-Julien l'hospitalier*, *Hérodias*) the novelist returned to his romantic vein, his love for colourful violence. 'Je suis un vieux romantique enragé,' he wrote to his friends, and he remained one to the end.

In an oft-quoted article on *Madame Bovary*, Sainte-Beuve had detected, and appeared to denounce, the prevalence in the literature of

1850–65 of 'anatomists and physiologists', all observers and dissectors of the human brain and heart, and shatterers of many illusions. The scientific spirit of objective observation, historical impartiality, explanation through quantitative factors and through causes, invaded Europe after the middle of the nineteenth century. France counted an especially large number of scientists who were also excellent writers and, in several cases, who were close to men of letters: Pasteur (1822–95), Berthelot (1827–1907), Renan's lifelong friend, Claude Bernard (1813–78) and a medical man who was also an eminent lexicographer and a champion of positivism, Littré (1801–81). The most rapturous hymn to science, and especially to historical and philological sciences and the new vision of the human past they afforded, was written in 1848 (but published only in 1890) by Renan (1823–92). Trained for the priesthood, the young Breton scholar lost his faith when studying exegetically the Semitic languages and the evidence against accepting the Bible as a revealed book. He voraciously devoured several languages (Hebrew, Aramaic, Arabic, ancient classical and modern tongues), studied archaeology, epigraphy, comparative mythology and undertook the history of the most momentous phenomenon in human history: the replacement of the Greco-Roman culture by Christianity, the origins and slow unfolding of Christian religion and its preparation by the Jewish people. Tirelessly, and in spite of a violent outcry against him as a desecrator of faith and an Antichrist, Renan devoted twenty-five years of labour to his twelve-volume enterprise: the *Histoire des origines du christianisme*, from the *Vie de Jésus* (1863) to *Marc-Aurèle* (1881) and the *Histoire du peuple d'Israël* (1887–93). These learned volumes rest on an immense mass of precise research, but they are also written with art, often with grace; they aim, like Michelet's history, with less imaginative fire and in a softer, more allusive and insinuating manner, at resurrecting a remote past. The scenery in which the Hebrew prophets, Christ and St Paul lived, the collective moods of those ages when imaginative dreams, superstitions, *élans* of the heart and protests against social injustice counted for more than the observation of facts or the logical reasonings of philosophers are very skilfully brought back to life by Renan. Often he is led to conjecture and to reinvent, since precise documentation is not available. With a subtlety which sometimes displays itself too complacently, he practises what he called the art 'de solliciter doucement les textes'. These volumes exercised a far-reaching influence in France and elsewhere for decades: they instilled into many unbelievers a new sense for the poetry of Christianity and the eagerness, if dogmas, rites and theology are to be thrown overboard in our time, to preserve at least the sensibility and the idealism which Christian faith had for centuries embodied for the West.

Renan is also a master of the philosophical essay, urbane, mellow, written in elegant, mellifluous prose, fond of suggesting paradoxes and of indulging in dreams on the future of mankind. Several are written in the form of dialogues or of dramas, dear to the author who enjoyed the dialectical clash of ideas. His literary masterpieces are to be found in a remarkable series of historical, biographical and 'moral' studies – moral connoting the psychological meditations on the meaning of life and on the guidance of men by generous ideas, as the adjective often does in French. Those masterpieces of the genre of the essay, probably the finest in French since Montaigne, are scattered in *Études d'histoire religieuse* (1857), *Essais de morale et de critique* (1859), *Souvenirs d'enfance et de jeunesse* (1883) and *Feuilles détachées* (1892).

Renan encountered, in his reflections on the Jewish people, the notion of race, which puzzled or seduced every historian of the last century. He was for a time half-tempted by some of the speculations on the subject indulged by Arthur de Gobineau (1816–82), in his *Essai sur l'inégalité des races humaines* (1851–5). Gobineau's factual errors, his venturesome conclusions and his dogmatism on the subject soon repelled the subtler and more balanced mind of Renan. The utilization made, chiefly in Germany, of Gobineau's theory that there once existed a pure Aryan race, which racial mixture had brought to degeneracy, should not make us underestimate the dazzling intelligence and the terse, ironical style of the author. He has been praised by British connoisseurs of the East as the author of the most penetrating stories ever laid in Asia, *Nouvelles asiatiques* (1876); his reports and letters from Iran, where he served as a French diplomat, his stories on *La Renaissance* (1877) and his novel *Les Pléiades* (1874) are works of a very rare, perhaps of a very great, talent.

Taine (1828–93) exercised in the last decades of the nineteenth century, along with Renan, a profound influence on French psychologists, critics and novelists, such as Ribot, Barrès, Bourget, Brunetière and Maurras. After an early volume of comic and scathing irony on the superficial philosophers who had preceded him in France, *Les Philosophes français du XIXe siècle* (1857), and a rigidly dogmatic attempt to explain La Fontaine through his 'race' and his 'milieu', Taine published a remarkable series of essays entitled *Essais de critique et d'histoire*

(1858, 1866), few of which have lost their freshness and their force of conviction after a century, and the most famous of his critical achievements, his five-volume *Histoire de la littérature anglaise* (1864, completed in 1869). The chapters on Chaucer, Shakespeare, Swift and Byron, controversial as they are, are still thought-provoking today. The doctrine of its introduction is too rigorous and fails to make an allowance for the unpredictable originality of one brother in a family, of one author among a thousand who were moulded in the same 'race', environment and time. But it constituted a bold and coherent attempt to understand literary and artistic works and not merely to enjoy them in a dilettante way.

Taine subsequently turned to history. The defeat of France at the hands of Prussia in 1870 shattered many of his dreams, as it did those of Michelet and Renan. The sight of the Parisian mob, enraged by the defeat and the siege, seizing power with the 1871 Commune, destroying and burning buildings, then savagely punished by the reaction which defeated them, strengthened Taine's profound pessimism on human nature. He ceased to have any faith in democracy. He regretted the Revolution, the vain conquests of Napoleon and the political instability of the French. He envied the reforming and moderate spirit of the British monarchy. In order to understand his countrymen and his own age, Taine undertook to explore *Les Origines de la France contemporaine* (1875–93) in six brilliant, dogmatic and partial volumes. His generalizations on the regrettable consequences for France of the 'classical spirit', allegedly abstract, doctrinaire, unmindful of the empirical lessons of facts, have had a powerful appeal for the political thinkers of France who, in large numbers, have criticized parliamentary democracy. It was probably a misfortune for the country that, after Michelet's revolutionary enthusiasm, most of the eminent political thinkers of France were hostile, or implacably severe, to democracy.

The fall of Napoleon III in September 1870 marked for France the closing of an era which had experimented in a number of political regimes without finding stability but which had at last effected an industrial revolution and brought economic welfare to a larger number of citizens. But literature, as always, stood in opposition to the spread of those material forces and collective trends which strengthened the State and the administration and threatened to restrict the freedom of the creative individual. Literary and artistic works were either a means of escape from too crushing a reality or a bitter criticism of things as they were (in fiction, drama, history). With Hugo, Leconte de Lisle or Baudelaire as with Stendhal or Flaubert, the nobleness of the writer's profession lay in his calling everything in question and in protesting against the injustice (of the social order and more generally of the human condition) in the name of an ideal, however dimly conceived. Under a wide diversity of shapes, the revolt of the Romantics, first asserted by their predecessors such as Diderot and Rousseau, had echoed throughout the years 1800–70. It has hardly ever been silenced since.

Bibliography

The titles listed here are necessarily very few, in relation to the huge number of volumes which have, within the last fifty years, been devoted to the interpretation and criticism of French literature in its modern periods. Very specialized works and works not readily accessible, or not available in the two languages taken to be familiar to the users of this volume (English and French) have been left out. For the French titles for which no place of publication is mentioned, Paris is to be understood.

SECOND HALF OF THE EIGHTEENTH CENTURY: VOLTAIRE, DIDEROT, ROUSSEAU

The writers of the age of Enlightenment had suffered relative neglect during the century which followed, partly as a reaction against the French Revolution and the movement of ideas which had seemed to prepare it, partly because the seventeenth century had been set up by academic critics as the classical century *par excellence* and the one best fit to provide models for the youth. Historians of the Revolution like Michelet, historians of arts and manners like the Goncourt brothers, had started a rehabilitation of the literature of the Regency and of the reign of Louis XV. A new and more scientific study of the 'Philosophic Spirit' was started by G. Lanson on the eve of the First World War. The empirical spirit of that age, its admiring attitude toward English thinkers and novelists, its impact upon the American Founding Fathers, have since made it a favourite period of study for English-speaking scholars.

Among the general or inclusive works which have reappraised the thought of the eighteenth century (chiefly in its second half), the following are especially relevant: C. Becker, *The Heavenly City of the Eighteenth Century Philosophers* (New Haven, 1955); I. Berlin, *The Eighteenth Century Philosophers, The Age of Enlightenment* (London and New York, 1956); E. Cassirer, *The Philosophy of the Enlightenment* (Princeton, 1951; appeared in German in 1932); L. Crocker, *An Age of Crisis: Man and World in Eighteenth Century French Thought* (Baltimore, 1959) and *Nature and Culture: Ethical Thought in the French Enlightenment* (Baltimore, 1963); M. Duchet, *Anthropologie et histoire au siècle des Lumières* (1971); J. Ehrard, *L'Idée de nature en France à l'aube des Lumières* (1970); G. Elton, *The Revolutionary Idea in France 1789–1871* (London, 1923); J. Fabre, *Lumières et romantisme: Energie et nostalgie*

(Klincksieck, 1963); P. Gay, *The Enlightenment, an Interpretation*, 2 vols (New York, 1966 and 1969); F. C. Green, *Minuet, a Critical Survey of French and English Literary Ideas in the Eighteenth Century* (London, 1935); G. Havens, *The Age of Ideas: From Reaction to Revolution in Eighteenth Century France* (New York, 1955); G. Lanson, *Essais de méthode, de critique et d'histoire littéraire* (1965); R. Mauzi, *L'Idée du bonheur au XVIIIe siècle* (1960); R. Mortier, *Clartés et ombres au siècle des Lumières* (Geneva, 1969); R. Niklaus, *The Eighteenth Century: 1715–89* (London, 1970); J. Roger, *Les Sciences de la vie dans la pensée française du dix-huitième siècle* (1963); J. Starobinski, *L'Invention de la liberté* (Geneva, 1964); K. Mannheim, *Ideology and Utopia* (London, 1936, and New York, 1960); A. Viatte, *Les Sources occultes du romantisme, 1770–1820* (1938). On the idea of progress more particularly, C. Becker, *Progress and Power* (Stanford, 1936); J. B. Bury, *The Idea of Progress* (London and New York, 1955; first published 1932); C. Frankel, *The Faith of Reason* (New York, 1948); F. L. Tuveson, *Millennium and Utopia* (Berkeley, 1949).

On Voltaire, a number of the many volumes of *Studies on Voltaire and the Eighteenth Century*, published by T. Besterman in Geneva and subsequently in Banbury, Oxfordshire, have added greatly to our knowledge of the eighteenth century. Among the mass of significant works on Voltaire, the following will be found especially useful: H. N. Brailsford, *Voltaire and Reform in the Light of the French Revolution* (London and New York, 1959; first appeared 1935); P. Gay, *Voltaire's Politics* (Princeton, 1959); G. Lanson, *Voltaire* (1906), translated into English with substantial additions (New York, 1966); A. Maurois, *Voltaire* (1935); R. Naves, *Le Goût de Voltaire* (1938); R. Pomeau, *La Religion de Voltaire* (1969; first published 1956) and *Voltaire par lui-même* (1955); J. Sareil, *Voltaire et la critique* (Englewood Cliffs, N. J., 1966).

On Diderot, several volumes of *Diderot Studies*, edited by Otis Fellows and other Columbia University scholars, have appeared in Geneva since 1949. See also L. Crocker, *Two Diderot Studies: Ethics and Esthetics* (Baltimore, 1952); H. Dieckmann, *Cinq leçons sur Diderot* (Geneva, 1959); R. Pomeau, *Diderot, sa vie et son œuvre* (1967); J. Proust, *Diderot et l'Encyclopédie* (1962); A. M. Wilson, *Diderot* (New York, 1972, new ed.).

On Rousseau, biographical, political, ethical, literary and philosophical aspects of his controversial personality and writings have long been discussed in book after book. Among the recent titles: P. Burgelin, *La Philosophie de l'existence de Rousseau* (1952); E. H. Dobinson, *Rousseau: his Thought and its Relevance Today* (London, 1969); F. C. Green, *Rousseau: a Critical Study of his Life and Writings* (Cambridge, 1955); R. Grimsley, *Rousseau: a Critical Study of Self-Awareness* (Cardiff, 1961); R. D. Masters, *The Political Philosophy of Rousseau* (Princeton, 1968); M. Raymond, *Rousseau: la quête de soi et la rêverie* (1962); J. Starobinski, *La Transparence et l'obstacle* (1957); C. E. Vaughan, *The Political Writings of Rousseau* (Cambridge, 1915).

A few sundry titles on other thinkers and on novelists and dramatists are grouped here: J. Bouissounouse, *Julie de Lespinasse* (New York, 1962); R. Desné, *Les Matérialistes français* (1965); J. Fabre, *Chénier, l'homme et l'œuvre* (1951); R. Hubert, *Les Sciences sociales dans l'Encyclopédie* (Lille, 1923); R. Niklaus, *Beaumarchais, le Barbier de Séville* (London, 1968). On Condorcet, J. Schapiro, *Condorcet and the Rise of Liberalism* (New York, 1934); on Turgot, D. Dakin, *Turgot and the Ancien*

Régime (London, 1939); On the eighteenth century novelists: M. Blanchot, *Lautréamont et Sade* (1949); P. Brooks, *The Novel of Worldliness* (Princeton, 1969); G. Gorer, *The Life and Ideas of the Marquis de Sade* (London, 1953, new ed.), and G. Lély, *Sade: étude sur sa vie et ses œuvres* (1967); A. Malraux, *Le Triangle noir* (1970); G. May, *Le Dilemme du roman au dix-huitième siècle* (New Haven, 1963); V. Mylne, *The Eighteenth Century French Novel: Techniques of Illusion* (Manchester, 1965); E. Showalter, *The Evolution of the French Novel, 1641–1782* (Princeton, 1972); P. Stewart, *Imitation and Make-Believe in the French Novel, 1700–50* (New Haven, 1969); E. Sturm, *Crébillon fils et le libertinage au XVIIIe siècle* (Nizet, 1970).

ROMANTICISM

There exists a whole library on the Romantic movement in France and in other countries of Europe. Romanticism can be variously conceived as starting in the middle of the previous century (with Rousseau, Diderot, Goethe, Ossian and others), as a movement culminating in 1820–45, or as a revolution of sensibility and of thought whose impact was felt over the whole nineteenth century and is still powerful today. The following titles are selected as the most relevant: M. H. Abrams, *The Mirror and the Lamp, Romantic Theory and the Critical Tradition* (New York, 1953); R. M. Adams, *Nil: Episodes in the Literary Conquest of Void During the Nineteenth Century* (New York, 1966); F. Baldensperger, *Le Mouvement des idées dans l'émigration française, 1789–1815* (1925); A. Béguin, *L'Âme romantique et le rêve* (1963, new ed.); J. Bousquet, *Les Thèmes du rêve dans la littérature romantique* (1964) and *Anthologie du dix-huitième siècle romantique* (1972); R. Bray, *Chronologie du romantisme (1804–30)* (1932); M. J. Durry, *La Vieillesse de Chateaubriand, 1830–48* (1933); L. Emery, *L'Âge romantique*, 2 vols (Lyon, 1960); D. O. Evans, *Social Romanticism in France, 1830–48* (Oxford, 1951); L. Guichard, *La Musique et les lettres au temps du romantisme* (1955); P. Guiral, *La Société française 1815–1914, vue par les romanciers* (1969); H. J. Hunt *Le Socialisme et le romantisme en France* (Oxford, 1935) and *The Epic in Nineteenth Century France* (Oxford, 1941); H. Lefebvre, *Musset dramaturge* (1955); M. Milner, *Le Diable dans la littérature française*, 2 vols (1960) and *Le Romantisme, I (1820–43)* (1973); A. Monglond, *Le Préromantisme français* (Grenoble, 1930); P. Moreau, *Le Classicisme des romantiques* (1932) and *Le Romantisme* (1957); D. Mornet, *Le Romantisme en France au XVIIIe siècle* (1912); A. R. Oliver, *Nodier Pilot of Romanticism* (Syracuse, 1964); H. Peyre, *Literature and Sincerity* (New Haven, 1963) and *Qu'est-ce que le romantisme?* (1971); M. Praz, *The Romantic Agony* (Oxford, 1951; first ed. in Italian in 1930).

THE NOVEL

The novel of the nineteenth century has been studied from many a point of view in all the standard volumes on the craft of fiction, such as the well-known ones by P. Lubbock, E. M. Forster, G. Lukács. Among more recent ones, the most useful may be the following: P. Castex, *Le Conte fantastique en France de Nodier à Maupassant* (1951); I. Howe, *Politics and the Novel* (New York, 1964); H. Levin, *The Gates of Horn* (New York and London, 1963); M. Turnell, *The Art of French Fiction* (London, 1951, and New York, 1958). Stendhal has been the subject of a great many works since 1920 or so. Among them those by M. Bardèche, *Stendhal romancier* (1947); V. Brombert, *Stendhal et la voie oblique* (1954); A. Caraccio,

Stendhal, l'homme et l'œuvre (1951); G. Durand, *Le Décor mythique de la Chartreuse de Parme* (1961); F. C. Green, *Stendhal* (Cambridge, 1939); F. Hemmings, *Stendhal, a Study of his Novels* (Oxford, 1964); F. Marill, *Le Naturel chez Stendhal* (1956); J. Prévost, *La Création chez Stendhal* (1951); J. Starobinski, 'Stendhal pseudonyme', in *L'Œil vivant* (1961).

Studies on Balzac have been hardly less numerous: M. Bardèche, *Balzac romancier* (1941); P. Bertault, *Balzac, l'homme et l'œuvre* (1968; first ed. 1948); F. Hemmings, *Balzac, an Interpretation of La Comédie humaine* (New York, 1967); H. J. Hunt, *Balzac's Comédie humaine* (London, 1959); P. Laubriet, *L'Intelligence de l'art chez Balzac* (1961); D. F. McCormick, *Les Nouvelles de Balzac* (1973); A. Maurois, *Prometheus, the Life of Balzac* (London and New York, 1965); G. Picon, *Balzac par lui-même* (1956). On the third of the giants of French fiction before 1870, Flaubert, the best works are those by V. Brombert, *The Novels of Flaubert* (Princeton, 1966) and *Flaubert par lui-même* (1971); C. Digeon, *Flaubert* (1970); J. P. Sartre, *L'Idiot de la famille*, 3 vols (1971–3); E. Starkie, *Flaubert, the Making of the Master* and *The Master*, 2 vols (London and New York, 1967 and 1971); A. Thibaudet, *Flaubert* (1935).

On other novelists, only a few significant titles may be mentioned: A. Oliver, *Benjamin Constant: écriture et conquête du moi* (1970); P. Delbouille, *Genèse, structure et destin d'Adolphe* (1972); B. Jasinski, *L'Engagement de B. Constant* (1971). J. Bornecque, *Les Années d'apprentissage de Daudet* (1951); M. Sachs, *The Career of Daudet, a Critical Study* (Cambridge, U.S.A., 1965).

POETRY

A reappraisal of the French Romantic poets has taken place since 1930 or so, when the centenary of Romanticism was celebrated in France and the lasting impact of the Romantic 'mal du siècle' over the post-Second-World-War generations appeared as giving relevance to the visionary poets of 1820–50. Among the general studies on that poetry, the following are notable: A. M. Boase, *The Poetry of France, Vol. 3, 1800–1900* (London, 1967; first published 1952); A. E. Carter, *The Idea of Decadence in French Literature* (Toronto, 1958); A. Cassagne, *La Théorie de l'art pour l'art en France* (1959; first published 1905); E. Estève, *Byron et le romantisme français* (1929; first published 1907); M. Gilman, *The Idea of Poetry in France* (Cambridge, U.S.A., 1958); J. P. Houston, *The Demonic Imagination: Style and Theme in French Romantic Poetry* (Baton Rouge, Louisiana, 1969); M. Moraud, *Le Romantisme français en Angleterre, 1814–48* (1933); J. P. Richard, *Poésie et profondeur* (1955) and *Études sur le romantisme* (1970); H. Riffaterre, *L'Orphisme dans la poésie romantique* (1970).

A very few among the important works on the individual poets are: H. Guillemin, *Le Jocelyn de Lamartine* (1936) and *Lamartine, l'homme et l'œuvre* (1940); G. Bonnefoy, *La Pensée religieuse et morale d'A. de Vigny* (1944); F. Germain, *L'Imagination de Vigny* (1961); E. Lauvrière, *Vigny*, 2 vols (1946). P. Albouy, *La Creation mythologique chez Hugo* (1963); J. B. Barrère, *La Fantaisie de Hugo*, 3 vols (1949–60), *Hugo l'homme et l'œuvre* (1952) and *Hugo devant Dieu* (1965); L. Emery, *Vision et pensée chez Hugo* (Lyon, n.d.); J. Gaudon, *Hugo, le temps de la contemplation* (1969); H. Guillemin, *Hugo par lui-même* (1951); A. Maurois, *Olympio ou la Vie de Hugo*, 2 vols (1954); H. Peyre, *Hugo philosophe* (1972); D. Saurat, *La Religion de V. Hugo*

(1929); P. Zumthor, *Hugo poète de Satan* (1929). P. Gastinel, *Le Romantisme de Musset* (1933). S. Fauchereau, *Th. Gautier* (1972); J. Richardson, *Gautier, his Life and Times* (London, 1958). A. Béguin, *Nerval ou la Descente aux enfers* (1945); P. Bénichou, *Nerval et la chanson folklorique* (1971); P. Castex, *Aurelia* (1971); L. Cellier, *Nerval, l'homme et l'œuvre* (1956); R. Chambers, *Nerval et la poétique du voyage* (1969); R. Jean, *Nerval par lui-même* (1964); J. Richer, *Nerval et les doctrines ésotériques* (1947). E. Estève, *Leconte de Lisle* (1923); A. Fairlie, *Leconte de Lisle's Poems on the Barbarian Races* (Cambridge, 1947); I. Putter, *Le Pessimisme de Leconte de Lisle*, 2 vols (Berkeley, 1954 and 1961). L. Austin, *L'Univers poétique de Baudelaire* (1956); P. Emmanuel, *Baudelaire devant Dieu* (1967); A. Fairlie, *Les Fleurs du mal* (London, 1960); M. Gilman, *Baudelaire the Critic* (New York, 1943); J. Hubert, *L'Esthétique des Fleurs du mal* (Geneva, 1953); C. Pichois and W. Bandy, *Baudelaire devant ses contemporains* (1967, new ed.); J. P. Sartre, *Baudelaire* (1947); E. Starkie, *Baudelaire* (London, 1971, new ed.). M. Blanchot, *Lautréamont et Sade* (1963); R. Faurisson, *A-t-on lu Lautréamont?* (1972).

ESSAYISTS, HISTORIANS AND CRITICS

The nineteenth century has been called the golden age of the essay, critical and historical. The greatest historians of France meditated on the past in order to understand the present and often to prophesy or to prepare the future. Only a very summary selection among the many works dealing with the French thinkers and historians can be attempted here. Among the general surveys and studies, I. Babbit, *The Masters of French Criticism* (New York, 1963; first appeared 1912); D. G. Charlton, *Positivist Thought in France During the Second Empire* (Oxford, 1959) and *Secular Religions in France, 1815–70* (London, 1963); E. Faguet, *Politiques et moralistes du dix-neuvième siècle*, 3 vols (1891–1900; Vol. 3 appeared in English translation, London, 1928); E. Wilson, *To the Finland Station* (New York, 1970). On Sainte-Beuve: R. Fayolle, *Sainte-Beuve et le dix-huitième siècle* (1972); A. G Lehmann, *Sainte-Beuve, a Portrait of the Critic, 1804–42* (Oxford, 1962); M. Leroy, *La Pensée de Sainte-Beuve* (1940); L. F. Mott, *Sainte-Beuve* (New York and London, 1925); H. Nicolson, *Sainte-Beuve* (London, 1957); M. Regard, *Saint-Beuve* (1960). On Renan; R. Chadbourne, *Renan* (New York, 1968) and *Renan as an Essayist* (Ithaca, N. Y., 1959); R. Galand, *L'Âme celtique de Renan* (1959); K. Gore, *L'Idée de progrès dans la pensée de Renan* (1970); G. Guisan, *Renan et l'art d'écrire* (Geneva, 1962); L. F. Mott, *Renan* (New York, 1921); H. Peyre, *Sagesse de Renan* (1966) and *Renan et la Grèce* (1973); J. Pommier, *Renan* (1923); H. W. Wardman, *Renan, a Critical Biography* (London, 1964). On Michelet: R. Barthes, *Michelet par lui-même* (1954); J. Gaulmier, *Michelet devant Dieu* (1968); P. Viallaneix, *La Voie royale* (1959). On Taine: A. Chevrillon, *Taine, formation de sa pensée* (1932); R. Gibaudan, *Les Idées sociales de Taine* (1928); S. J. Kahn, *Science and Aesthetic Judgment: a Study in Taine's Critical Method* (London, 1953); P. Lacombe, *Taine historien et sociologue* (1909); F. C. Roe, *Taine et l'Angleterre* (1923). On Tocqueville: H. Brogan, *Tocqueville* (London, 1973); J. Lively, *The Social and Political Thought of Tocqueville* (Oxford, 1962); J. P. Mayer, *Tocqueville, a Biographical Essay in Political Science* (London and New York, 1940). On Gobineau: J. Buenzod, *La Formation de la pensée de Gobineau* (1967); J. Gaulmier, *Spectre de Gobineau* (1965).

9 French Literature since 1870

JOHN CRUICKSHANK

The date 1870 is more obviously significant for the political evolution of France than for its literary development. This is the year in which the Franco-Prussian war brought the Second Empire under Napoleon III to a no doubt deservedly inglorious end. It saw the crushing nature of the French defeat highlighted by capitulation at Sedan and the siege of Paris. Nevertheless, 1870 is also the year in which two contrasting works, both significant in the history of literature, were completed: Taine's psychological essay, *De l'intelligence*, and Verlaine's collection of love poems, *La Bonne Chanson*. Taine wrote from a firm belief in exact and scientific determinism as the proper basis for a study of human nature. Verlaine, on the contrary, sought to express human truth through a private sensibility and conscious imprecision at odds with rational analysis. The closing decades of the nineteenth century were to elaborate and diversify further these two attitudes. In terms both of intellectual debate and literary practice, they received their most striking expression in naturalism and symbolism respectively.

Naturalism

Nineteenth-century 'scientism' was a broad set of beliefs, materialist, determinist and atheist in spirit, to which Comte, Renan and Taine made particularly important contributions. Auguste Comte (1798–1857) elaborated a 'philosophy of positivism' which divided the development of the human mind into three historical stages: the theological, the metaphysical, and the scientific or positivist. In this scheme scientific positivism clearly represented intellectual maturity and Comte, who saw evidence of analytical precision already ousting philosophic generalities in various spheres, was anxious to apply scientific method to all areas of human speculation. In particular, he argued the need for strict observation and experiment in the study of society ('la physique sociale') and may be seen, for good or ill, as a founding father of modern sociology. In a similar spirit Ernest Renan (1823–92) held science to be the only acceptable religion ('il n'y a pas de surnaturel'), while Hippolyte Taine (1828–93) attributed the determining role of heredity and environment to three factors: 'race', 'milieu' and 'moment'.

These are some of the general ideas, not always fully understood, from which the naturalist movement drew inspiration. Émile Zola (1840–1902), the most gifted novelist of the group and its chief theoretician, was familiar with contemporary scientific ideas (including Darwinism) and also read more specialized works including Prosper Lucas's *Traité philosophique et physiologique de l'hérédité naturelle* (1847–50), Claude Bernard's *Introduction à l'étude de la médecine expérimentale* (1865) and Charles Letourneau's *Physiologie des passions* (1868). He combined these scientific interests with a strong social sense and his novels often apply the conclusions of science to the ills of society in a spirit of radical analysis.

In a theoretical justification of his practice as a novelist (*Le Roman expérimental*, 1880) he refers to himself and his fellow naturalists as 'moralistes expérimenteurs'. He made the extravagant claim that the naturalist novelist places his characters in a particular social milieu and then, like a chemist in a laboratory, observes the interaction of temperament and environment which he finally 'writes up'. Zola sees the novelist as the amanuensis of his characters. More seriously, most of the novels use the temperament/environment interaction to suggest that even the most reprehensible characters are not so much innately 'bad' as victims of hereditary and social conditioning – the only acceptable conclusion for what he called, more chillingly than he intended, 'un siècle de science et de démocratie'.

These ideas had already been applied in *Thérèse Raquin* (1867). In 1871 Zola drew the logical consequences of his theories by planning the twenty-volume 'Rougon-Macquart' cycle (1871–93). He was later to write two further, though smaller, groups of novels, *Les Trois Villes* (1894–8) and *Les Quatre Évangiles* (1899–1903), but these are second rate and overtly didactic works. His reputation rests on the 'Rougon-Macquart' series – a grandiose fresco of the Second Empire in which various members of the two related families experience their inherited taints in a variety of situations that include Parisian slum life (*L'Assommoir*, 1877), the world of the *demi-mondaine* (*Nana*, 1880), a strike in a mining community (*Germinal*, 1885), rural poverty (*La Terre*, 1887) and the Franco-Prussian war (*La Débâcle*, 1892). Such novels combine conscientious documentation with a heavy concentration on the more bestial human manifestations. They were severely condemned as prurient and pornographic, while also being widely read and enjoyed.

No aesthetic formula could satisfactorily accommodate Zola's conception of a strictly 'experimental' novel, and the scientific value of the 'Rougon-Macquart' series is almost nil. At the same time, Zola's failure as a scientist is the source of his artistic strength. By temperament he was a poet and visionary, and if the tension between romance and science encouraged some ill-judged melodramatic writing it also created some of the most powerfully imagined scenes in his work. His strong visual response to physical detail and collective movement helped to expand the scope of late nineteenth-century fiction beyond the traditional limits of internalized and individualized psychological analysis.

The Goncourt brothers (Edmond, 1822–96, and Jules, 1830–70), famous for the *Journal* which they began in 1851, first made a reputation as art critics and historians. In the 1860s they collaborated on a number of novels, clearly naturalist in spirit, published before Zola codified naturalistic doctrine. Their early training enabled them to write carefully documented accounts of contemporary society and they also took a particular interest in analysing mental abnormality, e.g. hysteria in *Germinie Lacerteux* (1865) and religious mania in *Madame Gervaisais* (1869). Their approach is typified by a *Journal* entry for 1860, discussing the novel *Sœur Philomène* (1861) and its hospital setting, in which they resolve to study the background 'sur le vrai, sur le vif, sur le saignant'.

The other major figure associated with naturalism is Guy de Maupassant (1850–93) whose first published story, *Boule de suif*, appeared in Zola's collection of *nouvelles*, *Les Soirées de Médan* (1880). Other contributors, apart from Zola himself, were Paul Alexis (1847–1901), Joris-Karl Huysmans (1848–1907), Léon Hennique (1851–1935) and Henry Céard (1851–1924) whose novel, *Une Belle Journée* (1881), dealt with what he himself called 'cette loi de la médiocrité universelle qui, pareille à la gravitation et despotique autant que la pesanteur, ploie le monde et le soumet à son ordonnance'. As for Maupassant, he is the genuine entertainer among the naturalists, a cynical, amusing observer of human folly whose 300 or so short stories show an astonishing range of narrative skill and artistic versatility. In the preface to the best of his six novels, *Pierre et Jean* (1888), he rightly describes himself as probing, with detachment, 'le sens profond et caché des événements'.

Mention should also be made of Alphonse Daudet (1840–97) though he is best remembered today for the comic and ironic stories collected in *Lettres de mon moulin* (1866), *Tartarin de Tarascon* (1872). etc. The deliberate naturalism of such novels as *Jack* (1876), *Le Nabab* (1877), *Numa Roumestan* (1881) and *Sapho* (1884) contains an element of sentimentality suggesting that Daudet was attracted to the movement more by human sympathy with naturalist subject-matter than from artistic instinct. He rightly described himself as a *homo duplex*.

In the 1880s naturalism scored some success in the theatre with stage adaptations of novels by Zola, the Goncourts, Daudet and others. Between 1887 and 1896 Antoine's Théâtre Libre developed in the same direction, putting on plays by Alexis, Hennique and Céard and such important foreign 'naturalists' as Hauptmann, Ibsen and Strindberg. Ironically, the one French naturalist play of genuine quality, *Les Corbeaux* (1882) by Henry Becque (1837–99), failed completely when first performed at the Comédie Française.

Symbolism

Daudet's dual output suggests that not all writers classed as naturalists fit completely into this category. A striking example is Joris-Karl Huysmans whose early association with naturalism, seen in such novels as *Les Sœurs Vatard* (1879) and *En ménage* (1881), was prompted less by scientific conviction than by a Céard-like pessimism before the irremediable vulgarity of a world in which 'seul le pire arrive'. A fastidious temperament and refined artistic sense led Huysmans to reject the dominant 'scientism' of the day. His best-known novel, *A rebours* (1884), shows the hero, Des Esseintes, escaping from sordid materialism into aestheticism and recherché 'spiritual' experiences. The opening pages of *Là-bas* (1891) discuss the shortcomings of the naturalist novel and the hero, Durtal, is fascinated and repelled by satanism. Huysmans' own development, through aestheticism and satanism to the Catholic faith, is plotted in these two books and in such later novels as *En route* (1895), *La Cathédrale* (1898) and *L'Oblat* (1903).

Significantly, Des Esseintes in *A rebours* reads Mallarmé's poetry – hinting that the symbolist movement with which Mallarmé is associated, and the revival of religious values of which Huysmans's later novels are only one example, represent a common dissatisfaction with the intellectual and artistic assumptions of naturalism. Symbolist doctrine and the Catholic revival possess fundamental differences, but they share a central belief in an *au-delà* beyond immediate material reality.

Symbolism is primarily associated with poetry and with Baudelaire's description of the world as a 'forêt de symboles'. In its final doctrinal form it is a complicated and sometimes pretentious theory though its effects on poetic technique have been important and lasting. The symbolists held the poet to be uniquely equipped to convey to others the truth of the Idea – a world of transcendent reality symbolized in the more immediately accessible world of material objects. This is so because of the poet's sensibility and because words have magical properties which make possible their use as 'symbols' rather than 'dictionary equivalents'. For the symbolist, therefore, the naturalist both failed to recognize the potential power of language and concentrated, in his subject-matter, on appearance rather than reality.

Among the precursors of symbolism Verlaine and Rimbaud are important figures. Paul Verlaine (1844–96) was originally associated with the Parnassian reaction against Romantic rhetoric and subjectivity but his earliest collections of poems, *Poèmes saturniens* (1866) and *Fêtes galantes* (1869), give evidence of the suggestive evocation of mood and the haunting verbal music which were to become important elements in the symbolists' art:

> Les sanglots longs
> Des violons
>   De l'automne
> Blessent mon cœur
> D'une langueur
>   Monotone.

Perhaps his finest collection is *Romances sans paroles* (1874). In the same year in which it appeared he wrote 'Art poétique', a poem setting out his aesthetic ideas at this period. He emphasizes musicality ('De la musique avant toute chose') and points out another symbolist ideal with his call for a poetry of suggestion rather than statement, creating a reality free from definition or discursive comment ('. . . la chanson grise / Où l'Indécis au Précis se joint'). The religious poems collected in *Sagesse* (1881) mark his conversion to Catholicism and seek atonement for his disreputable life. Some are deeply moving (e.g. 'Ô mon Dieu, vous m'avez blessé d'amour') but many will seem maudlin or tasteless to the average modern reader.

Verlaine and Rimbaud were related on the scandalous level of a stormy homosexual relationship. A more lasting and significant link between them is to be found in their individual contributions to the revolutionizing of late nineteenth-century poetry. Arthur Rimbaud (1854–91) had a brief and meteoric literary career, had turned his back on poetry by the age of twenty ('l'art est une sottise'), and died after ten years in Abyssinia as trader, explorer and gun-runner. His poetry, like his life, was a continuing attack on most forms of convention. The earliest poems hit out indiscriminately at all manifestations of authority from God to the local librarian. A vision of limitless freedom is expressed in poems such as 'Sensation' or 'Ophélie' and reaches a climax in the lurching, fascinating imagery of 'Le Bateau ivre':

> J'ai vu des archipels sidéraux! et des îles
> Dont le cieux délirants sont ouverts au vogueur:
> – Est-ce en ces nuits sans fonds que tu dors et t'exiles,
> Million d'oiseaux d'or, ô future Vigueur? –

Shortly afterwards Rimbaud rejected rhyme and completed the poetic prose of his two major works: *Les Illuminations* (probably written 1872) and *Une Saison en enfer* (written 1873).

Like his symbolist contemporaries, Rimbaud strove in these works to capture the reality which is absent from the familiar world. Characteristically, he chose extreme means. Having asserted that the poet must be a seer, 'un voyant', he added: 'Il s'agit d'arriver à l'inconnu par le dérèglement de tous les sens.' If this disordered sensory ferment is the means of experiencing ultimate reality, its literary expression depends on verbal magic. This explains the quite marvellous use of language in *Les Illuminations* and *Une Saison en enfer*. It also accounts for the failure of his ambitions. Rimbaud walked alone to the utmost frontier of symbolism, found that language could not capture his vision, and renounced poetry.

The life of Stéphane Mallarmé (1842–98) was the opposite of Rimbaud's or Verlaine's in its respectable uneventfulness. A literary ascetic and a master-craftsman, he pursued the absent reality of the Idea through the intellect rather than the senses and wrote poems that are beautifully finished and highly enigmatic verbal structures. A few early poems such as 'Brise marine' are not difficult. Others, including such well-known sonnets as 'Le vierge, le vivace et le bel aujourd'hui' or 'Ses purs ongles très haut dédiant leur onyx', have given rise to many different interpretations. Perhaps his most outstanding achievement is to be found in the longer poems such as the unfinished *Hérodiade* (1864–7),

L'Après-midi d'un faune (1876) and *Un Coup de dés jamais n'abolira le hasard* (1897). He states the theory behind such poems as follows: 'Nommer un objet, c'est supprimer la jouissance du poème, qui est faite du bonheur de deviner peu à peu; le suggérer, voilà le rêve. C'est le parfait usage de ce mystère qui constitue le symbole.' This statement (which Verlaine might have signed), together with Mallarmé's distinction between language as 'signe' and as 'organisme dépositaire de la vie', may remind us that his poetry demands a response that goes beyond the limits of logical discourse and strictly rational meaning.

Among the many other poets associated with the symbolist movement three in particular deserve mention. The Comte de Lautréamont – pseudonym of Isidore Ducasse (1846–70) – wrote a set of strikingly original and hallucinatory prose-poems, *Les Chants de Maldoror* (1868). Their mixture of fantasy and fury, blasphemy and sadism, later caused the surrealists to rehabilitate Lautréamont as a precursor, a 'figure éblouissante de lumière noire' as Breton described him. Tristan Corbière (1845–75) is best remembered for his collection, *Les Amours jaunes* (1873), the work of a 'poète maudit' who wrote of himself: 'Son goût était dans le dégoût'. He wrote sardonic, staccato poems in which love and seafaring are the main themes. As for Jules Laforgue (1860–87), his ironical melancholy, his highly personal and unconventional poetic vocabulary, and his use of free verse – e.g. *Les Complaintes* (1885) – influenced a number of later poets including the young T. S. Eliot.

Symbolism also had an impact on the theatre, partly by way of reaction against commercial plays and *pièces à thèse*. The new drama found a sympathetic response in the 1890s from Paul Fort's relatively short-lived Théâtre de l'Art and Lugné-Poë's Théâtre de l'Oeuvre. The two playwrights of lasting interest associated with the movement are Villiers de l'Isle-Adam (1838–89) and Maurice Maeterlinck (1862–1949). The former's *Axël* (1890) combines symbolist qualities with the trappings of decadent Romanticism. The latter's *Pelléas et Mélisande* (1892) has the strengths and weaknesses of symbolist aesthetics when practised in the theatre.

Public Themes and Private Concerns

Looking back on a given historical period one is struck by the number of writers whose published work fails to fit any of the major categories suggested by historians of literature. This is true of many relatively minor literary figures active during the closing decades of the nineteenth century and the early years of the twentieth. Nevertheless, such novelists as Vallès, Bourget and Renard, while neither naturalists nor symbolists, share an intense dissatisfaction with the public standards of their age.

It has been said of Jules Vallès (1832–85) that 'la bohème et l'anarchie composaient son univers'. He led an impoverished life as journalist and political agitator and his fiercely uncompromising left-wing attitude is reflected in all that he did and wrote – from participation in the Republican 'manifestations' at Nantes in 1848 (at the age of fifteen) to his fictional trilogy, *Jacques Vingtras* (1879–86). In some ways he was a kind of prose Rimbaud, though moved to violent and revolutionary positions by social rather than metaphysical anger. The three 'Jacques Vingtras' novels, *L'Enfant* (1879), *Le Bachelier* (1881) and *L'Insurgé* (1886), express savage indignation at the society of his day and a fierce pity for the socially oppressed.

Paul Bourget (1852–1935) was a very different kind of writer who, towards the end of his life, sympathized with the highly conservative Catholicism of the Action Française. The dominant influence of Taine is clear in his two series of *Essais de psychologie contemporaine* (1883 and 1886), but his subsequent writings, particularly his best-known novels, *Le Disciple* (1889) and *L'Étape* (1902), reject the conclusions of progressive positivism. A certain kind of 'freethinking' ethic, related to materialistic and atheistic assumptions, causes misery and tragedy in both *Le Disciple* and *L'Étape*. It was Bourget's ambitious aim to establish an intellectual position which would reveal 'l'identité entre la loi de l'Église et la loi de la réalité, entre l'enseignement de l'éxpérience et celui de la Révélation'.

We return, with Jules Renard (1864–1910), to social rather than philosophical dissatisfaction, particularly in the one novel by which he is still remembered, *Poil de carotte* (1894). This story of an unhappy boyhood becomes the vehicle for an attack on the adult society of his day. Nevertheless, Renard lacked the energetic anger of a Vallès and his ambiguous position – part critical and part escapist – is illustrated by the *Histoires naturelles* (1896) – portraits of birds and animals to which he brought outstanding gifts of observation, fantasy and humour.

There is an element of Romantic *évasion* in the exotic novels of Pierre Loti – pseudonym of Julien Viaud (1850–1923) – whose career as a sailor took him to many parts of the world. Travel and writing became forms of temporary distraction from the ineluctable fact of death. The two activities resulted in novels which convey a richly poetic picture of faraway settings for unhappy love-affairs, e.g. *Aziyadé* (1879), *Le Mariage de Loti* (1880), *Rarahu* (1880), *Madame Chrysanthème* (1887), *Ramuntcho* (1897) and *Les Désenchantées* (1906). These romantic stories enjoy little favour nowadays, though Loti's novel of Breton fishing life, *Pêcheur d'Islande* (1886), remains a minor classic. Escape of a somewhat different kind into the world of childhood make-believe and adolescent love is found in another, later minor classic. This is *Le Grand Meaulnes* (1913) by Alain-Fournier, pseudonym of Henri-Alban Fournier (1886–1914). Fournier's aim, and eventual achievement, in the novel are put succinctly in a letter of 1906: 'Mon credo en art et en littérature: l'enfance. Arriver à la rendre sans aucune puérilité, avec sa profondeur qui touche les mystères.'

Two poets who developed along very different paths are the Belgian Verhaeren and the Béarnais Jammes. Émile Verhaeren (1855–1916) has often been compared with Walt Whitman both on account of his handling of free verse and his vision of democratic fraternity. He wrote some fine love poetry towards the end of his life but is usually associated with more public themes, inspired by socialist ideals and the problems and achievements of industrial progress, to be found in such collections as *Les Villes tentaculaires* (1895), *Les Forces tumultueuses* (1902) and *La Multiple Splendeur* (1906). He was a poet who could justifiably claim: 'Mon cœur, je l'ai rempli du beau tumulte humain.' Francis Jammes (1868–1938), on the contrary, is above all a poet of private simplicities filtered through a tender, melancholy, humorous and original sensibility. He writes of humble people and country life in *De l'angélus de l'aube à l'angélus du soir* (1898). A rediscovered Christian faith adds a further dimension to *Les Géorgiques chrétiennes* (1911) which seek to convey 'la beauté que Dieu donne à la vie ordinaire'.

In the history of the French theatre the closing years of the nineteenth century were a relatively impoverished period. One may mention the well-made, essentially superficial, plays of Victorien Sardou (1831–1908), the sometimes pretentious psychological dramas of Georges de Porto-Riche (1849–1930), the mechanical, farcical comedies of Georges Courteline (1858–1929) and Georges Feydeau (1862–1921), and the neo-Romantic theatre of Edmond Rostand (1868–1918) including *Cyrano de Bergerac* (1897) and *L'Aiglon* (1900).

Politics and Polemics

In 1894 Captain Alfred Dreyfus was arrested, tried and convicted on a charge of passing French military secrets to the Germans. The famous 'Affair' which followed lasted until 1906. In the years leading up to the quashing of the 1894 verdict Dreyfus, who was Jewish, became a symbol around which the contending forces of Left and Right waged a fierce ideological battle. The anti-military, anti-clerical Left – the Dreyfusards – pressed for revision. Zola, Proust, Renard, Péguy and Anatole France, among many others, were identified in varying degrees with Dreyfusism. The conservative, Catholic Right defended authority and the honour of the army, claiming that the nation was in danger of being undermined by atheists, Jews and freemasons. Among prominent anti-Dreyfusards were Barrès, Déroulède, Maurras and the critic Jules Lemaître. The turn of the century thus became a period of intense social and political conflict and its leading literary figures were France, Péguy, Barrès and Bloy.

It has never been seriously questioned that Anatole France, pseudonym of Anatole-François Thibault (1844–1924), was a master of clear and stylish French prose. Nevertheless he has often been dismissed – perhaps too easily – as a shallow, smiling sceptic of very limited moral and intellectual qualities. There is some justification for this judgement in his early work, but a notable change occurred after 1895 under the impact of the Dreyfus case. Apart from *L'Affaire Crainquebille* (1902), a novel about wrongful imprisonment, the four novels forming *L'Histoire contemporaine* (1896–1901) pillory the army, the Church, royalist politics and the anti-Semitism of the day. However, France's humane and rational socialism itself became qualified, in the three major novels of his maturity, by increasing pessimism about man. *L'Île des pingouins* (1908) despairs of social progress; *Les Dieux ont soif* (1912) finds an appalling human capacity for fanatical cruelty exemplified by the Jacobins during the French Revolution; *La Révolte des anges* (1914) bitterly satirizes Christianity.

Charles Péguy (1873–1914) was also prominent in the Dreyfusard cause and lived through the intellectual confrontations of the age with exemplary honesty. It was in fact this honesty, not lack of integrity, which compelled him to step across party divisions and espouse apparently opposite causes: internationalism and patriotism, anti-clericalism and devout Catholicism, republicanism and political conservatism. This pluralism of outlook marks the *Cahiers de la quinzaine* (1900–14) in which he published work by Anatole France, Romain Rolland and others, as well as his own major journalism and poetry. In *Notre Jeunesse* (1910) he defended the Dreyfusism of his earlier years while attacking those Dreyfusards who reduced this *mystique* to a *politique*, i.e. to the vulgar level of political manœuvring. Before his death in battle in 1914 he gave passionate mystical expression to his patriotism and deep religious sense in poems of epic length such as *Ève* (1914), and in three prose poems: *Le Mystère de la charité de Jeanne d'Arc* (1910), *Le Porche du mystère de la deuxième vertu* (1911) and *Le Mystère des saints innocents* (1912).

The most influential and gifted writer in the anti-Dreyfusard camp was Maurice Barrès (1862–1923). His journalism and novels confront socialist collectivism with a passionate defence of individual independence (in his trilogy, *Le Culte du moi*, 1888–91) and later of traditionalist and nationalist values (in a second trilogy, *Le Roman de l'énergie nationale*, 1897–1902). Though not possessing Péguy's profound religious sense, Barrès saw Catholicism as a necessary element both of traditionalism and nationalism. Also, as a Lorrainer, he preached a war of revenge for the lost provinces of Alsace and Lorraine. The articles written during World War I were in the same spirit. Barrès was instrumental in providing his generation with a partly rational, partly mystical, basis for right-wing views. The genuinely original literary gifts which he brought to this task are seen at their best in one of his later and finest novels, *La Colline inspirée* (1913).

Like Péguy and Barrès, Léon Bloy (1846–1917) was a man of passionate conviction. Though much less directly involved in political polemics, his unorthodox Catholicism proved fiercely intransigent in social and moral matters. He stigmatized contemporary society as 'athée, renégate, apostate, sacrilège, parricide, infanticide'. When a fire at the Bazar de la Charité in 1897 resulted in 125 members of high society being burned alive, he only regretted that the number of victims had not been greater. Such violent hatred can be explained, though not excused, by his horror of contemporary materialism, his feeling for the despair of the socially oppressed, his mystical cult of poverty as necessary to salvation. These themes dominate his chaotic and visionary novels, *Le Désespéré* (1886) and *La Femme pauvre* (1897). In this last novel Clotilde Maréchal formulates Bloy's own conviction when she exclaims: 'Il n'y a qu'une tristesse, c'est de N'ÊTRE PAS DES SAINTS'. His conception of sanctity, however, was the reverse of the *bien-pensant*'s cosy vision.

Four New Masters

Proust, Gide, Valéry and Claudel, all born within four years of one another, came to maturity in the 1890s and dominated the first three decades of this century. With the possible exception of Gide, they are all major writers of European importance.

The early life of Marcel Proust (1871–1922) gave little indication that he was destined to become the greatest French novelist of the twentieth century. During the 1890s he appeared to be a rather affected frequenter of various fashionable Parisian *salons*, an aesthete and dilettante who suffered from ill-health and wrote intelligent but essentially ephemeral essays on art, literature and high society. These articles were eventually collected in *Les Plaisirs et les jours* (1896), *Pastiches et mélanges* (1919) and the posthumously published *Chroniques* (1927). He also underwent a period of intense enthusiasm for Ruskin's 'religion of beauty'. His translations of Ruskin, done with considerable difficulty, are *La Bible d'Amiens* (1904) and *Sésame et les lys* (1906). We now know that during this early period Proust was also observing, with a sharp and often satiric eye, the very social circles with which he himself was most closely identified. They were to provide much of the material for his study of the transformation of French society between the 1880s and the end of World War I – a study which is an important element in his vast novel. With his mother's death in 1905, and his own increasing ill-health, he retired to the famous cork-lined room in the Boulevard Haussmann and wrote the fifteen volumes of *A la recherche du temps perdu*.

The relatively late discovery of two collections of manuscripts – a novel, *Jean Santeuil* (1952) and some critical essays and imaginative prose, *Contre Sainte-Beuve suivi de Nouveaux mélanges* (1954) – makes it clear that Proust had actually begun work on his masterpiece some time in the 1890s. His deep emotional relationship with his mother probably proved an inhibiting factor, and he experienced other problems, but after 1905 he worked with increasing success, finished a first version in 1912 and published the opening section (*Du Côté de chez Swann*) at his own expense in 1913. Further publication was interrupted by the war but he revised his text until it grew from something like 1,200 pages to approximately 4,000. He continued to work on it right up to his death.

Proust's purpose in *A la recherche du temps perdu* (1913–27) can be summed up by Ruskin's phrase in *Stones of Venice*: '. . . what we want art to do for us is to stay what is fleeting, and to enlighten what is incomprehensive, to incorporate the things that have no measure, and immortalize the things that have no duration.' The Proustian world is one of flux and mystery, reflecting in artistic terms the contemporary rejection of rationalism and scientism by Bergson. The novel's narrator gradually learns to arrest time through the phenomenon of involuntary memory and, eventually, through his art. As he elucidates the previously hidden associations of some sense impression (eating a *madeleine* dipped in tea, gazing at a hawthorn hedge, etc.) he solves a mystery, relives a piece of the past, establishes the enduring nature of the self, and later discovers the creative principle of his novel. The self is also explored in relation to the phenomenon of love (both heterosexual and homosexual) which Proust analyses as a supreme form of self-deception rendered more bitter by inevitable jealousy and the failure to make genuine contact with another human being. As these explorations and discoveries progress through the novel they are linked with many counterpointed themes: art and life, society and the self, impressionism and symbolism, painting and music. Satire and humour, poetry and analytical intelligence, are used to create a remarkable range of fictional characters. Above all, Proust displays his greatness as a novelist through his creation of an autonomous, imaginative world to which we readily surrender yet which also illuminates profoundly our everyday experience. This illumination depends on language and style, as well as on vision. The importance which Proust gives to style, and his conception of it as an integral part of truth in art, are both evident when he writes in the final volume of his novel: '. . . la vérité ne commencera qu'au moment où l'écrivain prendra deux objets différents, posera leur rapport . . . et les enfermera dans les anneaux nécessaires d'un beau style'.

Proust and Gide (in common with Valéry) possessed outstanding gifts of intellectual analysis and artistic sensibility. Inevitably, these gifts took different forms. Whereas Proust died in his early fifties yet suggests a prematurely old man recapturing and reinterpreting the past, Gide died in his eighties yet possesses the attitudes and interests of a permanently young man probing and anticipating the future. Ironically, however, it was the reputation of the apparently forward-looking Gide which declined shortly after his death. Fashionable radicalism is notoriously transient and public attitudes, as well as public events, have overtaken Gide. His arguments against puritanism and colonialism, and in favour of sexual and social freedom, are now largely taken for granted. The 'liberator of youth' appears irrelevant to those who have long since lost their chains.

André Gide (1869–1951) had a strict Protestant upbringing and his frequently stated desire to 'disturb' his readers springs from a need to free himself from the inhibitions and prohibitions of a late nineteenth-century adolescence. His earliest writings show affinities with the symbolists, and his work of 'moral subversion' is first explicit in *Les Nourritures terrestres* (1897). Visits to North Africa in the preceding years had contributed much to his liberation from asceticism, and in the lyrical pages of *Les Nourritures* he exhorts an imaginary young man, Nathanaël, to rid himself of the Christian sense of sin and cultivate the life of the senses. He also teaches intensity of living ('Nathanaël, je t'enseignerai la ferveur'), horror of settled habits ('Ne *demeure* jamais, Nathanaël') and a comprehensive individualism ('Assumer le plus possible d'humanité'). Some assertions made by Gide in the book (e.g. 'Les idées nettes sont les plus dangereuses' or 'Il faut agir sans juger si l'action est bonne ou mauvaise') appear naïve or irresponsible viewed from the post-Auschwitz, post-Hiroshima world.

The puritan conscience is not easily eradicated, however, and Gide did not liberate himself completely. Much of his best writing, in fact, reflects a tension between the pagan and the puritan, between the teachings of Nietzsche and of the Bible. Two of his best *récits*, *L'Immoraliste* (1902) and *La Porte étroite* (1909), deal respectively with the themes of self-indulgence and self-denial. The conflict between them, causing a mixture of hypocrisy and self-deception, is movingly and delicately explored in *La Symphonie pastorale* (1919). The play, *Le Roi Candaule* (1901), swings right away from the viewpoint of *Les Nourritures* whereas the satirical and sometimes farcical tales which Gide termed *soties* – *Paludes* (1896), *Les Caves du Vatican* (1914), etc. – praise moral nonconformity. The latter work also contains the most notorious example of the famous Gidean *acte gratuit* – a murder committed for reasons of emotional and intellectual curiosity.

The term *roman* is applied to only one of the fictional works: *Les Faux-Monnayeurs* (1926). This is a clever, indeed over-clever, novel in which Gide breaks away from traditional French forms by means of a deliberately loose, untidy structure and characters which he refuses to 'explain' comprehensively to his readers. Distinctions between art and life are blurred by the fact that one of the characters, Édouard, is himself writing a novel entitled *Les Faux-Monnayeurs* and is keeping a literary diary which has the same title as that which Gide himself actually published: *Journal des Faux-Monnayeurs* (1926). Despite a determination to convey the 'openness' and disorder of actual experience, Gide's literary pyrotechnics finally produces an impression of extreme artificiality.

Gide's social conscience was first seriously stirred by his experience as a juror at a Criminal Assize Court in Normandy (*Souvenirs de la cour d'assises*, 1914). His conscience was further sharpened by ten months spent in Central Africa and his *Voyage au Congo* (1928) is sharply critical of European colonialism. The book has since been attacked for criticizing the *results* of colonialism rather than the *system* as such, and most of the judgements made are more moral than political, e.g. 'Moins le blanc est intelligent, plus le noir lui paraît bête'. The disillusion following Gide's short-lived admiration for communism is explained in *Retour de l'U.R.S.S.* (1936) and *Retouches à mon Retour de l'U.R.S.S.* (1937). Fundamentally, Gide was intensely self-absorbed and, in addition to an indirect apologia for his own homosexuality in *Corydon* (1923), he wrote a fascinating autobiography, *Si le grain ne meurt* (1926), and noted his reflexions on his reading and on his contemporaries in the *Journal* extending from 1889 to 1949.

Among the major European poets of this century – Rilke, Yeats, T. S. Eliot, etc. – Paul Valéry (1871–1945) is not the least important figure. It was due to the encouragement of Gide and Pierre Louÿs that he moved to Paris from his native Midi in the early 1890s. This was a crucial moment in his life since it brought him into direct contact with Mallarmé. The latter was to exercise a potent influence on Valéry's work and his early poems, later collected in *Album des vers anciens* (1920), display the intricate verbal melody and severe intellectuality of symbolism:

> Été, roche d'air pur, et toi, ardente ruche,
> Ô mer! Éparpillée en mille mouches sur
> Les touffes d'une chair fraîche comme une cruche,
> Et jusque dans la bouche où bourdonne l'azur . . .

Lines such as these remind us that Valéry's Apollonian severity does not exclude Dionysian elements containing a rich sensuality.

Despite some early success, Valéry was dissatisfied both with his own poetry and with literature in general. In 1892 he underwent an intellectual crisis in Genoa, the so-called 'nuit de Gênes', and for the next twenty years wrote almost no poetry. This 'silence' has been explained in several ways, but it seems most likely that Valéry decided to explore and cultivate the resources of his own mind rather than continue writing poetry. From an early date he had been interested in a wide range of subjects including psychology, mathematics and architecture; he even attempted to unify all human knowledge by means of mathematics. He possessed formidable intellectual tastes ('Les choses du monde ne m'intéressent que sous le rapport de l'intellect') and, though he produced no philosophical system, the workings of his mind can be followed in detail in the famous *Cahiers* (twenty-nine large volumes) begun in 1894. Two prose works, *Introduction à la méthode de Léonard de Vinci* (1895) and *La Soirée avec Monsieur Teste* (1896), show how much he was fascinated by intellectual universality. Other prose writings include two fine dialogues on Socratic lines, *Eupalinos ou l'architecte* (1921) and *L'Âme et la danse* (1921), while ten years later he published his acute *Regards sur le monde actuel.* In 1919 he had written a brief but penetrating essay on the contemporary world, 'La Crise de l'esprit', with its famous opening sentence: 'Nous autres, civilisations, nous savons maintenant que nous sommes mortelles.'

In 1912, under pressure from Gide among others, Valéry began to revise his early poems for collective publication (the eventual *Album des vers anciens*). He also started work on a long poem published in 1917 as *La Jeune Parque* and dedicated to Gide. This has been called the most difficult poem in the French language. According to its author, it is an attempt to achieve in words something akin to modulation in music. Verbal modulations catch the changes of a human consciousness during the course of a night, partly through the figure of a young woman ('La Jeune Parque') faced with problems of love and death. The kind of poetry that results, and the impossibility of reducing it to rational, discursive terms, are both suggested by Valéry's statement: '. . . plus un poème est conforme à la Poésie, moins il peut se penser en prose sans périr.'

Apart from some verse passages in *Mon Faust* (1941), Valéry's last significant poetry is contained in *Charmes* (1922). The title comes from the Latin *carmina*, songs or incantations, and the collection consists of twenty-one poems including such famous pieces as 'Fragments du Narcisse', 'Ébauche d'un serpent' and 'Le Cimetière marin'. Valéry considered that eight lines from the first of these three poems represented his most successful attempt to reach his own ideal of 'la poésie pure':

> Ô douceur de survivre à la force du jour,
> Quand elle se retire enfin rose d'amour,
> Encore un peu brûlante, et lasse, mais comblée,
> Et de tant de trésors tendrement accablée
> Par de tels souvenirs qu'ils empourprent sa mort,
> Et qu'ils la font heureuse agenouiller dans l'or,
> Puis s'étendre, se fondre, et perdre sa vendange,
> Et s'éteindre en un songe en qui le soir se change.

Generally, the poems of *Charmes* have a classical regularity justified by Valéry's claim that 'les exigences d'une stricte prosodie sont l'artifice qui confère au langage naturel les qualités d'une matière résistante'. They are poems written to endure by conferring formal perfection on a profound response to experience.

It is through his discovery of a completely satisfying spiritual and artistic inspiration within the limits of Roman Catholic orthodoxy that Paul Claudel (1868–1955) differs most significantly from his three distinguished contemporaries. The great certainties of the faith, as well as its central mysteries, pervade his best work both as poet and dramatist. According to his own account, Claudel was first made conscious of the *existence* of a supernatural world, and incidentally freed from nineteenth-century scientism, by reading Rimbaud's *Les Illuminations* and *Une Saison en enfer*. He found the *meaning* of this supernatural world in the Bible and Catholic teaching, particularly during the four years following a mystical experience in Notre-Dame-de-Paris while the 'Magnificat' was being sung on Christmas Day 1886. Later, his careful study of Thomist philosophy was to have a profound influence on his work. He also acknowledged different forms of indebtedness to Aeschylus, Dante, Shakespeare, Dostoevsky, etc.

Claudel was a diplomat by profession and his experience of the Far East prompted an outstanding prose-poem, *Connaissance de l'Est* (1900). This kind of writing, rather than the self-imposed formal severity of a Valéry, suited his genius best, and his poetry is almost all written in *versets*, irregular and cunningly used lines of which he wrote: 'Le verset est une ligne qui s'arrête, non parce qu'elle est arrivée à une frontière naturelle, et que l'espace lui manque, mais parce que son chiffre intérieur est accompli et que sa vertu est consommée.' The use to which he put the *verset* can be studied at its best in *Cinq Grandes Odes* (1910) and *Cantate à trois voix* (1914). In the following lines from the first of these collections Claudel's rich and buoyant lyricism issues in praise of God's immanence in the beauty and wonder of the physical and human worlds:

> Je vous salue, ô monde libéral à mes yeux!
> Je comprends par quoi vous êtes présent,
> C'est que l'Éternel est avec vous, et qu'où est la Créature,
>   le Créateur ne l'a point quittée.
> Je suis en vous et vous êtes à moi et votre possession est la
>   mienne,

Et maintenant en nous à la fin
Éclate le commencement,
Éclate le jour nouveau, éclate dans la possession de la source
je ne sais quelle jeunesse angélique!

Though a gifted lyric poet, Claudel is admired above all as an epic dramatist, combining the spoken exchanges of the theatre with high rhetorical forms in the tradition of Corneille. In view of the 'dialectic of salvation', the struggle between the flesh and the spirit which is central to Christianity, it is not surprising that he should have found the theatre a congenial medium. He writes in the interesting *Positions et propositions I* (1928): 'La foi fait vivre tout homme moderne dans un milieu essentiellement dramatique. . . . La vie est pour lui, non pas une série incohérente de gestes vagues et inachevés, mais un drame précis qui comporte un dénouement et un sens.' Of the dozen or so plays which he wrote (sometimes in two versions), the best are probably *Partage de midi* (1906), *L'Annonce faite à Marie* (1912) and *Le Soulier de satin* (1929 and 1944). These are not so much 'realistic' works as rhetorical meditations on religious themes. Although some of the plays fail to convince us as psychology, *Partage de midi* is both a moving portrayal of adulterous love and an exploration of the means whereby sexual love may be transmuted into love of God. Mesa's return to God, through Ysé, causes him to exclaim in Act III:

Ah! je sais maintenant
Ce que c'est que l'amour! et je sais ce que vous avez
endurée sur votre croix, dans ton Cœur,
Si vous avez aimé chacun de nous
Terriblement comme j'ai aimé cette femme, et le râle,
et l'asphyxie, et l'étau . . .

This 'evangelization of the flesh' is also a central theme in *Le Soulier de satin* – a lengthy, ambitious work which projects the drama of body and spirit on to an enormous canvas that includes sixteenth-century Europe, Africa and America. The beautifully written *L'Annonce faite à Marie* has a medieval setting of miracles, mysteries and exemplary self-immolation. The events of the play are held together by the doctrine of substitution, the idea that all human beings live in a state of spiritual interdependence which gives purpose and meaning to suffering and evil.

The Growth of the Avant-Garde

The closing years of the nineteenth century are notable for change and innovation in many spheres of French life. With the founding of the trade-union movement, the Confédération Générale du Travail, in 1895, industrial society came of age. By the end of the century the bitter conflicts and unsavoury revelations of the Dreyfus Affair had dealt severe blows to the authority of both the army and the Church. At the same time, applied science was making rapid progress. In 1900, when the Eiffel Tower had already dominated the Parisian skyline for eleven years, the electric light bulb appeared at the International Exhibition and the Paris *métro* began its underground life. Significant co-operation between technology and art dates from the same year when Georges Méliès set up a film studio at Montreuil.

In the early 1870s Rimbaud had declared: 'Il faut être absolument moderne.' Even earlier, Lautréamont had given lessons in modernity to a restricted audience. Nevertheless, the growth of the artistic avant-garde is chiefly associated with the decade preceding World War I. In music, Satie and Roussel were active. In painting, the Salon d'Automne of 1905 revealed fauvism, Picasso completed 'Les Demoiselles d'Avignon' in 1907, and almost immediately afterwards he and Braque developed their particular forms of cubism. In literature, modernism was chiefly associated with poetry. New attitudes and new forms were cultivated by Jacob, by Cendrars and, above all, by Apollinaire. Literary innovation was made easier, however, by the earlier work of Alfred Jarry (1873–1907) whose play *Ubu Roi* (1896) remains a notable avant-garde landmark.

Ubu Roi, one of several 'Ubu' works, has the virtues and faults of a certain kind of avant-garde writing. It is a violent farce which caricatures human greed, cruelty and cowardice. The atmosphere suggests both the blind destructiveness and the freewheeling imagination of an ungovernable child. Ferocity and fantasy, crude language and lavatory jokes, combine to place it in a curious no-man's-land between precocious adolescence and retarded manhood. Jarry's posthumously published *Gestes et opinions du Docteur Faustroll* (1911) is his other claim to fame. This 'neo-scientific' prose fantasy outlines his doctrine of 'pataphysics' (a science going as far beyond metaphysics as metaphysics extends beyond physics) and was later much admired by the surrealists.

The work by Jarry was enthusiastically acclaimed by Guillaume Apollinaire (1880–1918) for its 'débauches de l'intelligence'. This response was in keeping with his own role as, in André Billy's phrase, 'prince de l'esprit moderne'. As prose-writer and art critic, as well as poet, Apollinaire sought to understand and reflect the scientific advances and intellectual innovations of the new century. His collection of stories, *Le Poète assassiné* (1916), explores the significance and status of poetry in the modern world. Essays such as *Les Peintres cubistes* and *L'Esprit nouveau et les poètes* explain and advocate modernism. Surrealist fantasy, recalling Jarry, animates his play *Les Mamelles de Tirésias* (1917).

Apollinaire's first collection of poems, *Alcools* (1913), apart from its experimental aspect, also contains traditionalist poetic forms with symbolist overtones and reveals him as a major love poet. His range varies from the lyric perfection of 'Le Pont Mirabeau' to the positive modernity of 'Zone' ('Bergère ô tour Eiffel le troupeau des ponts bêle ce matin'). Unexpected juxtapositions, simultaneity and discontinuity, a conversational tone and surrealist imagery, are all techniques of modernism carried over into *Calligrammes* (1918) which, as the title suggests, contains poems set out typographically in pictural form. The final poem of the collection, 'La Jolie Rousse', is a moving poetic testament suggesting that Apollinaire wished to be a 'modern' without vilifying an earlier literary tradition:

> Soyez indulgents quand vous nous comparez
> A ceux qui furent la perfection de l'ordre
> Nous qui quêtons partout l'aventure
>
> Nous ne sommes pas vos ennemis
> Nous voulons vous donner de vastes et d'étranges domaines
> Où le mystère en fleurs s'offre à qui veut le cueillir

Apollinaire's innovations were later surpassed by those of the Dadaist and surrealist movements. Nevertheless, he invented the term 'surrealism' and Breton's *Manifeste du surréalisme* (1924) was dedicated to him. He is a genuine experimenter who deservedly became a classic.

Two other poets, Max Jacob (1876–1944) and Blaise Cendrars – pseudonym of Frédéric Sauser (1887–1961) – should be mentioned. Jacob was an early friend of Apollinaire and Picasso, sharing their avant-garde struggles. He opposed reason and tradition in art with irony and humour, parody and burlesque. He is best known for the prose poems of *Cornet à Dès* (1917). Conversion to a highly personal and unconventional faith prompted him to live in seclusion from 1921 onwards. His otherworldliness is summed up in the last two lines of a poem written some time before his death in the Drancy concentration camp:

> Je suis mourant d'avoir compris
> que notre terre n'est d'aucun prix.

Cendrars wrote a number of novels including *Moravagine* (1926) and *Les Confessions de Dan Yack* (2 vols: 1927, 1929). Many of his poems, like his novels, reflect his wide travels. The title poem of the collection *Prose du Transsibérien* (1913) is also a literary collage using techniques of juxtaposition, discontinuity and simultaneity which recall Apollinaire. These techniques create an impression of confused and animated city life in the following lines:

> Il pleut des globes électriques
> Montrouge Gare de l'Est Métro Nord-Sud bateaux-mouches
>   monde
> Tout est halo
> Profondeur
> Rue de Buci on crie *l'Intransigeant* et *Paris-Sports*
> L'aérodrome du ciel est maintenant, embrasé, un tableau
>   de Cimabué.

Literature and World War I

World War I broke out at a moment when intensive patriotism was already a notable theme among some of the most influential French writers. In an earlier section reference was made to Péguy's mystical love of France and Barrès's call for the return of Alsace and Lorraine. To these names should be added that of Ernest Psichari (1883–1914) whose novels, particularly *L'Appel des armes* (1913), seek a common order and tradition in the established values of the army and the Church. *L'Appel des armes* was dedicated to Péguy and owes a clear literary debt both to him and to Barrès. The fact that patriotic and military sentiments were widespread among young Frenchmen in the immediate pre-war years was confirmed and analysed in *Les Jeunes Gens d'aujourd'hui* published by Henri Massis and Alfred de Tarde in 1913. It is not surprising that the effect of war itself was to sharpen such feelings. Patriotic verse and prose became the order of the day. On the other hand, such writing rarely achieves high literary quality. In particular, poetry and patriotism coexist at the expense of the former – at least in the modern world – and evidence of this can be found in such collections as Jammes's *Cinq Poèmes pour le temps de la guerre* (1916), Verhaeren's *Les Ailes rouges de la guerre* (1917), Rostand's *Le Vol de la Marseillaise* (1919) and Claudel's *Poèmes de guerre 1914–1916* (1922). The fact that Claudel attempted to read a fundamental spiritual meaning into the conflict between France and Germany did not save him from either bombast or bathos.

Poetry of protest against the war, such as that written in England by Wilfred Owen or Siegfried Sassoon, scarcely existed in France. There is no major French war poet and the best poetry written on the battlefield turns out, surprisingly perhaps, to be that of Apollinaire. The poems he wrote at the front are mainly collected in *Calligrammes* (1918) and the posthumously published *Ombre de mon amour* which appeared in 1948. The experience of war heightened Apollinaire's sense of mortality, intensified his love affairs, and provided a new range of aesthetic experiences. The opening stanza of a poem from this period brings together his pathos and his aestheticism:

> Si je mourrais là-bas sur le front de l'armée,
> Tu pleurerais un jour, ô Lou, ma bien-aimée,
> Et puis mon souvenir s'éteindrait comme meurt
> Un obus éclatant sur le front de l'armée,
> Un bel obus semblable aux mimosas en fleur.

The last three lines of the same poem show that Apollinaire, the conscious manipulator of words and typography, could also express with simplicity and economy the fearful destiny of his generation:

> La nuit descend,
> On y present
> Un long, un long destin de sang.

It is clear that something at once as unique and appalling as trench warfare provided novelists with a new subject for realistic description as well as arousing moral horror and revulsion. These two responses are present in what was undoubtedly the major French novel of warfare at this period – *Le Feu* (1916) by Henri Barbusse (1873–1935). It is a violent book on a violent subject, containing a Zola-like sense of physical detail together with anger at 'des choses épouvantables faites par 30 millions d'hommes qui ne le veulent pas'. Later, Barbusse developed much further the mixture of pacifism and revolutionary Marxism already implicit in this novel. His post-war writings, however, stayed at the level of radical journalism and ended ingloriously with adulatory biographies of Lenin and Stalin. Another war novel which made a considerable impact on publication is *Les Croix de bois* (1919) by Roland Dorgelès – the pseudonym of Roland Lecavelé (1886–1973). Dorgelès's descriptive powers recall those of Barbusse though they are accompanied by a certain sentimentality foreign to *Le Feu*. Authentic non-heroism also has its place, summed up by the statement: 'J'trouve que c'est une victoire, parce que j'en suis sorti vivant.' Perhaps the most humane protest – one which saw the war as a terrible failure on the part of Western civilization – is to be found in *Vie des martyrs* (1917) and the ironically entitled *Civilisation* (1918) by Georges Duhamel (1884–1966). Such novels illustrate 'l'illusion perdue d'une culture européenne' of which Valéry wrote. Among the many other novelists who published during the war, mention should be made of Maurice Genevoix (b. 1890). Five of his novels were collected and reprinted in 1950 under the title *Ceux de 14*.

Inevitably, a number of writers preferred to digest their experiences more slowly and published retrospective novels aiming at something more intellectually ambitious than direct reportage or instant protest. Three such writers are Henry de Montherlant (1896–1972), Jules Romains (the pseudonym of Louis Farigoule, 1885–1972) and Roger Martin du Gard (1881–1958). Montherlant's *Le Songe* (1922) is a distinctive, often lyrical, meditation on the themes of love, war and death as well as an exploration of the relationship between thought and action. Characteristically, his reaction to the experience of war combines the contrasting emotions of exultation and horror. War provides the main descriptive set-pieces of *Le Songe*, yet something of its wider scope is suggested by the question on which it ends: 'Le désir est incomplet. L'amitié manque de viscères. L'amour tel qu'on l'entend d'ordinaire est une infériorité. Qui me tirera une tendresse qui vient du fond de mes entrailles et que j'approuve pourtant de toute ma raison?' In the case of Jules Romains, the novels *Prélude à Verdun* (1937) and *Verdun* (1938) form part of an enormous *roman-fleuve* – *Les Hommes de bonne volonté* (1932–46) – in which the war is related to wider aspects of French society and history between 1908 and 1933. Roger Martin du Gard was also the author of a *roman-fleuve* – *Les Thibault* (1922–40). The section of this work entitled *L'Été 1914* (1936) dramatically evokes Europe on the brink of war. For Martin du Gard the experience of 1914–18 both made him an ardent pacifist and destroyed the faith in progressive rationalism which had characterized his first major novel, *Jean Barois* (1913).

Surrealism

The fact that Apollinaire invented the adjective *surréaliste* serves as a reminder that this movement of conscious irrationality had its roots in the pre-war avant-garde. The further fact that the most glorious days of surrealism spanned the decade following World War I suggests a connection between this attack on logic and reason and the crisis of confidence in the established order brought about by the events of 1914–18. In fact, as early as 1916, a group of young writers and artists, mostly pacifists and revolutionaries by instinct, had launched the so-called Dadaist movement from Zürich in neutral Switzerland. The *Manifeste Dada 1918* by Tristan Tzara (1896–1963) proclaimed the liberation of literature and art from all logic, scorned bourgeois notions of order and meaning, and characterized the contemporary world as one of disaster and decomposition. These now familiar ideas were warmly welcomed by André Breton (1896–1966), the future leader of French surrealism, and his associates including Philippe Soupault (b. 1897) and Louis Aragon (b. 1897). After the war Breton and Tzara joined forces in Paris but disagreements developed between them. In 1924 the first issue of the periodical *La Révolution surréaliste* (1924–9) marked both the end of Dadaism and the foundation of surrealism as a distinctive movement.

Breton's first *Manifeste du surréalisme* (1924) is a statement, appropriately iconoclastic and incoherent, of the movement's aims. These were neo-Dadaist in so far as they sought to ridicule the cultural certainties of a society which had ended in the cataclysm of 1914–18. The inherent violence and absurdity of this rational, ordered society were to be countered by violence and absurdity in art. More particularly, Breton had been influenced by Freud's ideas and he elaborated a theory of the truth and freedom to be obtained by automatic writing (liberated from all moral and aesthetic constraints) and the cultivation of dreams. Later, in *Le Surréalisme et la peinture* (1928), Breton extended his theories to the visual arts and with his second manifesto a year later identified the surrealist adventure with the aims of Marxism. This manifesto, published in the only issue of *La Révolution surréaliste* to appear in 1929, marks the beginning of Breton's ultimately unsuccessful attempt to reconcile the authoritarian programme of the French Communist Party with the mysticism and imaginative freedom inherent in surrealist theory and practice. This mysticism is indicated – it could hardly be precisely defined – in a famous passage in the manifesto:

> Tout porte à croire qu'il existe un certain point de l'esprit d'où la vie et la mort, le réel et l'imaginaire, le passé et le futur, le communicable et l'incommunicable, le haut et le bas, cessent d'être perçus contradictoirement. Or c'est en vain qu'on chercherait à l'activité surréaliste un autre mobile que l'espoir de détermination de ce point.

In fact, Breton's later theoretical works stick to this position and move away from that 'conformisme stalinien' with which he taxed the Communist Party in 1935. Similarly, when Aragon broke with surrealism to become a totally committed Communist, Benjamin Peret – co-editor with Pierre Naville of *La Révolution surréaliste* – described the move as one from the status of *poète* to that of *agent de publicité*.

As might be guessed, the temperaments of writers attracted by surrealism tended to break them up into warring factions or encouraged them to pursue highly individual paths. Individuals differed a good deal in their ideas and in the manner in which these ideas were expressed. In many ways, the movement remains more impressive as a collective phenomenon than as a series of separate, individual achievements. Indeed, the movement has tended to denounce the cult of personal authorship. It may also be said that the chief manifestations of surrealism have been in poetry, painting and the cinema. Nevertheless, a tradition of novel-writing also exists. Raymond Roussel (1877–1933) laid the foundations of the surrealist novel (and drama) with such early works as *Impressions d'Afrique* (1910), *Locus solus* (1914) and *L'Étoile au front* (1925). The tradition was continued by Aragon's *Le Paysan de Paris* (1926) and Breton's *Nadja* (1928), while more recent surrealist fiction includes *Au Château d'Argol* (1939), *Un Beau ténébreux* (1945), *Le Rivage des Syrtes* (1951) by Julien Gracq (b. 1910) and *Le Lis de mer* (1956) and *La Motocyclette* (1963) by André Pieyre de Mandiargues (b. 1909).

As regards poetry, one of the most constant features has been the bringing together of unexpected and apparently unconnected images. In *L'Amour la poésie* (1929) Paul Éluard (1895–1952), the major poet of the movement, wrote: 'Les ressemblances ne sont pas en rapport. Elles se heurtent.' Something of his own achievement can be seen in a short love poem from an earlier collection, *Capitale de la douleur* (1926):

> Ta chevelure d'oranges dans le vide du monde,
> Dans le vide des vitres lourdes de silence
> Et d'ombre où mes mains cherchent tous tes reflets.

La forme de ton cœur est chimérique
Et ton amour ressemble à mon désir perdu.
Ô soupirs d'ambre, rêves, regards.

Mais tu n'as pas toujours été avec moi. Ma mémoire
Est encore obscurcie de t'avoir vue venir
Et partir. Le temps se sert de mots comme l'amour.

Such poetry does not simply reflect a mood; it creates an independent, self-authenticating aesthetic structure. It also creates a 'surreality' which is offered as the royal road to a new knowledge spanning (as in much primitive art) the traditional gap between subjective and objective reality.

Surrealism has always had both its serious and its leg-pulling aspects. Writers as diverse as Breton and Éluard, Roussel and Soupault, René Crevel (1900–35) and Robert Desnos (1900–45) have produced pessimism and *le merveilleux*, blasphemy and *humour noir*, praise of insanity and a *beauté convulsive*. Today, the success of surrealism may be measured by the extent to which it has become an integral part of our contemporary sensibility. Its failure lies in the fact that it has proved a symptom rather than a cure, reflecting and reinforcing the social and moral confusion against which it originally reacted.

Inter-War Theatre

The period 1918–39 was one of original producers and enterprising dramatists. The former category includes Jacques Copeau, Jacques Hébertot and the anti-naturalist 'Cartel des quatre': Georges Pitöeff, Charles Dullin, Louis Jouvet and Gaston Baty. The dramatists who have lasted best are Jean Giraudoux (1882–1944), Jean Cocteau (1889–1963) and Jean Anouilh (b. 1910). Producers and playwrights combined to encourage poetic drama, fantasy and mime, to simplify or stylize stage scenery, to regard the 'well-made' play with suspicion, to create what Baty called 'une zone de mystère'.

It is no exaggeration to say, however, that the French stage was dominated, at least during the 1930s, by Giraudoux and Jouvet – a collaboration that began with the production of *Siegfried* (1928) and extended to *La Folle de Chaillot* (1945). It also included *Amphitryon 38* (1929), *Intermezzo* (1933), *La Guerre de Troie n'aura pas lieu* (1935), *Électre* (1937) and *Ondine* (1939). Giraudoux's qualities are indicated by the adjectives most commonly used by French critics to describe his talent: 'paradoxal', 'raffiné', 'précieux'. His is above all a theatre of verbal magic, a literary theatre clothed in original, poetic language. Beneath a brilliant surface created by irony and wit, verbal subtlety and delicate, luminous speech, there exist a preoccupation with fundamental human qualities and what is often a tragic vision. Such concerns are fed by the subject-matter which Giraudoux mostly derived from mythological, classical or biblical sources. The conflict between human and supernatural values is the central theme of *Amphitryon 38*, while questions of war and peace, of sacred and profane love, of freedom and compromise, pervade *La Guerre de Troie*, *Judith* (1931) and *Électre* respectively. Something of Giraudoux's pride in human limitation is seen in the opening lines of Alcmène's statement to Jupiter in *Amphitryon 38*:

> Je ne crains pas la mort. C'est l'enjeu de la vie. Puisque ton Jupiter, à tort ou à raison, a créé la mort sur la terre, je me solidarise avec mon astre. Je sens trop mes fibres continuer celles des autres hommes, des animaux, même des plantes, pour ne pas mourir tant qu'il n'y aura pas un légume immortel. Devenir immortel, c'est trahir, pour un humain . . .

This passage, though incomplete, also reminds us that Giraudoux created a theatre of eloquent monologues. The lengthy *tirade* has a major role in his work as in the verbal encounters between Hector and Ulysse that are a memorable feature of *La Guerre de Troie*. In many of the plays these long speeches exchanged between characters are less a debate than what has been called 'an aesthetic equilibrium between contrary definitions'. Ultimately, the characters use language to account for the world in terms that reach the mind through the imagination.

Jean Cocteau possessed an astonishingly rich diversity of talents. His achievements include those of poet, playwright, actor, film director, choreographer, book illustrator and artist in glass and ceramics. He fulfilled a variety of innovating roles on the inter-war scene and must be regarded as an important and gifted *animateur* who finally lacked that intense concentration of talent which characterizes most of the greatest artists. As a man of the theatre, he began with a number of ballets, particularly *Parade* (1917) of which he wrote the scenario with settings by Picasso, music by Satie and choreography by Massine. For *Les Mariés de la Tour Eiffel* (1921) Cocteau himself provided the choreography with music by 'les Six' (i.e. Auric, Durey, Honegger,

Milhaud, Poulenc and Taillefer). In *La Machine infernale* (1934) – a witty reworking of the Oedipus legend – and in other plays such as *Les Chevaliers de la Table Ronde* (1937) and *Les Parents terribles* (1938), as well as in a series of experimental films from *Le Sang d'un poète* (1932) to *Orphée* (1949), Cocteau displays imagination, sophistication and technical ingenuity as he explores the role of the poet, the tragic nature of love, the traps set by life for youth, purity and idealism.

It was from Giraudoux rather than Cocteau that Anouilh learnt 'qu'on pouvait avoir au théâtre une langue poétique et artificielle qui demeure plus vraie que la conversation sténographique.' Inventiveness and stylization mark his plays and, although a less gifted poet than either of his seniors, Anouilh outstrips them in terms of a quite brilliant mastery of stage technique. In splendidly constructed plays he uses comedy and tragedy, wit and cynicism, to convey his disenchanted vision – and particularly the imperious, yet finally fruitless, rebellion of the young on behalf of purity and against mediocrity, ugliness and compromise. Characteristic works among the earlier plays are such 'pièces roses' or 'pièces brillantes' as *Le Bal des Voleurs* (1932), *Le Rendez-vous de Senlis* (1937), *La Répétition* (1950) and such 'pièces noires' as *La Sauvage* (1934) and *Antigone* (1944). In some other plays, particularly *Le Voyageur sans bagage* (1937), *Léocadia* (1939) and *L'Invitation au château* (1947), the bitterness, whether expressed as comedy or tragedy, gives way to what appears as a scarcely logical happy ending – a reflection of Anouilh's claim that art itself can impose satisfactory form on a fatally flawed existence. Plays written after 1950 and deserving mention are *L'Alouette* (1952), a lyrical treatment of the Joan of Arc theme, *Pauvre Bitos* (1956), an attack on ideological murder by tyrants of both Left and Right, and *Becket, ou l'Honneur de Dieu* (1959), a superficial work when compared with Eliot's *Murder in the Cathedral.*

Among the many other plays written during this period, mention should be made of the comedies of Jules Romains – e.g. *Monsieur Le Trouhadec saisi par la débauche* (1923), *Knock, ou le Triomphe de la médecine* (1923) and *Donogoo* (1930); the farces of Fernand Crommelynck (1888–1970) – e.g. *Le Cocu magnifique* (1921); the delicate, understated 'theatre of silence' of Jean-Jacques Bernard (1888–1972) – *Le Feu qui reprend mal* (1921); the homely yet poetic handling of biblical material by André Obey (b. 1892) – e.g. *Noé* (1931) and *Lazare* (1952); the fantasy, satire and metaphysical unease of Armand Salacrou (b. 1899) – e.g. *L'Inconnue d'Arras* (1935), *La Terre est ronde* (1938) and *Les Nuits de la colère* (1946).

An Age of Fiction

Both Giraudoux and Cocteau also wrote a number of novels. In the case of Giraudoux, his fiction possesses many of the qualities of his drama. His satire and wit are at their best in *Bella* (1926), a devastating picture of the French political scene of his day. His gifts of poetry and humorous fantasy give a very distinctive flavour to such novels as *Simon le pathétique* (1918), *Suzanne et le pacifique* (1921) and *Juliette au pays des hommes* (1924). *Siegfried et le limousin* (1922), a novel on Franco-German relations, reached the stage as *Siegfried* in 1928. As regards Cocteau, he wrote fewer novels than Giraudoux and is best remembered for *Thomas l'imposteur* (1923), *Le Grand Écart* (1923) and *Les Enfants terribles* (1929). A short passage from the first of these novels, describing military defences on the Belgian coast during World War I, is typical of Cocteau's amusing inventiveness:

> On se trouvait ému devant ce paysage féminin, lisse, cambré, hanché, couché, rempli d'hommes. Car ces dunes n'étaient désertes qu'en apparence. En réalité, elles n'étaient que trucs, décors, trompe-l'œil, trappes et artifices. La fausse dune du colonel Quinton y faisait un vrai mensonge de femme. Ce colonel, si brave, l'avait construite sous une grêle d'obus, qu'il recevait en fumant dans un rocking-chair. Elle dissimulait, en haut, un observatoire d'où l'observateur pouvait descendre en un clin d'œil, par un toboggan. En somme, ces dunes aux malices inépuisablement renouvelées, côté pile, présentaient, côté face, aux télescopes allemands, un immense tour de cartes, un bonneteur silencieux.

A different kind of lyricism, focused on the world of sense impressions, on young love, on animals and on life in the theatre, is to be found in the novels of Sidonie-Gabrielle Colette (1873–1954). Thinly veiled autobiography provides the subject-matter of the 'Claudine' series, of which *La Maison de Claudine* (1922) is perhaps the best, and *Sido* (1930). More objective novels include *La Vagabonde* (1910), *Chéri* (1920) and *La Fin de Chéri* (1926), *Le Blé en herbe* (1923) with its delicate portrait of adolescent love, *La Chatte* (1933) in which a cat significantly affects the life of a young married couple, and *Gigi* (1945). Colette registered the world of physical sensation, both inside and outside human beings, with poetic precision. She has been described as an 'amie de l'instinct' and wrote of what she herself called 'mon désir de posséder par les yeux les merveilles de la terre'. With that honesty which was one of her most obvious qualities, she also wrote – in elegiac rather than tragic terms – of physical decay and the relative brevity of sensual life. Her talent, if minor, was perfect of its kind, and she possessed outstanding gifts as a stylist.

Whereas Colette lived to be more than eighty, Raymond Radiguet (1903–23) died at the age of twenty. He was an astonishingly precocious youth, known by his friends as 'le miracle de la Marne' because of his talent and the place of his birth. Although owing much to the friendship of Cocteau and Max Jacob, Radiguet had distinct literary views of his own. He wrote two novels which have been widely admired, *Le Diable au corps* (1923) and *Le Bal du comte d'Orgel* (1924). Both show his mastery of a 'classical' prose style – at once precise and analytical. In each novel there is an admirable woman who loves two men in different ways. However, whereas the emphasis in *Le Diable au corps* is on the confusion and pain of an adolescent's love for an older woman, *Le Bal du comte d'Orgel* is a conscious reworking of the dilemma posed in the seventeenth century by Madame de La Fayette's *La Princesse de Clèves*.

With Henri Bosco (1888–1976) and Jean Giono (1895–1970) we return, though in a somewhat different spirit, to Colette's 'merveilles de la terre'. Bosco and Giono have deep roots in different parts of the Midi and write of the countryside and its peasant inhabitants with profound understanding. A few lines from Bosco's best novel, *Le Mas Théotime* (1945), sum up his basic attitude: 'Cette terre est forte et nourricière d'âme . . . car elle satisfait à ce besoin inné de lenteur solennelle et d'éternel retour que seuls la croissance du blé ou le verdissement des vignes offrent à l'homme qui est aux prises avec la grandeur et les servitudes agricoles.' The gifts of poetic evocation and mythic patterning which distinguish other novels by Bosco, including *L'Âne culotté* (1937) and *Malicroix* (1948), are sometimes accompanied by weaknesses of plot. Despite inevitable individual differences, Giono's early work was similar in spirit with its study of primitive peasants in the Basses-Alpes seen against a background of elemental powers and what he calls 'cette force qui ne choisit pas, mais qui pèse d'un poids égal sur l'amandier qui veut fleurir, sur la chienne qui court sa course, et sur l'homme.' The most remarkable novels of this type are those forming the 'Pan' trilogy: *Colline* (1928), *Un de Baumugnes* (1929) and *Regain* (1930). After World War II Giono's novels underwent a considerable change in substance and form. Such works as *Le Hussard sur le toit* (1951) and *Le Moulin de Pologne* (1952) show a broadening of scope, as well as a concision of style, that contrast sharply with the earlier lyrical paganism.

A very different group of novelists is constituted by those who wrote between the wars from a position of firm religious belief. Major novelists of the period whose fiction reflects their Catholic convictions are François Mauriac (1885–1970), Georges Bernanos (1888–1948) and Julien Green (b. 1900). These writers were all faced with a particular difficulty – that of doing justice to their belief in divine oversight of human affairs while making such a belief acceptable, at least within the terms of their novels, to the generality of readers. They were aware of the problem facing them as they attempted to portray what Green calls 'la région secrète où Dieu travaille'. Bernanos asserted that 'l'expérience de l'amour divin n'est pas du domaine du roman' while Mauriac found 'rien de moins saisissable que le doigt de Dieu dans le cours d'une destinée'. Nevertheless, all three are the authors of an impressive body of fiction which, while hardly constituting what could be called 'the Catholic novel', indicates the rich variety of forms that can be taken by 'novels written by Catholics'.

For Mauriac, as for Proust, the memory of childhood impressions is a major creative principle. His best works are set in the Landes surrounding his native Bordeaux. A striking sense of place is achieved by repeated references to vineyards, pine forests, the flatness of the countryside, sultry weather, heavily shuttered houses, etc. These physical details create an appropriate atmosphere for his study of human sinfulness ('l'abîme qu'ouvre, dans le monde moderne, l'absence de Dieu'). Young people are torn between purity and evil, while the 'middle-aged' sins of complacency, materialism, insensitivity, hypocrisy and scandal-mongering are attributed to the *bien-pensants* – Mauriac's 'worm-eaten pillars of the Church'. Up to 1930 he appears to side, against the *bien-pensants*, with characters who remain outside the Church – e.g. the heroine in *Thérèse Desqueyroux* (1927) who attempts to poison her husband. Other major novels of the same period – *Le Baiser au lépreux* (1922), *Genitrix* (1923), *Le Désert de l'amour* (1925) – attack Catholic conformism with almost anti-clerical vehemence while also emphasizing the vanity of human love and displaying Mauriac's reaction to what he regards as the bestial nature of sex. Some of his later novels, including *Le Mystère Frontenac* (1933) and *La Fin de la nuit* (1936), are artistic failures precisely because Mauriac attempted to 'purify the source' and treated bourgeois Catholic orthodoxy much more sympathetically. Even as good a novel as *La Pharisienne* (1941) suffers from an overtly 'improving' conclusion. *Le Nœud de vipères* (1932), however, remains a remarkably successful attempt to portray the process of religious conversion in psychologically convincing and spiritually moving terms.

The fictional world of Georges Bernanos is the work of a powerful, visionary gift. He renders experience in terms of a titanic struggle between good and evil which is more uncompromising and dramatic than in Mauriac. Miracles occur, Satan takes human form, heroic individuals struggle to the utmost limits of pure grace or pure malignity, and violence – in both its moral and physical forms, including murder, suicide and rape – is an integral part of the characters' life. All these features are present in two of Bernanos' best-known novels, *Sous le soleil de Satan* (1926) and *Journal d'un curé de campagne* (1936). Also, each has as its central figure a priest of little practical competence, but possessing great spiritual power, recalling the 'saintly fools' of Dostoevsky. Sainthood is also achieved by Chantal de Clergerie, the heroine of *La Joie* (1929), whereas single-minded evil characterizes Abbé Cénabre in *L'Imposture* (1927) and the horrifying, haunting hero of *Monsieur Ouine* (1943). In these novels, as in the starkly impressive *Nouvelle Histoire de Mouchette* (1937), extreme suffering is often part of a pattern through which Bernanos suggests modern versions of Christ's Passion and the way in which the torment of one individual may possess redemptive power for another.

Julien Green also writes of violence – murder and rape, madness and suicide – in a way that recalls Bernanos. At the same time, and although he writes in a distinctly personal idiom, his reaction to sexuality and his picture of a loveless, faithless world remind one of Mauriac. Such novels as *Adrienne Mesurat* (1927), *Léviathan* (1929) and *Épaves* (1932) powerfully convey this 'monde de désespérés'. Green had an early Protestant upbringing, became a Catholic convert but lost the faith, was deeply influenced by Buddhism, and finally embraced Catholicism in 1939. The main novels reflecting his Buddhist phase – *Le Visionnaire* (1934), *Minuit* (1936) and *Varouna* (1940) – added a dimension of mysticism and fantasy to his earlier vision. His specifically Christian preoccupations are central to one of his best-known novels, *Moïra* (1950), with its American student hero who tragically fails to sustain the consequences of his belief in God. Conflict between the flesh and the spirit is also present in *Chaque homme dans sa nuit* (1960) where, for once, the atmosphere of gloom is lightened by a suggestion of meaning and hope extending beyond the suffering and solitude, cruelty and fear, which characterize his view of the human condition.

It should be added that Mauriac, Bernanos and Green have all had success in the theatre. Of Mauriac's five plays, *Asmodée* (1938) and *Les Mal Aimés* (1945) are perhaps the best. Two of Green's three plays, *Sud* (1953) and *L'Ennemi* (1954), have been particularly admired, while Bernanos wrote a moving film script, *Dialogues des Carmélites* (1949), based on the guillotining of a community of nuns during the French Revolution and set to music by Poulenc.

A novelist who is attracted by the more austerely contemplative demands of religion and art, yet also strongly solicited by action and sexuality, is Henry de Montherlant. Reference has already been made to his early novel, *Le Songe*, but he is the author of numerous other works of fiction insufficiently appreciated outside France. Bullfighting and adolescent love are humorously counterpointed in *Les Bestiaires* (1926); irony and compassion create memorable characterization in *Les Célibataires* (1934); the artist's need both for sexual stimulation and ascetic detachment is explored with wit and intelligence in the four volumes of *Les Jeunes Filles* (1936–9). Major novels appearing more recently are *Le Chaos et la nuit* (1963), an imaginative study of an aged Spanish anarchist exiled in France; *La Rose de sable* (1968), an indictment of French colonialism in North Africa; *Les Garçons* (1969), a moving evocation of a liberal Catholic school in Paris on the eve of World War I.

Three other novelists who have combined action and contemplation in their work are André Malraux (1901–76), Antoine de Saint-Exupéry (1900–44) and Louis-Ferdinand Céline – pseudonym of Dr L.-F. Destouches (1894–1961). Malraux is the major figure among these three. His work marks the coming of age of what might be called 'the novel of the human condition', and this metaphysical dimension has proved a major influence in modern French fiction. Malraux's novels, with the exception of *La Voie royale* (1930), have also reflected some of the major political events of his lifetime: revolution in China in *Les Conquérants* (1928) and *La Condition humaine* (1933); Nazi Germany in *Le Temps du mépris* (1935); the Spanish Civil War in *L'Espoir* (1937); World Wars I and II in *Les Noyers de l'Altenburg* (1948). In an early essay, *La Tentation de l'Occident* (1926), a young Chinese expresses Malraux's own view when he writes to his French correspondent: 'La réalité a été pour vous Dieu, puis l'homme; mais *l'homme est mort*, après Dieu, et vous cherchez avec angoisse celui à qui vous pourriez confier son étrange héritage.' This is the post-Nietzschean drama which Malraux has explored in his novels and lengthy writings on art, a drama intensified by Spengler's pessimistic view of Western civilization. In turbulent novels of fresh psychological insight and outstanding narrative skill Malraux probes beneath the political surface of his story to uncover human solitude in the face of death and what he terms the 'royaumes métalliques de l'absurdité'. These metallic kingdoms are peopled by characters vainly seeking self-validation in heroism, collective political action, drugs, eroticism, mythomania and art.

The world of action in Saint-Exupéry's novels is that of the commercial pilot, pioneering routes to West Africa and South America – *Courrier Sud* (1928), *Vol de nuit* (1931), *Terre des hommes* (1939) – and that of the combat pilot in World War II – *Pilote de guerre* (1942). Like Malraux, Saint-Exupéry considered the life of thought to be sterile without the accompaniment of difficult or dangerous action. His novels combine stories of his own and his friends' adventures with lyrical passages on the wonder of life, the dignity of human beings, and what he calls the authentic luxury of human relations. These are loosely constructed but beautifully written works in which ideas of sacrifice and duty, heroism and fraternity, contribute to a mystical humanism rather less attractively presented in the posthumously published collection of notes and impressions, *Citadelle* (1948).

A very different atmosphere pervades Céline's novels. He sees no salvation for man (whom he judges to be cowardly, hypocritical, selfish) and considers the truth of the world to be death. The title of his first and finest novel, *Voyage au bout de la nuit* (1932), is an apt description of Céline's literary and spiritual journey. He was a romantic nihilist who made literature out of his disgust for human beings and developed a scathing, colloquial prose style which has influenced a number of later writers. After *Mort à crédit* (1936) he produced a series of increasingly strident, often anti-Semitic, and virtually self-parodying novels including *Bagatelles pour un massacre* (1938), *Féerie pour une autre fois I* (1952), *Normance* (*Féerie pour une autre fois II*) (1954), and a horrifying trilogy reflecting the collapse of Nazi Germany: *D'un château l'autre* (1957), *Nord* (1960) and the posthumously published *Rigodon* (1969).

In this 'age of fiction' in inter-war France many other novelists were active. Georges Duhamel extended his immediate post-war reputation with two novel cycles: *Vie et aventures de Salavin* (1920–32) and *Chronique des Pasquier* (1933–44). Jacques de Lacretelle (b. 1888) achieved popular success with *Silbermann* (1922) and *Retour de Silbermann* (1930). Marcel Jouhandeau (b. 1888) is a self-tormenting and unorthodox Catholic whose many novels analysing marriage and human relations include *Monsieur Godeau intime* (1926), *Monsieur Godeau marié* (1933) and *Chamindour* (1934). Drieu la Rochelle (1893–1945) reflected the moral malaise of the twenties and thirties in various novels and collections of short stories including *L'Homme couvert de femmes* (1925), *Le Feu follet* (1931) and *Gilles* (1939), while Marcel Aymé (1902–67) first achieved success as a comic satirist with a robust account of provincial and peasant *mores* in *La Jument verte* (1933).

Two other novelists, both of strong left-wing views, should be mentioned. Paul Nizan (1905–40) had his reputation renewed by Sartre's preface to the 1960 edition of *Aden Arabie* (1931). A member of the Communist Party, Nizan wrote fluent political novels, including *Antoine Bloyé* (1933), *Le Cheval de Troie* (1935) and *La Conspiration* (1938), designed to show that 'toute la société bourgeoise est en proie à la mort'. A more wide-ranging novelist is Louis Guilloux (b. 1899), a non-Marxist revolutionary whose novels express the metaphysical and social anger and scepticism of Cripure in *Le Sang noir* (1935): 'Je détruis toute idole, et je n'ai pas de Dieu à mettre sur l'autel. . . . Les paradis humanitaires, les Édens sociologiques, hum!' Guilloux's earlier novels, including *La Maison du peuple* (1927), were autobiographical and populist. Much later, in *Le Jeu de patience* (1949), he showed a readiness to combine social preoccupations with interesting technical experiments.

World War II: Resistance and Liberation

The successive experiences of military defeat, enemy occupation, resistance to this occupation, and final liberation inevitably had a profound effect on the population of France, including French writers, between 1940 and 1944. A mood of moral and social guilt under the Vichy regime gradually gave way to patriotic affirmation and heroism. This, in its turn, was followed by the memoirs and apologias, the explanations and radical revisions, of the post-Liberation period.

Political and moral confusion and uncertainty, already evident in the years immediately preceding World War II, were intensified by the signing of the armistice in France and the establishment of the Vichy government. Its supporters included patriotic traditionalists who put their faith in Marshal Pétain (e.g. the aged Charles Maurras), anti-Semites and Fascists who admired Nazi ideology, pacifists who preferred occupation to war, ideologues who regarded Hitler as the only effective bulwark against the spread of Communism in Europe, religious traditionalists who hoped for much-needed moral regeneration and a Catholic revival. Inevitably, these were not the views of a majority of intellectuals and the literature associated with these various attitudes is limited in both quantity and interest. Writers already mentioned who favoured collaboration with Nazism include Drieu la Rochelle and Céline. Two other novelists should be mentioned. Alphonse de Châteaubriant (1877–1951) responded with a kind of romantic lyricism to Nazi mythology and directed the collaborationist journal *La Gerbe*. Much earlier he had published two widely praised novels, *Monsieur des Lourdines* (1911) and *La Brière* (1923). Robert Brasillach (1909–45) wrote some good literary criticism and several novels including *Les Sept Couleurs* (1939). With Drieu la Rochelle he is the most admirable figure associated with collaboration – honest, idealistic, courageous. He was tried, imprisoned and shot in 1945 and his *Poèmes de Fresnes* were posthumously published in 1949.

Under the Occupation certain symbolic gestures were possible. Parisian audiences were able to interpret Sartre's *Les Mouches* (1943) and Anouilh's *Antigone* (1944) in Resistance terms. Generally speaking, however, the clandestine conditions imposed on dissident writers by the fact of enemy occupation did not make for large output or lasting quality. Writing often took the form of polemics or patriotic essays contributed to such initially roneo-typed periodicals as *Résistance*, *La Pensée libre* and the important *Lettres françaises*. Contributors included Aragon, Éluard, Mauriac and Sartre. A clandestine publishing house, Les Éditions de Minuit, had also been established. It published such texts as Mauriac's *Le Cahier noir*, a *nouvelle* by Elsa Triolet, *Les Amants d'Avignon*, poems by Aragon and Éluard, and *33 Sonnets composés au secret* by Jean Cassou. The most famous publication was a short novel, *Le Silence de la mer* (1942), by Vercors – pseudonym of Jean Bruller (b. 1902). This is a humane and finely drawn study of the relations between two French people and a German officer billeted on them during the Occupation.

It is not surprising that much clandestine literature took the relatively intense and economical form of poetry. Aragon and Éluard became outstanding Resistance poets, the former in *Le Crève-cœur* (1941) and *Le Musée Grévin* (1943), the latter in *Poésie et vérité* (1942), *Au rendez-vous allemand* (1944), and particularly in his famous litany to 'Liberté'. Among many other poets writing at this time were Robert Desnos who had broken with surrealism before his death in a concentration camp in 1945, and Pierre Emmanuel (b. 1916). Emmanuel is a Catholic poet whose wartime collections include *Jour de colère* (1942) and *La Liberté guide nos pas* (1943) and who wrote: 'La guerre me révéla cette *sensibilité spirituelle* que je n'ai pas cessé de traduire depuis.'

With the Liberation the novelists came back into their own with a vast amount of fiction dealing with war, deportation, occupation and resistance. There is only space to list a few of the more interesting works. On the war itself, Robert Merle gave a tough, graphic account of Dunkirk in *Week-end à Zuydcoote* (1949) and Jules Roy, in *La Vallée heureuse* (1946), provided the bomber pilot's pendant to Saint-Exupéry's *Pilote de guerre*. Roger Nimier's *Le Hussard bleu* (1950) covered the final phases of the war in Europe. Deportation and the world of the concentration camps is the subject of David Rousset's *L'Univers concentrationnaire* (1946) and *Les Jours de notre mort* (1948) as well as of Francis Ambrière's *Les Grandes Vacances* (1946) and Robert Antelme's *L'Espèce humaine* (1947). Moving poetry born of these experiences will be found in Jean Cayrol's *Miroir de la Rédemption* (1944) and *Poèmes de la nuit et du brouillard* (1946). Occupation and resistance are treated in many different ways in *Drôle de jeu* (1945) by Roger Vailland, *Les Forêts de la nuit* (1947) by Jean-Louis Curtis, *Les Épées* (1948) by Roger Nimier, *Uranus* (1948) by Marcel Aymé, *Bande à part* (1951) by Jacques Perret, and *Au bon beurre* (1952) by Jean Dutourd.

Humanism and Existentialism

The search for an authentic humanism which Albert Camus shared in some measure with Gide and Malraux, and the brand of atheistic existentialism which Jean-Paul Sartre described as a form of humanism, both have their roots in a tradition of intellectual dissent and rebellion of which the outrage of Lautréamont and Rimbaud, or the anti-rationalism of the surrealists, offer particularly striking literary expressions. Perhaps it is therefore not surprising that Camus (1913–60) and Sartre (b. 1905) were both classed as existentialists in 1945 although Camus explicitly rejected this classification and Sartre pointed out important differences between them. What they had most obviously in common was a sense of the absurd or irrational nature of man's experience of the world and an acute feeling of his solitary, isolated position facing the finality of death in a universe without God. At the same time, whereas Camus located irrationality not in the world as such but in the confrontation between the human mind and that world, Sartre argued that the physical universe itself is absurd in the sense that it can be given no *a priori* philosophical justification. These ideas are reflected in different ways in the essays, novels and plays of both writers. They led Camus to look for an alternative philosophy to both Christianity and Marxism; they have prompted Sartre to regard Marxism as alone providing a coherent set of solutions.

After an honourable career in clandestine journalism during the Occupation, Camus rapidly emerged as a major literary figure with two plays, *Le Malentendu* (1944) and *Caligula* (1945), and a striking first novel, *L'Étranger* (published in 1942 but only widely read after 1945). All these works explored, in terms of individual experience, that sense of 'the absurd' which Camus also discussed on a more philosophical level in a long essay, *Le Mythe de Sisyphe* (1942). The plays proved less successful than the novel in which, through the personality of Meursault, Camus conveyed the 'feeling' of a contemporary brand of nihilism with which he had undoubted temperamental affinities yet which he was mainly concerned to overcome. His own rebellion against nihilism, in the name of justice and human fraternity, is given imaginative form in his second major novel, *La Peste* (1947), with its elaborate and suggestive symbolic structure, and in two further plays, *L'État de siège* (1948) and *Les Justes* (1950). In another influential essay, *L'Homme révolté* (1951), he contrasted his own idea of moral and metaphysical rebellion with the Marxist doctrine of violent politico-historical revolution which he saw as running counter to true humanism. He achieved an outstanding measure of moral and artistic integrity which perhaps reached their culminating point in his third novel, *La Chute* (1956), and in the short stories – which are also a set of fascinating stylistic exercises – collected under the title *L'Exil et le royaume* (1957).

By professional training Sartre is a teacher of philosophy. His earliest published works, which appeared before World War II, consisted of philosophical papers together with his best-known novel, *La Nausée* (1938), and a collection of short stories, *Le Mur* (1939). From this point onwards his novels and plays continued to centre around certain themes first set out at great length in *L'Être et le néant* (1943), a philosophical work which remains the major statement in French of atheistic existentialism. For Sartre there is no God, no objective system of universal values, and therefore no 'given' or established religious or secular morality. The individual is totally free and therefore totally responsible. He must exercise his freedom by constant, responsible choice, avoiding the pitfalls of evasive 'bad faith' and refusing to fulfil roles which others seek to impose upon him in order to deprive him of his freedom.

Unlike Camus, Sartre has been a more successful playwright than novelist and some of the ideas just mentioned are given dramatic form, and handled with considerable theatrical skill, in *Les Mouches* (1943), *Morts sans sépulture* (1946), *La Putain respectueuse* (1946), *Les Mains sales* (1948), *Les Séquestrés d'Altona* (1959), etc. In what is probably his most ambitious play, *Le Diable et le bon Dieu* (1951), existentialist themes are combined with an imaginative projection of the conflict between ends and means which reminds us of his political preoccupations and of the fascination which Communism holds for him. Existentialism and Communism are also central to his most ambitious work of fiction, the three volumes of *Les Chemins de la liberté* (1945–9). Thus in *L'Âge de raison* (1945) the central figure, Mathieu, is pulled in opposite directions by his demand for individual freedom and his sense of collective efficacy. Of the other two volumes, *Le Sursis* (1947) uses techniques of simultaneity to convey a complex picture of Europe during the Munich crisis while *La Mort dans l'âme* (1949) has the Fall of France as its subject. Sartre's most sustained – and opaque – attempt to relate existentialism and Marxism at a philosophical level will be found in *Critique de la raison dialectique* (1960).

The literary status of Simone de Beauvoir (b. 1908), closely associated with Sartre both personally and intellectually, has been the subject of some debate. A long, untidy novel, *Les Mandarins* (1954), evokes the Parisian intellectual circles of the 1940s to which she belonged and contains thinly fictionalized portraits of Camus and Sartre among others. Like Sartre, she has written philosophical essays on existentialism and on the need to divorce ethics from religious or metaphysical absolutes – *Pour une morale de l'ambiguité* (1947), etc. – as well as a lengthy and sometimes alarmingly humourless book on the status and rights of women, *Le Deuxième Sexe* (1949). Her best novels are *L'Invitée* (1943) and *Le Sang des autres* (1944). The former deals with the existentialist idea of the individual achieving freedom through a genuinely autonomous act. It is not without significance that the act in this particular instance is the murder of another human being. The latter is a dramatic and sometimes moving novel about the 1930s and the French Resistance movement. The intellectual world which Sartre and Simone de Beauvoir represent, and which Camus came to reject with increasing firmness, is portrayed in her three autobiographical volumes, *Mémoires d'une jeune fille rangée* (1958), *La Force de l'âge* (1960) and *La Force des choses* (1963).

New Forms in the Theatre

Montherlant's plays belong to this section more by historical accident than aesthetic affinity. Although he had established his reputation as a novelist and essayist in the inter-war period, he did not begin his public career as a dramatist until the writing and production of *La Reine morte* in 1942. This play immediately struck what was to become the authentic Montherlantian note in the theatre – a searching account of psychological and moral dilemmas associated with exaltation and grandeur and expressed in richly rhetorical terms. These qualities, together with the fact that he has written a number of 'costume' tragedies, place Montherlant in a tradition that goes back through Claudel, and the Musset of *Lorenzaccio*, to the plays of Corneille and Racine. His conception of the theatre, and the world created by his drama, are unique in the post-war period and represent a new form in this sense, however far removed they may be from the 'theatre of the absurd' and the laconic anti-heroism of Beckett or Ionesco.

Montherlant's main 'costume' tragedies, in addition to *La Reine morte*, are – with their dates of publication rather than performance – *Malatesta* (1946), *Le Maître de Santiago* (1947), *Port-Royal* (1954), *Don Juan* (1958), *Le Cardinal d'Espagne* (1960) and *La Guerre civile* (1965). In all these plays character polarities predominate and Montherlant matches the tragic inevitability inherent in his historical material with a tightly woven theatrical structure. His non-historical plays, written in less lyrical and more everyday language, include *Fils de personne* (1944) and *La Ville dont le prince est un enfant* (1951). The former is a moving tragedy of the failure of a father and (illegitimate) son to understand each other despite goodwill on both sides. The latter dramatizes material skilfully reworked eighteen years later in the novel *Les Garçons*.

Although he differs from Montherlant in almost every respect, Jean Genet (b. 1910) shares with him the ability to manipulate language with outstanding skill and to clothe his ideas in rich and sonorous prose. Genet uses this gift of language, however, to praise evil and hymn the virtues of murder, betrayal, theft and violent crime generally. He spent much of his early life in jail in various European countries and faced life imprisonment in 1947. He was eventually pardoned, largely through the intervention of the Parisian literary world. By this time he had written a number of novels glorifying his criminal associations and homosexual relationships. Artistic skill and often repulsive subject-matter come together in *Notre-Dame des fleurs* (1944), *Miracle de la rose* (1946), *Pompes funèbres* (1947) and *Querelle de Brest* (1947).

It was also in 1947 that Genet first turned to the theatre and it is Genet the dramatist who speaks most convincingly with an original and authentic literary voice. He condemns Western drama for its trivial realism and seeks to create a ritualized theatre inspired by Japan, Bali and China. The result is a theatre of ceremony in which, at least in the later plays, symbols in human form take the place of traditional, psychologically motivated characters. It was ideas like these which prompted him to describe the elevation of the host during the Mass as a piece of genuine theatrical effectiveness. His own first play, *Haute Surveillance* (1947), can in fact be interpreted as a perverse Mass acted out by three prisoners. *Les Bonnes* (1947) was a breakthrough in his work in so far as it moved away from the world of homosexually obsessed criminals. In common with *Le Balcon* (1956) it introduces a number of existentialist themes including the human tendency towards role-playing and the acting out of private fantasies. *Le Balcon*, with its brothel or 'house of illusions', also mirrors the falseness and hollowness of society. Two later plays, *Les Nègres* (1958) and *Les Paravents* (1961), are violent, ritualistic pieces closer to Voodoo ceremonies than to Noh theatre.

The writings of Samuel Beckett (b. 1906), with their bitter sense of the absurdity of existence and of a world predicated on death and physical decay, suggest a desperate rewriting of some of Camus's earliest work. Unlike the fundamentally classical Camus, however, Beckett sees language itself as a manifestation of irrationality. This fact both contributes to the distinctive resonance of his plays and links them in terms of expression as well as attitude to the 'theatre of the absurd' in general. The play which made Beckett a world-renowned figure, *En attendant Godot* (1952), opens on a deserted country road with a single, stunted tree. Under this tree two tramps talk to one another, achieve no meaningful communication, and await the mysterious Godot who fails to appear. This play creates talk without meaning, and movement without development. The wit, the humour and the punning are often tragic and painful. With some justification Beckett's plays have been described as constituting a 'théâtre-limite' and most of them, since *En attendant Godot*, show a progressive paring down of character, action and speech. *Fin de partie* (1957) takes place in a bare room; Hamm cannot stand, Clov cannot sit, and Hamm's legless parents, Nagg and Nell, occupy two dustbins. In *Krapp's Last Tape* (1959), translated into

French as *La Dernière Bande* (1959), man-become-animal confronts a machine. *Happy Days* (1961), translated into French as *Oh! les beaux jours* (1963), has a heroine who is buried up to the waist in earth. The crude, the farcical and the incoherent are all essential elements in Beckett's desperate and despairing response to life. His sometimes barely human characters, subject to extremes of physical humiliation, drag out a meaningless existence in a physical waste dominated by the fact of suffering and the eroding action of time.

The plays of Eugène Ionesco (b. 1912) also reflect a world in which man is dehumanized and alienated. Again, they mirror the breakdown of language. However, Ionesco differs from Beckett in his response to this situation which often takes the form of wildly funny and 'absurd' fantasy. He emphasizes his own conception of the theatre as one based on the private imagination and in which inventiveness is much more important than any specific message: 'C'est dans mes rêves, dans mes angoisses, dans mes désirs obscurs, dans mes contradictions intérieures que, pour ma part, je me réserve le droit de prendre cette matière théâtrale.' From this personal basis, which provides him with a set of near-surrealist images, he exposes the mechanical and the ready-made in behaviour and speech. Thus his first major play, *La Cantatrice chauve* (1950), shows up the routine conformity and pomposity of an English couple through the inanities of their conversation:

> M. SMITH. Un médecin consciencieux doit mourir avec le malade s'ils ne peuvent pas guérir ensemble. Le commandant d'un bateau périt avec le bateau, dans les vagues. Il ne lui survit pas.
>
> MME SMITH. On ne peut comparer un malade à un bateau.
>
> M. SMITH. Pourquoi pas? Le bateau a aussi ses maladies; d'ailleurs ton docteur est aussi sain qu'un vaisseau; voilà pourquoi encore il devait périr en même temps que le malade comme le docteur et son bateau.
>
> MME SMITH. Ah! Je n'y avais pas pensé . . . C'est peut-être juste . . . et alors, quelle conclusion en tires-tu?
>
> M. SMITH. C'est que tous les docteurs ne sont que des charlatans. Et tous les malades aussi. Seule la marine est honnête en Angleterre.
>
> MME SMITH. Mais pas les marins.
>
> M. SMITH. Naturellement.

Among Ionesco's numerous plays *La Leçon* (1951), *Les Chaises* (1952), *Amédée, ou Comment s'en débarrasser* (1954), *Le Nouveau Locataire* (1957),

Tueur sans gages (1959) and *Rhinocéros* (1960) all bear testimony to his imagination and inventiveness – and to his outstanding gift for making tragedy comic and comedy tragic. *Rhinocéros*, in particular, points to another aspect of his theatre – the fact that his inventiveness is sometimes a means of making social or political comment in symbolical terms. Thus Bérenger, who appears in other plays in addition to *Rhinocéros*, is the lone survivor in a society of men that has become a herd of dangerous rhinos, i.e. an authoritarian society lacking intellectual refinement but possessing potentially lethal power. The application to twentieth-century dictatorships, whether of the Right or the Left, is obvious.

Other writers for the theatre who may be classed in the same avant-garde tradition as Beckett and Ionesco include Jacques Audiberti (1899–1965), author of *Quoat-Quoat* (1946), *Le Mal court* (1947), *La Fête noire* (1948) and *Les Naturels du Bordelais* (1953); Jean Tardieu (b. 1903), whose *Théâtre de chambre* was published in 1955 and his *Poèmes à jouer* in 1960; Arthur Adamov (b. 1908), author of *Le Professeur Taranne* (1953) and *Le Ping-Pong* (1955); Fernando Arrabal (b. 1932), whose *Théâtre I* and *Théâtre II* were published in 1958 and 1961 and his *Théâtre panique* in 1965. One can find in most of these dramatists, as in Genet, Beckett and Ionesco, traces of the theories set out so forcibly by Antonin Artaud (1896–1948) – theories to do with ritual, spectacle and anti-rationalism – in *Le Théâtre et son double* (1938).

Some Post-War Poets

One of the most accessible French poets still writing after World War II was Jules Supervielle (1884–1960). Within the general development of twentieth-century poetry he saw himself as pioneering 'une poésie moins ardue, plus proche de chacun de nous'. At the same time, this poetry was calculated to lead the reader 'dans les lointains et les abîmes'. In fact, Supervielle was a spiritual idealist who wrote about the mysterious beauty of the physical world and the organic relationship between man and nature. Many poems are devoted to this theme and the opening stanza of 'Arbres dans la nuit et le jour', published in 1945, is typical:

> Candélabres de la noirceur,
> Hauts-commissaires des ténèbres,
> Malgré votre grandeur funèbre
> Arbres, mes frères et mes sœurs,

Nous sommes de même famille,
L'étrangeté se pousse en nous
Jusqu'aux veinules, aux ramilles,
Et nous comble de bout en bout.

Delicacy and charm, simplicity and humour, are features of Supervielle's poetry as of his short stories on mythical and biblical themes (e.g. *L'Arche de Noé* (1938) and *Le Petit Bois et autres contes* (1947)). Some of his most characteristic verse – poems on animals which recall La Fontaine and whimsical poems on the relationship between God and man – will be found in *Gravitations* (1925), *Le Forçat innocent* (1930), *La Fable du monde* (1938) and *Oublieuse mémoire* (1949). Another collection, *Poèmes de la France malheureuse* (1941), consists of poems written in Uruguay (where he was born) and passed from hand to hand in Occupied France.

With Pierre-Jean Jouve (1887–1976) we approach more closely to the mainstream of modern French poetry since he recognizes a considerable debt to Baudelaire and has in turn influenced poets younger than himself – e.g. Emmanuel and Bonnefoy. Jouve dates his poetic maturity from *Les Mystérieuses Noces* (1925). He had become a convert to Roman Catholicism shortly before, as well as showing a deep interest in psychoanalytic theory, and much of his verse from this point onwards centres around the problem of good and evil interpreted by means of a distinctive, and fundamentally pessimistic, mixture of theological and Freudian imagery. His poems reveal the 'neuves férocités et lâchetés anciennes' of man. Apart from *Les Mystérieuses Noces*, his many volumes of poetry include *La Symphonie à Dieu* (1930), *Sueur de sang* (1934), *Gloire* (1940) and *La Vierge de Paris* (1945). Although his poetic vigour sometimes leads to formlessness, Jouve is often a master of language and something of his ability to transmute his faith into memorable verse can be seen in these lines from the final poem in *La Symphonie à Dieu*:

Témoin des lieux insensés de mon cœur
Tu es né d'une vierge absolue et tu es né
Parce que Dieu avait posé les mains sur sa poitrine,
Et tu es né
Homme de nerfs et de douleur et de semence
Pour marcher sur la magnifique dalle de chagrin

Et ton flanc mort fut percé pour la preuve
Et jaillit sur l'obscur et extérieur nuage
Du sang avec de l'eau.

Saint-John Perse – pseudonym of Alexis St Léger Léger (1887–1975) published his first book of verse as long ago as 1909. His best-known long poem, *Anabase* (1924), was translated into English by T. S. Eliot in 1930, yet his world-wide reputation only dates from the award of the Nobel Prize for Literature in 1960. With ceremonious formality, and in often difficult imagery, Saint-John Perse celebrates the rich variety of the natural world. He writes: '. . . par son adhésion totale à ce qui est, le poète tient pour nous liaison avec la permanence et l'unité de l'Être' – and he adds: 'Poète est celui qui rompt pour nous l'accoutumance.' Both these poetic functions are typically present in this short extract from *Amers*:

Ô mon amour au goût de mer, que d'autres paissent loin de mer l'églogue au fond des vallons clos – menthes, mélisse et méliot, tiédeurs d'alysse et d'origan – et l'un y parle d'abeillage et l'autre y traite d'agnelage, et la brebis feutrée baisse la terre au bas des murs de pollen noir. Dans le temps où les pêches se nouent, et les liens sont triés pour la vigne, moi j'ai tranché le nœud de chanvre qui tient la coque sur son ber, à son berceau de bois. Et mon amour est sur les mers! et ma brûlure est sur les mers! . . .

Saint-John Perse's celebration of Being emphasizes plenitude, regeneration, purification, energy and love in *Éloges* (1911), *Pluies* (1943), *Neiges* (1944), *Vents* (1946) and *Amers* (1957). Exile in America during World War II inspired *Exil* (1942) and old age *Chronique* (1960).

If a poet with as individual a voice as Saint-John Perse had to be classified we should probably place him, at least technically, in the symbolist tradition. Pierre Reverdy (1889–1960), on the other hand, owes a clear debt to surrealism like so many of his contemporaries. Both these poets shunned publicity and left their poetry to speak for itself. Reverdy, indeed, lived the life of a recluse at Solesmes from 1926 until his death, vainly seeking a solution to his religious problems. The circumscribed but very real quality of Reverdy's verse was only generally recognized with the republication of his poems for the period 1915–22 in *Plupart du temps* (1945). Other major collections include *Les Épaves du ciel* (1924) and *Liberté des mers* (1960). Reverdy's characteristic combination of haunting sadness and a strong plastic sense is seen in 'Fausse porte ou portrait' from *Les Épaves du ciel*:

> Dans la place qui reste là
> Entre quatre lignes
> Un carré où le blanc se joue
> La main qui soutenait ta joue
> Lune
> Une figure qui s'allume
> Le profil d'un autre
> Mais tes yeux
> Je suis la lampe qui me guide
> Un doigt sur la paupière humide
> Au milieu
> Les larmes roulent dans cet espace
> Entre quatre lignes
> Une glace

Like Reverdy, René Char (b. 1907) served an apprenticeship to surrealism, and the collection *Artine* (1930) has been called a 'classic' of the movement. His poems published since 1945 are different in manner and mood though a certain obscurity, and a sometimes dazzling use of imagery, recall his literary origins. Char is both the poet of that sensibility which his friend and admirer Camus called 'the absurd' (he defines the poet as a 'magicien de l'insécurité'), and a writer whose humanity and sensibility have deep and permanent roots in his native Vaucluse. The following lines, from a poem on the river Sorgue in the collection *Fureur et mystère* (1948), indicate something of his qualities:

> Rivière de l'âme vide, de la guenille et du soupçon,
> Du vieux malheur qui se dévide, de l'ormeau, de la compassion.
>
> Rivière des farfelus, des fiévreux, des équarisseurs,
> Du soleil lâchant sa charrue pour s'acoquiner au menteur.

Char has increasingly used the prose-poem as a medium for taut, aphoristic writing with which to illuminate deep and elusive truths about human experience. An excellent anthology of his poems, chosen by himself, was published as *Commune Présence* in 1964.

Inevitably, the five poets named so far, while they are probably major figures in post-war French poetry (along with Éluard), do not exhaust either the number or variety of poets whose work deserves to be mentioned. At one extreme of sensibility there is the radical pessimism of Henri Michaux (b. 1899) for whom: 'Tout s'enfonce, rien ne libère / Le suicidé renaît à une nouvelle souffrance'. He sees the world in Kafkaesque terms and has sought to exorcize it through mescalin and art. Representative collections of his work are *Épreuves, Exorcismes* (1945) and *Passages* (1950). At another extreme Francis Ponge (b. 1899) devotes many prose poems to physical objects, particularly in *Le Parti pris des choses* (1942), in a manner recalling the *chosisme* of the 'new novelists'. Indeed, Ponge might be speaking for Robbe-Grillet when he writes: '. . . je me fais tirer, par les objets, hors du vieil humanisme, hors de l'homme actuel et en avant de lui.' Very different again, both from these poets and from one another, are Jacques Prévert (b. 1900) and Raymond Queneau (b. 1903) who have both written clever, witty and humorous verse and who made their names with *Paroles* (1946) and *Si tu t'imagines* (1952) respectively. We return to the expression of nihilism, often vigorously and memorably expressed, in the poetry of André Frénaud (b. 1907). The title of his most representative collection of poems, *Il n'y a pas de paradis* (1962), is significant.

Two other poets have established considerable reputations: Patrice de la Tour du Pin (b. 1911) and Yves Bonnefoy (b. 1923). La Tour du Pin has been underrated by some critics, perhaps because of the largely traditionalist and classical qualities of his verse. An enormous work, *Une Somme de poésie* (1946), to which he added further lengthy volumes in 1959 and 1963, is inevitably of uneven quality though impressive in scope and ambition. The best passages reveal an outstanding ability to handle religious themes and the experience of love. La Tour du Pin is also acutely conscious of the spiritual paucity of the post-Christian world.

> Nous n'avons plus d'idoles . . .
> Après celles de pierre ont croulé celles d'âme.
> Les derniers sens d'adoration se sont défaits.
> D'ailleurs, qui s'en étonne?
> Plus on touche à la mort et plus on prend ses traits.

As regards Bonnefoy, he is also a less consciously avant-garde poet than many of his contemporaries, but he carries out an anguished interrogation of a world in which death is the overriding reality. His best-known collections are *Du mouvement et de l'immobilité de Douve* (1954) and *Hier régnant désert* (1958).

Towards a New Novel

The various terms *nouveau roman, anti-roman, école du regard* or *chosisme* suggest that the phenomenon to which they refer is neither obviously homogeneous nor easily defined. The novelists in question share the conviction that it is inappropriate today, for social, philosophical or aesthetic reasons, to write novels indistinguishable in form and attitude from those of the nineteenth century. Nevertheless, there is a vast difference between the fierce nihilism of Beckett, the psychological subtleties of Sarraute or Duras, the objectivity and formalism of Robbe-Grillet.

A clear break with the traditional novel, and one which anticipates later ideas, is to be found in a work on the theory of fiction, *Lazare parmi nous* (1950), by Jean Cayrol (b. 1911). Cayrol's experiences during three years spent in prisons and concentration camps during World War II convinced him that suffering is a necessary precondition of redemption. He entertains some ultimate hope for man, but sees him as conditioned by solitude, dereliction and estrangement. A social outcast, resembling a secular Christ taking on himself the world's misery, is the protagonist of his trilogy *Je vivrai l'amour des autres* (1947–50). Themes of estrangement and absence continue to haunt such later novels as *La Noire* (1949), *Le Vent de la mémoire* (1952), *L'Espace d'une nuit* (1954), *Les Corps étrangers* (1959), etc.

The world of the human or sub-human outcast is something which Cayrol and Beckett have in common though Beckett, as we saw in the case of his plays, wholly lacks that belief in the possibility of redemption which is central to Cayrol. Another surface similarity between their desolate fictional worlds is the fact that the balance between people and objects is precarious in two senses: people are often reduced by these novelists to the status of 'things' haunting the very fringes of existence; furthermore, objects can take on major significance in this world of depersonalized human creatures. Neither Cayrol nor Beckett treats objects with the scientific detachment aimed at by Robbe-Grillet or Butor. Rather, material things are necessary points of reference in a world of desolation and flux – a pair of old socks, riddled with holes, in the opening volume of Cayrol's *Je vivrai l'amour des autres*, or the sucking-stones in Beckett's *Molloy* (1951). This last work forms part of a trilogy of which the other volumes are *Malone meurt* (1951) and *L'Innommable* (1953). The increasing tendency in these novels to withdraw from the physical world of bodies and objects into the flux of demented consciousness and confusions of language reaches a climax in *Comment c'est* (1961) in which the elemental Bom and Pim crawl naked through the slime and darkness of existence.

The nineteenth-century conception of the novel is challenged in a different way in the fiction of Nathalie Sarraute (b. 1902). Plot and character portrayal are replaced by situations existing between people whose inner movements and underlying reactions compose a network of relationships beyond the reach of any socio-psychological approach to character. One is reminded of Dostoevsky, and more particularly of Virginia Woolf. In a collection of literary essays, *L'Ère du soupçon* (1956), Nathalie Sarraute explains her 'suspicion' of traditional accounts of human nature and therefore of the fictional characters portrayed by most nineteenth-century novelists. In the early *Tropismes* (1939), and in later novels such as *Portrait d'un inconnu* (1946), *Martereau* (1953), *Le Planétarium* (1959) and *Les Fruits d'or* (1963), she shows authentic personality expressing itself, and true relations between people being established, by silences, gestures, inflections and oblique meanings often totally at variance with the words spoken.

The network of relationships between people is also explored, with a distinctive dialectic of absence and presence, silence and words, passivity and revolt, by Marguerite Duras (b. 1914). Tone, texture and subtle counterpointing are brilliantly handled in such novels as *Les Petits Chevaux de Tarquinia* (1953), *Le Square* (1955), and *Moderato cantabile* (1958) in which a laconic workman and his boss's wife act out in imagination an adulterous passion shot through with the obsessive overtones of a *crime passionnel* which each had witnessed separately. Later works include the film scenario *Hiroshima mon amour* (1960) and the novels *Le Vice-consul* (1966) and *L'Amante anglaise* (1967).

Claude Simon (b. 1913), Alain Robbe-Grillet (b. 1922) and Michel Butor (b. 1926) are generally regarded as the quintessential 'new novelists'. Simon is a distinctive writer concerned with the destructive nature of time in novels of dizzying chronology and confused consciousness that recall the American William Faulkner. Difficulties and uncertainties assail the reader of such novels as *Le Vent* (1957), *L'Herbe* (1958), *La Route des Flandres* (1960) and *Le Palace* (1962).

Difficulties and unresolved doubts are also created by the novels of Robbe-Grillet and Butor. Coherence and meaning, characters and plot, give way to a puzzling pattern of inconsistencies and ambiguities, hints and half-truths. Robbe-Grillet argues that 'coherent' nineteenth-century forms of character and plot reflected a social order which no longer exists and a set of social values in which we no longer believe. With character and plot lacking intellectual respectability, we must find different forms while being forced to concern ourselves increasingly with objects. Such objects will be seen as 'being present' rather than as 'having meaning beyond themselves'. Hence the detached formalism and the ambiguities of character and story in *Les Gommes* (1953), *Le Voyeur* (1955), *La Jalousie* (1957), *Dans le labyrinthe* (1959) and *La Maison de rendez-vous* (1963).

Michel Butor's novels have contained more varied types of experiment. An early novel such as *L'Emploi du temps* (1956) has many of the characteristics attributed to Robbe-Grillet above. With *La Modification* (1957), however, although the plot has an almost traditional clarity, unusual effects are achieved by the use of the vocative form throughout the whole narrative. Ambitious experiments with the presentation of space and time are made in *Degrés* (1960) and in the literary collage entitled *Mobile* (1962).

It may be argued that most 'new novelists' are too self-consciously intellectual, and too much in love with technique and theory, to be truly creative. One is tempted to suggest that their theoretical writings provide more entertaining fiction than is found in many of their novels. Generally speaking, the middle decades of the twentieth century have been a period of intelligent agitation in literature rather than one of permanent accomplishment. Even novels as well contrived as *La Route des Flandres*, *La Jalousie* or *La Modification* may become curios, not classics. Nevertheless it is on experiment in drama and poetry, no less than in fiction, that genuine growth and future achievement in literature depend.

Structuralism and Semiology

The theory and practice of both structuralism and semiology have played an increasingly prominent role in French intellectual debate during the 1960s and 1970s.[1] The theory is not always easy to grasp and the practice is often characterized by a difficult and highly technical vocabulary. However, as regards the links between structuralism and semiology (or semiotics), these have had an important effect on current conceptions of literature and literary criticism. Put in the simplest terms, structuralism is concerned with the interplay of elements in a

[1] Cf. Chapter 6, pp. 310 ff., for an outline of structuralist thought.

given organized whole. It defines a single element in terms of the whole of which that element is an integral part. In this way structuralism provides a framework or a model for the study of phenomena which may be termed semiological, that is, which have to do with the creation or perception of meaning through a system of signs. Language is the primary semiological phenomenon, but the structure of sign systems has also been studied in literature, in the other arts, in psychology and anthropology. Indeed, Roland Barthes (b. 1915) has used structuralism and semiotics to analyse in an entertaining and penetrating way such varied phenomena as advertising, fashion and all-in wrestling. Relevant works by Barthes, in ascending order of difficulty, include *Mythologies* (1957), *Système de la mode* (1967) and *Éléments de sémiologie* (1965).

The founding father of modern structuralism is generally agreed to be the Swiss linguist Ferdinand de Saussure (1857–1913). His posthumously published *Cours de linguistique générale* (1916) emphasized the view of language as a system of relations between such elements as sounds, words, etc. – a system in which each element is understood in terms of its relationship to a larger 'structure'. For Saussure, meaning involves structure (whether it be the various uses of a word or interpretations of a sentence), but he was particularly concerned to refute the view that meanings *precede* words. There are no ideas prior to words. The concept involved in the word (*le signifié*) and its sound or form (*le signifiant*) are inseparable.

This is a view which reappears in structuralist literary criticism. Barthes, for example, argues that literary texts do not contain a prior moral truth or pre-existent information about a particular society or historical period. He regards literary works as objects created from signs. These objects are, in effect, codes which set ideas in motion in the reader's mind. In other words, thought is coeval with language. The medium *is* the message. As a result, Barthes argues against 'realism' or 'mimesis' as a literary theory and against those forms of criticism which seek to understand a work better by referring to the biography of the author and the history of his times.

Structuralists are not generally noted for intellectual tolerance. Structuralist critics have severely attacked other critical traditions, and their total rejection of traditional 'university' criticism and scholarship can be studied in the celebrated and fascinating controversy between Barthes and Raymond Picard on the subject of Racine. Key texts in the argument are Barthes's *Sur Racine* (1963), his *Critique et vérité* (1966) and Picard's *Nouvelle critique ou nouvelle imposture* (1965). Fundamentally, Barthes seeks to refute any theory of literature as mimesis and a belief in language as communication. At a more general level, he even asserts that 'le discours n'a aucune responsabilité envers le réel' and argues that society can only be radically transformed if language and signs, as we have traditionally known and used them, are finally destroyed.

The work of a number of structuralists in fields other than literature has influenced literary theory and practice. The major figure here is Claude Lévi-Strauss (b. 1908) whose professional works include *Anthropologie structurale* (1958), *La Pensée sauvage* (1962) and *Le Cru et le cuit* (1964). His largely autobiographical *Tristes tropiques* (1955) contains an interesting account of certain aspects of post-war intellectual life in France. Other distinguished structuralists working in primarily non-literary fields include Jacques Lacan (b. 1901), Louis Althusser (b. 1918) and Michel Foucault (b. 1926). In the field of literary analysis the group associated with the review *Tel Quel* (founded in 1961 by Philippe Sollers) has exerted considerable influence through its combination of Marxism and formalism. Other leading structuralist literary critics include Gérard Genette (b. 1930) and Tzvetan Todorov (b. 1940).

Structuralist theory, which has links with the practice of certain 'new novelists', appears to be regarded by its most enthusiastic devotees as a philosophy of life. Indeed, it is seen by some as having ousted existentialism and shown up its inadequacies. From the point of view of the Sartrean existentialist, however, it is criticized as a static, ahistorical doctrine. Also, its emphasis on structures leaves little room for the existentialist concept of freedom. The psychoanalyst Lacan, for example, holds that 'l'inconscient est structuré comme un langage'. The individual's freedom is the relative freedom of movement within predetermined structures.

Two final comments on structuralist literary criticism are worth making briefly. The temptation to use highly technical language (not to say barbaric jargon) is very strong. A page of *Tel Quel* can prove a formidable linguistic obstacle race as the following short extract suggests:

> Les processus sémiotiques qui introduisent l'errance, le flou dans le langage et a fortiori le langage poétique, sont, d'un point de vue synchronique, des marques des processus pulsionnels (appropriation/rejet, oralité/analité, amour/haine, vie/mort), et, d'un point de vue diachronique, remontent aux archaîsmes du corps sémiotique qui,

avant de se reconnaître comme identique dans un miroir et par conséquent comme signifiant, est dans une dépendance vis-à-vis de la mère. Pulsionnels, maternels, ces processus sémiotiques préparent l'entrée du futur parlant dans le sens et la signification (dans le symbolique).

There is no doubt that structuralist critics often provide a subtle and revealing analysis of texts, but there are occasions when they cannot escape the charge either of unnecessary obfuscation or of expressing the ordinary or the obvious in gratuitously difficult formulations. Furthermore, some of the basic emphases of structuralism (e.g. a rejection of biography or an insistence on the self-sufficiency of the literary work) are much less original than is often suggested or assumed. Structuralist criticism shares a number of fundamental insights with the work, published in the 1920s and 1930s, by the American 'New Critics' and such English critics as I. A. Richards, William Empson and Wilson Knight. The Anglo-Saxon world has long been familiar with arguments emphasizing the autonomy of the written text and denouncing the 'intentional fallacy'. In particular, poems have frequently been analysed as self-justifying entities, divorced from their historical background and from the poets' own ideas and aims. Those who are familiar with such criticism will find that it has reappeared, heavily disguised and yet still identifiable, in the writings of many structuralists. Old wine, as it were, in new bottles of particularly opaque glass.

Bibliography

The development of French literature since 1870 is a complex subject as well as a lengthy one. This has two obvious results where the present bibliography is concerned. In the first place, general studies of the period are inevitably selective and tend to present their material in terms of somewhat arbitrary patterns. Secondly, it has only been possible to mention a few of the most helpful titles from among the many critical works devoted to various sections into which the preceding chapter has been divided.

GENERAL STUDIES

A detailed, traditional literary history in English will be found in P. E. Charvet, *A Literary History of France: the Nineteenth and Twentieth Centuries, 1870–1940* (London, 1967). This book, which does not deal with post-war writing, extends from naturalism to existentialism and includes accounts of all the main literary figures. The best French history of the subject is H. Clouard, *Histoire de la littérature française du symbolisme à nos jours*, 2 vols (Paris, 1962). Particularly valuable is the attention paid to philosophy, history, literary criticism and memoirs during the period. A wider canvas, in the sense that it deals with Europe generally and not only France, can be found in R.-M. Albérès, *L'Aventure intellectuelle du XXe siècle, 1900–1950* (Paris, 1950). A more selective approach is contained in J. Cruickshank (ed.), *French Literature and its Background*, Vols 5 and 6 (London, 1969 and 1970). Vol. 5 *The Late Nineteenth Century*, includes chapters on 'Symbolism and Mallarmé' and 'Literature and Ideology, 1880–1914'; Vol. 6, *The Twentieth Century*, apart from essays on the main authors, contains chapters on such subjects as 'The Birth of the Modern, 1885–1914', 'Surrealism', 'Vichy France, 1940–1944' and 'The "Nouveau roman" '. W. Fowlie, *Climate of Violence* (London, 1969), is still more selective and includes an interesting section on poets and painters at the turn of the century.

NATURALISM

One of the leading French authorities on naturalism (and realism) is R. Dumesnil. His *Le Réalisme et le naturalisme* (Paris, 1955) is a large and comprehensive treatment of the subject. As regards naturalism, parts 3–6 are particularly relevant, especially the sections dealing with 'scientisme', 'naturalisme' and the theatre between 1850 and 1890. P. Martino is perhaps a more old-fashioned historian of literature but his *Le Roman réaliste sous le Second Empire* (Paris, 1913) and his *Le Naturalisme français* (Paris, 1923) are very informative and worth consulting. Another sound and detailed work is C. Beuchat, *Histoire du naturalisme français*, 2 vols (Paris, 1949).

SYMBOLISM

The theory and practice of the symbolist movement in France are well set out and discussed in A. G. Lehmann, *The Symbolist Aesthetic in France, 1885–1895*, 2nd ed. (Oxford, 1968). The same subject is dealt with at length, and in considerable detail, in two works by G. Michaud. His *La Doctrine symboliste* (Paris, 1947) and *Message poétique du symbolisme*, 3 vols (Paris, 1947) are essential reading for a scholarly understanding of symbolism. This is also true of M. Décaudin, *La Crise des valeurs symbolistes* (Paris, 1960), which is only useful for those who are already familiar with basic symbolist doctrine. As regards the theatre, its development through the phases of naturalism and symbolism is excellently studied in J. A. Henderson, *The First Avant-Garde (1887–1894): Sources of the Modern French Theatre* (London, 1971). Apart from accounts of Antoine, Paul Fort and Lugné-Poe, attention is paid to mime, marionettes, etc.

PUBLIC THEMES AND PRIVATE CONCERNS

Several of the ideas and authors mentioned in this section are very readably discussed in V. Brombert, *The Intellectual Hero: Studies in the French Novel, 1880–1955* (Philadelphia and New York, 1961). This book also contains an interesting essay on the development of the concept of 'the intellectual' in France. Those who seek more detailed knowledge of Bourget or Loti should consult M. Mansuy, *Paul*

Bourget (Paris, 1961), or K. G. Millward, *L'Œuvre de Pierre Loti et l'esprit fin de siècle* (Paris, 1955). The drama of the period is discussed in J. R. Taylor, *The Rise and Fall of the Well-Made Play* (London, 1967).

POLITICS AND POLEMICS

M. Tison-Braun, *La Crise de l'humanisme*, Vol. I (Paris, 1958), offers a very full and challenging account of the major writers of the second half of the nineteenth century who also had some political importance or, like Bloy, were passionate critics of Belle Époque society. Much of the same subject-matter, but with an emphasis on the main Catholic polemicists of the period, is covered in R. Griffiths, *The Reactionary Revolution: the Catholic Revival in French Literature, 1870–1914* (London, 1966). The anti-rationalism and political conservatism of the period are excellently described and analysed. These ideas are also briefly but usefully discussed in chapter 3 of P.-H. Simon, *L'Esprit et l'histoire* (Paris, 1954).

FOUR NEW MASTERS

One of the best introductory approaches to Proust remains A. Maurois, *A la recherche de Marcel Proust* (Paris, 1949). A short but illuminating study in English is A. King, *Proust* (London, 1968). We are presented with a most intelligent and sophisticated analysis of *A la recherche du temps perdu* by I. Bersani, *Marcel Proust: the Fictions of Life and of Art* (New York, 1965), and mention should also be made of J. M. Cocking, *Proust* (London, 1956), and J. Mouton, *Proust* (Paris, 1968).

G. W. Ireland, *Gide* (London, 1963), offers a clear and concise general guide to Gide's work. As further reading on the subject both G. Brée, *André Gide, l'insaisissable Protée* (Paris, 1953), and A. J. Guérard, *André Gide*, 2nd ed. (Cambridge, Mass., 1969), are to be recommended. J. Delay has made an impressive psychological study of the young Gide in *La Jeunesse d'André Gide*, 2 vols (Paris, 1956–8).

Among the many books on Valéry, helpful general works include H. A. Grubbs, *Paul Valéry* (New York, 1968), W. N. Ince, *The Poetic Theory of Paul Valéry* (London, 1961), F. Scarfe, *The Art of Paul Valéry* (London, 1954), and P. O. Walzer, *La Poésie de Valéry* (Geneva, 1953).

As regards Claudel, essential reading would include J. Madaule, *Le Drame de Paul Claudel* (Paris, 1947), H. Colleye, *La Poésie catholique de Claudel* (Liège, 1945), and J. Chiari, *The Poetic Drama of Paul Claudel* (London, 1954).

THE GROWTH OF THE AVANT-GARDE

The development of the early avant-garde theatre is comprehensively and authoritatively studied in H. Béhar, *Étude sur le théâtre dada et surréaliste* (Paris, 1967). A more general, somewhat journalistic, but thoroughly entertaining account of the early avant-garde is R. Shattuck, *The Banquet Years: the Arts in France, 1885–1918* (London, 1958). There are chapters on the paintings of Henri Rousseau and the music of Satie, as well as on Jarry and Apollinaire.

LITERATURE AND WORLD WAR I

Basic works include J. N. Cru, *Témoins* (Paris, 1929), and the relevant chapters in M. Tison-Braun, *La Crise de l'humanisme*, Vol. II (Paris, 1967), and M. Rieuneau,

Guerre et révolution dans le roman français 1919–1939 (Paris, 1974). There are useful chapters on the French literary reaction to the war in P.-H. Simon, *L'Esprit et l'histoire* (Paris, 1954), and H. Klein (ed.), *The First World War in Fiction* (London, 1976).

SURREALISM

A very readable account of the phenomenon of surrealism will be found in A Balakian, *Surrealism: the Road to the Absolute* (New York, 1959). An essential work is M. Nadeau, *Histoire du surréalisme*, 2 vols (Paris, 1945–7). The second of these volumes contains a fascinating collection of documents, manifestos, broadsheets, etc. Other helpful and important contributions to the subject include M. Raymond, *De Baudelaire au surréalisme* (Paris, 1933), F. Alquié, *Philosophie du surréalisme* (Paris, 1955), and M. Carrouges, *André Breton et les données fondamentales du surréalisme* (Paris, 1950).

INTER-WAR THEATRE

Most immediately relevant are P. Brisson, *Le Théâtre des années folles* (Geneva, 1943), and D. Knowles, *French Drama in the Inter-War Years, 1918–1939* (London, 1967). This latter work is a mine of factual information enthusiastically presented. Among many other books which include sections on this period, mention should be made of J. Guicharnaud, *Modern French Theatre* (New Haven, Conn., 1961), D. I. Grossvogel, *Twentieth Century French Drama* (New York, 1958), J. Jacquot (ed.), *Le Théâtre moderne:* Vol. I, *Hommes et tendances* (Paris, 1958), and P. Surer, *Le Théâtre français contemporain* (Paris, 1964).

AN AGE OF FICTION

All the novelists mentioned in this section are the subject of many separate studies, either whole books or substantial essays. Attempts to cover more generally the most significant fiction of the period are also numerous. The most full and detailed treatment will be found in H. Peyre, *The Contemporary French Novel* (New York, 1955), and G. Brée and M. Guiton, *An Age of Fiction* (London, 1957). An important work in French is P. de Boisdeffre, *Métamorphoses de la littérature*, 2 vols (Paris, 1963). There is a section on the French novel between the two World Wars in M. Raimond, *Le Roman depuis la Révolution* (Paris, 1967), and essays on Bernanos, Malraux and some theoretical aspects of the age of fiction in J. Cruickshank (ed.), *The Novelist as Philosopher: Studies in French Fiction 1935–1960* (London, 1962).

WORLD WAR II: RESISTANCE AND LIBERATION

Essential to a general understanding of the Resistance are H. Michel, *Histoire de la Résistance*, 2nd ed. (Paris, 1958), and the same author's *Les Courants de pensée de la Résistance* (Paris, 1962). Resistance writing is discussed in Vercors, *La Bataille du silence: souvenirs de minuit* (Paris, 1967), and, more narrowly and at second hand, in H. Josephson and M. Cowley, *Aragon, Poet of the French Resistance* (London, 1945). It is perhaps worth adding that the writings of collaborators are dealt with in P. Sérant, *Le Romantisme fasciste* (Paris, 1959).

HUMANISM AND EXISTENTIALISM

The general literature on this subject is vast. Among general studies, mention should be made of P. Foulquié, *L'Existentialisme* (Paris, 1949), R. Grimsley, *Existentialist Thought* (Cardiff, 1955), R. Pierce, *Contemporary French Political Thought* (London, 1966), and C. Smith, *Contemporary French Philosophy* (London, 1964). It is only possible to list a very few of the many books published on Sartre and Camus. Two of the clearest and most penetrating shorter books on Sartre are: I. Murdoch, *Sartre* (London, 1953), and M. Cranston, *Sartre* (London, 1962). Among longer studies A. R. Manser, *Sartre: a Philosophic Study* (London, 1966), and P. Thody, *Sartre: a Literary and Political Study* (London, 1960), are both to be recommended. On Camus, two of the first studies in English are J. Cruickshank, *Albert Camus and the Literature of Revolt* (London, 1959), and P. Thody, *Albert Camus 1913–1960: a Biographical Study* (London, 1961). A sound general treatment will be found in P. H. Rhein, *Albert Camus* (New York, 1969), and Camus is excellently studied as a 'committed' writer in E. Parker, *Albert Camus: the Artist in the Arena* (Madison, 1965). In connection with French existentialist writing, mention should also be made of G. Gennari, *Simone de Beauvoir* (Paris, 1959).

NEW FORMS IN THE THEATRE

Two basic introductory studies in English are M. Esslin, *The Theatre of the Absurd* (London, 1961), and L. C. Pronko, *Avant-Garde: the Experimental Theatre in France* (Berkeley and Los Angeles, 1962). Other books well worth consulting include L. Abel, *Metatheatre: a New View of Dramatic Form* (New York, 1963), P. L. Mignon, *Le Théâtre d'aujourd'hui de A jusqu'à Z* (Paris, 1966), G. Serreau, *Histoire du nouveau théâtre* (Paris, 1966), and G. E. Wellworth, *The Theatre of Protest and Paradox* (London, 1964).

SOME POST-WAR POETS

Selections from all the leading post-war French poets, together with some most illuminating critical comments, will be found in C. A. Hackett, *An Anthology of French Poetry* (Oxford, 1952), and the same editor's *New French Poetry: an Anthology* (Oxford, 1973). Other useful introductions to this general field are A. M. Boase (ed.), *The Poetry of France, Vol. 4: 1900–1965* (London, 1969), and J. Rousselot, *Panorama critique des nouveaux poètes français* (Paris, 1953). There are some outstanding critical insights in J.-P. Richard, *Onze études sur la poésie moderne* (Paris, 1964), and there are articles on Jouve, Reverdy, Aragon, Desnos and the modern *poème en prose* in E. M. Beaumont, J. M. Cocking and J. Cruickshank (eds), *Order and Adventure in Post-Romantic French Poetry: Essays presented to C. A. Hackett* (Oxford, 1973).

TOWARDS A NEW NOVEL

The best introduction in English is undoubtedly J. Sturrock, *The French New Novel* (London, 1969). Another highly intelligent book, and one which is also sympathetic towards the aims of the *nouveaux romanciers*, is L. Janvier, *Une Parole exigeante* (Paris, 1964). A more hostile view is taken by J. Bloch-Michel, *Le Présent de l'indicatif* (Paris, 1963). The whole phenomenon is discussed, useful factual information is given, and brief extracts in English translation from more than a dozen 'new novelists' are provided by L. Lesage, *The French New Novel: an Introduction and a Sampler* (Pennsylvania, 1962).

STRUCTURALISM AND SEMIOLOGY

Among the increasing number of volumes of structuralist literary criticism, particular mention should be made of G. Genette, *Figures*, 3 vols (Paris, 1966, 1969, 1972), T. Todorov, *Littérature et signification* (Paris, 1967), and R. Barthes, *S/Z* (Paris, 1970). Basic works on the theory and practice of structuralism and semiotics include J. Culler, *Structuralist Poetics* (London, 1975), T. Hawkes, *Structuralism and Semiotics* (London, 1977), and M. Lane, *Structuralism: a Reader* (London, 1970). J.-M. Auzias, *Clefs pour le structuralisme* (Paris, 1967), is clear and helpful. Much more demanding is J.-M. Benoist, *La Révolution structurale* (Paris, 1975). Mention should also be made of P. Pettit, *The Concept of Structuralism: a Critical Analysis* (Dublin, 1975).

10 French Painting, Sculpture and Architecture since 1500

ANTHONY BLUNT

The Sixteenth Century

In the years 1530–40 there occurred in French painting one of those complete breaks which are very rare in the history of art. On his return from captivity in Madrid, François I set about achieving his ambition to create in France an intellectual and artistic centre which should rival the great courts of Italy, the beauties of which he had savoured during the Italian campaigns.[1]

The focal point of his activities was Fontainebleau, which, from being a small hunting lodge, became within a few years one of the most splendid palaces in Europe. Two Italian artists were called to France to decorate it. One, Giovanni Battista Rosso (1494–1540), was a Florentine; the other, Francesco Primaticcio (1504–70), was trained in Bologna and Mantua. Their achievement can be judged from the decoration surviving in the Galerie François I, now freed from the nineteenth-century restoration which for long disfigured it.

What is unusual about the achievement of the First School of Fontainebleau, as it is called, was that the two Italian artists did not produce a slightly second-hand version of what they had learnt in Italy, but created a completely new manner of decoration which was to spread over the whole of Europe, and even to exercise influence in northern Italy on artists of the calibre of Palladio. Its essential novelty lay in a brilliant combination of high-relief stucco work with large painted

[1] Owing to the general scheme of the book in which this essay was first published, this section had to be produced without illustrations, and the author was therefore forced to concentrate on the more general characteristics of French art. In this new edition a few plates are included but these can only give a taste of the pleasures which the subject provides.

panels, and its hallmark was a type of decoration called strap-work, which consists of elements looking like pieces of leather or parchment cut and curled over in the form of scrolls. Panels of this strap-work were copied in engravings which were circulated throughout Europe and helped to spread the style. In their actual paintings Rosso and Primaticcio created novel variations on the style called 'Mannerism', which had recently been evolved in Italy by the members of Raphael's studio in Rome and Mantua. It was characterized by extreme elegance of forms and of gestures, elongation of proportions, and ingenuity of iconography, all features to be seen in the frescoes of the Galerie François I.

Rosso and Primaticcio swept the board as far as decorative and historical painting were concerned, but in portraiture a naturalistic style, deriving partly from Flanders and partly from Italy, continued to be practised. Much the most distinguished representative of this style was Jean Clouet (active 1516; d. 1540), who is known by a few paintings and miniatures, and by a magnificent series of portrait drawings in the Musée Condé at Chantilly. The tradition of portraiture was carried on by his son, François (before 1520–72), who was brilliantly successful in his rendering of costume but lacked the grasp of monumental form which characterized the work of his father, and by Corneille de Lyon (d. 1574), an enigmatic figure to whom a number of small and delicately painted portraits are ascribed.

In architecture the change was much less abrupt. During the first quarter of the sixteenth century French soldiers and diplomats taking part in the Italian campaigns had brought back from Lombardy, and even sometimes from further south, sculptors and craftsmen capable of executing fine Italianate decoration on the buildings then going up, which were still in a late Gothic style. The combination is sometimes awkward but can be surprisingly harmonious, as in churches such as Saint-Pierre at Caen, built by Hector Sohier between 1528 and 1545 or Saint-Eustache in Paris (begun 1532), in the châteaux like Chambord (begun in 1519), Azay-le-Rideau (1518–27) and Chenonceaux (begun 1515), and in smaller town houses, of which many are also to be found in the Loire Valley (e.g. the Hôtel Pincé at Angers and the Hôtel d'Alluye at Blois (before 1508)), or further south at Toulouse.

The first architect to bring a more consciously classical style of architecture into France was Sebastiano Serlio (1475–1554), who arrived in 1540 or 1541. The house which he built for the Cardinal of Ferrara at Fontainebleau, called 'Le grand Ferrare', is now known only from engravings, but it set a pattern, which was followed for more than a century, consisting of a principal *corps-de-logis* at the back of a courtyard which was flanked by lower wings and closed by a wall containing the main entrance. His only surviving building, the Château of Ancy-le-Franc near Tonnerre (*c.* 1546), is the first 'regular' building to be put up in France. It was not, however, much copied as a model, and Serlio's influence was exercised much more powerfully through his *Treatise*, which appeared in parts between 1537 and 1554, and which was used as a textbook by French architects for the remainder of the sixteenth century.

The formation of the School of Fontainebleau is an example of a phenomenon relatively common in the history of the visual arts, which for obvious reasons can hardly ever happen in the history of literature: a complete change of direction caused by the arrival of foreign artists. In literature the language barrier is inevitably so strong that the temptation to a poet to settle in another country is not great, and such emigrations usually only occur for external, probably political or religious, reasons.[1] Even the influence of foreign writers through their books, read in the original or in translation, has not quite the same immediacy as the physical presence of artists who set up their studios, take in pupils, execute commissions for patrons, and on occasion transform the art of the country of their adoption. Examples of such 'invasions' are not rare – Holbein and Van Dyck in England are obvious examples – though they hardly occur after the sixteenth century in France, but another aspect of the same phenomenon continued to be of importance. Till at any rate the beginning of the nineteenth century Italy – and above all Rome – continued to be the goal of every French artist, whether painter, sculptor, or architect, and all those who were able went there to study, either sent by a rich patron or, later, with a Prix de Rome. In this way they acquired a knowledge of Italian art which often exercised a decisive influence on their style. If they went to Rome, their principal aim would be to see the works of ancient art – which they studied just as writers read the classics – but they were also influenced by the art of Raphael or Annibale Carracci, or – more rarely – the great artists of the baroque, and they came back to France armed with drawings after the works they particularly admired, which they kept in their studios and to which they referred constantly as the standards at which they themselves aimed in their own productions. In

[1] The phenomenon occurs in music, but less frequently than in painting. The cases of Lully, Piccini and Gluck are the most obvious.

the later periods they were also kept in touch with what was taking place or had taken place abroad by means of engravings, which by the later seventeenth century had attained a high level of accuracy as reproductions. Finally, from the last years of Louis XIV's reign onwards, artists could see original works of older masters in the Royal Collection and in other private collections in Paris.

It must not be supposed that this constant reference to the works of ancient Roman or more recent Italian art implies any limitation in the French artists of the sixteenth and seventeenth centuries. On the contrary, what they learnt from their studies in Rome served only to enrich their minds and enabled them, if they had any innate imaginative power, to give richer and fuller expression to their own ideas. The history of French art at this time is largely that of the new and personal interpretation of ideas, formal and iconographical, learnt from the ancients or the great masters of the Renaissance. Poussin – the most personal and perhaps the most purely French of French classical artists – would have been the first to admit this. He declared himself the pupil of antiquity and Raphael, but no one would deny that he was one of the most original artists of the whole seventeenth century.

The way in which French artists of the mid-sixteenth century transformed what they had learnt from Italy into a national style is an example of this phenomenon. The transformation was due to two men: Pierre Lescot (*c.* 1510–78) and Philibert de l'Orme (*c.* 1510–70). In the same year that Serlio planned Ancy-le-Franc, Lescot began work on rebuilding the Square Court of the Louvre, which replaced the medieval château. It was originally planned to be of about the same size as the medieval building, but at an early stage the project was enlarged so that each side of the court was to contain two wings of the original scale with a large central pavilion between them. Building proceeded very slowly, and the central feature which we see today, the Pavillon de l'Horloge, was built by Lemercier in about 1640. Lescot's style is a characteristically French variation on Italian models. Each floor is articulated by an order of half-columns, as would be normal in an Italian palace, but the treatment of architectural detail would to Italian eyes seem rather free, and the architect has indulged in a richness of surface decoration which would be unusual in Rome. This decoration was executed by the finest sculptor of the day, Jean Goujon (*c.* 1510–? 1568), whose work has an almost Hellenistic elegance. He also decorated the Hôtel Carnavalet, the only town house of the period surviving in Paris, which was almost certainly designed by Lescot –

where Madame de Sévigné later lived – and carved the exquisite reliefs on the Fontaine des Innocents (now in the Louvre).

Philibert de l'Orme was a much more inventive architect, who combined great skill in structure, derived from the tradition of medieval masons, with the use of classical forms which he learnt during a long stay in Rome. Little of his work survives, but the fragments of the château of Anet (begun *c.* 1549; the frontispiece has been moved to the École des Beaux-Arts, Paris) show his talents both as a builder and as a decorator. His treatise on architecture gives a remarkable insight into the way architects worked in the sixteenth century. De l'Orme was a friend of Rabelais, and the architectural details of the Abbaye de Thélème were probably supplied by him.

Art at the court of the last Valois, particularly Henri III, was of great, perhaps excessive, refinement. The paintings of Antoine Caron (*c.* 1520–*c.* 1600), who worked largely for Catherine de Medici, exaggerate the elongation of forms of the First School of Fontainebleau and go even further in the use of fantastic iconography, including references to alchemy and the most obscure ancient historians, all directed towards the flattery of the queen and her courtiers. The one great artist of the period was the sculptor Germain Pilon (before 1530–90), whose bronze figures from the tomb of the chancellor René de Birague (now in the Louvre) are among the most profound expressions of the spirit of the Counter-Reformation to be found in French art.

The wars of religion limited activities in architecture. Charles IX planned a vast château called Charleval, Catherine de Medici began the palace of the Tuileries and a few courtiers imitated her; but little came of it and almost nothing remains. A few houses still stand in Paris, of which the most important is the Hôtel d'Angoulême, later the Hôtel de Lamoignon.

In many provincial cities, however, there was great activity in the arts during the second half of the sixteenth century. In Toulouse and many other towns the rich bourgeois built a series of splendid private houses, and in Limoges there was a remarkable revival of the art of enamel painting which had been one of the glories of the city during the Middle Ages.

The Seventeenth Century

After the pacification of France, Henri IV quickly set about improving the city of Paris. His two great creations there, the Place Royale, now the Place des Vosges, and the Place Dauphine on the point of the Île de la Cité, are much in advance of town planning elsewhere and embody Henri's desire to put up buildings of practical use to the citizens of Paris rather than monuments to his own glory.

During the reign of Henri IV painting was at a low ebb, and the painters employed by the king to decorate his palaces, who formed the Second School of Fontainebleau, were mainly of mediocre ability, though one, Toussaint Dubreuil (1561–1602), showed some sensibility. There was much more activity at the court of Lorraine, the art of which is best represented by the work of two etchers, Jacques Bellange (act. 1600–17), a Mannerist of unusual dramatic power, and Jacques Callot (1592–1635), who learnt his art in Florence but came back to Nancy for the last years of his life. His etchings range from witty renderings of court life to deeply felt records of the Thirty Years War, such as the *Grandes Misères de la Guerre* (1633).

In Paris much the most important event in painting in the early part of the century was the return in 1627 of Simon Vouet (1590–1649) from Italy, where he had spent some thirteen years, mainly in Rome. He brought back with him a knowledge of baroque painting as it was being developed in Rome by artists such as Giovanni Lanfranco and Pietro da Cortona. He soon established himself as the most popular painter with the king and with the great officers of the court, for whom he executed decorations for their châteaux and town houses, and altar-pieces for churches of which they were patrons. All the most important painters of the next generation – in the first instance Charles Lebrun – learnt their art in his studio. Vouet was not an artist of great originality, but he supplied French patrons with a form of moderate baroque style which exactly suited their needs. His paintings were striking and decorative, but they did not have the intense rhetorical emotionalism of Roman baroque art.

As *premier peintre du Roi* Vouet was the most powerfully placed artist in Paris, but both before and after his return from Rome there were other artists working in manners independent of his influence. Claude Vignon (1593–1670) had also spent some years (1616–24) in Rome, where he was influenced by Elsheimer and the Caravaggisti. His interest lay in richness of colour and texture rather than in the conventional formulas of the baroque. He was also influenced by the Dutch painters whom Rembrandt studied in his youth, and he was even in touch with Rembrandt himself, whose etchings he seems to have made known in Paris.

During the 1630s and 1640s there were certain painters who, though influenced by Vouet, yet moved away from his style towards a calmer, more classical, manner. Of these the most attractive was Jacques Blanchard (1600–38), whose cool silvery tones contrast with the strong, sometimes rather brash colouring of Vouet. Laurent de la Hire (1606–56), who is said to have trained himself by the study of the painters of Fontainebleau, produced small paintings, mainly of religious subjects, which are markedly classical in style and in a sense prepared the Parisian public for the works of Poussin.

Other artists, notably Eustache Le Sueur (1616–55) and Sébastien Bourdon (1616–71), formed part of this classicizing group and were in their later works directly influenced by Poussin. Le Sueur was trained in Vouet's studio and for a time followed his style, but in his later works he was influenced by Poussin's religious painting of the 1640s. His series of canvases illustrating the life of St Bruno (Louvre), painted for the cloister of the Chartreux of Paris, have a quality of *recueillement* which is appropriate to the contemplative life of this order. Sébastien Bourdon spent some years in Rome, where he was influenced by the Dutch painters of popular scenes, called the *Bamboccianti*, but on his return to Paris took up religious painting in a more personal style. The works of his last years are in a cold version of Poussin's classical style.

More independent were the three brothers Le Nain, who were born in Laon but spent their working lives in Paris, where they established a successful studio for painting large religious compositions. They are now, however, mainly remembered for their small naturalistic paintings of interiors, sometimes with groups of bourgeois sitters, sometimes with peasants. The eldest, Antoine (before 1600–48), painted very small pictures, sometimes on copper, of endearing simplicity but no great artistic merit. Mathieu, the youngest (1607–77), became a more fashionable artist and painted more polished groups, sometimes with figures from the Paris militia to which he belonged. By far the most distinguished is the middle brother, Louis (after 1600–48), whose paintings of peasants – sometimes in their kitchens, but sometimes in a landscape setting – have a classical dignity and detachment, avoiding the extremes of caricature or sentimentality which so often mark paintings of peasant subjects. It remains a mystery by whom these peasant groups were commissioned. There is no record of any collector owning a painting by any of the Le Nains till the 1760s, when, in the age of *sensibilité*, their works had a sudden success. It is unlikely that they painted for the great nobles or the very rich bourgeois because their works would be recorded in the inventories of their collections, and it may be surmised – with every hesitation – that they worked for real middle-class patrons, whose forebears may have come from the country not many generations earlier. But this is a pure guess.

A less grand kind of naturalism is to be seen in the engravings of Abraham Bosse (1602–76), which are of historical value as giving the best available picture of everyday life in Paris in the mid-seventeenth century, but which also have great technical skill and show a classical sense of design.

The work of Bosse and the Le Nain brothers has analogies with the naturalism of Dutch and Flemish art of the same period, but does not seem to derive directly from it. Philippe de Champaigne (1602–70) on the other hand was born in Flanders and partly trained there. He came to Paris as a young man in 1621 and spent the rest of his life there. Although he was originally trained as a landscape painter, his most important works are religious compositions and portraits. In his earlier years he was closely connected with the court and was commissioned by the Queen Mother to paint a number of altar-pieces for convents in which she was interested, notably the Carmelites of the Rue Saint-Jacques, and he also executed official portraits for Louis XIII. His most personal works were in a different vein and for different patrons. In the early 1640s he came into contact with the Jansenists, and his outlook on life and art was profoundly influenced by their teachings. His daughter became a nun at Port-Royal and Philippe himself remained in close touch with the group, painting the altar-piece for the abbey and portraits of many prominent Jansenists. Some of these are portraits from life – Arnauld d'Andilly, La Mère Agnès Arnauld – but others were certainly commemorative portraits, executed at or after the death of the subjects. They were images of the saints of Jansenism – Jansen himself, the first Saint-Cyran, and others – and it is certainly no chance that they have a remarkable similarity to the *chef* reliquaries made in the Middle Ages to house the relics of particularly venerable saints. Champaigne's grandest expression of his devotion to Jansenism is the portrait of La Mère Agnès Arnauld and Champaigne's own daughter, painted to celebrate the miraculous cure of the latter brought about in 1662 by the prayers of the nuns of Port-Royal. It is perhaps the calmest and most classical rendering of a miracle in seventeenth-century art.

Paris was the main centre of artistic activity in France at this time, but in centres such as Toulouse and Aix-en-Provence there existed schools which were to some extent independent of the capital. Most of these were undistinguished, but Nancy produced one great artist in Georges de la Tour (1593–1652), who gave to the naturalism and the dramatic use of light which had been the great innovation of Caravaggio a monumentality and a stillness which have justifiably led to the word 'classical' being applied to his art.

It is a paradox that the two greatest French painters of the seventeenth century spent their whole working lives in Rome. Nicolas Poussin (1594–1665) was born in Normandy and spent his youth in Paris, but in 1624 he settled in Rome, only leaving it for an unhappy visit to Paris in 1640–2. Claude Gellée, Le Lorrain (1600–82), was born in Lorraine but went to Rome as a boy, staying there for the rest of his life, apart from a visit to Nancy in 1625.

Poussin arrived in Rome at the moment when the baroque style was reaching a sudden maturity, but, except in one or two early experimental works, he set his face against this movement and, working outside the mainstream of official painting in Rome, evolved a style which is among the purest expressions of the classical spirit. From his first years in Rome his approach to his art was deeply influenced by the circle of friends among whom he moved and for whom he worked. This was centred round Cassiano dal Pozzo, a patron of the arts, a passionate admirer of antiquity, a learned archaeologist, and a student of both philosophy and the natural sciences. From Pozzo and his friends Poussin soon acquired a knowledge not only of ancient art, but also of ancient history and philosophy, which was to be a vital factor in his artistic creation. Poussin is one of the rare instances of an artist who painted primarily to express his ideas, but he believed that the idea must be expressed in a form which is beautiful in itself and perfectly suited to it. It was to the pursuit of this ideal that he devoted his life, avoiding public acclaim in order to work quietly in his own studio, rejecting the tricks and virtuosity of his baroque contemporaries, and seeking only to satisfy his own scrupulous sensibility.

During the late twenties and the first half of the thirties his themes were chosen mainly from Greek and Roman mythology, above all from Ovid's *Metamorphoses*, and these he embodied in a series of small poetical canvases, warm in colour and free in handling, in a style inspired by the *Bacchanals* of Titian, which he studied and even copied in Rome. These early paintings appeal immediately by their atmosphere and their technical brilliance, but they generally have more complex associations than appears at first sight. The *Arcadian Shepherds* (Chatsworth) is an allegory on the frailty of human happiness, and many of the mythological paintings were almost certainly intended to have allusions to the cyclical processes of nature, particularly the alternation of day and night, and some, such as the *Death of Adonis* (Caen), refer to familiar ancient symbols of death and resurrection.

In the second half of the thirties Poussin's work began to be known in Paris. Cardinal Richelieu commissioned two famous *Bacchanals* for the Château de Richelieu, but Poussin's main patrons in France were drawn from a group of serious though not very wealthy bourgeois civil servants, small bankers, silk manufacturers, and so on, some of whom visited Rome and were in contact with the circle of Pozzo. It was for them that Poussin produced in the 1640s and early 1650s the paintings for which he was most famous in his own day and for the remainder of the seventeenth century.

The themes of these paintings were drawn mainly from the *Lives* of Plutarch or from the New Testament. Poussin's letters make it abundantly clear that he was a keen admirer of Stoic philosophy – indeed his own life was lived in accordance with it – and he found inspiration for some of his finest works in the stories of Phocion, Scipio Africanus and other heroes of Plutarch. On the other hand he was a sincere Christian, sometimes making light of the outward ceremonies of the Church of Rome, but believing profoundly in her basic doctrines. But, as was often the case in the seventeenth century, there was no conflict between his two creeds, and in some of his most remarkable works of this period, notably the *Seven Sacraments* (Duke of Sutherland collection, on loan to the National Gallery of Scotland), the two are combined in a kind of syncretism not uncommon at the time.

Stylistically there is a marked change in these works. Poussin now conceives of painting as a rational art, appealing to the mind, not the eye, and he jettisons all the sensuous attractions of his earlier work in his pursuit of the clearest, most explicit, and most concentrated expression of his theme. Forms are sharp and moulded like Roman sculpture; colours are clear and unbroken; space is defined with the utmost clarity; gestures are used solely to express the action and emotion of the participants in the scene; architecture and other archaeological details are minutely thought out. The result is an art without surprises, but with rare lucidity and harmony.

In the same period Poussin developed his interest in landscape painting, usually as a setting for a Stoic story, such as that of Phocion (two paintings, belonging to the Earl of Derby and the Earl of Plymouth). Here the figures are relatively small and nature plays the major role, but it is an orderly nature, drawn to the scale of man, and it is almost certain that Poussin had in mind the Stoic idea that the greatest manifestations of the λόγος were the harmony of nature and the virtues of man. In his last years Poussin's landscapes change in character: nature becomes rich, luxuriant and powerful, and man becomes a worm. The almost pantheistic feeling in these paintings was apparently inspired by the doctrines of Tommaso Campanella, but Poussin also incorporates in them certain mythological themes which had been used by late antique Stoic philosophers, such as Macrobius, as allegories for the processes of nature. Poussin therefore returns to themes which he had treated in his youth, but he does so in a very different spirit. The last paintings, such as the *Apollo and Daphne* (Louvre), are the meditation of an ageing philosopher, not the romantic out-pourings of a young painter; they carry one to a world of intellectual dreaming, in which Poussin's ideas find their purest and most poetic expression.

Claude Lorrain is in many respects the exact opposite of Poussin. He only painted landscapes and never figure compositions. Poussin sprang from the tradition of ancient art and of Italian High Renaissance painting; Claude belongs to the line of naturalist landscape painters from Flanders, Holland and Germany who worked in Rome. Even in their treatment of landscape painting their approaches are different. Poussin's landscapes are closed and rationally ordered; Claude's are open to the horizon and evocative. They recall the beauty of the Campagna round Rome, which was usually the subject of his landscapes; but they do not evoke it only visually; they call up the legends which had grown up in it, the nymphs and country deities who haunted it in Virgil and still haunt it today, the stories of Aeneas sailing up the Tiber and landing at Pallanteum to found the city of Rome. Sometimes Claude paints religious subjects or themes from Ovid, but these, too, he sets in the Campagna. Claude loved the sun and the sea. No painter has suggested so vividly the ripples of the Mediterranean disappearing towards the horizon, and no painter before him had had the courage actually to paint the sun in the sky.

Claude's landscapes show us a quintessence of the Campagna in generalized form, but they are based on a minute study of the actual scenery which he painted. His drawings are unequalled for their subtle observation of the silhouettes formed by trees against the sky and of the effects of light, direct or *à contre-jour*, which he observed in the Campagna. His early biographers tell us that he went out before dawn to draw and often lingered till sunset, and many of his paintings embody his observation of the long shadows of early morning and late evening, and sometimes even of the effects of moonlight. The Dutch painters of Claude's time observed nature with as much care as he did, but their approach was more prosaic. He penetrated more deeply into the spirit of nature, and it is no chance that he was so much admired by the Romantic poets. His paintings have much in common with the poetry of Keats, who wrote a very moving description of one of them, the *Enchanted Castle* (C. Loyd collection, Lockinge, Berkshire).

The middle decades of the seventeenth century were also a period of great glory in French architecture. The movement begins with Salomon de Brosse (1571–1626), who, though trained in the school of the Androuet du Cerceau family, rejected their ornate and tortured style and brought French architecture back to the line of classicism inaugurated by Philibert de l'Orme. Much of his work has been destroyed, but the Luxembourg Palace, built for Marie de' Medici (begun 1615), and the façade of the Palais du Parlement de Bretagne at Rennes (now the Palais de Justice) reveal a feeling for simple masses which had been lost in the late sixteenth century in the pursuit of surface ornament.

The most successful architect of the next generation was Jacques Le Mercier (1585–1654), who, after a period of training in Rome, became first architect to the king and, what was even more important, the favourite architect of Cardinal Richelieu, for whom he built the châteaux at Richelieu and Rueil, the Palais Royal and the Sorbonne. Of these works only the church of the Sorbonne survives and shows Le Mercier to have been a competent but unimaginative architect. The true successor to Salomon de Brosse was François Mansart (1598–1667). He created the first maturely classical style of French architecture and, in the subtlety of his interpretation of antiquity, as well as the refinement of his designs, he forms a close parallel to Poussin. In spite of the fact that he almost certainly never visited Italy, his works reveal a far truer understanding of the architecture of the Italian Renaissance than those of Le Mercier, who spent many years in Rome.

Like Poussin, Mansart worked mainly for the bourgeoisie rather than the great noble families, but, architecture being a more expensive art than painting, it was among the very rich members of the class that he found his patrons. They were often the rich *partisans* who had made their fortunes through the exploitation of the State taxes, or the most powerful - and probably most corrupt – members of the legal caste, but they had the taste to appreciate his art and the patience to put up with his arrogant and wayward character.

In his earliest surviving work, the Château de Balleroy, near Bayeux, Mansart breaks with the French tradition of building châteaux round a central courtyard and creates a free-standing block divided into three harmoniously related sections. In this he was following the example set by de Brosse in the destroyed Château of Blérancourt, but in his two major works of this kind, the Orléans wing of the Château de Blois (1635–8) and the château of Maisons, now Maisons-Laffitte (1642–6), near Paris, he goes far beyond his master.

At Blois the effect depends mainly on the scrupulous manner in which he respects the surface of the walls, only broken by light pilasters, which are carefully disposed so as not to interfere with the sharpness of the corners which define the blocks. At Maisons the main block is broken up in a much bolder manner, leading in a series of stages to the tall central frontispiece, composed of three superimposed groups of coupled columns, each floor being treated in a different manner. The effect of variety is increased by the presence of two one-storeyed wings which project at each end of the block. Inside the château the most remarkable feature is the staircase, one of the first to be built in France round an open well, so disposed that the spectator can grasp at a single glance the whole space and the movement of the staircase itself. The detail at Maisons is of superb quality. The orders are treated with a correctness hitherto unknown in France; some of the carved decoration, which was executed by Jacques Sarrazin (1588–1660) and the brothers François (1604–69) and Michel Anguier (1617–86), foreshadows the classicism of the style of Louis XVI; and the wrought-iron grilles, which originally filled the entrance doors but are now in the Galerie d'Apollon in the Louvre, show an incredibly high level of craftsmanship.

Although Mansart was essentially a great classical architect, there are certain features in his work which come close to the baroque. At Maisons he used concave oval bays on the outside of the projecting wings, and even more complex shapes occur in his designs for the east front of the Louvre. Moreover, if his whole schemes for Blois and Maisons had been carried out, they would have created enormous vistas of a kind which are characteristic of the baroque: at Blois a great forecourt leading down into the town on one side, and, on the other, gardens carried on a huge bridge over the ravine behind the château; at Maisons long avenues leading at right angles to each other into the

Forêt de Saint-Germain. Here and in the Château of Fresnes, near Meaux – now destroyed – Mansart also used many forms of garden layout the invention of which is generally attributed to André Le Nôtre.

Mansart was also involved in the building of several churches, but many of them have been modified or destroyed. The Visitation in the Rue Saint-Antoine is an early work, ingenious in plan and decoration, but unfortunately the Val-de-Grâce, which would have been his masterpiece, was not completed according to his designs. The plan is his, and he carried the actual building up to the level of the cornice; but the commission was then taken away from him and given to Le Mercier, on account of Mansart's extravagance and his refusal to stick to any plan he had made if he thought of an improvement to it. This difficult temperament caused him also to lose the commission for the east wing of the Louvre, and probably also prevented him from carrying out the chapel which Louis XIV planned to build at the east end of Saint Denis to form a mausoleum for the Bourbon dynasty, grander than the Valois chapel begun by Catherine de Medici for her husband, herself and their children, attached to the transept of the same church.

The third architect of this group, Louis Le Vau (1612–70), was a younger man and leads over into the period of Versailles. He began his career as a brilliant designer of town houses, and the Hôtel Lambert, on the point of the Île Saint-Louis (begun 1640), is one of the best examples of ingenuity in the exploitation of a difficult site. His great opportunity came when he was commissioned by Fouquet to build the Château of Vaux-le-Vicomte, near Melun. The château itself lacks the *finesse* of Maisons, and the great achievement of Fouquet and Le Vau was the organization of a team of artists of all kinds to collaborate in a great whole, including the gardens as well as the house, sculpture and painting as well as architecture, and even the art of music. The team only gave one full performance, the great fête of 17 August 1661, given by Fouquet to the king, which precipitated the Minister's downfall. Here, in a château designed by Le Vau and painted by Charles Lebrun, set in gardens designed by Le Nôtre with sculptures after models by Poussin, the first performance of Molière's *Les Fâcheux* was given, with a prologue by La Fontaine and interludes by Lully. When Fouquet was arrested, Colbert had only to take over this team to serve the king and prepare the art of Versailles.

The Personal Reign of Louis XIV

Louis XIV did not finally decide to abandon the Louvre in favour of Versailles till about 1668, and during the 1660s Colbert, who was still hoping to persuade the king to remain in Paris, was concerned with the completion of the Square Court of the Louvre by adding the east wing which was to contain the principal entrance to the palace. After Mansart's designs had been rejected, the king asked various Italian architects to submit designs and eventually invited Bernini to come to Paris to supervise the actual execution of the building. For various reasons – not least the fact that Bernini took no account of French taste or the requirements of the king – the project was abandoned, and the designs are now known only from engravings. The event was of great significance as symbolizing the fact that France was no longer subservient to the dictates of Rome in matters of taste, but was establishing its own standards and indeed preparing to create a style which was to dominate Europe. This style was fully elaborated only at Versailles, but many of its essential features are to be seen in works executed on Colbert's orders at the Louvre: the Galerie d'Apollon, redecorated by Lebrun after a fire in 1661, and the Colonnade, built between 1667 and 1670 after designs prepared by a committee of three, Le Vau, Charles Perrault and Lebrun of whom the first two played the most important parts in the production of the design.

French art of the period from 1661 till the death of Colbert in 1683 is dominated by two factors: the taste of the king – and more particularly his ideas on the function of the arts in an absolute monarchy – and the ability of Colbert and Lebrun (1619–90) to give these ideas practical expression. For Louis XIV the main function of the arts was to provide an appropriate setting for his person and his court and to record his actions and the glories of his reign. For this purpose the team of artists taken over from Fouquet formed an admirable starting-point, but a clear formal organization was needed. This was achieved by two means: the reorganization of the Academy and the creation of the Gobelins. The Académie de Peinture et de Sculpture had been formed in 1648 by a group of artists under the protection of the Chancellor, Séguier, primarily to free themselves from the old *maîtrise*, the Guild of St Luke, which was in many ways out of date and restrictive. In 1663 Lebrun was put in charge of the Academy and undertook a complete reform of its organization. Its function was double: to train young painters and sculptors, and to define the correct doctrine about the arts, just as the Académie Française was responsible for the principles of language and literature. The training was carefully organized under a team of professors, who were also compelled, often against their will, to give lectures on individual paintings in the Royal Collection, in which they laid down the principles according to which artists should work. The Gobelins was designed to fulfil a more practical function. Under the direction of Lebrun a superb group of craftsmen was brought together who could design and execute everything that was necessary for the decoration of a palace: furniture, wood-carving, tapestry, and silver-work. Only carpets were excluded, and they were made in a separate factory at the Savonnerie. For all these works Lebrun supplied at least small sketches, which were worked up and then put into execution by the individual craftsmen.

Versailles had originally been a small château built by Louis XIII as a hunting lodge, and when Louis XIV decided to make it the seat of the court and the centre of the State administration, drastic enlargements were necessary. The first alterations, begun by Le Vau in 1669, involved building two flights of rooms on the outside of the existing château, one for the king's *appartement*, the other for the queen's. These ended on the garden front in two pavilions, between which ran a terrace at first-floor level. At the end of the 1670s the king decided to fill in this terrace, in order to build the Galerie des Glaces, the Salon de la Paix, and the Salon de la Guerre. Soon afterwards the palace was extended by the addition of two long wings, which gave the garden façade a length of more than 1,800 feet. Le Vau had died in 1670, and the alterations were carried out by Jules Hardouin-Mansart (1646–1708), the great-nephew of François Mansart, who exercised supreme power over the royal buildings for more than thirty years. Unfortunately he did not take into account the effect which the vast increase in length would have on the façade as a whole, and he simply repeated Le Vau's design with a small order for the principal floor, which was in scale with the original front but has a certain meanness when repeated over the central part of the façade, no longer broken by the terrace, and the whole length of the wings.

The two *Grands Appartements* are the most magnificent manifestation of the art of Louis XIV's reign; or, it would be truer to say, they were such a manifestation at the time of their creation, because many of their essential elements have vanished. The marbled panels of the walls, the stuccoed and painted ceilings, and the carved doors survive, but the marble floors were taken up after a short time for practical reasons, many of the tapestries were sold and – the greatest loss of all – the silver furniture was all sent to the mint to be melted down in 1689 during the war of the League of Augsburg. Unhappily there are no adequate visual records of what these rooms looked like when completely furnished, and it requires a considerable effort of the imagination to visualize their splendour.

The gardens of Versailles are as splendid as the palace. Here Le Nôtre, who had developed the new style of garden design on a small scale at Vaux and the Tuileries, had the opportunity of working in the grand manner and to lay out a complex of parterres, *allées* and canals, punctuated by sculptures and fountains, on a scale hitherto unknown. To twentieth-century eyes the gardens of Versailles seem formal, but in fact Le Nôtre's object was to break away from the even more artificial Italian type of garden, which was composed mainly of pergolas and knot-gardens, and to make his park more 'natural'.

Lebrun was in the first place a superb organizer, but he was also a fine artist in his own right. He was something of a prodigy and was already providing mature works of considerable originality and great force before he went to complete his studies in Rome in 1643 at the age of twenty-four. In the execution of the painted ceilings at Versailles and the huge canvases commissioned by the king, such as the *Histoire d'Alexandre*, he of necessity made use of assistants, but evidently executed much of the work with his own hand. His real talents as an artist appear at their best in a small group of very moving works, painted for his own pleasure during the years after the death of Colbert, when he was in effect pushed aside by Louvois and prevented from obtaining any official commissions.

The Academy laid down strict rules for the teaching of its students. The young painter began by copying, first from engravings or drawings and then after paintings by the accepted masters, and finally from casts of ancient sculpture. By this process he was supposed to learn what was beautiful in nature, according to the accepted standards, which meant in effect according to the practice of the ancient Romans, Raphael and Poussin. Only after he had fixed in his mind the principles according to which these artists worked, above all in so far as they concerned the proportions of the human figure, was the young artist allowed to draw directly from nature, for only then would he be in a position to judge what was truly beautiful in nature, what was in accordance with the ideal which, according to Aristotle, nature always seeks but never attains in any one work. Lebrun also laid great stress on the importance of the correct expression of the emotions, and in his treatise on the subject laid down rules on how the features of the face were affected by different emotions, examining the physiological causes for the changes and further investigating the analogies which exist between the various types of human face and the heads of different animals.

The doctrine of the Academy, based as it was on the models of antiquity, Raphael and Poussin, further laid down that drawing was the true basis of painting, because it appealed to the mind, and that colour, which only appealed to the eye, was of altogether minor importance. This doctrine soon aroused opposition and led to a series of violent discussions between the supporters of drawing, called the *Poussinistes*, and the partisans of colour, called the *Rubénistes*, because they set up Rubens as the equal of the great French painter on account of his mastery of colour. The drawing-colour quarrel was in many ways a parallel to the Quarrel of the Ancients and Moderns, in that it involved a challenge to the supremacy of ancient sculpture and of the masters who based their art on the study of it. It was also connected with a new naturalism in painting, because one of the arguments in favour of colour was that it produced a more complete imitation of natural objects than was possible by drawing alone. In the end the supporters of colour, led by the critic Roger de Piles, won the day, and the tradition of classical idealism inaugurated by Poussin and carried on by Lebrun and the Academy gave way to a quite different conception of painting.

This change was to have its most important effects in the early eighteenth century on painting not directly connected with the king, but even the art of Versailles underwent changes in the last decades of Louis XIV's reign. In painting a more baroque spirit and a stronger feeling for colour appeared in the work of Charles de la Fosse (1626–1716), who executed some paintings for Versailles and decorated the dome of the Invalides in an illusionistic baroque idiom. This tendency was even more marked in the work of Antoine Coypel (1661–1722), for instance in the vault of the chapel at Versailles, but the most brilliant ceiling painting of this transitional period is that of the Salon d'Hercule, also at Versailles (1733–36), by François Lemoyne (1688–1737), in which the artist gives up the heavy illusionist architecture introduced by earlier decorators and opens up the whole ceiling to the sky, producing an effect which can almost be called rococo.

In portraiture artists began to break away from the old formality

1. Anet. Château. Entrance.

2. Fontainebleau. Galerie François I.

3. Paris. Place Royale (Place des Vosges).

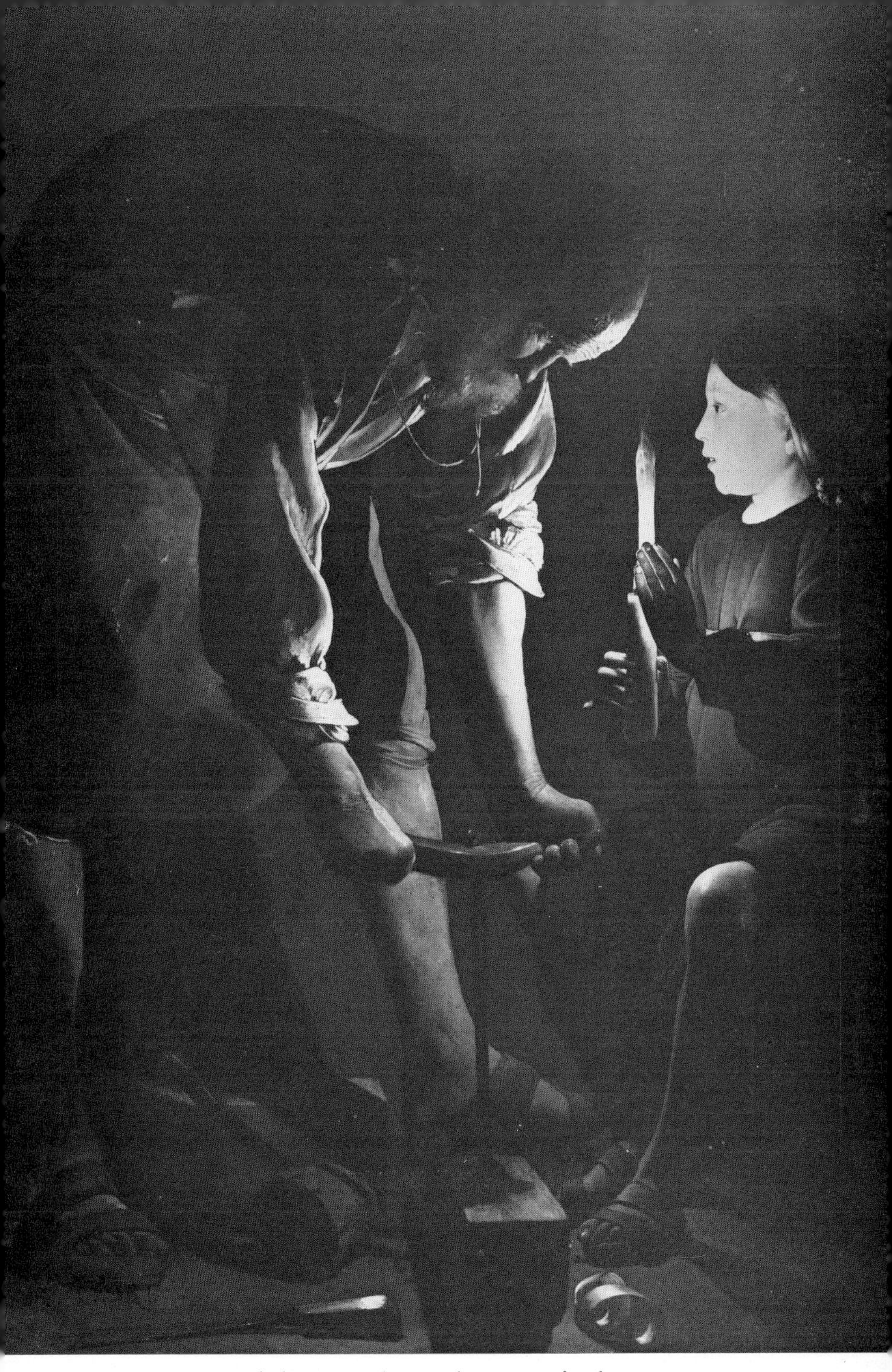

4. Georges de la Tour. *Christ in the Carpenter's Shop*. Louvre.

5. Versailles. Galerie des Glaces.

6. Maisons-Lafitte. Château.

7. Poussin. *Ordination.* Duke of Sutherland Collection (on loan to National Gallery of Scotland, Edinburgh).

8. Claude Lorrain. *The Rape of Europa*. Royal Collection.

9. Antoine Watteau. *Le Concert*. Wallace Collection.

10. François Boucher. *The Triumph of Amphitrite.* National Museum, Stockholm.

11. Jean-Baptiste-Siméon Chardin. *L'Écureuse*. Hunterian Museum, Glasgow University.

12. Jacques-Louis David. *The Death of Marat*. Musée des Beaux-Arts, Brussels.

13. Versailles. The Petit Trianon.

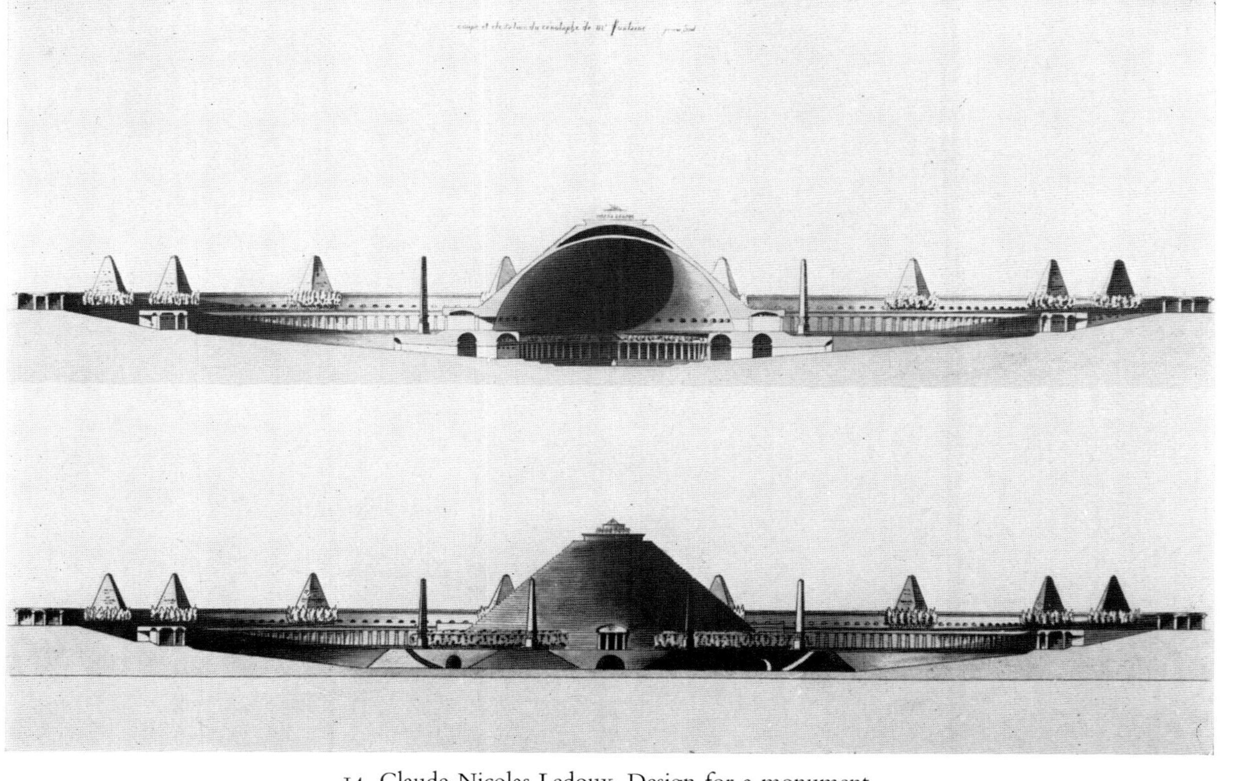

14. Claude-Nicolas Ledoux. Design for a monument.

15. Eugène Delacroix. *La Liberté aux barricades*. Louvre.

16. Théodore Géricault. *Le Radeau de la Méduse*. Louvre.

17 Camille Corot. *Palace of the Popes, Avignon*. National Gallery.

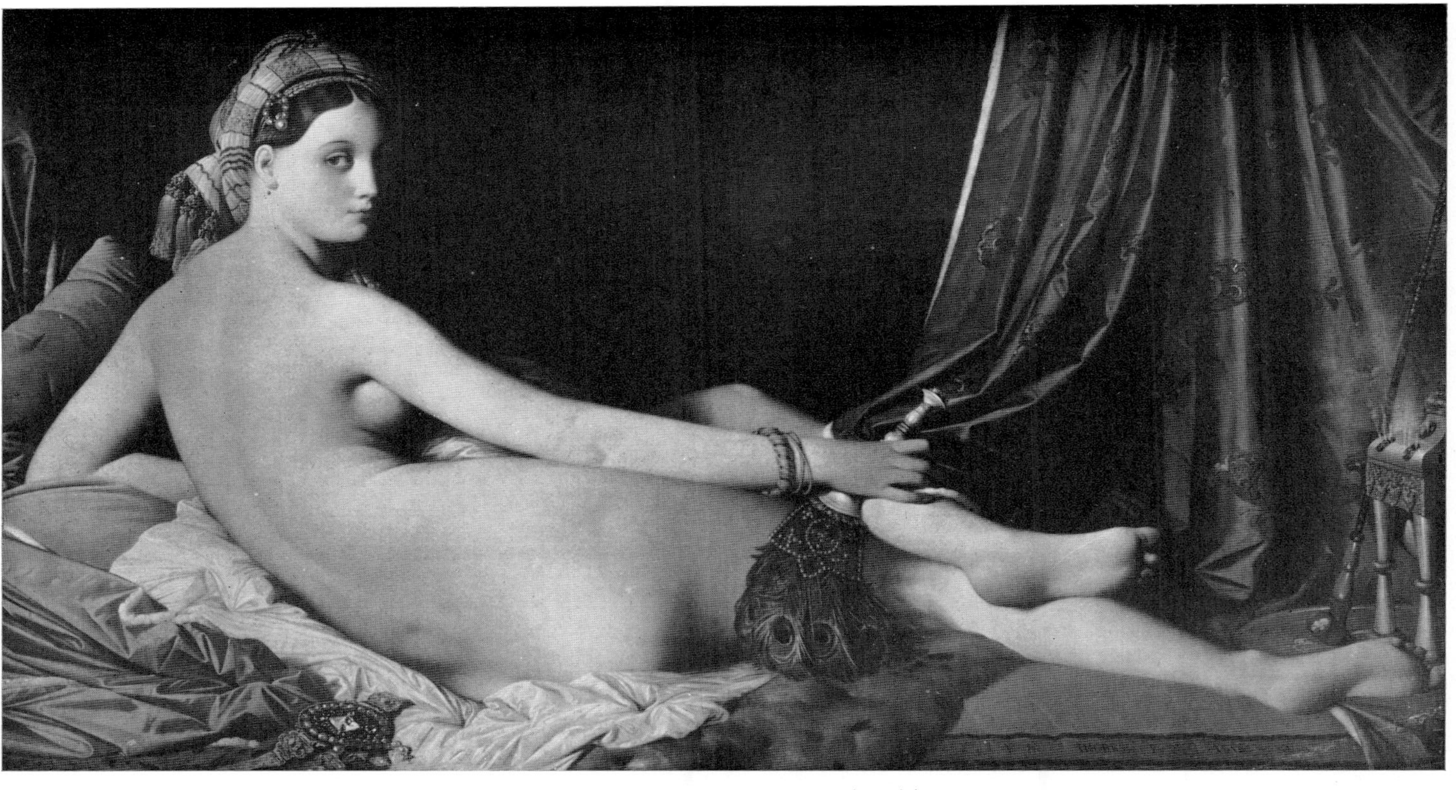

18. Jean-Baptiste-Dominique Ingres. *La Grande Odalisque*. Louvre.

19. Honoré Daumier. *Bons Confrères*. Burrell Collection, Glasgow.

20. Gustave Courbet. *L'Enterrement à Ornans*. Louvre.

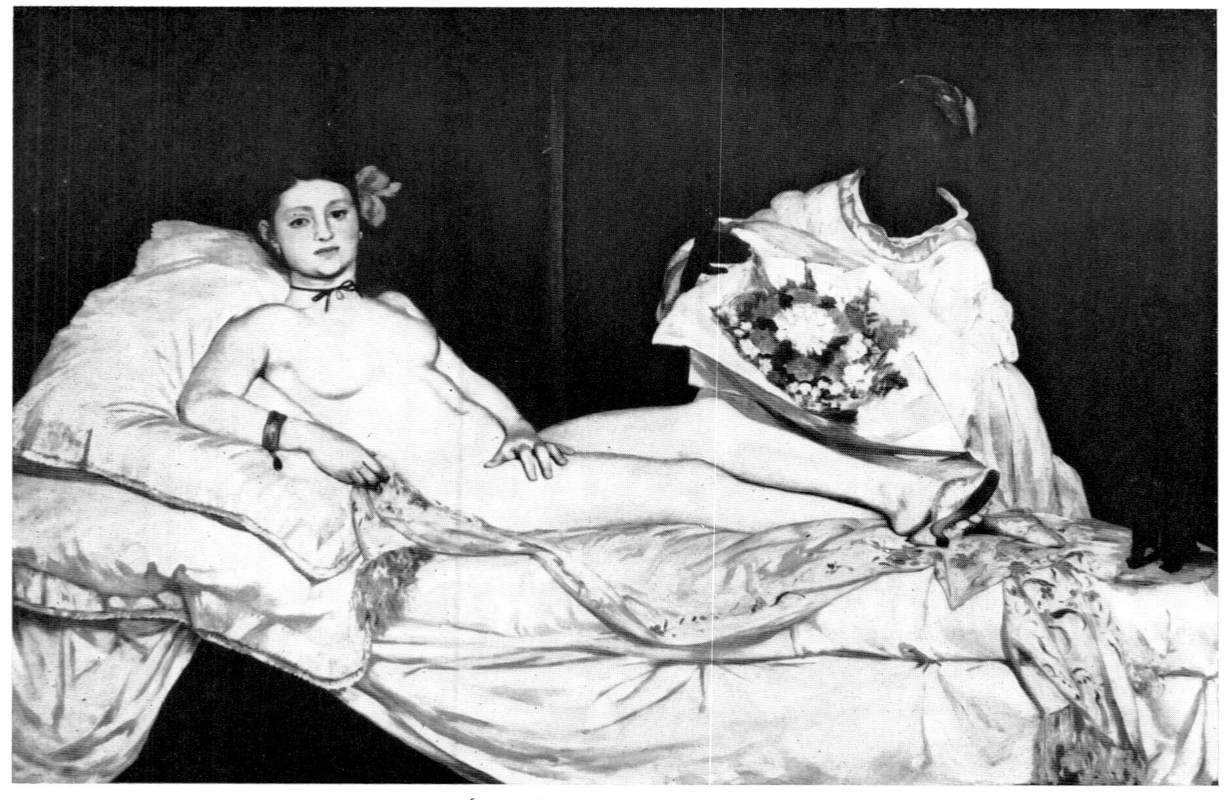

21. Édouard Manet. *Olympia*. Louvre.

22. Edgar Degas. *Le Foyer de l'Opéra.* Burrell Collection, Glasgow.

23. Pierre-Auguste Renoir. *Le Coup de Vent*. Fitzwilliam Museum, Cambridge.

24. Claude Monet. *Antibes*. Courtauld Institute Galleries.

25. Paul Cézanne. *La Montagne Sainte-Victoire*. Courtauld Institute Galleries.

26. Vincent van Gogh. *An Orchard near Arles*. Courtauld Institute Galleries.

27. Paul Gauguin. *Nevermore.* Courtauld Institute Galleries.

28. Georges Seurat. *Une Baignade à Asnières.* National Gallery.

29. Henri Matisse. *La Danse*. Hermitage, Leningrad.

30. Pablo Picasso. *Les Saltimbanques.* National Gallery, Washington.

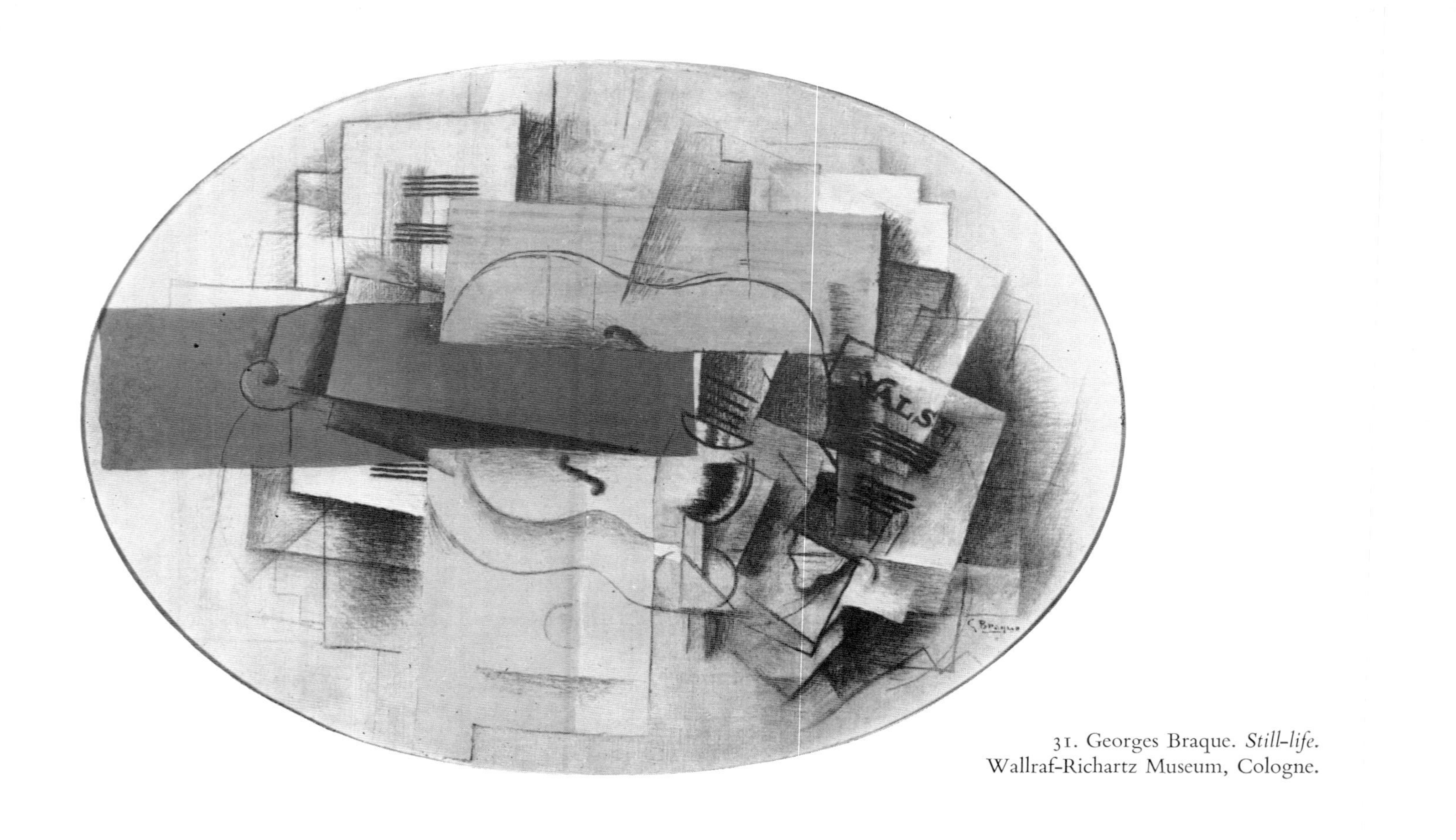

31. Georges Braque. *Still-life.*
Wallraf-Richartz Museum, Cologne.

32. Pablo Picasso. *Guernica*. Museum of Modern Art, New York.

33. Nicolas de Staël. *Étude de Paysage.* The Tate Gallery.

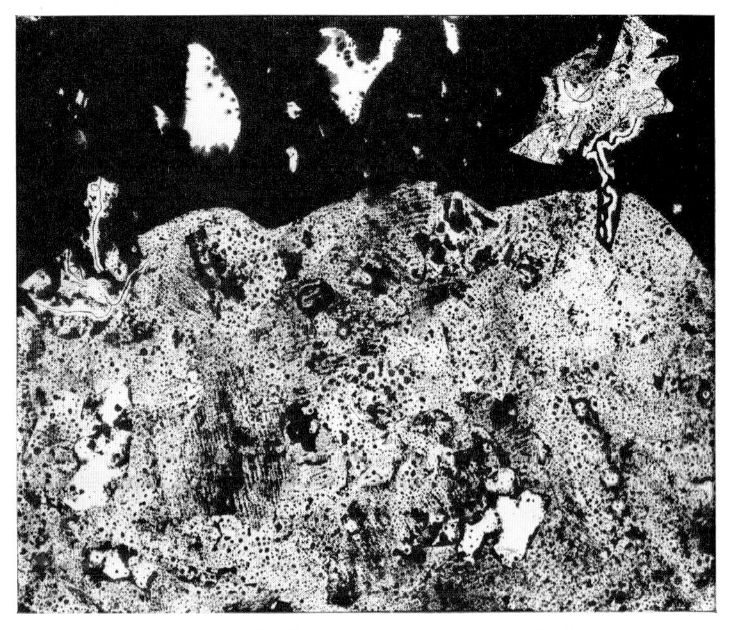

34. Jean Dubuffet. *Paysage aux Nuages tachetés.*

of Pierre Mignard (1612–95), and in the hands of Hyacinthe Rigaud (1659–1743) and Nicolas Largillierre (1656–1746) the art took on a new vigour and a new naturalism, partly derived from the study of Dutch and Flemish models. At the same time a certain lightness appears in the paintings commissioned by the king for the Grand Trianon and for some smaller buildings at Versailles, such as the Ménagerie, which was decorated for the Duchesse de Bourgogne. The grandeur and formality of the previous phase disappears, and in some respects these paintings prepare the way for the rococo.

Other tendencies, not directly connected with the court and partly inspired by the art of the Low Countries, led in the same direction. The Academy had laid down a strict hierarchy of the arts, headed by history painting, which included mythological and religious subjects as well as historical themes in the normal sense, and with the other genres – portraits, battles, domestic scenes, landscape, animal painting, and still life – in lower positions in descending order of importance. The claim of the *Rubénistes*, that the imitation of natural appearances was the first object of painting, led naturally to less emphasis being laid on the *sujet noble*, and the minor genres rose to a higher status. The change can be traced in the lists of paintings shown at the Salon, which was inaugurated in 1673 and held very irregularly till the 1730s. In the early Salons almost all the paintings would have been classed as 'history', but in 1704 the balance had changed so much that there were more pictures of domestic scenes and still lifes than of religious or historical subjects. Animal painting had always held a certain importance at the court, where François Desportes (1661–1740) and later Jean-Baptiste Oudry (1686–1755) were commissioned to paint the king's dogs and the animals in the Ménagerie; Adam Frans van der Meulen (1632–90) had been employed to paint the campaigns of the reign; and flower paintings had been used as decorations for overdoors in the royal palaces; but now all the minor genres became popular with the public and were treated in a much more naturalistic spirit.

The painting of battle-scenes was transformed by Joseph Parrocel (1646–1704), who learnt his art in Venice instead of Rome, and whose use of colour has the richness and brilliance of Delacroix. Equally striking examples of the change in taste are the landscape studies of Desportes (mainly in the Château de Compiègne), made primarily for his own enjoyment, which foreshadow the early sketches of Corot in their direct and sensitive rendering of the countryside of the Île-de-

France. In the early years of the eighteenth century Claude Gillot (1673–1732) revived an aspect of the art of Callot in his drawings and paintings of the Italian Comedy. At the same time artists and collectors turned their attention to the Flemish and Dutch schools. The Duc de Richelieu had brought together a magnificent group of paintings by Rubens, which incited Frenchmen to look – curiously enough almost for the first time – at the series of canvases which he had painted in the Luxembourg Palace for Marie de' Medici. Rembrandt, too, was 'discovered' by artists such as Rigaud, who owned several canvases by him and imitated him in style in his rare religious compositions.

Sculpture went through similar changes. The art of François Girardon (1628–1715), who had been the principal designer of the sculpture which ornamented the gardens at Versailles and had made portraits of the king and his courtiers in a formal classical style, gave way to the livelier manner of Antoine Coysevox (1640–1720), who was capable of baroque swagger in his official portraits, of penetrating psychological observation in busts of his friends, and of a near-rococo lightness and elegance in his portrayals of the Duchesse de Bourgogne (Louvre). Pierre Puget (1620–94), who was born in Aix-en-Provence and worked mainly in Genoa, Toulon and Marseille, enjoyed a sudden burst of favour after the death of Colbert, when his almost purely baroque groups, such as the Milo of Crotona (Louvre), were placed in the gardens at Versailles; but his style was too strong meat for the court, and after a short time his contact with Versailles ceased and he continued to work for patrons in his native Provence.

In architecture there is a marked change in the buildings designed for the king by Hardouin-Mansart, of which the most important are the chapel at Versailles and the new church of the Invalides. The first (begun in 1688 but not finished till 1710) is a brilliant solution to the problem presented by the designing of a court chapel, in which the emphasis has to be as much on the royal gallery at the west end on the first floor as on the altar on the lower floor at the east, but it was criticized at the time for its unusually high proportions, which were said to be 'Gothic', and indeed from the outside the apse, with its buttresses and its high-pitched roof, looks almost like the *chevet* of a Gothic cathedral. The Église du Dôme at the Invalides (1676–91), though partly based on François Mansart's designs for the Bourbon Chapel at Saint-Denis, is one of the most explicitly baroque buildings put up in France in the seventeenth century, particularly in the treatment of the dome, which internally is cut off, so that the eye passes through to

La Fosse's fresco of St Louis received into heaven, lit by windows concealed by the lower dome. There is some reason to think that Louis XIV originally planned this church as a mausoleum for himself and his family, but, if this is so, the project was altered and no tomb was erected till the ashes of Napoleon were enshrined there in the nineteenth century.

At the same time domestic architecture was also moving away from the formal classicism of the 1670s and 1680s, but in a different direction. The new style is first visible in certain rooms at Versailles and the Grand Trianon, remodelled in about 1700. In these rooms the decoration becomes lighter; pilasters are no longer used; cornices take on more broken forms, and looking-glasses with slender frames replace the traditional heavy overmantels.

The Eighteenth Century

The changes which took place in painting, sculpture and architecture in the years around 1700 led up to the rococo, the style which dominated French art roughly between 1715 and 1750.[1] The origin of the style has often been connected with a reaction against the formality of Versailles which followed the death of Louis XIV and, although this is an over-simplification, since many of the crucial steps towards the rococo were taken at Versailles, it is true that in its early phase the rococo was often connected with Paris, which at this period began once more to assert its independence of the court in matters of taste as well as in politics. It was the period when the Faubourg Saint-Germain was being developed as a residential centre by the nobility and by the newly enriched bourgeoisie, who built there a series of *hôtels* which represent one of the high points in domestic architecture. Owing to the fact that there was more space than in the crowded quarters of the old city, architects were able to make their buildings spread horizontally, and the traditional arrangement with the house built in three or four storeys round a relatively small court was replaced by a plan with the main *corps-de-logis* spread along a wide façade of two or sometimes only one floor, while at the back a large garden provided space and air

[1] The style is usually called by French writers 'le style Louis XV', in spite of the fact that it originated before the death of Louis XIV and was well developed under the Regency. In the same way most of the elements which make up the transitional style called 'Style Régence' were invented before 1700 by artists such as Jean Bérain (1640–1711) and Daniel Marot (1663–1752).

on a scale unknown in earlier houses. The rooms were planned in a much more convenient manner than previously. For the first time a special room was set aside as a dining-room, and attention was paid to the advantages of having the kitchen near it rather than on the other side of the court. The bedroom, which under Louis XIV had been the scene of all formal functions, now became a private room for the use of the owner of the house, and a series of *salons* and *boudoirs* were included to be used for formal or intimate occasions. The rooms are now often circular or oval in shape, and these forms are varied by the addition of curved niches or alcoves. The decoration takes on a lightness and an elegance in harmony with these new ideas of intimacy and convenience. The old system of ceilings with a mixture of stucco and painted decoration and walls divided into panels by an order of pilasters vanishes, and the whole room is decorated with a light network of curvilinear patterns which play across the flat or slightly curved ceiling and over the doors and walls in a low relief which hardly interrupts the plane surfaces. Generally the walls were panelled in oak or pine, usually painted white picked out in gold, and the ceiling was decorated in stucco of the same colours. Sometimes, however, the wall panels were painted with flowers, grotesques, or *singeries*, and occasionally paintings were introduced as overdoors. The decoration of the room was completed by looking-glasses, crystal chandeliers, and furniture, often inlaid and ornamented with ormolu, on which would be displayed porcelain imported from the Far East, known as *Compagnie des Indes* from the organization through which it reached Europe.

In this period there was no one figure who dominated architecture as Hardouin-Mansart had done in the previous phase, and these exquisite ensembles were created by a group of talented architects who had mostly received their training in his office, the best known being Robert de Cotte (1656–1735), who decorated the Galerie Dorée at the Hôtel de Toulouse (now the Banque de France) in 1714–15; Pierre Cailleteau, called L'Assurance (1655–1723) and Germain Boffrand (1667–1754), who was responsible for the two oval *salons* at the Hôtel de Soubise (now the Archives Nationales; 1735–6).

In painting the period produced one artist of genius, Antoine Watteau (1684–1721), who died of consumption at the age of thirty-seven. He was born and partly trained in Valenciennes, a town which had only recently become French and was still dominated by its cultural affiliation to Flanders, and his early style was largely formed by the study of Flemish genre painters, such as the younger Teniers. When he came to Paris at the age of eighteen, he joined the studio of Gillot and learnt from him a witty style of draughtsmanship and an interest in painting fancy subjects connected with the theatre. In Paris he saw and studied the paintings of Rubens and the Venetians, which transformed his approach towards the use of colour. From these elements he composed a style of almost unparalleled elegance and delicacy, combining a crisp and witty touch in drawing with an almost romantic treatment of landscape. His subjects were mainly *fêtes galantes*, or scenes enacted by the people of his own time but in a fancy dress which owed something to the theatre and something to the traditions of the pastoral. In the greatest of these, the *Embarquement pour Cythère* (Louvre), he also incorporated a type of love-allegory which goes back to the *Carte de Tendre* and the tradition of the Hôtel de Rambouillet. The *fête galante* became fashionable with the rich financiers for whom Watteau worked – the most sympathetic were the younger Crozat and Jean de Julienne, who looked after the artist in his last illness – and Watteau had many imitators, such as Nicolas Lancret (1690–1743) and Jean-Baptiste Pater (1695–1736), but they never attained the same imaginative level as Watteau. They were brilliant *virtuosi* who turned out their works in an almost mechanical manner; he was an artist of deep feeling and of penetrating observation. Particularly in his drawings, but also in his paintings, he can make the turn of a head or the gesture of a hand express something of deep significance which creates a mood rare in eighteenth-century painting. The poetical power of his art is seen at its most noble in the life-size painting of *Gilles* in the Louvre, and at the other extreme his naturalism and his sense of design enabled him to paint the *Enseigne de Gersaint* (Dahlem Museum, Berlin), a monumental record of a contemporary scene; but these are exceptions, and Watteau will always be regarded as the creator of the lyrical paintings of the *fêtes galantes*, which sum up in quintessential form the culture of early eighteenth-century Paris, recorded with almost equal sensibility in the comedies of Marivaux.

A second stage of rococo painting is represented by François Boucher (1703–70), a brilliant performer, but altogether lacking the profundity of Watteau. He replaced the *fête galante* by the *bergerie*, a much more artificial genre, in which the erotic element is more marked than in the painting of the previous generation. It could be argued that Boucher was at his best in portraiture, and his small full-length of Madame de Pompadour (Wallace Collection) sums up to perfection the mannered elegance of the mid-century, better in fact than the work of the professional portrait painter of the period, Jean-Marc Nattier (1685–1766), in whose paintings the character of the sitter is lost in the pink waxen complexion and the brilliance of silks and laces. A far finer observer of character was Maurice Quentin de la Tour (1704–88), whose portraits record not only the ladies of the court, but with magnificent penetration the intellectuals (Voltaire, Diderot), the actresses (Mademoiselle Fels) and, even more movingly, his own plain but lively face. The third portrait painter of the time, Jean-Baptiste Perronneau (1715–83), was particularly successful in the depiction of older women. His portraits are somewhat akin in their dignity and also in their technique to the works of Gainsborough.

The delicate art of the rococo was not suited to large-scale works or to stone as a medium, and it is therefore not surprising that little monumental sculpture of importance was produced in France during the first half of the eighteenth century. The most notable exceptions were the Chevaux de Marly (1740–45) by Guillaume Coustou (1677–1746), which now stand at the entrance to the Champs Élysées, and Robert le Lorrain's (1666–1743) relief of the horses of Apollo over the stables of the Hôtel de Rohan (1740), a brilliant example of low-relief decoration on architecture. Jean-Baptiste Lemoyne (1704–78) made a series of portraits, mainly equestrian, of Louis XV for the great provincial towns of France. These were all destroyed in the Revolution, but some are known from small bronze versions. The most baroque artists of the middle of the century were Jean-Baptiste Pigalle (1714–85), whose famous statue of Voltaire in the nude is in the Institut de France, and Étienne-Maurice Falconet (1716–91), who designed the impressive equestrian statue of Peter the Great, commissioned in 1766 by Catherine the Great for St Petersburg.

Falconet's other works illustrate the taste for small delicate statuettes, which was characteristic of the mid-century, particularly of Madame de Pompadour, who, appropriately, made Falconet head of the Sèvres porcelain factory. Claude Michel, called Clodion (1738–1814), specialized in small terracotta figures in the same vein. Perhaps the greatest achievement of the age in sculpture lay in portraiture. Almost all the artists mentioned above executed fine work in this genre, but it reached its greatest height towards the end of the century with the busts of Augustin Pajou (1730–1809) and Jean-Antoine Houdon (1741–1828), who portrayed all the great men of their day – Voltaire, Rousseau, Diderot and even Washington – with brilliant observation of features and pose.

The elegance of the period is reflected in the elaborately veneered and inlaid furniture associated with the reign of Louis XV, of which the greatest master was Charles Cressent (1685–1768), the Gobelins and Beauvais tapestries after the designs of Boucher and Jean-François de Troy (1679–1752), the fine carpets from the Savonnerie factory, and the products of the china factories of Vincennes and Sèvres.

Neoclassicism and Romanticism

About the middle of the eighteenth century a change began to be evident in all the arts. Artists and patrons began to react against the frivolity of the rococo and turn to more serious subjects and more restrained forms. A new style was born, known as *le style Louis XVI*, because, although it was created well before the death of Louis XV, it dominated the whole reign of his successor.

The change was partly due to the more serious atmosphere which prevailed in intellectual circles in France under the influence of the *Encyclopédistes*, but in the arts it was directly sponsored by the Marquis de Marigny, brother of Madame de Pompadour, who was appointed Surintendant des Bâtiments in succession to his uncle, Lenormont de Tournehem, in 1751. Marigny's artistic education had been furthered by a long visit to Italy which Madame de Pompadour had arranged for him in 1749, accompanied by the engraver Nicolas Cochin, the architect Soufflot, and the Abbé Leblanc. This visit was carefully planned to enable Marigny to see the great works of ancient art, first in Rome and then in the paintings and sculpture newly excavated at Herculaneum and Pompeii. He came back inspired with enthusiasm for the grandeur of ancient Rome and for the ideals of classical art.

On his return he set about transforming the organization of the arts in France. In painting and sculpture he established a series of competitions with set subjects drawn from history, that is to say, the kind of noble subjects which had been normal in the later seventeenth century but which had been almost entirely displaced by semi-erotic mythological themes and *bergeries* in the first half of the eighteenth century.

The change of subject in painting was accompanied by a change in style, which also affected the painting of religious and domestic subjects. The contrast between the old and new manners is admirably brought out by Diderot in his *Salon* of 1767, in which he makes a detailed comparison between the *Miracle des Ardents* by François Doyen (1726–1806) and the *St Denis prêchant la foi* by Joseph-Marie Vien (1716–1809), both painted for the church of St Roch, the former a bombastic baroque *grande machine*, full of ecstatic figures, putti, and clouds, the latter a calm, carefully thought-out composition in which each figure plays a specific role, made easily intelligible by his gestures and facial expression.

The victory of the new style was not, however, immediate, and many painters went on working in the old manners. Carle van Loo (1705–65) continued to produce baroque mythologies – violently attacked by Diderot – till his death, and Jean-Honoré Fragonard (1732–1806), who survived the Revolution, evolved a new kind of rococo eroticism, which is saved from being banal by the brilliance of the handling and colour. Pierre-Paul Prud'hon (1758–1823), who lived also till after the Revolution, worked in a style which owed much to Correggio technically and had also some of his soft sensuality. Other painters, such as Nicolas Lavreince (1737–1807) and Louis-Léopold Boilly (1761–1845), specialized in small works of a mildly salacious character.

An even more radical change was taking place in the painting of domestic subjects, which was deeply affected by *sensibilité*, already popular in the novel and in the theatre. The great exponent of the new style was Jean-Baptiste Greuze (1725–1805), whose sentimental and moralizing scenes are the equivalent in painting of the *drames* of Diderot, the great supporter and exponent of his art. The paintings of Greuze fall into two main categories: the strictly moralizing paintings, such as the *Malédiction paternelle* or the *Mauvais fils puni* (Louvre), which roused Diderot to some of his most splendid pieces of imaginative criticism, and his portraits of girls, with doves, cats, or a *cruche cassée*, which appealed equally strongly to his sensibility and his sensuality. Greuze is indeed typical of the ambiguity of the epoch – manifested with equal clarity in the writings of Diderot – with its desire to reform, but also its determination to enjoy the pleasures of the senses.

The paintings of Greuze are the most complete expression of *sensibilité* in the visual arts, but other artists painted scenes of domestic life with a certain touch of sentimentality. One of these, Bernard Lépicié (1734–84), was a painter of considerable skill, with a delicate sense of colour, who would probably be better known if he had not been completely overshadowed by Jean-Baptiste-Siméon Chardin (1699–1779). Chardin's genre scenes have a delicacy and a subtlety of observation unparalleled in the eighteenth century. He never points a moral, nor are his paintings ever sensual. He is a pure observer, noting little scenes of domestic life with humour and detachment, fascinated – almost like Degas – with the poses of women scouring pans or working a churn, and amused by the naïve and sometimes prim actions of children. But above all he is supreme in the rendering of light falling on the surface of clothes in his figure subjects, or on fruit and pots in his still lifes. Unlike the Dutch masters of the seventeenth century, he is not interested in painting silks or fine china; his preference is for the rougher surfaces of wool or linen and for the coarse pottery of the kitchen; but from these he constructs compositions with a monumentality and a simplicity that can properly be called classical.

It is not surprising that a generation which admired Greuze and Chardin should have been interested in the paintings of the Le Nain brothers, but it is interesting to notice that of the two most important collections of their paintings one belonged to a member of a great noble family, the Duc de Choiseul, and the other to a rich bourgeois, Poullain. The same is true of Greuze and Chardin: their themes and even the sentiment which inspired them may have been bourgeois in origin, but their works appealed to aristocratic collectors as much as to their more recently enriched competitors.

Diderot was almost as much moved by the landscapes of Claude-Joseph Vernet (1714–89) as by the figure paintings of Greuze, and largely for the same reason. In the seventeenth century landscape had been the setting either for grand historical themes, as with Poussin, or for idyllic subjects, as with Claude. Vernet regarded nature as the reflection of the moods of man and of the drama of his existence. He was the first French painter to depict the horror of mountains, the violence of waterfalls, and the power of nature to dominate and destroy man. He had a predecessor in the Italian Salvator Rosa, but, whereas Rosa populates his landscapes with shepherds or bandits, almost without action, Vernet depicts actual human tragedy: the bridge carried away by the mountain stream and hurling the coach into the abyss, the ship wrecked near the shore, watched by the terror-stricken families of the crew. Sometimes his mood is calmer and in many of his coast-scenes he shows fishermen peacefully seated round a fire under the light of the moon – but always the human message dominates, and the message is that of Jean-Jacques Rousseau or Bernardin de Saint-Pierre.

Other types of landscape were, however, also painted. Hubert Robert (1733–1808) studied in Italy and came back with his sketchbook filled with drawings of the ruins of Rome and the decaying villas of Frascati and Tivoli. These he used as a basis for compositions which are reflections on the passage of time and the decay which overcomes even the greatest civilizations. He extended this idea in one unexpected direction by painting a series of pictures showing the Louvre and other modern French buildings as they would look in a state of ruin, thus projecting nostalgic admiration for ruins into the future. In his themes Robert paid tribute to *sensibilité*, but his treatment of them was markedly classical, particularly in its restrained range of cool colours. Another exponent of this approach to colour in landscape was Louis-Gabriel Moreau, called Moreau le Vieux (1739–1805), whose views of French parks and châteaux develop the discoveries of Desportes and lead up, through his immediate successor, Pierre-Henri Valenciennes (1750–1819), to the landscapes of Corot.

The architecture of this phase is magnificently represented by the work of Ange-Jacques Gabriel (1698–1782), who led a movement towards classicism based partly on a return to the style of François Mansart. His most important commission was the designing of the Place Louis XV, now the Place de la Concorde (1754). With its two palaces on the north side, it is one of the finest examples of large-scale layout in the whole eighteenth century, carrying on the example set by his father in the Place Royale at Bordeaux. It must have been even finer when it had the equestrian statue of the king in the middle and the moats round the central space hollowed out. The interiors of the two palaces, and also that of the École Militaire (planned 1751), show the change in decoration which accompanied the general move towards classicism. The curves of the rococo give way to straight lines, and details are freely borrowed from ancient models, but a strong element of the delicacy and refinement of the rococo phase lingers on, till it was finally banished by the severity of the Empire style. Gabriel's skill in planning and the delicacy of his decoration on an intimate scale are seen to perfection in the Opéra at Versailles (planned 1763) and at the Petit Trianon, begun in 1761 for Madame du Barry and later remodelled for Marie-Antoinette.

Jacques-Germain Soufflot (1713–80), a younger man than Gabriel, went still further towards classicism. Following the theories propounded by the Abbé Laugier, he banished the use of arches over columns and replaced them, in accordance with ancient practice, with a flat entablature. His most famous building, the church of Sainte-Geneviève, now the Panthéon (begun 1757), reflects the renewed feeling of classicism in its huge free-standing portico, based on the Roman Pantheon, and in the severe lines of its dome.

In the two decades before the Revolution architecture went through a curious phase, which combined a stricter classicism in detail with a fantasy of invention which can only be called Romantic. The most interesting architect of this phase, Claude-Nicolas Ledoux (1736–1800), began work in the tradition of Gabriel, but in 1775 he was commissioned to design a complete new town at the salt-mines of Chaux, near Besançon. He designed it on a circular plan, with the administrative buildings at the centre and houses for the workers on radiating and concentric streets. The effect of the whole is very impressive, and the detail is lively, consisting of a mixture of ancient Roman motives, with elements taken from the architecture of Michelangelo. Ledoux was also responsible for designing the customs houses at the gates of Paris in the new Enceinte des Fermiers-Généraux, built between 1784 and 1789, of which three survive: the little Rotonde in the Parc Monceaux, the massive block at the Barrière d'Enfer, and the cylindrical building at the Porte de La Villette.

In his later years Ledoux found it difficult to obtain commissions, but he produced a series of projects which embodied his Rousseauist social ideas and his passion for pure geometrical forms, which sometimes led him to design buildings in the form of spheres. Not unnaturally these projects were never executed, but they are recorded in a series of engravings by the architect himself, published in 1806 with the characteristic title: *L'Architecture considérée sous le rapport de l'art, des mœurs et de la législation.* A similar mixture of grandiose ideas and classical detail is to be found in the designs of Ledoux's contemporary, L. E. Boullée (1728–99), of which very few were actually carried out.

By far the most important figure of the neoclassical phase in France is the painter Jacques-Louis David (1748–1825). David was trained in the mildly classical idiom of Vien, but the vital factor in his formation was his stay of eleven years in Rome, from 1774 to 1785. Here he came under the influence of the group which had been formed round Winckelmann and Anton Raphael Mengs, who had set up a quite new classical ideal, based on admiration not only for the heroic times of the Roman Republic, but also for ancient Greece. In 1784 David painted what was the first great manifesto of the new school, *Le Serment des Horaces* (Louvre). In this picture he returned to the ideals of Poussin, both in his choice of subject and in his style, which has the noble severity of Poussin's works of the 1640s. The painting, which had an enormous success when it was shown in the artist's studio in Rome, was certainly intended to convey a lofty moral message, but it is doubtful if David really meant to give it the political implications which were read into it when it was shown on his return to Paris in 1785, where it was seen as a panegyric of patriotism and of a display of courage in the defence of a democratic state. During the Revolution David became in effect dictator in matters connected with the arts. He was responsible for organizing the *fêtes* given by the Republic, but he made his most significant contribution to the art of the Revolution by his painting of *La Mort de Marat* (Brussels). This is a picture of the most dramatic simplicity and a novelty in the history of painting in that it portrays a contemporary historical event in direct terms, without the use of allegory which was traditional in subjects of this kind. Formally it is moving by the bold simplicity of the design, divided into two almost equal parts by the edge of the bath, the upper half being largely a blank wall, and by the beauty of the cool colour and the nervous brushwork. At the fall of Robespierre David was arrested, but was soon released and retired to the country, where he painted two portraits of his hosts, Monsieur and Madame Sériziat (Louvre), which are among the most accomplished portraits of the period.

When Napoleon came to power, he appointed David as his official painter, and the artist executed many portraits of him as General, First Consul and Emperor. He was also commissioned to paint the great ceremonies of the Empire, of which the *Sacre de Napoléon I* (Louvre) is the most celebrated. It lacks the fervour of the *Marat*, but the artist has solved in a masterly way the problem of combining into a coherent design several hundred figures, most of which had to be accurate portraits. In 1815 David, being known to have voted for the death of Louis XVI, fled to Brussels, where he continued to paint portraits and occasionally mythological subjects.

The other painter officially employed to record the events of the Napoleonic period was Baron Gros (1771–1835). He learnt his style not like David from classical models but principally from the study of Rubens, and his paintings, of which the *Pestiférés de Jaffa* (Louvre) is perhaps the most successful, have something of the robust naturalism of this master. The neoclassical tendency was represented at this time by Pierre-Narcisse Guérin (1774–1833) and Anne-Louis Girodet-Trioson (1767–1824), whose *Atala* (Louvre; 1808) was one of the most famous paintings inspired by Chateaubriand's novel.

The first half of the nineteenth century is dominated in art as in literature by the struggle between neoclassicism and Romanticism, with the difference that, whereas in literature the weight of the Romantic attack left their opponents fairly well crushed, in painting the struggle was more equal, as the classical party had among them one great painter, Jean-Baptiste-Dominique Ingres (1780–1867), who, like his rival Eugène Delacroix (1798–1863), the leader of the Romantics, lived on till long after their quarrel had been forgotten in the new battle over realism.

Ingres did not become a pure classical artist all at once. He was a pupil of David and, when in his studio, belonged to the group who called themselves *les Primitifs* and advocated a return to a simpler form of art than the over-polished classicism of their day. In some of his early works Ingres drew on sources which are more akin to Romanticism than to classicism, notably in the painting of *Le Songe d'Ossian* (1813; Montauban) and, to a lesser degree, the *Paolo and Francesca*, based on Dante. Surprisingly enough some of his early nudes, such as the *Baigneuse de Valpinçon* (Louvre), shown in Paris in 1808, provoked attacks from traditional critics, because the nude was thought to be ugly, on the grounds that it did not conform to the standards established by the generation of Guérin and Girodet-Trioson, but soon Ingres 'purified' his style and established himself as the successor to David and the champion of the ideals of the ancients, Raphael and Poussin. Ingres's conception of female beauty was based not on fifth-century-B.C. Greek sculpture, which was still hardly known – the Elgin marbles had been brought to England in 1816 but were not available to French artists – but on late Hellenistic models, and his art lacks altogether the virile quality of David's classicism. He excels, however, in the pursuit of a harmonious contour, which is not only beautiful in itself, but which perfectly describes the volume which it encloses. His innumerable studies from the nude are evidence of the persistence with which he pursued this search. At first sight Ingres's drawings and paintings of the nude seem to be entirely naturalistic, but their appearance is in fact deceptive, and he often takes great liberties with human anatomy for expressive or formal reasons, as with the famous neck of Thetis in *Jupiter et Thétis* (1811).

Ingres was also a great portrait painter. During his early years in Rome he made portrait drawings of visitors and their families, which, in addition to being interesting social records, have a remarkable crispness of drawing, but he also painted some vigorous oil portraits of members of the French Civil Service in Rome, of which the *Monsieur de Norvins* in the National Gallery is typical. Later he evolved a magnificent and luxurious type of female portrait, in which dress and setting are as important as the sitter. Portraits like the *Madame Moitessier* of 1856 (National Gallery) convey the opulence of Second Empire society to perfection. The magnificent portrait of the rich and influential journalist Louis-François Bertin, founder of the *Journal des Débats* (1832; Louvre), records with equal vividness the tougher aspect of the period in finance and politics.

The success of Ingres was predictable, because he had all the skills necessary to please the society for which he painted, but the career of Delacroix is more puzzling. The paintings which he submitted to the Salon in the 1820s aroused the most violent attacks in the press and among the public, but in spite of this they continued to be accepted, and the *Barque de Dante* was actually bought by the State. It was said at the time that this was due to the influence of Talleyrand, who was believed, probably with reason, to have been his father.

Delacroix bore the brunt of the fight to establish Romantic painting, but the first shots were fired by a slightly older artist, Théodore Géricault (1791–1824), who, if he had lived, would have been an artist of almost equal importance. He was trained in the studios of Carle Vernet and Guérin, but at the age of twenty-five he went to Rome, where he studied ancient art in the spirit of the neoclassical artists, but he was also inspired by the scenes that he saw in the city, particularly by the race of riderless horses which took place once a year down the Corso. Some of his paintings of this are designed like Greek bas-reliefs, but they have a fire very different from the rather feeble classicism of his French masters, and in others he paints the whole setting of the scene with a naturalism unusual at that date. When he returned to France in 1818, he continued to paint horses, which were one of the great passions of his life, but in a different context. His subjects were taken from the Napoleonic Wars, but he chose to paint individual anonymous soldiers rather than the victories of generals, as in his *Cuirassier blessé* (Louvre; 1814), which has an energy and an individualism that are close to Romanticism. His greatest work, the *Radeau de la Méduse* (Louvre; 1819), was painted in a consciously political spirit, the subject being a naval disaster of which the Liberals had made a stick to beat the Government. It is a magnificent work of mixed characteristics: its composition is *mouvementé* and baroque, owing much to Rubens; its gruesome detail is naturalistic, but in its treatment of the nude there are still strong traces of Géricault's study of ancient sculpture.

In 1820 Géricault brought the *Méduse* to be exhibited in London, and on this occasion he was struck by the naturalism and free handling of English painting, particularly in the work of the animal painters, including Ward and the young Landseer. On his return to Paris he produced a few lithographs which show these influences, and it is likely that, if he had not died in 1824 as the result of an accident while out riding, he would have developed in the direction later taken by Courbet. A similar tendency, though combined with a Romantic interest in the abnormal, is to be seen in a series of studies of various types of insanity which he made with the help of a well-known alienist.

The death of Géricault left Delacroix as the leader of the Romantic school. During the 1820s he asserted his personality through a number of paintings shown in the Salon. In 1822 the *Barque de Dante* (Louvre) shocked the critics and the public by the grimness of its subject and the freedom of its handling, based on a study of Rubens, which was thought to be due to mere lack of finish. In 1824 the *Massacre de Scio* (Louvre) caused an even greater sensation, partly for the same reasons, and partly because of the freshness of colouring which Delacroix introduced at the last moment as the result of seeing Constable's *Haywain* in Paris earlier in the same year. In 1827 his *Sardanapale* (Louvre), one of his most accomplished paintings, was also thought to be unnecessarily brutal, though its technical skill could not be ignored.

The literary sources on which Delacroix drew are significant. First Dante in the *Barque*, then Byron in *Sardanapale*, and Shakespeare in a number of small paintings and lithographs. In 1825 he paid a visit to London and was deeply impressed by the rich colouring and impasto of Lawrence's portraits, and also by the genre painting of Wilkie, in which he admired the power of observation and the liveliness of touch. He was also a regular visitor to the theatre, where he saw both Kemble and Kean in Shakespeare, greatly preferring the nervous and lively acting of the latter to the declamation of the former.

In 1832 he went to Morocco, where he was impressed by the dignity of the Arabs, whom he regarded as the Romans of the nineteenth century, and where he was stimulated by the strong light and the intense colours which it gave by reflection to objects in shadow. The exploration of colour was in fact Delacroix's great contribution to French painting. He learnt much from Rubens and Constable, but the richness of his harmonies is all his own. In his last years, particularly in the frescoes of the Chapelle des Anges in Saint-Sulpice (1853–61), he goes even further and in his use of little touches of pure brilliant colours comes near to the bolder experiments of the impressionists.

The interest in painting everyday scenes, which is implicit in some of Géricault's last works, was the foundation of the realism which was to be the most important movement of the mid-nineteenth century. In the work of Honoré Daumier (1810–79) it took a special form owing to his preoccupation with politics, in which he was a strong supporter of the Left throughout his career. He earned his living mainly by doing caricatures for *Le Charivari* and other opposition papers. In the early stages these consisted of direct attacks on Louis-Philippe and his Ministers, but, when this proved too dangerous, he turned to satire on the middle classes. At the time of the Commune he once again became quite explicit in his support of left-wing views. He is now principally remembered for his social satires, which present a vivid picture of the smugness of middle-class life, but in his relatively rare paintings he is more positive, and those which represent workers at their occupations, painted with sympathy but without sentimentality, are perhaps his most imaginative creations.

Landscape painting also moved towards a more naturalistic approach in the early nineteenth century. The first to break with a neoclassical type of landscape based on the study of Poussin and represented by Bertin (1755–1842) and Michallon (1796–1822) was Georges Michel (1763–1843), who turned for inspiration to the art of Rembrandt and the scenery that he saw in the suburbs of Paris, particularly in the then deserted hill of Montmartre with its windmills; but the main change was effected by the Barbizon School, called after the village on the edge of the Forest of Fontainebleau where it was established. Its original members were Théodore Rousseau (1812–67), Charles-François Daubigny (1817–78), Constant Troyon (1810–65) and Narcisse-Virgile Diaz (1808–76), but both Camille Corot (1796–1875) and Jean-François Millet (1814–75) were attached to it for a time. Their main principle was the direct study of nature, though in practice they saw it through the eyes of seventeenth-century Dutch painters, such as Hobbema or Jacob Ruisdael, and English artists of the previous generation, above all Constable, whom they took as models instead of the classical landscape painters, Claude and Poussin, admired by their predecessors. They continued to paint their finished pictures in the studio, but they made drawings and small oil-sketches in front of the actual scene they were to paint.

Corot spent many years in Italy, where he painted small landscapes of extraordinary calm and luminosity directly inspired by the Roman Campagna. Later he made a great success with his silvery landscapes, composed of frail wispy trees and peopled by shepherds or nymphs, but he continued to paint more spontaneous canvases, both of landscape and of figures, to the end of his career. Millet also differed from his companions in that he painted not only landscapes but compositions with peasant scenes, of which the most famous are the *Angelus* and *Les Glaneuses* (Louvre). Diaz came near to the Barbizon painters in his landscapes, but he was more at home in the painting of romantic, pastoral or mythological scenes in rich colours and thick impasto, a technique derived from the study of Venetian painting and of Watteau. Adolphe Monticelli (1824–86) scored a more popular success by painting *fêtes champêtres* in a similar but even more succulent technique.

Realism and Impressionism

The most explicit and vocal champion of realism was Gustave Courbet (1819–77). He was something of a megalomaniac, and in his early self-portraits he painted himself as a Romantic bohemian hero. Soon, however, he was caught up by the socialist movement and became a friend of Proudhon, whose theories he purported to embody in his painting. His enormous *Enterrement à Ornans* caused a scandal at the Salon of 1850, and at the International Exhibition of 1855 his works, which included the *Atelier du Peintre* (Louvre), were so badly hung that Courbet removed them and exhibited them in a room specially hired for the purpose, thus inaugurating the 'one-man show'.

Whether or not the *Enterrement* fulfils the programme set out by Proudhon in his pamphlet *Du Principe de l'art et de sa destination sociale*, it is undoubtedly a revolutionary work. The mere fact of painting an ordinary funeral on the scale usually reserved for history was a break with a well-established tradition, but the artist sinned further in neglecting all the classical rules of composition in favour of a long drawn-out procession which straggles across the composition, and in painting the figures with no attempt at embellishment and in a rough and vigorous technique. In some of his later paintings, such as *Les Casseurs de pierres* (1853; Dresden), Courbet continued to treat subjects with obvious social implications, but the works that were to influence his successors were his landscapes and his still lifes. Here his heavy greens and earth colours, applied in broad strokes, often with the palette-knife, gave his paintings a boldness of structure lacking in the productions of the Barbizon School. A more romantic spirit appears in his sea-scapes, particularly in the several versions which he painted of *La Vague*, in which he conveys the power of the ocean with a quite novel intensity.

Édouard Manet (1832–83) was mainly influenced in his early work by his study of Velasquez and other Spanish painters of the seventeenth century, whose works he knew in French private collections even before his brief visit to Spain. In this vein he painted a number of picturesque figures in subdued tones of greys and browns, with a subtle observation of tonal values, but in the early 1860s he struck out on a new line, which caused an even greater storm than the more deliberately revolutionary paintings of Courbet – much to Manet's distress, because he was at heart a conservative and would have enjoyed popular success. His paintings were rejected at the Salon of 1863, but some were shown in the famous Salon des Refusés in the same year. The *Déjeuner sur l'herbe* (1863; Louvre) and *Olympia* (1865; Louvre) shocked the public by their subjects, the first because it showed a naked woman seated with clothed men – although it was pointed out that Giorgione had done the same in his much admired *Concert champêtre* – the latter because it depicted a little French tart and not a Venus, and because the black cat and the black servant were thought to have sinister erotic implications. However, the technique was thought to be equally outrageous, because Manet had broken with the tradition of sombre colour rising from a dark background and had painted in flat areas of bright colours on white ground, a formula which he derived partly from the study of Japanese prints, which were beginning to be known in Paris. In the 1870s Manet, who was a friend of the impressionists, was influenced by their discoveries in the painting of light, and his last works, particularly the *Bar aux Folies-Bergère* (Courtauld Institute Galleries, London), combine his love of flat areas of colour, particularly black, with a dazzling treatment of the effect of light on glasses, bottles and flowers.

The impressionist group was formed in the early 1870s and held its first exhibition in 1874. The founders were Claude Monet (1840–1926) and Auguste Renoir (1841–1919), who were later joined by Camille Pissarro (1830–1903). Round them were grouped certain painters of less originality, such as Alfred Sisley (1839–99), who remained constant to the principles of impressionism all their lives; others, like Paul Cézanne (1839–1906), who were influenced by their principles for a time but moved on to different ideals at a later date; yet others, like Edgar Degas (1834–1917), who sympathized with the aims of the group but stood slightly apart.

In the first half of the sixties Monet was painting in a manner principally influenced by Manet, with broad areas of strong colours, but by about 1867 he became insistent on the principle that open-air scenes, whether pure landscape or figure groups, must be painted on the spot and not in the studio. In 1869 he was joined by Renoir and Pissarro, and all three painted a series of views at a point on the Seine called La Grenouillère, in which they attempted to capture the fleeting effects of light on trees and water. In the early seventies they carried the idea further, using purer colours and developing the discovery, hinted at by Delacroix and Manet, but only fully worked out by Monet and his friends, that shadows on an object are not merely darker than the part in light, but actually different in colour. Monet insisted that the landscape painter must not only record a particular view, but record it at a particular moment of the day and in particular light, and in the 1880s he painted two great series of canvases to establish his point, one of haystacks and one of the façade of Rouen Cathedral (several versions in the Louvre). In these paintings he allows the light almost to dissolve the solid forms on which it falls. In his later years he concentrated on painting the water-lily pond in his garden at Giverny and, in two magnificent series of decorative canvases of this (Orangerie), carried the dissolution of solid forms so far that they have been claimed – probably without justification – as one of the sources of abstract art.

Pissarro continued for many years to work in the idiom of impressionism, but he was always more interested than Monet in figure painting, and his greater concern for social problems – he was by conviction an anarchist – often led him to choose peasant subjects for his compositions. In the 1890s he was attracted for a few years by the ideas of neo-impressionism and modified his technique accordingly.

Degas started as a classical painter, influenced by Ingres and the study of Raphael, but in the 1870s he became interested in seizing the quickly changing poses of horses and dancers in movement. In thus concentrating on a single instant his method presents an analogy with the impressionist's treatment of light, but he never turned, like them, to the painting of landscape. He also differed from the pure impressionist in having a keen interest in the problems of space-construction. In his later years, as his eyesight began to fail, he changed his technique and his subjects. He found he could control the pure colours of pastel better than the more subtle tones attainable in oils, and he chose subjects which did not involve the observation of rapid movement. In this phase he made principally studies of women washing or drying after a bath. His superb draughtsmanship enabled him to give monumental grandeur to a series of poses in themselves clumsy and even ugly. He also made brilliant wax statuettes of dancers and horses which, after his death, were cast in bronze.

The appearance of impressionism confirmed the breach which had been growing between fashionable art and 'advanced' art, or, as we should say, between lowbrow and highbrow art. The Salon fostered various brands of fashionable art, of which the portraiture of Léon Bonnat (1833–1922), the sensuality of Adolphe Bouguereau (1825–1905) and the minute craftsmanship of Ernest Meissonier (1815–91) were the most popular. On the other hand the division between the two factions was never complete. Bonnat was a close friend of Degas; Fantin-Latour (1836–1904), who enjoyed great popular success with his flower paintings, painted a composition entitled *Hommage à Delacroix*, in which he included portraits of Manet and Baudelaire; the models that Cézanne studied most carefully were the great Venetians of the sixteenth century, who would also have been acclaimed in the Beaux-Arts; and most of the impressionists went on trying to get their paintings accepted by the Salon jury, even though they disapproved of most of the work exhibited there.

In sculpture the opposition was even less sharp. Jules Dalou (1838–1902), who started as a fashionable sculptor, held strong left-wing views in politics, and during his exile in England after the Commune evolved a very serious kind of naturalism; Antoine-Louis Barye (1796–1875), who enjoyed international success, learnt much from Géricault and Delacroix in the depiction of animals; and Auguste Rodin (1840–1917), by far the greatest sculptor of the period, was technically much influenced by Jean-Baptiste Carpeaux (1827–75), although he applied the virtuosity of the latter to much grander and more monumental works. His rough treatment of the surface of the clay in which he modelled his figures produced an effect of varied light and shade which has some analogy with the methods of the impressionist painters.

The most important innovations in nineteenth-century French architecture took place in town-planning and in the development of new materials for building. The new layout of Paris was begun by

Napoleon I, who was responsible for the western part of the Rue de Rivoli (by Charles Percier (1764–1838) and Pierre-François Fontaine (1762–1858); begun in 1802), the Arc de Triomphe de l'Étoile (mainly Chalgrin (1739–1811); begun 1806), and the Madeleine (Pierre Vignon (1762–1828); begun 1808), but the great transformation of Paris was carried out under the Second Empire by Baron Haussmann, Prefect of the Seine, who replanned the Cité and laid out boulevards linking the new stations (Gare de l'Est and Gare du Nord) and the Opéra with the centre of Paris. At the same time the Rue de Rivoli was completed and the Louvre extended along it to link up with the Tuileries, on the designs of Louis Visconti (1791–1853) and Hector Lefuel (1810–80). The Opéra, designed by Charles Garnier (1825–98), and decorated on the outside with Carpeaux's famous group, *La danse*, was the most spectacular symbol of Second Empire luxury.

Meanwhile architecture of a different kind was being evolved, based on the use of iron for the structure of buildings. The first mature example of the new technique was the Bibliothèque Sainte-Geneviève, built in 1843–50 by Henri Labrouste (1801–75), who later built the reading room of the Bibliothèque Nationale, but it was soon adopted by ecclesiastical architects, as in Saint-Augustin (1860–1) by Louis-Auguste Boileau (1812–96). The International Exhibition of 1889 provided the opportunity for the two greatest manifestations of the new technique in the Hall des Machines, built by Ferdinand Dutert (1845–1906) and Henri Contamine (1810–97), which had a span of 385 feet, and the Eiffel Tower, a thousand feet high, constructed by Gustave Eiffel (1832–1923). In the last decade of the century reinforced concrete was introduced by Anatole de Baudot (1834–1915) in Saint-Jean-de-Montmartre (1894–9). In the structure of this church Baudot followed the lines of Gothic vaulting, but the new material was used in a manner more in accordance with its real nature by Auguste Perret (1874–1954) in his block of flats at 25 bis Rue Franklin (1902–3). At the turn of the century the use of iron was adapted to the art-nouveau style, which scored a great success in the decorative arts as well as in architecture. Of the most famous monuments in this manner, the Métro stations designed by Hector Guimard (1867–1942) in 1900, very few now remain.

The Gothic Revival, which was essentially a northern movement, produced relatively little effect in France, though Sainte-Clotilde (1846–57) by Franz Christian Gau (1790–1853) and Théodore Ballu (1817–74) is a prominent example of the style, the virtues of which were enthusiastically expounded by Viollet-le-Duc (1814–79) in his theoretical writings, which also contain many ideas foreshadowing modern functionalism. His bad reputation for over-restoring medieval churches and châteaux has been exaggerated, and in fact he did much to save buildings which would otherwise have perished.

The Late Nineteenth Century

The impressionist painters continued to work till the early years of the twentieth century, but after 1876 they ceased to exhibit as a group and their position in the vanguard of the advanced school was taken in the 1880s by other artists, who had learnt much from them but later modified or even rejected their principles. These artists are loosely described as the post-impressionists, but they never formed a coherent group and indeed were far from unanimous in their admiration for each other's work.

Cézanne, after an early Romantic phase, when he applied the dark colouring of early Manet and the heavy brushwork of Courbet to erotic themes, worked very closely with Pissarro for several years in the early 1870s and absorbed the new impressionist technique, but in the eighties he settled down in Aix-en-Provence and devoted himself to an unremitting study of the effect of light on his native landscape and of the interaction of colours and shapes in still lifes carefully disposed in his studio. These subjects he studied with a fixed intensity which often revealed relationships which the more rapid observation of the impressionists had overlooked. His observation showed not only that colours juxtaposed affect each other, but that forms can behave in the same manner, and this discovery led him to a series of subtle adjustments of contours which have often been put down to systematic distortion. In fact continuous refinement of his forms caused his compositions – when they were fully *poussées*, as he would have said – to have a meticulous organization in space and on the surface undreamt of by the impressionists and rare in the work of any artist. In his last years his palette became richer and the breaking-up of forms more pronounced; but in his landscapes, still lifes and portraits he never departed from his strict observation of nature. In his *Baigneuses* the case was different, as he was unable to bring himself to paint from the naked model, and there is about them an arbitrariness lacking in his other works. The fact that he painted in seclusion at Aix had the result that his work was little known in Paris, and it was not till the great retrospective exhibition in 1904 that the younger generation came to appreciate his achievement.

Early in the 1880s Renoir was affected by the dissatisfaction with impressionism felt by many of his friends, and the sight of the great masterpieces of Renaissance painting on a visit to Italy in 1881–2 made him feel that he must submit himself to a more severe discipline, particularly in drawing. The result was a series of cold figure paintings, in which he almost seems to be emulating Ingres, but he emerged from this 'reformation' with a new method of painting the nude in a series of grand and simplified masses and in a rich colouring which gradually changed from an almost impressionist palette to much hotter tones in his very last works, such as the big *Baigneuses* in the Louvre.

Though Vincent van Gogh (1853–90) was born and bred in Holland, his most important works were painted in France and he cannot be left out of any history of French painting. As a young man his aim was to enter the Church, but in this he failed, and after a short period working among the miners of Le Borinage in Belgium he decided to devote his whole energies to painting. The sight of impressionist and neo-impressionist paintings in Paris, where he spent about a year in 1886–7, caused him to abandon the sombre style which he had learnt from Dutch painters like Josef Israels and to adopt a brilliant palette, composed solely of pure colours. This tendency was confirmed by his admiration for the rather crude Japanese prints which were beginning to be known in Paris. In the spring of 1888 he moved to Arles, attracted by the sun and the cheapness of living. Soon afterwards he was joined by Gauguin, whom he attempted to kill in an attack of madness. In spite of recurring crises he continued to paint, first in a lunatic asylum at Saint-Rémy, and later under the care of Dr Gachet at Auvers, near Pontoise. He used the brilliant palette which he had learnt in Paris for purposes quite foreign to the inventors of the technique. For him colours had a meaning of their own, and he used them to express his feelings about people or places, irrespective of whether they conformed to nature. These colours were applied in vigorous brush-strokes, in the form of commas or S-shapes, which make the surface of his canvases vibrate, and the result is a kind of painting which conveys the fervour of his emotions about people, trees or flowers. The works painted in Arles are permeated with the brilliant sun of Provence, but in those executed at Saint-Rémy his palette becomes cooler. While he was confined there he had difficulty in getting models, and he often copied engravings after Rembrandt or Gustave Doré, translating them wholly into his own language. In the last few months of his life, spent at Auvers, his handling became almost frantic and his colours wild and dramatic, but there was no sign whatsoever that his talent was exhausted, and these paintings are among the most moving works that he ever produced. On 29 July 1890, in a fit of despair, he shot himself.

Like Van Gogh, Gauguin (1848–1903) came to painting late, though from a different background. Till the age of thirty-five he worked as a stockbroker, but then, having come into contact with impressionism, he threw up his career and abandoned his family in order to devote himself to art. He soon found the impressionist doctrine unsatisfying and developed ideas on the symbolical value of colours which were allied to those of Van Gogh. His method of painting, however, was quite different and, instead of torturing the canvas with nervous touches of colour, he laid it on in large almost unbroken areas, arguing that 'if you want to paint green, a metre of green is greener than a centimetre'. He left Paris for Brittany, where he found it cheaper to live, and at Pont-Aven founded with Émile Bernard (1868–1941) a colony of artists who espoused his ideas, of which the most important was that a painting was essentially a flat surface decorated with areas of colour which must possess their own decorative coherence, irrespective of their relation to the natural objects depicted. In 1891 Gauguin went to live in Tahiti, partly for reasons of economy, and partly because he was attracted to the simple life of the natives and the exotic beauty of the island, which in fact supplied the ideal subject-matter for his rich, decorative compositions. Many of these were based on the beliefs of the natives, which Gauguin found more congenial than the conventional religion and over-intellectualized philosophy which he had left behind in Europe. In 1901, having quarrelled with the French administration over his attempts to stand up for the rights of the natives, he moved to the Marquesas islands, where he died in extreme misery two years later.

The painters just mentioned all worked according to a series of personal ideas – Cézanne talked of his *petite sensation*, Renoir believed in the sensuousness of painting, Van Gogh and Gauguin in the value of colour – but they all worked essentially from instinct and none of them consciously evolved an aesthetic doctrine. This was left for Georges Seurat (1859–91), the inventor of neo-impressionism or *pointillisme*. Seurat's starting-point was the impressionist use of strong pure colours and their discovery of coloured shadows, but, whereas they applied their ideas empirically, Seurat, under the influence of new discoveries in optics, particularly those of Chevreul and Clark-Maxwell as popularized by Charles Blanc, worked out an almost scientific approach towards colour. He believed that in any group of objects on which light falls there are three kinds of colour: the local colour, or colour which the object would have under white light; the colour which it receives from the source of light (e.g. yellow, if the source is sunlight); and a third colour due to the fact that one colour juxtaposed to another induces its complementary in it (e.g. yellow induces purple, green red). Seurat applied the three kinds of colour separately in minute dots, so that the fusion takes place optically, on the retina and not on the canvas. In addition Seurat evolved theories about the emotional effect of lines in composition – those rising from a base line conveying joy, those sinking sorrow, and so on – and was deeply interested in the application of certain mathematical proportions, particularly the Golden Section. He did not come to these theories immediately, and in some of his earlier works, like *Une Baignade* (1884; National Gallery), although the proportions are carefully calculated, the *pointillisme* is perceptible only in certain areas which the artist retouched later. The method was fully developed in the *Grande Jatte* (1886; Chicago) and the *Poseuses* (1888; Barnes Foundation, Merion, Pa.), and in the *Poudreuse* (1889–90; Courtauld Institute Galleries, London). The result is a kind of painting which at times seems cold but which is infinitely satisfying in the perfection of its harmony and in the monumentality of its forms. Seurat has been compared with Piero della Francesca, and the comparison is neither silly nor accidental, because Seurat knew and studied copies after Piero in the École des Beaux-Arts. In his last works, *Le Chahut* (1889–90; Otterlo, Holland) and *Le Cirque* (1890–1; unfinished, Louvre), he seems to be breaking away from the rigid rectangular compositions of his earlier paintings and to be introducing new curved forms, partly influenced by art-nouveau.

By the first years of the nineties the impulse of impressionism was spent; Van Gogh and Seurat were dead, Cézanne and Gauguin were in hiding, and Renoir could never have become a *chef d'école*. It is not surprising, therefore, that the lead passed from them, not to another single group but to several individual artists or groups whose ideas and methods had little in common.

Of the individual artists the most remarkable was Henri de Toulouse-Lautrec (1864–1901). Lautrec lived in and painted exactly the over-sophisticated world that Gauguin had gone to Tahiti to escape, and he produced the most vivid and yet the most detached commentary on bohemian life in Montmartre in the nineties. Deformed as the result of a riding accident, he was unable to fulfil the ambitions of his aristocratic parents, with which in any case he did not sympathize, and he spent most of his short life among the music-halls and brothels of Paris, which provided the subjects for almost all his paintings, drawings and lithographs. His brilliant draughtsmanship was partly learnt from the study of Degas – modified by the curves of art-nouveau – but his approach was entirely different. Degas was interested in a detached way in the curious movements of human beings engaged in their everyday occupations. Lautrec was fascinated by the human implications of what he saw and was intent on recording his reactions. These varied according to the type of subject that he treated. He was savage to the rich clients of the Moulin Rouge, appreciative, perhaps with a touch of irony, of the talents of a Jane Avril or an Yvette Guilbert, and moving when he depicted the boredom and squalor of the life led by the prostitutes in the *maisons-closes*. In his desire to treat in paintings human types and human problems – albeit of a rather specialized type – he stands apart from his contemporaries, the post-impressionists, and is nearer in spirit to the great social satirists, Goya and Daumier.

Another painter active in the nineties who does not fit into any category is Henri Rousseau (1844–1910), generally known as Le Douanier Rousseau. Till he was forty he was an employee in one of the customs offices at the fortifications of Paris (a painting of the *Octroi* is in the Courtauld Institute Galleries, London), and painting was for him only a hobby, but on his retirement in 1885 it became his main occupation. His work was 'discovered' by Signac and Gauguin and later appreciated by Picasso and Apollinaire for the spontaneity and freshness of the artist's vision. Rousseau's paintings are, however, far from being naïve. They are the result of very careful thought and are based on a long study of the Old Masters in the Louvre. Admiration for Rousseau started a fashion for 'primitive' painting, but unfortunately none of the artists who claimed to belong to this category had anything of the true imaginative power which saves Le Douanier's work from being trivial.

The most prominent group in French art of the nineties was that of the symbolists, but they were far from being united in their views. Some drew their ideas from Gauguin's conception of colour, and others, like Gustave Moreau (1826–98) and Puvis de Chavannes (1824–98), were inspired by religious and mythological themes, but they treated them in wholly different manners, Moreau in rich jewel-like colours, Puvis in a decorative style derived from the study of Renaissance frescoes. The most imaginative of them, Odilon Redon (1840–1916), built up his compositions round more allusive and more poetical ideas, often taken from Poe or from ancient legend or mythology. What they had in common was a belief that a painting was above all an object which must be beautiful in itself, in its colour, and in its craftsmanship, and that these elements serve to convey a spiritual beauty beyond that of the material world. As Aurier wrote, their art was to be 'ideal, symbolical, synthetic, subjective and decorative'. Eugène Carrière (1849–1906) was a friend of the symbolists and shared their view of painting as a spiritual art, but his themes were simple domestic subjects, often taken from his own family life, painted in very subdued tones, almost in monochrome, and in a soft technique without sharp outlines.

In some ways Carrière forms a link with the second group in the nineties, the Nabis, who belonged to a younger generation. Their name was taken from the Hebrew word for prophet, and in their earlier stage they shared many of the beliefs of the symbolists and of Gauguin, to which they were introduced by Paul Sérusier (1863–1927). Maurice Denis (1870–1943) applied the theory primarily to religious art and learnt much from early Italian painting; Ker Xavier Roussel (1867–1944) was inspired by classical mythology, but the two most significant members of the group, Pierre Bonnard (1867–1947) and Edouard Vuillard (1868–1940), soon abandoned the literary associations of this early phase and developed a style, sometimes called intimist, which they used for small paintings of domestic scenes. They retained the symbolist idea that a picture must be a painted area attractive to the eye and coherent in itself by eliminating all effect of depth and treating the canvas almost as if it were a tapestry or an embroidery. In many of their works of the nineties they embody the sinuous curves of art-nouveau as the basis of their surface patterns. In their early works both artists used a restricted palette of subdued and delicate tones; Vuillard continued to work in this vein, but Bonnard, in his later work, employed a palette of warm, glowing tones, dominated by reds, oranges and luminous purples. Though limited in their range compared with many twentieth-century artists, they were gifted with a high degree of sensibility. Maurice Utrillo (1883–1955) was never a member of the Nabi group, but his early views of Paris streets are in a palette closely allied to theirs and have a somewhat similar intimacy.

In sculpture the transition to the twentieth century is marked by the career of Aristide Maillol (1861–1944). He began as a tapestry designer under the influence of Gauguin and was for a time in touch with the Nabis, but in about 1900 he turned to sculpture, in which he evolved a formula for carving monumental figures of women in a style which owed something to Rodin, but much more to the study of Greek sculpture.

The Twentieth Century

The years between 1900 and the outbreak of the First World War were among the most eventful in the history of French art. They witnessed the establishment of *fauvisme* and the revolution brought about by the invention of cubism.

Fauvisme, of which the leading exponent was Henri Matisse (1869–1954), became a coherent school about 1904–5 and made its début at the Salon d'Automne of 1905. In certain respects the ideas of the *fauves* were based on immediately preceding doctrines. They accepted the importance of colour, they believed that a painting must be a coherent two-dimensional object, and they rejected classical canons of draughtsmanship. But they went much further than their predecessors: their colours were not merely pure, they were savage; they eliminated traditional perspective altogether, and they allowed themselves a quite new freedom in the distortion of the human figure for expressive or decorative purposes. Above all they entirely rejected the literary elements in painting, which had been vital to the symbolists and implicit in the art of Van Gogh and Gauguin. For them a painting was simply a painting; content was of quite secondary importance, and its relation to nature almost fortuitous. In fact the *fauves* applied in practice, and ruthlessly, what their predecessors had proclaimed in theory but had only carried out timidly. The result was a movement of quite extraordinary vitality which absorbed almost all the younger talent of the day. Matisse set the pace and created the first masterpieces in the new style: *Luxe, calme et volupté* (1904–5), which is still *pointilliste* in technique, *Bonheur de vivre* (1905–6; Barnes Foundation, Merion, Pa.), in which the flattening of forms and abolition of perspective are worked into an almost art-nouveau arabesque, and the two versions of *Le Luxe* (1907–8; Musée d'Art Moderne and Copenhagen) much grander in scale and more daring in their distortions. But other artists were infected by the enthusiasm of the moment and produced their own variations of the manner. Albert Marquet (1875–1947) worked in a style very close to Matisse, but Georges Braque (1882–1963), André Derain (1880–1954) and Maurice de Vlaminck (1876–1958) painted landscapes in simplified forms combined with fiery colours, and even painters of altogether minor talent, such as Kees van Dongen (1877–1968), Raoul Dufy (1877–1953), Henri Manguin (1874–1943) and Othon Friesz (1874–1949), applied the new methods with seriousness and individuality.

One painter of great power, Georges Rouault (1871–1958), was associated with the *fauve* group, although his style was fundamentally different from theirs. He was a devout Catholic and a pupil of Gustave Moreau. In his earliest works he imitated the style of his master, but by about 1905 he moved to a quite different conception of art. Obsessed by the evil and hyprocrisy of conventional society, he showed up its weaknesses in a series of savagely painted pictures of smug bourgeois couples, judges and prostitutes, executed with the comminatory vehemence of an Old Testament prophet.

Amadeo Modigliani (1884–1920), an Italian who early settled in Paris, belonged to no group, but his flat, linear paintings of elongated figures and his rich, warm colouring embody some of the principles of the *fauves*, and he shared with them an interest in African art, on which many of his faces are modelled. His work has, however, a certain monotony which indicates a lack of invention.

Of the various artists just named most never went on from *fauvisme* to break new ground. Some, like Van Dongen and Dufy, became purely frivolous, while Derain, Vlaminck and Othon Friesz sank into academic repetition. In the years just before the First World War Matisse went on to a splendid phase, in which the violence of early *fauvisme* was tempered by a certain intellectual control, which led him to produce some of the richest and most beautifully organized compositions in early twentieth-century art. After the end of the war, he went through an almost rococo phase with his lightweight paintings of interiors at Nice, but in the mid-thirties he recovered much of his early vitality, and the *papiers découpés* of his last years are thought by many to be among his finest works.

Braque alone went on to a completely new phase and collaborated with Picasso in the creation of cubism. Pablo Picasso (1881–1973) had already shown his astonishing talent and versatility in the paintings of the Blue and Pink periods, of which the former have some affinity with symbolism in their melancholy atmosphere, and the latter some relation to *fauvisme* in their flat, decorative quality; but he had been working in some isolation and in styles more conventional than *fauvisme*. In the famous *Demoiselles d'Avignon* (1906–7; Museum of Modern Art, New York), however, he broke through conventions which even the *fauves* had respected and at once took the position of leader among a slightly stunned group of colleagues. The *Demoiselles* was begun in a relatively conventional manner with a number of sketches in which the artist gradually refined the composition, but when the painting was half finished Picasso suddenly introduced completely new elements. He redrew one of the figures, so that the body and legs are seen from the back but the head is turned round so as to be seen almost full-face, thus breaking with the age-old convention of the single viewpoint. Secondly, he repainted several of the heads in a completely new idiom, based on the study of African masks, which Picasso and his friends had recently 'discovered'. The interest in African sculpture was in part due to a reaction against the over-sophistication of contemporary European culture, similar to that which drove Gauguin to Tahiti, but on Picasso it had a further effect because he was impressed by the manner in which Negro artists simplified the shapes of their images, reducing them to almost geometrical forms. It was this aspect of Negro sculpture rather than its savage or magical qualities which contributed to the development of cubism. It was about this time that Picasso and Braque began to work very closely together, each making his contribution to the new style. Through Braque Picasso came to study the late work of Cézanne, the lessons of which he applied in a series of landscapes painted in the summer of 1909 at Horta de Ebro. In these he made two further innovations: the abandoning of a single source of illumination, so that light and shade are applied in an arbitrary manner for purely formal reasons, and the rejection of central perspective, which in a sense was implied in the rejection of a single viewpoint introduced in the *Demoiselles d'Avignon*. In the following years, 1909–10, Picasso and Braque went further and further in the application of these principles, so that the forms of nature almost disappear as they are analysed into small facets seen from different angles and in different perspectives. Eventually these facets are extended, so that they almost take on a life of their own, and the same method of analysis is applied to the background, so that figure or still life merges with it into a single complex bas-relief, painted in a very restrained palette of grey-browns and greens. Then, in 1911, just as Braque and Picasso seemed on the point of breaking off all contact with the visible world, they began to re-establish it by the introduction of details painted in an almost *trompe l'œil* style, of words from newspaper headings or popular songs, and finally of actual objects such as matchboxes and cigarette packets. These *collages* introduced the phase of cubism called synthetic, as opposed to the earlier analytical type.

Cubism was essentially the invention of Picasso and Braque, but other artists of great talent joined the group and made their own contribution. Some, like Albert Gleizes (1881–1953) and Jean Metzinger (1883–1956), were more distinguished as theorists than as creative artists, but their writings are of interest since they are the earliest expositions of cubist doctrine, apart from Apollinaire's articles brought together under the title *Les Peintres cubistes*. The most original painters were the Spaniard Juan Gris (1887–1927), whose approach to art had something of the intellectualism of Seurat but whose best paintings have also great delicacy, and Fernand Léger (1881–1955), a more robust artist, whose cubist paintings are stronger in colour and contain more direct allusions to nature than the works of Picasso and Braque.

Although cubism was essentially concerned with painting, Picasso and Braque also made 'constructions' in order to try out some of their formal experiments which involved three-dimensional effects. Hardly any of these constructions have survived, owing to the fact that they were made in perishable materials, such as cardboard and paper, but a few artists, of whom Lipschitz (b. 1891) and Laurens (1885–1954) were the most interesting, produced cubist sculpture in more permanent materials.

Cubism was the dominant school in Paris in the years before the First World War, but there were other groups influenced by their ideas though working towards different ends. One of these, called the Orphists, and led by Robert Delaunay (1885–1941), wanted to escape from the extreme intellectualism of cubism and to introduce light and colour. In Delaunay's early paintings the forms of nature are dissolved by light, not into the vague forms of impressionism but into facets like those of cubist painting, though less rigorously patterned. Later he went further and painted abstract compositions based on rectangles or circles of pure colour, transfixed by rays of light. The Orphists formed the nucleus of a group called *La Section d'Or*, which in 1911–12 attracted most of those artists who were on the fringe of cubism, including Léger and Gris, and others of great talent who had not committed themselves to any specific creed. The movement was joined by theoretically minded painters, such as Gleizes, Metzinger, André Lhote (1885–

1962), but also by more spontaneous painters, like Roger de la Fresnaye (1885–1925), whose works are among the most attractive if not the most original products of the group. The half-brothers Jacques Villon (1875–1963) and Marcel Duchamp (1887–1968) also made very personal contributions. Villon's paintings have been described as being composed of 'frozen light', and this well defines their crystalline beauty. Duchamp was interested in movement rather than light and came closer than any other French painter to the ideas of the Italian futurists, with their cult of the machine and their admiration for the speed of modern life. During the First World War he lived in New York, where, with Francis Picabia (1879–1953), he founded a branch of the Dadaist school which had arisen in Central Europe, largely as a reflection of the despair felt by intellectuals at the collapse of the old order of society. Dadaism, which in its original form was a purely destructive creed, never really took root in Paris, but was later to be of great importance in the formation of surrealism.

The 1914–18 war inevitably marked an interruption in artistic activity in France. Most of the leading artists were called up and, although Picasso and Gris, being neutrals, continued to paint, they did not make any revolutionary innovations. In the years immediately after the Peace of Versailles a number of new factors can be traced, of which perhaps the most important is the increased internationalism of the École de Paris, for up to 1914, with a few exceptions, all the leading figures in the school had been French, and Paris as a whole had been curiously unaware of, or aloof from, artistic movements in other countries, such as expressionism in Germany or futurism in Italy.

After the war certain groups of artists continued along the lines mapped out before 1914. One example of this was purism, which was in a sense a development of the *Section d'Or*. Under the leadership of Amédée Ozenfant (1886–1966) and Edouard Jeanneret (1887–1965), better known in the field of architecture as Le Corbusier, the purists emphasized the colder, more intellectual aspects of cubism, basing their art on an admiration for the machine. They were joined by Léger, who produced a series of paintings in which the clear colour and steely sharpness of machines are used as the raw material for compositions of great subtlety and harmony. Picasso's cubist paintings of the same years have analogies with the works of the purists, and even his great figure paintings of the period share with them the classical calm which characterized certain aspects of French culture at this time, notably the music of *Les Six*.

Purism was also of great importance in connection with architecture, to which Le Corbusier applied many of the principles which he had learnt in connection with painting. Le Corbusier, who was Swiss by birth but lived in Paris from 1917 onwards, avoided the methods of training usual in architecture at the time, that is to say, study at the Beaux-Arts combined with apprenticeship in an architect's studio, but as a young man he met almost all the European architects of the older generation who were leading the way towards functionalism, and from them he learnt the foundations of his art. His own contribution was double: first a feeling for pure, simple forms and, secondly, a new and carefully reasoned conception of what was practically necessary in architecture in the twentieth century. Formally his buildings owe much to the principles of purism in the shapes and materials used and in the rejection of ornament. On the practical side he went far beyond his predecessors in town-planning, such as Tony Garnier (1869–1948) and the Italian Sant'Elia, because they worked out principles which were suitable for small units, whereas he planned for modern industrial cities with millions of inhabitants. His famous definition of a house as 'une machine pour vivre' was first applied to small houses in the suburbs of Paris (Villa Savoye, Poissy), but later to apartment blocks (Marseille) and public buildings (Maison Suisse, Cité Universitaire, Paris; Supreme Court, Chandigarh) and by extension to the designing of whole cities. His most celebrated work since the Second World War, the church of Notre-Dame-du-Haut at Ronchamp, is in a quite different vein, and the forms that the architect uses seem to be those of a surrealist sculptor rather than a purist architect.

The artistic scene in Paris in the 1920s was to a considerable extent affected by the fact that a number of artists from central and eastern Europe settled in France just before or just after the war and produced an infusion of quite different styles. Marc Chagall (b. 1887) brought with him from Russia via Germany an art which at its best employs Russian and Jewish symbols to create remarkable fantasies, but which often sinks into a mere whimsy, and Chaim Soutine (1894–1943) introduced a violent form of expressionism, partly based on the study of Van Gogh, which was quite contrary to the paintings of the School of Paris at the time.

In the middle-twenties the surrealists transformed the anti-rationalism of Dadaism into something more positive by asserting the supremacy of the imagination and the value of dreams, and of certain other non-rational phenomena, particularly automatic writing and drawing.

Their theories probably applied more completely to literature than to the visual arts, but certain painters, such as the German Max Ernst (b. 1891), the Spaniard Joan Mirò (b. 1893), the Belgian René Magritte (1898–1967) and the Frenchman André Masson (b. 1896) produced paintings which fully expressed the doctrines of the school. Among the founder-members of the surrealist group was the Swiss sculptor and draughtsman Hans Arp (1887–1966), who had been an active Dadaist in Switzerland but settled in France in 1922, where he produced compositions built up of forms which, though non-representational, suggest organic growth. The surrealist painters admitted a debt to Picasso, and he was certainly influenced by their ideas in his *Three Dancers* (1925; Tate Gallery) and in his metamorphic paintings of 1929–30.

At the other extreme abstract art, originally an invention of Central and Eastern European artists, took a hold in Paris. Wassily Kandinsky (1866–1944), a Russian who had evolved an imaginative form of abstraction in Munich just before the war, and Piet Mondriaan (1872–1944), the leading Dutch abstract painter, both lived in Paris for some years, and the sculpture of the Romanian Constantin Brancusi (1876–1957) and the Russian Alexander Archipenko (1877–1964) enjoyed a sudden success. Artists who were French by birth did not, however, in general take kindly to abstract art, and the movement never really took root in Paris.

Some of the older artists who had been leaders in the creation of fauvism and cubism went on painting in modifications of their old style, but others continued to develop. The most conspicuous of these was Picasso, who in the thirties produced a new synthesis which combined the imaginative intensity of surrealism with a personal symbolism based on the bullfight to produce some of his most forceful paintings and engravings. Under the impulse of the Spanish Civil War he produced in *Guernica* (1937; Museum of Modern Art, New York) what could be considered the last great masterpiece in a long tradition of European paintings which commemorate through mythological, religious or historical symbolism the great tragedies of humanity.

The Second World War caused an even greater break than the first in the history of French art. Picasso continued to paint, and many of his works, notably the *Femme se coiffant* (1940), reflect the grimness of the situation in France under the German occupation. Other members of the older generation went on working in the provinces, particularly in the south of France before it was occupied by the Germans, but clearly the state of the country prevented the appearance of a new movement.

When after 1945 conditions began to return to normal, the position of the School of Paris had radically changed. The most important single factor affecting it was the rise of the School of New York. This was due partly to the fact that many Central European artists, who had taken refuge in Paris during the thirties, moved to America just before or during the war, but New York had also produced its own movement of abstract expressionism or action painting, created by Jackson Pollock (1912–56), which combined the automatism of surrealism with the vigour of expressionism. The vitality of the School of Paris had already begun to wane in the 1930s, and it lacked the buoyant confidence of the *fauve* or cubist periods, the passionate destructiveness of Dada, or the emotional enthusiasm of surrealism. After the Second World War, however, a feeling of actual provincialism began to appear, and it could be argued that Paris made little real contribution to the development of art, though all the avant-garde idioms of contemporary art were taken up and developed with skill and wit. There were, of course, artists of distinction and originality working: Nicolas de Staël (1914–51) was still creating his luminous abstract paintings and Jean Dubuffet (b. 1901) developed a kind of fantasy painting which, though it owes much to Paul Klee, is completely personal. But generally speaking it must be admitted that for the first time for a century and a half Paris was no longer the artistic centre of the world, and the goal of young artists was New York. Now there are signs that this situation is changing, and the pendulum seems to be swinging back towards Europe.

Bibliography

There is no satisfactory single history of French art for the whole period from 1500 to the present day, though Louis Gillet's highly personal but very vivid *Histoire de l'art français*, first published fifty years ago, has been reprinted, slightly brought up to date and with good plates (Paris, 1978). Much of the subject is covered by the relevant volumes in the Pelican History of Art, all of which have full bibliographies: the present writer's *Art and Architecture in France 1500–1700*, 2nd ed. (1970), M. Levey and W. von Kalnein, *Art and Architecture of the Eighteenth Century in France* (1972), F. Novotny, *Painting and Sculpture in Europe 1780–1880* (1960), G. H. Hamilton, *Painting and Sculpture in Europe 1880–1940* (1967), R. Hitchcock, *Architecture: Nineteenth and Twentieth Centuries* (1958). For architecture L. Hautecœur, *L'Histoire de l'architecture classique en France* (Paris, 1943; a revised edition is appearing) is a valuable book of reference for the period up to the mid-nineteenth century, though not always accurate in detail and with poor plates. The volumes by A. Châtelet and J. Thuillier, *La Peinture française de Fouquet à Poussin* (Geneva,

1963) and *La Peinture française de Le Nain à Fragonard* (Geneva, 1964), provide an excellent survey up to the late eighteenth century.

Much valuable information about all fields of French art in the sixteenth century is to be found in the catalogue of the exhibition 'L'École de Fontainebleau', held in the Grand Palais in 1972–3. For the painting of the period the reader should also consult Sylvie Béguin, *L'École de Fontainebleau* (Paris, 1960). For Jean Clouet, see P. Mellen, *Jean Clouet* (London, 1971), and for the other portrait painters of the sixteenth century, see L. Dimier, *Histoire de la peinture de portrait en France* (Paris, 1924–5), and E. Moreau-Nélaton, *Les Clouet et leurs émules* (Paris, 1924). For Primaticcio, see L. Dimier, *Le Primatice* (Paris, 1900 and 1928).

For Vouet see W. R. Crelly, *The Paintings of Simon Vouet* (New Haven and London, 1962), and for La Tour see B. Nicolson and C. Wright, *Georges De La Tour* (London, 1974). For Poussin see A. Blunt, *Nicolas Poussin* (London, 1967–8) and W. Friedlaender and A. Blunt, *The Drawings of Nicolas Poussin* (London, 1939–74); and for Claude see M. Roethlisberger, *Claude Lorrain: The Paintings* (London, 1961) and *Claude Lorrain: The Drawings* (Berkeley, 1968).

The architecture of the late sixteenth and early seventeenth centuries is well covered in R. Coope, *Salomon de Brosse and the Development of the Classical Style in French Architecture from 1565 to 1630* (London, 1972). For François Mansart see P. Smith and A. Braham, *François Mansart* (London, 1974). P. Verlet's *Versailles* (Paris, 1961) provides a convenient and reliable account of the complicated building history of that palace. Philippe de Champaigne has been covered by B. Dorival in a long monograph (Paris, 1977) which gives much information but is in many respects unreliable (see the present writer's review in the *Burlington Magazine*, CXIX (1977), p. 574). For the high period of Louis XIV's reign, see the catalogues of the Lebrun exhibition at Versailles (1963) and *Les Collections de Louis XIV* at the Orangerie (1977). For the end of the reign, see A. Schnapper, *Jean Jouvenet* (Paris, 1974), which gives a new conspectus of the painting of the period. F. Souchal's *French Sculptors of the 17th and 18th Centuries*, of which the first volume appeared in 1977 (Oxford), will be the authoritative work on the subject.

The first half of the eighteenth century has been neglected by scholars of the twentieth century but much useful information is to be found in L. Dimier's unfinished *Les Peintres français du XVIIIe siècle* (Paris, 1928, 1930). For Watteau's paintings see J. Ferré, *Watteau* (Madrid, 1972), and for his drawings K. T. Parker and J. Mathey, *Antoine Watteau, catalogue complet de son œuvre dessiné* (Paris, 1957). A good short account of his work is given by A. Brookner, *Watteau* (London, 1967).

Useful monographs exist on the following artists: for Lancret, G. Wildenstein (Paris, 1924); for Pater, F. Ingersoll-Smouse (Paris, 1928); for Chardin, P. Rosenberg, catalogue of the Chardin exhibition, Grand Palais, Paris, 1979; for C. J. Vernet, F. Ingersoll-Smouse (Paris, 1926); and for Greuze, A. Brookner (London, 1972).

For the taste of the mid-eighteenth century the essential document is Diderot's *Salons*, ed. J. Seznec (Oxford, 1957–67), but much can be gleaned from J. Locquin, *La Peinture d'histoire en France de 1747 à 1785* (Paris, 1912). There is still no satisfactory history of French sculpture in the eighteenth century, and for this and other aspects of French art of the period the most up-to-date information is to be found in the catalogues of the James A. de Rothschild collection at Waddesdon Manor, particularly *Sculpture* by T. Hodgkinson (Fribourg, 1970), *Sèvres Porcelain* by S. Eriksen (Fribourg, 1968) and *Furniture* by G. de Bellaigue (1974). Pierre Verlet's volume on the Savonnerie carpets, which will contain a history of the Savonnerie factory, is due to appear in 1979. For architecture the most useful book is C. Tadgell, *Ange-Jacques Gabriel* (Zwemmer, 1978).

The most useful survey of neo-classicism is H. Honour's *Neo-classicism* (Harmondsworth, 1969) but the reader should also consult R. Rosenblum, *Transformations in Late 18th Century Art* (Princeton, 1967). Much detailed information and a good corpus of plates are to be found in the voluminous catalogue of the exhibition of neo-classical art held in London in 1972. For J. L. David see L. Hautecœur (Paris, 1954) and A. Brookner, *J. L. David: A Personal Interpretation* (London, 1974); and for Ingres, R. Rosenblum (London, 1967) and N. Schlenoff, *Ingres, ses sources littéraires* (Paris, 1956).

The literature on Romanticism is vast but of uneven quality. The best short survey is W. Vaughan, *Romanticism* (London, 1978), but the reader should also consult Wakefield, *Stendhal and the Arts* (London, 1973) and *Charles Baudelaire critique d'art*, ed. C. Pichon (Paris, 1965). For Géricault see Clément (Paris, 1868) and L. E. A. Eitner, *Géricault's 'Raft of the Medusa'* (London, 1972). Delacroix's *Journal* and *Correspondance* have been published by A. Joubin (Paris, 1932 and 1935). For a general treatment of him as an artist see L. Johnson (London, 1963) and F. A. Trapp, *The Attainment of Delacroix* (Baltimore, 1971). T. Clark's *The Absolute Bourgeois* (London, 1973) and *The Image of the People* (London, 1973) give a stimulating account of the realist movement under the July Monarchy and the Second Republic. For Daumier see K. Maison (London, 1967–8) and for Courbet, the catalogue of the Courbet exhibition at the Royal Academy, January 1978.

The most complete accounts of impressionism and post-impressionism are J. Rewald, *The History of Impressionism* (New York, 1961) and *Post Impressionism* (New York, 1962), but the reader should also consult Phoebe Pool's briefer *Impressionism* (1967). For neo-impressionism see R. L. Herbert, catalogue of the neo-impressionist exhibition at the Guggenheim Museum, New York, 1968. On symbolism see the catalogue of the exhibition *French Symbolist Painters* at the Hayward Gallery (London, 1973). Monographs exist on all the principal painters of the period as follows: for Manet, see Anne Coffin Hanson, *Manet and the Modern Tradition* (Yale University Press, 1977); for Monet, W. C. Seitz (London, 1960); for Degas, P. Cabanne (London, 1958); for Pissarro, L. R. Pissarro and L. Venturi (Paris, 1939); for Renoir, M. Drucker (Paris, 1949); for Cézanne, L. Venturi (Paris, 1937), M. Schapiro (New York, 1952), and the *Letters*, ed. J. Rewald (Paris, 1937–49, and London, 1941); for Gauguin, G. Wildenstein (Paris, 1964) and R. S. Goldwater (London, 1957); for Van Gogh, J. B. de la Faille (revised edition, 1970), and J. Leymarie (Paris, 1951) and the complete correspondence (New York, 1958); for Seurat, H. Dorra and J. Rewald (Paris, 1959) and J. Russell (London, 1965); for Toulouse-Lautrec, D. Cooper (London, 1955); for Moreau and Redon, J. Rewald and D. Ashton in the catalogue of the exhibition of Redon, Moreau and Bresdin (Museum of Modern Art, New York, 1962). For Henri Rousseau see J. Bouret (London, 1961); for Rodin, A. E. Elsen (New York, 1963); for Bonnard, J. and H. Dauberville (Paris, 1960) and J. Rewald (New York, 1948); for Vuillard, John Russell (London, 1971).

The best account of fauvism is to be found in J. Elderfield, *The 'Wild Beasts': Fauvism and its Affinities* (New York, 1976). For Matisse see his *Écrits sur l'art*, ed.

D. Fourcade (Paris, 1972) and A. Barr (New York, 1951); for Derain, D. Sutton (London, 1959).

For surveys of cubism see J. Golding (London, revised ed. 1968) and R. Rosenblum, *Cubism and Twentieth Century Art* (New York, 1966). Of the huge literature on Picasso the most useful biography is by R. Penrose (London, revised ed. 1971) and the best analysis of his work up to 1930 is by A. Barr, *Picasso: Fifty Years of his Art* (New York, 1932). The most complete set of reproductions of his work is to be found in C. Zervos (Paris, 1932 – still appearing). For the most recent views on his art see *Picasso 1881–1973: Essays Edited by R. Penrose and J. Golding* (London, 1973). Monographs on the principal cubist and allied artists are as follows: on Braque, J. Leymarie (Geneva, 1961); on Gris, D. Cooper and M. Potter (Paris, 1977); on Léger, R. L. Delevoy (London, 1962). For Brancusi see the catalogue of the exhibition at the Guggenheim Museum, New York, 1965, by S. Geist. For purism see the catalogue of the exhibition of Léger and purist Paris at the Tate Gallery, 1970 (J. Golding and C. Green). For Orphism, V. Spate (Oxford, 1979). For Le Corbusier see C. Jencks (London, 1973). for Marcel Duchamp, see J. Golding, *Marcel Duchamp: The Bride Stripped Bare of her Bachelors, even* (London, 1973).

For Dadaism and surrealism see W. S. Rubin, *Dada, Surrealism and their Heritage* (New York, 1968), M. Jean, *History of Surrealist Painting*, English ed. (London, 1960), M. Nadeau, *Histoire du Surréalisme* (Paris, 1958), and the catalogue of the exhibition *Dada and Surrealism Reviewed* held at the Hayward Gallery, London, January 1978.

The student in search of original works of French art will of course find the largest and finest collections in Paris – in the Louvre for painting and sculpture up to the middle of the nineteenth century (with important works by Courbet, Dalou and others in the Petit Palais), in the Jeu de Paume and the Musée Marmotton for impressionism and post-impressionism, and the Musée d'Art Moderne at the Centre Pompidou for more recent periods. Separate museums exist in Paris showing the works of certain individual artists, such as Gustave Moreau and Rodin, and a Picasso museum is being installed in the Hôtel Aubert de Fontenay in the Marais.

Outside Paris most of the great cities have museums with representative collections of French art from the sixteenth century onwards, of which the most notable are perhaps Rouen, Lyon, Grenoble, Dijon and Lille. Arras has many of the large religious paintings of the seventeenth and eighteenth centuries; Toulouse has fine examples of the local school; Montaubon has paintings bequeathed by Ingres; and Montpellier fine paintings by Courbet and other artists of the mid-nineteenth century. In addition there are certain museums devoted to individual artists: Toulouse-Lautrec at Albi, Matisse at Cimiez (Nice) and in the chapel at Vence, Picasso at Antibes, and Léger at Biot.

In England the most important general collection of French painting is to be found in the National Gallery, London (up to the end of the nineteenth century), the Tate Gallery (for more recent periods) and the Courtauld Institute Galleries (impressionism and post-impressionism). The Wallace Collection and the James A. de Rothschild Collection at Waddesdon Manor (National Trust, near Aylesbury) have magnificent collections of French works of art, mainly of the eighteenth century, including furniture and china as well as paintings and sculpture. The National Gallery of Scotland has important French paintings of the seventeenth and eighteenth centuries, including Poussin's *Seven Sacraments* (on loan from the Duke of Sutherland), and the municipal gallery at Kelvingrove, Glasgow, houses the nineteenth-century paintings from the Burrell Collection. The National Museum of Wales has a small but fine group of paintings by nineteenth-century French artists bequeathed to it by the Misses Davies.

11 French Music since 1500

HUGH MACDONALD

At the end of his *Lettre sur la musique française*, published in 1753 in the thick of the so-called *Querelle des Bouffons*, Rousseau declared:

> I think I have shown that there is neither measure nor melody in French music, because the language is not capable of them; that French singing is a continual squalling, insupportable to an unprejudiced ear; that its harmony is crude and devoid of expression and suggests only the padding of a pupil; that French airs are not airs, that French recitative is not recitative. From this I conclude that the French have no music and cannot have any; or that if they ever have, it will be so much the worse for them.

Rousseau saw himself as the champion of Italian music, whose melodiousness and simplicity could teach a lesson to the old-fashioned *tragédie-lyrique*, at that time personified in Rameau. As a professional music copyist and the composer of a not negligible comic opera *Le Devin du village* staged at Fontainebleau in 1752, Rousseau was musician enough to be taken seriously, and the Encyclopedists as a body fell in behind him in condemning what they saw as the sterility of French music. The issue was perhaps narrowly partisan in that the *coin de la reine* (as Rameau's opponents were labelled) were seeking to introduce some novelty and modernity to replace what they saw as a moribund art; none the less every now and again the serious question was raised: are the French, or are they not, a musical nation? In the early eighteenth century cultivated Frenchmen were painfully aware of the supremacy of Italian music then dominant right across Europe from Madrid to St Petersburg, and they examined the reasons for their own apparent inferiority in countless pamphlets and tracts, of which Rousseau's *Lettre* is the most famous.

A hundred and fifty years later the rival was not Italy but Germany, whose political and cultural strength threatened to stifle French artistic creativity. Again the question kept being asked: are the French inherently more or less musical than the Germans, or anyone else? While Saint-Saëns, d'Indy, Debussy and many others embraced the cause of national music, it was Romain Rolland who remained detached enough to examine the question of cultural identity and to ask himself what makes French music French. Some even believed that the conflict could be settled by force of arms, speaking of the 'victory of French music', a phrase which came to sound ironically hollow in 1918.

Such periodic bouts of national self-appraisal mark the history of French music from the earliest times, ever since the Notre-Dame school led the way in the twelfth century. If France has never again been so clearly the leader of Europe in musical matters, she has many times aspired – and still aspires today – to head the league, as if to match her achievements in literature and painting. The pendulum swings from exclusiveness to cosmopolitanism, from jealously nourishing peculiarly French forms and attitudes to welcoming musicians and styles from all points of the globe. This strange alternation has produced that characteristic French product, a typically French genre created by foreigners yet commandeered and hallowed by the French themselves. Lully, Gluck and Meyerbeer all came from outside to establish what became an exclusively French operatic style. Small wonder that the French have so often questioned wherein their true identity lies.

French ambivalent regard for other nations' music is in telling contrast with England, for whereas here we have always welcomed foreign music, often in snobbish disdain for our own, the French have imported forms and styles only with reluctance, and sometimes not at all. It was a remarkable feat, for example, to resist the tide of Italian opera in the early eighteenth century when every other nation was consumed by it. This was the effect of Louis XIV's deliberate policy, initiated half a century earlier, of fostering national arts since they served to create the image of power and glory for all the world to see and admire, in keeping with the magnificence which so evidently characterized the monarchical style. Neither the king nor Colbert could themselves tell their poets and musicians what to write, but by supervising all stage spectacles and encouraging like-minded artists, much could be achieved, and was. Lully was the chosen instrument of Louis's musical glory, and, though he was himself an Italian who came to France in the 1640s at the age of ten or twelve, no French music exemplifies better than his this distinctly national sense of superiority to other nations. Once established as the most powerful musician in France, Lully opposed any kind of innovation from outside.

For similarly political motives German music was suppressed during the First World War. Those who loved Beethoven had either to pretend that he was in fact Flemish and therefore an expression of 'the purest form of the French genius' or else to play his music in private, as Marliave and his friends did at the front. Insularity of a more general kind extends to the French awareness, or ignorance rather, of musical developments in other countries, especially northern lands such as Scandinavia and England, much to the chagrin of many lovers of English music who are astonished that the French never hear, for example, the *Dream of Gerontius*. Most French admirers of Italian music have been literary men like Rousseau and Stendhal, while the three greatest figures in French music – Rameau, Berlioz and Debussy – have shown no more than scant interest in Italian music.

The readiness of the French to adopt and absorb foreign musicians on the other hand gives Parisian musical life a cosmopolitan distinction rarely rivalled by other cities. Many of the composers of the greatest French operas, as we have already observed, have been foreign: Lully, Gluck, Cherubini, Spontini, Rossini, Meyerbeer and Offenbach. In the 1830s the international flavour of Paris was incredible, with Liszt, Chopin, Hiller, Kalkbrenner, Cherubini, Moscheles, Hallé, Habeneck, Fétis, Sor, Schlesinger, Spontini, Rossini and Meyerbeer all more or less resident there and only Berlioz representing the host nation with any distinction. Yet no Frenchman voiced disquiet at this situation until Louis-Philippe's reign was over. A similar spirit prevailed in the 1920s, when Stravinsky embodied Parisian international modishness and men like Prokofiev and Martinů found such surroundings congenial. Even today Boulez's Ircam project is staffed by Englishmen, Americans, Germans, Yugoslavs and Japanese, with no thought for national interests.

Before the Revolution

SONG, BALLET AND OPERA

It is a curious fact that, while in the fifteenth century Italy was the cultural centre of Europe, that pre-eminence was notably missing in the field of music. Italy had few composers and imported freely from the extraordinary galaxy of musical talent that grew up in the Burgundian provinces, especially in the Netherlands. France, like Italy, was fallow at the same time, for it would perhaps be fair to regard the great Netherlands school, comprising men so outstanding as Binchois, Busnois, Dufay, Obrecht, Ockeghem and Josquin Després, as separate from the French tradition. By the beginning of the sixteenth century Josquin was the supreme figure of the age and on this tradition was built the great flowering of sacred and secular music in late sixteenth-century Italy.

In contrast France's great musical treasure of the sixteenth century was the chanson, whose lightness and simplicity were effected by chordal textures and rapid repeated notes. Its sectional structure revealed a sharp contrast with the more intricately woven music of the Burgundian school and relied largely on the direct impact of verse in a brilliantly immediate setting; Marot's verse provided exactly the right material. The two great masters of the French chanson were Clément Janequin (d. *c.* 1560) and Claudin de Sermisy (*c.* 1490–1562). Janequin was appointed composer-in-ordinary to the king in 1555 and wrote nearly 300 chansons, to texts by Marot, Ronsard, François I himself and others. His greatest fame rests on those pieces which convey realistic action, such as galloping horses, singing birds or the clamour of battle, as in his famous *La Guerre*, describing the Battle of Marignano of 1515, at which Janequin was present. *L'Alouette* and *Le Caquet des femmes* are typical Janequin titles, and not only did their naïve charm win immediate popularity in their own day, but they also look forward to the similar descriptive pieces of the clavecinistes nearly 200 years later. Claudin's preference was for more madrigalian subjects, for songs of unrequited love and tender passion, expressed in a simple chordal style with plentiful repetition. Gradually, in mid-century, the more complex Netherlands manner crept in, and the next generation of chanson composers included Arcadelt, Willaert and Lassus, all of them northerners who worked far afield, Arcadelt and Willaert in Italy, Lassus mostly in Munich. The use of chanson melodies in mass compositions of the time testifies to their wide and welcome circulation.

The chanson thrived on two sources of strength: one was the energy and skill of French music printers, chief among them Pierre Attaingnant (d. 1552), whose output was enormous in bulk and fine in quality, followed by Adrien Le Roy (d. *c.* 1589) and Robert Balard (d. 1600), founder of a great dynasty of French music printers. Attaingnant's publications included, besides vocal pieces, lute music and instrumental dances, many of them derived from chansons. These attest to the growth of domestic and amateur performance of secular music.

The other source of strength was the verse, since the French attached considerable importance to the clarity and form of sung words, as they have consistently done in every generation to this day, whether the music is by Lully or Debussy. The aesthetic aims of the Pléiade, articulated by Du Bellay and Ronsard, were to restore the nobility of French poetry by the imitation of Greek and Roman models, such as Horace and Pindar. Ronsard emphasized the importance of writing poetry that could not be submerged in polyphonic textures. Baïf's Académie de Poésie et Musique, founded in 1570, devised a more systematic approach, with strict treatment of long and short quantities on the analogy of classical verse, and the application of rules both to music and to verse ensured a unified art-form in which neither obscured the other. Baïf's *vers mesurés* required music in which all voices sing the words at the same time, a severe limitation at a time when polyphonic styles were flourishing in both sacred and secular music. Claude Le Jeune (*c.* 1525–1600) may be credited with largely overcoming these limitations through his harmonic and rhythmic resourcefulness, but the sterile application of theory is none the less apparent in much of his work, and *musique mesurée* enjoyed a relatively brief period of cultivation. The more general preoccupation with musical stress and metre and the matching of language to music, on the other hand, was of far-reaching importance, extending well beyond the sixteenth century.

We should here consider the origins of French opera, for while, like English opera, it was much later than its Italian equivalent in reaching what we recognize as a distinctly operatic form, it has a rich prehistory in the sixteenth and seventeenth centuries in the chanson, the *mascarade* and the *ballet de cour*, the latter two being entertainments in which music was by no means the most important element. Poetry, dancing, singing, playing and spectacle were all indispensable, and they were generally a close reflection of royal aspirations or fancy. François I brought numerous Italian decorators, dancers and musicians to Fontainebleau, and their shows generally included some kind of triumphal procession in which music and recitation made allusion to classical and mythological subjects. Catherine de Medici's ballet in honour of the Polish ambassadors in 1573 was described by Brantôme as 'le plus beau ballet qui fust jamais faict au monde', and a similarly magnificent ballet was staged for the marriage of Henri de Navarre and Marguerite de Valois in 1572. For this creation, entitled *Paradis d'amour*, Ronsard wrote the words, and the influence of Baïf and his friends was pervasively felt in the setting of words to music, in the *ballet de cour* as in the chanson.

The most celebrated of these grand ballets, with their long ancestry in the *fêtes* of the Renaissance, was the *Ballet comique de la reine*, also entitled *Circé* and composed in 1581 for the marriage of the queen's sister to the Duc de Joyeuse. The dancing master Balthasar de Beaujoyeulx was the 'author' of the piece, though the music, which has happily survived, was contributed by various hands. The entertainment lasted from 10 p.m. to 4 a.m. and has a definite plot concerning Circe, Mercury and Minerva, with much humanistic symbolism and endless dancing and processing. The music, considered on its own, is solid and dull, with, as one might expect, the stress and accent of the words ponderously articulated. Spectacular machinery came into vogue, and on it rode gods and zephyrs, armies and nymphs; Jupiter descended, Hades yawned, storm clouds billowed. The spectacular, which was to remain fundamental to French opera for many centuries, was largely the province of Italian machinists and designers, first the Florentine Francini and later the great Torelli.

For the betrothal of Louis XIII to the Spanish Infanta in 1612 a grand ballet was mounted in the Place Royale, the scope and scale of which may be grasped from Isherwood's description:

> A model palace was decorated with symbols of the sun and other allegorical figures. The defenders of the palace, the knights of glory, were carried to the scene on a chariot drawn by giants and lions accompanied by the lyre of Amphion. The first quadrille depicted Orpheus drawing toward him by the magic of his lyre a forest of laurel trees and the knights of the sun. The music also summoned the chariot of Apollo, a symbol of the union of the French and Spanish crowns, bearing Time, the Seasons, the Hours of the Day. A race by the knights of the lily was then held, followed by an equestrian ballet. In subsequent quadrilles mythological themes were depicted, including the legends of Amadis of Gaul and Perseus, laced with all the elements of ballet: récits, musical intermezzos, dances and every conceivable legendary figure, from Hercules to Jason, who could be likened to members of the royal family. After three days, the carrousel concluded with a final triumphal entry of Roman warriors, leading the captive kings of Africa and Asia mounted on elephants. The palace went up in a blaze of fireworks and a fanfare of trumpets.[1]

La Délivrance de Renaud (1617) was another elaborate ballet, based on Tasso, in which Louis XIII himself took part. The music, by

[1] Robert M. Isherwood, *Music in the Service of the King* (Ithaca, NY, 1973), p. 95.

Guédron, required sixty-four singers, twenty-eight string players and fourteen lutes. The unspoken purpose of these shows was the glorification of the monarchy and the entertainment of the nobility and they generally referred to contemporary events such as the expansion of commerce, the Thirty Years War or the revolt of the Huguenots. The *Ballet de la marine* (1635) recorded Richelieu's establishment of a co-ordinated and powerful navy, and in 1641, for the *Ballet de la prospérité des armes de France* (whose title reveals all), Richelieu brought Torelli's mechanical wizardry to Paris for the first time.

Louis XIV not unexpectedly delighted in the court ballet. He was trained in music and had some ear for it. He adored dancing and was often thought in his youth to be devoting an unhealthy amount of time to it. Mazarin encouraged the king's pleasures and brought Italian opera to France for the first time, grafting on to Luigi Rossi's *Orfeo* in 1645 a suitable panegyric (in Italian) in praise of the king. Most adept at flattery and adulation was Isaac Benserade, author of numerous ballets in the 1650s and collaborator with Torelli and Lully, before the latter's more important and extensive collaboration with Quinault in *tragédie-lyrique*. The *ballet à machines* became a popular genre. Corneille said of his *Andromède* (1650): 'I have employed music only to satisfy the ear while the eyes are looking at the machines, but I have been careful to have nothing sung that is essential to the understanding of the play because words are generally badly understood in music.' Music even served as a method of covering the noise of the machinery in motion.

Thus a long history of elaborate ballets, strictly for court consumption, and a short-lived attempt to introduce Italian opera to France in the 1640s provide the background to the eventual creation of a true French opera, and it was undoubtedly a great achievement. A common reaction to Italian opera, voiced for example by Saint-Évremond, was a distaste for Italian recitative, so the feeling was widespread that the French should have a more literary type of musical drama. It was not Lully who wrote the first French opera, for he was apparently committed to ballets, but Perrin and Cambert, whose *Ariane* in 1669 was permitted by *lettres-patentes* allowing an 'Académie d'opéras ou représentations en musique en langue française sur le pied de celles d'Italie'. Cambert's *Pomone* followed in 1671, but financial difficulties laid the way open for Lully to take over, and by a series of manœuvres of questionable integrity he ensured that the initiative, the control and finally the monopoly were all in his own hands. The patent granted on 13 March 1672 allowed Lully to 'establish a Royal Academy of Music, in order to perform some productions before us'. It prohibited all persons from 'singing any piece entirely in music, either in French verse or other languages, without the permission in writing of the said Sieur Lulli, in penalty of 10,000 livres fine'. Even Molière was limited to only six musicians at the Palais Royal. Further extensions of the privilege widened Lully's powers, even to the extent of forbidding performances of opera anywhere in the kingdom without Lully's consent, and making the privilege hereditary.

Between 1673 and his death in 1687 Lully wrote about one opera a year, and these works were to dominate the French repertory for nearly a century. It was remarkable that this should have so come about, since Lully's music has never had abundant admirers and could never be compared in genius to contemporaries such as Purcell or Alessandro Scarlatti, nor to his great successor Rameau. Since the eighteenth century his operas have remained quite dead, untouched even by the modern taste for baroque revivals. This perhaps indicates how indissolubly the Lullian *tragédie-lyrique* was linked to the tastes and circumstances of its time and its nation, representing an aspect of the *grand siècle* that cannot again be brought to life. The monarchy is itself present in the music, for Quinault, who supplied Lully with a dozen libretti, would submit certain subjects, usually drawn from Ovidian mythology, to the king, who would select one which he approved. The Prologue in these works is an undisguised panegyric of the king, often making reference to notable events of the day and elevating his heroic virtues: triumphant in war, generous in peace. The action of the operas circles round themes of glory and love. Monsters are overcome and enemies are magnanimously defeated. In the Preface to *Persée* (1682) Lully declared: 'I understand that in describing the favourable gifts which Persée has received from the Gods and the astonishing enterprises which he has achieved so gloriously, I am tracing a portrait of the heroic qualities and the wonderful deeds of Your Majesty.'

Lully based his style on the breadth and firmness that magniloquence demands, best seen in the opening sections of his overtures. Although he perhaps drew it from an Italian model, Lully's 'French overture' became accepted all over Europe with its bracing dotted rhythms followed by fugal or flowing second sections. Handel adopted it without question, and Bach, too, in his suites. Lully also devised a distinct style of recitative based on theatrical declamation, entirely different from that of Italian opera. He took pains to reproduce the flow and accent of tragic declamation. 'If you wish to sing my music correctly,' he said, 'go and hear la Champmeslé.' Since he studied Champmeslé's performances of Racine in the 1670s, he must owe much to Racine's own intonation, though he never set Racine's verse to music. Lully's recitative constantly alternates in time signature and bar length in order to catch the stress of the words, using a strictly syllabic style, and he was adept at alternating recitative and air or *ariette* in a way which Italians, with their stricter segregation of recitative and aria, would never accept. French opera did not allow singers and singing to dominate the stage as they did in Italy, and the extensive dramatis personae of the Lullian *tragédie-lyrique*, often incorporating numerous deities or minor personages, reflects much more care for theatrical than vocal splendour. None the less characteristic French voices were cultivated. Where the Italians had their splendid *castrati*, the usual heroic voice in France was the *haute-contre*, singing in the highest tenor range, not unlike the English counter-tenor in range but less artificial in quality. The *haute-contre* survived into the nineteenth century as the high lyric tenor, even after the arrival of the heavier heroic tenor for principal roles, and French choral writing long preserved its characteristic preference for dividing the male rather than the female voices. The plummy contralto, familiar enough to English choral societies, is a voice unheard and unrecognized in France.

Lully's first operas included comic scenes (*Cadmus et Hermione* and *Alceste*, both of 1673), but most of them present worthy themes in a dignified but spectacular manner. In *Alceste* Hercules represents the true hero, *Thésée* (1675) applauds glory and love, *Bellérophon* (1679) the virtues of moderation, *Amadis* (1684) the king's glorious repulsion of envious enemies. Storm and battle scenes and the slaughter of dragons and giants provide spectacular grand scenes to give the *tragédie* both its grandeur and its popular appeal. For audiences were not, at the Palais Royal, confined to the nobility as is often supposed; Lully had a considerable bourgeois following, and this was one factor contributing to his immense wealth and power.

Lully's death in 1687 occurred at a time when the king's personal interest in opera was declining, perhaps under Madame de Maintenon's influence. But the *tragédie-lyrique* remained, like the monarchy itself, highly resistant to change and outside influence. Lully's works dominated the repertory, and younger composers, now allowed to trespass in Lully's territory, adopted his models. Pascal Colasse (1649–1709) was most closely Lully's successor, and his *Thétis et Pélée* (1689) remained on the boards for sixty-five years. Campra (1660–1744) and Destouches

(1672–1749) were the leading French composers of opera until the arrival of Rameau, and they both wrote *tragédies-lyriques* as well as the *opéras-ballets* that became a vogue of the period. In the *opéra-ballet* dramatic continuity is sacrificed to scenic or balletic interest, with a preference for exotic settings in neatly formal balance. Campra's fine *L'Europe galante* (1697), for example, has the customary prologue, followed by four *entrées* representing France, Spain, Italy and Turkey in turn, with song and dance in equilibrium. Destouches's *Issé*, of the same year, goes further afield with its Act V *entrées* depicting Europeans, Americans, Egyptians and Chinese. Campra's *Tancrède* (1702) includes Saracens and Syrians. *Divertissement* was considerably more desired than drama, although most of the *opéras-ballets* retained a light vestige of plot. Meanwhile *tragédies-lyriques* continued to uphold the virtues of heroism and magnanimity in such works as Destouches's *Amadis* (1712) and Campra's *Idoménée* (1725), later to be set and immortalized by Mozart.

Jean-Philippe Rameau (1683–1764) turned to the stage at the age of fifty, and his first *tragédie-lyrique*, *Hippolyte et Aricie*, was unquestionably the greatest offering in the form to that date, and perhaps the greatest of any date. Rameau was known to Frenchmen first as an organist, then as a claveciniste, then, and principally, as a theorist, certainly not as one who would have any feeling for the theatre. Admiration for Rameau's harmonic skill was tinged with scorn, such as is often reserved for 'clever' composers. But his skill was not confined to harmony, the central focus of his theoretical writings. He also had a brilliant feeling for instruments, a gift of melody and superfine dramatic judgement. His opponents persisted in seeing in Rameau only a sack of dry bones, mistaking the real countenance for the music, but his genius flowered in an unbroken series of fine works until his death in 1764.

He composed five *tragédies-lyriques* – *Hippolyte et Aricie* (1733), *Castor et Pollux* (1737), *Dardanus* (1739), *Zoroastre* (1749) and *Abaris ou les Boréades* (1764) – and about twenty other stage works: *opéras-ballets*, *comédies-lyriques*, *pastorales*, and so forth. It is a magnificent corpus, still too little known, perhaps because his style comes uneasily to ears brought up on Bach and Handel, his great contemporaries. It is wholly French in its traditional forms, its close attention to verbal declamation, and its emphasis on spectacle, movement and colour, yet Rameau's invention far exceeds that of earlier French composers for the stage. As in Lully, Rameau's operas are drawn from mythology and deal with an endless cycle of tragic and amorous themes. Figures such as Neptune,

Jupiter, Niobe, Apollo and Bacchus continue to appear; words like 'chaînes' and 'voler' always attract illustrative setting, often to magical effect. 'Triomphes', 'Amours', 'Sommeils', 'Fêtes' abound; so do *ariettes, divertissements* and the usual final *chaconnes*. The novelty in Rameau's music lay in its harmonic richness and its skilful attention to detail. Campra observed that in *Hippolyte et Aricie* there was music enough to supply ten operas; Rameau's critics, on the other hand, spoke of his music as 'baroque' and 'barbare', 'trop chargée', 'trop travaillée'. Perhaps they found the *Trio des Parques* in Act II of *Hippolyte et Aricie* too richly harmonized, but they should not have mistaken the incomparable dramatic force of Phèdre's great scene in that opera, or the orchestral inventiveness of the scenes depicting thunder, stormy seas or monsters. No one in the early eighteenth century used the orchestra so richly as Rameau, not unlike Berlioz a century later.

His fundamental aim was, again like Berlioz, to match words and dramatic essence with the appropriate music. 'The expression of thought, sentiment and passions should be the true aim of music,' he wrote. 'Few have attempted to do more than provide amusement and diversion with this art. . . . One often has occasion to admire a singer's performance or an instrumentalist's skill, but what is there here to do with *expression*?'

Rameau was largely untouched by the critical controversies that raged around him, and his final work, *Abaris* (which has never been staged and was only played for the first time in recent years), is as masterly as any, yet still within the *tragédie-lyrique* formula that had survived nearly a century. It was an old-fashioned formula, still redolent of seventeenth-century principles, yet given life by Rameau's genius and in some details distinctly modernized. The grandiloquent prologues, for example, had vanished, and much greater dramatic continuity was achieved by Rameau's use of repeated motives and themes, and by integrating action and *divertissement*. Cahusac, Rameau's principal librettist, was himself concerned to use dancing as an element in the dramatic plan, and Rameau came to use the overture not as a curtain-raiser but more as a preview of what is to come. The overture to *Zaïs* depicts the unravelling of chaos; in the *Pygmalion* overture we hear the chisel chipping at stone, and in *Zoroastre* Rameau gives a veritable descriptive symphony as an overture.

After Rameau's death in 1764 the Académie offered few new works and relied largely on their inherited repertory. Younger composers were in any case more drawn to the *opéra-comique*. Critical opinion regarded the *tragédie-lyrique* as a defunct form, fit only for old men capable of standing up for three long hours. When the Palais Bourbon, where the Opéra had been housed, caught fire, the wits remarked that the shortage of water buckets was hardly surprising: no one had expected a glacier to catch fire. Yet the arrival of Christoph Willibald Gluck (1714–87) in 1774 breathed new life into serious opera, and his immediate success with *Iphigénie en Aulide* heralded the fine series of operas which included French versions of *Orfeo* and *Alceste* (with *haute-contres* replacing *castrati*) and new operas written for Paris: *Armide* (1777) and his masterpiece *Iphigénie en Tauride* (1779). Gluck's reform was based on a revulsion from Italian opera, from its domination by singers and from its lack of dramatic feeling. In raising naturalness and simplicity of expression to places of importance Gluck was only exalting traditional French virtues, so that his operas matched a particular French sensibility and gave French opera a modern form of *tragédie-lyrique* stripped of baroque detail and set to music of startling simplicity, even plainness. For the expression of pathos or mourning Gluck's style was unequalled. 'Nature', which had earlier embraced the most artificial and elaborate of styles, now took on its more Rousseauesque implications as an ideal of purity and simplicity, full of feeling and expression but free from ornament and display.

Gluck was forced into controversy with the Italian Piccinni, though both composers respected each other's work. Critics such as Marmontel and La Harpe upheld Piccinni's music as 'claire, transparente', more evenly shaped and poetic; Gluck they regarded as a 'prosateur'. Once again the divisions hardly reflect real differences of musical style. Gluck was infinitely more inventive and subtle than Piccinni, and there the matter must rest. Gluck's real rival was not any other composer of his own type but the *opéra-comique*, which flourished extraordinarily in mid-century growing out of the *vaudeville* and the plays of Favart, with music no more sophisticated than the popular *ariette*, with spoken dialogue. Village stories about blacksmiths, woodcutters, and the like, were popular. François-André Philidor (1726–95) and Pierre-Alexandre Monsigny (1729–1817) led the way in the 1760s and 1770s, with Philidor's *Tom Jones* (1765) and Monsigny's *Le Déserteur* (1769) providing successful examples of the type. André-Ernest Grétry (1714–1813) declared himself bored by Rameau's music and enflamed by Pergolesi's and, when Monsigny retired from composing, Grétry led the field until the Revolution with a profusion of *opéras-comiques*. *Richard cœur de lion* (1784), though not by any means typical of the genre, pointed the way to a more elevated form with numerous adumbrations of romantic opera. It told a heroic story of rescue and deliverance, and Blondel's song, supposedly of troubadour origin, runs through the opera to fine dramatic effect.

CHURCH MUSIC

It was in secular music – in particular the chanson – that France's most distinctive contribution to European music of the sixteenth century was made. In sacred music she had no composer to equal Lassus, Palestrina, Victoria or Byrd when Renaissance polyphony reached its apogee at the end of the century. The dearth of French sacred music to compare with, say, Tudor church music may be explained by a lack of surviving sources (either printed or manuscript), by a humanistic preference for secular music in cultivated literary circles, and by the continuous religious conflict that beset the century. Claude Goudimel (d. 1572) composed in a style which, like the chanson, preferred melodic brevity and syllabic clarity to polyphonic complexity, and he is best known for his settings of the psalm tunes in the Genevan psalter, an austere musical medium if ever there was one. Calvin himself preferred devout, unadorned melodies, so that Goudimel was displaying an adventurous spirit in devising four-part settings, only occasionally venturing into more elaborate textures. Most notable is his giving of the tune to the top, treble line instead of to the habitual tenor part, a practice which clearly reveals the composer's desire to put singability and clarity above traditional practice and which ensured the popularity of his settings for many years to come.

Goudimel also wrote four masses, five motets and three magnificats, although in the field of the motet Lassus dominated the repertory of French churches at the end of the sixteenth century just as Josquin had at the beginning. French names in this field are unquestionably minor, though for their small but real efforts their names at least should be mentioned – men such as Mauduit and Maillard, who worked in the service of the Church at a difficult period. Du Caurroy's *Preces ecclesiasticae* (1609) use double choirs in a manner which was then probably a novelty in France. Instrumental accompaniment was also slow to be introduced; in fact sacred music remained stubbornly conservative throughout the beginning of the seventeenth century despite new styles then emerging from Italy. Instrumental accompaniment and the *basso continuo* were late to be adopted, yet when a distinctive style did finally evolve it reflected the ethos of the *grand siècle* with great splendour.

Nicolas Formé (1567–1638) and Thomas Gobert (d. 1672), successive *sous-maîtres* of the royal chapel after Du Caurroy, developed the larger-scale double-choir motet, and Jean Veillot (d. 1662) added instrumental symphonies. The *État actuel de la musique du roi et des trois spectacles de Paris* of 1772 attributed the introduction of instruments into the mass to the king himself: 'Occupied constantly with the idea of grandeur, born with the most decided spirit for music, having acquired some extraordinary knowledge in this art through the new genre of composition which the great Lully employed in his Opera, the king imagined that he could introduce the symphony of violins into the motet.' Henry Du Mont (1610–84) is the composer most clearly responsible for establishing the *grand motet*, for securing Louis XIV's imprimatur and thus setting a model for younger men much as Lully was to do with the *tragédie-lyrique*. One type of conservatism thus replaced another, none the less bringing into being a large corpus of music – extending from the middle of the seventeenth to the middle of the eighteenth centuries – which is still very little known. The *grand motet* comprised a series of episodes for solo voice or voices between music for choir, with instrumental symphonies and *ritournelles*, not unlike the Purcellian verse-anthem. The intricacy of the part-writing was one of the glories of the *grand motet*, whether by Du Mont, Lully or the greatest master of the genre Michel-Richard Delalande (1657–1726), who devoted his life to royal service and whose seventy-one motets are one of the great unexplored treasure-stores of the French baroque. Another contemporary of similar distinction was Marc-Antoine Charpentier (1634–1704) whose rich variety of music for the church is scarcely better known. He was trained in Italy and adopted Italian mannerisms, yet he was sometimes almost English in his harmonic audacity, using dissonance, as Purcell did, as an aid to expressiveness. He was a man of distinctly modern outlook, versatile and productive, working mainly in the field of sacred music. He ventured into *tragédie-lyrique* (not very successfully) with his *Médée* in 1693.

The king's conception of divine service was as an extension of court life, so that glorification of the monarch played as much part as glorification of the deity. He showed a marked increase in piety towards the end of his long reign. After 1715 religious music became ever more secular in spirit, perhaps in anticipation of Voltaire's baleful influence. The grand gestures of the previous reign survived in somewhat meaningless form, and the growth of anti-clericalism drove the best composers away from these too sterile pastures. Rameau and Leclair renounced writing for the Church in due course; Couperin's heart was elsewhere, even though his psalm verses and his *Leçons de ténèbres*, composed between 1713 and 1717, are intense and deeply felt. Composed for one or two solo voices and continuo accompaniment (which might be harpsichord or organ), and using recitative and closed forms, they are never far from the vocabulary of opera and cantata. Rather than the massive dignity of Lully and Delalande, Couperin's music is more intimate in scale and expression. Rameau's relatively slight interest in sacred music (four *grands motets* survive) similarly reflects the decline of church music and its almost total neglect in the reigns of Louis XV and XVI. At the period when Handel's oratorios found profound and permanent sympathy in England, nothing comparable was attempted or possible in France.

INSTRUMENTAL MUSIC

The later eighteenth century is similarly bleak in French instrumental music, though it followed a great flowering in the clavecinistes. They in their turn had their roots in the sixteenth century, in the vogue for playing chansons on the organ or on groups of instruments, viols and suchlike, and in the new dances such as *gavottes*, *branles*, *allemandes* and *courantes* which emerged at the end of the sixteenth century as the newest type of piece for keyboard or lute or viols. Dances, then as now, stepped giddily in and out of fashion, so that *pavanes* and *gaillardes* for one generation became the *courantes* and *sarabandes* for the next. What is most significant is that the majority of these dances were adopted across Europe under French names, suggesting already the supremacy of French dance, even when they were of Italian or Moorish or Spanish origin, as they often were. Observe the very names *allemande* and *écossaise*. Arbeau's celebrated *Orchésographie* of 1588 probably confirmed the authority of French dancing, and while dancing was strictly a social rather than artistic accomplishment its musical by-product was a corpus of fine instrumental music. Its chosen instrument in the early seventeenth century was the lute, described by Mersenne as the noblest of instruments, and we find magnificent collections of lute music containing all manner of court dances as well as the *fantaisies* and *préludes* which allowed a freer invention than the more strict rhythmic and formal demands of the dance. Antoine Francisque's *Le Trésor d'Orphée* (1600) and Jean-Baptiste Besard's *Thesaurus harmonicus* (1603) are two such collections. The greatest master of the lute was Denis Gaultier (*c*. 1603–72) whose manuscript volume *La Rhétorique des dieux* of about

1640 shows the wonderfully intricate textures of lute music at its height. The so-called *style brisé* ingeniously enabled the lute to reproduce polyphonic textures and moving inner parts, decked out with ornaments and *agréments* that offered the lutenist every opportunity to display his taste and skill. Several members of the Gaultier family were lutenists of distinction, for music was a family trade at that period, in France as elsewhere. Gaultiers, Couperins, Forquerays, Philidors, though never as numerous as the Bachs, served the French court over many generations.

What most strikes the newcomer to the instrumental music of Louis XIV's reign is its elaborate ornament and its profusion of fanciful titles. Ornament was of course part of the way of life – in architecture, in dress, in gesture and in speech – and in music it found expression in an elaborate harpsichord idiom, based on that of the lute, which came to perfection in the magnificent suites, or *ordres*, of François Couperin (1668–1733). The clavecinistes gradually supplanted the lutenists in the middle of the seventeenth century, beginning with Jacques de Chambonnières (*c.* 1602–72), Louis Couperin (d. 1661), Nicolas Antoine de Le Bègue (1630–1702) and Jean-Henri d'Anglebert (1635–91). Chambonnières's *Pièces de clavecin* were published in 1670 with an explanatory table of ornaments, such was their richness and complexity, and this practice was often followed in later publications. François Couperin's treatise *L'Art de toucher le clavecin* (1716) likewise laid great stress on the correct interpretation of ornaments and their function in articulating the music. His advocacy of modern rational fingering is also essential to the study of his own four books of harpsichord pieces, published between 1713 and 1730. These contain altogether twenty-seven *ordres*, comprising over 240 pieces, some of them dance movements of no great weight, some decorative, fanciful pieces, some grand formal compositions such as the great *Passacaille* in the eighth *ordre*. The titles are provocatively elusive, such as *Les Barricades mystérieuses* or *Le Drôle de corps* or *L'Évaporée* or *Les Brimborions*, which must have stimulated as much argument and speculation then as they do now. Couperin's descriptive skill and his immense range make him one of the leading figures of the French baroque, comparable in his field to Rameau in opera, and prophetic too of Debussy's imaginative works for the keyboard. Rameau's own output for the harpsichord was much slenderer, but it was of exceptional quality. His first book appeared in 1706, his second in 1724 and a third in 1728, all before his first opera was written. Like Couperin he could write tenderly or naïvely, or build large energetic movements out of the harpsichord's rhythmic punch. His character pieces are even more sharply descriptive than Couperin's, as for example *La Boiteuse*, depicting a cripple, or *La Poule*.

Couperin wrote no operas but there are many concerted pieces, trio sonatas and concertos, such as the *Concerts royaux* and *Les Goûts-réunis*, essentially concertos for various combinations of instruments. Rameau's pieces of this type are perhaps finer, notably the *Pièces de clavecin en concerts* of 1741. It was this music which represented the *goût français* in Europe at a time when Italian music was indisputably in the ascendant. The French style was recognized as such by German and English musicians and was carefully distinguished from the Italian. The contrast is clearly seen in Couperin's *L'Apothéose de Corelli* (1722) and *L'Apothéose de Lully* (1725). The French style is well exemplified in Bach's four orchestral suites, thoroughly French in manner and idiom, with their dotted-rhythm overtures and profusion of French dances – *bourrées*, *gavottes*, and so on. Foreign opinion was expectedly mixed: Dr Burney declared that Couperin's music was 'so crowded and deformed by beats, trills and shakes, that no plain note was ever left to enable the hearer of them to judge whether the tone of the instrument on which they were played was good or bad', while Georg Muffat, who had studied in Paris, pointed out that French ornamentation was condemned only because it was never performed accurately.

Although it never matched its Italian rival, the French violin school boasted some fine practitioners and composers, such as Duval, Francœur, Senaillé and the greatest of the group, Jean-Marie Leclair (1697–1764), whose forty-nine sonatas for solo violin and continuo and numerous trio sonatas are impressive testament to a vigorous school of violin virtuosi. Leclair had absorbed the brilliant Italian technique of Corelli and Vivaldi and he displayed in many respects, such as the variety of bowing technique and the precise ornamentation, an independently inventive mind. Boismortier, Mondonville and Guillemain carried the violin school further into mid-century. Flute and cello sonatas are also found in profusion. Most characteristic of French conservatism at this time is the survival of the bass viol (or viola da gamba) at a time when it was already obsolescent elsewhere. Marin Marais (1656–1728) and the two Forquerays, father and son, Antoine (1671–1745) and Jean-Baptiste (1700–82), were the leading virtuosi at court on an instrument that required stylish, elegant playing rather than brilliance, and the bass viol was indispensable in chamber ensembles and opera orchestras of the time.

One further branch of French music had a distinct and healthy vitality in the baroque age – that of organ music, a sphere in which national differences were then particularly marked. The French school grew on the foundation laid by Jehann Titelouze (1563–1633) who worked in Rouen and whose plainsong hymns are highly refined polyphonic compositions, with a clear dependence on the characteristic *plein jeu* sonority of French organs. Carefully specified registration and a concern for contrast and quality of sound are recurrent features of French classical organ music, and particular solo stops are often required. The organ books of Nivers, Le Bègue, Raison, d'Anglebert, Grigny and many others constitute a rich repertory, often archaic in its use of modes and polyphonic textures, but leaning also to dances and instrumental pieces such as those found in the harpsichord books of the period. Ornamentation is, of course, fundamentally important. François Couperin's early *Pièces d'orgue* (1690) consist of two masses each containing twenty-one pieces for the liturgy based both on Gregorian melodies and popular dances, such as the *gigue* and *marche* in the Gloria of the parish mass. Clérambault and Marchand are but two of the many names associated with this genre, composing liturgical suites with a strong secular flavour. Burney was surprised to find, later in the century, when Balbastre was playing at Saint-Roch church, that 'when the magnificat was sung he played likewise between each verse several minuets, fugues, imitations and every species of music, even to hunting pieces and jigs, without surprising or offending the congregation'.

The French baroque style, with its elaborate mannerisms and courtly *allure*, survived well past the middle of the eighteenth century. The newest ideas in music were then coming from Italy (in the overtures and finales of *opera buffa*), Vienna (the 'reform' opera of Gluck) and Germany (the *Empfindsamkeit* of C. P. E. Bach and the bracing orchestral style of the Mannheimers). Outside opera French music showed little interest in these newer forms, so that while symphonies were cropping in hundreds in German and Austrian cities the native French symphony showed a distinctly poor harvest. Performance and publication of foreign symphonies in Paris was prolific, yet with the exception of François-Joseph Gossec (1734–1829) few French composers contributed to this most abstract of musical forms. The 'Concert Spirituel' was the celebrated institution that fostered instrumental music at the time. It was initiated in 1725 by Anne Danican-Philidor, who had to pay a heavy royalty to Lully's son-in-law to contravene Lully's draconian privilege, and though it was originally devoted to religious music it soon provided a platform for all kinds of instrumental and vocal music, both French and foreign, and survived sixty-six years until 1791. It was here that Mozart's 'Paris' Symphony was first heard in 1778, and, though Mozart disliked Paris and had little opinion of Parisians, French music left its mark on him, especially on *Idomeneo*. He wrote to his father from Paris: 'to expect the French to realize that their own music is bad or at least to notice the difference – Heaven preserve us! And their singing! Good Lord! Let me never hear a Frenchwoman singing Italian arias . . .' Haydn's six 'Paris' Symphonies (Nos 82–7) were commissioned in 1784 by a different organization, the Concerts de la Loge Olympique.

Since the Revolution

The Revolution affected musical life in France almost immediately, and its influence was felt most directly in two spheres: in the music of ceremonial and popular hymns, and in the opera. Concert music, already relatively precarious an institution in eighteenth-century France when compared to England or Germany, sank into further oblivion for a few decades, perhaps because it was unable to carry the nationalist and popular sentiments expressed so enthusiastically in vocal music. Patriotic songs were the order of the day. The best known of all, the *Marseillaise*, Rouget de Lisle's stirring battle song, was written in April 1792 at the proclamation of war; it was taken up by the Marseilles soldiery on their entry into Paris in July 1792, so winning its name and its fame. It was one of many patriotic songs and hymns that poured from composers in the wake of the Revolution. The great ideological outpouring of those momentous years produced a crop of revolutionary music which was as much designed to supersede the bad old style as the republic was a replacement of the *ancien régime*. Rameau's elaborate mannerisms had already been drastically simplified by the advent of Gluck, but that was as nothing compared to the root-and-branch return to musical fundamentals preached by the composers of the Revolution. These were Berton, Catel, Cherubini, Le Sueur, Méhul and the most prolific, Gossec. Méhul and Gossec were the chief among them, propounding a new style in which plain keys, plain chords and plain progressions abound and in which chromaticism, modulation and counterpoint were proscribed. We may study this extraordinary outpouring of ideological music in the copious volumes of Constant Pierre, lovingly compiled and edited at the turn of the present century. Much of this music is assuredly dull and relies for its effect, as do the *Marseillaise* and Méhul's comparably successful *Chant du départ*, on a certain crude excitement and sentimental appeal. But it was designed not for professional musicians but for 'all that have heart and voice'; and that frequently meant the enormous crowds that gathered in the Champ de Mars and elsewhere in the 1790s for the large-scale outdoor ceremonies and *fêtes*, where massed bands and choirs played and sang in honour of the Republic and all its works. Reports speak of 'armies' of side-drums. Sometimes these large numbers were laid out in antiphonal groups. Méhul's magnificent *Chant national du 14 juillet 1800* was for three choruses and three orchestras, while Le Sueur's *Chant du 1er vendémiaire* of a little later in the same year calls for four of each. New instruments were designed after Roman models, such as the buccin and the tuba corva; the tam-tam was introduced for moments of solemnity; the ophicleide came into being at this time. Wind and percussion were indispensable for this grand outdoor music, and a tradition of military music was established which persisted through the nineteenth century. The greatest exponent of this kind of music, Berlioz, was not even born when the Bastille fell, but in three of his works – the *Grande messe des morts* (1837), the *Symphonie funèbre et triomphale* (1840) and the *Te Deum* (1849) – the simplistic gestures of the real revolutionary composers were brought to a high point of fulfilment without losing sight of their popular ethos.

The other great focus of modern sentiment was the opera, especially the *opéra-comique*, since the Académie was fatally associated with the discredited monarchy. *Opéra-comique* had already become a vehicle for noble sentiments in Grétry's *Richard cœur de lion* (1784), as we have seen. Cherubini's *Lodoiska* (1791) took the idea of a heroic rescue a stage further, still with spoken dialogue but with a much more advanced musical style. Indeed it anticipated many things in Beethoven's *Fidelio*, with its strongly political background, a wicked baritone villain, a noble tenor hero and the clear triumph of right over wrong. *Les Deux Journées* (1800) was of all Cherubini's operas the one to attach itself most strongly to the ideal of the common man, and it was extremely successful. It concerns the unselfish heroism of a Savoyard water-carrier whose nobility of spirit is stressed by the fact that it is an aristocrat whom he rescues from the wicked machinations of Cardinal Mazarin. Another theme of the opera is conjugal love and the elevation of domestic virtue.

Under the Consulate and Empire this new type of popular, moralist opera fused with the grander tradition, *tragédie-lyrique* in effect, to give birth to grand opera, one of France's great contributions to nineteenth-century culture. In grand opera great deeds are done against the epic backdrop of natural or historical cataclysm. Instead of individual virtue in a domestic scene, the new opera offered the heroic deeds of nations and peoples, usually in the face of tyrannical oppression, conceived on an epic scale. The personal dilemmas of individuals are seen against the greater interests of nations and are thus never explored for their own sake.

Ossian ou les bardes, by Jean-François Le Sueur (1760–1837), first performed in 1804, tells of the struggle of Caledonians and Scandinavians, with imprisonment, heroism, rescue, dreams and festivities filling a broad, spectacular canvas. His *La Mort d'Adam* (1809) was based on a blend of *Paradise Lost* and *Genesis* with an apocalyptic vision that embraced heaven, hell and the whole human race. Le Sueur, with his obsession for reviving both the spirit and the letter of antiquity, was a startling, original figure, but he lacked the dramatic and musical gifts of Gasparo Spontini (1774–1851), yet another Italian, like Cherubini, whose contribution to French opera was decisive. *La Vestale* (1807) bridges the gap between Gluck and Berlioz. Julia, the Vestal heroine, caught in the true Romantic dilemma between love and duty, has music of superb expressiveness and passion. His *Fernand Cortez* (1809) was a spectacular opera wherein shipwrecks and battles form the background to strongly expressed human passions. Neapolitan revolution in Auber's *La Muette de Portici* (1828) (whose heroine, being dumb, mimes her part – a superbly contrived opportunity for expressive programme music), Swiss nationalism in Rossini's *Guillaume Tell* (1829) (another imported Italian), medieval superstition in Meyerbeer's *Robert le diable* (1831), religious fanaticism in his *Les Huguenots* (1836) and Halévy's *La Juive* (1836) – these are the typical recipes that provided the new opera-going public with the *frisson* and entertainment they loved. Grand processional scenes and opulent staging were essential, and the present Paris Opéra, the Palais Garnier, opened in 1874 (it is no coincidence that it stands at the central point of all Paris's traffic systems), is sufficient alone to bring to mind the elaborate staginess of French nineteenth-century opera and its extraordinary social standing.

In 1830, at the height of theatrical and musical Romanticism, all eyes were focused on the Opéra, with its social and financial benefices. But it was not just opera composers like Rossini, Meyerbeer (successfully) and Wagner (unsuccessfully) who came from abroad to seek success in

Paris. Paris was also the world's capital of the salon. Young ladies played the fashionable harp, young gentlemen the guitar, and the brilliant sonority of the new pianoforte produced a rash of studies, caprices, concertos, fantasies, preludes, sonatas and variations, and a clutch of virtuosi to compose and play them. Kalkbrenner, Moscheles, Liszt and Chopin all gathered there. The young Karl Halle (later to bestow his name and his energies on the city of Manchester) felt the lure of Paris and left Germany to seek his fortune there. Liszt and Chopin could scarcely have had more dissimilar personalities, and while Liszt's dazzling career seems archetypically cosmopolitan, Chopin does surely reflect the French genius in innumerable ways: his poetic sensitivity, his lyrical gift, his sensuous harmony, all these recur in Fauré and Debussy, even though his style was beyond the reach of imitators in his own day. Chopin was impervious to the great movements of his time (the cult of Beethoven, of the individual, of the macabre, and so on) and communicates merely by his deft, poetic fingers. One Frenchman, Charles-Valentin Alkan (1813–88), left an extraordinary output ot piano music in which the macabre and the pictorial are prominent. He was a friend and admirer of Chopin, lacking his melodic gift, but endowed with a superhuman technique and the capacity to compose for the piano on an enormous scale. His reclusive, misanthropic nature and a streak of obsessive neurosis in the music, not to mention its inaccessibility and difficulty, has cast it into shadow, by no means its merited fate.

The one outstanding figure of French Romanticism was neither foreign nor able to establish his fame in the opera house or the salon. Hector Berlioz (1803–69) gave his first concert in Paris in 1828, and it was in the concert hall both in Paris and abroad that Berlioz's public activity as a composer was to be seen. He was to become one of the first modern conductors too. His concert work was significant in that Beethoven's symphonies provided a powerful impetus and the model for the *Symphonie fantastique* (1830), his first great work, but also misleading in that Berlioz's great achievement was to dispense with conventional categories of music-making. He wrote no pure operas, no pure symphonies, no pure oratorios, no piano music, no chamber music. All his works seek to match their subject-matter with musical forms and genres best suited to their expression. Expression is the key to his music, since everything he wrote relates to literary or personal experience, and this was more important than form or conventional codes of beauty. In addition Berlioz, being a highly articulate writer, left the clearest exposition of what his music is about. It is more than ironic that despite this his works were consistently misunderstood in his lifetime and remained so until recent years. His acute sense of sound, his capacity for intense feeling, his mastery of orchestral technique and his rhythmic élan all contribute to a highly individual sound-world that has its roots in eighteenth-century French opera – Rameau and Gluck – but which is infused through and through with Romantic feeling.

Shakespeare provided much of his material: a symphony on *Romeo and Juliet* (1839), an overture on *King Lear* (1831), a comic opera on *Much Ado About Nothing* (*Béatrice et Bénédict*, 1862), various pieces on *Hamlet*. Goethe gave him the *Huit scènes de Faust* (1829), later to be enriched and expanded into *La Damnation de Faust* (1846); Virgil, his childhood passion, emerged eventually in 1856–8 in *Les Troyens*, the culmination of French epic opera and the summation of all Berlioz's work, a fine balance of classical beauty and Romantic feeling. The actress Harriet Smithson, whom he later married, inspired the passionate drama of the *Symphonie fantastique*. No composer allowed his life and thoughts so profoundly to pervade his music; he *is* the artist, whose sufferings are recounted in the *Symphonie fantastique*, he *is* Lélio, the protagonist of its semi-dramatic sequel *Le Retour à la vie* (1832), he *is* Harold in his second symphony *Harold en Italie* (1834), he *is Benvenuto Cellini* the artist-hero fighting obstructive jealousy and blind bureaucracy, he *is* the ever-suffering, ever-feeling Faust. His writings are an extension of his music, his music an extension of his life. He was music critic for the *Journal des débats* for thirty years and wrote volumes of criticism of composers, performers, inventors, cranks great and small. This gave him an unequalled awareness of the absurdities of French musical life, especially when he compared them with what he encountered on his many successful concert tours abroad, and his *Mémoires* are an unmatched picture of that experience. *Les Soirées de l'orchestre* (1852) and *Les Grotesques de la musique* (1859) are less concerned with his own doings than with those of others, and it is clear that he was protected from despair by his unremitting sense of irony and his unfailingly witty pen.

Berlioz, dying in 1869, was spared the sufferings of the Siege and Commune, and by that time new initiatives were desperately needed to save French music from a general mediocrity of taste (from which Berlioz is to be excepted) similar to that which gripped England at the same time. Meyerbeer's hegemony at the Opéra and Offenbach's at the Bouffes-Parisiennes seem to belong definitively, in retrospect, to the

Second Empire. The form that the renewal took in the Third Republic was a vigorous turning to chamber and symphonic music with the deliberate aim of creating a national repertory of concert music. Pasdeloup's *Concerts populaires* were already under way when the Société Nationale de Musique, founded by Saint-Saëns and Bussine in 1871, took for its motto *ars gallica* and devoted itself exclusively to French music. No foreign music was heard in its programmes until 1886 and its achievement in bringing forward younger French composers was very positive. An abundance of composers of decent stature – Bizet, Lalo, Duparc, Dukas, Lekeu, Chausson, Bruneau and of course Saint-Saëns himself and the older César Franck – form the nucleus of a national school only rarely equalled in numbers and productivity at other periods of history. Saint-Saëns, Lalo and Fauré had to turn for their models for chamber music to Germany, to Beethoven, Mendelssohn and Schumann, and much of their music has an invigorating energy that is often thought to be lacking in French music. Two tendencies proved difficult to resist: one towards sentimentality and the other towards Wagner. Sentimentality characterized the early nineteenth-century *Romance* and became pervasive in Gounod and his followers, especially Massenet, wickedly nicknamed 'la fille de Gounod'. A dilettantish delight in oriental subjects was made fashionable by Félicien David with his enormously popular 'ode-symphonie' *Le Désert* in 1844, recurring in Bizet's *Les Pêcheurs de perles* (1863), Delibes's *Lakmé* (1883) and elsewhere. Both Georges Bizet (1838–75) and Delibes (who had a lot in common) were capable of rising above any suspicion of mediocrity, Delibes in his finely wrought ballets and Bizet in his last works, crowned by the immortal *Carmen* (1875). Bizet's genius shines fitfully through all his music, however frequently he descended into the vulgar, sentimental or commonplace. His melodic gift, related to that of Gounod, was extraordinary, and his dramatic sense, at least in *Carmen*, was far beyond anything that his French contemporaries could offer. His works have been consistently misrepresented in print and in performance to this day. Contemporary critics often accused him of Wagnerism (as they did anyone showing any kind of harmonic audacity), while Nietzsche went to the other extreme and elevated *Carmen* to the rank of antidote to the Wagnerian sickness.

Wagnerism in France was a powerful force even though Wagner's music was only rarely heard there. *Die Meistersinger* was not staged in France until 1897, *Tristan und Isolde* not until 1899 and *Der Ring des Nibelungen* not until 1911. The débâcle of *Tannhäuser* at the Opéra in

1861, the Franco-Prussian War and Wagner's disastrously tactless pamphlet *Eine Kapitulation*, published in 1873, full of unconcealed venom against the French, effectively banished his influence until the 1880s, when Saint-Saëns's weakening interest in the Société Nationale de Musique and the growing magnetism of Bayreuth brought about a surge of literary Wagnermania foreshadowed by Baudelaire and embodied in the *Revue wagnérienne* whose editors were men of letters and whose open cult of Wagnerism laid stress on symbolism and the newest literary trends. The *Revue* lasted from 1885 to 1887 and Frenchmen began to flock to Bayreuth. Catulle Mendès and Élimir Bourges wrote Wagnerian novels; d'Indy and Chausson wrote Wagnerian symphonic poems. Franck's pupils, with their ready inclination towards rich chromaticism, were the first to succumb to this irresistible force from Outrerhin, and a whole body of music came into being which instantly refutes the notion that French music is, typically, willowy and effeminate: César Franck (1822–90) could never be so described, certainly not in his full-bodied organ and piano works, not even in the delicate and masterly Violin Sonata. His pupils were of similar inclination. Chausson, Lekeu and that passionate Franco-Irishwoman Augusta Holmès wrote music rich in red corpuscles, leaning on Beethoven (in the case of Lekeu), Franck and the new Wagnerian vocabulary to generate a characteristically powerful style. Chausson's B flat Symphony, superior to Franck's better-known D minor Symphony in so many respects, is a fine example, and the symphonic poems of Holmès and d'Indy and the symphonies of Magnard and Dukas should be catalogued here.

There were wayward spirits who conformed exactly to neither line of thought. Emmanuel Chabrier (1841–94), whose gift was for witty and delicately poised compositions, subtle in understatement and delightful in style, fell for Wagner and composed a number of works, in particular his opera *Gwendoline* (1886), in an unabashedly Wagnerian manner, uncharacteristic of him though it was. Alfred Bruneau (1857–1934) developed a vein of naturalism which may in part have been due to the spell of *Carmen* but which was certainly stimulated more by his close contact with Daudet and Zola. *L'Attaque du moulin* (1893) is probably Bruneau's best work despite the oblivion in which it all now reposes. Then Gabriel Fauré (1845–1924), who has never been out of favour, ploughed his patient, personal furrow in quiet disregard of the blasts and counterblasts of musical fashion. His music *is* willowy and effeminate, but he should never be regarded as the archetype of his age. His sensitivity to words, his delicate feeling for harmony and his impulsive touches of modality make him the finest composer of *mélodies* and piano music before Debussy. His music flows like water without colour and without violent or even unsuspected interferences. In Verlaine he found poetry to inspire his finest songs, beginning with *Clair de lune* (1887) and followed shortly afterwards by such masterpieces as *En sourdine*, *Green* and the nine songs of *La Bonne Chanson*. In middle life, after growing out of the somewhat facile music of his early years (with which we must include the Requiem) and before his music succumbed to the structural disintegration of deafness and old age, Fauré was master of a private language, quiet and poetic and without any need for brilliance, bombast or academic severity. Except where his style infiltrated the new piano style of Debussy and Ravel, Fauré stands well away from the centre of modish music at the end of the century. With Fauré we should mention the small but exquisite group of songs by Henri Duparc (1848–1933), models of sensitive word-setting and poetic feeling. The fourteen songs on which his reputation rests were all composed in the years 1868 to 1884, after which Duparc lapsed into enigmatic silence for nearly fifty years.

Camille Saint-Saëns (1835–1921) sought his own refuge from the Wagnerian malaise by preaching principles of order and health. These he found in Mozart and, taking classical principles to their roots, in Greece. Even though very little was – and still is – known about ancient Greek music, Saint-Saëns more than dabbled in neo-Hellenism and in one work at least, his incidental music to *Antigone* composed in 1894, he attempted a thoroughgoing re-creation of Greek music. Saint-Saëns was an exceedingly intelligent musician whose facility and skill actually impeded the development of his powers, since he was too aware of what he wanted to avoid to carve out a niche of his own, and he simply lacked invention on a scale to equal his musicianship. 'The artist who does not feel thoroughly satisfied with elegant lines, harmonious colours or a fine series of chords does not understand art,' he once said, and he stuck to these high principles. In addition, he wrote both poetry and prose, and he loved the salon world. In the *Carnaval des animaux*, written for that milieu, he displayed a streak of wit and invention rarely to be found in his or anyone else's music of that time, and he was characteristically embarrassed by this brilliant *jeu d'esprit*. Fauré too felt drawn to the Hellenistic world and composed his *Prométhée* in 1900 for the theatre at Béziers, a project intended, with Saint-Saëns's active support, to offer a French rival to Bayreuth.

Not only the Greek revival but also a quest for the elegant world of

French neoclassicism runs through this very rich period of French music. It was partly *fin-de-siècle* nostalgia, partly a belief in the aesthetic virtues of the baroque in the face of an overpowering surge of Romanticism past its zenith. The movement goes back to shadowy figures of the mid-century like Reber and Delsarte (Bizet's uncle), and it surfaces plainly in Saint-Saëns (consider his *Sarabande et Rigaudon* of 1892 and his various preludes and fugues), Delibes (the exquisite suite of rococo dances for *Le Roi s'amuse* of 1882) and many others, eventually of course Debussy and Ravel. But it was not pure nostalgia, for it was also inspired by a desire to put forward classical French music as a counterpoise to the great stature of Bach and Handel. What seems like an honest artistic movement was accelerated, like so much else, by national fervour, and some notable archaeological projects were put in hand. One was the series of *Chefs d'œuvre classiques de l'opéra français*, publications of Lully, Campra, Rameau, etc., initiated by Théodore Michaelis in 1880. Another was the luxurious Rameau edition to which notable figures like d'Indy, Dukas and Saint-Saëns lent their authority and energy.

Vincent d'Indy (1851–1931) is an important and ambivalent figure in this gallery. He was a passionate nationalist, anti-Dreyfusard and antisemite, a member of the Action Française and an admirer of Wagner. The Schola Cantorum, which he founded with Bordes and Guilmant in 1894, was a school of severely dogmatic mien, upholding the finest musical heritage of the Catholic Church, especially Gregorian chant, Josquin, Palestrina, Lassus and Victoria, and pursuing the saintly example of Franck. Yet he admired Bach and had to find an excuse for the Lutheran element: 'If he is great it is not *because* but *in spite* of the dogmatic, enervating spirit of the Reformation.' The Schola Cantorum's most notable pupils, Satie and Roussel, were neither of them representative of its main principles, but its influence was nevertheless wide and powerful. D'Indy's own music has a lot of strength and character, though inhibited in range and utterance by his somewhat rigid outlook.

As the century turned, Paris, like Vienna, displayed a dazzling wealth of cultural activity deeply embedded in a society which felt intoxicated by its own momentum. If Proust's picture of Parisian *mœurs* reflects these heady decades with most penetration, Romain Rolland's vast novel *Jean-Christophe* brings us close to the musical life of the period as only fiction can. Rolland's hero is a German composer working in Paris amid the riches and follies of French musical life which he can only ever surmount by resorting to his Beethoven-like tenacity of will and lofty detachment. One of its most telling passages recounts the furore over Debussy, whose *Pelléas et Mélisande* was given to the world in 1902, generating fervid debate between the work's champions and enemies. The view of history places Claude Debussy (1862–1918) securely as the leading French composer of this period, and, when we consider how heterogeneous in style and direction the previous generation had been, his achievement in gathering a host of diverse strands into a single web and in laying down hints and pointers to the future is truly remarkable. Debussy was exposed to every kind of musical influence and absorbed them all; he was attracted by turns to Chopin, Gounod, Massenet, Tchaikovsky, Grieg, Franck, Palestrina, plainchant, Mussorgsky, Wagner, Satie, Javanese *gamelang*, American ragtime, folksong, modality – never to Beethoven, never to Berlioz, never to the teaching of the Conservatoire. And these were only the musical infusions. His literary and artistic sympathies were wide and deep, and they undoubtedly hold a key to an understanding of his mind. He preferred the company of poets and painters to that of musicians, and felt profoundly convinced of music's poetic and colouristic qualities, whether setting words or not. It was the symbolic and sensuous properties of words that attracted him, and in Mallarmé, Verlaine, Villiers de l'Isle-Adam and Maeterlinck he found lines that most perfectly drew from him music whose sensuality resided in harmony and in orchestral colour, and which eschewed suggestions of emphatic, cadential squareness.

To speak of Debussy's impressionism is to draw a comparison with painting, but it also describes strictly musical techniques in which he was a pioneer. By extending the vocabulary of harmony and by treating chords as valid for their own sake, for their inherent beauty or effect, Debussy stepped right against the assumption of musical tradition that chords belong linearly to progressions and cadences. His music can develop a static, timeless quality, especially when he touches on the whole-tone scale with its deliberate lack of tonal focus. The *Prélude à l'après-midi d'un faune* (1894) most perfectly exemplifies the atmospheric and orchestral beauty of musical impressionism, for here the exotic and the veiled came into the orbit of musical expression, not of course for the first time, but with penetrating force. None the less it would be misleading to think of Debussy's music as predominantly motionless and weightless. Much of it has vigour and momentum, and there is a peculiarly heavy and forceful atmosphere in *Pelléas et Mélisande* which is far from the frail understatement of some of the piano pieces, the *Arabesques* for example. *La Mer* is constant movement; *Mouvements* speaks for itself.

Debussy's equivocal response to Wagner is evident in every page of *Pelléas et Mélisande*. There is an important but not systematic network of leitmotifs; the musical interest is entirely in the orchestra, never in the vocal line; the symbolic world of *Parsifal* is magically re-created. Yet Debussy always prefers to leave things suggested or implied in direct contrast to Wagner's habitual overstatement, and his setting of words is much more akin to that of *Boris Godunov* with its naturalistic vocal rhythms and strictly syllabic setting. It has often been said that Debussy, like Beethoven and Mussorgsky, could only compose a single opera since that one work embodied all his dramatic ideals so perfectly and so unrepeatably. Ultimately Debussy turned to the austere ideals of classicism and devoted his declining years to three sonatas (there were to have been six) – for cello, for flute, viola and harp, and for violin – which defy ready understanding and remain stubbornly wayward. In Martin Cooper's apt words, this music has 'a certain breathlessness, an inability to rise to the old flights as of a mortally wounded bird, which has a beauty and pathos of its own'. Léon Vallas spoke of its 'ardent impotence'.

Would that it were possible to treat Ravel anywhere but under the shadow of Debussy, yet chronology and style make it inevitable. Maurice Ravel (1875–1937) has suffered greatly from poor-relation criticism, for he did borrow and share much of Debussy's language, beyond denial. He has suffered too from the jibes always addressed to artists whose consummate technique is so brilliantly obvious. The profundities of existence interested Ravel less than perfection of form and detail, and cuckoo-like he needed the stimulus of a borrowed idiom – whether Spanish, neo-baroque, Greek, Viennese, Negro, and so forth – on which to graft his fastidious textures. Ravel's understanding of harmony was even more advanced and subtle than Debussy's, his instrumental inventiveness, whether for piano or for orchestra, more striking. There is nothing careless or shabby in his music; it is often breathtakingly skilful. But fascinating though *Daphnis et Chloé* (1912) is for its technical brilliance and for its magical evocation of the Greek world, the large scale of the work defeated him, and his finest pieces are brief, like the *Valses nobles et sentimentales* or the *Tombeau de Couperin*. For some reason (which has never been satisfactorily analysed) Ravel turned himself in mid-career into a different kind of composer, seeking linear austerity when his orchestral and harmonic resourcefulness was obviously unlimited. Perhaps his genius simply expended itself in the great flow of masterpieces from *Jeux d'eau* (1902) to *La Valse* (1920), although it is with painful reluctance that the two late piano concertos are placed in a lower grade.

Ravel's admiration for Erik Satie (1866–1925) may partly explain his later preference for thinner, more ambling textures. Yet the two men could not have been more unlike, artistically speaking, Satie's craftsmanship being almost non-existent. Satie stimulated the young Debussy to seek new, irrational chord arrangements and may truly be godfather to some of the later music of both Debussy and Ravel. Yet his own music seems to deny more than it affirms. Before the First World War his iconoclastic nonconformism seemed merely eccentric, but after it he became a cult figure in the new aesthetic propounded by Cocteau and his friends. Cocteau's wry tract *Coq et Harlequin*, published in 1918, dismisses Wagner, Debussy and all the 'isms' of the late nineteenth century, and proclaims 'musique d'ameublement' to be the highest goal of art. 'Music is not all the time a gondola or a racehorse or a tightrope. It is sometimes a chair as well.' 'Satie is the opposite of an improviser. His works might be said to have been completed beforehand, while he meticulously unpicks them note by note. Satie teaches us what, in our age, is the greatest audacity – simplicity.' It was odd for Satie to have greatness thus thrust upon him since that was what he least aspired to; hit-and-miss music like the ballets *Parade* and *Relâche*, wonderful documents of the Zeitgeist though they are, must be allowed to miss as much as they hit.

Of Satie's disciples Milhaud and Poulenc had the most to offer to the next generation. Darius Milhaud (1892–1974) was able to absorb jazz and Latin-American music much more fruitfully than Ravel ever did, though the extreme modishness of the 1920s makes much of their work seem bewilderingly shallow. It is sometimes hard to believe that the composer of *Le Bœuf sur le toit* and *La Création du monde*, for example, can have a heart, especially when he was unremittingly prolific throughout his life in every genre of music. For Milhaud, as for Koechlin, his older, more reclusive contemporary, writing music was a daily activity not unlike breathing and eating; occasionally he put his soul into a bigger work like the opera *Christophe Colomb* or his music for the *Oresteia* trilogy, both inspired by his long friendship with Paul Claudel. Francis Poulenc's (1899–1963) superb literary sensibility made him a song-writer *par excellence*, preferring Éluard, Apollinaire and

Max Jacob, and jumping from café frivolity to numinous contemplation at a quaver's distance. Poulenc's music is steeped in irony and mockery, constantly poignant and sensuous. He represents a particular type of French artist who stands in total polarity to the momentous new music that came out of Vienna between the wars. Poulenc admired Schoenberg but could never have composed music in that way. Of his operas neither the sombre tragedy of *Le Dialogue des Carmélites* nor the remarkable monodrama *La Voix humaine* brings out Poulenc's abundant gifts so clearly as *Les Mamelles de Tirésias*, with seriousness and fun inextricably intertwined; Apollinaire's play seems perfectly made for music of this kind.

Since Debussy French music has become focused more and more on major individual figures and less on a profusion of talent. Of 'les Six' only Milhaud, Poulenc and the Swiss, Honegger, have retained any stature; of 'Jeune France', a group which emerged in the 1930s, only Olivier Messiaen. In the next generation Boulez enjoys splendid isolation. Individualists such as Roussel and Koechlin must not be overlooked. Albert Roussel (1869–1937) threw off the heritage of impressionism and his early love of oriental culture and turned in later life to a hard, wiry style full of energy and motion like Stravinsky, but more instinctive and irrational. Roussel is strictly a musician's musician and his lack of literary contact has cost him much potential following in France. Charles Koechlin's (1867–1950) vast *œuvre* is inaccessible since neither he nor his publishers, nor even his admirers, have ever promoted his works with vigour, with the single exception of *Les Bandarlog*, an untypical but clever satire on contemporary music. Koechlin, like Roussel, absorbed both the Orient and impressionism by turns, and developed a dense, modal style, predominantly linear in texture, but without intelligible formal development. His miniatures are consequently his most admirable pieces, though an assessment of his work as a whole is still impossible to make.

Eastern culture has again left its mark on the leading figure in contemporary French music, Olivier Messiaen (b. 1908), another individualist who is also influential as a teacher. As in Debussy one may easily catalogue the constituent elements of Messiaen's style, yet to convey the striking individuality of his synthesis is a more forbidding task. An elaborate technical microstructure supports his expression of religious and mystical belief. His extraordinarily cosmic sense of time (many of his works are very long) is counterbalanced by a metric scheme that takes account of the smallest units of musical time, with proportions and rhythms demanding extreme mathematical exactitude. His preoccupation with apocalyptic vision finds frequent expression, similar to that of Skriabin but more closely based on religious faith. Like Skriabin Messiaen is drawn to colours both as symbols and as constituent musical metaphors. His music is indeed highly coloured, by its high tessitura and brilliant sonority, by his idiosyncratic taste for instruments like the Ondes Martenot and gongs (as in *Et expecto resurrectionem mortuorum*, for example), and in his brilliant repertory for the organ. Here he may be linked to a distinctive French tradition – for the organ has bred a notable generation of French composers like Dupré and Alain in succession to Vierne and Widor – yet Messiaen has eschewed the more obvious superficialities of their music and infused his organ works with his unmistakable brand of Catholic faith.

In 1944, before his most important works had been written, Messiaen published his *Technique de mon langage musical* wherein he expounded his complex system of modal and rhythmic technique. Strictly delineated musical techniques remind us of Rimsky-Korsakov, again of Skriabin, or of Schoenberg, perhaps of Rameau. He pursued his interest in technique further in a period after the Second World War when the rigid control of dynamics, rhythm and pitch became the basis of *Canteyodjaya* and *Modes de valeurs et d'intensités* (1949), a work which proved seminal for Boulez, Stockhausen and the development of advanced serial techniques in the 1950s. However, Messiaen himself soon abandoned this approach, possibly under his overwhelming attraction to birdsong. Thereafter (and indeed before) birdsong is at the centre of his inspiration, meticulously catalogued and translated into musical notation. Even a work like *Chronochromie* (1960), whose title betrays its absorption with matters of time and colour, has an uplifting passage of dense, entrancing birdsong in its midst.

Messiaen's pupil Pierre Boulez (b. 1925) is a commanding figure in French musical life, a man of extreme musical intelligence and the sworn enemy of anything parochial or narrowly chauvinistic in French music. As a composer he commands respect rather than discipleship and has written relatively few works. This undoubtedly reflects the dilemma of the post-war avant-garde confronted with the appetite for artistic expression but without being able to escape the burgeoning technical complexity of the language. It also reflects Boulez's tireless energy as a conductor, in which role he has done an enormous amount to stimulate interest in twentieth-century music, especially that of Debussy and the second Viennese school. His Domaine Musicale concerts in the early

1960s, in which Boulez was assisted by Bruno Maderna, Gilbert Amy and others, were a pioneering effort to bring contemporary music into Parisian concert life, but Boulez left France in 1966 after a disagreement with Malraux, then Minister of Culture, and did not return until 1977 when he was persuaded to head the newly founded Ircam (Institut de Recherche et de Coordination Acoustique/Musique). Part of the enormous Centre Georges Pompidou, Ircam is unquestionably the focal point of the musical avant-garde in France and it provides young composers with the resources and the opportunity to explore new paths of music. The assumption is that these new paths will be grounded more in technology than in inspiration, itself a defiant challenge to the lessons of history. If this is so, we have to replace our traditional image of the French composer's background: no longer the *rive-gauche* garret and *la vie de Bohème*, but instead the *rive-droite* soundproofed subterranean acoustic chambers of Ircam.

Certain elements of French music recur consistently over the pages of history, and, from such observations of succeeding generations as we can make, more general conclusions about French culture may be tentatively drawn. Some features are embedded in the French character, some are derived from external conditions which are themselves subject to wider historical forces. The effect of France's highly centralized government and culture, for example, has been to elevate fashion to a place of great importance and to give easy dominance to leading figures and groups, with the result that French music has a tendency to present only one face at a time. For long decades the Opéra has been effectively the hub of dramatic music, and the Conservatoire that to musical instruction, just as the Comédie-Française has held the theatrical limelight. This is a partial misrepresentation, of course, since provincial music has often displayed a healthy independence from Paris, especially in Lyon and Strasbourg, with their own music schools, opera house, publishers and traditions. There are at present no less than thirty provincial conservatoires. But all the great figures in French music have yielded to the magnetism and power of Paris as though the monarchical gravity of the *ancien régime* had never lost its force.

French composers resist the onrush of current fashion at their peril. Berlioz is the clearest example of one who stood aside from the accepted moulds of his age and paid dearly for it. Rameau in old age did the same. The moulds can be forceful and new, as they were in the

1790s and the 1920s, or they can be stifling and worn, as in the 1760s and the 1860s, but they exert an inescapable attraction.

If centralization is a powerful factor in taste, it is equally so in education, for the country has a top-heavy system which has concentrated much more on the professional musician than on the amateur, a figure who is far less familiar in France than in England or Germany. Choral singing has never enjoyed much vogue, except under the successful Orphéon movement in the mid-nineteenth century. There is a notable absence of encouragement and teaching of music in French schools, and it still remains more a parental than an educational matter whether a child is introduced to music or not, with the result that rudimentary musical education is all too rare. This is surprising, for not only has French education since Napoleonic times prided itself on its broad and generous social outlook, but also higher musical training has been well served in an institution of state, the Paris Conservatoire, which holds a prominent and vital place in French and indeed in European musical history. The very word 'Conservatoire' has crossed frontiers. The Conservatoire has, it is true, been notorious for its stuffiness and bureaucratic immobility, against which both Berlioz and Debussy railed, but it has had fine musicians like Cherubini and Fauré at its head and has nurtured a sizeable proportion of France's leading musicians. One institution of the Académie des Beaux-Arts that has left a characteristic mark on French music is the Prix de Rome, adjudicated every year throughout the nineteenth century and well into the twentieth. The prize was instituted in 1803 in order to encourage young French artists (painters, sculptors, engravers and composers) to learn from the relics of classical antiquity and to allow their talents to flower in the Villa Medici's elegant gardens in Rome. For sculptors at least, the idea is unimpeachable, and although the composers generally objected to any Italian music they were exposed to, a sojourn in Italy often widened the horizons of their art in ways they could not expect or recognize, for Gounod and Debussy especially. On the other hand the bigoted rejection of Ravel in 1905 after four attempts to win the Prix de Rome is one of the darker pages in the Conservatoire's history.

Any survey of French music should pay tribute to French craftsmanship in instrument manufacture and in music printing. The achievements of Attaingnant and the Balards in the latter sphere have already been mentioned. As instrument makers there have been notable dynasties such as the Blanchets making harpsichords and the Hotteterres making wind instruments in the seventeenth and eighteenth centuries, both contributing to the distinctive timbre of French baroque music, and the Vuillaumes making violins in the nineteenth. The French baroque organ was a characteristic instrument too, though the most celebrated builder of French organs supplied a very different type. The work of Cavaillé-Coll (1811–99) was outstanding in the creation of the large symphonic organ, the instrument for which Franck's music is conceived. His instruments are to be found today in the churches of the Madeleine, Saint-Sulpice, Saint-Clotilde and elsewhere. Pleyel and Érard are the names most associated with the piano in France, and although they have not held their ground against the great German piano manufacturers, Érard was a pioneer of new techniques of piano escapement and also of the double-action harp at a time when the harp enjoyed enormous favour as a domestic instrument. It was for Érard pianos that Chopin composed, yet we scarcely ever hear his music on those instruments today. French orchestras still preserve their distinctive timbre, most noticeable today in the sound of bassoons, horns and trombones, all of which have largely resisted the larger, plummier sounds made by German and American instruments. In military bands the name of Adolphe Sax (of Belgian birth) is sufficient to remind us of the importance and currency of French innovations.

It should scarcely be necessary to draw attention to the long association of music with dancing and the essential role of ballet in the French conception of opera. In Renaissance *fêtes*, as in *tragédie-lyrique* and grand opera, dancing has played an integral role. Saint-Évremond tells us that gentlemen were taught to 'ride, dance, play the lute, swordsmanship, a little mathematics, and that's all', with an even narrower definition of life's necessities from Clérambaûlt: 'When I come to court, I am persuaded that in order to be an upright man, it is necessary to know only how to dance.' We can see how dancing in a formal musical entertainment differed little from dancing in a purely social context, bridging the proscenium and revealing operas to be little more than an extension of real life. Ballet was primarily *divertissement*, even in Lully's expert hands, for he, like Leclair after him, was first a dancer before becoming a musician. Noverre's great achievements in the eighteenth century may well be likened to Gluck's in revealing the expressive potential of ballet and hence its role as a purveyor of drama, and until the coming of Diaghilev France led the world in the cultivation of ballet and so, incidentally, in the provision of music for ballet. It is difficult not to think of Diaghilev's legacy as rooted firmly in France, for it was there that Stravinsky's principal ballets were created, making France the capital of international ballet in the twentieth century as it had been of opera in the nineteenth. It was no coincidence that that type of opera contained decorative ballets as an essential ingredient and that many of the Opéra's *habitués* were more interested in fine dancing than in fine singing.

Even more obvious is the unmistakably literary and visual quality of French music at all periods. Composers themselves have consistently expounded their ideas, both technical and ethical: Rameau and Messiaen expound theory and technique, Berlioz is unsurpassed as critic and memoirist. French composers with no literary inclinations, like Lully and Ravel, are rare. Controversy about musical matters is as commonplace in France as it is rare in Italy. Figures such as Boileau, Rousseau or Cocteau – literary men with ardent views on music – are a regular feature of French criticism. The *tragédie-lyrique* in its early years was regarded strictly as a branch of poetic drama with certain very special concessions allowable, since music had been admitted as supporting decoration. Throughout the eighteenth century controversy either simmered or raged, always about opera and the relationship of words and music, about tradition and innovation, about declamation and stress. Although the French are not obviously a nation of singers, as the Italians are, and the language is not obviously easy to sing, as Italian is, it is opera that has claimed the attention of criticism and gossip over the centuries, since its literary dimension exposes it to all and sundry, to all who have opinions to offer, in other words to everyone. Opera has always attracted the unmusical, but never more than in France. Only there could the notorious Jockey Club have held such sway as they did in the Second Empire, as powerful and undiscriminating in their approval and disapproval as Roman emperors at the games.

At the same time the literary quality of French music is one of its chief glories. One can truly use the epithet 'poetic' to describe Berlioz's *Roméo et Juliette* or Debussy's *Prélude à l'après-midi d'un faune*. A gift for apt and touching illustration marks Janequin's chansons and Couperin's *ordres*. For the clavecinistes a fondness for descriptive and literary titles derives in part from the English virginal school, and their whimsicality has more than just charm. When it comes to literal description, one could scarcely go further than Marin Marais when he composed a musical description of the surgical removal of a gall-stone in one of his *Pièces* of 1725.

The point is more securely made by drawing attention to the relative scarcity of abstraction in French music. The symphony is by no means a neglected form in France, but it has never had the centrality it enjoys in Germany. There was some cultivation of sonata and symphony in eighteenth-century France, and these works are by no means negligible, but no French composer has emerged to the top rank without poetic, literary or visual allusion in his work. Saint-Saëns might well have hankered after independence from extra-musical ideas, Roussel undoubtedly did, but the profound link between abstract musical expression and the inner recesses of the human soul, of which perhaps Beethoven gives the clearest evidence, has been generally closed to the French, as it has too to the English and the Italians. Fontenelle's famous question 'Sonate, que me veux-tu?' might fairly encapsulate a perennial French attitude to the abstract forms.

The desire to link words and music is not then a condemnation of French musicality but a powerful source of inspiration. A less admirable aspect of French attitudes to music – which likewise exhibits their penchant for words – is their inclination to talk about music rather than play it. They are unadventurous as performers and impatient as listeners. Otherwise the extraordinary treasures of older music would have been revealed years ago. Lully remains unrevived, Delalande's music is scarcely known, Berlioz and Bizet have been culpably misrepresented for years. The latest, fashionable music is discussed today, as it always was, in noisy arguments and lengthy feuilletons; 'pour ou contre?' is always a vital issue, and 'contre' is often, regrettably, the vote. It is impossible to escape an awareness of anti-musical bias in the French mind that recurs at distressingly frequent intervals and which seems quite independent of the magnificent creative richness of French composers. In 1687 the *Mercure galant*, in discussing an opera, said: 'I shall not speak of the music because music has no *point de beauté* as other things do.' In 1704 the *Journal des savants* declared that the *effects* of music are pleasing, 'but one cannot speak favourably of music itself'. Could this be the same prejudice as that which led Malraux to declare, in 1965, 'France is not a musical nation'? Is there a certain unease with music which leads the French to envelop their operas with spectacle and ballet, their clavecin music with teasing titles, their symphonies with programmes, their songs with exquisite verse, their organ music with mystical allusion? The answer must be that the famed rationality of the French intellect does not extend to music, for the abstraction of a self-contained, rationally constructed art-form has little appeal. French music is sensuous, pictorial, elegant, allusive, decorative, imaginative, ritualistic, poetic, and many other things besides, but scarcely ever rational. 'La musique française, c'est la clarté, l'élégance, la déclamation simple et naturelle' – these are the words of a composer whose claim to speak authoritatively for the French race is beyond question: Claude Debussy.

Bibliography

Much will be found to place French music in its historical and European context in the standard series histories of music, such as the Norton series, the Prentice-Hall series, the New Oxford History of Music and the Pelican History of Music. In the Norton series Gustave Reese's *Music in the Middle Ages* (London, 1941), the same author's *Music in the Renaissance* (London, 1959) and Manfred F. Bukofzer's *Music in the Baroque Era* (London, 1948) are voluminous and wide-ranging. The more recent Prentice-Hall series includes *Music in the Medieval World* by Albert Seay, *Renaissance Music* by Howard Brown, *Baroque Music* by Claude Palisca, *Music in the Classic Period* by Reinhard G. Pauly and *Nineteenth-Century Romanticism in Music* by Rey M. Longyear. Howard Brown's book gives a particularly useful perspective of French music in the Renaissance. Charles van den Borren's chapter on the French chanson is a notable section in Volume IV of the New Oxford History of Music (London, 1968), and in the Pelican History Brian Trowell's chapter 'The Early Renaissance' is to be recommended as an introduction to the work of the Burgundian school: *Renaissance and Baroque* (London, 1963).

For the English reader two books will provide a full and informative background to early French music: Isabelle Cazeaux's *French Music in the Fifteenth and Sixteenth Centuries* (Oxford, 1975) with a broad picture of the social milieu in which it was created; James R. Anthony's *French Baroque Music* (London, 1973), subtitled *From Beaujoyeulx to Rameau*, is now recognized as a standard work in an increasingly popular field.

Two large series are devoted to the specialist study of early French music, with too many titles to be individually listed. The *Recherches sur la musique classique française*, begun in 1960 under the editorship of Norbert Dufourcq, covers a wide range of topics in pre-revolutionary music, and the series of books published by the Centre National de la Recherche Scientifique includes many important titles, such as *Musique et poésie au XVIe siècle* (Paris, 1954), *Les Fêtes de la renaissance*, 2 vols (Paris, 1960), *La Vie musicale en France sous les rois Bourbons* (Paris, 1954), *Musiques de cour – chapelle, chambre, écurie, 1661–1733* (Paris, 1971) and *Versailles et les musiciens du roi 1661–1733* (Paris, 1971), both the last two edited by Marcelle Benoit.

On the chanson one should read James Haar's *Chanson and Madrigal 1480–1530* (Harvard, 1964), François Lesure's essays in *Musique et musiciens français du XVIe siècle* (Geneva, 1969), and Brian Jeffery's two volumes of *French Chanson Verse* (London, 1971 and 1976). On the *ballet de cour* Henry Prunières, *Le Ballet de cour en France* (Paris, 1914), is a classic study which may be supplemented by Margaret M. McGowan's *L'Art du ballet de cour en France 1581–1643* (Paris, 1963). On opera there are three long-established books of central importance: Arthur Pougin's *Les Vrais Créateurs de l'opéra français* (Paris, 1881), Romain Rolland's *Musiciens d'autrefois* (Paris, 1914) and Henry Prunières's *L'Opéra italien en France avant Lulli* (Paris,

1913). Robert M. Isherwood's *Music in the Service of the King* (Ithaca, NY, 1973) is a fine study of French seventeenth-century court music. Instrumental music is the subject of Lionel de la Laurencie's definitive three volumes on *L'École française de violon* (Paris, 1922–4), and church music of a useful collection *La Musique religieuse française de ses origines à nos jours* published by the *Revue musicale* in 1954. Louis Striffling's *Goût musical en France au XVIIIe siècle* (Paris, 1912) is a superbly lucid summary of eighteenth-century thought on music, while Alfred Richard Oliver's *The Encyclopedists as Critics of Music* (New York, 1947) concentrates on the *Querelle des Bouffons* and its attendant controversies. Constant Pierre's *Histoire du Concert Spirituel 1725–1790* (Paris, 1975) is a fully documented account of a famous and important institution.

On individual composers one may recommend: La Laurencie's *Lully* (Paris, 1911), Prunières's *Lully* (Paris, 1909; rev. ed. 1927), Girdlestone's *Jean-Philippe Rameau* (London, 1957), Paul-Marie Masson's *L'Opéra de Rameau* (Paris, 1930) and Wilfrid Meller's *François Couperin and the French Classical Tradition* (London, 1950).

In the post-revolutionary period general studies of French music include Constant Pierre's monumental collections *Musique des fêtes et cérémonies de la révolution française* (Paris, 1899) and *Les Hymnes et chansons de la révolution* (Paris, 1904), Winton Dean's useful article 'Opera under the French Revolution' in *Proceedings of the Royal Musical Association 1967–68*, René Dumesnil's *La Musique romantique française* (Paris, 1944), L. Rohizinsky's collection *Cinquante ans de musique française de 1874*, 2 vols (Paris, 1925), Martin Cooper's excellent *French Music from the Death of Berlioz to the Death of Fauré* (London, 1951), Ursula Eckart-Bäcker's study of French criticism *Frankreichs Musik zwischen Romantik und Moderne* (Regensburg, 1965), and René Dumesnil's very useful *La Musique en France entre les deux guerres 1919–1939* (Paris, 1946). Frits Noske's *French Song from Berlioz to Duparc* (New York, 1970; originally in French, Paris, 1954) contains a wealth of interesting information on the *mélodie*; in this connection Pierre Bernac's *The Interpretation of French Song* (London, 1970) provides authoritative insights from a renowned interpreter.

The absorbing theme of Wagner's influence in France may be studied in George Servières's *Richard Wagner jugé en France* (Paris, 1887), 'Wagner en France', special number of the *Revue musicale* (Paris, 1923), and Elliott Zuckerman's *The First Hundred Years of Wagner's Tristan* (New York, 1964). The resurgence of French nationalism after 1870 is the subject of Hugh Macdonald's 'Un Pays où tous sont musiciens . . .' in *From Parnassus: Essays in Honor of Jacques Barzun* (New York, 1976). The rich artistic life of turn-of-the-century Paris is vividly evoked in Roger Shattuck's *The Banquet Years* (London, 1959), with a special section on Satie.

The literature by and on individual composers is abundant. The best introduction to Berlioz is through his own *Memoirs*, superbly translated and edited by David Cairns (London, 1969). His other writings and letters are to be found in scholarly modern French editions. Jacques Barzun's *Berlioz and the Romantic Century* is a vast and comprehensive study of Berlioz and his background. The catalogue of the Victoria and Albert Museum's exhibition *Berlioz and the Romantic Imagination* (London, 1969) is much to be recommended for a re-creation of Berlioz's life and work.

The Master Musicians series includes very useful studies of French composers:

Arthur Hedley on Chopin (1947), Winton Dean on Bizet (1948; rev. ed. 1975), Edward Lockspeiser on Debussy (1936), Roger Nichols on Ravel (1977). On Bizet one should also read Mina Curtiss's fascinating picture of the age in *Bizet and his World* (London, 1959). On Debussy there are also Lockspeiser's classic two volumes *Debussy: His Life and Mind* (London, 1962–5) and Roger Nichols's brief but penetrating study of the music *Debussy* (London, 1972). Debussy's writings are admirably translated and presented by Richard Langham Smith in his *Debussy on Music* (London, 1977).

Of numerous other biographies one should include the following: James Harding's biographies of Gounod (1973), Saint-Saëns (1965) and Massenet (1970), Rollo Myers's biographies of Chabrier (1969), Ravel (1960) and Satie (1948). César Franck was the subject of something near to hagiography in Vincent d'Indy's life of his teacher (Paris, 1907); Laurence Davies's *César Franck and his Circle* (London, 1970) is more discursive.

On more recent music in France one may profitably consult Rollo Myers's *Modern French Music* (Oxford, 1971) or the wider-ranging *Concise History of Modern Music* by Paul Griffiths (London, 1978). André Hodeir's *Since Debussy* (London, 1961) discusses Messiaen, Boulez and Barraqué in their twentieth-century setting. For Messiaen one should read Claude Samuel's *Entretiens avec Olivier Messiaen* (Paris, 1967), and in English the choice is between Robert Sherlaw Johnson's detailed study *Messiaen* (London, 1975) and Roger Nichols's briefer and less technical *Messiaen* (London, 1975). *Boulez on Music Today* (1971) is a useful compendium of Boulez's complex writings, edited by Susan Bradshaw and Richard Rodney Bennett.

12 Contemporary France: Politics, Society and Institutions

J. BLONDEL

Introduction

Although a decade has elapsed since De Gaulle left office in the spring of 1969, following a major wave of unrest in the previous year, it is too early to be sure about the political and social stability of a country which has known sixteen constitutions in less than 200 years and in which only one regime, that of the Third Republic, succeeded in maintaining itself for a substantial period. Yet the 1970s seemed marked by rather more stability than would probably have been predicted by most observers of the pre-1968 period. Admittedly, the periodic waves of unrest which characterize France and originate, not merely from students, but from shopkeepers and peasants as well as from workers, help to raise doubts about the ability of the regime to maintain itself for more than a short period. In the past, some systems which were apparently very stable were quickly toppled: predictions are hazardous given the extent to which the French are prone to plunge suddenly, and even perhaps unwittingly, into a revolutionary mood. But the fundamental social changes which have occurred in the post-war period at least suggest that France may have now begun to enter a new era, and they constitute a potential base for greater stability.

It is this curious combination of an explosive surface and of more profound social transformations that we propose to examine here. We cannot of course examine this problem in all its ramifications. Even if all the answers were known, it would not be possible to describe fully the social context, the legal arrangements and the political process of a country of 53 million inhabitants with such a long and complex history. Nor could we consider in detail the attitudinal and behavioural characteristics of the population and of its élites. But a broad picture of the social and political system indicates the tensions which exist in a society which shares many characteristics in common with other western European countries and yet does show – and does still show – some striking differences. We shall have therefore to assess the extent to which the profound social and economic changes that France underwent in the last few decades have had an impact on the stability of the political system.

In the first section, we shall consider the main characteristics of modern French society and attempt to weigh the relative strength of the traditional elements, such as the inward-looking and stable peasantry, the Parisian middle class and the urban proletariat, in relation to the new 'classes' and the new outlook which economic modernization, increased mobility and the development of a more complex group structure have given to the society. The weighing will have to leave many questions unsettled, not only because the pace of future transformations cannot easily be predicted but also because social transformations in one sector often raise difficulties in another: successively, shopkeepers, peasants and students have been at the root of major disturbances or been the cause of much rethinking.

Secondly, we shall examine the basic political structures of French society and consider the attitudes of Frenchmen and the way in which these attitudes become, successfully or unsuccessfully, articulated in a number of political parties.

Thirdly, we shall look at government and politics in the Fifth Republic, under De Gaulle, Pompidou and Giscard, ascertain the extent of change from previous Republics and thereby attempt to gauge whether the system is likely to be better able to meet the demands of Frenchmen, and to satisfy their aspirations.

Fourthly, we shall return to society by looking at the relationship between the State machine and that society and the extent to which it can still be said to be characterized by a form of enlightened despotism, given the special role which the civil service has played in French life, at least since Napoleon and already under the kings. Of all the Western countries, France is *par excellence* the country which can be described as an 'administrative state' or a 'technocracy', in that more than anywhere else civil servants have played a part in developing the economy and constituted a pole of attraction for the private sector, for academic thinking and for the society at large. French modernization since the forties was first and foremost a public service effort; its impact on society was striking and will remain so for many generations. Despite some current half-hearted efforts at regionalism and decentralization, French society is clearly at least as much the product of the French bureaucracy as of the French government, though the French administrative system does reflect some basic traits in French society. French political and social life, its outbursts as well as its regularities, are in large part the result of the bureaucracy which runs counter to the basic individualism of the French, and helps both to contain it and to exacerbate it. Only if reform is assessed in relation to French bureaucratic structures can the overall impact of change be determined and the future of French society correctly ascertained.

A Changing Social Order

Of all the Western European countries, France is probably the one which underwent the most profound social and economic transformations since the early 1950s. Historians of the coming centuries will tell whether the last thirty years constituted a turning-point for a society which had hitherto been characterized by individualism, an inward-looking parochialism in many parts of the provinces and a fear of economic change. But for the contemporary observer, many aspects of the social system have been radically modified. Whether one looks at material well-being, demographic characteristics, educational development or class distribution, the basic features which often shaped France throughout the Third Republic (1870–1940) no longer describe the state of the country thirty years later. And, while change has come about much more slowly in many aspects of the interest-group structure of the country, new attitudes have begun to emerge in many organizations. From the family to the trade unions, from the Church to student organizations, the French have begun to eschew the distrust of associations which had been one of their main characteristics since the Revolution of 1789.

TRADITIONAL SOCIETY

Admittedly, much of traditional society is still apparent, commonly discussed, and at the root of social problems. For a century or more, while slowly industrializing and gradually becoming part of the contemporary mass society, France remained a peasant nation topped by a highly intellectualized and cultured middle class. The population remained at forty million for generations, and Italian and Spanish immigration barely succeeded in maintaining the adult working force at a constant level. At times, particularly in the 1850s and 1860s, under Napoleon III, and at the beginning of the twentieth century, industrial production rose rapidly, but the effects were too short or too limited in scope to affect the society as a whole. There were migrations from the land, but almost exclusively to Paris and not in sufficiently large numbers to switch the centre of gravity of the nation from the peasantry to the urban working class. Thus, with a third or more of the population living from the land and with over two-fifths of the population living in rural areas at the outbreak of the Second World War, France was scarcely a modern 'developed' nation. But, unlike the less developed parts of southern and eastern Europe, rural France was not inhabited by landless agricultural workers, but by a property-owning peasantry, neither rich nor very poor, not very educated but not illiterate, distrustful of the rest of society and of Paris in particular, but internally democratic and self-sufficient. Hence a basic stability and a solid common sense despite many movements on the surface, but hence also a fear of social transformations unknown to other countries of the industrialized world. This had gradually come about through a very slow social evolution. Admittedly, the Revolution of 1789 was instrumental in abolishing aristocratic privileges on the land as well as titles of nobility; but the development of a peasantry had already taken place long before; indeed, 1789 would not have been possible and its effects would not have been so easily accepted, had French society not already become in part, and even in large part, a rural democracy. In many areas, peasants had acquired the land in all but in name and the end of many estates, and particularly the end of Church property, mainly enabled peasants to acquire a little more, and in a wholly secure fashion, of what they already had come to have. Later, the drain on resources, human and financial, of the Revolutionary and Napoleonic wars half-froze this society. Industrialization was slow and those who left the land kept ties with their rural origins. Meanwhile, in the towns and in particular in Paris, the middle class inherited the reputation and some of the values of the nobility and French bourgeois culture remained less tainted than elsewhere with 'commercialism' and the pursuit of profit.

The existence of a large peasantry explains in part why France remained less profoundly united than most other European countries despite the powers of the central government; indeed, the centralization of the administration was introduced by the French kings and maintained since the Revolution precisely because France was a divided country. The roots of these divisions stem from the profound cultural diversity of the country: from north to south and from east to west, France is composed of a variety of cultural, linguistic and even ethnic groups. North-eastern Frenchmen are linguistically and culturally close to the Germans and the Flemings; south-eastern Frenchmen are close to Italians, and the whole of the southern half of the country is predominantly Latin in character. Though French kings slowly and patiently endeavoured to 'assimilate' the whole of the country and to impose the French language over the territory, dialects and even languages survived to the present day; some efforts are even currently made to revive them. This is particularly true of Breton, but this applies also to a lesser extent to some of the dialects of *occitanie* (the area of the *langue d'oc* or southern half of France), while many Alsatians continue to use their language in their daily life and indeed in their dealings with their Swiss and German neighbours.

Cultural and linguistic diversity diminishes everywhere with industrialization and urbanization; but since France remained largely a peasant nation up to the Second World War, variations remained more profound than elsewhere in western Europe. Though a unified educational system helped to develop a united vision of France, the traditions of the villages and small towns remained strong enough to maintain a lively belief in the superiority of the *petite patrie* in which one happens to live and in which new arrivals are treated as 'foreigners' for years and even decades, even if they come from a nearby district. Indeed, until very recently, it was rare for men or women to move to a village, even in order to retire, unless they had some family connection with that village. A climate of suspicion prevailed about the outside world: the State, the Government, the administration, other parts of the country were included in this suspicion: one preferred to be left alone and to have as few dealings as possible with the surrounding areas and with the government; as we shall see, this climate of suspicion and these limited horizons had a strong impact on the traditional nature of French politics and explain the slow build-up of a modern party system.

One national cleavage had been inherited from the Revolution, however, but this cleavage did not contribute to simplify politics: this was the issue of the role of the Church in society. France was traditionally a Catholic nation (the 'elder daughter of the Church'). It is indeed still overwhelmingly Catholic, at least nominally. After an upsurge of Protestantism – mainly Calvinism – religious wars broke out in the second half of the sixteenth century; these were followed by a period of uneasy truce for about a century, but, eventually, in 1685, Protestantism was banned altogether and repression occurred: many Protestants fled while others went underground or abandoned their faith. But just when Protestantism seemed crushed, Catholicism was attacked from another angle: eighteenth-century 'philosophers' questioned the Church and indeed established religion in general. Their impact was such among the French political and social élite that the religious issue became one of the major problems of the Revolution, which first attacked the material privileges of the Catholic Church and, in a second stage, even attempted to impose a new deist 'faith' designed to replace Christianity. This led to civil war in parts of the country, particularly in the west (the Vendée), where the population had remained strongly attached to both its priests and its nobility. Not surprisingly, the return of the monarchy in 1815 marked a 'revenge' of the Catholic Church. The association of the 'old order', represented by the monarchy, the aristocracy and the Church, became sealed: the Republic became likewise increasingly associated with 'anticlericalism'. By the middle of the nineteenth century, the issue was truly dividing the nation, with some areas of the country – those where nobles and priests were jointly disliked – being profoundly 'republican' under the leadership of members of the liberal professions (lawyers, doctors and above all teachers). Overall, the north, east and west, as well as parts of the south-west, remained broadly Catholic, while the centre and the bulk of the south were 'anti-clerical'.

For most of the period between 1870 and 1940, the Church-anti-Church cleavage mobilized the population and the parties. At the local level, the division was embodied in the opposition between the parish priest and the primary school teacher; at the national level, the game of groups and parties was based on the fundamental notion that no dialogue could take place with men of the 'other side' – a situation which restricted the scope for compromise and resulted in a marked slowdown in the solution of the increasingly important social and economic problems resulting from industrialization.

Of course, France was not merely a nation of small peasants divided by the Church issue: many nineteenth-century novels portray the lack of taste of the new bourgeoisie and the difficult living conditions of the urban working class. France, like England, had her rich, highly moralistic 'Victorian' families and her poor labourers earning pitiful wages in dark and dirty factories. By the end of the nineteenth century, industrialization had profoundly marked the nation, socially and politically. Yet the intellectualized Parisian élite and the self-centred and independent peasant still continued to shape French society more firmly and more profoundly than the oppressed working class and the aspiring businessmen, as if the two extremes of society, Paris and the village, were really determinant. By not having any other city even approaching the size of Paris, by not having a large industrial conurbation such as the Ruhr, Lancashire or the West Midlands (the north of France never was an equivalent pole of attraction), France maintained into the twentieth century more of the values of the eighteenth than any of its neighbours. The base of society – the peasantry – was not poor, it was not politically and socially dominated; it corresponded, albeit imperfectly, to the ideal of the traditional social 'community'. The top Parisian élite was sufficiently large and open not to seem to be an intolerable oligarchy, its culture was sufficiently real to be recognized, abroad as well as at home, and its domination was cushioned by the large bureaucracy of the kings and Napoleon, by the respect given to education, and by the prestige of the metropolis. Thus there were, in effect, two different nations, not really antagonistic because they had little in common; they found it possible to join in order to resist, and if necessary to crush (as in June 1848, in 1871 and in a more diffused fashion in the early years of the century), the revolutionary demands made by or for the working class. France is the only Western nation in which an alliance between the peasantry and the bourgeoisie persisted for so long, despite relatively few real and positive gains (though peasants did benefit to some extent from the alliance, as over tariffs in the 1890s and in general through various kinds of subsidies, this was more to prevent their economic decline than to create conditions for a genuine economic growth on the land). What suggests a basic social revolution in the 1970s is not so much that this alliance no longer exists (the June 1968 election, coming after the May 'Revolution' of that year, had some of the characteristics of the old 'alliance') but that so many changes have taken place that neither by its size, nor by its attitudes, can the peasantry any longer be said to be the backbone of the country and that a new configuration of social forces has come into being.

THE NEW SOCIAL FORCES

The new social equilibrium arose from four main factors: sudden demographic changes, the decrease of the peasantry, extensive urbanization, in particular outside Paris, and a rapid rise in secondary and higher education. By the combined operation of these four elements, France can be said to have truly become a 'modern' mass society and to have effectively lost most of the characteristics which made the country 'unique' among Western countries.

The Population Explosion

The stagnation of the population throughout the second half of the nineteenth century and up to the Second World War had come to be a cause for concern in the inter-war years. Low birth-rates (a *de facto* very effective form of birth control) combined with the effect of the First World War (one and a half million dead); there was effective depopulation, though the return of Alsace-Lorraine in 1919 and immigration helped to mask the decline. Governments were sufficiently worried by 1939 to introduce a new 'family code' designed by various means, and in particular family allowances, to check the effects of this depopulation. The policy fitted the ideology of the right-wing Pétain regime under the German occupation and it was continued; it was further pursued after 1945 so that an increased birth-rate marked not only the early post-war years but the 1950s and most of the 1960s. Static for almost a century at 40 million, the population had reached 45 million at the end of the 1950s; helped by the repatriation of almost one million Frenchmen from Algeria in 1962, the population jumped to 50 million at the end of the 1960s.

The rise has now markedly slowed down, as in other Western countries. Dreams, scarcely justified even on the more optimistic projection, of 100 million Frenchmen which De Gaulle once allowed himself to entertain are clearly without foundation. Indeed, some are again worried that a very low birth-rate should once more characterize the country: with a drop in birth-rate of 1·5 per cent (from 18·1 in 1964 to 16·6 in 1969) the natural increase dropped from over 7 per cent to less than 6 per cent at the end of the 1960s. It declined markedly in the 1970s to about 14 per cent. But there is still natural population growth and in an age where overpopulation becomes an increasing problem, France's decreasing birth-rate is still not a cause for worry.

The Changing Social Structure

While France's population explosion has now come to an end, changes in the occupational structure are likely to continue and to extend their consequences well into the coming decades. As we noted earlier, the percentage of the population living from the land had decreased only slowly throughout the nineteenth century and the early part of the twentieth. But, by the early 1950s, about 50,000 people were leaving the rural areas every year; by the early 1960s, this number had doubled; in the second half of the 1960s, the land was being depopulated at the rate of 3·8 per cent a year. A third of the French people were engaged in agriculture in 1939; the figure had dropped to a quarter in the late 1950s, a fifth in the middle 1960s, a tenth at the end of the 1970s. Meanwhile, the much smaller agricultural population had profoundly changed its mode of existence: at the outbreak of the Second World War, mechanization of the farm was still rare, except in relatively large farms in the plains of the Paris region and of northern France; by the early 1960s, still only two-fifths of the farms were equipped with tractors: in 1967, the proportion had grown to two-thirds. Other mechanical equipment was being used, often on a co-operative basis by most smallholders. Peasants, once economically conservative and famous for their gold savings, had become part of the financial circuit, incurred debts in banks and credit companies and were concerned with problems of capital goods depreciation and the market structure. The self-sufficient peasant had given way to the industrialized farmer, with a larger income, but often greater insecurity and a greater dependence on the whole economy.

Changes also affected the distribution sector and turned the once numerous small shopkeepers and self-employed artisans into one of the more vociferous opponents of the new society. Their numbers declined at the rate of 1·5 per cent a year throughout the 1960s and 1970s; supermarkets and chain stores developed, despite periodic legislative measures designed to allay shopkeepers' fears. French consumers were becoming increasingly price-conscious and, through the increased mobility provided for by car ownership, less dependent on the local shop, whether in villages or in towns. Thus, despite many rearguard actions due to recurring waves of unrest, France was becoming increasingly a nation of wage-earners (more than four-fifths in the mid-1970s): the age of the small independent man was over.

Perhaps the most profound and least discussed aspect of the change is that which affects the worker himself. This change has not been studied systematically; and the analysis is complicated by the existence of ideological standpoints which tend to superimpose ready-made interpretations. It is also difficult to disentangle long-term trends from short-term variations arising from special circumstances or from particular events. Three broad points seem to emerge, however. First, as in many Western European countries, immigration has modified the nature of the problem: 15 per cent of the French manual working force is now composed of men coming, not so much from Italy and Spain, but from Portugal, Greece, Turkey and of course Algeria. These provide much of the unskilled labour which the country requires and for which few Frenchmen can be found. As immigrant labour is necessarily less vocal than the French work-force and as foreigners do not participate in politics (unless they become naturalized), the result is both a disfranchisement of a part of the working class and a tendency for groups and parties to concentrate on the relatively more affluent sections of the society. In common with other Western European countries, France has tended to create a 'sub-proletariat' which is divorced from the organized proletariat and, like the Blacks in the United States until recently, cannot make its voice heard.

OCCUPATIONAL BACKGROUND OF THE FRENCH POPULATION

	Percentage of the active population			
	1954	*1962*	*1967*	*1975*
Farmers and farm labourers	26·5	24·0	16·0	9·4
Owners of businesses	12·0	10·0	9·0	7·8
Higher management and professions	3·0	4·0	5·0	6·7
Middle management	6·0	7·5	10·0	12·7
White-collar workers	11·0	12·0	14·0	17·6
Manual workers	33·5	35·0	37·0	37·6
Service workers	5·0	5·0	5·5	4·7
Other (army, police, etc.)	3·0	2·5	3·5	3·5
	100·0	100·0	100·0	100·0
Total (millions)	19·3	20·1	20·7	21·7

Second, the country in general and the working class in particular have become more affluent. France remains an inegalitarian country, with salaries at the top sometimes twenty or thirty times higher than those of the very poor and with a relatively low level of direct taxation and thus a limited amount of redistribution. Yet the wages of the working class increased markedly as the economy became more prosperous. The guaranteed minimum wage jumped throughout the 1970s; social security benefits, and in particular family allowances and retirement pensions, are universal and generous: thus the less wealthy parts of the population can achieve living standards equal or even superior to those of their counterparts elsewhere in Europe. If it is still the case that France lags in the number of its telephones, working-class housing has improved beyond recognition and the various 'gadgets' of the consumer society – from television to motor cars – are now purchased by the working class on an even more avid basis than in other Western European countries.

Third, the attitudes of the working class are also slowly changing, though care must be taken neither to overstate nor to underestimate developments. On the surface, there often seems to be little change. Indeed, France appeared to be 'revolutionary' in 1968. For three weeks the country was almost at a standstill: triggered by discontent in the universities, the (very peaceful) shutdown extended to most if not all aspects of industrial life; public services stopped, large factories were closed, and even at times occupied. Workers seemed to rediscover with a vengeance the attitudes of militants in relation to capitalism, the profit motive, changes in industrial structure, productivity, etc. The French worker has always found factory life more difficult to accept than the American worker, and the routinization of many jobs as a result of modernization has made many material changes gained in the last two decades look less attractive. This explains why strikes have tended to be relatively numerous in France: these are often spontaneous and short-lived (although some are now harder); but they recur as if the country was composed of a large segment which, at best, does not accept the current order and, at worst, is profoundly alienated.

Yet, behind this apparent 'anarchism' of the French working class, many have also noted an equally engrained belief in hard work and a solid common sense. Furthermore, the attitudes of the working class seem to be affected by greater affluence. Studies of the French worker have shown that the percentage of those who believe that their lot has improved in recent years and will continue to improve in the future is appreciably larger than those who believe that their condition is static or deteriorating. Even the outward manifestations of discontent seem to be decreasing. It is true that the events of 1968 indicated a profound level of discontent; but it is equally true that, immediately after the end of the three weeks of 'great holidays' which the French had offered themselves, the country came back to normality with greater speed and ease than had been predicted. Except for students, who continued their agitation for a period, the population went back to work; production increased at an even faster rate. Since 1968, efforts made by left-wing trade-unionists and intellectuals to 'mobilize' the working class have ended in failure. At three successive occasions, in 1973, 1974 and 1978, despite increasing hopes among the Left that a 'popular coalition' could and would win, those who inherited the government from De Gaulle were confirmed in power. These results seem due in part to the fact that at least important segments of the working class are not revolutionary. The pace of change may be so slow that the leaders of the working class do not perceive it, but their lack of success in undermining the 'capitalist' system in the 1970s seems to indicate that there is indeed a greater acceptance by all sections of the society of the social and political conditions and therefore a greater unity of the nation than in the past.

The Growth of Towns

Overall, a new France, based on manual workers (38 per cent in 1975) and white-collar employees (18 per cent in 1975) has started to ease the century-long hold of the peasantry and the traditional bourgeoisie. Meanwhile, for the first time, France has really begun to be faced with the problems of suburban life. Before 1939, Paris, Marseille and Lyon were the only large French cities; and indeed the last two had less than a million inhabitants and did not constitute the centres of conurbations. French cities thus remained cities in the old sense, the expansion of suburbs being sufficiently slow to allow for a gradual integration of new areas around the original centre. From the 1950s, on the contrary, many French provincial towns have started to boom, while the growth of Paris has been less than average: from 1962 to 1968, the growth of Paris and of its region has been of about 8 per cent, while many other cities have grown at between 11 per cent and 15 per cent. The Paris region is now declining, while some cities are close to the half-million range, and the Lille conurbation has joined Lyon and Marseille at the one million level. The physical shape of provincial France has markedly changed. Large high-rise apartment blocks have multiplied at the periphery of most middle-sized cities. Although there are still no real regional centres comparable to those of many other Western countries, and while efforts at industrial decentralization have been only half-successful, a new attitude has begun to develop in relation to provincial life: Paris used to be the universal attraction; it is now no longer the case. Political decentralization may still remain limited, as we shall see; cultural decentralization may still be something of a token affair. But the trend of the 1960s and 1970s towards the medium-sized and relatively large cities became sufficiently pronounced to suggest that, by necessity or by choice, Frenchmen have begun to live in suburbia. Conurbation problems began to be felt elsewhere than in Paris with the result that slowly, but perceptibly, the provincialism of what was once called the 'French desert' has begun to decline and differences between Paris and the provinces are felt less acutely.

The Educational Revolution

It is often not sufficiently realized, even by Frenchmen, how narrow the base of the education system was, at least beyond the primary-school universal foundation. The Third Republic gave all Frenchmen a modicum of education (though the movement had already progressed markedly before the 1880s). Yet not only was education beyond fourteen limited to a minority but the State system divided sharply (and still to some extent continues to divide) between those who were destined for higher education (and went to *lycées*) and those who finished their education at the primary-plus level. The system was democratic, in the sense that it was free and based on merit; indeed the emphasis on intellectual achievement has always been more marked in France than in other educational systems, and outstanding children of working-class or peasant origins were channelled to secondary schools and universities (or indeed in most cases to the technical *grandes écoles*, such as the École Polytechnique which did pride itself in being open precisely to those children). But numbers were limited: less than 10 per cent of each age group finished secondary education before the war and the total university population was only 60,000.

In the course of the 1950s, the number of children attending secondary schools began to increase rapidly, both because of the high birth-rates of the 1940s and because more children stayed at school beyond the compulsory age: where only about one child in nine took the *baccalauréat* in 1960 (and thus finished secondary school), about one in four did so ten years later. 763,000 students were in higher education in 1975, twelve times more than in the pre-war years. But this development was not planned for and led to numerous crises at all levels and particularly in higher education, because of the lack of infrastructure, of teachers, of facilities generally, as well as because of the obvious psychological problems of adjustment stemming from such a growth. In the Paris area in particular, which had 175,000 students in 1968, new campuses sprang up somewhat chaotically, difficulties being increased by the centralized character of the educational system which was proving unable to provide academic leadership and yet led to the insistence on bureaucratic procedures which slowed down developments and irritated both students and teachers. The student explosion has of course taken place in all Western countries and it corresponds to the difficulties encountered by these societies in providing the young with a genuine challenge and an intellectually attractive employment; but it took in 1968–70 a dramatic (though not very violent) form in France, in part because the growth of the university population occurred in an academic environment that had always praised individualism and as a result did not provide (indeed deliberately refused to provide) the kind of community life which large numbers of students obviously need. The famous Nanterre campus, tucked away in the western outskirts of Paris with almost no social facilities and bad communications with the capital, became a wholly isolated 'ghetto', whose only contacts with the outside world were the slums of nearby immigrants in a grim industrial district. As we shall see, higher education reform, one of the few long-term consequences of the 1968 unrest, has moved the whole system some way towards decentralization and autonomy, though at the cost of much short-term administrative chaos: there are now thirteen universities in the Paris area. Yet, whatever its defects, the educational 'boom' has changed France intellectually and socially and has contributed to destroy the hitherto rather refined character of the cultural élite.

Since the mid-1970s, France has experienced industrial stagnation, inflation and unemployment as other industrial countries – less so than Britain, but more so than West Germany. Yet it is no paradox to say that the problems of the 1970s are in part the consequence of the rapid socio-economic changes of the 1950s and 1960s; indeed, the form of the reaction to the crisis is also a consequence of these changes. Young men and women are revolting against the constraints of the 'system'; shopkeepers and peasants are caught in a process of modernization for which generations of stagnation had made them ill prepared; workers and white-collar employees have begun to enjoy consumer goods, from cars (one for four inhabitants) to washing machines, and longer holidays (four weeks for a large percentage of the population, mainly taken in August and turning the country into a vast holiday camp), but they are increasingly confronted with the problems of suburban monotony in the *grands ensembles* (as reflected in J.-L. Godard's *Deux ou trois choses que je sais d'elle*); all segments of the population except a small fringe of pensioners and traditional peasants in outlying areas have embarked on a new life and are acquiring new attitudes towards society. Of course, older attitudes die hard: France is still in many ways a peasant nation, on which modern life has been superimposed. Hence perhaps more tensions than elsewhere and rather more difficult adjustments. Hence some difficulty in opening to the world and, if not xenophobia, at least a marked nationalism. But, in the post-war period, the French began to move out of individualism and became, through increased mobility and the mass media (radio and television though not the newspapers, which are still mainly regional), increasingly one nation. Social and economic change is achieving naturally what kings, Napoleon and the previous Republics, with their administrative centralization, had found difficult to impose.

THE GROUP STRUCTURE AND THE DEVELOPMENT OF MODERN ASSOCIATIONALISM

The reluctance of the French to join voluntary associations is legendary. Up to 1789, France had kept the old corporations of the Middle Ages and business and commerce were straitjacketed by compulsory groups. The Revolution having abolished corporations and the nation being organized around the bourgeoisie and the independent peasantry, the distrust for 'coalitions' became one of the leitmotives of most politicians; this enabled industrialists to resist, until late in the nineteenth century, the legalization of labour unions. Only in 1884 for trade unions and in 1901 for other associations did the law allow voluntary associations to develop easily and freely; but foundations have remained almost impossible to create, in contrast with the growth of these institutions in most Western countries.

One of the reasons for the delay in the liberalization of the laws on associations was because one group at least had successfully maintained itself throughout the nineteenth century, though by sheer power rather than through legislation. The Roman Catholic Church, having escaped from the Revolution's efforts first at 'nationalizing' it and then at destroying it, remained for a century largely paid for by State funds (ostensibly because its property had been taken over during the Revolution, but salaries were eventually given to the very much smaller Protestant and Jewish Churches); Roman Catholicism continued to play a major part in the social and political life of a country which was nominally 95 per cent Catholic. After the 1905 'separation' with the State and some tragi-comic episodes against some religious orders, the

Church's strength gradually declined as a hierarchical body. In some parts of the country (in the west and east, as well as in the south-east of the Central Massif) its following was still large; elsewhere, both in rural areas and in towns, Christianity became increasingly nominal, the teachings of the lay *instituteur* (primary-school teacher) having successfully undermined those of the village *curé*. The victory of the Republican State over the Church in 1905 was thus the final episode of the fight of the modern State against traditional groups; ironically, it took place at the very moment when voluntary associations were beginning to develop. A generation later, the Church had recovered sufficiently – though on a much more modern basis – to influence many progressive associations among workers and farmers.

The changes in the social structure that affected France in the 1950s and 1960s did not merely affect Church organizations, however; throughout the post-war period, one can trace a sizeable growth in voluntary associations, though partly because of the traditional legal restrictions and partly because of the classic individualism of Frenchmen, interest groups remain weaker, smaller in numbers and as a result more chaotic in their behaviour than their counterparts in other countries. Political (and even religious) considerations still account for divisions among trade unions, while the impact of modernization created tensions among farmers' and business organizations. It is still unclear when France will fully accept interest groups (De Gaulle was very critical of these when he came back to power in 1958 and reflected the attitudes of many Frenchmen in this respect) but the acceptance of the role and position of associations is unquestionably much more widespread than at any time since the Revolution.

Trade Unions

Divisions among trade unions mirror both the traditional divisions of the Left and the attitudinal differences that characterize modern French society. In the nineteenth century, legal restrictions on unions combined with the relative numerical weakness of the manual working class to account for the slow development of the Confédération Générale du Travail (CGT), which was created in 1895 and embarked on a militant policy against capitalism at its Amiens Congress in 1906. To this day, except during three very short periods (1919, 1936 and 1945), the CGT succeeded in attracting only a relatively small minority of the workers, although it consistently remained the largest trade-union organization. Since the Second World War, it became dominated by the Communist party (though some of its members and even some of its leaders are not Communist) and this cost the union some support among anti-Communists or simply non-Communists. Christians have tended to join the Confédération Française des Travailleurs Chrétiens (CFTC), renamed in 1964 the Confédération Française Démocratique du Travail (CFDT), which, though created in 1919, long before the CGT became Communist, grew appreciably after 1945, while Socialists formed a breakaway union in 1947, the CGT-Force Ouvrière. This politicization of the unions probably alienated many workers from trade unions with the result that French unions do not organize more than about 20 to 25 per cent of the total work-force, about 65 per cent of these being members of the CGT. Thus, although traditionally anti-capitalist and profoundly opposed to many aspects of society, the French working class tends to distrust union leaders and attempts – with some success – to benefit from the gains obtained without having to pay subscriptions or generally to be involved, while, mainly in small firms, employers succeeded in preventing the development of unions. Individualistic attitudes are thus latent among workers and account for many of the failures of the French working class.

The division between unions tends of course to reinforce this individualism. Yet, were it not for this division, the structure of the unions would be well-suited to modern industrial society. Both the CGT and the CFDT (and indeed the smaller unions as well) are organized on the basis of whole branches of industry (mining, engineering, chemicals, etc.): the CGT and the CFDT are 'confederacies' – as the name of these central organizations indicates – grouping a number of industrial unions. The structure is thus similar to that of American or German unions and is more appropriate to collective bargaining than the older craft unions or the general unions which one finds in Britain. But, unlike American or German unions, each of the industrial unions is relatively weak, while the power of the central organization is correspondingly greater. One reason for this relative strength of the central organizations is the 'politicization' of at least one of the unions, the CGT; another is the fact that, alongside industrial unions, each city or area with a large working-class segment forms the basis of a geographical grouping, known as the *bourse du travail*, where the policy of all the unions within the same confederacy is hammered out, at least in theory; and, third, the need for some collaboration between the various confederacies, and in particular between the CGT and the CFDT, leads to greater strength at both ends (at plant level and at confederacy level) than at the level of industrial unions. It is not uncommon for local strikes or other forms of union activity to take place after a joint agreement between unions, for instance if a particular problem affects a specific firm; it is not uncommon for the national leaders of the two major trade-union confederacies to meet and attempt to devise a common national policy, at least for a specific period. Strategies at the level of an industry are rarely adopted: the weight of trade unions is often more symbolic than real at industrial union level and union policy is in the end more directed at government policy in general than at private business.

In the post-war period, and in particular in the 1960s, the CFDT has attempted to break these attitudes. Though only half the size of the CGT, it has exercised greater drive and initiative in a number of fields and was in particular instrumental in developing collective bargaining (in the car industry especially) in the late 1950s. From the middle 1960s it launched a campaign aimed at breaking anti-trade-union attitudes in small firms by attempting to educate workers and the public about the role of trade unions. As a result it often appeared much more militant than the Communist CGT, in particular in May 1968, when it insisted, not merely on wage increases which the Government quickly became prepared to concede in order to stop the strikes, but on guarantees for unionization on the shop floor in firms where employers had been very hostile. Success had been limited and the penetration of unions is still slow in many sections and in many regions. But, as social attitudes develop gradually among workers and among the public as a whole, the ideas of the CFDT on union–employers relations should probably permeate gradually. They should result in an increase in union membership, though it is unlikely that the major stumbling-block – the division between CGT and CFDT – will disappear as long as the CGT remains dominated by the Communist party (Force Ouvrière remaining much smaller than the other two and being mainly concentrated among civil servants).

Employers' Organizations

The legacy from the past can also be felt, though naturally in a different fashion, in employers' organizations. Firstly, up to the Second World War, only a small number of relatively large firms joined the Confédération Générale de la Production Française (CGPF), renamed after the war the Conseil National du Patronat Français (CNPF). Moreover, the organization did not acquire until late, as it may not have acquired even by the 1970s, genuine recognition from business as a whole. Despite its growth, it suffered from not being really representative of the small firms whose leaders, for reasons similar to those of many workers, preferred not to join any organization; many large firms, having direct access to the Government and the civil service because of their national importance and because of their personal contacts, rarely used the CNPF as a channel for negotiations; and, as collective bargaining remained exceptional before the war and somewhat limited even afterwards, the CNPF was rarely involved in bargaining with unions on wages or work conditions.

The impact of modernization on large masses of French firms did lead to the gradual estrangement of one fraction of the French *patronat* which, under the Confédération Générale des Petites et Moyennes Entreprises (CGPME), attempted to resist changes in legislation or in the economy which effectively tended to limit the role of small business. The CGPME was not particularly radical in itself, but it was periodically undermined, in the 1950s and 1960s, by more militant associations of shopkeepers and small artisans.

The causes of the development of these more 'radical' movements of small businessmen lie in the rejuvenation of the French economy itself. The transformation which took place had the effect of undermining the traditional structure of business: even though France has relatively fewer large businesses (and in particular very large firms) than other Western European countries, concentration has taken place rapidly. This concentration affected industrial businesses in the first instance, but it spread gradually to commerce, and the 1950s and 1960s saw the development of department stores and 'hypermarkets' which increasingly attracted the ordinary customer by a policy of price cuts and discounts which small shopkeepers neither could afford nor indeed were psychologically ready to adopt. But the tradition of 'defence' of the 'small man' had been so engrained for generations that it became possible for shopkeepers to claim that their fight was of vital importance and to acquire as a result some – though admittedly only some – audience among the public. The first wave of shopkeeper discontent, in the 1950s, was very successful: it came at a time when the political system was under attack for its inability to solve the major problems of French society. Thus Pierre Poujade launched a movement, the Union de Défense des Commerçants et Artisans, UDCA, and attracted a large following: the use of direct action, in particular against tax offices and tax officials, was at least passively condoned by the population; at the 1956 general election, UDCA candidates even obtained over 10 per cent of the votes. Only the arrival of De Gaulle in 1958 broke the enthusiasm and silenced the 'protest' of the shopkeepers.

Protest was to start again in the late 1960s under the leadership of Léon Nicoud who founded the Comité d'Information et de Défense – Union Nationale des Artisans et des Travailleurs Indépendants, CID-UNATI. This seemed to revert to the same tactics as those of the UDCA, but, because of the stability of the Government, partly also because the 'consumer society' was better entrenched and the French population had become more price-conscious and more aware of its strength, the movement did not achieve the same popularity, nor indeed the same fame as its predecessor. Despite some hesitations, the CID-UNATI stopped short of political action. The relative setback of the second wave of shopkeepers' unrest seems to point, too, to the long-term psychological effects of French economic change.

Agricultural Organizations

Agriculture was, as we saw, one of the sectors of the French economy and of French social life in which change was most marked in the post-war period; in many ways, agricultural organizations were also those which showed the greatest degree of liveliness in the French polity. At the end of the Second World War, an attempt was made to bring under one umbrella, the Confédération Générale de l'Agriculture (CGA), the whole of the population engaged in agriculture. The organization failed, but one of its components, the Fédération Nationale des Syndicats d'Exploitants Agricoles (FNSEA), remained a lively defender of the interests of French peasants (though its membership was limited to about one-third of the total potential, this was more than the percentage of unionized workers). For a period the FNSEA tended to represent the larger and more mechanized farmers of northern France, but, from the late 1950s, some younger elements, in the Confédération Nationale des Jeunes Agriculteurs (CNJA), became increasingly influential within the FNSEA. As with the CFDT (and also as a result of the role of Christian leaders) an effort was made to reconsider the role of 'peasants' in French society and to obtain, possibly on a co-operative basis, a better deal for farmers who were compelled to change and improve their working methods. CNJA leaders even took over the FNSEA for a short period, but, although they were defeated by more conservative elements, a marked change in attitudes is noticeable in the organization. First, representation is better achieved than in the past, and although anomic outbursts occur periodically, especially in the poorer areas, the difficulties encountered by employers' or workers' unions in making themselves accepted by their own rank and file have not marred farmers' organizations. Secondly, the attitudes of the agricultural unions to the modernization process have been based on a broad co-operation with the Government in an attempt to improve life on the land, and a search for new ideas indeed sometimes led civil servants to rely on farmers' leaders for new arrangements and new methods.

Middle-Class and Student Groups

For a period in the 1950s, it seemed as if the only really representative organizations were, on the one hand, the middle-class group of teachers or doctors and, on the other, student organizations. As in many other Western countries, French doctors' associations have been militantly anti-socialistic and they succeeded for a long time in preventing the effective implementation of some aspects of social security by refusing to agree on the content of contracts for doctors' fees. Despite (or because of) generally high earnings, doctors insisted on their freedom to charge the price which they privately wished to charge and social security reimbursements remained as a result only a small proportion of the patients' expenditure. Even though, in the 1960s, the Government managed to pass contracts with doctors in many areas, the medical profession succeeded remarkably in maintaining its position, in sharp contrast with small business.

Student organizations were, for a time, even more remarkable. Indeed, teachers and students were almost the only groups which, at least for a period, succeeded in maintaining unity of representation among social categories notoriously divided in their ideology as well as over tactics. At the end of the 1950s, the Union Nationale des Étudiants de France (UNEF) was neither narrowly occupational and catering merely for the day-to-day services of students nor so markedly ideological that divisions among its members would cause disunity. Indeed, during the Algerian war of independence against France (1954–62) – a period as traumatic to France as the Vietnam war was to be for the United States – the UNEF appeared sometimes to be the only organized force able to unite the opposition to repression and to force the pace of liberalization. Perhaps because of this very participation against the Algerian war, however, divisions gradually grew and the increasing intervention of some of its leaders in favour of extremist policies led to the withdrawal of a large part of the rank and file. This in turn increased the hold of radical elements over the organization until the union finally collapsed: the last intervention of the UNEF in French public life was in May 1968, though in the May events it was often more reacting to actions of small student ginger groups than leading student policy. Splits and almost complete disorganization put students, at the time of their increased legal influence in university administration, in a wholly ineffective position; the rebuilding of the student organizations since 1968 has taken place on the basis of a division between a number of unions: the situation which prevails among students is thus comparable to that which characterizes workers' organizations, the Communist students' union having emerged in many universities both with a strong and with a somewhat moderating influence.

While students' organizations ceased to occupy the forefront of the stage, other groups emerged and even flourished in the 1960s and 1970s. These groups are the manifestation of the new 'associational' trends in French society. Perhaps the first of the modern associational groups should be traced back to the late 1950s and early 1960s when the Algerian war was by far the most important political issue, since it had led to the end of the Fourth Republic in 1958 and seemed for four long years to be intractable even to De Gaulle. Opposition to the war was widespread among the young and the intellectuals, but it remained diffuse; the organized groups – parties or trade unions – whether Communist or not, remained broadly silent because of the explosive character of the problem among their own ranks. The opposition to the war had therefore to take place outside traditional groupings; and new organizations were naturally created.

The direct effect of these new organizations on the duration of the war and its outcome was limited; but their effect on the nature of society was probably large. For the first time, perhaps, groups were pressing for the solution of a problem and putting pressure on the Government, the parties, the trade unions. At the same time, a number of political 'clubs' were formed in order to study the long-term future of French society and politics in the light of the changes brought about by the Fifth Republic and of the impossible return to the chaos of the Fourth Republic, however authoritarian the Fifth Republic may sometimes appear to be. Thus France became slowly accustomed to groups raising major questions about society. Later, in the 1960s, preservation societies, consumer bodies, anti-pollution groups came to express their views and attempted to influence opinion. Women's organizations, hitherto weak and entirely dominated by the political parties, became independent: the 'Estates General of Women' were convened in 1971. Finally, regionalist bodies began to mushroom in almost every part of the country. The Breton and Basque organizations had long existed, admittedly, but they had never been viewed as serious 'participants' in the political system; they were either deemed to be subversive (as threatening the unity of France) or assumed not to be serious. From the late 1960s, folklore elements subsided when other organizations appeared and started to demand the end of the 'colonization' of France by Paris and the central government. In the southern half of the country in particular, the *mouvement occitan* claimed to work for a 'liberation' whose terms remained vague – and whose appeal still remained weak – but which had sufficient significance to be widely discussed; their pressure contributed to a sense of general unease among the bureaucracy and the political parties about the tradition of centralization. The response may be slow; most Frenchmen may still be unaware of the overcentralized character of the nation. But groups of various kinds have begun the process of psychological change which is the prerequisite to real administrative change.

The Social Bases of French Politics and Political Parties

The inchoate character of French parties and the seemingly erratic nature of French voting patterns has always been linked to the individualism of Frenchmen. While in most other Western democracies, a fairly simple party system developed at the end of the nineteenth century and at the beginning of the twentieth, pre-war French Chambers of Deputies and post-war National Assemblies have been composed of a large number of segments lacking unity of purpose and common behaviour. This has not always been the case, however: for a period, at the turn of the century, the opposition between Church and State led to a crystallization of opinion which almost gave rise to a well-organized party system. But, soon afterwards, the arrival of the Socialist party on the scene in the years preceding the First World War created new types of divisions which tended to multiply during the inter-war period and to give to the French Republic a reputation of instability which was to continue after the Second World War.

With the advent of the Fifth Republic in 1958, the party system has become less obscure, less faction-ridden and less personalized. For a while, and indeed to some extent even now, it was difficult to distinguish the short-term impact of De Gaulle from the possible long-term transformations stemming from changes in the social structure. In the 1970s, however, it became increasingly clear that the traditional social bases on which parties were founded and the relationship between elected member and elector which used to characterize French politics were in the process of disappearing and that a new form of political life was beginning to emerge. The movement is far from complete: as we saw for groups in society, there are still many competing claims and attitudes of Frenchmen are not wholly modified. The right-wing Gaullist party, the Rassemblement pour la République (RPR), heir to the Union pour la Nouvelle République founded by De Gaulle in 1958, may have acquired a substantial hold on a large section of the electorate; but it has declined from its dominant position of the 1960s and is seriously challenged by other segments of the Centre-Right close to the President elected in 1974, Valéry Giscard d'Estaing. Meanwhile, despite many efforts which took place in the 1960s and 1970s, especially after 1972, the Left is more divided than in any Western country except Italy and Finland. Yet there are enough changes in attitudes to raise at least the question of the emergence of a new form of mass political behaviour among the majority of the French people.

A NEW MASS POLITICAL BEHAVIOUR?

Traditional Voting Patterns

The individualistic nature of French parties was – and to some extent still is – the reflection on the socio-political plane of the individualistic and unorganized nature of the French social structure. The key concept to understand in relation to this political and specifically electoral tradition is that of 'sectionalism'. This sectionalism is geographical in that the inhabitants of a particular area seem to share more attitudes in common than they do with inhabitants of other areas and they vote accordingly. As is well known, modern parties developed in western Europe around some common standpoints: for instance, socialist parties tended to appeal to workers in particular and to underprivileged groups generally, irrespective of the area in which these groups were found; the underlying bond uniting the supporters of these parties was thus the common factor of class. By contrast, sectional parties are those which appeal to some characteristics of the population in given areas; these were very common before industrialization in most of western

Europe and one long-lasting example is that of the Democratic party in the south of the United States: given certain attitudes (particularly relating to race) which are shared widely among whites in the American south, the Democratic party is in fact divided into two segments which are widely opposed and voting patterns in the Congress and even the process of selection of presidential candidates are affected as a result.

Geographical sectionalism is thus not a unique French phenomenon, but it has been more widespread and lasted longer in France because of the characteristics of the French social structure up to and indeed after the Second World War; in particular, the large French peasantry has helped to maintain sectionalism. We noted earlier that peasants (by opposition to farmers) are characterized by self-reliance, economic and cultural, a fear of the outside world and therefore little desire to associate with others, and indeed a desire to prevent the impact of outside change on the local community. These characteristics are common to peasants in all societies (though not to agricultural workers who are not independent and therefore not self-reliant and in any case too poor to have a genuine impact on the political system); it follows that, as France had a much greater percentage of peasants at the time of the Second World War than any other Western country, the sectional nature of politics was necessarily more marked in France than elsewhere. Moreover, as we also noted, the relatively small number of large towns and the predominance of village life associated within this sectionalism many shopkeepers, artisans, lawyers and members of other professions who lived in a rural environment and depended for their livelihood on the trade or services furnished to the peasants. As late as the early 1950s, perhaps half the French population was directly or indirectly participating in a type of social life which was likely to foster political sectionalism.

The political consequences of geographical sectionalism are vast. We noted earlier that some modern parties, and specifically socialist parties, were born from the desire to unite workers who were held to have common problems irrespective of their place of residence. Where geographical sectionalism is high, such parties will grow with difficulty. Moreover, even new parties are also affected: the French Socialist party and less so the French Communist party have had to pay attention to feelings in the localities more than similar parties elsewhere, with the result that these parties have been more divided internally or have been forced to engage to a greater extent in ideological gymnastics, and their effectiveness was limited as a result. But, more importantly, sectionalism has contributed to the maintenance, over a longer period, of the position of 'notables' and other prominent local personalities in French political life. It is sometimes suggested that party politics in developed societies are now more affected by leaders than by programmes; but such leaders emerge at the national level and their impact depends on support across the whole nation and not within the context of one constituency. On the contrary, traditional French politics have been characterized and are still characterized to some extent by the role of local leaders, both locally and at the national level.

Typically, the career of a successful politician will begin as mayor of the village or small town, then continue in the county council and culminate in the National Assembly. Gradually, a bond develops between constituents and *this* particular politician (more than between electors and parties). As a result, what is important for such a representative (or deputy to take the French expression) is to satisfy the desires of the local constituents (and in particular those of the more important of these constituents, such as other mayors and county councillors) rather than to follow the lead of a party. The political network is one which is (or was traditionally) based on a hierarchy of elected persons each of whom has a 'capital' of personal influence, rather than on a party hierarchy of national and local executives.

This is not to say that politics developed irrespective of ideology. The opposition between pro-Church and anti-Church supporters contributed to profound cleavages among deputies and in the population, including in rural areas, for a very long period; indeed, while the cleavage was most alive, at the turn of the century, it almost led to the development of a national party system. But it became increasingly less deeply felt while the other main cleavage, that which opposed rich to poor, and which had started with the Revolution, took a large variety of forms, and allowed for much localism. Smallholders, while owning their land, felt that they were poor (and indeed were poor) in many areas, either because of lasting grievances related to an aristocracy which had long since disappeared or because of new grievances against commerce, business and industry which, jointly with the State, were held to make their life difficult. But these poor were different from industrial workers and the 'alliance between workers and peasants' was a dream of some revolutionaries and not a reality of the land. Ideological politics refracted through personal and local idiosyncrasies made parties appear incoherent, and indeed act very tortuously. This explains why, as some observers noted, the French might have had basic leanings towards Right or Left, and yet feel little identity with actual political parties; and this accounts for more than a small part of the very unstable nature of politics at the national level.

The New Mass Politics

Sectionalism is likely to persist only if the mobility of the population is low and if the purpose of politics is to maintain entrenched interests. This was precisely the case in France as long as a large peasantry had very limited horizons and was essentially concerned to prevent encroachments from the wider market economy. But, as we saw, the 1950s and 1960s showed a marked decrease of the rural population and consequently a marked physical mobility; new attitudes grew among farmers. Smallholders who favour the policies of the CNJA and modernization generally are unlikely to be concerned with purely sectional and local politics; they are interested in the future of the whole group of smallholders across the nation. Moreover, the growth of towns, including medium-sized towns, corresponds to an increase in the segment of the population which does not have deep roots in the locality and is therefore primarily concerned with its interests conceived as those of a national social group. Mobility and the sharp development of a new form of group identity have thus tended to replace old sectionalism by a form of national politics. In the business sector as well, the decline of small firms and the development of large businesses lead to increasingly national viewpoints among industrialists. For these a political system geared to the interests of a local clientele becomes unsatisfactory and unpredictable; thus national pressure groups acting on the Government are likely to replace more localized actions. The 1950s and 1960s created therefore the conditions for the end of geographical sectionalism and for the development of what has to be called a form of 'nationalization' of political attitudes and political behaviour.

But such a development takes time (which explains the lag between the flight from the land in the 1950s and the gradual nationalization of politics in the 1960s). It also requires the intervention of some outside catalyst: it can be said that De Gaulle played this part in the 1960s by providing the electorate with a sharp national focus. There is also a need for cleavages other than purely local ones: national cleavages were hidden or refracted under sectional politics in the past, but they did exist, and it became possible for them to re-emerge under the new national conditions. We noted earlier that France had broad ideological divisions: for a long time, the division between Church and State provided such a cleavage; for an even longer period perhaps, the opposition between the 'small' and the 'big', which accounts for the strength of the Left (or a particular variety of the Left in some rural areas), provided another. Modern mass politics is thus slowly emerging out of the traditional cleavages.

The traditional geographical sectionalism dies hard. Unquestionably, the attitudes of Frenchmen *vis-à-vis* State and Government remain still affected by generations of relative withdrawal from the community at large. Mass politics is developing, however. The 1960s were a watershed in French politics in that for the first time a party emerged on the Right which swept aside most of the traditional party structures in urban and rural areas. It declined in the 1970s, but did not disappear. Perhaps as interestingly, the Centre–Right groups which were traditionally mere factions led by local notables had to unite and to become national bodies under the leadership of Giscard d'Estaing. Thus the three presidential elections of 1965, at which De Gaulle was re-elected, of 1969, at which the Gaullist Pompidou came to high office, and of 1974, which saw the victory of the Centre–Right candidate Giscard, have been three different steps in a similar development. At the first two elections, the French chose to crush the traditional loose groupings of the Right; at the third, they elected a non-Gaullist Conservative, but a new Conservative who embodied a style of leadership as distant from the local appeal of past notables as had been that of his two predecessors in 1965 and 1969.

Indeed, the transformations in the electoral behaviour of Frenchmen can also be shown by the effects of the electoral system, which throughout the 1960s and 1970s had different results on politics from those it had had in the past, and which it had been predicted it would have at the time. It was widely assumed by most political observers (and indeed by many political scientists) that the *scrutin d'arrondissement* which is the electoral system under which most French elections had been fought since the 1870s and which is a two-ballot (or, as the Americans would say a run-off) system in single-member constituencies, was largely the cause of the undisciplined character of the French party system. It was alleged that, because the constituencies were relatively small (to elect one deputy only), the system favoured people who were locally known. And it is true that, contrary to what is usually thought outside France, France rarely had proportional representation: it was introduced only twice, on a limited basis, in 1919 and 1945; in neither case was it introduced fully and in neither case did it last for more than about a decade. But it is usually forgotten that Britain and other Commonwealth countries also have single-member constituencies (though without second ballot) and that politics do not become sectional as a result. More importantly for France, the same two-ballot system was reintroduced in 1958 and did not have the effect of increasing the localization of politics, but, on the contrary, elections became fought for the first time on a truly national basis, more so than they had been after 1945 while proportional representation was in force. The change in the social basis of politics led to the appearance of mass politics, and the voting patterns were changed, despite the same electoral system, breaking a century-long sectionalism.

THE RIGHT AND CENTRE: 'GAULLISTS', 'GISCARDIENS' AND 'CENTRISTS'

There was a time when politics on the Right was almost impossible to describe in terms of political parties: up to the Second World War, the various segments of the French Right and Centre were so divided that it was more accurate to talk in terms of factions, each led by one or more prominent politicians, than to talk of party alignments. This situation was indeed at the root of French political instability, though it was rarely perceived in this manner; nor were serious efforts made to bring about more modern party structures.

The post-war period did open a new phase, during which efforts were made at periodic intervals to streamline the Right, first under the banner of a vastly expanded Christian Democratic Party, later, and at two successive occasions, under the banner of Gaullism. The cause for each of these three waves of streamlining was somewhat accidental, however, and these accidents proved in every case not to be strong enough to break altogether the traditions of 'factionalism' and indiscipline on the Right. There is hope that the decline of the Gaullist Party in the 1970s will not have the same consequences, as the social structure has changed and as the Constitution of the Fifth Republic enhanced the powers of the President; but a repetition of the disintegration of previous Conservative parties cannot be altogether ruled out.

The Christian Democrats (Mouvement Républicain Populaire, MRP) had a wave of success in 1945 because many Conservative candidates of the pre-war period were prevented from entering electoral contests, legally or *de facto* as a result of their association with the Pétain regime of occupied France. While the Christian Democrats had scored only minor successes before 1939 in Brittany and Alsace, they became for a while in 1946 the largest French party with slightly over a quarter of the electorate. But the MRP was not Conservative in ideology and leadership, while its electorate was Conservative; it became suspect to most of its electors by associating with Communists and Socialists in a governmental coalition known as *tripartisme* (it also voted in favour of many nationalizations), by being specifically associated with a new Constitution (that of the Fourth Republic) which was held to be too radical by many Conservative electors. Having been the subject of very strong attacks by De Gaulle from 1946, the MRP began to lose votes and to lose some of its leaders and deputies; a process of disintegration of the party started while traditional Conservative groups began to recover.

This recovery of the traditional Right was checked for a while by the launching of a party organization by De Gaulle in 1947. His Rassemblement du Peuple Français (RPF) won major successes at the municipal elections of that year and began acquiring a vast following among the population – larger than any party had before or since (one million members at the height of success). For several years it seemed that the party would sweep the country at the parliamentary elections, a prospect which most deputies of the Right and Centre viewed with considerable worry. They endeavoured to stem the tide and were helped by the fact that the general election did not have to be called before 1951; by then, the Gaullist Party, although still strong, had declined: it gained only a fifth of the votes among the population; and Gaullist deputies were later successfully split as a result of the popularity of a Conservative Prime Minister, Antoine Pinay, in 1952. De Gaulle concluded that his efforts had been in vain and he disbanded his party in 1953.

By the mid-1950s, the French Conservatives seemed effectively to have returned to power with the same characteristics as in the 1930s. There were three major Conservative groups in Parliament, as well as a number of smaller units. The main group was that of the 'Independents', whom their leader had tried unsuccessfully to organize into a more streamlined body but who succeeded in keeping their independence in that almost no voting discipline could be applied to them; these deputies owed their strength to the local personal influence they enjoyed, not to the party. Other Conservative groups had similar characteristics. Indeed, the disintegration of the MRP and of the RPF had been due to the fact that many deputies of these two parties had

FRENCH GENERAL ELECTIONS SINCE THE SECOND WORLD WAR

			Percentage of votes cast						
			Communists	*Socialists*	*Radicals*	*MRP*	*Indep. Conserv.*	*Gaullists*	*Other*
1945			26·5	24	11	25	13	—	0·5
1946	*June*		26	21	11·5	28	13	—	0·5
1946	*November*		28	18	11	26	16	—	1
1951			26	14·5	10·5	13	12	22·5	1·5
1956			26	15	15·5	11	15	4	13·5 (*mainly Poujadists*)
1958	*1st ballot*		19	15·5	11·5	11·5	23	17·5	2
	2nd ballot		20·5	14	8	7·5	23·5	26·5	—
1962	*1st ballot*		22	15	8	9	15	32	—
	2nd ballot		21·5	16·5	7	5	9·5	40·5	—
				Left Federation and other Left		*Dem. Centre*			
1967	*1st ballot*		22·4	21·0		12·8	37·8		6·0
	2nd ballot		21·4	25·0		7·1	42·6		3·9
1968	*1st ballot*		20·0	20·5		10·5	4	44·0	1
	2nd ballot		20·0	22·0		8·0	3·5	45·6	—
1973	*1st ballot*		21·2	23·6		12·4	38·4		4·1
	2nd ballot		20·6	26·4		6·1	46·3		0·6
		Extr. L.							
1978	*1st ballot*	3·3	20·6	24·7		23·8		22·6	4·9
	2nd ballot		18·6	30·7		26·1		23·1	1·4

well-entrenched electoral positions in their constituencies and could flout the leadership with total impunity. These deputies, together with some of the deputies of the Centre parties, played an increasing part in the shifting coalitions of the 1950s; but the lack of voting discipline in Parliament and the lack of continuous support given by deputies to the Governments they had chosen a few months earlier was in large part instrumental in the downfall of the Fourth Republic in 1958.

The third attempt at streamlining the Right came about in 1958 when, as a result of the crisis created by the Algerian war and in particular by the threat of military take-over (on 13 May 1958, French generals seized power in Algiers and declared that they would not obey the regular Paris Government), De Gaulle was called by the politicians to 'save the Republic'. His price was high: a new Constitution was to be drafted which would bring about political stability. But a party was also needed to mobilize support around De Gaulle's name among the population at the general election which was to take place in late 1958. This second version of the Gaullist Party, appropriately named Union for the New Republic (UNR), was to be the instrument of De Gaulle's power during his eleven years as President, from 1958 to 1969. It was even to be for a while a genuinely dominant party, attracting 40 per cent or more of the votes at the general elections of 1962, 1967 and 1968. But, with De Gaulle's departure in 1969, a slow process of decline took place: by 1973, the party was only one of a configuration of groups in the 'governmental majority', a situation which was to be repeated, indeed more strongly, at the 1978 election; like the Gaullist Party of 1951, the Gaullist Party of the 1970s, the RPR, could only master less than a quarter of the electorate. The third post-war attempt at streamlining the Right had not been more successful than the previous two.

The Gaullist Party in the 1960s and 1970s: UNR, UDR, RPR

The history of the Gaullist Party since 1958 is most revealing in terms of the characteristics of French politics and of the development of political parties. To a large extent, De Gaulle was both the instrument of the success of the party and of its relative downfall, although the factors which contributed to the division of the French Right – localism, in particular – also played a part. Unlike Adenauer who, in West Germany, ensured the dominance of the Christian Democrats on the Right by his systematic policy of merger of small parties, De Gaulle wished to remain somewhat aloof from the UNR and never involved himself too closely in the problems of internal party organization and in the tactical trade-offs or deals which are the stuff of daily politics. Indeed, De Gaulle was adamant not to give his party too strong an organization. He had failed in the early 1950s with the RPF, despite the fact that he had given that party a strong, even a somewhat militaristic structure. He overreacted perhaps and, fearing that the UNR of 1958 might be taken over by right-wing extremists, wished that the party might become only a group of reliable men in Parliament who would owe to him, and him alone, their political position. Candidates at the 1958 election were chosen mainly among inexperienced men, often loyal Gaullists of the war years, usually not prominent in the RPF of the 1940s, and unlikely to betray De Gaulle later. There were few members of the Party. The danger of take-over of the organization was therefore avoided, but the risk was also that the party would remain 'above' the mass of the population and would not therefore break the hold of the traditional Right.

This inherent danger was concealed throughout the 1960s because of the presence of De Gaulle and because of the boost given to the UNR by the electoral result of 1962. The general election of that year was indeed to be a major event in the evolution of the French Right, though, as it turned out, not a final break with the past. By October 1962, as the war in Algeria was over, the major problem which had forced the leaders of the Fourth Republic to give way to De Gaulle was solved: efforts were therefore soon made to shake De Gaulle's hold and to return to more 'traditional' politics. Although the UNR had been the largest party at the 1958 general election, it did not control a majority in Parliament and De Gaulle needed the support of the 'Independent Conservatives'. A coalition made of the Left, many traditional Conservatives and some ex-Gaullists who resented De Gaulle's Algerian settlement succeeded in censuring the Government and thus seemed to threaten the disappearance of the new 'style' of politics. But, having dissolved the Assembly, the President was given a new mandate by the people. The parties of the Left increased their parliamentary strength, but many Conservatives were defeated; those of the Gaullist deputies who had left the UNR over Algeria were also defeated, usually by unknown Gaullist candidates. The electorate, repeating and amplifying the gesture of 1958, had clearly voted for a united party, largely because of De Gaulle, admittedly, but, in doing so, it had crushed the local 'notables' who were the traditional leaders of the Conservatives.

Thus the election of 1962 gave France a majority party for the first time and, although the 1967 election was a setback for the Government, the controlling influence of the UNR over the electorate did not diminish; it was indeed expanded at the election which took place in 1968 following the student 'revolution' of that year. By then it seemed that the UNR (renamed UDR – Union des Démocrates pour la République) had come to be the 'natural' dominant party of the Right, with the smaller Conservative groups being merely either satellites or confined to an ineffective opposition.

It seemed that the Gaullist Party was slowly introducing a new style into French politics. It had been commonplace to criticize the UNR as De Gaulle's poodle in the early years: no programme could seemingly be ascribed to the party as such. It was noted that the about-turn on Algeria (from a defence of the 'integrity' of French Algeria in 1958 to the acceptance of independence four years later) left few scars within the party, as if it was effectively placing loyalty to the leader above any policy considerations: most observers were indeed surprised at the time that the UNR should have remained so united; it was expected, on the contrary, that, as previous parties on the Right before, De Gaulle's party would quickly break up. On all aspects of policy, whether on foreign affairs or on home affairs, on defence, on social security or on workers' participation (one of De Gaulle's main planks in the realm of employer–worker relations) the UDR could be counted on to vote as requested and to make no or few complaints against the leaders' decisions. Yet, over the years, the UDR gradually developed an outlook of its own. It also developed a 'style', more reminiscent of the British Conservatives than of French right-wing and Centre groups of the past: this style was based on basic loyalty to the leaders combined with the recognition that the party had many strands which needed to be accommodated. The charismatic bond of De Gaulle over the party seemed to forecast that the UNR would either be ruled in an authoritarian fashion or disintegrate after the founder had left; in fact, although loyalty was transferred to Pompidou when he became President, discussion began to flourish more actively in the party, within the context of the broad 'Gaullist' ideology of nationalism and 'populism'. Small groups of dissenters were tolerated; the leadership was often flexible, on the understanding that the party could be expected to rally if extreme tension occurred.

Yet, at this very moment, the party was entering a process of decline, largely as a result of Pompidou's decision, when he became President in 1969, to 'open up the basis of the Government' and to call in, not only

Giscard d'Estaing and his group of Independent Conservatives who had remained on the sidelines during the last years of De Gaulle's Presidency, but some of the leaders of the Centre parties. Pompidou's policy was to be the exact opposite to that of Adenauer in Germany. The small parties of the Right and Centre were not slowly integrated in the UDR; they came gradually to assert their independence and to insist that the Government be controlled not by the UDR alone. By 1973 the UDR proper was only an element in the electoral coalition which supported the Government. The death of Pompidou in 1974 precipitated this process: Giscard d'Estaing was elected against the regular Gaullist candidate, Chaban-Delmas; he split the Gaullists on the question of lending him support, some, under Jacques Chirac, being among the main promoters of his cause. Although Chirac was to be rewarded for a while with the Prime Ministership, the trend towards the build-up of a rival organization of the Centre continued. While Chirac attempted rather belatedly to refurbish the Gaullist Party (once more by giving it a new name – RPR – in 1977), he only succeeded in preventing a catastrophe at the 1978 election: with about 22 per cent of the votes and a quarter of the seats in Parliament, the Gaullist Party had unmistakably lost its position of prominence.

Giscardiens and Centrists

Until the Gaullist Party came to modify the panorama of political forces, it was customary to discuss French politics in terms of six main forces. Two were on the Right, namely the Gaullists and the various Conservative groups; two were on the Left, namely the CP and the Socialist Party; the last two were in the Centre and appeared to play a larger part than their strength warranted. One of them was the MRP which, as we saw, was drained of its electors by the combined action of the Gaullists and Conservatives; indeed, the party officially ceased to exist, though some of its leaders helped to create, together with some anti-Gaullist Conservatives, a Democratic Centre which came to be renamed as Progrès et Démocratie Moderne (PDM). The other Centre party was the Radical and Radical-Socialist Party, which, unlike the MRP, was anti-clerical by tradition and economically conservative by realism: because it had always been anti-Church, it allied with the Socialists; but its generally conservative economic views led to many quarrels with the Left both before the war and afterwards. Over all, these Centre groups seemed in the late 1960s to be crushed between the Gaullist Party and the Left which, despite its internal disunity, was at least at one in its opposition to the Government of the Fifth Republic.

The Centre groups were to receive a new lease of life from an unexpected ally – Giscard d'Estaing, who had maintained up to the mid-1960s an uneasy alliance with the Gaullist Party but had become increasingly critical of the Government after he lost the position of Minister of Finance in 1966. Giscard was originally a man without party: he was merely one of the very few Conservatives who, in 1962, sensed that there was little future in opposing De Gaulle; he was rewarded by being re-elected to Parliament and by becoming a Minister. But he never joined the Gaullist Party; nor was he altogether in agreement with Gaullist policies, both internal and external. Support for Giscard grew as Gaullism declined; Pompidou's approach being more 'pragmatic', Giscard's influence became larger. Meanwhile, the group of men whom Giscard led formed the nucleus of a party, both before and after Giscard's election to the Presidency in 1974. The Republican Party was formally launched in 1976 only, however: it aimed at obtaining mass popular support for Giscard's brand of conservatism; it obtained over 10 per cent of the votes at the 1978 general election.

These developments were both to be helped by and to help the other groups of the Centre. Previous efforts at constructing a party of the Centre had proved short-lived and rather unsuccessful, as had the efforts at reconstruction of the old Radical Party. The election of Giscard to the Presidency was to be a boost for the Centre parties, as they could for the first time rally round a leader who did not belong to the Gaullist Party. As the UDR had failed in the 1960s to establish itself locally in many areas, the Centre politicians and the Giscardiens could count on the support of many leaders in the provinces, and indeed enrolled many of them in their organizations. By 1978, the electoral alliance between Giscardiens and Centrists had been sealed under the name of the Union pour la Démocratie Française (UDF): this alliance was to obtain almost as many votes and almost as many seats as the Gaullist Party at the 1978 election.

The 1973 and 1978 elections thus marked the return to a more 'normal' situation: there are now at least two, and perhaps more, groups on the Government side, and no party can claim to command a controlling position. To this extent, the efforts of the Gaullists have failed, possibly because the French electorate is still relatively sectional in its attitudes, but surely also because De Gaulle was not sufficiently concerned with his party and even more because Pompidou chose to ally with Giscardiens and Centrists rather than steamroll them with the might of the UDR. Whether this division of the Right will eventually lead to a return to classic French instability is still not a foregone conclusion, however, both because the political institutions are different and because the social structure has changed. But it is a possibility, and one which is reinforced by the character of the Left, which emerged from the 1978 election more divided than it had been for almost a decade.

A PERMANENTLY DIVIDED LEFT?

The UDR gained between 40 and 45 per cent of the votes at the second ballot at each of the three general elections of the 1960s; the Left had difficulty in reaching the same level, although it was supported by more than half the electorate in 1945. In the 1970s the Left increased its share to about 47 per cent in 1973 and to very near victory both at the presidential election of 1974 and at the general election of 1978. Yet it failed, by one or two per cent, to reach a commanding position. Unquestionably, this failure has to be attributed to the division of the Left, and specifically to the fear which the Communist Party inspires among large sections of the electorate, not only on the Right but in the Socialist Party as well.

The Communist Party

The strength and character of the Communist Party are unquestionably among the main paradoxes of French politics; they are also old problems, dating from the 1930s: in 1936, the French CP emerged with 15 per cent of the votes and was a source of difficulties for the first Socialist Government. From that date, the CP maintained a substantial working-class base (about half the French manual workers vote for the party) and a foothold in many other groups. It is not insignificant among peasants, and it consistently champions the cause of smallholders and rural democracy; it has some strength among white-collar workers and technicians, particularly where they are unionized, as well as among teachers and other professionals. Drawing its appeal from the old battle cry of 'no enemy to the Left', in part being associated with anti-clerical radicalism, the French CP succeeded in becoming a large organization, not only by its membership (which is relatively small, at about half a million, but is none the less the largest of any French party), but through its ancillary and dependent structures, primarily of course the CGT, as well as among the young, women, tenants or intellectuals. It has a press, which has also declined, except for the popular and somewhat 'sensational' *Humanité-Dimanche*, co-operative organizations, a banking system (much of the French trade with eastern Europe goes through a bank which is allied to the CP and provides the party with much revenue). It does give a section of the French people a way of life, a social environment, and this largely accounts for the fact that, despite almost forty years of very limited gains and a decade of slight decline, it has remained an impressive organization, with some appeal among the population, although it successfully thwarted any attempts at liberalization and internal democracy.

The Communist Party has indeed a very tight organization; it is the only French party which has a truly nation-wide structure and whose antennae extend deeply into the urban and rural areas. The basis of the local organization is the *cell*, composed in principle of a few members only; efforts have been made repeatedly to develop the *cellules d'entreprise*, or factory cells, but these constitute a minority of the primary organizations, most of which, on the contrary, are based on residence rather than on the place of work. Above the cell is the section, which groups the various cells in a given town or district. These are in turn grouped into departmental federations (the *département* being the local government structure equivalent to the English county), despite the fact that, since 1958, the parliamentary constituency is smaller than the *département*: the Communist Party views its activities as extending beyond the electoral process and as being directed towards the general education of the masses and of the working class in particular.

At the national level, the party is dominated by a strong secretariat: the secretary general of the French Communist Party plays a similar part to that of the secretary general of the Communist Party of the Soviet Union. Maurice Thorez, who became secretary general in the middle 1930s and was to remain in this post for over twenty years, gave strength to the institution of the secretariat: like his Soviet counterparts he used his position to control the apparatus of the party and to eliminate (from the party, if not physically) those of his subordinates who appeared to come too close to becoming heirs apparent. His successors, and in particular the current secretary general, Georges Marchais, have been less outwardly authoritarian, but the basic principles of rule without opposition remain. The representative organs of the party, culminating in the Party Congress (which meets in principle every two years), the Central Committee of about a hundred members and the Executive of about twenty, never appear to be more than ratification bodies: if there are divisions of opinion among the various leaders, these never come out in the open, unless the expulsion of one of them is about to follow.

The rigidity of the party is maintained by a high degree of centralization. The secretaries at each level (section or federation) are entrusted with the supervision of the organizations at the lower level (cell or section). The principle of 'democratic centralism', imported from the Communist Party of the Soviet Union, entails that decisions which have been officially adopted by the party may no longer be discussed, but must on the contrary be implemented with enthusiasm. Admittedly, the party did have to pay a price to keep such a rigid structure. The 1950s and 1960s have been characterized by periodic, though always limited, purges, the demotion of Roger Garaudy in 1970 at the Party Congress being only the last of a series of prior demotions which regularly affected in the past the heirs-apparent of the Secretary-General! More importantly perhaps, the party has gradually attracted fewer intellectuals (Sartre's battles with the party have been numerous and few well-known intellectuals have remained consistently loyal).

With the development of the extreme Left, the party may be facing even greater problems: it had been successful in the past in preventing the development of a radical Left, but the slow growth of the United Socialist Party (PSU), which emerged originally from the Socialist Party, may provide the CP with its first major challenge. Radicalism has hitherto been mainly limited to students and, to a small extent, to some younger workers. Communist students have therefore sometimes appeared to be the best defenders of law and order in the revolting universities in the late 1960s, but this is not a position which the CP can hold for very long without endangering its own reputation as a left-wing party.

Moreover, the close association of the CP with the Soviet Union may have been an asset (though perhaps somewhat ironically) at the time when, under Stalin, the Soviet Union appeared to most radicals as the country of socialism, to be supported at all costs despite its obvious defects; this has become less true when China and even Cuba form alternative poles of attraction and when radical elements among the young appear committed, if not to 'bourgeois liberalism', at least to libertarian values which neither the Soviet Union nor the French CP are known to endorse. The timid opposition of the French CP to Soviet intervention in Czechoslovakia (contrasting with the much greater independence of the Italian CP) has done little to increase the reputation of the Communists for courage and independence of thought. In the mid-1970s, the party seemed to go further, at the height of the alliance with the Socialists: after having endorsed a 'Common Programme of the Left' in 1972 and supported the Socialist candidate at the 1974 presidential election, it seemed to engage in a process of ideological revisionism. Criticisms of the Soviet Union and of other Eastern European Communist States became more widespread; perhaps encouraged by the strength of 'Euro-Communism' in Spain, the French CP seemed to eschew some of its most traditional Marxist doctrinal points. It even formally abandoned its support for the dictatorship of the proletariat and agreed to the idea of alternance in government. But it made a dramatic volte-face in the autumn of 1977 when it broke with the Socialist Party, probably because it felt that it was not benefiting electorally from these concessions. Thus the 1978 election showed the French Communist Party once more true to its traditions – including that of contributing to the defeat of the Left.

The Socialist Party

One of the ways in which the Left suffered from the CP's attitude and behaviour has been through the fact that unity has been impossible to obtain, even despite the fact that such divisions entailed large losses in seats in the course of the Fifth Republic. The PSU has still little electoral appeal: it polled only 2 to 3 per cent of the electorate although one of its candidates was the popular ex-Premier of the 1950s, Pierre Mendès-France, who disentangled France from the Vietnam problem. In fact, the PSU is more the result of the division and inadequacies of both the Communist and Socialist Left than, at least up to now, a serious alternative. But the same is not true of the Socialist Party which, after a long period of decline, entered a period of new development under the leadership of François Mitterrand.

Unlike the Communist Party, the French Socialist Party has always been characterized by a high degree of internal democracy; this, however, did exacerbate divisions which date back from the pre-First World War period when Marxists and non-Marxists coexisted uneasily within the ranks of the party. The growth of the CP in the inter-war period led to a relative stagnation of the Socialist Party: its hour of triumph did come as a result of the 1936 general election which led to the first French Socialist Government, headed by Léon Blum; but it was also the beginning of a long decline. From obtaining about a quarter of the votes in 1936 and about the same percentage ten years later, the party dropped to about 15 per cent at the time of De Gaulle's return to power in 1958. This seemed to be partly the result of the policy of coalitions with centre and right-wing parties, a policy forced on the Socialists by their desire to preserve liberal government when it came under the joint pressure of the Communists on the Left and of the Gaullists (and later Poujadists) on the Right. But the decline of the Socialist Party was also the consequence of the gradual 'bureaucratization' of the party structure, under the secretary general of the time, Guy Mollet: the number of members decreased (to less than 50,000 in 1960 from a peak of several hundred thousands after the Second World War); a large fraction of the electorate came from agricultural areas, from economically declining parts of the country, and from older segments of the population. Dynamism seemed to have vanished, and the party did not appear any longer able to resist further inroads into its traditional support from its old enemy on the Left, the Communist Party.

Indirectly, and perhaps somewhat paradoxically, De Gaulle's return to power and the consequential development of a strong Gaullist Party helped to lay the foundations of the rejuvenation of the Socialist Party. Socialists no longer needed to participate in governments; nor was there any desire on the part of De Gaulle to accommodate, even in a token fashion, the goals of Socialism. Forced into opposition soon after the start of the Fifth Republic, the Socialist Party had to reconsider its role in the panorama of French politics – and its electoral appeal. Given the streamlining of the Right, the party had to conclude alliances with the other parties of the Left: an arrangement had to be made with the Communist Party – even if this was only to be an electoral pact; an attempt to establish formal ties with the Radical Party (the nearest equivalent to the British Liberal Party) seemed also natural: a merger was even contemplated – with little success – for a short period in the 1960s.

Yet the new strength of the French Socialist Party comes probably from the emergence of a new leader, François Mitterrand, whose power and influence was enhanced by the 'presidential' character of the new Constitution. This one-time Minister of the Fourth Republic came to be the presidential candidate, in 1965, thanks to all the other candidates on the Left being, for a variety of reasons, unacceptable to one of the parties or groups. During his presidential campaign, Mitterrand exploited the situation by appearing as the 'leader of the Left': the Communist Party had agreed not to field a candidate and was forced to support him; the Socialist bureaucracy was grudgingly obliged to back him. With 45 per cent of the votes against De Gaulle's 55 per cent, Mitterrand had clearly come to be, by the end of the campaign, *the* leader of the opposition – a position which no one had held in France for generations.

The Socialist bureaucracy did not give in to Mitterrand immediately: for four further years, efforts were made by the traditional leaders to circumvent Mitterrand's influence (who was not a member of the Socialist Party, but belonged to a small centre-left group); these were indirectly supported by the Communist Party who viewed with disfavour the growth of the popularity of a non-Communist leader among left-wing voters. When De Gaulle resigned, in 1969, neither party chose to select Mitterrand as their candidate. But the division of the Left led to a straight fight between Pompidou and a leader of the Centre Party, at the second ballot, after all left-wing candidates had been eliminated at the first, and after the Socialist candidate made such a poor showing that the Socialist Party seemed to be on the verge of disappearing altogether. The defeat of the Socialist Party shook the rank-and-file: the choice of Mitterrand as the leader became a necessity if the party was to be saved from total collapse.

Mitterrand had seen that the future of the Socialist Party depended on a determined effort to reconquer some of the positions lost to the Communists in the previous decades; such a strategy should be based, not on 'anti-Communism' and an alliance with the Right, but on an alliance with the Communist Party combined with a rejuvenation of the Socialist Party. A close look at the post-war elections did indeed show that, while the Socialists had markedly declined, the Communist Party, too, had lost votes: from a peak of 28 per cent in 1946, it had fallen to about 20 per cent during the Fifth Republic; the opportunity could therefore be seized to redress the balance if an effort was made to develop the organization, to eschew backdoor compromises, and to adopt a posture of defence of the working class and of the poorer sections of the population. To symbolize this change, Mitterrand pressed for, and obtained in 1970 the dissolution of the old party and its reconstitution on slightly different lines, in order that it might include some of the smaller left-wing groups which, in Mitterrand's view, would bring greater life to the declining body.

The strategy did pay off in the 1970s, though not quite to a sufficient extent to enable the party to reach the dominant position which it expected to achieve. After the 1973 general election, for the first time in thirty years the party ceased to decline; indeed it redressed its fortunes so dramatically that it obtained almost as many votes as the Communist Party while gaining more seats, thanks to the significantly different behaviour of left-wing voters faced with Communist or Socialist candidates. While Communist electors voted Socialist in their great majority in constituencies where a Socialist candidate stood, the converse was not true; nor did electors of the Centre show the same tendency to vote Communist as they did to vote Socialist if they wished to register their protest against the Gaullist Party. At the 1974 presidential election, success was even closer, as Mitterrand polled 49 per cent of the votes. For four further years the Socialist Party increased its efforts by developing its organization, by building the image of Mitterrand as a leader and by making its programme better known. It scored successes at by-elections and at local elections and was generally granted a markedly greater strength than the Communist Party. But the success was too rapid; the Communists were frightened and began attacking the Socialist Party for not remaining sufficiently to the Left, thereby forcing Mitterrand to make some concessions which in turn alienated crucial marginal voters of the Centre. While the 1978 election showed the Socialist Party to be, for the first time in forty years, electorally more popular than the CP (23 per cent versus 20·5 per cent), the lead was not sufficient to give the Socialist Party a real margin over its left-wing ally, let alone a near-majority of seats in Parliament. As a result, the problems of the division of the Left became as acute as ever: the CP must decline further, and the Socialist Party grow stronger, if a Government of the Left is to become a reality.

French electoral behaviour has thus changed somewhat, but only somewhat, in the 1960s and 1970s. Gaullists had their ups and downs; the non-Gaullist Right is more streamlined; the Socialists, not the Communists, are now the largest party on the Left. France emerges from the Gaullist and post-Gaullist era with a somewhat simplified and rather more manageable party system. But there are problems, most of which stem from the continued strength of localism and from the general weakness of parties as organizations (with the curious, indeed almost inexplicable exception of the Communist Party). The Gaullist Party resembles more the Tories of the early part of the nineteenth century than the British Conservatives of the 1970s; the Communist Party does not seem really to wish to provide a parliamentary alternative to conservatism; and battles between Communists and Socialists echo the problems of the Cold War more than the reality of modern Western democracies. Above all, parties have depended too much, and continue to depend too much, on individual leaders – such as De Gaulle, Pompidou, Chirac, Giscard, Mitterrand – to be assured of a healthy future. The changes of the 1960s and 1970s have given France an opportunity to move closer to stable political life; but this is still only an opportunity. Much has to be done before this opportunity becomes a permanent reality.

The Institutions of the Fifth Republic

While the party system that emerged from the first decade of the Fifth Republic was largely unintended by De Gaulle and indeed forced upon him to maintain his hold over politics, the constitution of the new regime has always been recognized by all to be De Gaulle's doing; many doubted that the new institutions would survive the departure of their founder. Indeed, despite the support expressed for the regime at elections and referendums since 1958, the events which took place in 1968 shook the institutions so strongly that their quick collapse suddenly became a distinct possibility. The revolutionary demands of students, combined with the frustrations of leaders of many traditional parties which the Fifth Republic had kept on the sidelines, created a situation that for a few days appeared to threaten the fabric of the new regime; and such developments must be seen against the background of the history of the country which, to say the least, has been politically volatile. Whether in the nineteenth century or in the twentieth, few prominent leaders have refrained from calling for major constitutional reform; for many, changes in the arrangement of State institutions have appeared as the panacea to cure France's evils, and De Gaulle is only one of the recent examples in a long tradition.

It is therefore difficult to be dogmatic about the longevity of institutions in a country that has known sixteen constitutions, some of which were admittedly not implemented at all or lasted barely a few years, but only one of which lasted long enough to have truly emerged with a political style. From 1789 to 1870, French political institutions seemed to follow cycles of constitutional monarchy, republic and dictatorial empire: this evolution was repeated twice, from 1789 to 1815 (when Napoleon was defeated at Waterloo) and from 1815 to 1870 (when Napoleon III, the nephew of Napoleon, resigned after his defeat in the Franco-Prussian war). From 1870 to 1940, France knew its one period of constitutional stability with the Third Republic (the First lasted a few years from 1793 to 1799, to be replaced by Napoleon and the Second from 1848 to 1851, to be replaced by Napoleon III). But the lack of cohesion of parties led to such a governmental instability in the 1930s, at a time when major economic problems and a serious external threat increased the regime's impotence, that the Third Republic ended with France's defeat in 1940, De Gaulle having blamed the French Government of the time ever since for not having left the country and fought from Algeria. Instead, powers were transferred (legally) to Pétain who ruled France dictatorially under German occupation. The Liberation of 1944 brought a return to democratic institutions under a new name and the Fourth Republic, created by referendum in 1945, saw its constitution approved in the following year, but with difficulty and after two further popular votes. But the same lack of party cohesion as in the Third Republic quickly beset the Fourth: unable to solve the Algerian problem and under the threat of military take-over, the National Assembly gave powers to De Gaulle in 1958 in a manner reminiscent of the transfer of powers to Pétain eighteen years earlier. De Gaulle did not, however, rule dictatorially: a constitution was quickly drafted and approved by the people in September of the same year by a four-to-one majority. It has already lasted longer than that of any other regime apart from the Third Republic.

Having originated in the midst of revolutionary tension and an Algiers uprising, the Fifth Republic might well suddenly collapse if, under weak leadership, some similar 'accident' occurred. For the regime to become established, two developments must take place, only one of which has hitherto, perforce perhaps, been present. Firstly, there must be enough stability and orderly transition to allow for politics to remain at a relatively low level of tension and to present unnecessary emotions from building up around the institutions, the government, or the procedures. Secondly, stability must be accepted and imposition must not have to be introduced to create an artificial predicament where otherwise chaos would take place. In the eyes of most Frenchmen, as polls have repeatedly shown, and as constitutional referendums confirmed, the case for the Fifth Republic is that of stability: unlike the previous two Republics, it has produced stable Governments; these have had fairly clear policies; and the electoral and party systems have allowed, for the first time in decades, choices to be made and decisions to be taken. But in many instances this had to be imposed, not in the ruthless dictatorial fashion which some opponents of De Gaulle, both at home and abroad, have sometimes stated that it was (De Gaulle's rule was neither dictatorial nor even authoritarian); but by using procedures and devices, by limiting the role of Parliament, by seemingly making the Constitutional Council an instrument of the executive's aims and extending its prerogative, the regime has given to many, and to many politicians in particular, a sense of daily frustration stemming from apparent impotence. Practices of previous periods may have led, as Gaullists repeatedly said, to habits of 'anarchy' which had to be corrected. But, as long as the 'correction' is imposed and new habits are not engrained, the regime runs risks. And after two decades of existence, the Fifth Republic has done more for the stability of the executive than for the genuine acceptance of the relative spheres of influence of the various institutions of the State.

A STRONG EXECUTIVE

On the surface at least, all Frenchmen agreed with De Gaulle, in the middle of the Algiers crisis, that the country lacked a strong executive. But a profound ambiguity divided the mass of the population from the dedicated Gaullists. What had made the French impatient and had worried many politicians were the repeated falls of Governments and the waste which these created. Not only was it customary, at least from the 1930s, for Prime Ministers to be replaced twice a year after repeated efforts at compromises which consumed much energy, but during their precarious existence, Cabinets felt so dependent on the will of the Assembly that they lacked leadership, initiative and often policy: survival was the main motto or, in many circumstances, the 'field' on which to fall was the extent of choice left to the Government. By having instilled cynicism at home and brought the regime into disrepute abroad, what was known as the *régime d'assemblée* was a manifest French disease which would at some point have to be cured if the country was to prosper and perhaps to survive. Few saw sufficiently clearly that parties, more than the constitution, were really at fault, as the indiscipline of deputies and the 'prima donna' attitudes of many leaders were at the root of 'assembly power'; often unaware of the real need for parties, Frenchmen looked for constitutional remedies that would miraculously give the desired stability.

De Gaulle's conception of executive strength was more exalted; it went beyond mere stability and aimed at national authority. Ever since 1940, when the President of the Third Republic refused to continue to fight and agreed to France's collapse, De Gaulle called for a leader who could, in emergencies, embody France's destiny and act as the country's steward. But, even less than governmental stability, national authority cannot be imposed by law; even if De Gaulle had been free to draft the constitution he wanted, whether back from Algiers in 1944 or at his return to power in 1958, no constitutional rule would have enabled him to implement his viewpoint. And neither in 1945 nor even in 1958 was he completely free. His exalted conception of the executive smacked of Bonapartism and even Fascism in the eyes of many, as indeed De Gaulle was often accused at the time of the RPF. When Frenchmen wanted stability, they thought of the whole executive, of the Government, of the Cabinet and Prime Minister; when De Gaulle aimed at national 'guidance', he aimed at the Presidency, which politicians had gradually weakened and which almost all concurred in seeing merely as a symbol of the nation and as a guardian of the republican idea.

Divisions run so deep that, even in the atmosphere of 1958 in which De Gaulle's authority was almost complete, neither the outgoing National Assembly allowed, nor did De Gaulle feel able to suggest a constitution where the President would have a full array of powers and would be directly elected by popular suffrage. Among the many French regimes, the one which had, in 1848, on the American model, allowed for popular presidential election, had led after only three years to Napoleon III's dictatorial take-over. Only in 1962, when De Gaulle's strength seemed assured through the Algerian settlement, when fears of his own take-over had been dissipated and politicians became more subdued, was the popular presidential election introduced by referendum in lieu of an election by local authority representatives, though the move, carried out in an improper constitutional fashion, created a major political stir. And the President, rather than impose full 'presidentialism', resolved to use the UDR to further his parliamentary strength.

The President of the Republic

It is therefore mistaken to view the President of the Fifth Republic, even at the apex of De Gaulle's prestige, as endowed with major *constitutional* strength, except in emergencies. Strictly, the Head of State, elected for seven years, remains in normal times, even since he became elected by popular suffrage, the guardian of the constitution and the arbiter of French politics. Nearly all of his powers existed in previous Republics and in particular the Third. There is nothing unusual in the fact that the President can choose the Prime Minister (though he may not dismiss him), that he can appoint Ministers on the proposal of the Prime Minister (but not others on his own), that he may ask Parliament to reconsider laws within two weeks of a final vote (but he cannot veto them), that he has to sign decrees and regulations (but they must be countersigned by Ministers), that he chairs the Council of Ministers and the High Councils of the Armed Forces, that he may send messages to the National Assembly, that he ratifies treaties and that he may pardon. There is nothing in this array of powers which gives him the leadership of the policy of the nation more than it would have given it to him under the Third Republic; and if chairing the Council of Ministers gives him the right to exercise influence, this is, by law at least, only an influence.

Where the constitution of the Fifth Republic departs significantly from previous republican regimes is in relation to four powers which deal with unusual or exceptional situations and which are given solely to the President and not to the Government. Yet three of these powers should not, at least on paper, give rise to much controversy, while the fourth is a legal attribute which the law itself can do little to implement. One of these presidential powers is the right of dissolution. Unlike most parliamentary systems, France had effectively remained, throughout the last hundred years, with no effective dissolution; and it was often suggested, during the Third Republic, that the curtailment of this right (*de facto*, because the President never dared, after a constitutional crisis which occurred in 1877, to ask permission from the Senate to dissolve the Lower House) had significantly contributed to the growth of 'Assembly power'. Yet the constitution of 1946, while introducing dissolution, had limited the conditions of its use and turned it into a very limited threat. Given to the President since 1958, but not more than once in twelve months, dissolution is scarcely a weapon which places the French President in an extraordinarily strong position. Nor are in theory at least two other powers which relate to referendums. One did not raise any controversy: it merely allows the President to dispense with a referendum, on constitutional matters, under certain conditions of procedure, and makes for speedier action on mainly technical matters. The other seemed also somewhat innocuous, as it merely gives the President the right to send some types of important laws for approval by the people; it was used twice for Algerian matters in a seemingly proper fashion, though the ambiguity (deliberate or not) of the clause made it possible for the President to send bills directly to the people *instead* of sending them to Parliament – and it was certainly assumed by most that the referendum would come *after* a parliamentary vote. But on two further occasions, both raising constitutional questions, De Gaulle used the same clause and bypassed the regular procedure to amend the constitution. In 1962, the people approved, in this form, of the election of the President by popular suffrage; but, in 1969, it effectively rejected De Gaulle by refusing to approve constitutional changes which would have affected the Senate and introduced a form of regionalism. Yet it was more the misuse of the power than its proper use which gave the President a say in policy matters; and while the threat of a referendum may help future Presidents, the actual use of the weapon has very narrow limits; of value in relation to Algeria, a problem which deeply divided the French and needed authority to be solved, it was not used, even by De Gaulle, on matters other than constitutional. It was used only once by Pompidou, in 1972, over British membership of the Common Market. It has not been used by Giscard.

We are thus left with one power, which, though forgotten gradually in the course of the 1960s, gave rise to considerable controversy at the time when the constitution was drafted but proved of little use when it was invoked by De Gaulle. This once famous article 16 of the French constitution decides, directly under De Gaulle's inspiration, that in time of emergency and specifically

> . . . when the institutions of the Republic, the independence of the nation, the integrity of its territory or the fulfilment of its international obligations are threatened in a grave and immediate manner, and when the regular functioning of the constitutional governmental authorities is interrupted, the President of the Republic shall take the measures commanded by the circumstances, after official consultation with the Premier, the Presidents of the Assemblies and the Constitutional Council.

This was the 'power' which, according to De Gaulle and his supporters, would enable the President of the Republic in future and dire circumstances to avoid the precedent of 1940 and to save at least the nation's honour. Unfortunately, not only was the clause limited by further clauses which stated that, in such circumstances 'Parliament would meet as of right' – a concession which De Gaulle had to make to those who claimed that such a power given to the President would be tantamount to legal dictatorship – but the very idea that it is possible both to legislate for emergencies and to legislate to give Presidents of the Republic 'moral fibre' or 'national authority' is somewhat legalistic, to say the least. Nothing except the lack of desire to do so prevented the last President of the Third Republic from doing what the Belgian Government or the Dutch Queen and Government did during the Second World War; indeed, the Belgian Government left for England while the king remained in Belgium. What simply happened was that the President of the French Republic chose not to exercise leadership, that the Government collapsed and that practically all the politicians were convinced that Nazi Germany would win the war. Article 16 cannot legislate to prevent such attitudes from developing. Nor does the clause appear more satisfactory in somewhat less extreme types of emergencies, as was indeed shown when De Gaulle chose to use it after an attempted *putsch* by four generals in Algiers in 1961. If and when the constitutional authorities do not collapse, except in some part of the territory, the measures which the President may take have then still to be channelled through the regular authorities; moreover, when article 16 ceases to be invoked, the question of the fate of the measures taken becomes a source of legal entanglements, as was shown by the problems raised by the creation of a special court set up in 1961 to try those who had been responsible for the Algiers military *putsch*. It may be argued that the use of article 16 was improper at the time, since there was a threat, but no interruption of the regular authorities; but if this is the case, it is unclear under what circumstances the clause can help, except perhaps to remind timid and vacillating Presidents that they have a duty to endeavour to save the nation when a full-scale calamity has occurred.

The Government

The real powers of the presidency do not stem from the constitution as such: they come almost entirely from the practice which under the first three Presidents of the Fifth Republic (De Gaulle, 1958–69; Pompidou, 1969–74; Giscard, 1974–81)[1] led to a symbiosis between President and Government and to what might be termed a 'duumvirate' between President and Prime Minister. In order to understand this practice, we need, however, to look first at the powers and position of the Government as a whole.

[1] De Gaulle was elected for a first term of seven years in 1958; he was re-elected in 1965, but resigned before his term ended in 1969, the French people having voted No to a referendum on regionalism which De Gaulle strongly supported; Pompidou was elected in 1969 for seven years but he died in office in 1974.

The constitution circumscribes fairly narrowly the powers of the President outside emergencies: it is clearly not valid to state that the 'executive branch', to use the American expression, is in the President's hands. Indeed, as if to reinforce this point positively, the constitution states: 'The Government shall determine and direct the policy of the nation. It shall have at its disposal the administration and the armed forces.' And: 'The Prime Minister shall direct the operation of the Government. He shall be responsible for national defence. He shall ensure the execution of the laws.' It is the Government, under the leadership of the Prime Minister, which is responsible for the conduct of the affairs of the nation. Almost certainly, De Gaulle's first choice might have been different, had he been free to draft 'his' own constitution. But there the constitution stands. While reinforcing the powers of the President at the edges and while bowing to De Gaulle's desire to strengthen the President in time of highly unusual emergencies, the framers of the constitution effectively maintained the tradition of collective governmental action while attempting to increase, but only in a limited fashion, the powers of the Prime Minister.

The leadership of the Prime Minister stems from the fact that he nominates the Ministers to the President and asks the President to terminate their functions. But his own authority is constitutionally independent from that of the President, as he owes his power to the continued confidence of the National Assembly and can put his Government in the balance after deliberation of the Council of Ministers. Though with limitations which we shall consider in the next subsection, the basis of the system is parliamentary and the limitations are aimed, not at enhancing the power and influence of the President, but the power and influence of the Government and Prime Minister. Only in one respect is the practice of most parliamentary systems not followed: at De Gaulle's specific instigation, it was decided to insert a clause stating that Ministers would have to resign their seats in Parliament on joining the Government. This was held to be a means of preventing deputies from wanting to overthrow Governments merely to become Ministers, as the penalty was in effect exclusion from the Chamber for a term; but this clause has for all intents and purposes been bypassed as it is becoming increasingly the practice for outgoing Ministers to find a deputy willing to resign to allow the Minister to return to Parliament.

Thus the constitution firmly establishes the Government as the executive and the authority of the Government and Prime Minister has to come from the Chamber, not from the President. This is in practice why De Gaulle had to make sure that the majority of the National Assembly was loyal to his policies and the development of the disciplined Gaullist party is thus a direct consequence of the existence of a parliamentary system. Given a conflict between President and Government, the President's only constitutional recourse is to appeal to the people (but only once) and, if defeated, to appoint a Premier who has the confidence of the Assembly. This might not prevent him from trying to manipulate parties and party leaders, as was indeed done in the Third and Fourth Republics. But a constitutional crisis would be opened (as was the case in 1877) if the President were to try to impose a Government and Prime Minister on an unwilling Assembly.

De Gaulle's strength (and his successors' strength) in the reality of policy-making lay therefore in the confidence of the majority of the Assembly, in the authority of the President which happens to be in practice greater than that of the Prime Minister: this is why he can really choose the Prime Minister and discuss with the Prime Minister the composition of the Cabinet. This enabled De Gaulle to be the effective decision-maker in at least two main fields, defence and foreign affairs (as well as, for as long as the problem arose, Algeria and the French Community). Given that De Gaulle's Prime Ministers, Debré, Pompidou and Couve de Murville, were willing to allow the President an area or areas of special interest (the 'presidential sphere' as Pompidou's first Prime Minister, Chaban-Delmas, stated in 1959), it became possible for a direct relationship to be established between President and Foreign Minister, and between President and Defence Minister. In fact, the area of intervention which characterized De Gaulle's presidency did extend further, and, depending on the urgency of the matter or the current interests of the President (as with the idea of workers' participation), the influence of the Elysée Palace was felt more or less markedly. For this purpose, De Gaulle surrounded himself with a large presidential secretariat which paralleled the secretariat of the Prime Minister and intervened in those matters for which the President happened to care particularly at a given moment, while they operated as watchdogs exercising constant surveillance on activities of all the Ministries. It even became suggested for a time that De Gaulle was attempting to dismantle the Cabinet altogether, not only through the considerable influence which he exercised at meetings, but also by seeing that civil servants were appointed to the Cabinet (about a third of the total) and by the creation of a number of committees composed of Ministers and higher civil servants which took decisions and bypassed the Cabinet. But this last practice slowly faded out, perhaps because economic and social questions became increasingly serious and De Gaulle remained always much less at ease in relation to these matters. Indeed, although De Gaulle's successors, Pompidou and Giscard, displayed greater interest in home affairs than De Gaulle and were less concerned in pursuing (or less able to pursue) an active foreign policy, the Government as a whole increased its strength, and the authority of the Prime Minister over his Ministers as co-ordinator and indeed leader has been markedly enhanced.

The practice of the new system thus led to the emergence of a form of dual leadership between President and Prime Minister which is both interesting *per se* and seemingly somewhat transitional. The very possibility of such a dual leadership hinges upon the recognition by the Prime Minister that he is mainly responsible for the policy of the nation and yet acts within the framework of authority which the President imparts upon him. The mechanism is complex, almost unique in contemporary western democracies, though it is spreading elsewhere. But it is also well suited to the transitional period which French politics underwent after 1958.

As we noted in our examination of the party system, and in particular in our assessment of the characteristics of the UDR in contrast to traditional parties of the Right, French political institutions needed new mechanisms able to develop stable patterns of leadership. In a cunning fashion, De Gaulle saw that, whatever the constitutional powers given to the President, a popular election would give the Head of State some of the needed authority. Meanwhile, as we also noted, active members and parliamentarians of the UDR came to accept that the function of the President was to provide the country with a strong Government able to govern. The special relationship between President and Prime Minister stems from these developments. Contrary to what was often believed in the early years of the regime, the Prime Minister is not merely an 'assistant' to the President: he directs the policy of the nation, though the President always played a major part in foreign affairs. The President does indeed need the Prime Minister because the President has to show the nation that the nation is governed. Thus the Prime Minister can count on the President if he has to establish his authority over Ministers and backbenchers of the majority parties.

Yet these arrangements have already undergone some strain since 1974; they have an even more uncertain future. The strain has been apparent after the election of Giscard in 1974 since, as we saw, the new President belonged to the 'governmental majority' but not to the Gaullist Party. Although Giscard appointed Chirac (who had been his main supporter in the Gaullist Party) as Prime Minister in 1974, the relationship became uneasy on a variety of issues and, perhaps more importantly, with respect to political style: the President dismissed his Prime Minister in 1976 and appointed a non-party man with strong leanings towards the President, Raymond Barre, to head the Government. It seemed that a smooth relationship between President and Prime Minister could not easily be maintained in the current conception of the two offices if their holders were not politically close.

Hence the uncertain future of the arrangement: despite considerable discussion in political circles, what would happen if President and Parliament were to clash over the composition of the Government and over the Prime Minister is far from clear. Both before the 1973 and 1978 elections, when the possibility – indeed the probability – of the victory of the Left seemed high, various alternative models were suggested. Pompidou had remained silent in 1973 as to what he would have done; Giscard said categorically in 1978 that he would appoint a Socialist Prime Minister if the parties of the Left won the election; but he also strongly urged the French not to vote for the Left. Had the Socialist–Communist alliance become the new majority, the relationship between President and Government would clearly have been strained and the Presidency as it has been known since 1958 would have had to change its character. In the long run (unless one assumes that by some strange historical accident presidents and parliaments will always be in accord, despite the fact that they are not elected in the same way or at the same time) the semi-presidential system which De Gaulle gave France in 1958 will have to be altered and a more traditional parliamentary regime will probably develop. Yet this transitional 'dualism' did help the country to achieve, for the first time in decades, stable government in a liberal context.

A SYSTEM OF LIMITED CHECKS

Given that the Fifth Republic establishes a Government which needs the confidence of the Assembly to survive, the maintenance of a stable Government is linked necessarily, at least as far as the constitution is concerned, to the setting-up of a number of devices which are designed to limit the ability, and if possible the propensity, of Parliament to overthrow and harass Governments. We noted already one of these devices, that of the interdiction made to Ministers to remain in Parliament, though its effectiveness has been questioned from the start. Several other pieces of 'constitutional engineering' are scattered throughout the constitution of 1958, though their effectiveness is also of some doubt.

The Régime d'Assemblée Before 1958

To understand both the overall reason and the detailed justifications for the introduction of a whole series of dams designed to stop encroachments by the Assembly, it is essential to appreciate the extent to which French Governments were subjected, and unquestionably exaggeratedly subjected, to Assembly pressure. Because of a fear of dictatorial or authoritarian executives, of which there have been a number throughout recent French history, but also because of the sectional attitudes which characterized French deputies, the Chamber of Deputies of the Third Republic, followed by the National Assembly of the Fourth, took upon themselves to exercise a very detailed and supercilious scrutiny of the legislation presented by the Governments and manifested almost no self-control over their own passionate outbursts in relation to nearly every aspect of governmental policy. In relation to legislation, the Lower House (as well as the Upper House) developed a highly intricate committee system, comparable to that of the American congress, to which all bills, governmental or coming from private members, had to go before being discussed on the floor. In these committees, bills were sometimes wholly rejected and often amended to a considerable extent; they then went to the whole Assembly in the shape that the committee wished and only after the Government had either made concessions or had exerted considerable pressure. Justifications on grounds of scrutiny were often covering the ambitions of individual deputies specializing in particular matters or originating from given areas, as was particularly the case with the notorious Committee on Beverages. Specifically, the ambitions of committee chairmen played a considerable part, as the passage of a piece of Governmental legislation often became the subject of a personal feud between Minister and committee Chairman, the latter hoping to become the Minister after the Cabinet's fall. While, in Great Britain, debates have typically tended to oppose Ministers and Shadow Ministers, the equivalent function was fulfilled in the French Assembly by debates between Ministers and committee Chairmen – but the latter, and not the former, were likely to have the confidence of the Assembly, at least as long as they did not in turn become Ministers.

While debates relating to legislation were thus major obstacles for the Governments, Ministers having often to bring back clauses which had been deleted in committee and as a result of which the bill had been markedly altered, a further series of hurdles was provided by the *interpellation* procedure: these were debates, often springing up suddenly, on any matter of policy which the Assembly cared to choose. They were particularly dangerous because, though ostensibly created to prevent the Government from engaging in policies behind the back of the Chamber, they often concerned matters of limited importance, were essentially negative in character and, by springing up suddenly, had the natural effect of completely upsetting the legislative timetable. Admittedly, *interpellations* took place only if the *Bureau* of the Assembly had agreed to them and, in the last resort, if the Assembly itself wished to debate them. But a form of solidarity between deputies tended to prevail, particularly as it became the practice for several *interpellations* to be 'blocked' together, a device which, instead of saving time, had the effect of increasing the potential opposition. As Governments could not count on the loyalty of all of their followers, given the nature of the party system which we examined earlier, the fear of *interpellations* forced Ministers and particularly Prime Ministers to forget substantive policies and to concentrate on tactics. Tension developed in the 'house without windows' which the French Assembly was, deputies seemingly believing that the world would cease to move and home affairs would lose importance as Governments were repeatedly challenged in the Palais Bourbon. What had started as an instrument of scrutiny of the 'general policy' of the Government had turned into a vicious technique which demoralized Ministers, reduced them to impotence and turned politics into a series of elaborate chess moves.

Ironically at first sight, but logically as a result, the time consumed by the French National Assembly on these manoeuvrings (as well as the physical harassment arising from prolonged night sittings) led to a decrease in the amount of real policy control by the people's representatives. The strength of the civil service, which we shall consider in the next section, stems in part from this failure. But the practical necessities of government became so compelling, and indeed the unpopularity of the measures called for became so troublesome that, from the 1920s, the French Parliament agreed increasingly to grant 'full powers' to those very Governments which it was harassing daily. In the last few years of the Third Republic, every new Government was given 'decree-law'-making powers at the time of its investiture, but these were then trimmed, squeezed or annihilated after a few months had elapsed and the Government was soon forced to resign through these contradictions. The abandonment of traditional legislative powers by the Chamber appeared so shocking that it was held responsible for the demise of the Republic in 1940; the constitution of 1946 attempted to prevent the return of such practices; but the behaviour of the Assembly remaining after 1945 what it was in the 1930s, 'outline laws' became once more the practice, while delays in the votes of estimates and the budget made it also necessary to vote 'provisional twelfths' for one, two or three months.

The Organization of Parliament in the Fifth Republic

The strength and stability of the executive thus seemed to require that Parliament be streamlined and its powers reduced on a scale which could not have been envisaged in the climate of the Fourth Republic. But, in doing so, the constitution-makers of the Fifth Republic might multiply interdictions and thus alienate even the supporters of the regime and encourage a *de facto* bypassing of the rules. Some of the arrangements of the new system have indeed come dangerously close to having a boomerang effect. Only the authority of De Gaulle over his new party prevented wholesale rebellions; and some of the discontent of 1968 can be attributed directly to the delayed effects of pressures on Parliament.

The Parliament of the Fifth Republic is composed, as that of the previous two Republics, of two Chambers, a National Assembly of about 500 deputies elected for five years (unless dissolved) by universal direct suffrage and a Senate of about 300 elected for nine years by local authority representatives on the basis of a complex formula, one-third of the senators retiring every three years. The election of the Senate by local authority representatives has been customary since the early years of the Third Republic, and the Upper Chamber was sometimes nicknamed the 'grand council of French communes'. Despite some changes, the Senate over-represented consistently the rural areas at the expense of towns so that both Communists and Gaullists are markedly under-represented. Throughout the Fifth Republic, the Senate became dominated by traditional Conservatives, Socialists and members of the Centre parties; it was thus a focus of opposition to De Gaulle; this explains why the President of the Senate was an opposition leader and why De Gaulle, whose 1962 referendum on the popular election of the President was attacked as unconstitutional by the then President of the

Senate, attempted unsuccessfully in 1969 to demote the Upper House. But this was not forecast in 1958 and the constitution did increase marginally the powers of the Senate, though ultimate decisions on legislation and the censure of the Government were left to the Lower House.

It is common to exaggerate the extent to which the Parliament of the Fifth Republic has become a rubber stamp, as comparisons tend to be made, not with Parliaments of other western European countries, but with the Parliaments of the Third and Fourth Republics. In reality, except in two, admittedly very important, respects, the legal restrictions placed on the French Parliament are no more serious than the restrictions placed, in fact, on the Parliaments of other countries. For instance, a clause of the constitution provides for the election of the President of the Assembly for the whole of the Parliament and thereby limits unnecessary disputes taking place every year. Others state that Government bills shall have priority, that they shall come to the floor of the Assembly on the basis of the text presented by the Government (and not disfigured as they used to be in committee), that the Government shall have the right to close the debate (by asking for a vote on the whole bill), that the Government shall have the right to ask for a power to legislate by ordinance for a limited period (as was previously the practice) but that these shall have to be ratified by Parliament at the end of the period stated, that deputies shall not be allowed to initiate measures designed to increase expenditure or decrease revenue and that the budget shall have to be voted within seventy days of it being tabled. Somewhat more dubiously, though, judging by British practice, not wholly without precedent abroad, a clause limits to six the number of standing committees. Finally, in order to reduce harassment, Parliament's total sittings are reduced to six months, instead of the usual nine, though extraordinary sessions can of course be called; but De Gaulle's interpretation of this power was so restrictive that only the Government seems still to have this right.

The two main new limitations which, though perhaps justifiable, are of doubtful psychological value and may thus cause a boomerang effect relate to the definition of the scope of legislation and to the technical conditions for the motion of censure. Determined to avoid encroachments by the Assembly in executive matters, and hoping thereby to reduce the scope for parliamentary guerrilla warfare, the constitution-makers introduced a long article 34 which purports to define the scope of legislation, which is passed by Parliament, and states that matters not mentioned in the list are in the executive's prerogative. Yet, as the article allows for changes, which is realistic, a belligerent Assembly could once more extend its role. Moreover, provisions are vague in that they distinguish between matters 'determined' by the law and those in which only 'fundamental principles' are to be decided by Parliament: the clause itself does not define what these 'principles' are; the scope for argument and conflict can once more become wide. Though adjudication of these matters, as on many questions relating to Parliament, is given to a Constitutional Council, the safeguard is incomplete: the Council may become increasingly inclined to give way to the Assembly's demands and its composition need not necessarily lead, as we shall see, to governmental supremacy.

While the restriction on the scope of legislation may be somewhat ineffective and does not seem to have affected the situation to a considerable extent, the limitations imposed on the motion of censure are unnecessarily stringent and would become intolerable if the procedure were frequently to be used. Admittedly, less drastic attempts made in 1946 to reduce the excesses of the *interpellation* technique had proved ineffective. Though the Fourth Republic Constitution stated not only that time had to elapse between the tabling of a censure motion and the voting on that motion but that an absolute majority was necessary for the motion to be carried, Governments resigned none the less, because they felt they did not have the confidence of the Assembly, or because their bills were defeated, even if these were only the result of minority votes. Thus the drafters of the 1958 constitution had to go further and they had to prevent the Government from even knowing the number of their followers, and they thus stipulated that only those favouring the censure would register their vote while supporters of the Government would be required to abstain. Thus abstainers would be effectively counted as being in the Government's camp. Such a negative system of support might have the advantage of maintaining Cabinets against freak oppositions, but an undue use of the technique would soon bring it into disrepute. If Governments did have unstable majorities and if, as a result, they were to table repeatedly such questions of 'confidence', the mechanism would soon appear unjust and cowardly. It is in fact because Governments of the Fifth Republic, generally sure of the result, have sparingly used the method to show the opposition's weakness that little capital has been made against this bizarre piece of procedure.

The Executive and the Balance of Powers

Even under De Gaulle, the institutional devices provided by the constitution to prevent parliamentary outbursts from overthrowing Governments have not often been used, and yet the Government sometimes came dangerously close to creating profound antipathy. In the summer of 1967, the use of ordinances to change social security arrangements created considerable opposition in the country and in Parliament and contributed in some part to the revolutionary mood of the following spring. Little effort has been made to debate foreign policy and defence matters and an analysis of parliamentary debates shows too much time devoted to secondary legislation by contrast with essential policy. Yet there have been enough cases in which the Government and the Prime Minister showed attention to the Assembly (though not to the Senate) to prevent the Lower House from living in permanent tension, particularly from the middle of the 1960s. By blandishments of individual deputies (often appointed as Ministers at the right period), by agreeing to amendments presented by others than the Government party supporters, by putting Government supporters, individually or in study groups, in the confidence of the Government, the second Prime Minister of the Fifth Republic did much to restore a confidence between Government and Parliament which had been much reduced during the early years of the Fifth Republic.

Indeed, as in many other aspects of the Fifth Republic, changes are gradually giving Parliament a new position and parliamentarians are gradually acquiring a new role. For a long period, the Parliament of the Fifth Republic was compared very unfavourably to that of the Fourth Republic. But too much emphasis was placed in these comparisons on the one real power of the National Assembly before 1958, that of overthrowing governments; too little stress was placed on the negative character of such a power: the fact was that the Assembly blocked legislation but was never able to initiate programmes or even pass laws of real significance.

In the early years of the Fifth Republic, many deputies were new, unsure of their role and markedly affected by the superior authority of the President. Parliament was not 'institutionalized' in the true sense of the word. New customs and new functions had to be elaborated; if Parliament was not to overthrow Governments, it seemed for a while that it could only be a rubber stamp of governmental decisions. Only with the passage of time could the new functions be gradually recognized. Like the British Parliament, the French Parliament could become increasingly a place where Government and Opposition debate in front of public opinion, where new ideas are aired and where the administrative machine is criticized. But these developments would only occur once members of Parliament dissociate the function of criticism from the desire to overthrow Governments and thus turn their back on what had been the main characteristic of French parliamentary life for generations.

The change is gradually taking place. It is true that the function of debate is still not developed enough, particularly in the fields of foreign affairs and defence where the Government has kept the upper hand. But in many other fields, parliamentary activity has prompted governmental action in subsequent periods, while occasional rebellions of the rank-and-file of the Government party have forced the Government to reconsider some aspects of its legislative programme. The Chambers of 1958 and 1962 marked the trial runs of the new 'generation' of French deputies: the 1970s are a period of transformation where the bulk of the deputies, not having known the Fourth Republic at first hand, and no longer obsessed by the desire to see a return of their former opportunities to practise the *gouvernement d'assemblée*, have come to settle for a different, less dramatic, but probably more useful activity – that of helping to introduce different viewpoints into the administrative machine and of deflecting, but not upsetting, the course of governmental action.

The constitutional devices provided by the Constitution may therefore be less important in the long run if deputies and indeed the Government agree on a *modus vivendi* by which the Government's right to initiate is recognized, while that of Parliament to criticize, air grievances and modify programmes is also accepted. For this view of politics to be fully accepted by all, more is required than constitutional arrangements limiting the powers of Parliament over legislation and over the motion of censure: the attitudes of men have to be changed. This cannot happen unless parties remain disciplined in the future as they have been since 1958. With the decline of the Gaullist Party since 1973, the danger of a return to sectionalism has also returned. The election of Giscard in 1974 clearly helped to maintain discipline and loyalty to the President among the non-Gaullist segments of the Centre and Right, while Gaullist Party members, imbued with the basic belief in the need to support the Presidency in the last resort, found it distasteful to split the majority. But there is, once more, potential for sectionalism and for the consequential erosion of Government majorities. If this were to increase, the dams set up by the constitution would soon give way; the Government would have to resort to the more drastic procedures and its position would appear increasingly weaker: committees would begin to reassert their power, closure of debate would be difficult, and the motion of censure would soon raise an outcry. Nor would the Constitutional Council itself provide a fool-proof protection, at least for very long: composed of nine members, three of whom are appointed by the President of the Republic and three each by the Presidents of the National Assembly and of the Senate, the Constitutional Council would soon reflect changes in the power position. Thus the interpretation of the constitution might become more tilted towards the Assembly: standing orders would be considered with less care and the scope of the law would once more be enlarged.

As has been noted for other constitutions, procedural engineering can redress only to an extent the customs and habits of members of Governments and Parliaments. The constitution of the Fifth Republic has been moderately successful only inasmuch as it has not really been put to the test, though it did benefit from the start from broad support among the French, from the new personnel which came with the Gaullist party and from a feeling among other deputies that previous practices had clearly brought the regime into disrepute and the liberal system very near total collapse. As these original feelings gradually die out, only a stabilization of the party system coupled with the elimination of some of the more objectionable clauses of the constitution can help to maintain the new edifice on a firm and permanent basis. The balance between Government and Parliament depends on these conditions. Only then will the constitution be accorded the respect which a constitution needs to survive and which no French constitution obtained since 1789 (except and only for a time that of the Third Republic). Social change brought about some alterations in the party system; the temporary dominance of the Gaullist Party gave the Constitution of 1958 a better start than that of 1946, which had been immediately and summarily condemned by the combined and often brutal attacks of Gaullists and Communists. But only one French Constitution has lasted more than a generation: great skill will have to be displayed if there is not to be once more impatience about the institutions and a desire, however unrealistic, to start a new regime afresh rather than reform gradually that of 1958.

An Administrative State?

It has often been noted that governmental instability was of little importance in a country such as France in which the strength and influence of the civil service appeared overwhelming. Depending on the standpoint chosen, this situation has been praised or deplored, but rarely denied. The Fifth Republic has appeared to some to have merely made this process official by bringing into the Government, as we noted earlier, a number of civil servants. Dating back at least from the seventeenth century, perfected by Napoleon, the administrative organization has remained, without major change, throughout the many regimes, used by kings and emperors alike and kept sometimes uneasily by republican Governments often too weak to engage in major reorganizations. Indeed, the French administrative structures, both centralized and extending their tentacles throughout the provinces, served as the instruments by which new Governments, including under the Republics, sought to protect themselves against those who threatened the regime: until recently at least, no regime was established enough to enable those in power to dispense with this help.

Administrative centralization did not merely give Governments a means to maintain law and order, however. From its origins, the French civil service was heavily technical in character: it built roads, developed industry, improved rural life. The French monarchy was *dirigiste* and considered as one of its main tasks to guide and lead the economy; it practised a form of 'enlightened despotism' which gave a sense of mission to the civil service and fostered an *esprit de corps*. By desire or necessity, Napoleon further expanded the service to serve the many new purposes of the enlarged Empire. Thus the French civil service developed its engineering activities and supervised commerce and industry on a renewed basis, and despite the economic liberalism prevailing in later decades, the French State continued to intervene on a scale unknown in other Western countries. From this stem the origins of modern French planning which, as one of the manifestations of French administrative inventiveness, has acquired at least perhaps more prestige abroad than it did in France itself.

The impact of the civil service on the life of the nation is thus probably greater than in other developed countries; it is deep and far-reaching. It has thus naturally been charged from time to time with having stifled initiative and being instrumental in the overdevelopment of Paris against the provinces. The lack of real autonomy of the small towns and villages, the centralized development of education and other social services have increasingly come to be questioned. Yet changes in the last twenty years have generally proved limited and patchy and stopped short of real reform. For some, the structure of the civil service is so rigid and so all-embracing that nothing short of revolution will free the society. Such a radical change is hard to imagine; but changes will have to come, and they will require a capital of political strength that even the Fifth Republic has not proved able to muster at the heyday of De Gaulle's power.

THE STRENGTHS AND SKILLS OF THE CIVIL SERVICE

The French civil service occupies a vastly more important position in the French nation than in other Western countries. Indeed, the position which the service occupied in the past was perhaps even more important than that of its counterparts abroad. The difference is due in part to the size of the service, which reached 200,000 a century ago, about four times that of the British civil service of the time. In the 1970s, with about a million members, the French civil service is proportionately twice as large as the British.

Size alone does not explain the weight of the service and its vast international reputation, however. Indeed, size is in turn partly explained by the fact that in France the civil service undertakes many activities which are the province of local government in other liberal democracies: teachers are State civil servants in France, for instance. But the real influence of the service stems even more from the combination of three factors which are embedded in the structure of the French bureaucracy. First, the service provides some of the best training which the nation can supply: élite schools help to staff the *grands corps*, or prestigious branches of the service which are concerned with the various aspects of policy-making. Second, heavy emphasis is placed on technical corps; the civil service includes some of the best engineers of the nation and these technicians are in a position to realize many of their dreams in the general context of an administrative culture in which there is belief in State action and State enterprise. Third, civil servants are posted throughout the country and can therefore influence local authorities and even private business on a scale rarely reached in other Western European countries.

The posting of large numbers of civil servants in the provinces has long been a characteristic of the French bureaucracy: the idea is that it should be close to the *administrés*. Practically all the departments are divided into central services, located in Paris, and external services, which can be found not only in main towns, but, for a number of departments at least, in literally hundreds of small urban areas. This has been of course particularly true of the Ministry of the Interior, which is in charge of the supervision of local authorities and of the maintenance of law and order, a role which, in France, has always been in part a State function and is delegated to a network of prefects and sub-prefects. But prefects, as we shall see, are also in charge of the executive branch of the *département* which is the upper-tier local authority; thus they have an ambivalent position which manifests the centralization imposed by Napoleon soon after the *départements* were created by the Revolution in 1789. Below the prefects and sub-prefects, civil servants extend the Ministry of the Interior's administrative presence in the provinces while, socially, the prefecture constitutes, or at least constituted for a long time, the centre and focus of the activities of many provincial towns. In the nineteenth century at least, the *Bal de la Préfecture* was an event to which the local bourgeoisie wanted to be invited. Social hierarchy is thus in part determined by and around prefects. The importance of the State and of the State civil service in the provinces is reinforced as a result.

Apart from the prefect and his administrators, representatives of nearly all the Ministries are posted in the *département*. In theory at least, these representatives are hierarchically subordinated to the prefect, who is deemed to be the head of all State services; in fact officials of the Ministry of Transport, of the Ministry of Agriculture, of the Ministry of Equipment or of the Ministry of National Education have become increasingly independent from the prefect and have direct lines of communication with the central services in Paris. They are also in direct contact with local authorities and local business, whether their function is to promote new industry, to build roads (most roads are in fact built by the Service des Ponts et Chaussées even though they are built in the name of local authorities), whether they are engaged in rural engineering or are State educators (teaching is a State function and all public school teachers are appointed and paid by the State, even though much school-building is a local-authority matter). Complex networks of vertical relationships are thus established between Paris and the smallest local authorities through civil servants, some of whom spend all their life in one *département*, but many of whom go to the provinces during their first years of civil-service life and move after a period to the Paris central services. As a result the presence of the civil service is felt physically by many in the provinces, while large numbers of civil servants acquire a real knowledge of provincial France, even though their ideal may be, as is that of many Frenchmen, to remain in Paris for the rest of their life. As this has been a long-standing practice, the civil service never really became divorced from the nation and isolated in an ivory tower; it has also provided a channel for upward mobility for many sons of peasants and lower-middle-class employees, if not perhaps as commonly for manual workers. Respect tainted with jealousy has thus been one of the main attitudes of Frenchmen towards those who belong to this large network and appear to share a segment of the power of the State.

Such a respect would not have developed locally, and *a fortiori* in Paris and abroad, if the civil service had not been renowned for its technical skill, traditionally in the fields of civil engineering, rural engineering, mining and increasingly in the field of economic planning and, though less so, in town and country planning. This, too, developed under Napoleon, but the origins can be traced back at least to the seventeenth century; the Corps des Ponts et Chaussées (Roads and Bridges) was created in the middle of the eighteenth century. The tradition of French *dirigisme* centred on the civil service stems in large part from the widely held belief that, unless the State intervenes, private business would not display enough entrepreneurial skills and would probably not acquire the knowhow nor amass the capital required to engage in the major industrial efforts needed to develop the nation. The theory of *laissez faire* never had profound roots in the country: the basic philosophy of the French bureaucracy and of a large section of the political and social élite always was more akin to the ideology which prevails in contemporary developing states. In the seventeenth and eighteenth centuries, the stress was on road-building, on drainage, on agricultural works; it was also on commercial and industrial undertakings, partly geared towards exports, as with china at Sèvres and tapestry at the Gobelins. Napoleon merely used and expanded an already existing base, partly as a result of the economic blockade which resulted from the European wars. The idea was then kept alive throughout the nineteenth century by the Saint-Simoniens, whose social philosophy was based on 'technocracy' – that is to say on the management and development of the State through the influence, not of elected representatives, but of men trained in the technical skills needed to solve economic and social problems.

This is why the role of technicians in the civil service is tied to the problem of training: since the State was to have a mission of initiative, the State was to ensure that its servants were better equipped than the rest of the nation. It was up to the State to create and maintain schools able to provide young men with the skills which were required. The oldest and in many ways most prestigious school is the École Polytechnique, which was founded in 1794 and moved increasingly away from its original function of training of artillery and engineering officers to that of preparing civil servants for technical services, particularly in the fields of road building, civil engineering and mining.

Gradually, the idea spread outside the technical fields, however, and the civil service created other schools for younger civil servants, in almost all aspects of government, though only in 1945 was a general school for administrators, the École Nationale d'Administration (ENA) constituted as a replica for administrators to the École Polytechnique. The younger men who staff the higher positions in the administrative parts of the civil (and foreign) service are trained in this school. With their emphasis on a very stringent academic record, these *grandes écoles* have contributed to a form of meritocracy which is increasingly challenged by the younger generation, but which has both contributed to upward social mobility and to intellectual and technical excellence in many parts of the service.

It has also accounted for the development of professionalism throughout the nation as well as contributed to the influence of the civil service in many walks of life. The meritocracy produced by the civil-service schools led to a sharp cleavage within the civil service between the top elements who belong to the *grands corps* and the rest of the service. Prefects, inspectors of finance, members of the Conseil d'État – the highest administrative court in the land as we shall see – members of the Court of Accounts, engineers of roads and bridges, and mining engineers are 'starred' by the civil service; they are hailed as the most brilliant members of their generation. As a result, big business began to look for many of its recruits and top executives among civil servants belonging to these corps. The process by which civil servants, sometimes at an early age, though more often in their thirties and forties, leave the service to join business is thus very common (so much so that the word *pantouflage* has been coined colloquially to indicate this process), but it gives the civil service a key role in the formation of the nation's élites. Many leaders of the economy have been through civil-service schools; they therefore often know each other well; they have acquired ideas in common and share a common outlook on life, though, in France as elsewhere, ex-civil servants who go into business complain about the civil service and joke about its character. This also contributed to lower the age at which French civil servants are in responsible positions: directors and directors-general of many Ministries (the highest civil service posts in the hierarchy) are often in their forties and then leave the service to lead large private businesses or nationalized industries.

The civil service, particularly through its *grands corps*, acts therefore in ways similar to public schools and Oxbridge colleges in the British élite formation system. But, in contrast with the more amateurish characteristics of British civil servants and indeed businessmen, French civil servants and businessmen have often a technical background and believe in professional training. Technicians play a role in the French civil service which is strikingly larger than in other countries. From technical training in a narrow sense, the emphasis on professionalism spread naturally to the administration at large, to economic management, to the social sciences. In the early part of the nineteenth century, some Frenchmen, often attached to or stemming from the École Polytechnique, developed ideas of social engineering which, under the label of saint-simonisme, had a wide impact on attitudes if not always on actions. Not surprisingly, economic and social planning developed as a result more easily in France than in other countries; not surprisingly, too, the civil service was in France at the centre of most economic development.

The French civil service is headed by a skilled bureaucracy; it pervades all walks of life; it moulds the nation. But the very success of the service has come into conflict with the principles of liberal democracy on which the nation is also based. For a very long time, the two principles survived uneasily side by side: the instability of Governments made the reliance on the civil service necessary; the relative weakness of private business and the relative backwardness of agriculture also justified the role of the bureaucracy. But the increased role of groups and the greater stability of the Government in the 1960s are now combining to precipitate the clash between the principle of technocracy embodied in the civil service and the principles of democracy and representative government. In the civil service itself, and among members of the *grands corps* in particular, there is growing unease about the position of the bureaucracy in the nation. The new mottos being 'participation' and 'consultation', it becomes increasingly difficult to justify the way in which the service can take decisions without being, in some way, 'responsible' to the nation. It is true that the service has a sense of mission; but it is also true that, in the context of the last decades of the twentieth century, demands from the many publics challenge the right of the civil service to 'know better' than the citizen what the nation should do. The nation owed in large part to the civil service its economic development during the post-war period; but some of the social troubles – including the 1968 troubles – can also be ascribed to the elevated position of the civil service. On the ability of the bureaucracy to combine its tradition of technical excellence with current desires for greater participation depends to a large extent the future wellbeing and social stability of the nation.

WEAK AND SOMEWHAT PASSIVE LOCAL AUTHORITIES

In contrast with the dynamic attitudes of the higher civil service and with its desire to mould the nation, local government has traditionally been weak, divided as it is in a multitude of very small units lacking money and human resources to put forward major plans and implement them. Cynics might suggest that this was deliberate policy of the civil service and Government and that little effort was made to force local authorities out of their parochialism, as the situation suited the expansionist desires of the higher administrators and indeed gave jobs to many younger civil servants having to work in the field. The reasons are of course complex, but it cannot easily be sustained rationally that 38,000 lower-tier authorities (the *communes*), with an average population of little over a thousand if large cities are excluded, constitute an efficient means of managing local services and that these bodies can have much scope for genuine autonomy.

On paper at least, these communes have far-reaching powers, though they are in many cases subjected to the supervision of the prefect or sub-prefect. They were created by the Revolution (on the basis of old villages), but the election of mayors and municipal councils was only finally established in the 1830s and powers were granted on a general basis by an Act of 1884 which decided that the municipal council was 'in charge of the affairs of the commune'. For a small village, this means typically the maintenance of local roads and of the local school and a skeleton welfare administration. In towns, housing, street-lighting and municipal transport are among the more important services, while education, police and even the fire services are largely in the hands of the prefectoral administration. Very little has been done to force communes to amalgamate: indeed, the only type of co-ordination which existed traditionally was that of joint boards, created for special purposes, such as drainage or sewerage, to which a number of villages decided to belong. In the 1960s, some attempts were made in relation to conurbations, first through the creation of joint organizations known as urban districts comprising a town and a number of neighbouring small communes (which do not cease to exist, however) and, later, through the creation of conurbation authorities for some of the major cities. Clearly, although the maintenance of the *status quo* is said to result from the desire of communes, the Government is in fact loath to create sizeable authorities which, being richer and better able to attract specialized and competent personnel, would be able to undermine the role of the civil service.

The case of Paris provides an example of this general governmental policy. First, Paris was only granted a mayor in 1977 (except for a few months in 1848) and was until then administered by two prefects, appointed by the Government; the elected municipal council is thus not implementing itself the decisions which it takes. Secondly, the growth of the Paris conurbation demanded the creation of a greater Paris area, the City of Paris being, with its two million inhabitants, a mere quarter to a third of the total urban region. Yet the solution that prevailed was not that of a 'Greater Paris'. A District of the Paris Region was created, admittedly, but with specific and indeed rather limited powers; its council is composed of representatives of local authorities and is not directly elected, and its executive agent, the Delegate General, is a civil servant appointed by the Government. But, more importantly, the day-to-day administration and most of the decisions are left to communes which are closely supervised, for co-ordination purposes or other reasons; and supervision was increased in the middle 1960s by the splitting of the old *départements* of Seine and of Seine-et-Oise into seven new *départements*, each of which has a prefectoral administration. The reorganization of the Paris area did not lead to unity, but to a greater division than was the case in the past. Clearly, the Government feared the constitution of a powerful Paris conurbation authority, not merely nor possibly even primarily because of the so-called Communist 'Red Belt' (Paris itself is right-wing and the Belt is 'Red' only in the northern, eastern and south-eastern suburbs) but because of the traditions of supervision and control which are deep-rooted in the civil service and in the Ministry of the Interior in particular (it has sometimes been suggested that the prefectoral corps was worried lest it found itself without jobs, were more autonomy to be granted to local bodies).

Above the commune, the upper-tier authority is the *département.* This is an ambivalent structure, as we said, since it is a local authority but corresponds also in large part to civil-service bodies. As a result of the Paris reorganization, there are now ninety-six *départements* (Corsica included) plus a number of similar bodies in parts of overseas France. The *département* never fully obtained autonomy, a law of 1871 having simply stated that the Council of the *département* (the general council) would vote the budget and decide on the services of the authority, but that the prefect would still run these services. Although political difficulties arise from time to time between prefects and general councils, relations are normally amicable, in part because a good prefect has to learn to manipulate his council and not to antagonize it, in part also because the electoral system to the general council is antiquated and favours heavily the small rural communes against urban areas; thus the prefect is more confronted with representatives of relatively poor districts dependent on State aid than with those of richer and more dynamic areas. General councillors are indeed known mainly for their functions of intermediaries: they try to obtain favours from the prefects and ministerial agencies and are therefore usually not in a position to act collectively and with determination; not surprisingly, it is in the general councils that one finds most of the remaining traces of the sectionalism which used to characterize politics at the national level; but at the level of the *département*, the result is to place the council in a position of dependence as the prefect's resources are broader than those of his county budget. Indeed, since the general council is responsible for a limited number of services, mainly roads and social welfare, the prefect can fairly easily use his power as provider of State subsidies in other fields to try to keep general councillors in line if they become restless.

The *département* has thus often been criticized for being run more as a subdivision of the State than as a local authority. It has also been accused of being too small for modern purposes. Indeed, the civil service recognized its smallness for its own purposes, though with some internal resistance, admittedly, since it was only in the 1960s that twenty standard regions were finally adopted as the normal subdivisions for all the Ministries. But these regions remained purely agencies for the central government. An advisory council, the Commission de Développement Économique Régional (CODER) was created in each region; it was composed of representatives of local authorities and of interest groups and was consulted from time to time on economic problems and specifically on the early stages of development of the national plan; but it had no powers of decision. Indeed, even within the civil-service structure, the region remained an organ of transmission, though regional prefects had been given various functions of co-ordination and some executive jurisdiction (as in police matters and in the allocation of some development funds).

It may of course be argued that the French were to blame for the limited role played by the regions, since the Government presented to the people in 1969 a referendum designed to turn the region into a local authority, and since the proposal was rejected by a 53 per cent majority (which led to De Gaulle's departure). But the referendum also included a reform of the Senate designed to diminish the powers of the Chamber – and this contributed to the defeat of the proposal. Moreover, the regional arrangements suggested were cautious and even timid – as many opponents of the reform were quick to point out. Yet it was a similarly timid reform which the Government presented in 1971, this time to Parliament, and which was approved without much enthusiasm. Thus, although France is now divided into a number of regions which are deemed to be the highest local authorities, these regions are neither truly autonomous nor really representative. There is no direct election to the regional councils; the *départements* have not been abolished nor have their powers been curtailed; and the administration of the region is in the hands of the regional prefect. Thus the region is organized on the model of the *département*; some role and influence are given to local representatives, but safeguards of various kinds ensure that State agents retain the upper hand. It is sometimes suggested that this move was merely a first step and that regions will gradually acquire a real autonomy; but the history of the development of the *département* shows that the second step may never be taken: it can reasonably be inferred that, faced with a larger unit and a potentially more powerful one, the Government will be even less inclined to come to give later a real autonomy to the various regions.

At the other end of the local-authority chain the reluctance to change still remains unbreakable at the level of communes. In this the Government is not alone to blame, as it is not evident that the Government and civil service would want to perpetuate very small authorities which are inefficient and expensive to run. Grass-roots demand for change is very limited indeed; the bulk of mayors and local politicians have naturally vested interests; and as Gaullism has often been accused of heavy-handedness and of favouring big business and big administration against smaller bodies, the Government probably preferred not to innovate in a field in which administrative gains are likely to be for the long term and political costs arise immediately. At last, from the early 1970s, an effort has been made to encourage small villages to regroup as one local authority, but the process is slow: a law passed in 1972 gives the Prefect, under certain conditions, the right to call for a local referendum on amalgamation, and some financial incentives are added to encourage local authorities to take advantage of the law. Yet, in practice, little change has occurred. It is understandable that local patriotism should run high, but it is surprising that demand for change should have remained so small as, unlike before the war, communes have become actively involved in various forms of capital work and come to be markedly in debt. The physical face of rural France was dramatically modified in the 1950s and 1960s, with the consequence that most local authorities have become highly conscious of their limited financial base while being pressed by the population to expand services, to attract industry and generally to appear modern and well equipped.

French local-government structures thus need massive reorganization; attitudes to local government need to be profoundly reformed, not only within the civil service (many sections of the civil service would welcome a more responsible and genuinely autonomous local government), but among the whole population (Parisians have tended to look down on the localities and the influence of Paris was such that the problem of local government was not given any real attention until the 1960s). So long as these attitudes are not changed, so long as there is no real demand stemming from the population for new forms of authorities both able and willing to act responsibly, reforms will not be made. But these reforms would also have profound consequences for many State services from planning to education and would entail a new division of labour which might tend to transform most administrative structures. Fortunately or unfortunately, these services have affected too many Frenchmen, and their level of achievement has been sufficiently high to have restricted the demand for change to a limited number of fields and, in most of these fields, to have made the demand for change a very recent affair.

The Judiciary

The French judiciary both suffers and benefits from the importance of the civil service in the nation. On the one hand, it is accused of not being sufficiently independent from the State: justice is viewed as a public service and the principles of hierarchy and career advancement obtain; many defects of the arrangements of criminal justice follow from these principles. On the other hand, the overriding influence of the bureaucracy led to the development of administrative courts, which came gradually to protect the citizen against undue interference by the central and local governments.

Ordinary Justice

The 'ordinary' judiciary – by opposition to administrative courts – is based on a network of courts which are expected to implement the law as it stands: case-law has no value *per se*, and French courts are indeed expressly prohibited by law from making pronouncements of a general character which could form the basis of future decisions. Of course, in practice, a decision taken by a court will tend to be followed in the future, especially if this decision was taken by one of the higher courts; but this is merely guidance and reversals of interpretation are neither exceptional nor unexpected. Nor are courts entitled to discuss the law in the name of higher principles or of the constitution: no appeal against an act of Parliament is allowed on grounds of 'unconstitutionality'. Though a constitutional council was created in 1946 and maintained in 1958, it has limited powers once the Act is published; and only the President of the Republic and the Speakers of the two Chambers can set a case for review to the constitutional council.

The hierarchy of courts follows closely the general principle that the administration should be as close as possible to the average citizen, though a reform of 1958 abolished many of the little-used smallest courts. There are lower courts dealing with the least important matters (civil and criminal) and, in each *département*, a court is concerned with the most important questions. Appeal (which is almost always of right) goes to Courts of Appeal of which there are 26, each covering approximately the area of an administrative region. In Paris sits the Supreme Court, known as Cour de Cassation, whose exclusive role is to see that the lower courts, including the Courts of Appeal, have interpreted the law in a regular fashion.

The system is broadly the same for civil and criminal cases and judges are often the same persons. But it is to criminal justice that most criticisms are being directed. First, unlike English courts, French courts operate the system of 'inquisitorial' justice, through which, at least in theory, the aim is to establish the truth, and not merely to see whether the prosecution has amassed enough evidence to convict the accused; in practice this principle leads in many cases to a general reduction of the rights of the accused. Second, and most importantly, the prosecution is a branch, albeit a separate branch, of the judiciary: it is not up to the police to find a lawyer and build up a case; the case made by the police is transferred to an examining magistrate (the *juge d'instruction*) who, if he is satisfied that the grounds for prosecution are strong, transfers the file to the prosecuting judge. This could of course ensure that the work of the police is closely supervised by men who are more 'neutral'; in practice the gap between police, examining magistrate, and prosecution is often very small. Though reforms have increased the rights of accused persons and though a jury of laymen is called to decide on guilt for the most serious crimes, the superior status of the prosecution remains almost untouched; nor is there much pressure for radical reform, except among some younger members of the judiciary.

Administrative Courts

The serious shortcomings of 'ordinary' justice are somewhat compensated by the development of administrative courts which have come to see their role as one of protection of the citizen against encroachments by the 'public powers'. The network of administrative courts developed gradually from their Napoleonic function of advice. At the national level, a Council of State was created to help the government draft its regulations and, though to a very limited extent, to receive complaints from citizens aggrieved by these regulations. It was also to help to draft, and to hear complaints about individual decisions made by the Ministers. In each *département*, a Council of *Préfecture* was to have the same functions with regard to prefects, their staff and local authorities.

The power to 'hear complaints' increased gradually throughout the nineteenth century, partly because the administration tended, as we know, to intervene markedly in the affairs of the nation, partly because Council of State and Councils of *Préfecture* took increasingly their role to be 'judicial'; but only in 1872 was this judicial power formally recognized and only in 1953 was the evolution complete. The Councils of *Préfecture* were renamed *tribunaux administratifs* and were to become lower-tier administrative courts; appeals of their judgements would go to the Council of State (hitherto overburdened), except for the most important regulations, taken by the whole government and known as *decrees*, about which plaintiffs would still go directly to the Council of State.

Two major consequences flow from these extensive powers of administrative courts. First they can investigate almost any action of the administration. Only a tiny number of decisions, mainly relating to foreign affairs, may not be examined by the Council of State. These courts do not merely oversee whether the decision keeps within the letter of the law: they look at the spirit of the decision and at the general conditions which were at its origin. Second, courts may quash both minor decisions of an administrative body as well as the most important and most general decrees of the entire Government. Thus, though the French Constitution does not entitle courts to annul acts of Parliament, administrative courts may – and indeed do – quash governmental decrees on grounds that they do not follow acts of Parliament or even the general 'principles' on which French society is held to be run. The procedure tends of course to be used only in extreme situations: but the existence of these courts has unquestionably given Frenchmen a powerful weapon against the bureaucracy and helped to check tendencies towards irresponsibility. While courts do not exactly correspond to the institutions of the 'parliamentary commissioners' or 'ombudsmen' which now exist in many liberal democracies (and of which an equivalent was indeed introduced in France in 1972), they have been and continue to be a powerful, cheap and easy way to curb the natural tendencies of the bureaucracy to extend its powers, particularly in a country where the role of the civil service has been so comprehensive for so long.

THE FRENCH WELFARE STATE

The French Welfare State is in many ways older, more patchy, more bureaucratic and more run from above than the British Welfare State. Its best achievement, though with reservations, is in economic planning, its worst result has been, hitherto at least, in the educational field, while the legally comprehensive social security system has shown itself to be beset with periodic difficulties and numerous financial setbacks.

Economic Planning

The traditions of State intervention led to economic planning after the Second World War, since the destructions of the war coupled with the low level of the economic infrastructure raised the question of the survival of France as a modern nation. At the start, planning was almost exclusively a civil service affair, and the First Plan, adopted in 1946, was scarcely even debated in the French Parliament. Its main emphasis was on infrastructure and the targets given to the economy for the turn of the 1950s affected essentially services which either had belonged to the State earlier (railways for instance) or were being nationalized (coal, gas, electricity in particular). It was thus possible for planners, grouped in the Commissariat Général au Plan under Jean Monnet, to have a direct impact on early developments, particularly as the major banks were also being nationalized and the financial market, traditionally weak in France, was at the time almost non-existent. With the years, planning entered gradually new fields. It was very successful for agriculture, through the priorities given to tractors and other equipment; it became less successful as it came to be concerned with sectors most left to free enterprise, though, for a time at least, the scarcity of private capital acted in its favour. Yet the Commissariat au Plan gradually acquired a reputation for its forecasts of economic trends and, having set its goals at indicative planning only, it did not antagonize more than to a limited extent the broad mass of businessmen who came to regard the Plan as a means of finding what competitors were likely to do and what suppliers and clients were likely to produce and demand. While achievements have clearly been exaggerated abroad, the Plan did help to transform attitudes, not only towards planning in general, but towards economic growth and dynamism in industry in a country which had at times been very malthusian.

Greater difficulties occurred in the 1960s, in part because, when Giscard was Finance Minister, the Government favoured for a time the financial market as an economic regulator and slowed the growth of the economy in an effort to turn the franc into an instrument of foreign policy, in part also because the original targets of economic planning became gradually complicated by newer goals of social improvement. Clearly, as the original problems of reconstruction and even of construction of the infrastructure were met, economic development came increasingly to raise questions of social priorities in the fields of urban design, educational, housing and hospital policy. In order to embody these goals in the Plan, the Commissariat began to involve in its machinery a series of specialized and regional committees, composed of representatives of local interest groups, which could advise on the requirements and could provide some legitimacy for the decisions to be taken. This was particularly noticeable in the preparation of the Fifth Plan (1966–9), with the paradoxical result, however, that criticisms against the Plan came increasingly to be levelled, not by the supporters of free enterprise opposed to the idea of planning, but by supporters of a socialized economy, who objected both to the priorities and to the extent and character of the consultation and participation process. A 'counter-plan' was even drafted which purported to demonstrate that, under different economic and social assumptions, economic growth could be greater and the priorities for various services could be different and more democratic. In the event, the economic difficulties of the late 1960s made most of the targets appear unrealistic. Social planning is still in its infancy and controversies about priorities are impossible to avoid. Clearly, to the extent that the Commissariat au Plan has tried to go beyond simple and mechanical tasks and showed a marked imagination, it has helped to maintain the high reputation of the civil service, even if it has become, as a result, an object of contention; though the future of planning came increasingly into question in the climate of economic depression of the second half of the 1970s, the idea remains alive and the Commissariat au Plan still retains much of the prestige of the earlier years.

Social Security and Social Welfare

Social security has also remained at the centre of many controversies, but for much less lofty reasons. A law of 1946 unified and generalized the patchy elements of the old system of social welfare and created a so-called 'general regime' run by a number of Boards (*Caisses*) mainly elected by the members of the social security system, employers as well as employees, entrusted with the running of what quickly became a large administrative machine. But supervision by the State remained very strict, both because the law and subsequent decrees decided on the level of contributions and on the extent of reimbursements and because periodic deficits led to repeated efforts at reorganization, the last having taken place in the summer of 1967 and, as we saw, having contributed in part to the climate of disgruntlement which led to the wave of strikes of 1968. The problems are many. Clearly, deficits arose to a large extent because the social security system enabled Frenchmen to be better cured, especially for major diseases, than they had been in the past. Moreover, the system of family allowances which was created in 1939 to remedy the demographic situation led to massive outgoings which account in part for the large difference between the costs of labour for employers and the size of the pay packets. But the attitudes of the medical and ancillary professions to the service have been a cause of constant political problems while giving to the citizens the impression that the system did not give the benefits which had been promised by law. Alleged infringements of the freedom of choice of doctors were cited as excuses for refusing to agree to fees fixed by the social security Boards and only after years of discussion was it possible in the 1960s to come gradually to a *modus vivendi* with which most doctors complied. Clearly, this is not a specifically French phenomenon. But whereas it is probably true that patients who are very ill (and are willing to go to public hospitals, where standards have markedly increased in recent years) can obtain extensive treatments and be free of financial worries, the bulk of smaller illnesses still raise minor problems and remain, at least to an extent, a drain on resources.

While health treatment was unsatisfactory, unemployment benefits and retirement pensions (except for civil servants) were for a long time almost non-existent. Only in the 1960s was a drastic improvement made in both fields, with the effect that it can at last be said that the social security and welfare benefits amount really to a comprehensive system of general insurance against most of the basic problems relating to health in modern society. But it does remain true that, on balance, the French system is somewhat less interested in ameliorating the situation of its citizens than it has been in taking care of the structure of the economy; this is in part due to the fact that, in 1939, the French standard of living was appreciably lower than that of many Western countries, and of Britain in particular. Economic growth and a general rejuvenation of the economy have made it possible for France to close the gap. It is noticeable that, not only the planners, but the public as a whole, appear to be significantly more concerned with social welfare than they were in the 1950s. But deep-rooted attitudes die hard; for a very long time, the family – and in particular the family on the farm – was a self-supporting unit which acted as a welfare organization; the decrease of the rural population and the gradual modernization of the country have rendered such a traditional system wholly anachronistic. An evolution of society, of the civil service and of the Government has taken place; but a gap still exists and improvements need to occur in the coming decades.

The Educational Revolution

We noted in the first section the extent to which education had spread to new social groups and the effects on the role of students in society. Yet developments took place wholly haphazard and within the old administrative structures during the post-war period. The process remained entirely led from above, in the Ministry of National Education;

practically no autonomy to experiment or even merely administer was accorded to universities and other institutions until 1968. After the revolt, the Government became so anxious to recover at least part of the goodwill that it had lost, not merely among students, but also among teachers, that a drastic reform of higher education was presented to Parliament at the end of 1968 and, significantly enough, was passed without one dissenter by the National Assembly. Meanwhile, new experiments had been attempted, particularly in the Paris area, which created major problems of organization but did at least constitute outlets for those of the new generation of teachers who were determined to experiment. Vincennes may have been a failure in many ways in a conventional academic sense; it was and still is a social experiment which helped to lower tension in some aspects of the French higher education system.

Little concrete change has taken place since the passing of the 1968 Education Act, except inasmuch as the administrative structures of the old universities have been replaced by new structures at the departmental and faculty level on which teachers and students participate and which allow for greater flexibility of subjects. But the main problem remains, as with local government, that of the scope of university autonomy. The French do not appear to be prepared to abandon the concept of national diplomas and degrees nor to abandon that of a national competition system from which university and college teachers have to be chosen; nor is it clear that they are prepared – or at any rate that the Ministry of National Education is prepared – to give a block grant to universities and allow these to run their affairs within this general budget. Yet, so long as these changes do not occur, teachers and students alike will not feel compelled to adopt more responsible attitudes towards educational reform. Meanwhile, levels of centralization in secondary and even primary schools remain very high indeed, not only because curricula are basically decided in Paris and little scope for initiative and experimentation exists at any level (even in private schools the French State alone distributes the diplomas which, for instance, allow for entry into the universities), but because school-teaching is also organized on a national or at best *département* basis and thus makes it impossible for headmasters to recruit individual teachers. Teachers being posted, not chosen, schools do not become communities and headmasters are unlikely to have much influence on the way the school is run.

These attitudes are so deep-rooted in the French educational system, they affect so profoundly teachers and the whole population, that it is unlikely that the current reforms will do more than modify the surface of the whole edifice. This is particularly so because, while France has come to be admired abroad for its planning mechanism and for its civil service structure in general, the French have traditionally been proud of their educational system and only recently have they come to recognize that it was antiquated both in content and structure. However, world-wide educational difficulties are more likely to lead the French to believe that there is something wrong with students in general than to feel that their own system would stand to gain by learning from abroad. Change will therefore be slow. It started in the late 1960s only, but given the pressure from students, and, though less so, from teachers, it will continue to occur. It may even affect, indirectly, attitudes to local government and thus increase the movement for participation which was one of the main mottoes of the 1968 'revolution'. Though France never was quite an administrative State in the past, changes which are currently taking place are likely to drive the country towards a healthier equilibrium between the 'enlightened despotism' of the civil servants and the impossible ideal of grass-roots democracy.

French administrative structures have always been independent in the past of the evolution of the political system. From Napoleon to the present day, one can trace the development of social institutions, of the educational network, of administrative courts, even to some extent of local government, without reference to the political superstructure. In the Fifth Republic, however, such a separation has become increasingly difficult, partly because the pressure from students and other groups on the administrative structures have had repeated effects on the stability of the regime as a whole and partly because the cry for participation and local autonomy leads to fundamental changes which, as we saw, cannot be achieved without relying on the strength of the political system. The influence of the administrative system on society has come to be fully perceived while the changes in the social bases of the French polity are beginning to have effects on administrative structures as well as on politics.

When analysing the new political life, we had repeated occasions to note that predictions about the future are hazardous in a country which is prone to erratic outbursts and has been undergoing for the first time a number of profound social changes. The revolution in the countryside and the new urban developments suggest that the Fifth Republic still has to undertake reforms, though the institutions are gradually being accepted by the bulk of the population and though even politicians have uttered rather less opposition than was often the case under previous regimes. But the administrative structures are being seriously challenged, perhaps for the first time; the perception of the bureaucratic nature of the society has become more general, in part because of the increased mobility of the population and because of the growth of the Welfare State itself. Thus, paradoxically, it may be the administrative structures, more than the political system, that will create difficulties for the French Government, as indeed the 1968 'revolution' already suggested and as discontent in relation to regionalism as well as the educational system have often indicated.

The question of the role of European institutions is a further unknown in the future development of the French Fifth Republic. With the broad support of the population, De Gaulle and his successors have tended to see Europe as a 'confederacy' of sovereign nation-states, in which the French Government would play a major part. The support for direct elections to the European Parliament was rather muted in the French public and the Bill to introduce these elections had to be railroaded through Parliament against marked opposition from the Gaullist and Communist Parties. The temptation, if not to go alone, at least to soft-pedal on devolving more powers to a United Europe remains alive in a country which has tended to pride itself on the fastest economic growth, on the greatest developments in advanced technology, and on the most skilled civil service among the states of the Community. While Europe was a challenge for French industry and the French economy in the late 1950s, it has tended to become, in the 1960s and 1970s, the platform from which French civil servants endeavour to spread their *dirigiste* ideas on their 'opposite numbers' who are generally more inclined towards economic liberalism. Whether this attitude will gradually give way to greater 'partnership', and a genuine desire to merge the economies and indeed the political life of the various nations, depends in large part on the extent to which other countries can successfully put pressure on the French Government. But it depends even more on the extent to which the French population is prepared to back the European ideal, not just as an alliance of a number of like-minded countries, but as one real community marked by a common goal.

The answer to this question will be given, like the answer to so many others, by the attitudes of the French people towards the role of the administration in the society. Yet the French administration is so old and so much part of French life that it is difficult for the population to conceive of new structures, to call for major changes and to adapt to these changes when they are brought about. Over all, despite the development of planning and the unquestioned skills of the French civil service, despite the fact that the French bureaucracy helped the Fourth Republic to transform the society and the Fifth to maintain the impetus, the future of the political system depends on an extent of gradual 'debureaucratization' of the country. It is not that the civil service should lose its sense of mission and cease to contribute to the training of much of the French élite; but responsibility for public affairs, locally and in the social services, must be shared more widely. Only in this way will the basic 'anarchism' of the French be used to better ends; only in this way will the stability of the society – and of the political system – be permanently assured.

Bibliography

The number of works on French politics and society is of course vast, both in English and in French. Given the variety of French political and social experience, given the instability of French institutions since 1789, given also the unique role of the bureaucracy in the fabric of French society, it is not surprising that the accounts should be diverse and at times contradictory. All authors recognize (at least have had to recognize by the early 1970s) that the Fifth Republic has brought about a decidedly different pattern of politics; but the new 'system' remains the object of major criticisms on the part of many while others emphasize the importance of the newly found stability of French politics. All authors recognize that the economic and social transformations of post-war France have altered the living conditions of Frenchmen as well as giving the country an enhanced position among major industrial nations; but many criticize in acerbic terms the impact of the bureaucracy and emphasize the consequences on participation and self-government, while others stress the role of the civil service in providing the world with what is perhaps the only successful *dirigiste* mixed economy. Even the shortest of bibliographies has to take into account these diverse currents, all of which are part of the overall understanding of French society.

It is difficult to assess contemporary French life without a detour into history. Perhaps the best concise introduction to the various ideological strands that have characterized French society since the eighteenth century can be found in D. Thompson, *Democracy in France* (London, 1958). A more detailed examination of the last hundred years can be found in D. W. Brogan, *The Development of Modern France* (London, 1940), which is a classic on the Third Republic (1870–1940); in P. M. Williams, *Crisis and Compromise* (London, 1964), which is the most comprehensive study of political life in the Fourth Republic (1946–58); and in P. M. Williams and M. Harrison, *Politics and Society in De Gaulle's Republic*

(London, 1971), which brings the analysis up to date. Those who are interested in the peculiar 'interregnum' of the German occupation would benefit by reading R. Aron's *Histoire de Vichy* (Paris, 1954), which examines dispassionately the characteristics of the authoritarian Pétain regime.

Studies devoted to various aspects of modern French society are numerous: perhaps the best introduction to the nature and characteristics of traditional France can be found in L. Wylie's *Village in the Vaucluse* (Cambridge, Mass., 1964), which, though primarily a detailed 'anthropological' study of a small rural community in the south of France, gives a vivid impression of the social and political bonds which existed in the past and shows the way in which these bonds have been modified under the impact of 'modernization'. Perhaps the best survey of French ills and their historical causes is R. Peyrefitte's *Le Mal français* (Paris, 1977), while a good and systematic introduction to the tensions and 'contradictions' in French contemporary society can be found in the collection of essays published by J. D. Raynaud under the title of *Tendances et volontés de la société française* (Paris, 1966), while J. Ardagh's *The New French Revolution* (London, 1968) covers extensively the various aspects of change in a somewhat less technical fashion. More controversial and somewhat idiosyncratic is the study of M. Crozier, *La Société bloquée* (Paris, 1970), which explains how, in the author's view, France suffers from being dominated by a civil service which constitutes to a large extent a society of its own: the book presents in a more popular fashion the thesis which had been carefully documented in *The Bureaucratic Phenomenon* (London 1964). Transformations affecting specifically the working class and the peasantry can be assessed by reading S. Mallet's *La Nouvelle Classe ouvrière* (Paris, 1964) and M. Gervais *et al.*'s *Une France sans paysans* (Paris, 1965). Finally, the characteristics of French planning are examined with great care in P. Bauchet, *Economic Planning: the French Experience* (London, 1963).

It is more difficult to make a choice among the numerous general texts on French politics in the Fifth Republic. A good introduction for a British audience can be found in P. Avril's *Politics in France* (Harmondsworth, 1969), as the author takes into account both the varied traditions and the impact of social forces on politics. A more detailed treatment of current French politics can be found in the two-volume study of D. Pickles, *The Government and Politics of France* (London, 1972 and 1973). But, as an understanding of current French politics and of future trends implies an assessment of the characteristics of the Gaullist party, an indispensable guide is J. Charlot's *The Gaullist Phenomenon* (London, 1971), which draws comparisons with Britain and is markedly helped by the author's knowledge of the nature of British politics. Indeed, those interested in examining in greater detail the structure of the Gaullist Party would consult with great profit the study on *L'UNR* (Paris, 1967) by the same author. No work of quite the same comprehensiveness exists on other parties, though anyone wishing to understand the peculiar phenomenon of Communist strength would benefit from reading A. Kriegel's study on *The French Communists* (Chicago, 1972) as well as A. Barjonet's study of the Communist trade union, *La CGT* (Paris, 1968). (A work on the Christian trade union, *La CFDT* (Paris, 1968), has also been published by the same author and would help to draw a parallel between the two main styles of trade-unionism.) Moreover, as one of the major changes of the new Republic concerns Parliament, which, according to some, has suffered a real demise, readers should consult both N. Leites's *On the Game of Politics in France* (Stanford, Calif., 1959), which shows the unreal character of parliamentary politics before De Gaulle, and P. M. Williams, *The French Parliament* (London, 1968), which provides detailed case-studies of the role of the new French Parliament in the context of legislation.

No survey of French society and politics is complete without an examination of the civil service. Perhaps the most detailed and comprehensive work on the French bureaucracy is F. Ridley's and J. Blondel's *Public Administration in France* (London, 1969), while R. Grégoire's study, *The French Civil Service* (Brussels, 1964), covers more extensively the characteristics and structure of the bureaucracy. B. Chapman's *Introduction to French Local Government* (London, 1953) remains a classic, despite the many changes which have affected the apparatus of local government in the last twenty years, particularly at the regional level. Finally, H. Ehrman's *Organised Business in France* (Princeton, N.J., 1957) illuminates by many examples the personal ties linking top civil servants with the leaders of French industry.

It is still not clear whether the events of 1968 were a 'missed revolution', 'great holidays', the last episode of a process of change in a society that had remained static during many decades or the first sign of a move towards 'participatory society'. But it is clear that 1968 played a sufficiently important part in the minds of many Frenchmen, from students to trade-unionists, and from the Government to highly volatile and minuscule extremist groups. Readers interested in contemporary French politics and society should at least examine some of the aspects of this 'revolution', even though, given the nature of the problem, accounts and conclusions are necessarily one-sided: of the works published in English perhaps the *Reflections on the Revolution in France* (London, 1970), edited by C. M. Posner, are the most comprehensive and varied testimonial. On this work, as on the whole of this bibliography, however, the point does apply that views on the present and future of France are almost as numerous as there are authors – which may seem bewildering but merely suggests that France continues to be a puzzle to insiders and outsiders alike, as it was to observers of previous generations.

Index

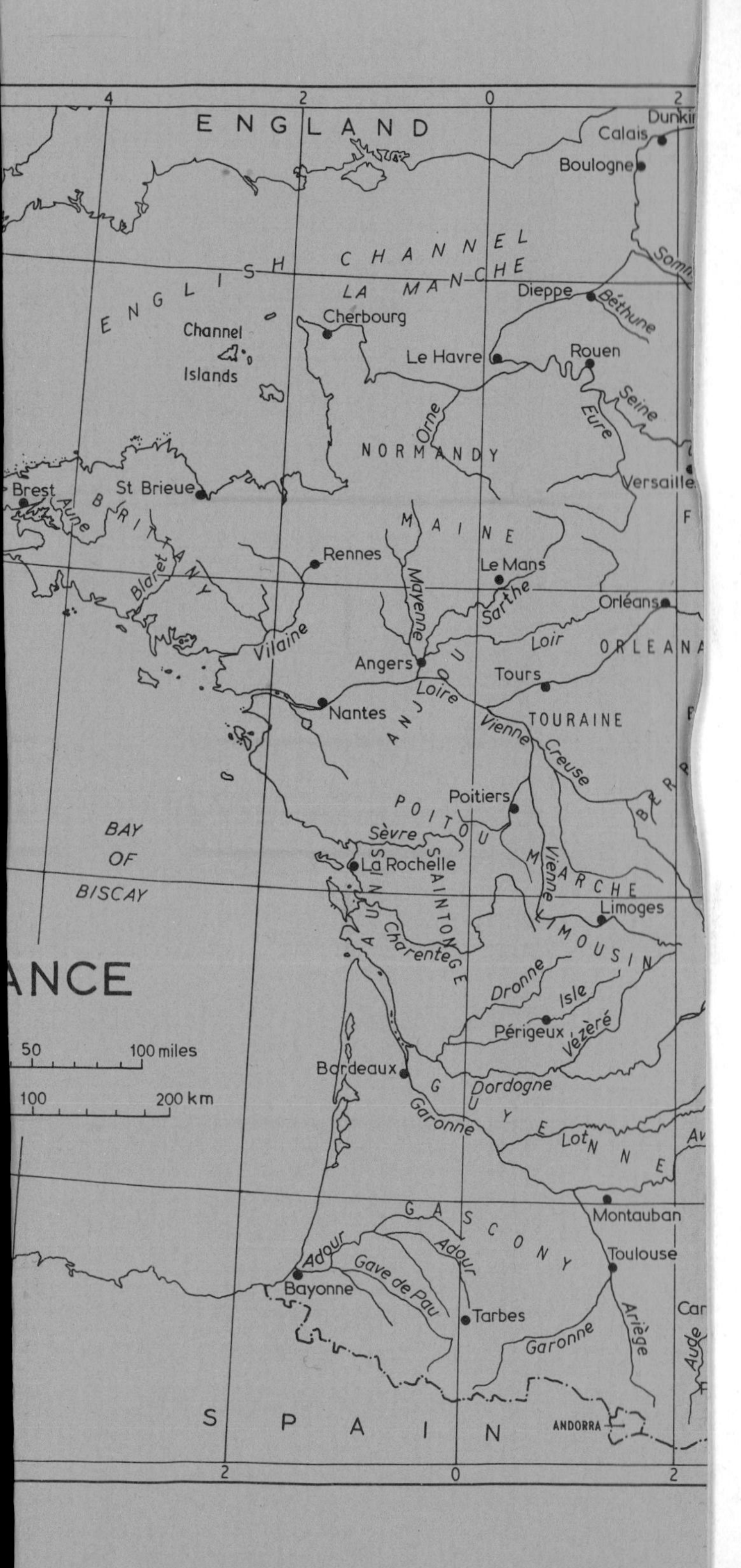
ENGLAND
Calais
Dunkir
Boulogne
ENGLISH CHANNEL
LA MANCHE
Somme
Dieppe
Béthune
Channel
Islands
Cherbourg
Le Havre
Rouen
Seine
Eure
Orne
NORMANDY
Versaille
Brest
St Brieuc
BRITTANY
Aune
Blavet
MAINE
Rennes
Mayenne
Le Mans
Sarthe
Orléans
Loir
ORLEANA
Vilaine
Angers
ANJOU
Tours
Loire
Nantes
TOURAINE
Vienne
Creuse
Poitiers
POITOU
BERRY
BAY
OF
BISCAY
Sèvre
La Rochelle
SAINTONGE
AUNIS
MARCHE
Vienne
Limoges
LIMOUSIN
Charente
ANCE
Dronne
Isle
Périgeux
Vezère
50
100 miles
100
200 km
Bordeaux
GUYENNE
Dordogne
Garonne
Lot
Montauban
GASCONY
Adour
Gave de Pau
Toulouse
Bayonne
Tarbes
Garonne
Ariège
Aude
SPAIN
ANDORRA
4
2
0
2

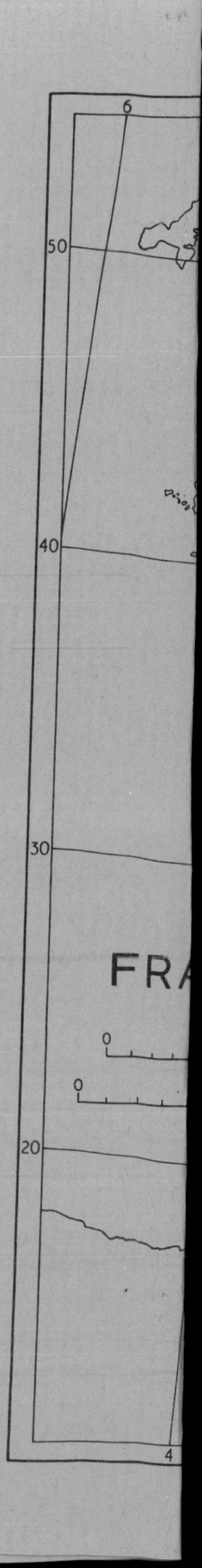
6
50
40
30
FRA
0
0
20
4